HISTORY

OF THE

WAR IN THE PENINSULA

AND IN THE

SOUTH OF FRANCE

FROM THE YEAR 1807 TO THE YEAR 1814

VOLUME VI

HISTORY

OF THE

WAR IN THE PENINSULA

AND IN THE

SOUTH OF FRANCE,

FROM THE YEAR 1807 TO THE YEAR 1814.

BY

W. F. P. NAPIER, C.B.

COLONEL H. P. FORTY-THIRD REGIMENT, MEMBER OF THE ROYAL SWEDISH
ACADEMY OF MILITARY SCIENCES.

VOL. VI.

CONSTABLE · LONDON

This edition first published in Great Britain 1993
by Constable and Company Limited
3 The Lanchesters, 162 Fulham Palace Road
London W6 9ER

Originally published in London in 1840
by Thomas and William Boone

ISBN 0 09 471890 3

Printed in Great Britain by
St Edmundsbury Press Ltd
Bury St Edmunds, Suffolk

TABLE OF CONTENTS.

BOOK XXI.

CHAPTER I.

Lord Wellington blockades Pampeluna, besieges St. Sebastian—Operations on the eastern coast of Spain—General Elio's misconduct—Sir John Murray sails to attack Taragona—Colonel Prevot takes St. Felippe de Balaguer—Second siege of Taragona—Suchet and Maurice Mathieu endeavour to relieve the place—Sir John Murray raises the siege—Embarks with the loss of his guns—Disembarks again at St. Felippe de Balaguer—Lord William Bentinck arrives—Sir John Murray's trial—Observations .   .   .   . Page 1

CHAP. II.

Danger of Sicily—Averted by Murat's secret defection from the emperor—Lord William Bentinck re-embarks—His design of attacking the city of Valencia frustrated—Del Parque is defeated on the Xucar—The Anglo-Sicilians disembark at Alicant—Suchet prepares to attack the allies—Prevented by the battle of Vittoria—Abandons Valencia—Marches towards Zaragoza—Clauzel retreats to France—Paris evacuates Zaragoza—Suchet retires to Taragona—Mines the walls—Lord William Bentinck passes the Ebro—Secures the Col de Balaguer—Invests Taragona—Partial insurrection in Upper Catalonia—Combat of Salud—Del Parque joins lord William Bentinck who projects an attack upon Suchet's cantonments—Suchet concentrates his army—Is joined by Decaen—Advances—The allies retreat to the mountains—Del Parque invests Tortoza—His rear-guard attacked by the garrison while passing the Ebro—Suchet blows up the walls of Taragona—Lord William desires to besiege Tortoza—Hears that Suchet has detached troops—Sends Del Parque's army to join lord Wellington—Advances to Villa Franca—Combat of Ordal—The allies retreat—Lord Frederick Bentinck fights with the French general Myers and wounds him—Lord William returns to Sicily—Observations .   . 33

CHAP. III.

Siege of Sebastian—Convent of Bartolomeo stormed—Assault on the place fails—Causes thereof—Siege turned into a blockade, and the guns embarked at Passages—French make a successful sally 65

TABLE OF CONTENTS.

CHAP. IV.

Soult appointed the emperor's lieutenant—Arrives at Bayonne—Joseph goes to Paris—Sketch of Napoleon's political and military situation—His greatness of mind—Soult's activity—Theatre of operations described—Soult resolves to succour Pampeluna—Relative positions and numbers of the contending armies described 86

CHAP. V.

Soult attacks the right of the allies—Combat of Roncesvalles—Combat of Linzoain—Count D'Erlon attacks the allies' right centre—Combat of Maya—General Hill takes a position at Irueta—General Picton and Cole retreat down the Val de Zubiri—They turn at Huarte and offer battle—Lord Wellington arrives—Combat of the 27th—First battle of Sauroren—Various movements—D'Erlon joins Soult who attacks general Hill—Second battle of Sauroren—Foy is cut off from the main army—Night march of the light division—Soult retreats—Combat of Dona Maria—Dangerous position of the French at San Estevan—Soult marches down the Bidassoa—Forced march of the light division—Terrible scene near the bridge of Yanzi—Combats of Echallar and Ivantelly—Narrow escape of lord Wellington—-Observations . . 109

BOOK XXII.

CHAP. I.

New positions of the armies—Lord Melville's mismanagement of the naval co-operation—Siege of St. Sebastian—Progress of the second attack . . 179

CHAP. II.

Storming of St. Sebastian—Lord Wellington calls for volunteers from the first fourth and light divisions—The place is assaulted and taken—The town burned—The castle is bombarded and surrenders—Observations . . 197

CHAP. III.

Soult's views and positions during the siege described—He endeavours to succour the place—Attacks lord Wellington—Combats of San Marcial and Vera—The French are repulsed the same day that San Sebastian is stormed—Soult resolves to adopt a defensive system—Observations 218

CHAP. IV.

The duke of Berri proposes to invade France promising the aid of twenty thousand insurgents—Lord Wellington's views on this subject—His personal acrimony against Napoleon—That monarch's policy and character defended—Dangerous state of affairs in Catalonia—Lord Wellington designs to go there himself, but at the desire of the allied sovereigns and the English government

TABLE OF CONTENTS.

resolves to establish a part of his army in France—His plans retarded by accidents and bad weather—Soult unable to divine his project—Passage of the Bidassoa—Second combat of Vera—Colonel Colborne's great presence of mind—Gallant action of lieutenant Havelock—The French lose the redoubt of Sarre and abandon the great Rhune—Observations . . . 239

CHAP. V.

Soult retakes the redoubt of Sarre—Wellington organizes the army in three great divisions under sir Rowland Hill, marshal Beresford, and sir John Hope —Disinterested conduct of the last-named officer—Soult's immense entrench·· ments described—His correspondence with Suchet—Proposes to retake the offensive and unite their armies in Aragon—Suchet will not accede to his views and makes inaccurate statements—Lord Wellington, hearing of advantages gained by the allied sovereigns in Germany, resolves to invade France— Blockade and fall of Pampeluna—Lord Wellington organizes a brigade under lord Aylmer to besiege Santona, but afterwards changes his design . 271

CHAP. VI.

Political state of Portugal—Violence, ingratitude, and folly of the government of that country—Political state of Spain—Various factions described, their violence, insolence, and folly—Scandalous scenes at Cadiz—Several Spanish generals desire a revolution—Lord Wellington describes the miserable state of the country—Anticipates the necessity of putting down the Cortez by force— Resigns his command of the Spanish armies—The English ministers propose to remove him to Germany—The new Cortez reinstate him as generalissimo on his own terms—He expresses his fears that the cause will finally fail and advises the English ministers to withdraw the British army . . . 295

BOOK XXIII.

CHAP. I.

War in the south of France—Soult's political difficulties—Privations of the allied troops—Lord Wellington appeals to their military honour with effect— Averse to offensive operations, but when Napoleon's disasters in Germany became known, again yields to the wishes of the allied sovereigns—His dispositions of attack retarded—They are described—Battle of the Nivelle— Observations—Deaths and characters of Mr. Edward Freer and colonel Thomas Lloyd 326

CHAP. II.

Soult occupies the entrenched camp of Bayonne, and the line of the Nive river —Lord Wellington unable to pursue his victory from the state of the roads— Bridge-head of Cambo abandoned by the French —Excesses of the Spanish troops—Lord Wellington's indignation—He sends them back to Spain—Various skirmishes in front of Bayonne—The generals J. Wilson and Vandeleur are wounded—Mina plunders the Val de Baygorry—Is beaten by the national

TABLE OF CONTENTS.

guards—Passage of the Nive and battles in front of Bayonne—Combat of the 10th—Combat of the 11th—Combat of the 12th—Battle of St. Pierre— Observations 363

CHAP. III.

Respective situations and views of lord Wellington and Soult—Partizan warfare —The Basques of the Val de Baygorry excited to arms by the excesses of Mina's troops—General Harispe takes the command of the insurgents—Clauzel advances beyond the Bidouze river—General movements—Partizan combats —Excesses committed by the Spaniards—Lord Wellington reproaches their generals—His vigorous and resolute conduct—He menaces the French insurgents of the valleys with fire and sword and the insurrection subsides—Soult hemns the allies right closely—Partizan combats continued—Remarkable instances of the habits established between the French and British soldiers of the light division—Shipwrecks on the coast 410

CHAP. IV.

Political state of Portugal—Political state of Spain—Lord Wellington advises the English government to prepare for a war with Spain and to seize St. Sebastian as a security for the withdrawal of the British and Portuguese troops—The seat of government and the new Cortez are removed to Madrid —The duke of San Carlos arrives secretly with the treaty of Valencay— It is rejected by the Spanish regency and Cortez—Lord Wellington's views on the subject 425

CHAP. V.

Political state of Napoleon—Guileful policy of the allied sovereigns—M. de St. Aignan—General reflections—Unsettled policy of the English ministers— They neglect lord Wellington—He remonstrates and exposes the denuded state of his army 440

CHAP. VI.

Continuation of the war in the eastern provinces—Suchet's erroneous statements —Sir William Clinton repairs Taragona—Advances to Villa Franca—Suchet endeavours to surprize him—Fails—The French cavalry cut off an English detachment at Ordal—The duke of San Carlos passes through the French posts —Copons favourable to his mission—Clinton and Manso endeavour to cut off the French troops at Molino del Rey—They fail through the misconduct of Copons—Napoleon recalls a great body of Suchet's troops—Whereupon he reinforces the garrison of Barcelona and retires to Gerona—Van Halen—He endeavours to beguile the governor of Tortoza—Fails—Succeeds at Lerida, Mequinenza, and Monzon—Sketch of the siege of Monzon—It is defended by the Italian soldier St. Jaques for one hundred and forty days—Clinton and Copons invest Barcelona—The beguiled garrisons of Lerida, Mequinenza, and Monzon, arrive at Martorel—Are surrounded and surrender on terms—Capitulation violated by Copons—King Ferdinand returns to Spain—His character —Clinton breaks up his army—His conduct eulogised—Lamentable sally from

TABLE OF CONTENTS.

Barcelona—The French garrisons beyond the Ebro return to France and Habert evacuates Barcelona—Fate of the prince of Conti and the duchess of Bourbon—Siege of Santona 475

BOOK XXIV.

CHAP. I.

Napoleon recalls several divisions of infantry and cavalry from Soult's army—Embarrassments of that marshal—Mr. Batbedat a banker of Bayonne offers to aid the allies secretly with money and provisions—La Roche Jacquelin and other Bourbon partizans arrive at the allies' head-quarter—The duke of Angoulême arrives there—Lord Wellington's political views—General reflections—Soult embarrassed by the hostility of the French people—Lord Wellington embarrassed by the hostility of the Spaniards—Soult's remarkable project for the defence of France —Napoleon's reasons for neglecting it put hypothetically—Lord Wellington's situation suddenly ameliorated—His wise policy, foresight, and diligence—Resolves to throw a bridge over the Adour below Bayonne, and to drive Soult from that river—Soult's system of defence—Numbers of the contending armies—Passage of the Gaves—Combat of Garris—Lord Wellington forces the line of the Bidouze and Gave of Mauleon—Soult takes the line of the Gave de Oleron and resolves to change his system of operation 505

CHAP. II.

Lord Wellington arrests his movements and returns in person to St. Jean de Luz to throw his bridge over the Adour—Is prevented by bad weather and returns to the Gave of Mauleon—Passage of the Adour by sir John Hope—Difficulty of the operation—The flotilla passes the bar and enters the river—The French sally from Bayonne but are repulsed and the stupendous bridge is cast—Citadel invested after a severe action—Lord Wellington passes the Gave of Oleron and invests Navarrens—Soult concentrates his army at Orthes—Beresford passes the Gave de Pau near Pereyhorade—Battle of Orthes—Soult changes his line of operations—Combat of Aire—Observations 536

CHAP. III.

Soult's perilous situation—He falls back to Tarbes—Napoleon sends him a plan of operations— His reply and views stated—Lord Wellington's embarrassments —Soult's proclamation—Observations upon it—Lord Wellington calls up Freyre's Gallicians and detaches Beresford against Bordeaux—The mayor of that city revolts from Napoleon—Beresford enters Bordeaux and is followed by the duke of Angoulême—Fears of a reaction—The mayor issues a false proclamation—Lord Wellington expresses his indignation—Rebukes the duke of Angoulême—Recalls Beresford but leaves lord Dalhousie with the seventh division and some cavalry—Decaen commences the organization of the army of the Gironde—Admiral Penrose enters the Garonne—Remarkable exploit of the commissary Ogilvie—Lord Dalhousie passes the Garonne and the Dordogne and defeats L'Huillier at Etauliers—Admiral Penrose destroys the French flotilla—The French set fire to their ships of war—The British seamen and marines land and destroy all the French batteries from Blaye to the mouth of the Garonne 580

TABLE OF CONTENTS.

CHAP. IV.

Wellington's and Soult's situations and forces described—Folly of the English ministers—Freyre's Gallicians and Ponsonby's heavy cavalry join lord Welton—He orders Giron's Andalusians and Del Parque's army to enter France—Soult suddenly takes the offensive—Combats of cavalry—Partizan expedition of Captain Dania—Wellington menaces the peasantry with fire and sword if they take up arms—Soult retires—Lord Wellington advances—Combat of Vic Bigorre—Death and character of colonel Henry Sturgeon—Daring exploit of captain William Light*—Combat of Tarbes—Soult retreats by forced marches to Toulouse—Wellington follows more slowly—Cavalry combat at St. Gaudens —The allies arrive in front of Toulouse—Reflections 603

CHAP. V.

Views of the commanders on each side—Wellington designs to throw a bridge over the Garonne at Portet above Toulouse, but below the confluence of the Arriege and Garonne—The river is found too wide for the pontoons—He changes his design—Cavalry action at St. Martyn de Touch—General Hill passes the Garonne at Pensaguel above the confluence of the Arriege— Marches upon Cintegabelle—Crosses the Arriege—Finds the country too deep for his artillery and returns to Pensaguel—Recrosses the Garonne—Soult fortifies Toulouse and the Mont Rave—Lord Wellington sends his pontoons down the Garonne—Passes that river at Grenade fifteen miles below Toulouse with twenty thousand men—The river floods and his bridge is taken up—The waters subside—The bridge is again laid—The Spaniards pass—Lord Wellington advances up the right bank to Fenouilhet—Combat of cavalry—The eighteenth hussars win the bridge of Croix d'Orade—Lord Wellington resolves to attack Soult on the 9th of April—Orders the pontoons to be taken up and relaid higher up the Garonne at Seilth in the night of the 8th—Time is lost in the execution and the attack is deferred—The light division cross at Seilth on the morning of the 10th—Battle of Toulouse . . . 624

CHAP. VI.

General observations and reflections 657

LIST OF APPENDIX.

No. I.
Lord William Bentinck's correspondence with sir Edward Pellew and lord Wellington about Sicily 691

No. II.
General Nugent's and Mr. King's correspondence with lord William Bentinck about Italy 693

No. III.
Extracts from the correspondence of sir H. Wellesley, Mr. Vaughan, and Mr. Stuart upon Spanish and Portuguese affairs 699

* Since colonel and surveyor-general of South Australia.

TABLE OF CONTENTS.

No. IV.

Justificatory pieces relating to the combats of Maya and Roncesvalles . 701

No. V.

Ditto   ditto   of Ordal 703

No. VI.

Official States of the allied army in Catalonia 704

No. VII.

Ditto   of the Anglo-Portuguese at different epochs   .   .   . 705

No. VIII.

Ditto   of the French armies at different epochs   707

No. IX.

Extract from lord Wellington's order of movements for the battle of Toulouse
709

No. X.

Note and morning state of the Anglo-Portuguese on the 10th of April, 1814   710

PLATES.

No. 1. Explanatory of the Catalonian Operations and plan of Position at Cape Salud.

2. Explanatory of Soult's Operations to relieve Pampeluna.

3. Combats of Maya and Roncesvalles.

4. Explanatory Sketch of the Assault of St. Sebastian.

5. Explanatory Sketch of Soult's and lord Wellington's Passage of the Bidassoa.

6. Explanatory Sketch of the Battle of the Nivelle.

7. Explanatory Sketch of the Operations round Bayonne, and of the Battle.

8. Explanatory Sketch of the Battle of the Nive, and Battle of St. Pierre.

9. Explanatory Sketch of the Battle of Orthes, and the Retreat of Soult to Aire.

10. Explanatory Sketch of the Operations against Tarbes, and the Battle of Toulouse.

To follow Page 689.

NOTICE.

T‍HIS volume was nearly printed when my attention was called to a passage in an article upon the duke of Wellington's despatches, published in the last number of the " British and Foreign Quarterly Review."

After describing colonel Gurwood's proceedings to procure the publication of the despatches the reviewer says,

" *We here distinctly state*, that no other person ever had access to *any* documents of the duke, by his grace's permission, for any historical or other purpose, and that all inferential pretensions to such privilege are not founded in fact."

This assertion, which if not wholly directed against my history certainly includes it with others, *I distinctly state to be untrue.*

For firstly, the duke of Wellington gave me access to the original morning states of his army for the use of my history ; he permitted me to take them into my possession, and I still have possession of them.

Secondly. The duke of Wellington voluntarily directed me to apply to sir George Murray for the " *orders of movements.*" That is to say the orders of battle issued by him to the different generals previous to every great action. Sir George Murray thought proper, as the reader will see in the justificatory pieces of this volume, to deny all knowledge of these " *orders of movements.*" I have since obtained some of them from others, but the permission to get them all was given to me at Strathfieldsaye, in the presence of lord Fitzroy Somerset, who was at the same time directed to give me the morning states and he did do so. These were documents of no ordinary importance for a history of the war.

Thirdly. Lord Fitzroy Somerset, with the consent of the duke of Wellington, put into my hands king Joseph's portfolio, taken at Vittoria and containing that monarch's correspondence with the emperor, with the French minister of war, and with the marshals and generals who at different periods were employed in the

Peninsula. These also were documents of no slight importance for a history of the war, and they are still in my possession.

When I first resolved to write this History, I applied verbally to the duke of Wellington to give me papers in aid of my undertaking. His answer in substance was, that he had arranged all his own papers with a view to publication himself—that he had not decided in what form they should be given to the world, or when, probably not during his lifetime, but he thought his plan would be to "*write a plain didactic history*" to be published after his death—that he was resolved never to publish anything unless he could tell the whole truth, but at that time he could not tell the whole truth without wounding the feelings of many worthy men, without doing mischief: adding in a laughing way "*I should do as much mischief as Buonaparte.*" Then expatiating upon the subject he related to me many anecdotes illustrative of this observation, shewing errors committed by generals and others acting with him, or under him, especially at Waterloo; errors so materially affecting his operations that he could not do justice to himself if he suppressed them, and yet by giving them publicity he would ungraciously affect the fame of many worthy men whose only fault was dulness.

For these reasons he would not, he said, give me his own private papers, but he gave me the documents I have already noticed, and told me he would then, and always, answer any questions as to facts which I might in the course of my work think necessary to put. And he has fulfilled that promise rigidly, for I did then put many questions to him verbally and took notes of his answers, and many of the facts in my History which have been most cavilled at and denied by my critics have been related by me solely upon his authority. Moreover I have since at various times sent to the duke a number of questions in writing, and always they have been fully and carefully answered without delay, though often put when his mind must have been harassed and his attention deeply occupied by momentous affairs.

But though the duke of Wellington denied me access to his own peculiar documents, the greatest part of those documents existed in duplicate; they were in other persons' hands, and in two instances were voluntarily transferred with other interesting papers to mine. Of this truth the reader may easily satisfy himself by referring to my five first volumes, some of which were published years before colonel Gurwood's compilation appeared. He will find in those volumes frequent allusions to the substance of the duke's private communications with the governments he served; and in the Appendix a number of his letters, printed precisely as they have since been given by colonel Gurwood. I could have greatly augmented the number if I had been disposed so to swell my work. Another proof will be found in the Justificatory Pieces of this volume, where I have restored the whole reading of a remarkable letter of the duke's which has been garbled in colonel Gurwood's compilation, and this not from any unworthy desire to promulgate what the duke of Wellington desired to suppress, but that having long before attributed, on the strength of that passage, certain strong opinions to his grace, I was bound in defence of my own probity as an historian to reproduce my authority.

W. F. P. NAPIER.

March 28*th*, 1840.

HISTORY

PENINSULAR WAR.

BOOK XXI.

CHAPTER I.

THE fate of Spain was decided at Vittoria, but on the fields of Lutzen and Bautzen Napoleon's genius restored the general balance, and the negociations which followed those victories affected the war in the Peninsula.

Lord Wellington's first intention was to reduce Pampeluna by force, and the sudden fall of the Pancorbo forts, which opened the great Madrid road was a favourable event; but Portugal being relinquished as a place of arms, a new base of operations was required, lest a change of fortune should force the allies to return to that country when all the great military establishments were broken up, when the opposition of the native government to British influence was become rancorous, and the public sentiment quite averse to English supremacy. The Western Pyrenees, in conjunction with the ocean, offered such a base, yet the harbours were few, and the English general desired to secure a convenient one, near the new positions of the army; wherefore to reduce San Sebastian was of more immediate importance than to reduce Pampeluna; and it was essential to effect this during the fine season because the coast was iron-bound and very dangerous in winter.

Pampeluna was strong. A regular attack required three weeks for the bringing up of ordnance and stores, five or six weeks more for the attack, and from fifteen to twenty thousand of the best men, because British soldiers were wanted for the assault; but an investment could be maintained by fewer and inferior troops, Spaniards and Portuguese, and the enemy's magazines were likely to fail under blockade sooner than his ramparts would crumble under fire. Moreover on the eastern coast misfortune and disgrace had befallen the English arms. Sir John Murray had failed at Taragona. He had lost the honoured battering-train intrusted to his charge, and his artillery equipage was supposed to be ruined. The French fortresses in Catalonia and Valencia were numerous, the Anglo-Sicilian army could neither undertake an important siege, nor seriously menace the enemy without obtaining some strong place as a base. Suchet was therefore free to march on Zaragoza, and uniting with Clauzel and Paris, to operate with a powerful mass against the right flank of the allies. For these reasons Wellington finally concluded to blockade Pampeluna and besiege San Sebastian, and the troops, as they returned from the pursuit of Clauzel, marched to form a covering army in the mountains. The peasantry of the vicinity were then employed on the works of the blockade which was ultimately intrusted to O'Donnel's Andalusian reserve.

July.

Confidently did the English general expect the

immediate fall of San Sebastian, and he was intent
to have it before the negociations for the armistice
in Germany should terminate; but mighty pains
and difficulties awaited him, and ere these can be
treated of, the progress of the war in other parts,
during his victorious march from Portugal to the
Pyrenees, must be treated of.

CONTINUATION OF THE OPERATIONS ON THE EASTERN COAST.

It will be remembered that the duke Del Parque _{Vol. V. p. 512.} was to move from the Sierra Morena, by Almanza, to join Elio, whose army had been reinforced from Minorca; the united troops were then to act against Suchet, on the Xucar, while sir John Murray sailed to attack Taragona. Del Parque received his orders the 24th of April, he had long known of the project and the march was one of twelve days, yet he did not reach his destination until the end of May. This delay resulted, partly from the bad state of his army, partly from the usual procrastination of Spaniards, partly from the conduct of Elio, whose proceedings, though probably springing from a dislike to serve under Del Parque, created doubts of his own fidelity.

It has been already shewn, how, contrary to his agreement with Murray, Elio withdrew his cavalry _{Vol. V. p. 460.} when Mijares was at Yecla, whence sprung that general's misfortune; how he placed the regiment of Velez Malaga in Villeña, a helpless prey for Suchet; how he left the Anglo-Sicilian army to fight the battle of Castalla unaided. He now persuaded Del Parque to move towards Utiel instead of Almanza, and to send a detachment under Mijares to Requena, thereby threatening

Suchet's right, but exposing the Spanish army to a
sudden blow, and disobeying his instructions which
prescribed a march by Almanza.

This false movement Elio represented as Del
Parque's own, but the latter, when Murray remonstrated, quickly approached Castalla by Jumilla,
declaring his earnest desire to obey Wellington's
orders. The divergence of his former march had,
however, already placed him in danger; his left
flank was so exposed, while coming by Jumilla,
that Murray postponed his own embarkation to
concert with Elio a combined operation, from Biar
and Sax, against Fuente de la Higuera where
Suchet's troops were lying in wait. Previous to
this epoch Elio had earnestly urged the English
general, to disregard Del Parque altogether and
embark at once for Taragona, undertaking himself
to secure the junction with his fellow-commander.
And now, after agreeing to cooperate with Murray
he secretly withdrew his cavalry from Sax, sent
Whittingham in a false direction, placed Roche
without support at Alcoy, retired himself to the
city of Murcia, and at the same time one of his
regiments quartered at Alicant fired upon a British
guard. Roche was attacked and lost eighty men, and
Del Parque's flank was menaced from Fuente de la
Higuera, but the British cavalry, assembling at
Biar, secured his communication with Murray on
the 25th, and the 27th the Anglo-Sicilians broke
up from their quarters to embark at Alicant.

The French were now very strong. Suchet unmolested for forty days after the battle of Castalla,
had improved his defensive works, chased the
bands from his rear, called up his reinforcements,
rehorsed his cavalry and artillery, and prepared

for new operations, without losing the advantage
of foraging the fertile districts immediately in front
of the Xucar. On the other hand lord William
Bentinck, alarmed by intelligence of an intended
descent upon Sicily, had recalled more British
troops; and as Whittingham's cavalry, and Roche's
division, were left at Alicant, the force actually
embarked to attack Taragona, including a fresh
English regiment from Carthagena, scarcely exceeded fourteen thousand present under arms. Of Appendix,
No. 6.
these, less than eight thousand were British or
German, and the horsemen were only seven hundred. Yet the armament was formidable, for the
battering train was complete and powerful, the materials for gabions and fascines previously collected at
Ivica, and the naval squadron, under admiral Hallowel, consisted of several line-of-battle ships, frigates,
bomb-vessels and gun-boats, besides the transports.
There was however no cordiality between general
Clinton and Murray, nor between the latter and his
quarter-master-general Donkin, nor between Donkin
and the admiral; subordinate officers also, in both
services, adopting false notions, some from vanity,
some from hearsay, added to the uneasy feeling
which prevailed amongst the chiefs. Neither
admiral nor general seem to have had sanguine
hopes of success even at the moment of embarkation, and there was in no quarter a clear understanding of lord Wellington's able plan for the
operations.

While Del Parque's army was yet in march,
Suchet, if he had no secret understanding with Elio
or any of his officers, must have been doubtful of
the allies' intentions, although the strength of the
battering-train at Alicant indicated some siege of

importance. He however recalled Pannetier's brigade from the frontier of Aragon, and placed it on
the road to Tortoza; and at the same time, knowing Clauzel was then warring down the partidas
in Navarre, he judged Aragon safe, and drew Severoli's Italian brigade from thence, leaving only
the garrisons, and a few thousand men under
general Paris as a reserve at Zaragoza: and this
was the reason the army of Aragon did not co-
operate to crush Mina after his defeat by Clauzel
in the valley of Roncal. Decaen also sent some
reinforcements, wherefore, after completing his garrisons, Suchet could furnish the drafts required by
Napoleon, and yet bring twenty thousand men into
the field. He was however very unquiet, and notwithstanding Clauzel's operations, in fear for his
troops in Aragon, where Paris had been attacked
by Goyan, even in Zaragoza; moreover now, for
the first time since its subjugation, an unfriendly
feeling was perceptible in Valencia.

On the 31st of May Murray sailed from Alicant.
Suchet immediately ordered Pannetier's brigade to
close towards Tortoza, but kept his own positions
in front of Valencia until the fleet was seen to pass
the Grāo with a fair wind. Then feeling assured
the expedition aimed at Catalonia, he prepared to
aid that principality; but the column of succour
being drawn principally from the camp of Xativa,
forty miles from Valencia, he could not quit the
latter before the 7th of June. He took with him
nine thousand men of all arms, leaving Harispe on
the Xucar, with seven thousand infantry and cavalry, exclusive of Severoli's troops which were
in full march from Teruel. Meanwhile sir John
Murray's armament, having very favourable weather,

anchored on the evening of the 2d in the bay of Taragona, whence five ships of war under captain Adam, and two battalions of infantry with some guns under colonel Prevot, were detached to attack San Felippe de Balaguer.

The strength and value of this fort arose from its peculiar position. The works, garrisoned by a hundred men, were only sixty feet square, but the site was a steep isolated rock, standing in the very gorge of a pass, and blocking the only carriage-way from Tortoza to Taragona. The mountains on either hand, although commanding the fort, were nearly inaccessible themselves, and great labour was required to form the batteries.

Prevot, landing on the 3d, was joined by a Spanish brigade of Copons' army, and in concert with the navy immediately commenced operations by placing two six-pounders on the heights south of the pass, from whence at six or seven hundred yards distance they threw shrapnel-shells ; but this projectile is, when used with guns of small calibre, insignificant save as a round shot.

On the 4th two twelve-pounders, and a howitzer, being brought to the same point by the sailors, opened their fire, and at night the seamen with extraordinary exertions dragged up five twenty-four-pounders and their stores. The troops then constructed one battery, for two howitzers, on the slope of the grand ridge to the northward of the pass, and a second, for four heavy guns, on the rock where the fort stood at a distance of one hundred and fifty yards. To form these batteries earth was carried from below, and every thing else, even water, brought from the ships, though the landing place was more than a mile and a half off.

Hence, as time was valuable, favourable terms were offered to the garrison, but the offer was refused. The 5th the fire was continued, but with slight success, the howitzer battery on the great ridge was relinquished, and at night a very violent storm retarded the construction of the breaching batteries. Previous to this colonel Prevot had warned Murray, that his means were insufficient, and a second Spanish brigade was sent to him. Yet the breaching batteries were still incomplete on the 6th, so severe was the labour of carrying up the guns, and out of three, already mounted, one was disabled by a shot from the fort.

Suchet, who was making forced marches to Tortoza, had ordered the governor of that place to succour San Felippe. He tried, and would undoubtedly have succeeded, if captain Peyton, of the Thames frigate, had not previously obtained from admiral Hallowel two eight-inch mortars, which, being placed just under the fort and worked by Mr. James of the marine artillery, commencing at daybreak on the 7th, soon exploded a small magazine in the fort, whereupon the garrison surrendered. The besiegers who had lost about fifty men and officers then occupied the place, and meanwhile sir John Murray had commenced the

SECOND SIEGE OF TARAGONA.

Although the fleet cast anchor in the bay on the evening of the 2d, the surf prevented the disembarkation of the troops until the next day. The rampart of the lower town had been destroyed by Suchet, but Fort Royal remained and though in bad condition served, together with the ruins of the San Carlos bastion, to cover the western front which was the weakest line of defence. The governor Bertoletti, an Italian, was supposed by Murray to be disaffected, but he proved himself a loyal and energetic officer; and his garrison sixteen hundred strong, five hundred being privateer seamen and Franco-Spaniards, served him well.

The Olivo, and Loretto heights were occupied the first day by Clinton's and Whittingham's divisions, the other troops remaining on the low ground about the Francoli river; the town was then bombarded during the night by the navy, but the fire was sharply returned and the flotilla suffered the most. The next day two batteries were commenced six hundred yards from San Carlos, and nine hundred yards from Fort Royal. They opened the 6th, but being too distant to produce much effect, a third was commenced six hundred yards from Fort Royal. The 8th a practicable breach was made in that outwork, yet the assault was deferred, and some pieces removed to play from the Olivo; whereupon the besieged, finding the fire slacken, repaired the breach at Fort Royal and increased the defences. The subsequent proceedings cannot be understood without an accurate knowledge of the relative positions of the French and allied armies.

Taragona though situated on one of a cluster of heights, which terminate a range descending from the northward to the sea, is, with the exception of that range, surrounded by an open country called Plan, No. 1. the *Campo de Taragona*, which is again environed by very rugged mountains, through which the several roads descend into the plain.

Westward there were only two carriage ways, one direct, by the Col de Balaguer to Taragona; the other circuitous, leading by Mora, Falcet, Momblanch and Reus. The first was blocked by the taking of San Felippe ; the second, although used by Suchet for his convoys during the French siege of Taragona, was now in bad order, and at best only available for small mountain-guns.

Northward there was a carriage way, leading from Lerida, which united with that from Falcet at Momblanch.

Eastward there was the royal causeway, coming from Barcelona, through Villa Franca, Arbos, Vendrills, and Torredembarra; this road after passing Villa Franca sends off two branches to the right, one passing through the Col de Cristina, the other through Masarbones and Col de Leibra, leading upon Braffin and Valls. It was by the latter branch that M'Donald passed to Reus in 1810 ; he had, however, no guns or carriages, and his whole army laboured to make the way practicable.

Between these various roads the mountains were too rugged to permit any direct cross communications; and troops, coming from different sides, could only unite in the Campo de Taragona now occupied by the allies. Wherefore, as Murray had, including sergeants, above fifteen thousand fighting men, and Copons, reinforced with two regiments sent by sea from Coruña, was at Reus with six thousand regulars besides the irregular division of Manso, twenty-five thousand combatants were in possession of the French point of junction.

The Catalans, after Lacy's departure, had, with the aid of captain Adam's ship, destroyed two small forts at Perillo and Ampolla, and Eroles had blockaded San Felippe de Balaguer for thirty-six days, but it was then succoured by Maurice Mathieu ; and the success at Perillo was more than

balanced by a check which Sarzfield received on
the 3d of April from some of Pannetier's troops.
The partida warfare had, however, been more active
in Upper Catalonia, and Copons claimed two considerable victories, one gained by himself on the 17th
of May, at La Bispal near the Col de Cristina, where
he boasted to have beaten six thousand French with
half their numbers, destroying six hundred, as they
returned from succouring San Felippe de Balaguer.
In the other, won by colonel Lander near Olot
on the 7th of May, it was said twelve hundred
of Lamarque's men fell.   These exploits are by
French writers called skirmishes, and the following
description of the Catalan army, given to sir John
Murray by Cabanes, the chief of Copons' staff,
renders the French version the most credible.

" *We do not*," said that officer, " *exceed nine or
ten thousand men, extended on different points of a
line running from the neigbourhood of Reus along
the high mountains to the vicinity of Olot.   The
soldiers are brave, but without discipline, without
subordination, without clothing, without artillery,
without ammunition, without magazines, without
money, and without means of transport*"!

Copons himself, when he came down to the
Campo, very frankly told Murray, that as his
troops could only fight in position, he would not join
in any operation which endangered his retreat into
the high mountains.   However, with the exception
of twelve hundred men left at Vich under Eroles,
all his forces, the best perhaps in Spain, were now
at Reus and the Col de Balaguer, ready to intercept the communications of the different French
corps, and to harass their marches if they should
descend into the Campo.   Murray could also cal-

culate upon seven or eight hundred seamen and marines to aid him in pushing on the works of the siege, or in a battle near the shore; and he expected three thousand additional troops from Sicily. Sir Edward Pellew, commanding the great Mediterranean fleet, had promised to divert the attention of the French troops by a descent eastward of Barcelona, and the armies of Del Parque and Elio were to make a like diversion westward of Tortoza. Finally, a general rising of the Somatenes might have been effected, and those mountaineers were all at Murray's disposal, to procure intelligence, to give timely notice of the enemy's approach, or to impede his march by breaking up the roads.

On the French side there was greater but more scattered power. Suchet had marched with nine thousand men from Valencia, and what with Pannetier's brigade and some spare troops from Tortoza, eleven or twelve thousand men with artillery, might have come to the succour of Taragona from that side, if the sudden fall of San Felippe de Balaguer had not barred the only carriage way on the westward. A movement by Mora, Falcet, and Momblanch, remained open, yet it would have been tedious, and the disposable troops at Lerida were few. To the eastward therefore the garrison looked for the first succour. Maurice Mathieu, reinforced with a brigade from Upper Catalonia, could bring seven thousand men with artillery from Barcelona, and Decaen could move from the Ampurdam with an equal number, hence twenty-five thousand men might finally bear upon the allied army.

But Suchet, measuring from the Xucar, had more than one hundred and sixty miles to march;

Maurice Mathieu was to collect his forces from
various places and march seventy miles after
Murray had disembarked; nor could he stir at all,
until Taragona was actually besieged, lest the allies
should reimbark and attack Barcelona. Decaen
had in like manner to look to the security of the
Ampurdam, and he was one hundred and thirty
miles distant. Wherefore, however active the
French generals might be, the English general
could calculate upon ten days' clear operations,
after investment, before even the heads of the enemy's columns, coming from different quarters, could
issue from the hills bordering the Campo.

Some expectation also he might have, that Suchet would endeavour to cripple Del Parque,
before he marched to the succour of Taragona;
and it was in his favour, that eastward and westward, the royal causeway was in places exposed
to the fire of the naval squadron. The experience
of captain Codrington during the first siege of
Taragona, had proved indeed, that an army could
not be stopped by this fire, yet it was an impediment not to be left out of the calculation. Thus,
the advantage of a central position, the possession
of the enemy's point of junction, the initial movement, the good will of the people, and the aid of
powerful flank diversions, belonged to Murray;
superior numbers and a better army to the French,
since the allies, brave, and formidable to fight in
a position, were not well constituted for general
operations.

Taragona, if the resources for an internal defence
be disregarded, was a weak place. A simple
revetment three feet and a half thick, without

ditch or counterscarp, covered it on the west; the
two outworks of Fort Royal and San Carlos, slight
obstacles at best, were not armed, nor even repaired until after the investment, and the garrison,
too weak for the extent of rampart, was oppressed
with labour.   Here then, time being precious to
both sides, ordinary rules should have been set
Appendix, aside and daring operations adopted.   Lord Wel-
No. 6. lington had judged ten thousand men sufficient to
take Taragona.   Murray brought seventeen thousand, of which fourteen thousand were effective.
To do this he had, he said, so reduced his equipments, stores, and means of land transport, that
his army could not move from the shipping; he
was yet so unready for the siege, that Fort Royal
was not stormed on the 8th, because the engineer
was unprepared to profit from a successful assault.

This excuse, founded on the scarcity of stores, was
not however borne out by facts.   The equipments
left behind, were only draft animals and commissariat
field-stores; the thing wanting was vigour in the
general, and this was made manifest in various
ways. Copons, like all regular Spanish officers, was
averse to calling out the Somatenes, and Murray
did not press the matter.   Suchet took San Felippe
de Balaguer by escalade.   Murray attacked in form,
and without sufficient means; for if captain Peyton
had not brought up the mortars, which was an after-
thought, extraneous to the general's arrangements,
the fort could not have been reduced before succour
arrived from Tortoza.   Indeed the surrender was
scarcely creditable to the French commandant, for
his works were uninjured, and only a small part of
his powder destroyed.   It is also said, I believe

truly, that one of the officers employed to regulate the
capitulation had in his pocket, an order from Murray
to raise the siege and embark, spiking the guns!
At Taragona, the troops on the low ground, did
not approach so near, by three hundred yards, as
they might have done; and the outworks should have
been stormed at once, as Wellington stormed Fort
Francisco at the siege of Ciudad Rodrigo. Francisco
was a good outwork and complete. The outworks
of Taragona were incomplete, ill-flanked, without
palisades or casements, and their fall would have
enabled the besiegers to form a parallel against the
body of the place as Suchet had done in the former
siege; a few hours' firing would then have brought
down the wall and a general assault might have
been delivered. The French had stormed a similar
breach in that front, although defended by eight
thousand Spanish troops, and the allies opposed by
only sixteen hundred French and Italians, soldiers
and seamen, were in some measure bound by honour
to follow that example, since colonel Skerrett, at the
former siege, refused to commit twelve hundred
British troops in the place, on the special ground
that it was indefensible, though so strongly garrisoned. Murray's troops were brave, they had
been acting together for nearly a year; and after
the fight at Castalla had become so eager, that an
Italian regiment, which at Alicant, was ready to go
over bodily to the enemy, now volunteered to lead
the assault on Fort Royal. This confidence was
not shared by their general. Even at the moment
of victory, he had resolved, if Suchet advanced a
second time, to relinquish the position of Castalla
and retire to Alicant!

It is clear, that, up to the 8th, sir John Murray's

proceedings were ill-judged, and his after operations, were more injudicious.

As early as the 5th, false reports had made Suchet reach Tortoza, and had put two thousand French in movement from Lerida. Murray then openly avowed his alarm and his regret at having left Alicant; yet he proceeded to construct two heavy counter-batteries near the Olivo, sent a detachment to Valls in observation of the Lerida road, and desired Manso to watch that of Barcelona.

On the 9th his emissaries said the French were coming from the east, and from the west; and would, when united, exceed twenty thousand. Murray immediately sought an interview with the admiral, declaring his intention to raise the siege; his views were changed during the conference but he was discontented; and the two commanders were now evidently at variance, for Hallowel refused. to join in a summons to the governor, and his flotilla again bombarded the place.

The 10th the spies in Barcelona gave notice that eight or ten thousand French with fourteen guns, would march from that city the next day. Copons immediately joined Manso, and Murray, as if he now disdained his enemy, continued to disembark stores, landed several mortars, armed the batteries at the Olivo, and on the 11th opened their fire, in concert with that from the ships of war.

This was the first serious attack, and the English general, professing a wish to fight the column coming from Barcelona, sent the cavalry under Lord Frederick Bentinck to Altafalla, and in person sought a position of battle to the eastward. He left orders to storm the outworks that night, but returned, before the hour appointed, extremely disturbed by intelligence that Maurice Mathieu was at Villa Franca with eight thousand combatants, and Suchet closing upon the Col de Balaguer. The infirmity of his mind was now apparent to the whole army. At eight o'clock he repeated his order to assault the outworks; at ten o'clock the storming party was in the dry bed of the Francoli, awaiting the signal, when a countermand arrived the siege was then to be raised and the guns removed immediately from the Olivo; the commander of the artillery remonstrated, and the general then promised to hold the batteries until the next night. Meanwhile the detachment at Valls and the cavalry at Altafalla were called in, without any notice to general Copons, though he depended on their support.

The parc and all the heavy guns of the batteries on the low grounds were removed to the beach for embarkation on the morning of the 12th, and at twelve o'clock lord Frederick Bentinck arrived from Altafalla with the cavalry. It is said he was ordered to shoot his horses, but refused to obey, and moved towards the Col de Balaguer. The detachment from Valls arrived next, and the infantry marched to Cape Salou to embark, but the horsemen followed lord Frederick, and were themselves followed by fourteen pieces of artillery; each body moved independently, and all was confused, incoherent, afflicting, and dishonorable to the British arms.

While the seamen were embarking the guns, the quarter-master-general came down to the beach, with orders to abandon that business and collect boats for the reception of troops, the enemy being supposed close at hand; and notwithstanding Murray's promise to hold the Olivo until night-fall, fresh directions were given to spike the guns there,

and burn the carriages.   Then loud murmurs arose
on every side, and from both services; army and
navy were alike indignant, and so excited, that it is
said personal insult was offered to the general.
Three staff-officers repaired in a body to Murray's
quarters, to offer plans and opinions, and the admiral who it would appear did not object to raising
the siege but to the manner of doing it, would not
suffer the seamen to discontinue the embarkation of
artillery.   He even urged an attack upon the column
coming from Barcelona, and opposed the order to
spike the guns at the Olivo, offering to be responsible for carrying all clear off during the night.

Thus pressed, Murray again wavered.   Denying
that he had ordered the battering pieces to be
spiked, he sent counter-orders, and directed a
part of Clinton's troops to advance towards the
Gaya river.   Yet a few hours afterwards he reverted
to his former resolution, and peremptorily renewed
the order for the artillery to spike the guns on the
Olivo, and burn the carriages.   Nor was even this
unhappy action performed without confusion.   The
different orders received by Clinton in the course of
the day had indicated the extraordinary vacillation
of the commander-in-chief, and Clinton himself,
forgetful of his own arrangements, with an obso-
lete courtesy took off his hat to salute an enemy's
battery which had fired upon him; but this waving
of his hat from that particular spot was also the con-
ventional signal for the artillery to spike the guns, and
they were thus spiked prematurely.   The troops were
however all embarked in the night of the 12th, and
many of the stores and horses were shipped on the 13th
without the slightest interruption from the enemy;
but eighteen or nineteen battering pieces, whose car-

riages had been burnt, were, with all the platforms,
fascines, gabions, and small ammunition, in view of
the fleet and army, triumphantly carried into the
fortress. Sir J. Murray meanwhile seemingly un-
affected by this misfortune, shipped himself on the
evening of the 12th and took his usual repose in bed.

1813.
June.

Admiral
Hallo-
wel's evi-
dence on
the trial.

While the English general was thus precipitately
abandoning the siege, the French generals, unable
to surmount the obstacles opposed to their junction,
unable even to communicate by their emissaries,
were despairing of the safety of Taragona. Suchet
did not reach Tortoza before the 10th, but a detachment from the garrison, had on the 8th attempted to succour San Felipe, and nearly captured the naval captain Adam, colonel Prevot, and
other officers, who were examining the country.
On the other side Maurice Mathieu, having gathered
troops from various places, reached Villa Franca
early on the 10th, and deceiving even his own people as to his numbers, gave out that Decaen, who he
really expected, was close behind with a powerful
force. To give effect to this policy, he drove Copons
from Arbos on the 11th, and his scouting parties
entered Vendrills, as if he was resolved singly to
attack Murray. Sir Edward Pellew had however
landed his marines at Rosas, which arrested
Decaen's march; and Maurice Mathieu alarmed at
the cessation of fire about Taragona, knowing nothing of Suchet's movements, and too weak to fight
the allies alone, fell back in the night of the 12th
to the Llobregat, his main body never having
passed Villa Franca

Suchet's operations to the westward were even
less decisive. His advanced guard under Panettier,
reached Perillo the 10th. The 11th not hearing

from his spies, he caused Panettier to pass by his left over the mountains through Valdillos to some heights which terminate abruptly on the Campo, above Monroig. The 12th that officer reached the extreme verge of the hills, being then about twenty-five miles from Taragona. His patroles descending into the plains, met with lord Frederick Bentinck's troopers reported that Murray's whole army was at hand, wherefore he would not enter the Campo, but at night he kindled large fires to encourage the garrison of Taragona. These signals were however unobserved, the country people had disappeared, no intelligence could be procured, and Suchet could not follow him with a large force into those wild desert hills, where there was no water. Thus on both sides of Taragona the succouring armies were quite baffled at the moment chosen by Murray for flight.

Suchet now received alarming intelligence from Valencia, yet still anxious for Taragona, he pushed, on the 14th, along the coast-road towards San Felippe de Balaguer, thinking to find Prevôt's division alone ; but the head of his column was suddenly cannonaded by the Thames frigate, and he was wonderfully surprised to see the whole British fleet anchored off San Felippe, and disembarking troops. Murray's operations were indeed as irregular as those of a partizan, yet without partizan vigour. He had heard in the night of the 12th, from colonel Prevôt, of Panettier's march to Monroig, and to protect the cavalry and guns under lord Frederick Bentinck, sent Mackenzie's division by sea to Balaguer on the 13th, following with the whole army on the 14th. Mackenzie drove back the French posts on both sides of the pass, the embarkation of the cavalry and artillery then commenced, and Suchet, still uncertain if Taragona had fallen, moved towards Valdillos to bring off Panettier.

At this precise period, Murray heard that Maurice Mathieu's column, which he always erroneously supposed to be under Decaen, had retired to the Llobregat, that Copons was again at Reus, and that Taragona had not been reinforced. Elated by this information, he revolved various projects in his mind, at one time thinking to fall upon Suchet, at another to cut off Panettier, now resolving to march upon Cambrills, and even to menace Taragona again by land ; then he was for sending a detachment by sea to surprise the latter, but finally he disembarked his whole force on the 15th, and being ignorant of Suchet's last movement decided to strike at Panettier. In this view, he detached See Plan, No. 1. Mackenzie, by a rugged valley leading from the eastward to Valdillos, and that officer reached it on the 16th, but Suchet had already carried off Panettier's brigade, and the next day the British detachment was recalled by Murray, who now only thought of re-embarking.

This determination was caused by a fresh alarm from the eastward, for Maurice Mathieu, whose whole proceedings evinced both skill and vigour, hearing that the siege of Taragona was raised, and the allies re-landed at the Col de Balaguer, retraced his steps and boldly entered Cambrills the 17th. On that day, however, Mackenzie returned, and Murray's whole army was thus concentrated in the pass. Suchet was then behind Perillo, Copons at Reus, having come there at Murray's desire to attack Maurice Mathieu, and the latter would have

suffered, if the English general had been capable of
a vigorous stroke. On the other hand it was fortunate for Mackenzie, that Suchet, too anxious for
Valencia, disregarded his movement upon Valdillos ;
but, taught by the disembarkation of the whole English army that the fate of Taragona, whether for
good or evil, was decided, he had sent an emissary
to Maurice Mathieu on the 16th, and then retired
to Perillo and Amposta. He reached the latter
place the 17th, attentive only to the movement of
the fleet, and meanwhile Maurice Mathieu endeavoured to surprize the Catalans at Reus.

Copons was led into this danger by sir John
Murray, who had desired him to harass Maurice
Mathieu's rear, with a view to a general attack, and
then changed his plan without giving the Spanish
general any notice. However he escaped. The
French moved upon Taragona, and Murray was left
free to embark or to remain at the Col de Balaguer.
He called a council of war, and it was concluded to
re-embark, but at that moment, the great Mediterranean fleet appeared in the offing, and admiral
Hallowel, observing a signal announcing lord
William Bentinck's arrival, answered with more
promptitude than propriety, " we are all delighted."

Sir John Murray's command having thus terminated, the general discontent rendered it impossible
to avoid a public investigation, yet the difficulty of
holding a court in Spain, and some disposition at
home to shield him, caused great delay. He was
at last tried in England. Acquitted of two charges,
on the third he was declared guilty of an error in
judgement, and sentenced to be admonished; but
even that slight mortification was not inflicted.

This decision does not preclude the judgement of

history, nor will it sway that of posterity. The court-martial was assembled twenty months after the event, when the war being happily terminated, men's minds were little disposed to treat past failures with severity. There were two distinct prosecutors, having different views; the proceedings were conducted at a distance from the scene of action, defects of memory could not be remedied by references to localities, and a door was opened for contradiction and doubt upon important points. There was no indication that the members of the court were unanimous in their verdict; they were confined to specific charges, restricted by legal rules of evidence, and deprived of the testimony of all the Spanish officers, who were certainly discontented with Murray's conduct, and whose absence caused the serious charge of abandoning Copons' army to be suppressed. Moreover the warmth of temper displayed by the principal prosecutor, admiral Hallowel, together with his signal on lord William Bentinck's arrival, whereby, to the detriment of discipline, he manifested his contempt for the general with whom he was acting, gave Murray an advantage which he improved skilfully, for he was a man sufficiently acute and prompt when not at the head of an army. He charged the admiral with deceit, factious dealings, and disregard of the service; described him as a man of a passionate overweening, busy disposition, troubled with excess of vanity, meddling with everything, and thinking himself competent to manage both troops and ships.

Nevertheless sir John Murray had signally failed, both as an independent general, and as a lieutenant acting under superior orders. On his trial, blending these different capacities together, with expert sophistry he pleaded his instructions in excuse for his errors as a free commander, and his discretionary power in mitigation of his disobedience as a lieutenant; but his operations were indefensible in both capacities. Lord Wellington's instructions, precise, and founded upon the advantages offered by a command of the sea, prescribed an attack upon Taragona, with a definite object, namely, to deliver Valencia.

" *You tell me*," said he, " *that the line of the Xucar, which covers Valencia, is too strong to force; turn it then by the ocean, assail the rear of the enemy, and he will weaken his strong line to protect his communication; or, he will give you an opportunity to establish a new base of operations behind him.*"

This plan however demanded promptness and energy, and Murray professed neither. The weather was so favourable, that a voyage which might have consumed nine or ten days was performed in two, the Spanish troops punctually effected their junction, the initial operations were secured, Fort Balaguer fell, the French moved from all sides to the succour of Taragona, the line of the Xucar was weakened, the diversion was complete. In the night of the 12th the bulk of Murray's army was again afloat, a few hours would have sufficed to embark the cavalry at the Col de Balaguer, and the whole might have sailed for the city of Valencia, while Suchet's advanced guard was still on the hills above Monroig, and he, still uncertain as to the fate of Taragona, one hundred and fifty miles from the Xucar. In fine Murray had failed to attain the first object pointed out by Wellington's instructions, but the second was within his reach;

instead of grasping it he loitered about the Col de
Balaguer, and gave Suchet, as we shall find, time
to reach Valencia again.

Now whether the letter or the spirit of Wellington's instructions be considered, there was here a
manifest dereliction on the part of Murray. What
was that officer's defence? That no specific period
being named for his return to Valencia, he was
entitled to exercise his discretion! Did he then
as an independent general perform any useful or
brilliant action to justify his delay? No! his tale
was one of loss and dishonour! The improvident
arrangements for the siege of San Felippe de Balaguer, and the unexpected fortune which saved him
from the shame of abandoning his guns there also
have been noted; and it has been shown, that when
the gain of time was the great element of success,
he neither urged Copons to break up the roads, nor
pushed the siege of Taragona with vigour. The
feeble formality of this latter operation has indeed
been imputed to the engineer major Thackary,
yet unjustly so. It was the part of that officer to
form a plan of attack agreeable to the rules of art,
it might be a bold or a cautious plan, and many
persons did think Taragona was treated by him with
too much respect; but it was the part of the commander-in-chief, to decide, if the general scheme
of operations required a deviation from the regular
course. The untrammelled engineer could then
have displayed his genius. Sir John Murray made
no sign. His instructions and his ultimate views
were withheld alike, from his naval colleague, from
his second in command, and from his quartermaster-general; and while the last-named functionary was quite shut out from the confidence of

Defence of
sir J. Murray in Phillipart's Military Calendar.

his commander, the admiral, and many others, both of the army and navy, imagined him to be the secret author of the proceedings which were hourly exciting their indignation. Murray however declared on his trial, that he had rejected general Donkin's advice, an avowal consonant to facts, since that officer urged him to raise the siege on the 9th and had even told him where four hundred draught bullocks were to be had, to transport his heavy artillery. On the 12th he opposed the spiking of the guns, and urged Murray to drag them to Cape Salou, of which place he had given as early as the third day of the siege, a military plan, marking a position, strong in itself, covering several landing places, and capable of being flanked on both sides by the ships of war : it had no drawback save a scarcity of water, yet there were some springs, and the fleet would have supplied the deficiency.

See Plan,
No. 1.

It is true that Donkin, unacquainted with Wellington's instructions, and having at Castalla seen no reason to rely on sir John Murray's military vigour, was averse to the enterprize against Taragona. He thought the allies should have worked Suchet out of Valencia by operating on his right flank. And so Wellington would have thought, if he had only looked at their numbers and not at their quality ; he had even sketched such a plan for Murray, if the attack upon Taragona should be found impracticable. But he knew the Spaniards too well, to like such combinations for an army, two-thirds of which were of that nation, and not even under one head ; an army ill-equipped, and with the exception of Del Parque's troops, unused to active field operations. Wherefore, calculating

Vol. V.
p. 512.

their power with remarkable nicety, he preferred the sea-flank, and the aid of an English fleet.

Here it may be observed, that Napoleon's plan of invasion did not embrace the coast-lines where they could be avoided. It was an obvious disadvantage to give the British navy opportunities of acting against his communications. The French indeed, seized Santona and Santander in the Bay of Biscay, because, these being the only good ports on that coast, the English ships were thus in a manner shut out from the north of Spain. They likewise worked their invasion by the Catalonian and Valencian coast, because the only roads practicable for artillery run along that sea-line; but their general scheme was to hold, with large masses, the interior of the country, and keep their communications aloof from the danger of combined operations by sea and land. The providence of the plan was proved by Suchet's peril on this occasion.

Sir John Murray, when tried, grounded his justification on the following points. 1°· That he did not know with any certainty until the night of the 11th that Suchet was near. 2°· That the fall of Taragona being the principal object, and the drawing of the French from Valencia the accessary, he persisted in the siege, because he expected reinforcements from Sicily, and desired to profit from the accidents of war. 3°· That looking only to the second object, the diversion would have been incomplete, if the siege had been raised sooner, or even relaxed ; hence the landing of guns and stores after he despaired of success. 4°· That he dared not risk a battle to save his battering train, because Wellington would not pardon a defeat. Now had he adopted a vigorous plan, or persisted until the

danger of losing his army was apparent, and then
made a quick return to Valencia, this defence would
have been plausible, though inconclusive.   But
when every order, every movement, every expression, discovered his infirmity of purpose, his plead-
ing can only be regarded as the subtle tale of an
advocate.

The fault was not so much in the raising of the
siege as in the manner of doing it, and in the feebleness of the attack.   For first, however numerous
the chances of war are, fortresses expecting succour
do not surrender without being vigorously assailed.
The arrival of reinforcements from Sicily was too
uncertain for reasonable calculation, and it was
scarcely possible for the governor of Taragona,
while closely invested, to discover that no fresh
stores or guns were being landed ; still less could
he judge so timeously of Murray's final intention
by that fact, as to advertize Suchet that Taragona
was in no danger.   Neither were the spies, if any
were in the allies' camp, more capable of drawing
such conclusions, seeing that sufficient artillery
and stores for the siege were landed the first week.
And the landing of more guns could not have deceived them, when the feeble operations of the
general, and the universal discontent, furnished
surer guides for their reports.

Murray designed to raise the siege as early as
the 9th and only deferred it, after seeing the
admiral, from his natural vacillation.   It was therefore mere casuistry to say, that he first obtained
certain information of Suchet's advance on the
night of the 11th.   On the 8th and 10th through
various channels he knew the French marshal was
in march for Tortoza, and that his advanced guard

menaced the Col de Balaguer.   The approach of
Maurice Mathieu on the other side was also known;
he should therefore have been prepared to raise the
siege without the loss of his guns on the 12th.
Why were they lost at all? They could not be
saved, he said, without risking a battle in a bad
position, and Wellington had declared he would
not pardon a defeat! This was the after-thought of
a sophister, and not warranted by Wellington's instructions, which on that head, referred only to the
duke Del Parque and Elio.

But was it necessary to fight a battle in a bad
position to save the guns? all persons admitted
that they could have been embarked before mid-
day on the 13th.   Panettier was then at Monroig,
Suchet still behind Perillo, Maurice Mathieu
falling back from Villa Franca.   The French on
each side were therefore respectively thirty-six and
thirty-four miles distant on the night of the 12th,
and their point of junction was Reus.   Yet how
form that junction? The road from Villa Franca by
the Col de Cristina was partially broken up by
Copons, the road from Perillo to Reus was always
impracticable for artillery, and from the latter place
to Taragona was six miles of very rugged country.
The allies were in possession of the point of junction, Maurice Mathieu was retiring, not advancing.
And if the French could have marched thirty-four
and thirty-six miles, through the mountains in one
night, and been disposed to attack in the morning
without artillery, they must still have ascertained
the situation of Murray's army; they must have
made arrangements to watch Copons, Manso, and
Prevôt, who would have been on their rear and
flanks; they must have formed an order of battle

and decided upon the mode of attack before they advanced. It is true that their junction at Reus would have forced Murray to suspend his embarkation to fight; but not, as he said, in a bad position, with his back to the beach, where the ships' guns could not aid him, and where he might expect a dangerous surf for days. The naval officers denied the danger from surf at that season of the year; and it was not right to destroy the guns and stores when the enemy was not even in march for Reus. Coolness and consideration would have enabled Murray to see that there was no danger. In fact no emissaries escaped from the town, and the enemy had no spies in the camp, since no communication took place between the French columns until the 17th. On the 15th Suchet knew nothing of the fate of Taragona.

The above reasoning leaves out the possibility of profiting from a central position to fall with superior forces upon one of the French columns. It supposes however that accurate information was possessed by the French generals; that Maurice Mathieu was as strong as he pretended to be, Suchet eager and resolute to form a junction with him. But in truth Suchet knew not what to do after the fall of Fort Balaguer, Maurice Mathieu had less than seven thousand men of all arms, he was not followed by Decaen, and he imagined the allies to have twenty thousand men, exclusive of the Catalans. Besides which the position at Cape Salou was only six miles distant, and Murray might with the aid of the draft bullocks discovered by Donkin, have dragged all his heavy guns there, still maintaining the investment; he might have shipped his battery train, and when the enemy ap-

proached Reus, have marched to the Col de Balaguer, where he could, as he afterwards did, embark
or disembark in the presence of the enemy. The
danger of a flank march, Suchet being at Reus,
could not have deterred him, because he did send
his cavalry and field artillery by that very road on
the 12th, when the French advanced guard was at
Monroig and actually skirmished with lord Frederick Bentinck. Finally he could have embarked
his main body, leaving a small corps with some
cavalry to keep the garrison in check and bring off
his guns. Such a detachment, together with the
heavy guns, would have been afloat in a couple of
hours and on board the ships in four hours; it
could have embarked on the open beach, or, if
fearful of being molested by the garrison, might
have marched to Cape Salou, or to the Col de
Balaguer; and if the guns had thus been lost, the
necessity would have been apparent, and the dishonour lessened. It is clear therefore that there
was no military need to sacrifice the battery pieces.
And those were the guns that shook the bloody
ramparts of Badajos!

Wellington felt their loss keenly, sir John Murray
spoke of them lightly. *" They were of small value, old
iron ! he attached little importance to the sacrifice of
artillery, it was his principle, he had approved of colonel
Adam losing his guns at Biar, and he had also desired
colonel Prevôt, if pressed, to abandon his battering
train before the Fort of Balaguer."* *" Such doctrine
might appear strange to a British army, but it was
the rule with the continental armies and the French
owed much of their successes to the adoption of it."*

Strange indeed! Great commanders have risked
their own lives, and sacrificed their bravest men,

charging desperately in person, to retrieve even a single piece of cannon in a battle. They knew the value of moral force in war, and that of all the various springs and levers on which it depends military honour is the most powerful. No! it was not to the adoption of such a doctrine, that the French owed their great successes. It was to the care with which Napoleon fostered and cherished a contrary feeling. Sir John Murray's argument would have been more pungent, more complete, if he had lost his colours, and pleaded that they were only wooden staves, bearing old pieces of silk!

CHAPTER II.

LORD William Bentinck arrived without troops, for, having removed the queen from Sicily, he feared internal dissension and Napoleon had directed Murat to invade the island with twenty thousand men, the Toulon squadron being to act in concert. Sir Edward Pellew admitted that the latter might easily gain twenty-four hours' start of his fleet, and lord William judged that ten thousand invaders would suffice to conquer. Murat however, opened a secret negociation, and thus, that monarch, Bernadotte, and the emperor Francis endeavoured to destroy a hero connected with them by marriage and to whom they all owed their crowns either by gift or clemency !

This early defection of Murat is certain, and his declaration that he had instructions to invade Sicily was corroborated by a rumour, rife in the French camps before the battle of Vittoria, that the Toulon fleet had sailed and the descent actually made. Nevertheless there is some obscurity about the matter. The negociation was never completed, Murat left Italy to command Napoleon's cavalry and at the battle of Dresden contributed much to the success of that day. Now it is conceivable that he should mask his plans by joining the grand army, and that his fiery spirit should in the battle forget everything except victory. But to disobey Napo-

leon's orders as to the invasion of Sicily and dare to
face that monarch immediately after, was so unlikely
as to indicate rather a paper demonstration to alarm
lord Wellington than a real attack.   And it would
seem from the short observation of the latter in
answer to lord William Bentinck's detailed communication on this subject, namely " *Sicily is in no
danger,*" that he viewed it so, or thought it put forward by Murat to give more value to his defection.
However it sufficed to hinder reinforcements going
to Murray.

Appendix,
No. 1.

Lord William Bentinck on landing was informed
that Suchet was at Tortoza with from eight to twelve
thousand men, Maurice Mathieu with seven thousand at Cambrils.   To drive the latter back and
re-invest Taragona was easy, and the place would
have fallen because the garrison had exhausted all
their powder in the first siege; but this lord William
did not know, and to renew the attack vigorously
was impossible, because all the howitzers and platforms and fascines had been lost, and the animals
and general equipment of the army were too much
deteriorated by continual embarkations, and disem-
barkations, to keep the field in Catalonia.   Wherefore he resolved to return to Alicant, not without
hope still to fulfil Wellington's instructions by
landing at Valencia between Suchet and Harispe.
The re-embarkation was unmolested, the fort of
Balaguer was destroyed, and one regiment of Whittingham's division, destined to reinforce Copons'
army, being detached to effect a landing northward
of Barcelona, the fleet put to sea; but misfortune continued to pursue this unhappy armament.
A violent tempest impeded the voyage, fourteen
sail of transports struck upon the sands off the

mouth of the Ebro, and the army was not entirely
disembarked at Alicant before the 27th. Meanwhile
marshal Suchet, seeing the English fleet under sail
and taught by the destruction of the fort of Balaguer,
that the allies had relinquished operations in Lower
Catalonia, marched with such extraordinary diligence as to reach Valencia in forty-eight hours
after quitting Tortoza, thus frustrating lord William's
project of landing at Valencia.

During his absence Harispe had again proved
the weakness of the Spanish armies, and demonstrated the sagacity and prudence of lord Wellington. That great man's warning about defeat was
distinctly addressed to the Spanish generals, because
the chief object of the operations was not to defeat
Suchet but to keep him from aiding the French
armies in the north. Pitched battles were therefore to be avoided their issue being always doubtful, and the presence of a numerous and increasing
force on the front and flank of the French was more
sure to obtain the end in view. But all Spanish
generals desired to fight great battles, soothing their
national pride by attributing defeats to want of
cavalry. It was at first doubtful if Murray could
transport his horsemen to Taragona, and if left
behind they would have been under Elio and Del
Parque, whereby those officers would have been
encouraged to fight. Hence the English general's
menacing intimation. And he also considered that
as the army of Del Parque had been for three
years in continued activity under Ballesteros without
being actually dispersed, it must be more capable
than Elio's in the dodging warfare suitable for
Spaniards. Moreover Elio was best acquainted
with the country between the Xucar and Alicant.

Wherefore Del Parque was directed to turn the enemy's right flank by Requeña, Elio to menace the front, which, adverting to the support and protection furnished by Alicant and the mountains behind Castalla, was the least dangerous operation.

But to trust Spanish generals was to trust the winds and the clouds. General Elio persuaded the duke Del Parque to adopt the front attack, took the flank line himself, and detached general Mijares to fall upon Requeña. And though Suchet had weakened his line on the 2d of June, Del Parque was not ready until the 9th, thus giving the French a week for the relief of Taragona, and for the arrival of Severoli at Liria.

At this time Harispe had about eight thousand men of all arms in front of the Xucar. The Spaniards, including Roche's and Mijares' divisions and Whittingham's cavalry, were twenty-five thousand strong; and the Empecinado, Villa Campa, and the Frayle, Nebot, waited in the Cuenca and Albaracyn mountains to operate on the French rear. Notwithstanding this disproportion, the contest was short, and for the Spaniards, disastrous. They advanced in three columns. Elio, by the pass of Almanza; Del Parque by Villena and Fuente de la Higuera menacing Moxente; Roche and the prince of Anglona from Alcoy, by Onteniente and the pass of Albayda, menacing San Felippe de Xativa and turning Moxente.

Harispe abandoned those camps on the 11th, and took the line of the Xucar, occupying the entrenchments in front of his bridges at Alcira and Barca del Rey, near Alberique; and during this retrograde movement general Mesclop, commanding the rear-guard, being pressed by the Spanish horsemen, wheeled round and drove them in great confusion upon the infantry.

On the 15th Mijares took the fort of Requeña, thus turning the line of the Xucar, and securing the defiles of Cabrillas through which the Cuenca road leads to Valencia. Villa Campa immediately joined him thereby preventing Severoli from uniting with Harispe, and meanwhile Del Parque, after razing the French works at Moxente and San Felippe, advanced towards Alcira in two columns, the one moving by the road of Cargagente, the other by the road of Gandia. General Habert overthrew the first with one shock, took five hundred prisoners, and marched to attack the other, but it was already routed by general Gudin. After this contest Del Parque and Harispe maintained their respective positions, while Elio joined Mijares at Requeña. Villa Campa then descended to Chiva, and Harispe's position was becoming critical, when on the 23d the head of Suchet's column coming from the Ebro entered Valencia, and on the 24th Del Parque resumed the position of Castalla.

Thus in despite of Wellington's precautions every thing turned contrary to his designs. Elio had operated by the flank, Del Parque by the front, and the latter was defeated because he attacked the enemy in an entrenched position. Murray had failed entirely. His precipitancy at Taragona and his delays at Balaguer were alike hurtful, and would have caused the destruction of one or both of the Spanish armies but for the battle of Vittoria. For Suchet, having first detached general Musnier to recover the fort of Requeña and drive back Villa Campa, had assembled the bulk of his forces in his old positions, of San Felippe and Moxente, before

the return of the Anglo-Sicilian troops ; and as
Elio, unable to subsist at Utiel, had then returned
towards his former quarters, the French marshal
was upon the point of striking a fatal blow against
him, or Del Parque, or both, when the news of
Wellington's victory averted the danger.

Here the firmness, the activity and coolness of
Suchet, may be contrasted with the infirmity of
purpose displayed by Murray. Slow in attack,
precipitate in retreat, the English commander always
mistimed his movements ; the French marshal dou-
bled his force by rapidity. The latter was isolated
by the operations of lord Wellington ; his communication with Aragon was interrupted, and that province placed in imminent danger ; the communication between Valencia and Catalonia was exposed
to the attacks of the Anglo-Sicilian army and the
fleet ; nearly thirty thousand Spaniards menaced
him on the Xucar in front ; Villa Campa, the Frayle
and the Empecinado could bring ten thousand men
on his right flank ; yet he did not hesitate to leave
Harispe with only seven or eight thousand men to
oppose the Spaniards, while with the remainder of
his army he relieved Taragona and yet returned in
time to save Valencia.

Such was the state of affairs when lord William
Bentinck brought the Anglo-Sicilian troops once
more to Alicant. His first care was to re-organize
the means of transport for the commissariat and
artillery, but this was a matter of difficulty. Sir
John Murray, with a mischievous economy, and
strange disregard of that part of Wellington's instructions, which proscribed active field operations
in Valencia if he should be forced to return from
Catalonia, had discharged six hundred mules, and

two hundred country carts, that is to say five-sixths of the whole field equipment, before he sailed for Taragona. The army was thus crippled, while Suchet gathered strong in front, and Musnier's division retaking Requeña forced the Spaniards to retire from that quarter. Lord William urged Del Parque to advance meanwhile from Castalla, but he had not means of carrying even one day's biscuit, and at the same time Elio pressed by famine went off towards Cuenca. It was not until the 1st of July that the Anglo-Sicilian troops could even advance towards Alcoy.

Lord William Bentinck commanded the Spanish armies as well as his own, and letters passed between him and Lord Wellington relative to further operations. The latter, keeping to his original views, advised a renewed attack on Taragona or on Tortoza, if the ordnance still in possession of the army would admit of such a measure; but supposing this could not be, he recommended a general advance to seize the open country of Valencia, the British keeping close to the sea and in constant communication with the fleet.

Lord William's views were different. He found the Spanish soldiers robust and active, but their regimental officers bad, and their organization generally so deficient that they could not stand against even a small French force, as proved by their recent defeat at Alcira. The generals however pleased him at first, especially Del Parque, that is, like all Spaniards, they had fair words at command, and Lord William Bentinck without scanning very nicely their deeds, thought he could safely undertake a grand stragetic operation in conjunction with them.

To force the line of the Xucar he deemed unad-

visable, inasmuch as there were only two carriage
roads, both of which led to Suchet's entrenched
bridges; and though the river was fordable the enemy's bank was so favourable for defence as to render

Lord Wil-
liam Ben-
tinck's
Correspon-
dence,
MSS.
the passage by force dangerous. The Anglo-Sicilians
were unaccustomed to great tactical movements,
the Spaniards altogether incapable of them. Wherefore, relinquishing an attack in front, Lord William
proposed to move the allied armies in one mass and
turn the enemy's right flank either by Utiel and
Requeña, or, by a wider march, to reach Cuenca
and from thence gaining the Madrid road to Zaragoza, communicate with Wellington's army and
operate down the Ebro. In either case it was
necessary to cross the Albaracyn mountains and
there were no carriage roads, save those of Utiel
and Cuenca. But the passes near Utiel were
strongly fortified by the French, and a movement
on that line would necessarily lead to an attack
upon Suchet which was to be avoided. The line
of Cuenca was preferable though longer, and being
in the harvest season provisions he said would not
fail. The allies would thus force Suchet to cross
the Ebro, or attack him in a chosen position where
Wellington could reinforce them if necessary, and
in the event of a defeat they could retire for shelter
upon his army.

Wellington, better acquainted with Spanish warfare, and the nature of Spanish co-operation, told
him, provisions would fail on the march to Cuenca,
even in harvest time, and without money he would
get nothing; moreover by separating himself from
the fleet, he would be unable to return suddenly to
Sicily if that island should be really exposed to
any imminent danger.

While these letters were being exchanged the Anglo-Sicilians marched towards Villena on Del Parque's left, and Suchet was preparing to attack when intelligence of the battle of Vittoria, reaching both parties, totally changed the aspect of affairs. The French general instantly abandoned Valencia, and Lord William entered that city.

Suchet knew that Clauzel was at Zaragoza, and desirous of maintaining himself there to secure a point of junction for the army of Aragon with the king's army, if the latter should re-enter Spain. It was possible therefore, by abandoning all the fortresses in Valencia and some of those in Catalonia, to have concentrated more than thirty thousand men with which to join Clauzel, and the latter having carried off several small garrisons during his retreat, had fifteen thousand. Lord Wellington's position would then have been critical, since forty-five thousand good troops, having many supporting fortresses, would have menaced his right flank at the moment when his front was assailed by a new general and a powerful army. But if this junction with Clauzel invited Suchet on the one hand, on the other, with a view of influencing the general negociations during the armistice in Germany, it was important to appear strong in Spain. On such occasions men generally endeavour to reconcile both objects and obtain neither. Suchet resolved to march upon Zaragoza and at the same time retain his grasp upon Valencia by keeping large garrisons in the fortresses. This reduced his field force, a great error, it was so proved by the result. But if the war in the north of Spain and in Germany had taken a different turn, his foresight and prudence would have been applauded.

BOOK
XXI.
1813.
July.

The army of Aragon now counted thirty-two thousand effective men. Four thousand were in Zaragoza,
two thousand in Mequinenza, Venasque, Monzons,
Ayerbe, Jaca, and some smaller posts. Twenty-six
thousand remained. Of these one hundred and
ten were left in Denia, with provisions for eight
months; twelve hundred and fifty in Saguntum,
where there were immense stores, eight months'
provisions for the garrison, and two months' subsistence for the whole army; four hundred with
provisions for a year, were in Peniscola, and in
Morella one hundred and twenty with magazines
for six months. Into Tortoza, where there was
a large artillery parc, Suchet threw a garrison of
nearly five thousand men and then destroying the
bridges on the Xucar, marched from Valencia
on the 5th of July, taking the coast road for
Tortoza.

Suchet's
Memoirs.

The inhabitants, grateful for the discipline he
had maintained, were even friendly, and while the
main body thus moved, Musnier retreated from
Requeña across the mountains towards Caspe, the
point of concentration for the whole army : but ere
it could reach that point, Clauzel's flight to Jaca,
unnecessary for he was only pursued from Tudela
by Mina, became known, and the effect was fatal.
All the Partidas immediately united and menaced
Zaragoza, whereupon Suchet ordered Paris to retire
upon Caspe, and pressed forward himself to Favara.
Musnier, meanwhile, reached the former town,
having on the march picked up Severoli's brigade
and the garrisons of Teruel and Alcanitz. Thus
on the 12th the whole army was in military communication but extended along the Ebro from Tortoza to Caspe. Mina had, however, seized the

Monte Torrero on the 8th, and general Paris evacuated Zaragoza in the night of the 9th, leaving
five hundred men in the castle with much ordnance. Encumbered with a great train of carriages
he got entangled in the defiles of Alcubiere, and
being attacked lost many men and all his baggage
and artillery. Instead of joining Suchet he fled to
Huesca, where he rallied the garrison of Ayerbe
and then made for Jaca, reaching it on the 14th at
the moment when Clauzel, after another ineffectual
attempt to join the king, had returned to that
place. Duran then invested the castle of Zaragoza,
and the fort of Daroca. The first surrendered on
the 30th, but Daroca did not fall until the 11th of
August.

This sudden and total loss of Aragon made Suchet
think it no longer possible to fix a base in that
province, nor to rally Clauzel's troops on his own.
He could not remain on the right bank of the Ebro,
neither could he feed his army permanently in the
sterile country about Tortoza while Aragon was in
possession of the enemy. Moreover, the allies
having the command of the sea, might land troops,
and seize the passes of the hills behind him, wherefore fixing upon the fertile country about Taragona
for his position, he passed the Ebro at Tortoza,
Mora, and Mequinenza, on the 14th and 15th,
detaching Isidore Lamarque to fetch off the garrisons
of Belchite, Fuentes, Pina, and Bujarola, and bring
the whole to Lerida. Meanwhile the bulk of the
army moving on the road from Tortoza to Taragona,
although cannonaded by the English fleet, reached
Taragona with little hurt and the walls were mined
for destruction, but the place was still held with a
view to field operations.

The general state of the war seems to have been too little considered by Suchet at this time, or he would have made a more vigorous effort to establish himself in Aragon. Had he persisted to march on Zaragoza he would have raised the siege of the castle, perchance have given a blow to Mina whose orders were to retire upon Tudela where Wellington designed to offer battle; but Suchet might have avoided this, and to have appeared upon Wellington's flank were it only for a fortnight, would, as shall be hereafter shewn, have changed the aspect of the campaign. Suchet's previous rapidity and excellent arrangements had left the allies in Valencia far behind, they could not have gathered in force soon enough to meddle with him, and their pursuit now to be described, was not so cautiously conducted but that he might have turned and defeated them.

The 9th of July, four days after the French abandoned Valencia, lord William Bentinck entered that city and made it his place of arms instead of Alicant. On the 16th, marching by the coast road, in communication with the fleet and masking Peniscola, a fortress now of little importance, he followed the enemy; but Suchet had on that day completed the passage of the Ebro, he might have been close to Zaragoza, and Del Parque's army was still near Alicant in a very disorderly condition. And though Elio and Roche were at Valencia, the occupation of that town, and the blockades of Denia and Murviedro, proved more than a sufficient task for them: the garrison of the latter place received provisions continually, and were so confident as to assemble in order of battle on the glacis when the allies marched past.

The 20th lord William entered Vinaros and remained there until the 26th. Suchet might then
have been at Tudela or Sanguessa, and it shall be
shewn that Wellington could not have met him at
the former place as he designed.

During this period various reports were received.
" *The French had vainly endeavoured to regain
France by Zaragoza.*" " *Taragona was destroyed.*"
" *The evacuation of Spain was certain.*" " *A
large detachment had already quitted Catalonia.*" The English general, who had little time
to spare from the pressure of Sicilian affairs, became eager to advance. He threw a flying bridge
over the Ebro at Amposta, and having before embarked Clinton's division with a view to seize the
Col de Balaguer, resolved to follow Suchet with
the remainder of his army, which now included
Whittingham's cavalry. A detachment from Tortoza menaced his bridge on the 25th, but the troops
were reinforced and the passage of the Ebro
completed on the 27th. The next day Villa Campa
arrived with four thousand men and meanwhile
the Col de Balaguer was secured.

On the 29th the cavalry being in march was
threatened by infantry from Tortoza, near the Col
de Alba, but the movements generally were unop-
posed, and the army got possession of the mountains
beyond the Ebro.

Suchet was at this time inspecting the defences of
Lerida and Mequinenza, and his escort was necessarily large because Copons was hanging on his
flanks in the mountains about Manresa; but his
position about Villa Franca was exceedingly strong.
Taragona and Tortoza covered the front ; Barcelona,
the rear; the communication with Decaen was

secure, and on the right flank stood Lerida, to which the small forts of Mequinenza and Monzon served as outposts.

The Anglo-Sicilian troops reinforced with Whittingham's cavalry did not exceed ten thousand effective men, of which one division was on board ship from the 22d to the 26th. Elio and Roche were at Valencia in a destitute condition. Del Parque's army thirteen thousand strong, including Whittingham's infantry, was several marches in the rear, it was paid from the British subsidy but very ill-provided and the duke himself disinclined to obedience. Villa Campa did not join until the 28th, and Copons was in the mountains above Vich. Lord William therefore remained with ten thousand men and a large train of carriages, for ten days without any position of battle behind him nearer than the hills about Saguntum. His bridge over the Ebro was thrown within ten miles of Tortoza where there was a garrison of five thousand men, detachments from which could approach unperceived through the rugged mountains near the fortress; and Suchet's well-organised experienced army was within two marches. That marshal however, expecting a sharp warfare, was visiting his fortresses in person, and his troops quartered for the facility of feeding were unprepared to strike a sudden blow; moreover, judging his enemy's strength in offence what it might have been rather than what it was, he awaited the arrival of Decaen's force from Upper Catalonia before he offered battle.

But Decaen was himself pressed. The great English fleet menacing Rosas and Palamos had encouraged a partial insurrection of the Somatenes, which was supported by the divisions of Eroles, Manso, and

Villamiel. Several minor combats took place on the
side of Besala and Olot, Eroles invested Bañolas, and
though beaten there in a sharp action by Lamarque
on the 23d of June the insurrection spread. To
quell it Decaen combined a double operation from
the side of Gerona upon Vich, which was generally
the Catalan head-quarters. Designing to attack by
the south himself, he sent Maximilian Lamarque,
with fifteen hundred French troops and some Mi-
guelets, by the mountain paths of San Felice de
Pallarols and Amias. On the 8th of July that
officer gained the heights of Salud, seized the road
from Olot and descended from the north upon Roda
and Manlieu, ·in the expectation of seeing Decaen
attacking from the other side. He perceived below
him a heavy body in march, and at the same time
heard the sound of cannon and musquetry about
Vich. Concluding this was Decaen he advanced
confidently against the troops in his front, although
very numerous, thinking they were in retreat, but
they fought him until dark without advantage on
either side.

In the night an officer came with intelligence,
that Decaen's attack had been relinquished in consequence of Suchet's orders to move to the Llobregat, and it then appeared that a previous despatch
had been intercepted, that the whole Catalan force
to the amount of six or seven thousand combatants
was upon Lamarque's hands, and the firing heard at
Vich was a rejoicing for lord Wellington's victories in Navarre. A retreat was imperative. The
Spaniards followed at daylight, and Lamarque getting
entangled in difficult ground near Salud was forced
to deliver battle. The fight lasted many hours, all
his ammunition was expended, he lost four hundred

men and was upon the point of destruction, when general Beurmann came to his succour with four fresh battalions, and the Catalans were finally defeated with great loss. After this vigorous action Decaen marched to join Suchet, and the Catalans, moving by the mountains in separate divisions, approached lord William Bentinck.

The allies having thus passed the Ebro several officers of both nations conceived the siege of Tortoza would be the best operation. Nearly forty thousand men, that is to say, Villa Campa's, Copons', Del Parque's, Whittingham's, some of Elio's forces and the Anglo-Sicilians, could be united for the siege, and the defiles of the mountains on the left bank of the Ebro would enable them to resist Suchet's attempts to succour the place on that side, and force him to move by the circuitous route of Lerida. Wellington also leaned towards this operation, but lord William Bentinck resolved to push at once for Taragona, and even looked to an attack upon Barcelona; certainly a rash proceeding, inasmuch as Suchet awaited his approach with an army every way superior. It does not however follow that to besiege Tortoza would have been advisable, for though the battering train, much larger than Murray's losses gave reason at first to expect, was equal to the reduction of the place, the formal siege of such a fortress was a great undertaking. The vicinity was unhealthy and it would have been difficult to feed the Spanish troops. They were quite inexperienced in sieges, this was sure to be long, not sure to be successful, and Suchet seeing the allies engaged in such a difficult operation might have marched at once to Aragon.

It would seem lord William Bentinck was at this

time misled, partly by the reports of the Catalans,
partly by lord Wellington's great successes, into a
belief that the French were going to abandon Catalonia. His mind also run upon Italian affairs, and
he did not perceive that Suchet judiciously posted
and able to draw reinforcements from Decaen was in
fact much stronger than all the allies united. The
two armies of Aragon and Catalonia, numbered
sixty-seven thousand men. Of these, about twenty-
seven thousand, including Paris' division then at
Jaca, were in garrison, five thousand were sick, the
remainder in the field. In Catalonia the allies were
not principals, they were accessories. They were to
keep Suchet from operating on the flank of the
allies in Navarre and their defeat would have been
a great disaster. So entirely was this lord Wellington's view, that the duke Del Parque's army was to
make forced marches on Tudela if Suchet should
either move himself or detach largely towards
Aragon. Lord William after passing the Ebro
conld have secured the defiles of the mountains with
his own and Villa Campa's troops, that is to say,
with twenty thousand men including Whittingham's
division. He could have insulted the garrison of
Tortoza, and commenced the making of gabions and
fascines, which would have placed Suchet in doubt
as to his ulterior objects while he awaited the
junction of del Parque's, Copons', and the rest of
Elio's troops. Thus forty thousand men, three
thousand being cavalry and attended by a fleet,
could have descended into the Campo, still leaving
a detachment to watch Tortoza. If Suchet then
came to the succour of Taragona the allies superior
in numbers could have fought in a position chosen

beforehand. Still it is very doubtful if all these corps would, or could have kept together.

Lord William Bentinck's operations were headlong. He had prepared platforms and fascines for a siege in the island of Yvica, and on the 30th quitting the mountains suddenly invested Taragona with less than six thousand men, occupying ground three hundred yards nearer to the walls the first day than Murray had ever done. He thus prevented the garrison from abandoning the place, if, as was supposed, they had that intention; yet the fortress could not be besieged because of Suchet's vicinity and the dissemination of the allies. The 31st the bridge at Amposta was accidentally broken, three hundred bullocks were drowned, and the head of Del Parque's army, being on the left of the Ebro, fell back a day's march. However Whittingham's division and the cavalry came up, and on the 3rd, the bridge being restored, Del Parque also joined the investing army. Copons then promised to bring up his Catalans, Sarzfield's division now belonging to the second army arrived, and Elio had been ordered to reinforce it with three additional battalions while Villa Campa observed Tortoza. Meanwhile Lord William seeing that Suchet's troops were scattered and the marshal himself at Barcelona, thought of surprizing his posts and seizing the mountain line of the Llobregat; but Elio sent no battalions, Copons, jealous of some communications between the English general and Eroles, was slow, the garrison of Tortoza burned the bridge at Amposta, and Suchet taking alarm suddenly returned from Barcelona and concentrated his army.

Up to this time the Spaniards giving copious but false information to lord William, and no information

at all to Suchet, had induced a series of faults on
both sides balancing each other, a circumstance
not uncommon in war, which demands all the
faculties of the greatest minds. The Englishman
thinking his enemy retreating had pressed rashly
forward. The Frenchman deeming from the other's
boldness the whole of the allies were at hand,
thought himself too weak, and awaited the arrival of
Decaen, whose junction was retarded as we have
seen by the combined operations of the Catalan
army and the English fleet.

In this state of affairs Suchet heard of new and
important successes gained in Navarre by lord Wellington, one of his Italian battalions was at the
same time cut off at San Sadurni by Manso, and
lord William Bentinck took a position of battle
beyond the Gaya. His left, composed of Whittingham's division, occupied Braffin, the Col de Liebra,
and Col de Christina, his right covered the great
coast-road. These were the only carriage ways
by which the enemy could approach, but they were
ten miles apart, Copons held aloof, and Whittingham thought himself too weak to defend the passes
alone ; hence, when Suchet, reinforced by Decaen
with eight thousand sabres and bayonets, finally
advanced, lord William who had landed neither
guns nor stores decided to refuse battle. For such
a resolute officer, this must have been a painful
decision. He had now nearly thirty thousand fighting men, including a thousand marines which had
been landed to join the advanced guard at Altafalla;
he had assumed the offensive, invested Taragona
where the military honour of England had suffered
twice before, in fine provoked the action which he
now declined. But Suchet had equal numbers of a

better quality; the banks of the Gaya were rugged to pass in retreat if the fight should be lost; much must have been left to the general officers at different points; Del Parque's was an uneasy coadjutor, and if any part was forced the whole line would have been irretrievably lost. His reluctance was however manifest, for though he expected the enemy on the 9th he did not send his field artillery and baggage to the rear until the 11th, the day on which Decaen reached Villa Franca.

The French general dreading the fire of the fleet endeavoured by false attacks on the coast road to draw the allies from the defiles beyond Braffin, towards which he finally carried his whole army, and those defiles were indeed abandoned, not as his Memoirs state because of these demonstrations, but because lord William had previously determined to retreat. On the 16th finding the passes unguarded, he poured through and advanced upon Valls thus turning the allies, but he had lost time and the latter were in full retreat towards the mountains, the left wing by Reus, the right wing by Cambrills. The march of the former was covered by lord Frederick Bentinck who leading the British and German cavalry defeated the fourth French hussars with a loss of forty or fifty men; and it is said that either general Habert or Harispe was taken but escaped in the confusion.

The Anglo-Sicilians and Whittingham's division now entrenched themselves near the Col de Balaguer, and Del Parque marched with his own and Sarzfield's troops to invest Tortoza, but the garrison fell upon his rear while passing the Ebro and some loss was sustained. Meanwhile Suchet, more swayed by the remembrance of Castalla than by his recent success, would not again prove the courage of the British troops on a mountain position. Contrary to the wishes of his army he returned to Taragona and destroyed the ancient walls, which from the extreme hardness of the Roman cement proved a tedious and difficult matter : then resuming his old positions about Villa Franca and on the Llobregat he sent Decaen to Upper Catalonia. This terminated lord William Bentinck's first effort and the general result was favourable. He had risked much on insufficient grounds, yet his enemy made no profit and lost Taragona with its fertile Campo, Tortoza was invested, and Suchet was kept away from Navarre.

It is strange that this renowned French general suffered his large force to be thus paralyzed at such a crisis. Above twenty-seven thousand of his sol- Imperial
Muster-
rolls.
MSS. diers if we include the isolated division of Paris were shut up in garrison, but thirty-two thousand remained with which he marched to and fro in Catalonia while the war was being decided in Navarre. Had he moved to that province by Aragon before the end of July lord Wellington would have been overpowered. What was to be feared? That lord William Bentinck would follow, or attack one of his fortresses? If the French were successful in Navarre the loss of a fortress in Catalonia would have been a trifle, it was not certain that any would have fallen, and lord William could not abandon the coast. Suchet pleaded danger to France if he abandoned Catalonia; but to invade France, guarded as she was by her great military reputation, and to do so by land, leaving behind the fortresses of Valencia and Catalonia the latter barring all the carriage roads was chimerical. Success in Navarre would have made an invasion by sea pass as a parti-

zan descent, and moreover France, wanting Suchet's
troops to defend her in Navarre, was ultimately invaded by Wellington and in a far more formidable
manner.   This question shall however be treated
more largely in another place, it is sufficient to
observe here, that Clarke the minister of war, a man
without genius or attachment to the emperor's
cause, discouraged any great combined plan of
action, and Napoleon absorbed by his own immense
operations did not interpose.

Lord William now intent upon the siege of Tortoza wished lord Wellington to attack Mequinenza
with a detachment of his army; but this the situation
of affairs in Navarre and Guipuscoa did not admit
of, and he soon discovered that to assail Tortoza was
an undertaking beyond his own means.   Elio when
desired to gather provisions and assist in the operations demanded three weeks for preparation; all
the Spanish troops were in want, Roche's division,
blockading Murviedro, although so close to Valencia
was on half rations; and the siege of Tortoza was necessarily relinquished, because no great or sustained
operation could be conducted in concert with such
generals and such armies.   Suchet's fear of them
was an illustration of Napoleon's maxim, that war is
an affair of discrimination.   It is more essential to
know the quality than the quantity of enemies.

It was difficult for lord William Bentinck to
apply his mind vigorously to the campaign he was
conducting, because fresh changes injurious to the
British policy in Sicily called him to that island,
and his thoughts were running upon the invasion of
Italy; but as the Spaniards, deceived by the movements of escorts and convoys, reported that Suchet
had marched with twelve thousand men to join

Soult, he once more fixed his head-quarters at Taragona, and, following lord Wellington's instruc- tions, detached Del Parque's troops by forced marches upon Tudela.

On the 5th of September the army entered Villa Franca, and the 12th, detachments of Calabrese, Swiss, German, and British infantry, a squadron of cavalry and one battery, in all about twelve hundred men under colonel Adam, occupied the heights of Ordal. At this place, ten miles in advance of Villa Franca, being joined by three of Sarzfield's battalions and a Spanish squadron they took a position; but it now appeared that very few French troops had been detached; that Suchet had concentrated his whole force on the Llobregat; and that his army was very superior in numbers, because the allies, reduced by the loss of Del Parque's troops, had also left Whittingham's division at Reus and Valls to procure food. Sarzfield's division was feeding on the British supplies, and lord William again looked to a retreat, yet thinking the enemy disinclined to advance desired to preserve his forward position as long as possible.

He had only two lines of operation to watch. The one menacing his front from Molino del Rey by the main road, which colonel Adam blocked by his position at Ordal; the other from Martorel, by San Sadurni, menacing his left; but on this route, a difficult one, he had pushed the Catalans under Eroles and Manso reinforcing them with some Calabrese; there was indeed a third line by Avionet on his right, but it was little better than a goat-path. He had designed to place his main body close up to the Ordal on the evening of the 12th, yet from some slight cause delayed it until the next day. Meanwhile he viewed the country in advance of that defile without discovering an enemy. His confidential emissaries assured him the French were not going to advance, and he returned, satisfied that Adam's detachment was safe, and so expressed himself to that officer. A report of a contrary tendency was indeed made by colonel Reeves of the twenty-seventh, on the authority of a Spanish woman who had before proved her accuracy and ability as a spy; she was now however disbelieved, and this incredulity was unfortunate. For Suchet thus braved, and his communication with Lerida threatened by Manso on the side of Martorel, was already in march to attack Ordal with the army of Aragon, while Decaen and Maurice Mathieu, moving with the army of Catalonia from Martorel by San Sardurni, turned the left of the allies.

COMBAT OF ORDAL.

The heights occupied by colonel Adam although rugged rose gradually from a magnificent bridge, by which the main road was carried over a very deep and impracticable ravine. The second battalion of the twenty-seventh British regiment was posted on the right, the Germans and De Roll's Swiss with the artillery, defended an old Spanish fort commanding the main road; the Spaniards were in the centre, the Calabrese on the left; and the cavalry were in reserve. A bright moonlight facilitated the movements of the French, and a little before midnight, their leading column under general Mesclop passing the bridge without let or hindrance, mounted the heights with a rapid pace and driving back the picquets gave the first

alarm. The allied troops lying on their arms in
order of battle were ready instantly and the fight
commenced. The first effort was against the twenty-
seventh, then the Germans and the Spanish battalions were vigorously assailed in succession as the
French columns got free of the bridge, but the Calabrese were too far on the left to take a share in
the action. The combat was fierce and obstinate.
Harispe who commanded the French constantly outflanked the right of the allies, and at the same time
pressed their centre, where the Spaniards fought
gallantly.

Colonel Adam was wounded very early, the
command devolved upon colonel Reeves, and that
officer seeing his flank turned and his men falling
fast, in short, finding himself engaged with a whole
army on a position of which colonel Adam had lost
the key by neglecting the bridge, resolved to retreat.
In this view he first ordered the guns to fall back,
and to cover the movement charged a column of
the enemy which was pressing forward on the high
road, but he was severely wounded in this attack
and there was no recognized commander on the spot
to succeed him. Then the affair became confused.
For though the order to retreat was given the
Spaniards were fighting desperately, and the twenty-
seventh thought it shame to abandon them ; wherefore the Germans and De Roll's regiment still held
the old fort and the guns came back. The action
was thus continued with great fury. Colonel Carey
now brought the Calabrese into line from the left,
and menaced the right flank of the French, but he
was too late ; the Spaniards overwhelmed in the
centre were broken, the right was completely turned,
the old fort was lost, the enemy's skirmishers got into

the allies' rear, and at three o'clock the whole dis-persed, the most part in flight; the Spanish cavalry were then overthrown on the main road by the French hussars and four guns were taken in the tumult.

Captain Waldron, with the twenty-seventh re-duced to eighty men, and captain Müller with about the same number of Germans and Swiss, breaking through several small parties of the enemy effected their retreat in good order by the hills on each side of the road. Colonel Carey endeavoured at first to gain the road of Sadurni on the left, but meeting with Decaen's people on that side he retraced his steps, and crossing the field of battle in the rear of Suchet's columns made for Villa Nueva de Sitjes. There he finally embarked without loss, save a few stragglers who fell into the hands of a flank-ing battalion of French infantry which had moved through the mountains by Begas and Avionet. The overthrow was complete and the prisoners were at first very numerous, but the darkness enabled many to escape, and two thousand men reached Manso and Eroles.

Suchet pursuing his march came up with lord William about eight o'clock. The latter retired skirmishing and with excellent order beyond Villa Franca, followed by the French horsemen some of which assailed his rear-guard while others edged to their right to secure the communication with Decaen. The latter was looked for by both parties with great anxiety, but he had been delayed by the resistance of Manso and Eroles in the rugged country between Martorel and San Sadurni. Suchet's cavalry and artillery continued however to infest the rear of the retreating army until it reached a deep baranco, near the Venta de Monjos, where the passage being dangerous and the French horseman importunate, that brave and honest soldier, lord Frederick Bentinck, charged their right, and fighting hand to hand with the enemy's general Myers wounded him and over-threw his light cavalry; they rallied upon their dragoons and advanced again, endeavouring to turn the flank, but were stopped by the fire of two guns which general Clinton opened upon them. Mean-while the cuirassiers, on the left, pressed the Bruns-wick hussars and menaced the infantry yet they were finally checked by the fire of the tenth regi-ment. This cavalry action was vigorous, the twentieth and the Germans although few in numbers lost more than ninety men. The baranco was how-ever safely passed and about three o'clock the army having reached Arbos the pursuit ceased. The Catalans meanwhile had retreated towards Igualada and the Anglo-Sicilians retired to Taragona.

It was now thought Suchet would make a move-ment to carry off the garrisons of Lerida and Tor-toza, but this did not happen, and lord William went to Sicily, leaving the command of the army to sir William Clinton.

OBSERVATIONS.

1°. Lord William Bentinck committed errors, yet he has been censured without discrimination. " *He advanced rashly.*"   " *He was undecided.*" " *He exposed his advanced guard without support.*" Such were the opinions expressed at the time. Their justness may be disputed. His first object was to retain all the French force in Catalonia; his second, to profit from Suchet's weakness if he

detached largely. He could do neither by remaining inactive on the barren hills behind Hospitalet,
because the Spaniards would have dispersed for
want of provisions and the siege of Tortoza was
found to be impracticable. It was therefore the
part of a bold and skilful general to menace his
enemy, if he could be sure of retreating again
without danger or dishonour. The position at Villa
Franca fulfilled this condition. It was strong in
itself and offensive; sir Edward Pellew's fleet was
in movement to create diversions in Upper Catalonia, and all the emissaries and Spanish correspon-
dents concurred in declaring, though falsely, that
the French general had detached twelve thousand
men.

It is indeed one of the tests of a sagacious general to detect false intelligence, yet the greatest
are at times deceived, and all must act, if they
act at all, upon what appears at the time to be
true. Lord William's advance was founded on
erroneous data, but his position in front of Villa
Franca was well chosen. It enabled him to feed
Whittingham's division in the fertile country about
Reus and Valls, and there were short and easy communications from Villa Franca to the sea-coast.
The army could only be seriously assailed on two
lines. In front, by the main road, which though
broad was from Molino del Rey to the heights of
Ordal one continued defile. On the left by San
Sardurni, a road still more rugged and difficult than
the other. And the Catalans were launched on this
side as their natural line of operations, because,
without losing their hold of the mountains they
protected the left of the allies, menacing at the
same time the right of the enemy and his com-

munications with Lerida. Half a march to the rear would bring the army to Vendrills, beyond which the enemy could not follow without getting under the fire of the ships; neither could he forestall this movement by a march through the Liebra and Cristina defiles, because the Catalans falling back on Whittingham's division could hold him in check.

2°. Ordal and San Sadurni were the keys of the position. The last was well secured, the first not so, and there was the real error of Lord William Bentinck. It was none however to push an advanced guard of three thousand five hundred men, with cavalry and artillery, to a distance of ten miles for a few hours. He had a right to expect the commander of such a force would maintain his post until supported, or at least retreat without disaster. An officer of capacity would have done so. But whoever relies upon the capacity of sir Frederick Adam either in peace or war will be disappointed.

In 1810 lord Wellington detached general Robert Craufurd with two or three thousand men to a much greater distance, not for one night but for many weeks. And that excellent officer, though close to Massena's immense army the very cavalry of which was double his whole numbers; though he had the long line of the Agueda a fordable river to guard; though he was in an open country and continually skirmishing, never lost so much as a patrole and always remained master of his movements for his combat on the Coa was a studied and wilful error. It was no fault therefore to push colonel Adam's detachment to Ordal, but it was a fault that lord William, having determined to follow with his whole force, should have delayed doing so for one night, or that delaying he did not send some supporting troops forward. It was a fault not to do so because there was good reason to do so, and to delay was to tempt fortune. There was good reason to do so as well to profit of the advantage of the position as to support Adam. Had lord William Bentinck been at hand with his main body when the attack on Ordal commenced, the head of Suchet's force which was kept at bay for three hours by a detachment so ill commanded would have been driven into the ravine behind, and the victorious allies would still have had time to march against Decaen by the road along which colonel Cary endeavoured to join Manso. In fine, Suchet's dispositions were vicious in principle and ought not to have succeeded. He operated on two distinct lines having no cross communications, and before an enemy in possession of a central position with good communications.

3°. It was another fault that lord William Bentinck disregarded the Spanish woman's report to colonel Reeves ; his observations made in front of the bridge of Ordal on the evening of the 12th accorded indeed with the reports of his own emissaries, but the safe side should always be the rule of precaution. He also, although on the spot, overlooked the unmilitary dispositions of colonel Adam on the heights of Ordal. The summit could not be defended against superior numbers with a small corps, and that officer had nevertheless extended the Calabrese so far on the left that they could take no share in the action, and yet could not retreat without great difficulty. A commander who understood his business, would have blocked up the

bridge in front of the heights, and defended it by
a strong detachment, supporting that detachment
by others placed in succession on the heights behind, but keeping his main body always in hand,
ready either to fall on the head of the enemy's
column of attack, or to rally the advanced detachments and retreat in order. There were plenty of
trees and stones to block the bridge its own parapet would have supplied materials, and the ravine
was so deep and rugged, that the enemy could not
have crossed it on the flanks in the dark.

It is no defence to say colonel Adam only took
his ground in the evening after a march ; that he
expected the main body up the next morning and
that lord William assured him he was safe from
attack. Every officer is responsible for the security of his own troops, and the precautions prescribed by the rules of war should never be dispensed with or delayed at an outpost. Now it does
not appear that colonel Adam ever placed an infantry picquet on the bridge, or sent a cavalry
patrole beyond it ; and I have been informed by a
French soldier, one of a party sent to explore the
position, that they reached the crest of the heights
without opposition and returned safely, whereupon
Mesclop's brigade instantly crossed the bridge and
attacked.

4°. Ordal might be called a surprize with respect
to the general-in-chief, yet the troops engaged
were not surprised ; they were beaten and dispersed
because colonel Adam was unskilful. The French
general's victory was complete ; but he has in his
Memoirs exaggerated his difficulties and the importance of his success, his private report to the emperor was more accurate. The Memoirs state that

the English grenadiers defended certain works
which commanded the ascent of the main road,
and in the accompanying atlas a perspective view
of well-conditioned redoubts with colours flying,
is given.   The reader is thus led to imagine these
were regular forts of a fresh construction defended
by select troops; but in the private report they
are correctly designated as ancient retrenchments,
being in fact the ruins of some old Spanish field-
works and of no more advantage to the allies than
any natural inequality of ground.   Again in the
Memoirs the attack of the French cavalry near
Villa Franca is represented as quite successful; but
the private report only says the rear was harassed
by repeated charges, which is true, and moreover
those charges were vigorously repulsed.   The whole
French loss was about three hundred men, that of
the allies, heavy at Ordal, was lightened by escape
of prisoners during the night and ultimately did
not exceed a thousand men including Spaniards.

CHAPTER III.

TURNING from the war in Catalonia to the operations in Navarre and Guipuscoa, we shall find lord
Wellington's indomitable energy overcoming every
difficulty. It has been already shown how, changing
his first views, he disposed the Anglo-Portuguese
divisions to cover the siege of San Sebastian and
the blockade of Pampeluna, at the same time attacking with the Spanish divisions Santona on the coast,
and the castles of Daroca, Morella, Zaragoza, and
the forts of Pancorbo in the interior. These operations required many men, but the early fall of Pancorbo enabled O'Donnel's reserve to blockade Pampeluna, and Don Carlos D'España's division, four
thousand strong, which had remained at Miranda
del Castanar to improve its organization when lord
Wellington advanced to the Ebro, was approaching
to reinforce him.

The harbour of Passages was the only port near
the scene of operations suited for the supply of the
army. Yet it had this defect, that being situated
between the covering and the besieging army, the
stores and guns once landed were in danger from
every movement of the enemy. The Deba river,
between San Sebastian and Bilbaō, was unfit for
large vessels, and hence no permanent depôt could
be established nearer than Bilbaō. At that port
therefore, and at St. Ander and Coruña, the great
depôts of the army were fixed, the stores being trans-

ported to them from the establishments in Portugal;
but the French held Santoña, and their privateers
interrupted the communication along the coast of
Spain while American privateers did the same
between Lisbon and Coruña. On the other hand
the intercourse between San Sebastian and the ports
of France was scarcely molested, and the most urgent
remonstrances failed to procure a sufficient naval
force on the coast of Biscay. It was in these circumstances Wellington commenced

THE SIEGE OF SAN SEBASTIAN.

This place was built on a low sandy isthmus
formed by the harbour on one side and the river
Urumea on the other. Behind it rose the Monte
Orgullo, a rugged cone nearly four hundred feet
high, washed by the ocean and crowned with the
small castle of La Mota. Its southern face overlooking the town, was yet cut off from it by a line of
defensive works and covered with batteries; but La
Mota itself was commanded, at a distance of thirteen
hundred yards, by the Monte Olia on the other side
of the Urumea.

The land front of San Sebastian was three hundred and fifty yards wide, stretching quite across the
isthmus. It consisted of a high curtain or rampart,
very solid, strengthened by a lofty casemated flat
bastion or cavalier placed in the centre, and by half
bastions at either end. A regular horn-work was
pushed out from this front, and six hundred yards
beyond the horn-work the isthmus was closed by
the ridge of San Bartolomeo, at the foot of which
stood the suburb of San Martin.

On the opposite side of the Urumea were certain
sandy hills called the *Chofres*, through which the

road from Passages passed to the wooden bridge
over the river, and thence, by the suburb of Santa
Catalina, along the top of a sea-wall which formed a
fausse braye for the horn-work.

The flanks of the town were protected by simple
ramparts. The one was washed by the water of the
harbour, the other by the Urumea which at high
tide covered four of the twenty-seven feet comprised in its elevation. This was the weak side of
the fortress, for though covered by the river there
was only a single wall ill-flanked by two old
towers, and by the half bastion of San Elmo
which was situated at the extremity of the rampart close under the Monte Orgullo. There
was no ditch, no counter-scarp, or glacis, the wall
could be seen to its base from the Chofre hills at
distances varying from five hundred to a thousand
yards, and when the tide was out the Urumea left a
dry strand under the rampart as far as St. Elmo.
However the guns from the batteries at Monte Orgullo especially that called the Mirador, could see
this strand.

The other flank of the town was secured by the
harbour, in the mouth of which was a rocky island,
called Santa Clara, where the French had established
a post of twenty-five men.

When the battle of Vittoria happened San Sebastian was nearly dismantled; many of the guns had
been removed to form battering trains or to arm
smaller ports on the coast, there were no bomb-
proofs nor pallisades nor outworks, the wells were
foul and the place was supplied with water by a
single aqueduct. Joseph's defeat restored its importance as a fortress. General Emanuel Rey
entered it the 22d of June, bringing with him the

BOOK
XXI.

1813.
June.
escort of the convoy which had quitted Vittoria the
day before the battle. The town was thus filled with
emigrant Spanish families, with the ministers and
other persons attached to the court; the population ordinarily eight thousand was increased to sixteen thousand and disorder and confusion were predominant.

Bellas'
Journal of
French
Sieges in
Spain.
Rey, pushed by necessity, immediately forced all
persons not residents to march at once to France
granting them only a guard of one hundred men ;
the people of quality went by sea, the others by land,
and fortunately all arrived safely for the Partidas
would have given them no quarter.

On the 27th general Foy while retreating before
sir Thomas Graham threw a reinforcement into the
place. The next day Mendizabal's Spaniards appeared on the hills behind the ridge of San Bartolomeo and on the Chofres, whereupon general Rey
burned the wooden bridge and both the suburbs,
and commenced fortifying the heights of San Bartolomeo. The 29th the Spaniards slightly attacked
San Bartolomeo, and were repulsed.

July.
Sir G. Col-
lier's De-
spatch.
The 1st of July the governor of Gueteria abandoned that place, and with detestable ferocity secretly
left a lighted train which exploded the magazine
and destroyed many of the inhabitants. His troops
three hundred in number entered San Sebastian,
and at the same time a vessel from St. Jean de Luz
arrived with fifty-six cannoneers and some workmen ;
the garrison was thus increased to three thousand
men and all persons not able to provide subsistence for
themselves in advance were ordered to quit the place.
Meanwhile Mendizabal, having cut off the aqueduct,
made some approaches towards the head of the
burned bridge on the right of the Urumea and
molested the workmen on the heights of Bartolomeo.

On the 3d, the Surveillante frigate and a sloop with some small craft arrived to blockade the harbour, yet the French vessels from St. Jean de Luz continued to enter by night. The same day the governor made a sally with eleven hundred men in three columns to obtain news, and after some hours' skirmishing returned with a few prisoners.

The 6th some French vessels with a detachment of troops and a considerable convoy of provisions came from St. Jean de Luz.

The 7th Mendizabal tried, unsuccessfully, to set fire to the convent of San Bartolomeo.

On the 9th Sir Thomas Graham arrived with a corps of British and Portuguese troops, and on the 13th the Spaniards marched, some to reinforce the force blockading Santona, the remainder to rejoin the fourth army on the Bidassoa.

At this time general Reille held the entrances to the Bastan by Vera and Echallar, but Wellington drove him thence on the 15th and established the seventh and light divisions there, thus covering the passes over the Peña de Haya by which the siege might have been interrupted.

Before general Graham arrived the French had constructed a redoubt on the heights of San Bartolomeo, and connected it with the convent of that name which they also fortified. These outworks were supported by posts in the ruined houses of the suburb of San Martin behind, and by a low circular redoubt, formed of casks on the main road, half-way between the convent and the horn-work. Hence to reduce the place, working along the isthmus, it was necessary to carry in succession three lines of defence covering the town, and a fourth at the foot of Monte Orgullo, before the castle of La Mota

could be assailed. Seventy-six pieces of artillery
were mounted upon these works and others were
afterwards obtained from France by sea.

The besieging army consisted of the fifth division
under general Oswald, and the independent Portuguese brigades of J. Wilson and Bradford reinforced
by detachments from the first division. Thus, including the artillery-men some seamen commanded
by lieutenant O'Reilly of the Surveillante and one
hundred regular sappers and miners, now for the
first time used in the sieges of the Peninsula, nearly
ten thousand men were employed. The guns available for the attack, in the first instance, were a new
battering train originally prepared for the siege of
Jones's
Journal of
British
Sieges.
Burgos, consisting of fourteen iron twenty-four
pounders, six eight-inch brass howitzers, four sixty-
eight-pound iron carronades, and four iron ten-inch
mortars. To these were added six twenty-four
pounders lent by the ships of war, and six eighteen
pounders which had moved with the army from Portugal, making altogether forty pieces commanded
by colonel Dickson. The distance from the depôt
of siege at Passages to the Chofre sand-hills was
one mile and a half of good road, and a pontoon
bridge was laid over the Urumea river above the
Chofres, but from thence to the height of Bartolomeo was more than five miles of very bad road.

Early in July the fortress had been twice closely
examined by Major Smith, the engineer who had
so ably defended Tarifa. He proposed a plan of siege
founded upon the facility furnished by the Chofre
hills to destroy the flanks rake the principal front
and form a breach with the same batteries, the works
being at the same time secured, except at low
water, by the Urumea. Counter-batteries, to be

constructed on the left of that river, were to rake
the line of defence in which the breach was to be
formed; and against the castle and its outworks he
relied principally upon vertical fire, instancing the
reduction of Fort Bourbon in the West Indies in
proof of its efficacy.   This plan would probably
have reduced San Sebastian in a reasonable time
without any remarkable loss of men, and lord Wellington approving of it, though he doubted the efficacy of the vertical fire, ordered the siege to be
commenced.   He renewed his approval afterwards
when he had examined the works in person, and all
his orders were in the same spirit; but neither
the plan nor his orders were followed, the siege,
which should have been an ordinary event of war
has obtained a mournful celebrity, and lord Wellington has been unjustly charged with a contempt
for the maxims of the great masters of the art.
Anxious he was no doubt to save time, yet he did
not for that urge the engineer beyond the rules.
*Take the place in the quickest manner, yet do not
from over speed fail to take it,* was the sense of his
instructions; but sir Thomas Graham, one of England's best soldiers, appears to have been endowed
with a genius for war intuitive rather than reflective; and this joined to his natural modesty and a
certain easiness of temper, caused him at times to
abandon his own correct conceptions, for the less
judicious counsels of those about him who advised
deviations from the original plan.

Active operations were commenced on the night
of the 10th by the construction of two batteries
against the convent and redoubt of San Bartolomeo.
And on the night of the 13th four batteries to contain twenty of the heaviest guns and four eight-inch

howitzers, were marked out on the Chofre sand-hills, at distances varying from six hundred to thirteen hundred yards from the eastern rampart of the town. The river was supposed to be unfordable, wherefore no parallel of support was made, yet good trenches of communications, and subsequently regular approaches were formed. Two attacks were thus established. One on the right bank of the Urumea entrusted to the unattached Portuguese brigades; one on the left bank to the fifth division; but most of the troops were at first encamped on the right bank to facilitate a junction with the covering army in the event of a general battle.

On the 14th a French sloop entered the harbour with supplies, and the batteries of the left attack, under the direction of the German major Hartman, opened against San Bartolomeo, throwing hot shot into that building. The besieged responded with musquetry from the redoubt, with heavy guns from the town, and with a field-piece which they had mounted on the belfry of the convent itself.

The 15th of July sir Richard Fletcher took the chief command of the engineers, but major Smith retained the direction of the attack from the Chofre Hills and lord Wellington's orders continued to pass through his hands. This day the batteries of the left attack, aided by some howitzers from the right of the Urumea, set the convent on fire, silenced the musquetry of the besieged, and so damaged the defences that the Portuguese troops attached to the fifth division were ordered to feel the enemy's post. They were however repulsed with great loss, the French sallied, and the firing did not cease until night-fall.

A battery for seven additional guns to play against Bartolomeo was now commenced on the

right of the Urumea, and the original batteries set
fire to the convent several times, but the flames were
extinguished by the garrison.

In the night of the 16th general Rey sounded the
Urumea as high as Santa Catalina, designing to pass
over and storm the batteries on the Chofres ; but
the fords discovered were shifting, and the difficulty
of execution deterred him from this project.

The 17th, the convent being nearly in ruins, the
assault was ordered without waiting for the effect of
the new battery raised on the other side of the
Urumea. The storming party was formed in two
columns. Detachments from Wilson's Portuguese,
supported by the light company of the ninth British
regiment and three companies of the royals, composed the right, which under the direction of general
Hay was destined to assail the redoubt. General
Bradford directed the left which being composed of
Portuguese, supported by three companies of the
ninth British regiment under colonel Cameron, was
ordered to assail the convent.

ASSAULT OF SAN BARTOLOMEO.

At ten o'clock in the morning two heavy six-
pounders opened against the redoubt ; and a sharp
fire of musquetry in return from the French, who
had been reinforced and occupied the suburb of
San Martin, announced their resolution to fight.
The allied troops were assembled behind the crest
of the hill overlooking the convent, and the first
signal was given, but the Portuguese advanced
slowly at both attacks, and the supporting companies of the ninth regiment on each side, passing
through them fell upon the enemy with the usual
impetuosity of British soldiers. Colonel Cameron

while leading his grenadiers down the face of the hill was exposed to a heavy cannonade from the hornwork, but he soon gained the cover of a wall fifty yards from the convent and there awaited the second signal. However his rapid advance, which threatened to cut off the garrison from the suburb, joined to the fire of the two six-pounders and that of some other field-pieces on the farther side of the Urumea, caused the French to abandon the redoubt. Seeing this, Cameron jumped over the wall and assaulted both the convent and the houses of the suburb. At the latter a fierce struggle ensued and captain Woodman of the ninth was killed in the upper room of a house after fighting his way p from below; but the grenadiers carried the convent with such rapidity that the French, unable to explode some small mines they had prepared, hastily joined the troops in the suburb. There however the fighting continued and colonel Cameron's force being very much reduced the affair was becoming doubtful, when the remaining companies of his regiment, which he had sent for after the attack commenced, arrived, and the suburb was with much fighting entirely won. At the right attack the company of the ninth, although retarded by a ravine by a thick hedge by the slowness of the Portuguese and by a heavy fire, entered the abandoned redoubt with little loss, but the troops were then rashly led against the cask redoubt, contrary to general Oswald's orders, and were beaten back by the enemy.

The loss of the French was two hundred and forty men, that of the allies considerable; the companies of the ninth under colonel Cameron, alone, had seven officers and sixty men killed or wounded, and the operation although successful was an error.

The battery erected on the right bank of the Urumea was not opened, wherefore, either the assault was precipitated or the battery not necessary; but the loss justified the conception of the battery.

When the action ceased the engineers made a lodgement in the redoubt, and commenced two batteries for eight pieces to rake the horn-work and the eastern rampart of the place. Two other batteries to contain four sixty-eight-pound carronades and four ten-inch mortars were also commenced on the right bank of the Urumea.

The 18th the besieged threw up traverses on the land front to meet the raking fire of the besiegers, and the latter dragged four pieces up the Monte Olia to plunge into the Mirador and other batteries on the Monte Orgullo. In the night a lodgement was made on the ruins of San Martin, the two batteries at the right attack were armed, and two additional mortars dragged up the Monte Olia.

The 19th all the batteries at both attacks were armed, and in the night two approaches being commenced from the suburb of San Martin towards the cask redoubt the French were driven from that small work.

On the 20th the whole of the batteries opened their fire, the greatest part being directed to form the breach.

Major Smith's plan was similar to that followed by marshal Berwick a century before. He proposed a lodgement on the horn-work before the breach should be assailed, but he had not then read the description of that siege and therefore unknowingly fixed the breaching-point precisely where the wall had been most strongly rebuilt after Berwick's

Notes of
the Siege
by sir C.
Smith,
MSS.

attack. This was the first fault, yet a slight one
because the wall did not resist the batteries very
long, but it was a serious matter that sir Thomas
Graham at the suggestion of the commander of the
artillery began his operations by breaching. Major
Smith objected to it, and sir R. Fletcher acquiesced
reluctantly on the understanding that the ruining
of the defences was only postponed, an understanding afterwards unhappily forgotten.

The result of the first day's attack was not satisfactory, the weather proved bad, the guns mounted
on ship carriages failed, one twenty-four pounder
was rendered unserviceable by the enemy, another
became useless from an accident, a captain of
engineers was killed, and the besiegers' shot had
little effect upon the solid wall. In the night however the ship-guns were mounted on better carriages,
and a parallel across the isthmus was projected;
but the greatest part of the workmen, to avoid a
tempest, sought shelter in the suburb of San Martin
and when day broke only one-third of the work was
performed.

The 21st the besiegers' batteries ceased firing to
allow of a summons, but the governor refused to
receive the letter and the firing was resumed. The
main wall still resisted yet the parapets and embra-
zures crumbled away fast, and the batteries on
Monte Olia plunged into the horn-work, although
at sixteen hundred yards distance, with such effect,
that the besieged having no bomb-proofs were forced
to dig trenches to protect themselves. The counter-
fire directed solely against the breaching batteries
was feeble, but at midnight a shell thrown from the
castle into the bay gave the signal for a sally, and
during the firing which ensued several French

vessels with supplies entered the harbour. This night also the besieged isolated the breach by cuts in the rampart and other defences. On the other hand the besiegers' parallel across the isthmus was completed, and in its progress laid bare the mouth of a drain, four feet high and three feet wide, containing the pipe of the aqueduct cut off by the Spaniards. Through this dangerous opening lieutenant Reid of the engineers, a young and zealous officer, crept even to the counterscarp of the hornwork, and finding the passage there closed by a door returned without an accident. Thirty barrels of powder were placed in this drain, and eight feet was stopped with sand-bags, thus forming a globe of compression designed to blow, as through a tube, so much rubbish over the counterscarp as might fill the narrow ditch of the horn-work.

On the 22d the fire from the batteries, unexampled from its rapidity and accuracy, opened what appeared a practicable breach in the eastern flank wall, between the towers of Los Hornos and Las Mesquitas. The counter-fire of the besieged now slackened, but the descent into the town behind the breach was more than twelve feet perpendicular, and the garrison were seen from Monte Olia diligently working at the interior defences to receive the assault: they added also another gun to the battery of St Elmo, just under the Mirador battery, to flank the front attack. On the other hand the besiegers had placed four sixty-eight pound carronades in battery to play on the defences of the breach, but the fire on both sides slackened because the guns were greatly enlarged at the vents with constant practice.

On the 23d the sea blockade being null the French

Plan 3.

vessels returned to France with the badly wounded men. This day the besiegers judging the breach between the towers quite practicable turned the guns, at the suggestion of general Oswald, to break the wall on the right of the main breach. Major Smith opposed this, urging, that no advantage would be gained by making a second opening to get at which the troops must first pass the great breach; that time would be thus uselessly lost to the besiegers, and that there was a manifest objection on account of the tide and depth of water at the new point attacked. His counsel was overruled, and in the course of the day, the wall being thin the stroke heavy and quick, a second breach thirty feet wide was rendered practicable.

The defensive fire of the besieged being now much diminished, the ten-inch mortars and sixty-eight pound carronades were turned upon the defences of the great breach, and upon a stockade which separated the high curtain on the land front, from the lower works of the flank against which the attack was conducted. The houses near the breach were soon in flames which spread rapidly, destroyed some of the defences of the besieged and menacing the whole town with destruction. The assault was ordered for the next morning. But when the troops assembled in the trenches the burning houses appeared so formidable that the attack was deferred and the batteries again opened, partly against the second breach, partly against the defences, partly to break the wall in a third place between the half bastion of St. John on the land front and the main breach.

During the night the vigilant governor expecting the assault mounted two field-pieces on the cavalier,

in the centre of the land front, which being fifteen
feet above the other defences commanded the high
curtain, and they still had on the horn-work a light
piece, and two casemated guns on the flank of the
cavalier. Two other field-pieces were mounted on
an entrenchment which crossing the ditch of the
land front bore on the approaches to the main
breach; a twenty-four pounder looked from the tower
of Las Mesquitas, between the main breach and
where the third opening was being made and consequently flanking both ; two four-pounders were
in the tower of Hornos ; two heavy guns were on
the flank of St. Elmo, and two others, placed on the
right of the Mirador, could play upon the breaches
from within the fortified line of Monte Orgullo. Thus
fourteen pieces were still available for defence, the
retaining sea-wall or *fausse braye* which strengthened
the flank of the horn-work, and between which and
the river the storming parties must necessarily advance, was covered with live shells to roll over on
the columns, and behind the flaming houses near
the breach other edifices were loop-holed and filled
with musqueteers. However the fire extending
rapidly and fiercely greatly injured the defences,
the French to save their guns withdrew them until
the moment of attack, and the British artillery
officers were confident that in daylight they could
silence the enemy's guns and keep the parapet clear
of men ; wherefore sir Thomas Graham renewed
the order for

THE ASSAULT.

In the night of the 24th two thousand men of
the fifth division filed into the trenches on the
isthmus. This force was composed of the third

battalion of the royals under major Frazer, destined
to storm the great breach; the thirty-eighth regiment under colonel Greville, designed to assail the
lesser and most distant breach; the ninth regiment
under colonel Cameron, appointed to support the
royals; finally a detachment, selected from the
light companies of all those battalions, was placed in
the centre of the royals under the command of lieutenant Campbell of the ninth regiment. This chosen
detachment, accompanied by the engineer Machel
with a ladder party, was intended to sweep the
high curtain after the breach should be won.

The distance from the trenches to the points of
attack was more than three hundred yards along
the contracted space lying between the retaining
wall of the horn-work and the river; the ground
was strewed with rocks covered by slippery sea-
weeds; the tide had left large and deep pools of
water; the parapet of the horn-work was entire as
well as the retaining wall; the parapets of the other
works and the two towers, which closely flanked
the breach, although injured were far from being
ruined, and every place was thickly garnished with
musqueteers. The difficulties of the attack were
obvious, and a detachment of Portuguese placed in
a trench opened beyond the parallel on the isthmus,
within sixty yards of the ramparts, was ordered to
quell if possible the fire of the horn-work.

While it was still dark the storming columns
moved out of the trenches, and the globe of compression in the drain was exploded with great effect
against the counterscarp and glacis of the horn-work.
The garrison astonished by the unlooked-for event
abandoned the flanking parapet, and the troops
rushed onwards, the stormers for the main breach

leading and suffering more from the fire of their
own batteries on the right of the Urumea than from
the enemy. Major Frazer and the engineer Harry
Jones first reached the breach. The enemy had
fallen back in confusion behind the ruins of the
still burning houses, and those brave officers rushed
up expecting that their troops would follow, but
not many followed, for it was extremely dark,
the natural difficulties of the way had contracted
the front and disordered the column in its whole
length, and the soldiers, straggling and out of wind,
arrived in small disconnected parties at the foot of
the breach. The foremost gathered near their gallant
leaders, but the depth of the descent into the town
and the volumes of flames and smoke which still
issued from the burning houses behind awed the
stoutest; and more than two-thirds of the storming
column, irritated by the destructive flank fire, had
broken off at the demi-bastion to commence a
musquetry battle with the enemy on the rampart.
Meanwhile the shells from the Monte Orgullo fell
rapidly, the defenders of the breach rallied and
with a smashing musquetry from the ruins and
loopholed houses smote the head of the column,
while the men in the towers smote them on the
flanks; and from every quarter came showers of
grape and hand-grenades tearing the ranks in a
dreadful manner.

Major Frazer was killed on the flaming ruins, the
intrepid Jones stood there awhile longer amidst a
few heroic soldiers, hoping for aid, but none came
and he and those with him were struck down. The
engineer Machel had been killed early and the men
bearing ladders fell or were dispersed. Thus the
rear of the column was in absolute confusion before

the head was beaten.   It was in vain that colonel
Greville of the thirty-eighth, colonel Cameron of
the ninth, captain Archimbeau of the royals, and
many other regimental officers exerted themselves to
rally their discomfited troops and refill the breach;
it was in vain that lieutenant Campbell, breaking
through the tumultuous crowd with the survivors of
his chosen detachment, mounted the ruins ; twice he
ascended, twice he was wounded, and all around
him died.   The royals endeavouring to retire got
intermixed with the thirty-eighth, and with some
companies of the ninth which had unsuccessfully
endeavoured to pass them and get to the lesser
breach.   Then swayed by different impulses and
pent up in the narrow way between the horn-work
and the river, the mass reeling to and fro could
neither advance nor go back until the shells and
musquetry, constantly plied both in front and flank,
had thinned the concourse and the trenches were
regained in confusion.   At day-light a truce was
agreed to for an hour, during which the French,
who had already humanely removed the gallant
Jones and the other wounded men from the breach,
now carried off the more distant sufferers lest they
should be drowned by the rising of the tide.

Five officers of engineers including sir Richard
Fletcher, and forty-four officers of the line with
five hundred and twenty men, had been killed,
wounded, or made prisoners in this assault the
failure of which was signal, yet the causes were
obvious and may be classed thus.

1°. Deviation from the original project of siege
and from lord Wellington's instructions.

2°. Bad arrangements of detail.

3°. Want of vigour in the execution.

In respect of the first, lord Wellington having visited the Chofre trenches on the 22d confirmed his former approval of Smith's plan, and gave that officer final directions for the attack finishing thus, " *Fair daylight must be taken for the assault.*" These instructions and their emphatic termination were repeated by major Smith in the proper quarter, but they were not followed, no lodgement was made on the horn-work, the defences were nearly entire both in front and flank, and the assault was made in darkness. Major Smith had also, by calculation and by consultations with the fishermen, ascertained that the ebb of tide would serve exactly at day-break on the 24th; but the assault was made the 25th, and then before daylight, when the water being too high contracted the ground, increased the obstacles, and forced the assaulting column to march on a narrow front and a long line, making an uneasy progress and trickling onwards instead of dashing with a broad surge against the breach. In fine the rules of art being neglected and no extraordinary resource substituted the operation failed.

The troops filed out of the long narrow trenches in the night, a tedious operation, and were immediately exposed to a fire of grape from their own batteries on the Chofres. This fire, intended to keep down that of the enemy, should have ceased when the globe of compression was sprung in the drain, but owing to the darkness and the noise the explosion could neither be seen nor heard. The effect of it however drove the enemy from the horn-work, the Portuguese on that side advanced to the ditch, and a vigorous escalade would probably have succeeded but they had no ladders. Again the stormers of the great breach marched first, filling

Notes on the siege, by sir C. Smith, MSS.

up the way and rendering the second breach, as
major Smith had foretold, useless, and the ladder-
bearers never got to their destination. The attack
was certainly ill-digested, and there was a neglect
of moral influence followed by its natural consequence want of vigour in execution.

The deferring of the assault from the 24th to the
25th expressly because the breach was too difficult
rendered the troops uneasy, they suspected some
hidden danger, and in this mood emerging from the
trenches they were struck by the fire of their own
batteries; then wading through deep pools of water,
or staggering in the dark over slippery rocks, and
close under the enemy's flanking works whence
every shot told with fatal effect, how could they
manifest their natural conquering energy? It is
possible that a second and more vigorous assault on
the great breach might have been effected by a
recognized leader, but no general or staff officer
went out of the trenches with the troops, and the
isolated exertions of the regimental officers were
unavailing. Nor were there wanting other sinister
influences. General Oswald had in the councils
earnestly and justly urged the dangers arising from
the irregular mode of attack, but this anticipation
of ill success, in which other officers of rank joined,
was freely expressed out of council, and it said even
in the hearing of the troops abating that daring
confidence which victory loves.

Lord Wellington repaired immediately to St.
Sebastian. The causes of the failure were apparent
and he would have renewed the attack, but wanting
ammunition, deferred it until the powder and additional ordnance which he had written for to England as early as the 26th of June should arrive.

The next day other events caused him to resort to a blockade and the battering train was transported to Passages, two guns and two howitzers only being retained on the Chofres and the Monte Olia. This operation was completed in the night of the 26th, but at day-break the garrison made a sally from the horn-work, surprised the trenches and swept off two hundred Portuguese and thirty British soldiers. To avoid a repetition of this disaster the guards of the trenches were concentrated in the left parallel, and patroles only were sent out, yet one of those also was cut off on the 1st of August. Thus terminated the first part of the siege of San Sebastian in which the allies lost thirteen hundred soldiers and seamen, exclusive of Spaniards during Mendizabal's blockade.

CHAPTER IV.

THE battle of Vittoria was fought on the 21st of
June.

The 1st of July marshal Soult, under a decree
issued at Dresden, succeeded Joseph as lieutenant
to the emperor, who thus shewed how little his mind
had been affected by his brother's accusations.

The 12th, Soult, travelling with surprising expedition, assumed the command of the armies of the
" *north*," the " *centre*" and the " *south*" now reorganised in one body, called " *the army of Spain*."
And he had secret orders to put Joseph forcibly
aside if necessary, but that monarch voluntarily
retired from the army.

At this period general Paris remained at Jaca,
as belonging to Suchet's command, but Clauzel had
entered France, and the " *army of Spain*," reinforced from the interior, was composed of nine
divisions of infantry, a reserve, and two regular
divisions of cavalry besides the light horsemen
attached to the infantry. Following the imperial
muster-rolls this army, including the garrisons and
thirteen German Italian and Spanish battalions not
belonging to the organisation, amounted to one
hundred and fourteen thousand men; and as the
armies of Catalonia and of Aragon numbered at

the same period above sixty-six thousand, the whole force still employed against Spain exceeded one hundred and eighty thousand men with twenty thousand horses; and of this number one hundred and fifty-six thousand were present under arms, while in Germany and Poland above seven hundred thousand French soldiers were in activity.

Such great forces, guided by Napoleon, seemed sufficient to defy the world, but moral power which he has himself described as constituting three-fourths of military strength, that power which puny essayists declaiming for their hour against the genius of warriors, are unable to comprehend although by far the most important part of the art which they decry, was wanting. One-half of this force, organized in peace and setting forth in hope at the beginning of a war, would have enabled Napoleon to conquer; but now, near the close of a terrible struggle, with a declining fate and the national confidence in his fortune and genius shaken, although that genius was never more surpassingly displayed, his military power was a vast but unsound machine. The public mind was bewildered by the intricacy and greatness of combinations the full scope of which he alone could see clearly, and generals and ministers doubted and feared when they should have supported him, neglecting their duty or coldly executing his orders when their zeal should have redoubled. The unity of impulse so essential to success was thus lost, and his numerous armies carried not with them proportionate strength. To have struggled with hope under such astounding difficulties was scarcely to be expected from the greatest minds, but like the emperor, to calculate and combine the most stupendous efforts with calmness and accuracy, to seize every favourable chance with unerring rapidity, to sustain every reverse with undisturbed constancy, never urged to rashness by despair yet enterprizing to the utmost verge of daring consistent with reason, was a display of intellectual greatness so surpassing, that it is not without justice Napoleon has been called, in reference as well to past ages as to the present, the foremost of mankind.

The suddenness, as well as the completeness, of the destruction caused by the snows of Russia, had shattered the emperor's military and political system, and the broken parts of the former, scattered widely, were useless until he could again bind them together. To effect this he rushed with a raw army into the midst of Germany, for his hope was to obtain by celerity a rallying point for his veterans, who having survived the Russian winter and the succeeding pestilence were widely dispersed. His first effort was successful, but without good cavalry victory cannot be pushed far, and the practised horsemen of France had nearly disappeared; their successors badly mounted and less skilful were too few and too weak, and thus extraordinary exertion was required from soldiers, whose youth and inexperience rendered them unfit even for the ordinary hardships of war.

The measure of value for Wellington's campaign is thus attained, for if Joseph had opposed him with only moderate ability and had avoided a great battle, not less than fifty thousand veterans could have been drawn off to reinforce and give stability to the young soldiers in Germany. On the side of Spain those veterans were indeed still numerous, but the spirit of the French people behind them

almost worn out by victory, was now abashed by
defeat, and even the military men who had acquired
grandeur and riches beyond their hopes, were with
few exceptions averse to further toil. Napoleon's
astonishing firmness of mind was understood by
few in high stations, shared by fewer ; and many
were the traitors to him and to France and to the
glories of both. However his power was still enormous, and wherever he led in person his brave
and faithful soldiers, fighting with the true instinct
of patriotism, conquered. Where he was not their
iron hardihood abated.

Marshal Soult was one of the few men whose
indefatigable energy rendered them worthy lieutenants of the emperor; and with singular zeal,
vigour and ability he now served. His troops, nominally above one hundred thousand men ninety-
seven thousand being present under arms with
eighty-six pieces of artillery, were not all available
for field operations. The garrisons of Pampeluna,
San Sebastian, Santona, and Bayonne, together
with the foreign battalions, absorbed seventeen
thousand ; and most of the latter had orders to
regain their own countries with a view to form the
new levies. The permanent " *army of Spain*" furnished therefore only seventy-seven thousand five
hundred men present under arms, seven thousand of
which were cavalry, and its condition was not satisfactory. The people on the frontier were flying
from the allies, the military administration was disorganized, and the recent disasters had discouraged
the soldiers and deteriorated their discipline. Under
these circumstances Soult was desirous of some
delay to secure his base and restore order ere he

attempted to regain the offensive, but his instructions on that point were imperative.

Napoleon's system was perfectly adapted for great
efforts, civil or military; but so rapid had been
lord Wellington's advance from Portugal, so decisive his operations that the resources of France
were in a certain degree paralyzed, and the army
still reeled and rocked from the blows it had received. Bayonne, a fortress of no great strength
in itself, had been entirely neglected, and the arming and provisioning that and other places was
indispensible. The restoration of an entrenched
camp originally traced by Vauban to cover Bayonne followed, and the enforcement of discipline,
the removal of the immense train of Spanish families, civil administrators, and other wasteful followers
of Joseph's court, the arrangement of a general
system for supply of money and provisions, aided
by judicious efforts to stimulate the civil authorities
and excite the national spirit, were amongst the
first indications that a great commander was in the
field. The soldiers' confidence soon revived and
some leading merchants of Bayonne zealously seconded the general; but the people of the south
were generally more inclined to avoid the burthen
of defending their country than to answer appeals
to their patriotism.

On the 14th Soult examined the line of military
positions, and ordered Reille, who then occupied
the passes of Vera and Echallar, to prepare pontoons for throwing two bridges over the Bidassoa at
Biriatou. That general as we have seen was driven
from those passes the next day, but he prepared his
bridges; and such was Soult's activity that on the

16th all the combinations for a gigantic offensive
movement were digested, the means of executing
it rapidly advancing, and orders were issued for
the preliminary dispositions.

At this time the French army was divided into
three corps of battle, and a reserve. Clauzel commanding the left wing was at St. Jean Pied de Port
and in communication, by the French frontier, with
general Paris at Jaca. Drouet, count D'Erlon,
commanding the centre, occupied the heights near
Espelette and Ainhoa, with an advanced guard
behind Urdax. General Reille commanding the
right wing was in position on the mountains overlooking Vera from the side of France. The reserve
under Villatte, comprising a separate body of light
horsemen and the foreign battalions, guarded the
banks of the Bidassoa from the mouth upwards to
Irun, at which place the stone bridge was destroyed. The division of heavy cavalry under
Trielhard, and that of light cavalry under Pierre
Soult, the Marshal's brother, were on the banks of
the Nive and the Adour.

The counter-disposition of the allies was as
follows.

Byng's brigade of British infantry, detached from
the second division and reinforced by Morillo's Spaniards, was on the extreme right. These troops had
early in June driven the French from the village
of Valcarlos in the valley of that name, and had
foraged the French territory, but finding no good
permanent position, retreated again to the rocks in
front of the passes of Roncesvalles and Ibañeta.

On the left of Byng, Campbell's brigade detached from Hamilton's Portuguese division, was

posted in the Alduides and supported by general
Cole, who was with the fourth division at Viscayret
in the valley of Urroz.

On the left of Campbell general Hill defended
the Bastan with the remainder of the second division, and with Hamilton's Portuguese, now commanded by Sylveira, Conde d'Amarante. Picton,
with the third division, was stationed at Olague as
a reserve to those troops and to Cole.

On the left of Hill the seventh and light divi-
sions occupied a chain of mountains running by
Echallar to Vera, and behind them at the town of
San Estevan was posted the sixth division.

Longa's Spaniards continued the line of defence
from Vera to general Giron's position, which extending along the mountains bordering the Bidassoa to the sea, crossed the great road of Irun.
Behind Giron was the besieging army under sir
Thomas Graham.

Thirty-six pieces of field artillery, and some regiments of British and Portuguese cavalry, were
with the right wing and centre, but the bulk of the
horsemen and the heavy guns were behind the
mountains, chiefly about Tafalla. The great hospitals were in Vittoria, the commissariat depôts were
principally on the coast, and to supply the troops
in the mountains was exceedingly difficult and
onerous.

Henry O'Donnel, Conde de la Bispal, blockaded
Pampeluna with the Andalusian army of reserve,
and Carlos D'España's division was on the march
to join him. Mina, Julian Sanchez, Duran, Empecinado, Goyan and some smaller bands, were on
the side of Zaragoza and Daroca, cutting the com-

munication between Soult and Suchet, and the
latter, thinking Aragon lost, was, as we have seen,
falling back upon Catalonia.

The whole force under lord Wellington's immediate command, that is to say in Navarre and Guipuscoa, was certainly above one hundred thousand
men, of which the Anglo-Portuguese furnished
fifty-seven thousand present under arms, seven
thousand being cavalry; but the Spanish regulars
under Giron, Labispal and Carlos d'España, including Longa's division and some of Mendizabal's
army, scarcely amounted to twenty-five thousand.
According to the respective muster-rolls, the troops
in line actually under arms and facing each
other, were, of the allies, about eighty-two thousand, of the French about seventy-eight thousand;
but as the rolls of the latter include every man and
officer of all arms belonging to the organization,
and the British and Portuguese rolls so quoted,
would furnish between ten and twelve thousand
additional combatants, the French force must be
reduced, or the allies augmented in that proportion.
This surplus was however now compensated by the
foreign battalions temporarily attached to Soult's
army, and by the numerous national guards, all
amountaineers, fierce warlike and very useful as
guides. In other respects lord Wellington stood at
a disadvantage.

The theatre of operations was a trapezoid, with
sides from forty to sixty miles in length, and having
Bayonne, St. Jean Pied de Port, St. Sebastian and
Pampeluna, all fortresses, in possession of the French
at the angles. The interior, broken and tormented
by dreadful mountains, narrow craggy passes, deep
water-courses, precipices and forests, would at first

Appendix
7.

Notes by
the Duke
of Wel-
lington,
MSS.

sight appear a wilderness which no military combinations could embrace, and susceptible only of irregular and partizan operations. But the great spinal
ridge of the Pyrenees furnishes a clue to the labyrinth of hills and valleys. Running diagonally
across the quadrilateral, it separated Bayonne St.
Jean Pied de Port and San Sebastian from Pampeluna, and thus the portion of the allied army which
more especially belonged to the blockade of Pampeluna, was in a manner cut off from that which
belonged to the siege of San Sebastian. They
were distinct armies, each having its particular
object, and the only direct communication between
them was the great road running behind the mountains from Toloza, by Irurzun, to Pampeluna.
The centre of the allies was indeed an army of
succour and connection, but of necessity very much
scattered, and with lateral communications so few,
difficult and indirect as to prevent any unity of
movement ; nor could general Hill's corps move at
all until an attack was decidedly pronounced against
one of the extremities, lest the most direct gun-
road to Pampeluna which it covered should be
unwarily opened to the enemy. In short the French
general, taking the offensive, could by beaten roads
concentrate against any part of the English general's
line, which, necessarily a passively defensive one,
followed an irregular trace of more than fifty miles
of mountains.

Wellington having his battering train and stores
about San Sebastian, which was also nearer and
more accessible to the enemy than Pampeluna, made
his army lean towards that side. His left wing, including the army of siege, was twenty-one thousand strong with singularly strong positions of

defence, and the centre, about twenty-four thousand strong, could in two marches unite with the left wing to cover the siege or fall upon the flanks of an enemy advancing by the high road of Irun ; but three days or more were required by those troops to concentrate for the security of the blockade on the right. Soult however judged that no decisive result would attend a direct movement upon San Sebastian ; because Guipuscoa was exhausted of provisions, and the centre of the allies could fall on his flank before he reached Ernani, which, his attack in front failing, would place him in a dangerous position. Moreover by means of his sea communication he knew that San Sebastian was not in extremity ; but he had no communication with Pampeluna and feared its fall. Wherefore he resolved to operate by his left.

Profiting by the roads leading to St. Jean Pied de Port, and covering his movement by the Nivelle and Nive rivers and by the positions of his centre, he hoped to gather on Wellington's right quicker than that general could gather to oppose him, and thus compensating by numbers the disadvantage of assailing mountain positions force a way to Pampeluna. That fortress once succoured, he designed to seize the road of Irurzun, and keeping in mass either fall upon the separated divisions of the centre in detail as they descended from the hills, or operate on the rear of the force besieging San Sebastian, while a corps of observation, which he proposed to leave on the Lower Bidassoa, menaced it in front and followed it in retreat. The siege of San Sebastian, the blockade of Pampeluna and probably that of Santona, would be thus raised, and the French army united in an abundant country, and its communication with Suchet secured, would be free either to co-operate with that marshal or to press its own attack.

In this view, and to mislead lord Wellington by vexing his right simultaneously with the construction of the bridges against his left, Soult wrote to general Paris, desiring him to march when time suited from Jaca by the higher valleys towards Aviz or Sanguessa, to drive the partizans from that side and join the left of the army when it should have reached Pampeluna. Meanwhile Clauzel was directed to repair the roads in his own front, to push the heads of his columns towards the passes of Roncesvalles, and by sending a strong detachment into the Val de Baygorry, towards the lateral pass of Yspegui, to menace Hill's flank which was at that pass, and the front of Campbell's brigade in the Alduides.

On the 20th Reille's troops on the heights above Vera and Sarre, being cautiously relieved by Villatte, marched through Cambo towards St. Jean Pied de Port. They were to reach the latter early on the 22d, and on that day also the two divisions of cavalry and the park of artillery were to be concentrated at the same place. D'Erlon with the centre meanwhile still held his positions at Espelette, Ainhoüe or Ainhoa, and Urdax, thus covering and masking the great movements taking place behind.

Villatte who including the foreign battalions had eighteen thousand troops on the rolls, furnishing about fifteen thousand sabres and bayonets, remained in observation on the Bidassoa. If threatened by superior forces he was to retire slowly and in mass upon the entrenched camp commenced at Bayonne, yet halting successively on the positions of Bordegain in front of St. Jean de Luz, and on the heights

of Bidart in rear of that town. He was especially
directed to shew only French troops at the advanced
posts, and if the assailants made a point with a
small corps, to drive them vigorously over the
Bidassoa again. But if the allies should in consequence of Soult's operations against their right retire, Villatte was to relieve San Sebastian and to
follow them briskly by Tolosa.

Rapidity was of vital importance to the French
general, but heavy and continued rains swelled the
streams, and ruined the roads in the deep country
between Bayonne and the hills ; the head-quarters,
which should have arrived at St. Jean Pied de Port
on the 20th, only reached Olhonce, a few miles Soult's
Official
short of that place, the 21st ; and Reille's troops Correspondence,
unable to make way at all by Cambo took the MSS.
longer road of Bayonne. The cavalry was retarded
in like manner, and the whole army, men and
horses, were worn down by the severity of the
marches. Two days were thus lost, but on the 24th
more than sixty thousand fighting men including
cavalry national guards and gensd'armes, with sixty-
six pieces of artillery, were assembled to force the
passes of Roncesvalles and Maya. The main road
leading to the former was repaired, three hundred
sets of bullocks were provided to draw the guns up
the mountain, and the national guards of the frontier on the left were ordered to assemble in the
night on the heights of Yropil, to be reinforced on
the morning of the 25th by detachments of regular
troops with a view to vex and turn the right of the
allies which extended to the foundry of Orbaiceta.

Such were Soult's first dispositions, but as mountain warfare is complicated in the extreme, it will
be well to consider more in detail the relative posi-

tions and objects of the hostile forces and the nature of the country.

It has been already stated that the great spine of
the hills, trending westward, run diagonally across
the theatre of operations. From this spine huge
ridges shot out on either hand, and the communications between the valleys thus formed on both sides
of the main chain passed over certain comparatively
low places called " *cols* " by the French, and *puertos*
by the Spaniards. The Bastan, the Val Carlos,
and the Val de Baygorry the upper part of which
is divided into the Alduides and the Val de Ayra,
were on the French side of the great chain; on the
Spanish side were the valleys of Ahescoa or Orbaiceta, the valley of Iscua or Roncesvalles, the valley
of Urros, the Val de Zubiri, and the valley of Lanz,
the two latter leading down directly upon Pampeluna which stands within two miles of the junction
of their waters. Such being the relative situations
of the valleys, the disposition, and force, of the armies,
shall now be traced from left to right of the French,
and from right to left of the allies. But first it must be
observed that the main chain, throwing as it were a
shoulder forward from Roncesvalles towards St.
Jean Pied de Port, placed the entrance to the Spanish valley of Ahescoa or Orbaiceta, in the power
of Soult, who could thus by Yropil turn the extreme
right of his adversary with detachments, although
not with an army.

Val Carlos.—Two issues led from this valley over
the main chain, namely the Ibañeta and Mendichuri
passes; and there was also the lateral pass of Atalosti leading into the Alduides, all comprised within
a space of two or three miles.

The high road from St. Jean Pied de Port to

Pampeluna, ascending the left-hand ridge or boundary of Val Carlos, runs along the crest until it
joins the superior chain of mountains, and then
along the summit of that also until it reaches the
pass of Ibañeta, whence it descends to Roncesvalles.
Ibañeta may therefore be called the Spanish end of
the pass; but it is also a pass in itself, because a
narrow road, leading through Arnegui and the
village of Val Carlos, ascends directly to Ibañeta
and falls into the main road behind it.

Clauzel's three divisions of infantry, all the artillery
and the cavalry were formed in two columns in front
of St. Jean Pied de Port. The head of one was
placed on some heights above Arnegui about two
miles from the village of Val Carlos; the head
of the other at the Venta de Orrisson, on the main
road and within two miles of the remarkable rocks
of Chateau Piñon, a little beyond which one narrow
way descended on the right to the village of Val
Carlos, and another on the left to the foundry of
Orbaiceta.

On the right-hand boundary of Val Carlos, near
the rock of Ayrola, Reille's divisions were concentrated, with orders to ascend that rock at daylight,
and march by the crest of the ridge towards a culminant point of the great chain called the Lindouz,
which gained, Reille was to push detachments
through the passes of Ibañeta and Mendichuri to
the villages of Roncesvalles and Espinal. He was,
at the same time, to seize the passes of Sahorgain
and Urtiaga immediately on his right, and even approach the more distant passes of Renecabal and
Bellate, thus closing the issues from the Alduides,
and menacing those from the Bastan.

Val de Ayra. The Alduides. Val de Baygorry. Plan, No, 2.

The ridge of Ayrola, at the foot of which Reille's troops were posted, separates Val Carlos from these valleys which must be designated by the general name of the Alduides for the upper part, and the Val de Baygorry for the lower. The issues from the Alduides over the great chain towards Spain were the passes of Sahorgain and Urtiaga ; and there was also a road running from the village of Alduides through the Atalosti pass to Ibañeta a distance of eight miles, by which general Campbell's brigade communicated with and could join Byng and Morillo.

Bastan. This district, including the valley of Lerins and the Cinco Villas, is separated from the Alduides and Val de Baygorry by the lofty mountain of La Houssa, on which the national guards of the Val de Baygorry and the Alduides were ordered to assemble on the night of the 24th, and to light fires so as to make it appear a great body was menacing the Bastan by that flank. The Bastan however does not belong to the same geographical system as the other valleys. Instead of opening to the French territory it is entirely enclosed with high mountains, and while the waters of the Val Carlos, the Alduides, and Val de Baygorry run off northward by the Nive, those of the Bastan run off westward by the Bidassoa, from which they are separated by the Mandale, Commissari, La Rhune, Santa Barbara, Ivantelly, Atchiola and other mountains.

The entrances to the Bastan with reference to the position of the French army, were by the passes of Vera and Echallar on its right ; by the Col de Maya and Arietta passes in the centre ; and on the left by the lateral passes of Yspegui, Lorrieta, and

Berderez, which lead from the Val de Baygorry and the Alduides. The issues over the principal chain of the Pyrenees in the direct line from the Maya entrances, were the passes of Renecabal and Bellate ; the first leading into the valley of Zubiri, the second into the valley of Lanz. There was also the pass of Artesiaga leading into the Val de Zubiri, but it was nearly impracticable, and all the roads through the Bastan were crossed by strong positions dangerous to assail.

The Col de Maya comprised several passages in a space of four miles, all of which were menaced by D'Erlon from Espelete and Urdax ; and he had twenty-one thousand men, furnishing about eighteen thousand bayonets. His communications with Soult were maintained by cavalry posts through the Val de Baygorry, and his orders were to attack the allies when the combinations in the Val Carlos and on the Houssa mountain should cause them to abandon the passes at Maya ; but he was especially directed to operate by his left, so as to secure the passes leading towards Reille with a view to the concentration of the whole army. Thus if Hill retreated by the pass of Bellate D'Erlon was to move by Berderez and the Alduides ; but if Hill retired upon San Estevan D'Erlon was to move by the pass of Bellate. Such being the dispositions of the French general, those of the allies shall now be traced.

General Byng and Morillo guarded the passes in front of Roncesvalles. Their combined force consisted of sixteen hundred British and from three to four thousand Spaniards. Byng's brigade and two Spanish battalions occupied the rocks of Altobiscar on the high road facing Chateau Piñon ;

one Spanish battalion was at the foundry in the
valley of Orbaiceta on their right; Morillo with the
remainder of the Spaniards occupied the heights of
Iroulepe, on the left of the road leading to the
village of Val Carlos and overlooking the nearest
houses of that straggling place.

These positions, distant only four and five miles
from the French columns assembled at Venta de
Orrisson and Arnegui, were insecure. The ground
was indeed steep and difficult of access but too extensive; moreover, although the passes led into the
Roncesvalles that valley did not lead direct to
Pampeluna; the high road after descending a few
miles turned to the right, and crossing two ridges
and the intervening valley of Urros entered the
valley of Zubiri, down which it was conducted to
Pampeluna: wherefore after passing Ibañeta in retreat the allied troops could not avoid lending their
right flank to Reille's divisions as far as Viscayret
in the valley of Urroz. It was partly to obviate
this danger, partly to support O'Donnel while

Welling-
ton's
Morning
States.
Clauzel's force was in the vicinity of Jaca, that the
fourth division, about six thousand strong, occupied
Viscayret, six miles from the pass of Ibañeta, ten
miles from Morillo's position, and twelve miles from
Byng's position. But when Clauzel retired to
France, general Cole was directed to observe the
roads leading over the main chain from the Alduides
district, and to form a rallying point and reserve for
Campbell, Byng, and Morillo, his instructions being
to maintain the Roncesvalles passes against a front
attack, but not to commit his troops in a desperate
battle if the flanks were insecure.

Ibid.
On the left of Byng and Morillo, Campbell's
Portuguese, about two thousand strong, were en-

camped above the village of Alduides on a mountain called Mizpira. They observed the national
guards of the Val de Baygorry, preserved the communication between Byng and Hill, and in some
measure covered the right flank of the latter.
From the Alduides Campbell could retreat through
the pass of Sahorgain upon Viscayret in the valley
of Urroz, and through the passes of Urtiaga and
Renacabal upon Eugui in the Val de Zubiri; finally
by the lateral pass of Atalosti he could join Byng
and the fourth division. The communication between all these posts was maintained by Long's
cavalry.

Continuing the line of positions to the left, general
Hill occupied the Bastan with the second British
division, Sylveira's Portuguese, and some squadrons
of horse, but Byng's and Campbell's brigades being
detached, he had not more than nine thousand
sabres and bayonets. His two British brigades under
general William Stewart guarded the Col de Maya;
Sylveira's Portuguese were at Erazu, on the right of
Stewart, observing the passes of Arrieta, Yspegui
and Elliorita; of which the two former were occupied by Major Brotherton's cavalry and by the
sixth Caçadores. The direct line of retreat and
point of concentration for all these troops was
Elizondo.

From Elizondo the route of Pampeluna over the
great chain was by the pass of Bellate and the
valley of Lanz. The latter running nearly parallel
with the valley of Zubiri is separated from it by a
wooded and rugged ridge, and between them there
were but three communications: the one high up,
leading from Lanz to Eugui, and prolonged from
thence to Viscayret in the valley of Urros; the

other two lower down, leading from Ostiz and Olague to the village of Zubiri. At Olague the third division, furnishing four thousand three hundred bayonets under Picton, was posted ready to support Cole or Hill as occasion required.

Continuing the front line from the left of Stewart's position at the Col de Maya, the trace run along the mountains forming the French boundary of the Bastan. It comprized the passes of Echallar and Vera, guarded by the seventh division under lord Dalhousie, and by the light division under general Charles Alten. The former furnishing four thousand seven hundred bayonets communicated with general Stewart by a narrow road over the Atchiola mountain, and the eighty-second regiment was encamped at its junction with the Elizondo road, about three miles behind the pass of Maya. The light division, four thousand strong, was at Vera, guarding the roads which led behind the mountains through Sumbilla and San Estevan to Elizondo.

These two divisions being only observed by the left wing of Villatte's reserve were available for the succour of either wing, and behind them, at the town of San Estevan, was the sixth division of six thousand bayonets, now under general Pack. Placed at equal distances from Vera and Maya, having free communication with both and a direct line of march to Pampeluna over the main chain of the Pyrenees by the *Puerto de Arraiz*, sometimes called the pass of *Dona Maria*, this division was available for any object and could not have been better posted.

Around Pampeluna, the point to which all the lines of march converged, the Spanish troops under O'Donnel maintained the blockade, and they were afterwards joined by Carlos D'España's division at a very critical moment. Thus reinforced they amounted to eleven thousand, of which seven thousand could be brought into action without abandoning the works of blockade.

Head-quarters were at Lesaca, and the line of correspondence with the left wing was over the Peña de Haya, that with the right wing by San Estevan, Elizondo and the Alduides. The line of correspondence between sir Thomas Graham and Pampeluna was by Goizueta and the high road of Irurzun.

As the French were almost in contact with the allies' positions at Roncesvalles, which was also the point of defence nearest to Pampeluna, it followed that on the rapidity or slowness with which Soult overcame resistance in that quarter depended his success ; and a comparative estimate of numbers and distances will give the measure of his chances.

Clauzel's three divisions furnished about sixteen thousand bayonets, besides the cavalry, the artillery, and the national guards menacing the valley of Orbaiceta. Byng and Morillo were therefore with five thousand infantry, to sustain the assault of sixteen thousand until Cole could reinforce them ; but Cole being twelve miles distant could not come up in fighting order under four or five hours. And as Reille's divisions, of equal strength with Clauzel's, could before that time seize the Lindouz and turn the left, it was clear the allied troops, although increased to eleven thousand by the junction of the fourth division, must finally abandon their ground to seek a new field of battle where the third division could join them from the valley of Lanz, and Campbell's brigade from the Alduides. Thus

raised to seventeen or eighteen thousand bayonets
with some guns, they might on strong ground oppose Clauzel and Reille's thirty thousand ; but as
Picton's position at Olague was more than a day's
march from Byng's position at Altobiscar, their junction could only be made in the valley of the Zubiri
and not very distant from Pampeluna.   And when
seven thousand Spaniards from the blockade, and
two or three thousand cavalry from the side of the
Ebro are added, we have the full measure of the
allies' strength in this quarter.

General Hill, menaced by D'Erlon with a very
superior force, and having the pass of Maya, half
a day's march further from Pampeluna than the
passes of Roncesvalles, to defend, could not give
ready help.   If he retreated rapidly D'Erlon could
follow as rapidly, and though Picton and Cole
would thus be reinforced with ten thousand men
Soult would gain eighteen thousand.   Hill could
not however move until he knew that Byng and
Cole were driven from the Roncesvalles passes ;
in fine he could not avoid a dilemma.   For if he
maintained the passes at Maya and affairs went
wrong near Pampeluna, his own situation would be
imminently dangerous ; if he maintained Irrueta,
his next position, the same danger was to be
dreaded ; and the passes of Maya once abandoned,
D'Erlon, moving by his own left towards the Alduides, could join Soult in the valley of Zubiri
before Hill could join Cole and Picton by the valley
of Lanz.   But if Hill did not maintain the position
of Irrueta D'Erlon could follow and cut the sixth
and seventh divisions off from the valley of Lanz.
The extent and power of Soult's combinations are
thus evinced.   Hill forced to await orders and ham-

pered by the operations of D'Erlon, required, it

might be three days to get into line near Pampeluna; but D'Erlon after gaining Maya could in one
day and a half, by the passes of Berderez and Urtiaga, join Soult in the Val de Zubiri. Meanwhile
Byng, Morillo, Cole, Campbell, and Picton would
be exposed to the operations of double their own
numbers; and however firm and able individually
those generals might be, they could not when suddenly brought together be expected to seize the
whole system of operations and act with that decision and nicety of judgment which the occasion
demanded. It was clear therefore that Hill's force
must be in some measure paralyzed at first, and
finally thrown with the sixth, seventh, and light
divisions, upon an external line of operations while
the French moved upon internal lines.

On the other hand it is also clear that the corps
of Byng, Morillo, Campbell, Cole, Picton, and
Hill were only pieces of resistance on Lord Wellington's board, and that the sixth, seventh, and
light divisions were those with which he meant to
win his game. There was however a great difference in their value. The light division and the
seventh, especially the former, being at the greatest
distance from Pampeluna, having enemies close in
front and certain points to guard, were, the seventh
division a day, the light division two days, behind
the sixth division, which was quite free to move at
an instant's notice and was, the drag of D'Erlon's
corps considered, a day nearer to Pampeluna than
Hill. Wherefore upon the rapid handling of this
well-placed body the fate of the allies depended.
If it arrived in time, nearly thirty thousand in-

fantry with sufficient cavalry and artillery would be established, under the immediate command of the general-in-chief, on a position of strength to check the enemy until the rest of the army arrived. Where that position was and how the troops were there gathered and fought shall now be shown.

CHAPTER V.

BATTLES OF THE PYRENEES.

Combat of Roncesvalles.—On the 23d Soult issued an order of the day remarkable for its force and frankness. Tracing with a rapid pen the leading events of the past campaign, he shewed that the disasters sprung from the incapacity of the king, not from the weakness of the soldiers whose military virtue he justly extolled, and whose haughty courage he inflamed by allusions to former glories. He has been, by writers who disgrace English literature with unfounded aspersions of a courageous enemy, accused of unseemly boasting as to his ultimate operations at this time, but the calumny is refuted by the following passage from his dispatch to the minister at war.

" *I shall move directly upon Pampeluna, and if I succeed in relieving it I will operate towards my right to embarrass the enemy's troops in Guipuscoa, Biscay, and Alava, and to enable the reserve to join me, which will relieve St. Sebastian and Santona. If this should happen I will then consider what is to be done, either to push my own attack or to help the army of Aragon, but to look so far ahead would now be temerity.*"

It is true that conscious of superior abilities he did not suppress the sentiment of his own worth as

CHAP.
V.
——
1813.
July.
Plan 3.

a commander, but he was too proud to depreciate brave adversaries on the eve of battle.

" *Let us not,*" he said, " *defraud the enemy of the praise which is due to him. The dispositions of the general have been prompt, skilful, and consecutive, the valour and steadiness of his troops have been praiseworthy.*"

Having thus stimulated the ardour of his troops he put himself at the head of Clauzel's divisions, and on the 25th at daylight led them up against the rocks of Altobiscar.

General Byng, warned the evening before that danger was near, and jealous of some hostile indications towards the village of Val Carlos, had sent the fifty-seventh regiment down there but kept the rest of his men well in hand and gave notice to general Cole who had made a new disposition of his troops.   Ross's brigade was now at Espinal two miles in advance of Viscayret, six miles from the pass of Ibañeta, and eleven from Byng's position, but somewhat nearer to Morillo.   Anson's brigade was close behind Ross, Stubbs' Portuguese behind Anson, and the artillery was at Linzoain.

Such was the exact state of affairs when Soult, throwing out a multitude of skirmishers and pushing forward his supporting columns and guns as fast as the steepness of the road and difficult nature of the ground would permit, endeavoured to force Byng's position; but the British general, undismayed at the multitude of assailants, fought strongly, the French fell fast among the rocks, and their rolling musketry pealed in vain for hours along that cloudy field of battle elevated five thousand feet above the level of the plains.   Their numbers however continually increased in front, and the national guards from Yropil, reinforced by Clauzel's detachments, skirmished with the Spanish battalions at the foundry of Orbaiceta and threatened to turn the right. The Val Carlos was at the same time menaced from Arnegui, and Reille's divisions ascending the rock of Airola turned Morillo's left.

About mid-day general Cole arrived at Altobiscar, but his brigades were still distant, and the French renewing their attack neglected the Val Carlos to gather more thickly on the front of Byng. He resisted all their efforts, but Reille made progress along the summit of the Airola ridge. Morillo then fell back towards Ibañeta, and the French were already nearer to that pass than the troops at Altobiscar were, when Ross's brigade, coming up the pass of Mendichuri, suddenly appeared on the Lindouz, at the instant when the head of Reille's column being close to Atalosti was upon the point of cutting the communication with Campbell. This officer's picquets had been attacked early in the morning by the national guards of the Val de Baygorry, but he soon discovered that it was only a feint and therefore moved by his right towards Atalosti when he heard the firing on that side. His march was secured by the Val d'Ayra which separated him from the ridge of Airola along which Reille was advancing, but noting that general's strength, and at the same time seeing Ross's brigade labouring up the steep ridge of Mendichuri, Campbell judged that the latter was ignorant of what was going on above. Wherefore sending advice of the enemy's proximity and strength to Cole, he offered to pass the Atalosti and join in the battle if he could be furnished with transport for his sick, and provisions on the new line of operations.

Before this message could reach Cole, the head of Ross's column, composed of a wing of the twentieth regiment and a company of Brunswickers, was on the summit of the Lindouz, where most unexpectedly it encountered Reille's advanced guard. The moment was critical, but Ross an eager hardy soldier called aloud to charge, and captain Tovey of the twentieth running forward with his company crossed a slight wooded hollow and full against the front of the sixth French light infantry dashed with the bayonet. Brave men fell by that weapon on both sides, but numbers prevailing these daring soldiers were pushed back again by the French, Ross however gained his object, the remainder of his brigade had come up and the pass of Atalosti was secured, yet with a loss of one hundred and forty men of the twentieth regiment and forty-one of the Brunswickers.

Appendix,
No. 3.

Previous to this vigorous action general Cole seeing the French in the Val Carlos and in the valley of Orbaiceta, that is to say on both flanks of Byng whose front was not the less pressed, had ordered Anson to reinforce the Spaniards at the foundry, and Stubbs to enter the Val Carlos in support of the fifty-seventh. He now recalled Anson to assist in defence of the Lindouz, and learning from Campbell how strong Reille was, caused Byng, with a view to a final retreat, to relinquish his advanced position at Altobiscar and take a second nearer the Ibañeta. This movement uncovered the road leading down to the foundry of Orbaiceta, but it concentrated all the troops, and at the same time general Campbell, although he could not enter the line of battle, because Cole was unable to supply his demands, made so skilful a display of his Portuguese as to impress Reille with the notion that their numbers were considerable.

During these movements the skirmishing of the light troops continued, but a thick fog coming up the valley prevented Soult from making dispositions for a general attack with his six divisions, and when night fell general Cole still held the great chain of the mountains with a loss of only three hundred and eighty men killed and wounded. His right was however turned by Orbaiceta, he had but ten or eleven thousand bayonets to oppose to thirty thousand, and his line of retreat being for four or five miles down hill and flanked all the way by the Lindouz, was uneasy and unfavourable. Wherefore putting the troops silently in march after dark, he threaded the passes and gained the valley of Urros. His rear-guard composed of Anson's brigade followed in the morning, general Campbell retired from the Alduides by the pass of Urtiaga to Eugui in the valley of Zubiri, and the Spanish battalion retreating from the foundry of Orbaiceta by the narrow way of Navala rejoined Morillo near Espinal. The great chain was thus abandoned, but the result of the day's operation was unsatisfactory to the French general; he acknowledged a loss of four hundred men, he had not gained ten miles, and from the passes now abandoned, to Pampeluna, the distance was not less than twenty-two miles, with strong defensive positions in the way where increasing numbers of intrepid enemies were to be expected.

Soult's combinations, contrived for greater success, had been thwarted, partly by fortune, partly by errors of execution the like of which all generals must expect, and the most experienced are the most resigned as knowing them to be inevitable. The interference of fortune was felt in the fog which rose at the moment when he was ready to thrust forward his heavy masses of troops entire. The failure in execution was Reille's tardy movement. His orders were to gain with all expedition the Lindouz, that is to say the knot tying the heads of the Alduides, the Val Carlos, the Roncesvalles, and the valley of Urroz. From that position he would have commanded the Mendichuri, Atalosti, Ibañeta and Sahorgain passes, and by moving along the crest of the hills could menace the Urtiaga, Renacabal, and Bellate passes, thus endangering Campbell's and Hill's lines of retreat. But when he should have

Pellot,Mé-
moires
des Cam-
pagnes des
Pyren-
nées.

ascended the rocks of Airola he halted to incorporate two newly arrived conscript battalions and to issue provisions, and the hours thus lost would have sufficed to seize the Lindouz before general Ross got through the pass of Mendichuri. The fog would still have stopped the spread of the French columns to the extent designed by Soult, but fifteen or sixteen thousand men, placed on the flank and rear of Byng and Morillo, would have separated them from the fourth division, and forced the latter to retreat beyond Viscayret.

Soult however overrated the force opposed to him, supposing it to consist of two British divisions, besides Byng's brigade and Morillo's Spaniards. He was probably deceived by the wounded men, who hastily questioned on the field would declare they belonged to the second and fourth divisions, because Byng's brigade was part of the former;

Official
Despatch
to the Mi-
nister of
war, MSS.

but that general and the Spaniards had without aid

sustained Soult's first efforts, and even when the
fourth division came up, less than eleven thousand
men, exclusive of sergeants and officers, were present in the fight. Campbell's Portuguese never
entered the line at all, the remainder of the second
division was in the Bastan, and the third division
was at Olague in the valley of Lanz.

On the 26th the French general put Clauzel's
wing on the track of Cole, and ordered Reille to
follow the crest of the mountains and seize the
passes leading from the Bastan in Hill's rear while
D'Erlon pressed him in front. That general would
thus, Soult hoped, be crushed or thrown on the
side of San Estevan; D'Erlon could then reach
his proper place in the valley of Zubiri, while the
right descended the valley of Lanz and prevented
Picton quitting it to aid Cole. A retreat by those
generals and on separate lines would thus be inevitable, and the French army could issue forth in
a compact order of battle from the mouths of the
two valleys against Pampeluna.

COMBAT OF LINZOAIN.

All the columns were in movement at day-break,
but every hour brought its obstacle. The fog still
hung heavy on the mountain-tops, Reille's guides,
bewildered, refused to lead the troops along the
crests, and at ten o'clock having no other resource
he marched down the pass of Mendichuri upon
Espinal, and fell into the rear of the cavalry and
artillery following Clauzel's divisions. Meanwhile
Soult, although retarded also by the fog and the
difficulties of the ground, overtook Cole's rear-
guard in front of Viscayret. The leading troops

struck hotly upon some British light companies incorporated under the command of colonel Wilson
of the forty-eighth, and a French squadron passing
round their flank fell on the rear; but Wilson
facing about, drove off these horsemen and thus
fighting, Cole, about two o'clock, reached the
heights of Linzoain a mile beyond Viscayret, where
general Picton met him with intelligence that
Campbell had reached Eugui from the Alduides,
and that the third division having crossed the hills
from Olague was at Zubiri. The junction of all
these troops was thus secured, the loss of the
day was less than two hundred, and neither wounded
men nor baggage had been left behind. However
the French gathered in front and at four o'clock
seized some heights on the allies' left which endangered their position, wherefore again falling
back a mile, Cole offered battle on the ridge
separating the valley of Urroz from that of Zubiri.
During this skirmish Campbell coming from Eugui
shewed his Portuguese on the ridges above the right
flank of the French, but they were distant, Picton's troops were still at Zubiri, and there was light
for an action. Soult however disturbed with intelligence received from D'Erlon, and perhaps doubtful what Campbell's troops might be, put off the
attack until next morning, and after dark the junction of all the allies was effected.

This delay on the part of the French general
seems injudicious. Cole was alone for five hours.
Every action, by increasing the number of wounded
men and creating confusion in the rear, would have
augmented the difficulties of the retreat; and the
troops were fatigued with incessant fighting and
marching for two days and one night. Moreover

the alteration of Reille's march, occasioned by the
fog, had reduced the chances dependant on the
primary combinations to the operations of D'Erlon's corps, but the evening reports brought the
mortifying conviction that he also had gone wrong,
and by rough fighting only could Soult now attain
his object. It is said that his expressions discovered a secret anticipation of failure, if so, his temper was too stedfast to yield for he gave the signal
to march the next day, and more strongly renewed
his orders to D'Erlon whose operations must now
be noticed.

That general had three divisions of infantry,
furnishing twenty-one thousand men of which
about eighteen thousand were combatants. Early
on the morning of the 25th he assembled two of
them behind some heights near the passes of Maya,
having caused the national guards of Baygorry to
make previous demonstrations towards the passes of
Arriette, Yspeguy, and Lorietta. No change had
been made in the disposition of general Hill's force,
but general Stewart, deceived by the movements of
the national guards, looked towards Sylveira's posts
on the right rather than to his own front; his division, consisting of two British brigades, was consequently neither posted as it should be nor otherwise prepared for an attack. The ground to be
defended was indeed very strong, but however
rugged a mountain position may be, if it is too extensive for the troops or those troops are not disposed with judgment, the very inequalities constituting its defensive strength become advantageous
to an assailant.

There were three passes to defend. Aretesque
on the right, Lessessa in the centre, Maya on the

left, and from these entrances two ways led to
Elisondo in parallel directions ; one down the
valley through the town of Maya, receiving in its
course the Erazu road ; the other along the Atchiola
mountain. General Pringle's brigade was charged to
defend the Aretesque, and colonel Cameron's brigade
the Maya and Lessessa passes. The Col itself was
broad on the summit, about three miles long, and on
each flank lofty rocks and ridges rose one above another; those on the right blending with the Goramendi
mountains, those on the left with the Atchiola, near
the summit of which the eighty-second regiment
belonging to the seventh division was posted.

Cameron's brigade, encamped on the left, had a
clear view of troops coming from Urdax ; but at
Aretesque a great round hill, one mile in front,
masked the movements of an enemy coming from
Espelette. This hill was not occupied at night,
nor in the daytime save by some Portuguese cavalry videttes, and the next guard was an infantry
piquet posted on that slope of the Col which
fronted the great hill. Behind this piquet of eighty
men there was no immediate support, but four
light companies were encamped one mile down the
reverse slope which was more rugged and difficult
of access than that towards the enemy. The rest
of general Pringle's brigade was disposed at various
distances from two to three miles in the rear, and
the signal for assembling on the position was to be
the fire of four Portuguese guns from the rocks
above the Maya pass. Thus of six British regiments furnishing more than three thousand fighting
men, half only were in line of battle, and those
chiefly massed on the left of a position, wide open
and of an easy ascent from the Aretesque side, and

their general, Stewart, quite deceived as to the
real state of affairs, was at Elisondo when about
midday D'Erlon commenced the battle.

COMBAT OF MAYA.

Captain Moyle Sherer, the officer commanding
the picquet at the Aretesque pass, was told by his
predecessor, that at dawn a glimpse had been obtained of cavalry and infantry in movement along
the hills in front, some peasants also announced the
approach of the French, and at nine o'clock major
Thorne, a staff-officer, having patroled round the
great hill in front of the pass discovered sufficient
to make him order up the light companies to support the picquet. These companies had just formed
on the ridge with their left at the rock of Aretesque,
when d'Armagnac's division coming from Espelette
mounted the great hill in front, Abbé followed, and
general Maransin with a third division advanced
from Ainhoa and Urdax against the Maya pass,
meaning also to turn it by a narrow way leading up
the Atchiola mountain.

D'Armagnac's men pushed forwards at once in
several columns, and forced the picquet back with
great loss upon the light companies, who sustained
his vehement assault with infinite difficulty. The
alarm guns were now heard from the Maya pass, and
general Pringle hastened to the front, but his regiments moving hurriedly from different camps were
necessarily brought into action one after the other.
The thirty-fourth came up first at a running pace,
yet by companies not in mass and breathless from
the length and ruggedness of the ascent ; the thirty-
ninth and twenty-eighth followed, but not immediately nor together, and meanwhile D'Armagnac,

closely supported by Abbé, with domineering numbers and valour combined, maugre the desperate
fighting of the picquet of the light companies
and of the thirty-fourth, had established his columns
on the broad ridge of the position.

Colonel Cameron then sent the fiftieth from the
left to the assistance of the over-matched troops,
and that fierce and formidable old regiment charging
the head of an advancing column drove it clear out
of the pass of Lessessa in the centre. Yet the
French were so many that, checked at one point,
they assembled with increased force at another; nor
could general Pringle restore the battle with the
thirty-ninth and twenty-eighth regiments, which,
cut off from the others were though fighting desperately forced back to a second and lower ridge
crossing the main road to Elizondo. They were
followed by D'Armagnac, but Abbé continued to
press the fiftieth and thirty-fourth whose natural
line of retreat was towards the Atchiola road on
the left, because the position trended backward
from Aretesque towards that point, and because
Cameron's brigade was there. And that officer,
still holding the pass of Maya with the left wings
of the seventy-first and ninety-second regiments,
brought their right wings and the Portuguese guns
into action and thus maintained the fight; but so
dreadful was the slaughter, especially of the ninety-
second, that it is said the advancing enemy was
actually stopped by the heaped mass of dead and
dying; and then the left wing of that noble regiment
coming down from the higher ground smote wounded
friends and exulting foes alike, as mingled together
they stood or crawled before its fire.

It was in this state of affairs that general Stewart,

Appendix,
No. 3.

returning from Elizondo by the mountain road, reached the field of battle. The passes of Lessessa and Aretesque were lost, that of Maya was still held by the left wing of the seventy-first, but Stewart seeing Maransin's men gathered thickly on one side and Abbé's men on the other, abandoned it to take a new position on the first rocky ridge covering the road over the Atchiola ; and he called down the eighty-second regiment from the highest part of that mountain and sent messengers to demand further aid from the seventh division. Meanwhile although wounded himself he made a strenuous resistance, for he was a very gallant man ; but during the retrograde movement, Maransin no longer seeking to turn the position, suddenly thrust the head of his division across the front of the British line and connected his left with Abbé, throwing as he passed a destructive fire into the wasted remnant of the ninety-second, which even then sullenly gave way, for the men fell until two-thirds of the whole had gone to the ground. Still the survivors fought, and the left wing of the seventy-first came into action, but, one after the other all the regiments were forced back, and the first position was lost together with the Portuguese guns.

Abbé's division now followed D'Armagnac on the road to the town of Maya, leaving Maransin to deal with Stewart's new position, and notwithstanding its extreme strength the French gained ground until six o'clock, for the British, shrunk in numbers, also wanted ammunition, and a part of the eighty-second under major Fitzgerald were forced to roll down stones to defend the rocks on which they were posted. In this desperate condition Stewart was upon the point of abandoning the mountain entirely,

when a brigade of the seventh division, commanded
by general Barnes, arrived from Echallar, and that
officer charging at the head of the sixth regiment
drove the French back to the Maya ridge. Stewart
thus remained master of the Atchiola, and the count
D'Erlon who probably thought greater reinforcements
had come up, recalled his other divisions from the
French offi-
cial report,
MSS.
Maya road and reunited his whole corps on the *Col.*
He had lost fifteen hundred men and a general; but
British offi-
cial return.
he took four guns, and fourteen hundred British
soldiers were killed or wounded.

Such was the fight of Maya, a disaster, yet one
much exaggerated by French writers, and by an
Southey.
English author misrepresented as a surprise caused
by the negligence of the cavalry. General Stewart
was surprised, his troops were not, and never did
soldiers fight better, seldom so well. The stern
valour of the ninety-second, principally composed of
Irishmen, would have graced Thermopylæ. The
Portuguese cavalry patroles, if any went out which
is uncertain, might have neglected their duty, and
doubtless the front should have been scoured in a
more military manner; but the infantry picquets,
and the light companies so happily ordered up by
major Thorne, were ready, and no man wondered
to see the French columns crown the great hill in
front of the pass. Stewart expecting no attack at
General
Stewart's
Official Re-
port.
Maya, had gone to Elisondo leaving orders for the soldiers to cook; from his erroneous views therefore the
misfortune sprung and from no other source. Having
deceived himself as to the true point of attack he
did not take proper military precautions on his own
front; his position was only half occupied, his troops
Welling-
ton's Des-
patches.
brought into action wildly, and finally he caused
the loss of his guns by a misdirection as to the road.

General Stewart was a brave, energetic, zealous,

indefatigable man and of a magnanimous spirit, but he possessed neither the calm reflective judgment nor the intuitive genius which belongs to nature's generals.

It is difficult to understand count D'Erlon's operations. Why, when he had carried the right of the position, did he follow two weak regiments with two divisions, and leave only one division to attack five regiments, posted on the strongest ground and having hopes of succour from Echallar? Certainly if Abbé's division had acted with Maransin's, Stewart who was so hardly pressed by the latter alone, must have passed the road from Echallar in retreat before general Barnes's brigade arrived. On the other hand, Soult's orders directed Soult's Official Despatch, MSS. D'Erlon to operate by his left, with the view of connecting the whole army on the summit of the great chain of the Pyrenees. He should therefore either have used his whole force to crush the troops on the Atchiola before they could be succoured from Echallar; or, leaving Maransin there, have marched by the Maya road upon Ariscun to cut Sylveira's line of retreat; instead of this he remained inactive upon the Col de Maya for twenty hours after the battle! And general Hill concentrating his whole force, now augmented by Barnes's brigade, would probably have fallen upon him from the commanding rocks of Atchiola the next day, if intelligence of Cole's retreat from the Roncesvalles passes had not come through the Alduides. This rendered the recovery of the Col de Maya useless, and Hill withdrawing all his troops during the night, posted the British brigades which had been engaged, together with one Portuguese brigade of

infantry and a Portuguese battery, on the heights
in rear of Irueta, fifteen miles from the scene of
action. The other Portuguese brigade he left in
front of Elizondo, thus covering the road of San
Estevan on his left, that of Berderez on his right,
and the pass of Vellate in his rear.

Such was the commencement of Soult's operations to restore the fortunes of France. Three considerable actions fought on the same day had each
been favourable. At St. Sebastian the allies were
repulsed; at Roncesvalles they abandoned the
passes; at Maya they were defeated; but the
decisive blow had not yet been struck.

Lord Wellington heard of the fight at Maya on
his way back from St. Sebastian, but with the false
addition that D'Erlon was beaten. As early as the
22d he had known that Soult was preparing a great
offensive movement, but the immovable attitude of
the French centre, the skilful disposition of their
reserve which was twice as strong as he at first
supposed, together with the preparations made to
throw bridges over the Bidassoa at Biriatou, were
all calculated to mislead and did mislead him.

Soult's complicated combinations to bring D'Erlon's divisions finally into line on the crest of the
great chain were impenetrable, and the English
general could not believe his adversary would
throw himself with only thirty thousand men into
the valley of the Ebro unless sure of aid from
Suchet, and that general's movements indicated a
determination to remain in Catalonia; moreover
Wellington, in contrast to Soult, knew that Pampeluna was not in extremity, and before the failure
of the assault thought that San Sebastian was.
Hence the operations against his right, their full

extent not known, appeared a feint, and he judged
the real effort would be to throw bridges over the
Bidassoa and raise the siege of San Sebastian. But
in the night correct intelligence of the Maya and
Roncesvalles affairs arrived, Soult's object was then
scarcely doubtful, and Sir T. Graham was ordered
to turn the siege into a blockade, to embark his
guns and stores, and hold all his spare troops in
hand to join Giron, on a position of battle marked
out near the Bidassoa. General Cotton was ordered
to move the cavalry up to Pampeluna, and O'Donnel
was instructed to hold some of his Spanish troops
ready to act in advance. This done Wellington
arranged his lines of correspondence and proceeded
to San Estevan, which he reached early in the
morning.

While the embarkation of the guns and stores
was going on it was essential to hold the posts at
Vera and Echallar, because D'Erlon's object was
not pronounced, and an enemy in possession of
those places could approach San Sebastian by the
roads leading over the Pena de Haya, a rocky
mountain behind Lesaca, or by the defiles of Zubi-
etta leading round that mountain from the valley of
Lerins. Wherefore in passing through Estevan on
the morning of the 26th, Wellington merely directed general Pack to guard the bridges over the
Bidassoa. But when he reached Irueta, saw the
reduced state of Stewart's division, and heard that
Picton had marched from Olague, he directed all
the troops within his power upon Pampeluna; and
to prevent mistakes indicated the valley of Lanz as Manuscript Notes
the general line of movement. Of Picton's exact by the
Duke of
position or of his intentions nothing positive was Wellington.

known, but supposing him to have joined Cole at Linzoain, as indeed he had, Wellington judged that their combined forces would be sufficient to check the enemy until assistance could reach them from the centre or from Pampeluna, and he so advised Picton on the evening of the 26th.

In consequence of these orders the seventh division abandoned Echallar in the night of the 26th, the sixth division quitted San Estevan at daylight on the 27th, and general Hill concentrating his own troops and Barnes's brigade on the heights of Irueta, halted until the evening of the 27th but marched during the night through the pass of Vellate upon the town of Lanz. Meanwhile the light division quitting Vera also on the 27th retired by Lesaca to the summit of the Santa Cruz mountain, overlooking the valley of Lerins, and there halted, apparently to cover the pass of Zubieta until Longa's Spaniards should take post to block the roads leading over the Pena de Haya and protect the embarkation of the guns on that flank. That object being effected it was to thread the passes and descend upon Lecumberri on the great road of Irurzun, thus securing sir Thomas Graham's communication with the army round Pampeluna. These various movements spread fear and confusion far and wide. All the narrow valleys and roads were crowded with baggage, commissariat stores, artillery and fugitive families; reports of the most alarming nature were as usual rife; each division, ignorant of what had really happened to the other, dreaded that some of the numerous misfortunes related might be true; none knew what to expect or where they were to meet the enemy, and one uni-

versal hubbub filled the wild regions through which
the French army was now working its fiery path
towards Pampeluna.

D'Erlon's inactivity gave great uneasiness to
Soult, who repeated the order to push forward by
his left whatever might be the force opposed, and
thus stimulated he advanced to Elizondo on the
27th, but thinking the sixth division was still at
San Estevan, again halted, and it was not until the
morning of the 28th, when general Hill's retreat
had opened the way, that he followed through the
pass of Vellate. His further progress belongs to
other combinations arising from Soult's direct operations which are now to be continued.

General Picton, having assumed the command
of all the troops in the valley of Zubiri on the
evening of the 26th, recommenced the retreat before dawn on the 27th, and without the hope or intention of covering Pampeluna. Soult followed in
the morning, having first sent scouts towards the
ridges where Campbell's troops had appeared the
evening before. Reille marched by the left bank
of the Guy river, Clauzel by the right bank, the
cavalry and artillery closed the rear and as the
whole moved in compact order the narrow valley
was overgorged with troops, a hasty bicker of
musketry alone marking the separation of the hostile forces. Meanwhile the garrison of Pampeluna
made a sally and O'Donnel in great alarm spiked
some of his guns, destroyed his magazines, and
would have suffered a disaster, if Carlos D'España
had not fortunately arrived with his division and
checked the garrison. Nevertheless the danger was
imminent, for general Cole, first emerging from
the valley of Zubiri, had passed Villalba, only

three miles from Pampeluna, in retreat ; Picton, following close, was at Huarte, and O'Donnel's Spaniards were in confusion ; in fine Soult was all but successful when Picton, feeling the importance of the crisis, suddenly turned on some steep ridges, which, stretching under the names of San Miguel Mont Escava and San Cristoval quite across the mouths of the Zubiri and Lanz valleys, screen Pampeluna.

Posting the third division on the right of Huarte he prolonged his line to the left with Morillo's Spaniards, called upon O'Donnel to support him, and directed Cole to occupy some heights between Oricain and Arletta. But that general having with a surer eye observed a salient hill near Zabaldica, one mile in advance and commanding the road to Huarte, demanded and obtained permission to occupy it instead of the heights first appointed. Two Spanish regiments belonging to the blockading troops were still posted there, and towards them Cole directed his course. Soult had also marked this hill, a French detachment issuing from the mouth of the Val de Zubiri was in full career to seize it, and the hostile masses were rapidly approaching the summit on either side when the Spaniards, seeing the British so close, vindicated their own post by a sudden charge. This was for Soult the stroke of fate. His double columns just then emerging, exultant, from the narrow valley, were arrested at the sight of ten thousand men which under Cole crowned the summit of the mountain in opposition ; and two miles further back stood Picton with a greater number, for O'Donnel had now taken post on Morillo's left. To advance by the Huarte road was impossible, and to stand

still was dangerous, because the French army contracted to a span in front was cleft in its whole
length by the river Guy, and compressed on each
side by the mountains which in that part narrowed
the valley to a quarter of a mile. Soult however,
like a great and ready commander, at once shot the
head of Clauzel's columns to his right across the
mountain which separated the Val de Zubiri from
the Val de Lanz, and at the same time threw one
of Reille's divisions of infantry and a body of ca- Soult's
valry across the mountains on his left, beyond the Official
Correspon-
Guy river, as far as the village of Elcano, to dence,
MSS.
menace the front and right flank of Picton's
position at Huarte. The other two divisions of infantry he established at the village of Zabaldica in
the Val de Zubiri, close under Cole's right, and
meanwhile Clauzel seized the village of Sauroren
close under that general's left.

While the French general thus formed his line
of battle, Lord Wellington who had quitted sir
Rowland Hill's quarters in the Bastan very early
on the 27th, crossed the main ridge and descended
the valley of Lanz without having been able to Notes by
Lord Wel-
learn any thing of Picton's movements or position, lington,
MSS.
and in this state of uncertainty reached Ostiz, a
few miles from Sauroren, where he found general
Long with the brigade of light cavalry which had
furnished the posts of correspondence in the mountains. Here learning that Picton having abandoned the heights of Linzoain was moving on
Huarte, he left his quarter-master-general with instructions to stop all the troops coming down the
valley of Lanz until the state of affairs at Huarte
should be ascertained. Then at racing speed he
made for Sauroren. As he entered that village

he saw Clauzel's divisions moving from Zabaldica
along the crest of the mountain, and it was clear
that the allied troops in the valley of Lanz were
intercepted, wherefore pulling up his horse he
wrote on the parapet of the bridge of Sauroren
fresh instructions to turn every thing from that
valley to the right, by a road which led through
Lizasso and Marcalain behind the hills to the village of Oricain, that is to say, in rear of the position now occupied by Cole. Lord Fitzroy Somerset, the only staff-officer who had kept up with
him, galloped with these orders out of Sauroren
by one road, the French light cavalry dashed in by
another, and the English general rode alone up the
mountain to reach his troops. One of Campbell's
Portuguese battalions first descried him and raised
a cry of joy, and the shrill clamour caught up by
the next regiments swelled as it run along the line
into that stern and appalling shout which the British soldier is wont to give upon the edge of battle,
and which no enemy ever heard unmoved. Lord
Wellington suddenly stopped in a conspicuous place,
he desired that both armies should know he was
there, and a double spy who was present pointed
out Soult, then so near that his features could
be plainly distinguished. The English general, it
is said, fixed his eyes attentively upon this formidable man, and speaking as if to himself, said,
" *Yonder is a great commander, but he is a cautious
one and will delay his attack to ascertain the cause
of these cheers; that will give time for the sixth
division to arrive and I shall beat him.*" And certain it is that the French general made no serious
attack that day.

The position adopted by Cole was the summit

of a mountain mass which filled all the space between the Guy and the Lanz rivers as far back as
Huarte and Villalba. It was highest in the centre,
and boldly defined towards the enemy, but the trace
was irregular, the right being thrown back towards
the village of Arletta so as to flank the high road
to Huarte. This road was also swept by some guns
placed on a lower range, or neck, connecting the
right of Cole with Picton and Morillo.

Overlooking Zabaldica and the Guy river was
the bulging hill vindicated by the Spaniards; it
was a distinct point on the right of the fourth division, dependent upon the centre of the position
but considerably lower. The left of the position
also abating in height was yet extremely rugged
and steep overlooking the Lanz river and the
road to Villalba. General Ross's brigade of the
fourth division was posted on that side, having a
Portuguese battalion, whose flank rested on a small
chapel, in his front. General Campbell was on the
right of Ross. General Anson was on the highest
ground, partly behind, and partly on the right of
Campbell. General Byng's brigade was on a second mass of hills in reserve, and the Spanish hill
was reinforced by a battalion of the fourth Portuguese regiment.

The front of battle being less than two miles was
well filled, and the Lanz and Guy river washed
the flanks. Those torrents continuing their course
break by narrow passages through the steep ridges
of San Miguel and Cristoval, and then flowing
past Huarte and Villalba meet behind those places
to form the Arga river. On the ridges thus cleft
by the waters the second line was posted, that is to
say, at the distance of two miles from, and nearly

parallel to the first position, but on a more extended front.   Picton's left was at Huarte, his
right strengthened with a battery stretched to the
village of Goraitz, covering more than a mile of
ground on that flank.   Morillo prolonged Picton's
left along the crest of San Miguel to Villalba,
and O'Donnel continued the line to San Cristoval;
Carlos d'España's division maintained the blockade
behind these ridges, and the British cavalry under
General Cotton, coming up from Tafalla and Olite,
took post, the heavy brigades on some open ground
behind Picton, the hussar brigade on his right.
This second line being on a wider trace than the
first and equally well filled with troops, entirely
barred the openings of the two valleys leading down
to Pampeluna.

Soult's position was also a mountain filling the
space between the two rivers.   It was even more
rugged than the allies' mountain and they were only
separated by a deep narrow valley.   Clauzel's three
divisions leaned to the right on the village of Sauroren, which was quite down in the valley of Lanz
and close under the chapel height where the left of
the fourth division was posted.   His left was prolonged by two of Reille's divisions, which also occupied the village of Zabaldica quite down in the
valley of Zubiri under the right of the allies.   The
remaining division of this wing and a division of
cavalry, were, as I have before stated, thrown forward
on the mountains at the other side of the Guy river,
menacing Picton and seeking for an opportunity
to communicate with the garrison of Pampeluna.
Some guns were pushed in front of Zabaldica, but
the elevation required to send the shot upward rendered their fire ineffectual and the greatest part of

the artillery remained therefore in the narrow valley
of Zubiri.

Combat of the 27*th.* Soult's first effort was to gain the Spaniards' hill and establish himself near the centre of the allies' line of battle. The attack was vigorous but the French were valiantly repulsed about the time lord Wellington arrived, and he immediately reinforced that post with the fortieth British regiment. There was then a general skirmish along the front, under cover of which Soult carefully examined the whole position, and the firing continued on the mountain side until evening, when a terrible storm, the usual precursor of English battles in the Peninsula, brought on premature darkness and terminated the dispute. This was the state of affairs at day-break on the 28th, but a signal alteration had place before the great battle of that day commenced, and the movements of the wandering divisions by which this change was effected must now be traced.

It has been shewn that the Lanz covered the left of the allies and the right of the French. Nevertheless the heights occupied by either army were prolonged beyond that river, the continuation of the allies' ridge sweeping forward so as to look into the rear of Sauroren, while the continuation of the French heights fell back in a direction nearly parallel to the forward inclination of the opposing ridge. They were both steep and high, yet lower and less rugged than the heights on which the armies stood opposed, for the latter were mountains where rocks piled on rocks stood out like castles, difficult to approach and so dangerous to assail that the hardened veterans of the Peninsula only would have dared the trial. Now the road by which

the sixth division marched on the 27th, after clear-
ing the pass of Doña Maria, sends one branch to
Lanz, another to Ostiz, a third through Lizasso and
Marcalain; the first and second fall into the road
from Bellate and descend the valley of Lanz to
Sauroren ; the third passing behind the ridges, just
described as prolonging the positions of the armies,
also falls into the valley of Lanz, but at the village
of Oricain, that is to say one mile behind the ground
occupied by general Cole's left.

It was by this road of Marcalain that Wellington
now expected the sixth and seventh divisions, but
the rapidity with which Soult seized Sauroren
caused a delay of eighteen hours. For the sixth
division, having reached Olague in the valley of
Lanz about one o'clock on the 27th, halted there
until four, and then following the orders brought
by lord Fitzroy Somerset marched by Lizasso to
gain the Marcalain road ; but the great length of
these mountain marches, and the heavy storm which
had terminated the action at Zabaldica sweeping
with equal violence in this direction, prevented the
division from passing Lizasso that night.   However
the march was renewed at daylight on the 28th,
and meanwhile general Hill, having quitted the
Bastan on the evening of the 27th, reached the
town of Lanz on the morning of the 28th, and rallying general Long's cavalry and his own artillery,
which were in that valley, moved likewise upon
Lizasso.   At that place he met the seventh division
coming from San Estevan, and having restored
general Barnes's brigade to lord Dalhousie, took a
position on a ridge covering the road to Marcalain.
The seventh division being on his right, was in military communication with the sixth division, and thus

lord Wellington's left was prolonged, and covered
the great road leading from Pampeluna by Irurzun
to Tolosa. And during these important movements,
which were not completed until the evening of the
28th, which brought six thousand men into the
allies' line of battle, and fifteen thousand more into
military communication with their left, D'Erlon
remained planted in his position of observation near
Elizondo!

The near approach of the sixth division early on
the morning of the 28th and the certainty of Hill's
junction, made Wellington imagine that Soult would
not venture an attack, and certainly that marshal,
disquieted about D'Erlon of whom he only knew
that he had not followed his instructions, viewed the
strong position of his adversary with uneasy anticipations. Again with anxious eyes he took cognizance of all its rugged strength, and seemed dubious
and distrustful of his fortune. He could not operate
with advantage by his own left beyond the Guy
river, because the mountains there were rough, and
Wellington having shorter lines of movement could
meet him with all arms combined; and meanwhile
the French artillery, unable to emerge from the Val
de Zubiri except by the Huarte road, would have
been exposed to a counter attack. He crossed the
Lanz river and ascended the prolongation of the
allies' ridge, which, as he had possession of the
bridge of Sauroren, was for the moment his own
ground. From this height he could see all the left
and rear of Cole's position, looking down the valley
of Lanz as far as Villalba, but the country beyond
the ridge towards Marcalain was so broken that he
could not discern the march of the sixth division; Soult's
Correspon-
dence,
MSS.
he knew however from the deserters, that Welling-

ton expected four fresh divisions from that side, that
is to say, the second, sixth, and seventh British, and
Sylviera's Portuguese division which always marched
with Hill.　This information and the nature of the
ground decided the plan of attack.　The valley of Lanz
growing wider as it descended, offered the means of
assailing the allies' left in front and rear at one moment, and the same combination would cut off the
reinforcements expected from the side of Marcalain.

One of Clauzel's divisions already occupied Sauroren, and the other two coming from the mountain
took post upon each side of that village.　The division
on the right hand was ordered to throw some flankers
on the ridge from whence Soult was taking his
observations, and upon a signal given to move in one
body to a convenient distance down the valley and
then, wheeling to its left, assail the rear of the allies'
left flank while the other two divisions advancing
from their respective positions near Sauroren assailed
the front.　Cole's left, which did not exceed five
thousand men, would thus be enveloped by sixteen
thousand, and Soult expected to crush it notwithstanding the strength of the ground.　Meanwhile
Reille's two divisions advancing from the mountain
on the side of Zabaldica, were each to send a brigade against the hill occupied by the fortieth regiment; the right of this attack was to be connected
with the left of Clauzel, the remaining brigades
were closely to support the assailing masses, the
divisions beyond the Guy were to keep Picton in
check, and Soult who had no time to lose ordered
his lieutenants to throw their troops frankly and at
once into action.

First battle of Sauroren.—It was fought on the
fourth anniversary of the battle of Talavera.

About mid-day the French gathered at the foot
of the position and their skirmishers rushing forward
spread over the face of the mountain, working upward
like a conflagration; but the columns of attack were
not all prepared when Clauzel's division in the valley
of Lanz, too impatient to await the general signal of
battle, threw out its flankers on the ridge beyond the
river and pushed down the valley in one mass.
With a rapid pace it turned Cole's left and was preparing to wheel up on his rear, when a Portuguese
brigade of the sixth division, suddenly appearing on
the crest of the ridge beyond the river, drove the
French flankers back and instantly descended with
a rattling fire upon the right and rear of the column
in the valley.   And almost at the same instant, the
main body of the sixth division emerging from
behind the same ridge, near the village of Oricain,
formed in order of battle across the front.   It was
the counter-stroke of Salamanca!   The French,
striving to encompass the left of the allies were themselves encompassed, for two brigades of the fourth
division turned and smote them from the left, the
Portuguese smote them from the right; and while
thus scathed on both flanks with fire, they were
violently shocked and pushed back with a mighty
force by the sixth division, yet not in flight, but
fighting fiercely and strewing the ground with their
enemies' bodies as well as with their own.

Clauzel's second division, seeing this dire conflict,
with a hurried movement assailed the chapel height
to draw off the fire from the troops in the valley, and
gallantly did the French soldiers throng up the
craggy steep, but the general unity of the attack was
ruined; neither their third division nor Reille's brigades had yet received the signal, and their attacks

instead of being simultaneous were made in succession, running from right to left as the necessity of
aiding the others became apparent.   It was however
a terrible battle and well fought.   One column dart-
ing out of the village of Sauroren, silently, sternly,
without firing a shot, worked up to the chapel under
a tempest of bullets which swept away whole ranks
without abating the speed and power of the mass.
The seventh Caçadores shrunk abashed and that part
of the position was won.   Soon however they rallied
upon general Ross's British brigade, and the whole
running forward charged the French with a loud
shout and dashed them down the hill.   Heavily
stricken they were, yet undismayed, and recovering
their ranks again, they ascended in the same manner
to be again broken and overturned.   But the other
columns of attack were now bearing upwards through
the smoke and flame with which the skirmishers had
covered the face of the mountain, and the tenth
Portuguese regiment fighting on the right of Ross's
brigade yielded to their fury ; a heavy body crowned
the heights and wheeling against the exposed flank
of Ross forced that gallant officer also to go back.
His ground was instantly occupied by the enemies
with whom he had been engaged in front, and the
fight raged close and desperate on the crest of the
position, charge succeeded charge and each side
yielded and recovered by turns ; yet this astounding
effort of French valour was of little avail.   Lord Wellington brought Byng's brigade forward at a running
pace, and sent the twenty-seventh and forty-eighth
British regiments belonging to Anson's brigade down
from the higher ground in the centre against the
crowded masses, rolling them backward in disorder and
throwing them one after the other violently down the

mountain side; and with no child's play; the two British regiments fell upon the enemy three separate times with the bayonet and lost more than half their own numbers.

During this battle on the mountain-top, the British brigades of the sixth division strengthened by a battery of guns, gained ground in the valley of Lanz and arrived on the same front with the left of the victorious troops about the chapel. Lord Wellington then seeing the momentary disorder of the enemy ordered Madden's Portuguese brigade, which had never ceased its fire against the right flank of the French column, to assail the village of Sauroren in the rear, but the state of the action in other parts and the exhaustion of the troops soon induced him to countermand this movement. Meanwhile Reille's brigades, connecting their right with the left of Clauzel's third division, had environed the Spanish hill, ascended it unchecked, and at the moment when the fourth division was so hardly pressed made the regiment of El Pravia give way on the left of the fortieth. A Portuguese battalion rushing forward covered the flank of that invincible regiment, which waited in stern silence until the French set their feet upon the broad summit; but when their glittering arms appeared over the brow of the mountain the charging cry was heard, the crowded mass was broken to pieces and a tempest of bullets followed its flight. Four times this assault was renewed, and the French officers were seen to pull up their tired men by the belts, so fierce and resolute they were to win. It was however the labour of Sysiphus. The vehement shout and shock of the British soldier always prevailed, and at last, with thinned ranks, tired limbs, hearts fainting,

and hopeless from repeated failures, they were so
abashed that three British companies sufficed to
bear down a whole brigade.

While the battle was thus being fought on the
height the French cavalry beyond the Guy river,
passed a rivulet, and with a fire of carbines forced the
tenth hussars to yield some rocky ground on Picton's
right, but the eighteenth hussars having better fire-
arms than the tenth renewed the combat, killed two
officers, and finally drove the French over the rivulet
again.

Such were the leading events of this sanguinary
struggle, which lord Wellington fresh from the fight
with homely emphasis called " *bludgeon work*." Two
generals and eighteen hundred men had been killed
or wounded on the French side, following their official
reports, a number far below the estimate made at the
time by the allies whose loss amounted to two thousand six hundred. These discrepancies between hostile calculations ever occur, and there is little wisdom
in disputing where proof is unattainable ; but the
numbers actually engaged were, of French, twenty-
five thousand, of the allies twelve thousand, and if
the strength of the latter's position did not save them
from the greater loss their stedfast courage is to be
the more admired.

The 29th the armies rested in position without
firing a shot, but the wandering divisions on both
sides were now entering the line.

General Hill, having sent all his baggage artillery and wounded men to Berioplano behind the
Cristoval ridge, still occupied his strong ground
between Lizasso and Arestegui, covering the Marcalain and Irurzun roads, and menacing that lead-

ing from Lizasso to Olague in rear of Soult's right.

His communication with Oricain was maintained by
the seventh division, and the light division was approaching his left. Thus on Wellington's side
the crisis was over. He had vindicated his position
with only sixteen thousand combatants, and now,
including the troops still maintaining the blockade,
he had fifty thousand, twenty thousand being British, in close military combination. Thirty thousand flushed with recent success were in hand, and
Hill's troops were well placed for retaking the
offensive.

Soult's situation was proportionably difficult.
Finding that he could not force the allies' position
in front, he had sent his artillery part of his cavalry and his wounded men back to France immediately after the battle, ordering the two former to
join Villatte on the Lower Bidassoa and there
await further instructions. Having shaken off this
burthen he awaited D'Erlon's arrival by the valley
of Lanz, and that general reached Ostiz a few
miles above Sauroren at mid-day on the 29th,
bringing intelligence, obtained indirectly during his
march, that general Graham had retired from the
Bidassoa and Villatte had crossed that river. This
gave Soult a hope that his first movements had disengaged San Sebastian, and he instantly conceived
a new plan of operations, dangerous indeed yet
conformable to the critical state of his affairs.

No success was to be expected from another
attack, yet he could not at the moment of being
reinforced with eighteen thousand men, retire by
the road he came without some hishonour; nor
could he remain where he was, because his supplies

of provisions and ammunition derived from distant magazines by slow and small convoys was unequal to the consumption. Two-thirds of the British troops, the greatest part of the Portuguese, and all the Spaniards were, as he supposed, assembled in his front under Wellington, or on his right flank under Hill, and it was probable that other reinforcements were on the march ; wherefore he resolved to prolong his right with D'Erlon's corps, and then cautiously drawing off the rest of his army place himself between the allies and the Bastan, in military connection with his reserve and closer to his frontier magazines. Thus posted and able to combine all his troops in one operation, he expected to relieve San Sebastian entirely and profit from the new state of affairs.

In the evening of the 29th the second division of cavalry, which was in the valley of Zubiri, passed over the position to the valley of Lanz, and joined D'Erlon, who was ordered to march early on the 30th by Etulain upon Lizasso, sending out strong scouting parties to his left on all the roads leading upon Pampeluna, and also towards Letassa and Irurzun. During the night the first division of cavalry and La Martiniere's division of infantry, both at Elcano

Plan 2.

on the extreme left of the French army, retired over the mountains by Illurdos to Eugui, in the upper part of the valley of the Zubiri, having orders to cross the separating ridge enter the valley of Lanz and join D'Erlon. The remainder of Reille's wing was at the same time to march by the crest of the position from Zabaldica to the village of Sauroren, and gradually relieve Clauzel's troops which were then to assemble behind Sauroren, that is to

say towards Ostiz, and thus following the march of
D'Erlon were to be themselves followed in like manner by Reille's troops. To cover these last movements Clauzel detached two regiments to occupy the
French heights beyond the Lanz river, and they
were also to maintain his connection with D'Erlon
whose line of operations was just beyond those
heights. He was however to hold by Reille rather
than by D'Erlon until the former had perfected
his dangerous march across Wellington's front.

In the night of the 29th Soult heard from the
deserters that three divisions were to make an offensive movement towards Lizasso on the 30th, and
when daylight came he was convinced the men
spoke truly, because from a point beyond Sauroren
he discerned certain columns descending the ridge
of Cristoval and the heights above Oricain, while
others were in march on a wide sweep apparently
to turn Clauzel's right flank. These columns were
Morillo's Spaniards, Campbell's Portuguese, and
the seventh division, the former rejoining Hill to
whse corps they properly belonged, the others
adapting themselves to a new disposition of Wellington's line of battle which shall be presently
explained.

At six o'clock in the morning Foy's division of
Reille's wing was in march along the crest of the
mountain from Zabaldica towards Sauroren, where
Maucune's division had already relieved Conroux's ; the latter, belonging to Clauzel's wing, was
moving up the valley of Lanz to rejoin that general,
who had, with exception of the two flanking regiments before mentioned, concentrated his remaining
divisions between Olabe and Ostiz. In this state of

affairs Wellington opening his batteries from the chapel height sent skirmishers against Sauroren, and the fire spreading to the allies' right became brisk between Cole and Foy. It subsided however at Sauroren, and Soult, relying on the strength of the position, ordered Reille to maintain it until night-fall unless hardly pressed, and went off himself at a gallop to join D'Erlon, for his design was to fall upon the division attempting to turn his right and crush them with superior numbers : a daring project, well and quickly conceived, but he had to deal with a man whose rapid perception and rough stroke rendered sleight of hand dangerous. The marshal overtook D'Erlon at the moment when that general, having entered the valley of Ulzema with three divisions of infantry and two divisions of heavy cavalry, was making dispositions to assail Hill who was between Buenza and Arestegui.

Combat of Buenza. The allies who were about ten thousand fighting men, including Long's brigade of light cavalry, occupied a very extensive mountain ridge. Their right was strongly posted on rugged ground, but the left prolonged towards Buenza was insecure, and D'Erlon who including his two divisions of heavy cavalry had not less than twenty thousand sabres and bayonets, was followed by La Martiniere's division of infantry now coming from Lanz. Soult's combination was therefore extremely powerful. The light troops were already engaged when he arrived, and the same soldiers on both sides who had so strenuously combated at Maya on the 25th were again opposed to each other.

D'Armagnac's division was directed to make a false attack upon Hill's right; Abbé's division,

emerging by Lizasso, endeavoured to turn the
allies' left and gain the summit of the ridge in the
direction of Buenza; Maranzin followed Abbé, and
the divisions of cavalry entering the line supported and connected the two attacks. The action
was brisk at both points, but D'Armagnac pushing
his feint too far became seriously engaged, and was
beaten by Da Costa and Ashworth's Portuguese
aided by a part of the twenty-eighth British regiment.
Nor were the French at first more successful on the
other flank, being repeatedly repulsed, until Abbé,
turning that wing gained the summit of the mountain and rendered the position untenable. General
Hill who had lost about four hundred men then
retired to the heights of Equaros behind Arestegui
and Berasin, thus drawing towards Marcalain with
his right and throwing back his left. Here being
joined by Campbell and Morillo he again offered
battle, but Soult whose principal loss was in D'Armagnac's division had now gained his main object;
he had turned Hill's left, secured a fresh line of
retreat, a shorter communication with Villatte by
the pass of Donna Maria, and withal, the great
Irurzun road to Toloza distant only one league and
a half was in his power. His first thought was to Soult's
seize it and march through Lecumberri either upon Official
despatch,
Toloza, or Andoain and Ernani. There was nothing MS.
to oppose except the light division whose movements shall be noticed hereafter, but neither the
French marshal nor general Hill knew of its presence, and the former thought himself strong
enough to force his way to San Sebastian and there
unite with Villatte, and his artillery which following his previous orders was now on the Lower
Bidassoa.

This project was feasible. Lamartiniere's division, of Reille's wing, coming from Lanz, was not far off. Clauzel's three divisions were momentarily expected, and Reille's during the night. On the 31st therefore, Soult with at least fifty thousand men would have broken into Guipuscoa, thrusting aside the light division in his march, and menacing sir Thomas Graham's position in reverse while Villatte's reserve attacked it in front. The country about Lecumberri was however very strong for defence and lord Wellington would have followed, yet scarcely in time, for he did not suspect his views and was ignorant of his strength, thinking D'Erlon's force, to be originally two divisions of infantry and now only reinforced with a third division, whereas that general had three divisions originally and was now reinforced by a fourth division of infantry and two of cavalry. This error however did not prevent him from seizing with the rapidity of a great commander, the decisive point of operation, and giving a counter-stroke which Soult trusting to the strength of Reille's position little expected.

When Wellington saw that La Martiniere's divisions and the cavalry had abandoned the mountains above Elcano, and that Zabaldica was evacuated, he ordered Picton, reinforced with two squadrons of cavalry and a battery of artillery, to enter the valley of Zubiri and turn the French left; the seventh division was directed to sweep over the hills beyond the Lanz river upon the French right; the march of Campbell and Morillo insured the communication with Hill; and that general was to point his columns upon Olague and Lanz threatening the French rear, but meeting as we have seen with D'Erlon was forced back to Eguaros.

The fourth division was to assail Foy's position, but respecting its great strength the attack was to be measured according to the effect produced on the flanks. Meanwhile Byng's brigade and the sixth division, the latter having a battery of guns and some squadrons of cavalry, were combined to assault Sauroren. La Bispal's Spaniards followed the sixth division. Fane's horsemen were stationed at Berioplano with a detachment pushed to Irurzun, the heavy cavalry remained behind Huarte, and Carlos d'España maintained the blockade.

Second battle of Sauroren. — These movements began at daylight. Picton's advance was rapid. He gained the valley of Zubiri and threw his skirmishers at once on Foy's flank, and about the same time general Inglis, one of those veterans who purchase every step of promotion with their blood, advancing with only five hundred men of the seventh division, broke at one shock the two French regiments covering Clauzel's right, and drove them down into the valley of Lanz. He lost indeed one-third of his own men, but instantly spreading the remainder in skirmishing order along the descent, opened a biting fire upon the flank of Conroux's division, which was then moving up the valley from Sauroren, sorely amazed and disordered by this sudden fall of two regiments from the top of the mountain into the midst of the column.

Foy's division, marching to support Conroux and Maucune, was on the crest of the mountains between Zabaldica and Sauroren at the moment of attack, but too far off to give aid, and his own light troops were engaged with the skirmishers of the fourth division; and Inglis had been so sudden and

vigorous, that before the evil could be well perceived it was past remedy.   For Wellington instantly pushed the sixth division, now commanded
by general Pakenham Pack having been wounded
on the 28th, to the left of Sauroren, and shoved
Byng's brigade headlong down from the chapel
height against that village, which was defended by
Maucune's division.   Byng's vigorous assault was
simultaneously enforced from the opposite direction
by Madden's Portuguese of the sixth division, and
at the same time the battery near the chapel sent
its bullets crashing through the houses, and booming up the valley towards Conroux's column, which
Inglis never ceased to vex and he was closely supported by the remainder of the seventh division.

The village and bridge of Sauroren and the
straits beyond were now covered with a pall of
smoke, the musquetry pealed frequent and loud, and
the tumult and affray echoing from mountain to
mountain filled all the valley.   Byng with hard
fighting carried the village of Sauroren, and fourteen hundred prisoners were made, for the two
French divisions thus vehemently assailed in the
front and flank were entirely broken.   Part retreated
along the valley towards Clauzel's other divisions
which were now beyond Ostiz; part fled up the
mountain side to seek a refuge with Foy, who had
remained on the summit a helpless spectator of this
rout; but though he rallied the fugitives in great
numbers, he had soon to look to himself, for by this
time his skirmishers had been driven up the mountain by those of the fourth division, and his left was
infested by Picton's detachments.   Thus pressed,
he abandoned his strong position, and fell back
along the summit of the mountain between the

valley of Zubiri and valley of Lanz, and the woods
enabled him to effect his retreat without much loss;
but he dared not descend into either valley, and thinking himself entirely cut off, sent advice of his situation to Soult and then retired into the Alduides by
the pass of Urtiaga. Meanwhile Wellington pressing
up the valley of Lanz drove Clauzel as far as
Olague, and the latter now joined by La Martiniere's
division took a position in the evening covering
the roads of Lanz and Lizasso. The English
general whose pursuit had been damped by hearing
of Hill's action also halted near Ostiz.

The allies lost nineteen hundred men killed and
wounded, or taken, in the two battles of this day,
and of these nearly twelve hundred were Portuguese,
the soldiers of that nation having borne the brunt of
both fights. On the French side the loss was enormous. Conroux's and Maucune's divisions were
completely disorganized ; Foy with eight thousand
men, including the fugitives he had rallied, was
entirely separated from the main body ; two thousand men at the lowest computation had been
killed or wounded, many were dispersed in the
woods and ravines, and three thousand prisoners were
taken. This blow joined to former losses reduced
Soult's fighting men to thirty-five thousand, of
which the fifteen thousand under Clauzel and Reille
were dispirited by defeat, and the whole were
placed in a most critical situation. Hill's force now
increased to fifteen thousand men by the junction of Morillo and Campbell was in front, and
thirty thousand were on the rear in the valley of
Lanz, or on the hills at each side ; for the third division finding no more enemies in the valley of Zubiri,

had crowned the heights in conjunction with the fourth division.

Lord Wellington had detached some of La Bispal's Spaniards to Marcalain when he heard of Hill's action, but he was not yet aware of the true state of affairs on that side. His operations were founded upon the notion that Soult was in retreat towards the Bastan. He designed to follow closely pushing his own left forward to support sir Thomas Graham on the Bidassoa, but always underrating D'Erlon's troops he thought La Martiniere's division had retreated by the Roncesvalles road; and as Foy's column was numerous and two divisions had been broken at Sauroren, he judged the force immediately under Soult to be weak and made dispositions accordingly. The sixth division and the thirteenth light dragoons were to march by Eugui to join the third division, which was directed upon Linzoain and Roncesvalles. The fourth division was to descend into the valley of Lanz. General Hill, supported by the Spaniards at Marcalain, was to press Soult closely, always turning his right but directing his own march upon Lanz, from whence he was to send Campbell's brigade to the Alduides. The seventh division which had halted on the ridges between Hill and Wellington, was to suffer the former to cross its front and then march for the pass of Doña Maria.

It appears from these arrangements, that Wellington expecting Soult would rejoin Clauzel and make for the Bastan by the pass of Vellate, intended to confine and press him closely in that district. But the French marshal was in a worse position than his adversary imagined, being too far advanced towards

Buenza to return to Lanz; in fine he was between
two fires and without a retreat save by the pass of
Doña Maria upon San Estevan. Wherefore calling
in Clauzel, and giving D'Erlon whose divisions,
hitherto successful were in good order and undismayed, the rear-guard, he commenced his march
soon after midnight towards the pass. But mischief
was thickening around him.

Sir Thomas Graham having only the blockade
of San Sebastian to maintain was at the head of
twenty thousand men, ready to make a forward
movement, and there remained besides the light
division under Charles Alten of whose operations
it is time to speak. That general, as we have seen,
took post on the mountain of Santa Cruz the 27th.
From thence on the evening of the 28th he marched
to gain Lecumberri on the great road of Irurzun; but
whether by orders from sir Thomas Graham or in
default of orders, the difficulty of communication
being extreme in those wild regions, I know not,
he commenced his descent into the valley of Lerins
very late. His leading brigade, getting down
with some difficulty, reached Leyza beyond the
great chain by the pass of Goriti or Zubieta, but
darkness caught the other brigade and the troops
dispersed in that frightful wilderness of woods and
precipices. Many made faggot torches waving
them as signals, and thus moving about, the lights
served indeed to assist those who carried them but
misled and bewildered others who saw them at a
distance. The heights and the ravines were alike
studded with these small fires, and the soldiers
calling to each other for directions filled the whole
region with their clamour. Thus they continued to
rove and shout until morning shewed the face of the

mountain covered with tired and scattered men and
animals who had not gained half a league of ground
beyond their starting place, and it was many hours,
ere they could be collected to join the other brigade
at Leyza.

General Alten, who had now been separated for
three days from the army, sent mounted officers in
various directions to obtain tidings, and at six
o'clock in the evening renewed his march. At
Areysa he halted for some time without suffering
fires to be lighted, for he knew nothing of the
enemy and was fearful of discovering his situation,
but at night he again moved and finally established
his bivouacs near Lecumberri early on the 30th.
The noise of Hill's battle at Buenza was clearly
heard in the course of the day, and the light division was thus again comprized in the immediate
system of operations directed by Wellington in
person. Had Soult continued his march upon Guipuscoa Alten would have been in great danger, but
the French general being forced to retreat, the light
division was a new power thrown into his opponent's
hands, the value of which will be seen by a
reference to the peculiarity of the country through
which the French general was now to move.

It has been shewn that Foy cut off from the main
army was driven towards the Alduides; that the
French artillery and part of the cavalry were again
on the Bidassoa, whence Villatte, contrary to the
intelligence received by Soult, had not advanced,
though he had skirmished with Longa, leaving the latter however in possession of heights above Lesaca.
The troops under Soult's immediate command were
therefore completely isolated, and had no resources
save what his ability and their own courage could

supply. His single line of retreat by the pass of
Doña Maria was secure as far as San Estevan, and
from that town he could march up the Bidassoa to
Elizondo and so gain France by the Col de Maya,
or down the same river towards Vera by Sumbilla
and Yanzi, from both of which places roads branch-
ing off to the right lead over the mountains to the
passes of Echallar. There was also a third moun-
tain-road leading direct from Estevan to Zagaramurdi and Urdax, but it was too steep and rugged
for his wounded men and baggage.

The road to Elizondo was very good, but that
down the Bidassoa was a long and terrible defile,
and so contracted about the bridges of Yanzi and
Sumbilla that a few men only could march abreast.
This then Soult had to dread; that Wellington
who by the pass of Vellate could reach Elizondo
before him would block his passage on that side;
that Graham would occupy the rocks about Yanzi,
blocking the passage there and by detachments
cut off his line of march upon Echallar. Then,
confined to the narrow mountain-way from San
Estevan to Zagaramurdi, he would be followed hard
by general Hill, exposed to attacks in rear and
flank during his march, and perhaps be headed at
Urdax by the allied troops moving through Vellate Elizondo and the Col de Maya. In this state,
his first object being to get through the pass of Doña
Maria, he commenced his retreat as we have seen
in the night of the 30th, and Wellington still deceived as to the real state of affairs did not take the
most fitting measures to stop his march, that is to
say, he continued in his first design, halting in the
valley of Lanz while Hill passed his front to enter

the Bastan, into which district he sent Byng's
brigade as belonging to the second division. But
early on the 31st, when Soult's real strength became
known, he directed the seventh division to aid Hill,
followed Byng through the pass of Vellate with the
remainder of his forces, and thinking the light division might be at Zubieta in the valley of Lerins,
sent Alten orders to head the French if possible at San
Estevan, or at Sumbilla, in fine to cut in upon their
line of march somewhere; Longa also was ordered
to come down to the defiles at Yanzi, thus aiding
the light division to block the way on that side, and
sir Thomas Graham was advertised to hold his army
in readiness to move in the same view, and it would
appear that the route of the sixth and third divisions
were also changed for a time.

Combat of Dona Maria.—At ten o'clock in the
morning of the 31st, general Hill overtook Soult's
rear-guard between Lizasso and the Puerto. The
seventh division, coming from the hills above Olague,
was already ascending the mountain on his right,
and the French only gained a wood on the summit
of the pass under the fire of Hill's guns. There,
however they turned and throwing out their skirmishers made strong battle. General Stewart,
leading the attack of the second division, now for
the third time engaged with D'Erlon's troops, was
again wounded and his first brigade was repulsed,
but general Pringle who succeeded to the command,
renewed the attack with the second brigade, and the
thirty-fourth regiment leading, broke the enemy at
the moment that the seventh division did the same on
the right. Some prisoners were taken, but a thick
fog prevented further pursuit, and the loss of the

French in the action is unknown, probably less than that of the allies which was something short of four hundred men.

The seventh division remained on the mountain, but Hill fell back to Lizasso, and then, following his orders, moved by a short but rugged way, leading between the passes of Dona Maria and Vellate over the great chain to Almandoz, to join Wellington, who had during the combat descended into the Bastan by the pass of Vellate. Meanwhile Byng reached Elizondo, and captured a large convoy of provisions and ammunition left there under guard of a battalion by D'Erlon on the 29th; he made several hundred prisoners also after a sharp skirmish and then pushed forward to the pass of Maya. Wellington now occupied the hills through which the road leads from Elizondo to San Estevan, and full of hope he was to strike a terrible blow; for Soult, not being pursued after passing Doña Maria, had halted in San Estevan, although by his scouts he knew that the convoy had been taken at Elizondo. He was in a deep narrow valley, and three British divisions with one of Spaniards were behind the mountains overlooking the town; the seventh division was on the mountain of Doña Maria; the light division and sir Thomas Graham's Spaniards were marching to block the Vera and Echallar exits from the valley; Byng was already at Maya, and Hill was moving by Almandoz just behind Wellington's own position. A few hours gained and the French must surrender or disperse. Wellington gave strict orders to prevent the lighting of fires the straggling of soldiers or any other indication of the presence of troops; and he placed himself amongst

some rocks at a commanding point from whence he could observe every movement of the enemy. Soult seemed tranquil, and four of his *"gensd'armes"* were seen to ride up the valley in a careless manner. Some of the staff proposed to cut them off; the
English general whose object was to hide his own presence, would not suffer it, but the next moment three marauding English soldiers entered the valley and were instantly carried off by the horsemen. Half an hour afterwards the French drums beat to arms and their columns began to move out of San Estevan towards Sumbilla. Thus the disobedience of three plundering knaves, unworthy of the name of soldiers, deprived one consummate commander of the most splendid success, and saved another from the most terrible disaster.

The captives walked from their prison but their chains hung upon them. The way was narrow, the multitude great, and the baggage, and wounded men borne on their comrades' shoulders, filed with such long procession, that Clauzel's divisions forming the rear-guard were still about San Estevan on the morning of the 1st of August, and scarcely had they marched a league of ground, when the skirmishers of the fourth division and the Spaniards thronging along the heights on the right flank opened a fire to which little reply could be made. The troops and baggage then got mixed with an extreme disorder, numbers of the former fled up the hills, and the commanding energy of Soult whose personal exertions were conspicuous could scarcely prevent a general dispersion. However prisoners and baggage fell at every step into the hands of the pursuers, the boldest were dismayed at the peril,

and worse would have awaited them in front, if
Wellington had been on other points well seconded
by his subordinate generals.

The head of the French column instead of taking
the first road leading from Sumbilla to Echallar,
had passed onward towards that leading from the
bridge near Yanzi; the valley narrowed to a mere
cleft in the rocks as they advanced, the Bidassoa
was on their left, and there was a tributary torrent
to cross, the bridge of which was defended by a
battalion of Spanish Caçadores detached to that
point from the heights of Vera by general Barceñas.
The front was now as much disordered as the rear,
and had Longa or Barceñas reinforced the Caçadores, those only of the French who being near
Sumbilla could take the road from that place to
Echallar would have escaped; but the Spanish
generals kept aloof and D'Erlon won the defile,
However Reille's divisions were still to pass, and
when they came up a new enemy had appeared.

It will be remembered that the light division was
directed to head the French army at San Estevan,
or Sumbilla. This order was received on the evening of the 31st, and the division, repassing the
defiles of the Zubieta, descended the deep valley
of Lerins and reached Elgoriaga about midday on
the 1st of August, having then marched twenty-
four miles and being little more than a league
from Estevan and about the same distance from
Sumbilla. The movement of the French along the
Bidassoa was soon discovered, but the division instead of moving on Sumbilla turned to the left,
clambered up the great mountain of Santa Cruz
and made for the bridge of Yanzi. The weather
was exceedingly sultry, the mountain steep and

hard to overcome, many men fell and died convulsed and frothing at the mouth, while others whose spirit and strength had never before been quelled, leaned on their muskets and muttered in sullen tones that they yielded for the first time.

Towards evening, after marching for nineteen consecutive hours over forty miles of mountain roads, the head of the exhausted column reached the edge of a precipice near the bridge of Yanzi. Below, within pistol-shot, Reille's divisions were seen hurrying forward along the horrid defile in which they were pent up, and a fire of musketry commenced, slightly from the British on the high rock, more vigorously from some low ground near the bridge of Yanzi, where the riflemen had ensconced themselves in the brushwood. The scene which followed is thus described by an eye-witness.

Captain
Cooke's
Memoirs.

" We overlooked the enemy at stone's throw, and from the summit of a tremendous precipice. The river separated us, but the French were wedged in a narrow road with inaccessible rocks on one side and the river on the other. Confusion impossible to describe followed, the wounded were thrown down in the rush and trampled upon, the cavalry drew their swords and endeavoured to charge up the pass of Echallar, but the infantry beat them back, and several, horses and all, were precipitated into the river ; some fired vertically at us, the wounded called out for quarter, while others pointed to them, supported as they were on branches of trees, on which were suspended great coats clotted with gore, and blood-stained sheets taken from different habitations to aid the sufferers."

On these miserable supplicants brave men could not fire, and so piteous was the spectacle that it

was with averted or doubtful aim they shot at the
others, although the latter rapidly plied their muskets in passing, and some in their veteran hardihood
even dashed across the bridge of Yanzi to make
a counter-attack. It was a soldier-like but a vain
effort! the night found the British in possession of
the bridge, and though the great body of the enemy
escaped by the road to Echallar, the baggage was
cut off and fell, together with many prisoners, into
the hands of the light troops which were still hanging on the rear in pursuit from San Estevan.

The loss of the French this day was very great,
that of the allies about a hundred men, of which
sixty-five were British, principally of the fourth
division. Nevertheless lord Wellington was justly
discontented with the result. Neither Longa nor
general Alten had fulfilled their mission. The
former excused himself as being too feeble to oppose the mass Soult led down the valley; but the
rocks were so precipitous that the French could not
have reached him, and the resistance made by the
Spanish caçadores was Longa's condemnation. A
lamentable fatuity prevailed in many quarters. If
Barceñas had sent his whole brigade instead of a
weak battalion, the small torrent could not have
been forced by D'Erlon; and if Longa had been
near the bridge of Yanzi the French must have
surrendered, for the perpendicular rocks on their
right forbade even an escape by dispersion. Finally
if the light division instead of marching down the
valley of Lerins as far as Elgoriaga, had crossed
the Santa Cruz mountain by the road used the
night of the 28th, it would have arrived much earlier at the bridge of Yanzi, and then belike Longa
and Barceñas would also have come down. Alten's

instructions indeed prescribed Sumbilla and San Estevan as the first points to head the French army, but judging them too strong at Sumbilla he marched as we have seen upon Yanzi; and if he had passed the bridge there and seized the road to Echallar with one brigade, while the other plied the flank with fire from the left of the Bidassoa, he would have struck a great blow. It was for that the soldiers had made such a prodigious exertion, yet the prize was thrown away.

During the night Soult rallied his divisions about Echallar, and on the morning of the 2d occupied the " *Puerto*" of that name. His left was placed at the rocks of Zagaramurdi; his right at the rock of Ivantelly communicating with the left of Villatte's reserve, which was in position on the ridges between Soult's right and the head of the great Rhune mountain. Meanwhile Clauzel's three divisions, now reduced to six thousand men, took post on a strong hill between the " *Puerto*" and town of Echallar. This position was momentarily adopted by Soult to save time, to examine the country, and to make Wellington discover his final object, but that general would not suffer the affront. He had sent the third and sixth divisions to reoccupy the passes of Roncesvalles and the Alduides; Hill had reached the Col de Maya, and Byng was at Urdax; the fourth, seventh, and light divisions remained in hand, and with these he resolved to fall upon Clauzel whose position was dangerously advanced.

Combats of Echallar and Ivantelly.—The light division held the road running from the bridge of Yanzi to Echallar until relieved by the fourth division, and then marched by Lesaca to Santa Barbara, thus turning Clauzel's right. The fourth division marched from Yanzi upon Echallar to attack his front, and the seventh moved from Sumbilla against his left; but Barnes's brigade, contrary to lord Wellington's intention, arrived unsupported before the fourth and light divisions were either seen or felt, and without awaiting the arrival of more troops assailed Clauzel's strong position. The fire became vehement, but neither the steepness of the mountain nor the overshadowing multitude of the enemy clustering above in support of their skirmishers could arrest the assailants, and then was seen the astonishing spectacle of fifteen hundred men driving, by sheer valour and force of arms, six thousand good troops from a position, so rugged that there would have been little to boast of if the numbers had been reversed and the defence made good. It is true that the fourth division arrived towards the end of the action, that the French had fulfilled their mission as a rear-guard, that they were worn with fatigue and ill-provided with ammunition, having exhausted all their reserve stores during the retreat, but the real cause of their inferiority belongs to the highest part of war.

The British soldiers, their natural fierceness stimulated by the remarkable personal daring of their general, Barnes, were excited by the pride of success; and the French divisions were those which had failed in the attack on the 28th, which had been utterly defeated on the 30th, and which had suffered so severely the day before about Sumbilla. Such then is the preponderance of moral power. The men who had assailed the terrible rocks above Sauroren, with a force and energy that all the valour of the hardiest British veterans scarcely sufficed to repel, were now, only five days after-

wards, although posted so strongly, unable to sustain the shock of one-fourth of their own numbers.
And at this very time eighty British soldiers, the
comrades and equals of those who achieved this
wonderful exploit, having wandered to plunder
surrendered to some French peasants, who lord
Wellington truly observed, *" they would under
other circumstances have eat up!"* What gross
ignorance of human nature then do those writers
display who assert, that the employing of brute
force is the highest qualification of a general!

Clauzel, thus dispossessed of the mountain, fell
back fighting to a strong ridge beyond the pass of
Echallar, having his right covered by the Ivantelly
mountain which was strongly occupied. Meanwhile the light division emerging by Lesaca from
the narrow valley of the Bidassoa, ascended the
broad heights of Santa Barbara without opposition,
and halted there until the operations of the fourth
and seventh divisions were far enough advanced to
render it advisable to attack the Ivantelly. This
lofty mountain lifted its head on the right, rising as
it were out of the Santa Barbara heights, and separating them from the ridges through which the
French troops beaten at Echallar were now retiring. Evening was coming on, a thick mist
capped the crowning rocks which contained a
strong French regiment, the British soldiers besides their long and terrible march the previous
day had been for two days without sustenance, and
were leaning, weak and fainting, on their arms,
when the advancing fire of Barnes's action about
Echallar indicated the necessity of dislodging the
enemy from Ivantelly. Colonel Andrew Barnard
instantly led five companies of his riflemen to the

attack, and four companies of the forty-third followed in support. The misty cloud had descended,
and the riflemen were soon lost to the view, but the
sharp clang of their weapons heard in distinct reply
to the more sonorous rolling musketry of the
French, told what work was going on. For some
time the echoes rendered it doubtful how the action
went, but the following companies of the forty-third
could find no trace of an enemy save the killed and
wounded. Barnard had fought his way unaided
and without a check to the summit, where his dark-
clothed swarthy veterans raised their victorious
shout from the highest peak, just as the coming night
shewed the long ridges of the mountains beyond
sparkling with the last musket-flashes from Clauzel's
troops retiring in disorder from Echallar.

This day's fighting cost the British four hundred
men, and lord Wellington narrowly escaped the
enemy's hands. He had carried with him towards
Echallar half a company of the forty-third as an escort, and placed a serjeant named Blood with a party
to watch in front while he examined his maps. The
French who were close at hand sent a detachment
to cut the party off; and such was the nature of the
ground that their troops, rushing on at speed, would
infallibly have fallen unawares upon lord Wellington, if Blood a young intelligent man, seeing
the danger, had not with surprising activity, leaping rather than running down the precipitous rocks
he was posted on, given the general notice, and as
it was the French arrived in time to send a volley
of shot after him as he galloped away.

Soult now caused count D'Erlon to re-occupy
the hills about Ainhoa, Clauzel to take post on
the heights in advance of Sarre, and Reille to

carry his two divisions to St. Jean de Luz in second line behind Villatte's reserve. Foy, who had rashly uncovered St. Jean Pied de Port by descending upon Cambo, was ordered to return and reinforce his troops with all that he could collect of national guards and detachments.

Wellington had on the 1st directed general Graham to collect his forces and bring up pontoons for crossing the Bidassoa, but he finally abandoned this design, and the two armies therefore rested quiet in their respective positions, after nine days of continual movement during which they had fought ten serious actions. Of the allies, including the Spaniards, seven thousand three hundred officers and soldiers had been killed wounded or taken, and many were dispersed from fatigue or to plunder. On the French side the loss was terrible and the disorder rendered the official returns inaccurate. Nevertheless a close approximation may be made. Lord Wellington at first called it twelve thousand, but hearing that the French officers admitted more he raised his estimate to fifteen thousand. The engineer, *Belmas*, in his Journals of Sieges, compiled from official documents by order of the French government, sets down above thirteen thousand. Soult in his dispatches at the time, stated fifteen hundred as the loss at Maya, four hundred at Roncesvalles, two hundred on the 27th, and eighteen hundred on the 28th, after which he speaks no more of losses by battle. There remains therefore to be added the killed and wounded at the combats of Linzoain on the 26th, the double battles of Sauroren and Buenza on the 30th, the combats of the 31st, and those of the 1st and 2d of August; finally, four thousand unwounded

prisoners. Let this suffice. It is not needful to ~CHAP.~ ~V.~
sound the stream of blood in all its horrid depths.

1813.

OBSERVATIONS.

1°. The allies' line of defence was weak. Was
it therefore injudiciously adopted?

The French beaten at Vittoria were disorganized
and retreated without artillery or baggage on
excentric lines; Foy by Guipuscoa, Clauzel by
Zaragoza, Reille by San Estevan, the King by
Pampeluna. There was no reserve to rally upon,
the people fled from the frontier, Bayonne and
St. Jean Pied de Port if not defenceless were certainly in a very neglected state, and the English
general might have undertaken any operation,
assumed any position, offensive or defensive, which
seemed good to him. Why then did he not establish
the Anglo-Portuguese beyond the mountains, leaving
the Spaniards to blockade the fortresses behind
him? The answer to this question involves the
difference between the practice and the theory of
war.

" *The soldiers, instead of preparing food and rest-* Welling-
ing themselves after the battle dispersed in the night ton's Dis-
to plunder, and were so fatigued that when the rain patches.
came on the next day they were incapable of march-
ing and had more stragglers than the beaten enemy.
Eighteen days after the victory twelve thousand five
hundred men, chiefly British, were absent, most of
them marauding in the mountains."

Such were the reasons assigned by the English
general for his slack pursuit after the battle of
Vittoria, yet he had commanded that army for six

years! Was he then deficient in the first qualification of a general, the art of disciplining and
inspiring troops, or was the English military system
defective? It is certain that he always exacted the
confidence of his soldiers as a leader. It is not so
certain that he ever gained their affections. The
barbarity of the English military code excited public
horror, the inequality of promotion created public
discontent; yet the general complained he had no
adequate power to reward or punish, and he condemned alike the system and the soldiers it produced. The latter " *were detestable for every thing
but fighting, and the officers as culpable as the men.*"
The vehemence of these censures is inconsistent
with his celebrated observation, subsequently made,
namely, " that he thought he could go any where
and do any thing with the army that fought on the
Pyrenees," and although it cannot be denied that
his complaints were generally too well founded,
there were thousands of true and noble soldiers,
and zealous worthy officers, who served their country
honestly and merited no reproaches. It is enough
that they have been since neglected, exactly in
proportion to their want of that corrupt aristocratic
influence which produced the evils complained of.

2°. When the misconduct of the troops had thus
weakened the effect of victory, the question of
following Joseph at once into France assumed a
new aspect. Wellington's system of warfare had
never varied after the battle of Talavera. Rejecting
dangerous enterprize, it rested on profound calculation both as to time and resources for the accom-
plishment of a particular object, namely, the
gradual liberation of Spain by the Anglo-Portuguese
army. Not that he held it impossible to attain that

object suddenly, and his battles in India, the passage of the Douro, the advance to Talavera, prove
that by nature he was inclined to daring operations;
but such efforts, however glorious, could not be
adopted by a commander who feared even the loss
of a brigade lest the government he served should
put an end to the war. Neither was it suitable to
the state of his relations with the Portuguese and
Spaniards; their ignorance jealousy and passionate
pride, fierce in proportion to their weakness and
improvidence, would have enhanced every danger.

No man could have anticipated the extraordinary
errors of the French in 1813. Wellington did not
expect to cross the Ebro before the end of the
campaign, and his battering train was prepared for
the siege of Burgos not for that of Bayonne. A
sudden invasion of France her military reputation
considered, was therefore quite out of the pale of
his methodized system of warfare, which was
founded upon political as well as military considerations; and of the most complicated nature, seeing
that he had at all times to deal with the personal
and factious interests and passions, as well as the
great state interests of three distinct nations two
of which abhorred each other. At this moment
also, the uncertain state of affairs in Germany
strongly influenced his views. An armistice which
might end in a separate peace excluding England,
would have brought Napoleon's whole force to the
Pyrenees, and Wellington held cheap both the
military and political proceedings of the coalesced
powers. " *I would not move a corporal's guard in
reliance upon such a system,*" was the significant
phrase he employed to express his contempt.

These considerations justified his caution as to

invading France, but there were local military reasons equally cogent. 1°. He could not dispense with a secure harbour, because the fortresses still in possession of the French, namely, Santona, Pancorbo, Pampeluna, and St Sebastian, interrupted his communications with the interior of Spain; hence the siege of the latter place. 2°. He had to guard against the union of Suchet and Clauzel on his right flank; hence his efforts to cut off the last-named general; hence also the blockade of Pampeluna in preference to siege and the launching of Mina and the bands on the side of Zaragoza.

3°. After Vittoria the nature of the campaign depended upon Suchet's operations, which were rendered more important by Murray's misconduct. The allied force on the eastern coast was badly organized, it did not advance from Valencia as we have seen until the 16th, and then only partially and by the coast, whereas Suchet had assembled more than twenty thousand excellent troops on the Ebro as early as the 12th of July; and had he continued his march upon Zaragoza he would have saved the castle of that place with its stores. Then rallying Paris' division, he could have menaced Wellington's flank with twenty-five thousand men exclusive of Clauzel's force, and if that general joined him with forty thousand.

On the 16th, the day lord William Bentinck quitted Valencia, Suchet might have marched from Zaragoza on Tudela or Sanguessa, and Soult's preparations originally made as we have seen to attack on the 23d instead of the 25th, would have naturally been hastened. How difficult it would then have been for the allies to maintain themselves beyond the Ebro is evident, much more so to hold

a forward position in France. That Wellington
feared an operation of this nature is clear from his
instructions to lord William Bentinck and to Mina;
and because Picton's and Cole's divisions instead
of occupying the passes were kept behind the
mountains solely to watch Clauzel; when the latter
had regained the frontier of France Cole was permitted to join Byng and Morillo. It follows that
the operations after the battle of Vittoria were well
considered and consonant to lord Wellington's
general system. Their wisdom would have been
proved if Suchet had seized the advantages within
his reach.

4°. A general's capacity is sometimes more taxed
to profit from a victory than to gain one. Wellington, master of all Spain, Catalonia excepted, desired
to establish himself solidly in the Pyrenees, lest a
separate peace in Germany should enable Napoleon
to turn his whole force against the allies. In this
expectation, with astonishing exertion of body and
mind, he had in three days achieved a rigorous
examination of the whole mass of the Western
Pyrenees, and concluded that if Pampeluna and
San Sebastian fell, a defensive position as strong as
that of Portugal, and a much stronger one than
could be found behind the Ebro, might be established.
But to invest those places and maintain so difficult
a covering line was a greater task than to win the
battle of Vittoria. However, the early fall of San
Sebastian he expected, because the errors of execution in that siege could not be foreseen, and also
for gain of time he counted upon the disorganized
state of the French army, upon Joseph's want of
military capacity, and upon the moral ascendancy
which his own troops had acquired over the enemy

by their victories. He could not anticipate the expeditious journey, the sudden arrival of Soult, whose rapid reorganization of the French army, and whose vigorous operations contrasted with Joseph's abandonment of Spain, illustrated the old Greek saying, that a herd of deer led by a lion are more dangerous than a herd of lions led by a deer.

5°. The duke of Dalmatia was little beholden to fortune at the commencement of his movements. Her first contradiction was the bad weather, which breaking up the roads delayed the concentration of his army at St. Jean Pied de Port for two days; all officers know the effect which heavy rain and hard marches have upon the vigour and confidence of soldiers who are going to attack. If Soult had commenced on the 23d instead of the 25th the surprise would have been more complete his army more brisk; and as no conscript battalions would have arrived to delay Reille, that general would probably have been more ready in his attack, and might possibly have escaped the fog which on the 26th stopped his march along the superior crest of the mountain towards Vellate. On the other hand the allies would have been spared the unsuccessful assault on San Sebastian, and the pass of Maya might have been better furnished with troops. However Soult's combinations were so well knit that more than one error in execution, and more than one accident of fortune, were necessary to baffle him. Had count D'Erlon followed his instructions even on the 26th general Hill would probably have been shouldered off the valley of Lanz, and Soult would have had twenty thousand additional troops in the combats of the 27th and 28th. Such failures however generally attend extensively combined movements, and it is by no means certain that the count would have been able to carry the position of the Col de Maya on the 25th, if all general Stewart's forces had been posted there. It would therefore perhaps have been more strictly within the rules of art, if D'Erlon had been directed to leave one of his three divisions to menace the Col de Maya while he marched with the other two by St. Etienne de Baygorry up the Alduides. This movement, covered by the national guards who occupied the mountain of La Houssa, could not have been stopped by Campbell's Portuguese brigade, and would have dislodged Hill from the Bastan while it secured the junction of D'Erlon with Soult on the crest of the superior chain.

6°. The intrepid constancy with which Byng and Ross defended their several positions on the 25th, the able and clean retreat made by general Cole as far as the heights of Linzoain, gave full effect to the errors of Reille and D'Erlon, and would probably have baffled Soult at an early period if general Picton had truly comprehended the importance of his position. Lord Wellington says that the concentration of the army would have been effected on the 27th if that officer and general Cole had not agreed in thinking it impossible to make a stand behind Linzoain ; and surely the necessity of retreating on that day may be questioned. For if Cole with ten thousand men maintained the position in front of Altobiscar, Ibañeta, and Atalosti, Picton might have maintained the more contracted one behind Linzoain and Erro with twenty thousand. And that number he could have assembled, because Campbell's Portuguese reached Eugui long before the evening of the 26th, and lord Wellington had directed O'Donnel to keep three thousand five hundred of

the blockading troops in readiness to act in advance,
of which Picton could not have been ignorant.   It
was impossible to turn him by the valley of Urroz
that line being too rugged for the march of an army
and not leading directly upon Pampeluna.   The
only roads into the Val de Zubiri were by Erro
and Linzoain, lying close together and both
leading upon the village of Zubiri over the ridges
which Picton occupied, and the strength of which
was evident from Soult's declining an attack on the
evening of the 26th when Cole only was before him.
To abandon this ground so hastily when the concentration of the army depended upon keeping it,
appears therefore an error, aggravated by the neglect
of sending timely information to the commander-in-
chief, for lord Wellington did not know of the retreat
until the morning of the 27th and then only from
general Long.   It might be that Picton's messenger
failed, but many should have been sent when a retrograde movement involving the fate of Pampeluna
was contemplated.

Original
Note by
the Duke
of Wel-
lington,
MSS.

It has been said that general Cole was the adviser
of this retreat which if completed would have ruined
lord Wellington's campaign.   This is incorrect,
Picton was not a man to be guided by others.
General Cole indeed gave him a report, drawn up
by colonel Bell one of the ablest staff-officers of the
army, which stated that no position suitable for a
very inferior force existed between Zubiri and Pampeluna, and this was true in the sense of the report,
which had reference only to a division not to an
army ; moreover, although the actual battle of Sauroren was fought by inferior numbers, the whole
position, including the ridges of the second line occupied by Picton and the Spaniards, was only main-

Note by
General
Cole,MSS.

tained by equal numbers; and if Soult had made
the attack of the 28th on the evening of the 27th
before the sixth division arrived, the position would
have been carried. However there is no doubt that
colonel Bell's report influenced Picton, and it was
only when his troops had reached Huarte and Villalba that he suddenly resolved on battle. That was
a military resolution, vigorous and prompt; and not
the less worthy of praise that he so readily adopted
Cole's saving proposition to regain the more forward
heights above Zabaldica.

7°. Marshal Soult appeared unwilling to attack
on the evenings of the 26th and 27th. Yet success
depended upon forestalling the allies at their point
of concentration; and it is somewhat inexplicable
that on the 28th, having possession of the ridge
beyond the Lanz river and plenty of cavalry, he
should have known so little of the sixth division's
movements. The general conception of his scheme
on the 30th has also been blamed by some of his
own countrymen, apparently from ignorance of the
facts and because it failed. Crowned with success
it would have been cited as a fine illustration of the
art of war. To have retired at once by the two
valleys of Zubiri and Lanz after being reinforced
with twenty thousand men would have given great
importance to his repulse on the 28th; his reputation as a general capable of restoring the French
affairs would have vanished, and mischief only have
accrued, even though he should have effected his
retreat safely, which, regard being had to the nar-
:owness of the valleys the position of general Hill on
his right and the boldness of his adversary, was not
certain. To abandon the valley of Zubiri and secure
that of Lanz; to obtain another and shorter line of

retreat by the Doña Maria pass; to crush general
Hill with superior numbers, and thus gaining the
Irurzun road to succour San Sebastian, or failing of
that, to secure the union of the whole army and give
to his retreat the appearance of an able offensive
movement; to combine all these chances by one
operation immediately after a severe check was
Soult's plan, it was not impracticable and was surely
the conception of a great commander.

To succeed however it was essential either to beat
general Hill off-hand and thus draw Wellington to
that side by the way of Marcalain, or to secure the
defence of the French left in such a solid manner
that no efforts against it should prevail to the detriment of the offensive movement on the right: neither
was effected. The French general indeed brought
an overwhelming force to bear upon Hill, and drove
him from the road of Irurzun, but he did not crush
him, because that general fought so strongly and
retired with such good order, that beyond the loss
of the position no injury was sustained. Meanwhile
the left wing of the French was completely beaten,
and thus the advantage gained on the right was
more than nullified. Soult trusted to the remarkable defensive strength of the ground occupied by
his left, and he had reason to do so, for it was nearly
impregnable. Lord Wellington turned it on both
flanks at the same time, but neither Picton's advance
into the valley of Zubiri on Foy's left, nor Cole's
front attack on that general, nor Byng's assault
upon the village of Sauroren, would have seriously
damaged the French without the sudden and complete success of general Inglis beyond the Lanz.
The other attacks would indeed have forced the
French to retire somewhat hastily up the valley of

the Lanz, yet they could have held together in mass secure of their junction with Soult. But when the ridges running between them and the right wing of the French army were carried by Inglis, and the whole of the seventh division was thrown upon their flank and rear, the front attack became decisive. It is clear therefore that the key of the defence was on the ridge beyond the Lanz, and instead of two regiments Clauzel should have placed two divisions there.

8°. Lord Wellington's quick perception and vigorous stroke on the 30th were to be expected from such a consummate commander, yet he certainly was not master of all the bearings of the French general's operations; he knew neither the extent of Hill's danger nor the difficulties of Soult, otherwise it is probable that he would have put stronger columns in motion, and at an earlier hour, towards the pass of Doña Maria on the morning of the 31st. Hill did not commence his march that day until 8 o'clock, and it has been shewn that even with the help of the seventh division he was too weak against the heavy mass of the retreating French army. The faults and accidents which baffled Wellington's after operations have been sufficiently touched upon in the narrative, but he halted in the midst of his victorious career, when Soult's army was broken and flying, when Suchet had retired into Catalonia, and all things seemed favourable for the invasion of France.

His motives for this were strong. He knew the armistice in Germany had been renewed with a view to peace, and he had therefore reason to expect Soult would be reinforced. A forward position in France would have lent his right to the enemy who

pivotted upon St. Jean Pied de Port could operate
against his flank. His arrangements for supply,
and intercourse with his depôts and hospitals, would
have been more difficult and complicated, and as
the enemy possessed all the French and Spanish
fortresses commanding the great roads, his need to
gain one, at least, before the season closed, was
absolute if he would not resign his communications
with the interior of Spain. Then long marches and
frequent combats had fatigued his troops destroyed
their shoes and used up their musquet ammunition ;
and the loss of men had been great, especially of
British in the second division where their proportion to foreign troops was become too small. The
difficulty of re-equipping the troops would have
been increased by entering an enemy's state, because
the English system did not make war support war
and his communications would have been lengthened.
Finally it was France that was to be invaded, France
in which every person was a soldier, where the
whole population was armed and organised under
men, not as in other countries inexperienced in war
but who had all served more or less. Beyond the
Adour the army could not advance, and if a separate
peace was made by the northern powers, if any misfortune befel the allies in Catalonia so as to leave
Suchet at liberty to operate towards Pampeluna, or
if Soult profiting from the possession of San Jean
Pied de Port should turn the right flank of the new
position, a retreat into Spain would become necessary, and however short would be dangerous from
the hostility and warlike disposition of the people
directed in a military manner.

These reasons joined to the fact, that a forward
position, although offering better communications

from right to left, would have given the enemy
greater facilities for operating against an army
which must until the fortresses fell hold a defensive and somewhat extended line, were conclusive
as to the rashness of an invasion ; but they do not
appear so conclusive as to the necessity of stopping
short after the action of the 2d of August.   The
questions were distinct. The one was a great measure
involving vast political and military conditions, the
other was simply whether Wellington should profit
of his own victory and the enemy's distresses ; and
in this view the objections above-mentioned, save
the want of shoes the scarcity of ammunition and
the fatigue of the troops, are inapplicable.   But in
the two last particulars the allies were not so badly
off as the enemy, and in the first not so deficient as
to cripple the army, wherefore if the advantage to
be gained was worth the effort it was an error to
halt.

The solution of this problem is to be found in the
comparative condition of the armies.   Soult had
recovered his reserve his cavalry and artillery, but
Wellington was reinforced by general Graham's
corps which was more numerous and powerful than
Villate's reserve.   The new chances then were for
the allies, and the action of the 2d of August
demonstrated that their opponents however strongly
posted could not stand before them ; one more victory would have gone nigh to destroy the French
force altogether; for such was the disorder that
Maucune's division had on the 2d only one thou- Soult's Of-
sand men left out of more than five thousand, and port, MSS.
on the 6th it had still a thousand stragglers besides
killed and wounded: Conroux's and La Martinière's
divisions were scarcely in better plight, and the

BOOK
XXI.
———
1813.
losses of the other divisions although less remarkable were great. It must also be remembered that general Foy with eight thousand men was cut off from the main body; and the Nivelle, the sources of which were in the allies' power, was behind the French. With their left pressed from the pass of Maya, and their front vigorously assailed by the Soult's Official Report, MSS. main body of the allies, they could hardly have kept together, since more than twenty-one thousand men exclusive of Foy's troops were then absent from their colours. And as late as the 12th of August Soult warned the minister of war that he was indeed preparing to assail his enemy again, but he had not the means of resisting a counter-attack, Appendix, 4. although he held a different language to his army and to the people of the country.

Had Cæsar halted because his soldiers were fatigued, Pharsalia would have been but a common battle.

BOOK XXII.

CHAPTER I.

AFTER the combat of Echallar Soult adopted a permanent position and reorganized his army. The left
wing under D'Erlon occupied the hills of Ainhoa,
with an advanced guard on the heights overlooking
Urdax and Zuguramurdi. The centre under Clauzel was in advance of Sarre guarding the issues
from Vera and Echallar, his right resting on the
greatest of the Rhune mountains. The right wing
under Reille composed of Maucune's and La Martinière's divisions extended along the Lower Bidassoa
to the sea ; Villatte's reserve was encamped behind
the Nivelle near Serres, and Reille's third division,
under Foy, covered in conjunction with the national
guards, St. Jean Pied de Port and the roads leading
into France on that side. The cavalry for the convenience of forage were quartered, one division
between the Nive and the Nivelle rivers, the other
as far back as Dax.

Lord Wellington occupied his old positions from
the pass of Roncesvalles to the mouth of the Bidassoa,
but the disposition of his troops was different. Sir
Rowland Hill, reinforced by Morillo, held the Roncesvalles and Alduides throwing up field-works at
the former. The third and sixth divisions were in
the Bastan guarding the Puerto de Maya, and the

CHAP.
I.

1813.
August.

Soult'sOffi-
cial Re-
port, MSS.

seventh division, reinforced by O'Donnel's army of
reserve, occupied the passes at Echallar and Zu-
garamurdi. The light division was posted on the
Santa Barbara heights having picquets in the
town of Vera; their left rested on the Bidassoa,
their right on the Ivantelly rock, round which a
bridle communication with Echallar was now made
by the labour of the soldiers. Longa's troops were
beyond the Bidassoa on the left of the light division;
the fourth division was in reserve behind him, near
Lesaca; the fourth Spanish army, now commanded
by general Freyre, prolonged the line from the left
of Longa to the sea; it crossed the royal causeway
occupied Irun and Fontarabia and guarded the
Jaizquibel mountain. The first division was in reserve behind these Spaniards; the fifth division was
destined to resume the siege of San Sebastian; the
blockade of Pampeluna was maintained by Carlos
d'España's troops.

This disposition, made with increased means, was
more powerful for defence than the former occupation of the same ground. A strong corps under a
single command was well entrenched at Roncesvalles; and in the Bastan two British divisions
admonished by Stewart's error were more than
sufficient to defend the Puerto de Maya. The
Echallar mountains were with the aid of O'Donnel's
Spaniards equally secure, and the reserve instead of
occupying San Estevan was posted near Lesaca in
support of the left, now become the most important
part of the line.

The castles of Zaragoza and Daroca had fallen,
the Empecinado was directed upon Alcanitz and he
maintained the communication between the Catalan
army, and Mina. The latter now joined by Duran

was gathering near Jaca from whence his line of
retreat was by Sanguessa upon Pampeluna; in this
position he menaced general Paris, who marched
after a slight engagement on the 11th into France,
leaving eight hundred men in the town and castle.
At this time lord William Bentinck having crossed
the Ebro was investing Taragona, and thus the
allies, acting on the offensive, were in direct military
communication from the Mediteranean to the Bay
of Biscay, while Suchet though holding the fortresses could only communicate with Soult through
France.

This last-named marshal, being strongly posted,
did not much expect a front attack, but the augmentation of the allies on the side of Roncesvalles and
Maya gave him uneasiness, lest they should force
him to abandon his position by operating along the
Nive river. To meet this danger general Paris took
post at Oleron in second line to Foy, and the fortresses of St. Jean Pied de Port and Navareins were
put in a state of defence as pivots of operation on
that side, while Bayonne served a like purpose on
the other flank of the army. But with great diligence the French general fortified his line from the
mouth of the Bidassoa to the rocks of Mondarain
and the Nive.

Lord Wellington, whose reasons for not invading
France at this period have been already noticed, and
who had now little to fear from any renewal of the
French operations against his right wing, turned his
whole attention to the reduction of San Sebastian.
In this object he was however crossed in a manner
to prove that the English ministers were the very
counterparts of the Spanish and Portuguese states-
men. Lord Melville was at the head of the board

of admiralty ; under his rule the navy of England for the first time met with disasters in battle, and his neglect of the general's demands for maritime aid went nigh to fasten the like misfortunes upon the army. This neglect combined with the cabinet scheme of employing lord Wellington in Germany, would seem to prove that experience had taught the English ministers nothing as to the nature of the Peninsular war, or that elated with the array of sovereigns against Napoleon they were now careless of a cause so mixed up with democracy. Still it would be incredible that lord Melville, a man of ordinary capacity, should have been suffered to retard the great designs and endanger the final success of a general, whose sure judgement and extraordinary merit were authenticated by exploits unparalleled in English warfare, if lord Wellington's correspondence and that of Mr. Stuart did not establish the following facts.

1°. Desertion from the enemy was stopped, chiefly because the Admiralty, of which lord Melville was the head, refused to let the ships of war carry deserters or prisoners to England ; they were thus heaped up by hundreds at Lisbon and maltreated by the Portuguese government, which checked all desire in the French troops to come over.

2°. When the disputes with America commenced, Mr. Stuart's efforts to obtain flour for the army were most vexatiously thwarted by the board of admiralty, which permitted if it did not encourage the English ships of war to capture American vessels trading under the secret licenses.

3°. The refusal of the admiralty to establish certain cruisers along the coast, as recommended by lord Wellington, caused the loss of many store-ships

and merchantmen, to the great detriment of the
army before it quitted Portugal. Fifteen were taken
off Oporto, and one close to the bar of Lisbon in
May. And afterwards, the Mediterranean packet
bearing despatches from lord William Bentinck
was captured, which led to lamentable consequences;
for the papers were not in cypher, and contained
detailed accounts of plots against the French in
Italy, with the names of the principal persons engaged.

4°. A like neglect of the coast of Spain caused
ships containing money, shoes, and other indispensable stores to delay in port, or risk the being taken
on the passage by cruizers issuing from Santona,
Bayonne, and Bordeaux. And while the communications of the allies were thus intercepted, the
French coasting vessels supplied their army and
fortresses without difficulty.

5°. After the battle of Vittoria lord Wellington
was forced to use French ammunition, though too
small for the English muskets, because the ordnance
store-ships which he had ordered from Lisbon to
Santander could not sail for want of convoy. When
the troops were in the Pyrenees, a reinforcement of
five thousand men was kept at Gibraltar and Lisbon
waiting for ships of war, and the transports employed to convey them were thus withdrawn from
the service of carrying home wounded men, at a
time when the Spanish authorities at Bilbao refused
even for payment to concede public buildings for
hospitals.

6°. When snow was falling on the Pyrenees the
soldiers were without proper clothing, because the
ship containing their great coats, though ready to
sail in August, was detained at Oporto until Novem-

ber waiting for convoy. When the victories of
July were to be turned to profit ere the fitting
season for the siege of San Sebastian should pass
away, the attack of that fortress was retarded sixteen days because a battering train and ammunition,
demanded several months before by lord Wellington, had not yet arrived from England.

7°. During the siege the sea communication with
Bayonne was free. " Any thing in the shape of a
naval force," said lord Wellington, " would drive
away sir George Collier's squadron." The garrison
received reinforcements artillery ammunition and
all necessary stores for its defence, sending away
the sick and wounded men in empty vessels. The
Spanish general blockading Santona complained at
the same time that the exertions of his troops were
useless, because the French succoured the place by
sea when they pleased; and after the battle of Vittoria not less than five vessels laden with stores and
provisions, and one transport having British soldiers
and clothing on board, were taken by cruizers
issuing out of that port. The great advantage of
attacking San Sebastian by water as well as by
land was foregone for want of naval means, and
from the same cause British soldiers were withdrawn from their own service to unload store-ships;
the gun-boats employed in the blockade were Spanish vessels manned by Spanish soldiers withdrawn from the army, and the store-boats were navi-
gated by Spanish women.

8°. The coasting trade between Bordeaux and
Bayonne being quite free, the French, whose military means of transport had been so crippled by
their losses at Vittoria that they could scarcely have
collected magazines with land carriage only, received

their supplies by water, and were thus saved trouble
and expense and the unpopularity attending forced
requisitions.

Between April and August, more than twenty applications and remonstrances, were addressed by lord Wellington to the government upon these points without producing the slightest attention to his demands. Mr. Croker, the under-secretary of the Admiralty, of whose conduct he particularly complained, was indeed permitted to write an offensive official letter to him, but his demands and the dangers to be apprehended from neglecting them were disregarded, and to use his own words, *" since Great Britain had been a naval power a British army had never before been left in such a situation at a most important moment."*

Nor is it easy to determine whether negligence and incapacity or a grovelling sense of national honour prevailed most in the cabinet, when we find this renowned general complaining that the government, ignorant even to ridicule of military operations, seemed to know nothing of the nature of the element with which England was surrounded, and lord Melville so insensible to the glorious toils of the Peninsula as to tell him that his army was the last thing to be attended to.

RENEWED SIEGE OF SEBASTIAN.

Villatte's demonstration against Longa on the 28th of July had caused the ships laden with the battering train to put to sea, but on the 5th of August the guns were re-landed and the works against the fortress resumed. On the 8th, a notion having spread that the enemy was mining under the cask redoubt, the engineers seized the occasion

to exercise their inexperienced miners by sinking a
shaft and driving a gallery. The men soon acquired expertness, and as the water rose in the
shaft at twelve feet, the work was discontinued when
the gallery had attained eighty feet. Meanwhile
the old trenches were repaired, the heights of San
Bartolomeo were strengthened, and the convent of
Antigua, built on a rock to the left of those heights,
was fortified and armed with two guns to scour
the open beach and sweep the bay. The siege
however languished for want of ammunition;
and during this forced inactivity the garrison received supplies and reinforcements by sea, their
damaged works were repaired, new defences constructed, the magazines filled, and sixty-seven
pieces of artillery put in a condition to play. Eight
hundred and fifty men had been killed and wounded
since the commencement of the attack in July, but
as fresh men came by sea, more than two thousand
six hundred good soldiers were still present under
arms. And to show that their confidence was unabated they celebrated the Emperor's birthday by
crowning the castle with a splendid illumination;
encircling it with a fiery legend to his honour in
characters so large as to be distinctly read by the
besiegers.

On the 19th of August, that is to say after a
delay of sixteen days, the battering train arrived
from England, and in the night of the 22d fifteen
heavy pieces were placed in battery, eight at the
right attack and seven at the left. A second battering train came on the 23d, augmenting the number of pieces of various kinds to a hundred and
seventeen, including a large Spanish mortar; but
with characteristic negligence this enormous arma-

ment had been sent out from England with no more
shot and shells than would suffice for one day's
consumption !

In the night of the 23d the batteries on the
Chofre sand-hills were reinforced with four long
pieces and four sixty-eight pound carronades, and
the left attack with six additional guns. Ninety
sappers and miners had come with the train from
England, the seamen under Mr. O'Reilly were again
attached to the batteries, and part of the field artillerymen were brought to the siege.

On the 24th the attack was recommenced with
activity. The Chofre batteries were enlarged to
contain forty-eight pieces, and two batteries for
thirteen pieces were begun on the heights of Bartolomeo, designed to breach at seven hundred yards
distance the faces of the left demi-bastion of the
horn-work, that of St. John on the main front, and
the end of the high curtain, for these works rising
in gradation one above another were in the same
line of shot. The approaches on the isthmus were
now also pushed forward by the sap, but the old
trenches were still imperfect, and before daylight
on the 25th the French coming from the horn-
work swept the left of the parallel, injured the sap,
and made some prisoners before they were repulsed.

On the night of the 25th the batteries were all
armed on both sides of the Urumea, and on the
26th fifty-seven pieces opened with a general salvo,
and continued to play with astounding noise and
rapidity until evening. The firing from the Chofre
hills destroyed the revêtement of the demi-bastion
of St. John, and nearly ruined the towers near the
old breach together with the wall connecting them ;

but at the isthmus, the batteries although they injured the horn-work made little impression on the main front from which they were too distant.

Lord Wellington, present at this attack and discontented with the operation, now ordered a battery for six guns to be constructed amongst some ruined houses on the right of the parallel, only three hundred yards from the main front, and two shafts were sunk with a view to drive galleries for the protection of this new battery against the enemy's mines, but the work was slow because of the sandy nature of the soil.

At 3 o'clock in the morning of the 27th the boats of the squadron, commanded by lieut. Arbuthnot of the Surveillante and carrying a hundred soldiers of the ninth regiment under captain Cameron, pulled to attack the island of Santa Clara. A heavy fire was opened on them, and the troops landed with some difficulty, but the island was then easily taken and a lodgement made with the loss of only twenty-eight men and officers, of which eighteen were seamen.

In the night of the 27th, about 3 o'clock, the French sallied against the new battery on the isthmus, but as colonel Cameron of the ninth regiment met them on the very edge of the trenches with the bayonet the attempt failed, yet it delayed the arming of the battery. At day-break the renewed fire of the besiegers, especially that from the Chofres sand-hills, was extremely heavy, and the shrapnel shells were supposed to be very destructive; nevertheless the practice with that missile was very uncertain, the bullets frequently flew amongst the guards in the parallel and one struck the field-officer. In the course of the day another sally was commenced,

but the enemy being discovered and fired upon did
not persist.   The trenches were now furnished with
banquettes and parapets as fast as the quantity of
gabions and fascines would permit, yet the work
was slow, because the Spanish authorities of Guipuscoa, like those in every other part of Spain,
neglected to provide carts to convey the materials
from the woods, and this hard labour was performed
by the Portuguese soldiers.   It would seem however
an error not to have prepared all the materials of
this nature during the blockade.

Lord Wellington again visited the works this
day, and in the night the advanced battery, which,
at the desire of sir Richard Fletcher had been constructed for only four guns, was armed.   The 29th
it opened, but an accident had prevented the arrival
of one gun, and the fire of the enemy soon dismounted another, so that only two instead of six
guns as lord Wellington had designed, smote at
short range the face of the demi-bastion of St. John
and the end of the high curtain; however the
general firing was severe both upon the castle and
the town-works and great damage was done to the
defences.   By this time the French guns were nearly
silenced and as additional mortars were mounted on
the Chofre batteries, making in all sixty-three pieces
of which twenty-nine threw shells or spherical
case-shot, the superiority of the besiegers was
established.

The Urumea was now discovered to be fordable.
Captain Alexander Macdonald of the artillery, without orders, waded across in the night passed close
under the works to the breach and returned safely.
Wherefore as a few minutes would suffice to bring
the enemy into the Chofre batteries, to save the guns

from being spiked their vents were covered with
iron plates fastened by chains; and this was also
done at the advanced battery on the isthmus.

This day the materials and ordnance for a battery
of six pieces, to take the defences of the Monte
Orgullo in reverse, were sent to the island of Santa
Clara; and several guns in the Chofre batteries
were turned upon the retaining wall of the horn-
work, in the hope of shaking down any mines
the enemy might have prepared there, without
destroying the wall itself which offered cover for
the troops advancing to the assault.

The trenches leading from the parallel on the
isthmus were now very wide and good, the sap was
pushed on the right close to the demi-bastion of the
horn-work, and the sea-wall supporting the high
road into the town, which had increased the march
and cramped the formation of the columns in the
first assault, was broken through to give access to
the strand and shorten the approach to the breaches.
The crisis was at hand and in the night of the 29th
a false attack was ordered to make the enemy spring
his mines; a desperate service and bravely executed
by lieutenant Macadam of the ninth regiment. The
order was sudden, no volunteers were demanded, no
rewards offered, no means of excitement resorted
to; yet such is the inherent bravery of British
soldiers, that seventeen men of the royals, the
nearest at hand, immediately leaped forth ready and
willing to encounter what seemed certain death.
With a rapid pace, all the breaching batteries playing
hotly at the time, they reached the foot of the breach
unperceived, and then mounted in extended order
shouting and firing; but the French were too steady
to be imposed upon and their musquetry laid the

whole party low with the exception of their commander, who returned alone to the trenches.

On the 30th the sea flank of the place being
opened from the half-bastion of St. John on the
right to the most distant of the old breaches, that is
to say, for five hundred feet, the batteries on the
Chofres were turned against the castle and other
defences of the Monte Orgullo, while the advanced
battery on the isthmus, now containing three guns,
demolished, in conjunction with the fire from the
Chofres, the face of the half-bastion of St. John's
and the end of the high curtain above it. The
whole of that quarter was in ruins, and at the same
time the batteries on San Bartolomeo broke the face
of the demi-bastion of the horn-work and cut away
the palisades.

The 30th the batteries continued their fire, and
about three o'clock lord Wellington after examining
the enemy's defence resolved to make a lodgement
on the breach, and in that view ordered the assault
to be made the next day at eleven o'clock when the
ebb of tide would leave full space between the horn-
work and the water.

The galleries in front of the advanced battery on
the isthmus were now pushed close up to the sea
wall, under which three mines were formed with
the double view of opening a short and easy way
for the troops to reach the strand, and rendering
useless any subterranean works the enemy might
have made in that part. At two o'clock in the
morning of the 31st they were sprung, and opened
three wide passages which were immediately connected, and a traverse of gabions, six feet high, was
run across the mouth of the main trench on the
left, to screen the opening from the grape-shot of

the castle.   Everything was now ready for the assault, but before describing that terrible event it will be fitting to shew the exact state of the besieged in defence.

Sir Thomas Graham had been before the place for fifty-two days, during thirty of which the attack was suspended.   All this time the garrison had laboured incessantly, and though the heavy fire of the besiegers since the 26th appeared to have ruined the defences of the enormous breach in the sea flank, it was not so.   A perpendicular fall behind of more than twenty feet barred progress, and beyond that, amongst the ruins of the burned houses, was a strong counter-wall fifteen feet high, loopholed for musquetry, and extending in a parallel direction with the breaches, which were also cut off from the sound part of the rampart by traverses at the extremities.   The only really practicable road into the town was by the narrow end of the high curtain above the half bastion of St. John.

In front of the counter wall, about the middle of the great breach, stood the tower of Los Hornos still capable of some defence, and beneath it a mine charged with twelve hundred weight of powder.   The streets were all trenched, and furnished with traverses to dispute the passage and to cover a retreat to the Monte Orgullo ; but before the assailants could reach the main breach it was necessary either to form a lodgment in the horn-work, or to pass as in the former assault under a flanking fire of musquetry for a distance of nearly two hundred yards.   And the first step was close under the sea wall covering the salient angle of the covered way, where two mines charged with eight

hundred pounds of powder were prepared to overwhelm the advancing columns.

To support this system of retrenchments and
mines the French had still some artillery in reserve.
One sixteen-pounder mounted at St. Elmo flanked
the left of the breaches on the river face; a twelve
and an eight-pounder preserved in the casemates of
the Cavalier were ready to flank the land face of
the half-bastion of St. John; many guns from the
Monte Orgullo especially those of the Mirador
could play upon the columns, and there was a four-
pounder hidden on the horn-work to be brought
into action when the assault commenced. Neither
the resolution of the governor nor the courage of
the garrison were abated, but the overwhelming fire
of the last few days had reduced the number of
fighting men; General Rey had only two hundred
and fifty men in reserve, and he demanded of Soult
whether his brave garrison should be exposed to
another assault. " The army would endeavour to
succour him" was the reply, and he abided his fate.

Napoleon's ordinance, which forbade the surrender of a fortress without having stood at least
one assault, has been strongly censured by English
writers upon slender grounds. The obstinate defences made by French governors in the Peninsula
were the results, and to condemn an enemy's system
from which we have ourselves suffered will scarcely
bring it into disrepute. But the argument runs,
that the besiegers working by the rules of art must
make a way into the place, and to risk an assault
for the sake of military glory or to augment the
loss of the enemy is to sacrifice brave men uselessly;
that capitulation always followed a certain advance
of the besiegers in Louis the Fourteenth's time, and

to suppose Napoleon's upstart generals possessed of superior courage or sense of military honour to the high-minded nobility of that age was quite inadmissible; and it has been rather whimsically added that obedience to the emperor's orders might suit a predestinarian Turk but could not be tolerated by a reflecting Christian. From this it would seem, that certain nice distinctions as to the extent and manner reconcile human slaughter with Christianity, and that the true standard of military honour was fixed by the intriguing, depraved and insolent court of Louis the Fourteenth. It may however be reasonably supposed, that as the achievements of Napoleon's soldiers far exceeded the exploits of Louis's cringing courtiers they possessed greater military virtues.

But the whole argument seems to rest upon false grounds. To inflict loss upon an enemy is the very essence of war, and as the bravest men and officers will always be foremost in an assault, the loss thus occasioned may be of the utmost importance. To resist when nothing can be gained or saved is an act of barbarous courage which reason spurns at; but how seldom does that crisis happen in war? Napoleon wisely insisted upon a resistance which should make it dangerous for the besiegers to hasten a siege beyond the rules of art, he would not have a weak governor yield to a simulation of force not really existing; he desired that military honour should rest upon the courage and resources of men rather than upon the strength of walls: in fine he made a practical application of the proverb that necessity is the mother of invention.

Granted that a siege artfully conducted and with sufficient means must reduce the fortress attacked;

still there will be some opportunity for a governor to display his resources of mind. Vauban admits of one assault and several retrenchments, after a lodgment is made on the body of the place; Napoleon only insisted that every effort which courage and genius could dictate should be exhausted before a surrender, and those efforts can never be defined or bounded before-hand. Tarifa is a happy example. To be consistent, any attack which deviates from the rules of art must also be denounced as barbarous; yet how seldom has a general all the necessary means at his disposal. In Spain not one siege could be conducted by the British army according to the rules. And there is a manifest weakness in praising the Spanish defence of Zaragoza, and condemning Napoleon because he demanded from regular troops a devotion similar to that displayed by peasants and artizans. What governor was ever in a more desperate situation than general Bizanet at Bergen-op-Zoom, when Sir Thomas Graham, with a hardihood and daring which would alone place him amongst the foremost men of enterprize which Europe can boast of, threw more than two thousand men upon the ramparts of that almost impregnable fortress. The young soldiers of the garrison frightened by a surprise in the night, were dispersed, were flying. The assailants had possession of the walls for several hours, yet some cool and brave officers rallying the men towards morning, charged up the narrow ramps and drove the assailants over the parapets into the ditch. They who could not at first defend their works were now able to retake them, and so completely successful and illustrative of Napoleon's principle was this counter-attack that the number of prisoners equalled that of the garrison. There are no rules to limit energy and genius, and no man knew better than Napoleon how to call those qualities forth ; he possessed them himself in the utmost perfection and created them in others.

CHAPTER II.

STORMING OF SAN SEBASTIAN.

To assault the breaches without having destroyed the enemy's defences or established a lodgment on the horn-work, was, notwithstanding the increased fire and great facilities of the besiegers, obviously a repetition of the former fatal error. And the same generals who had before so indiscreetly made their disapproval of such operations public, now even more freely and imprudently dealt out censures, which not ill-founded in themselves were most ill-timed, since there is much danger when doubts come down from the commanders to the soldiers. Lord Wellington thought the fifth division had been thus discouraged, and incensed at the cause, demanded fifty volunteers from each of the fifteen regiments composing the first, fourth, and light divisions, " *men who could shew other troops how to mount a breach.*" This was the phrase employed, and seven hundred and fifty gallant soldiers instantly marched to San Sebastian in answer to the appeal. Colonel Cooke and major Robertson led the guards and Germans of the first division, major Rose commanded the men of the fourth division, and colonel Hunt, a daring officer who had already won his promotion at former assaults, was at the head of the

fierce rugged veterans of the light division, yet
there were good officers and brave soldiers in the
fifth division.

It being at first supposed that Lord Wellington
merely designed a simple lodgment on the great
breach, the volunteers and one brigade of the fifth
division only were ordered to be ready; but in a
council held at night major Smith maintained that
the orders were misunderstood, as no lodgment
could be formed unless the high curtain was gained.
General Oswald being called to the council was of
the same opinion, whereupon the remainder of the
fifth division was brought to the trenches, and general Bradford having offered the services of his
Portuguese brigade, was told he might ford the
Urumea and assail the farthest breach if he judged
it advisable.

Sir James Leith had resumed the command of
the fifth division, and being assisted by general
Oswald directed the attack from the isthmus. He
was extremely offended by the arrival of the volunteers and would not suffer them to lead the assault; some he spread along the trenches to keep
down the fire of the horn-work, the remainder were
held as a reserve along with general Hay's British
and Sprye's Portuguese brigades of the fifth division. To general Robinson's brigade the assault
was confided. It was formed in two columns, one
to assault the old breach between the towers, the
other to storm the bastion of St. John and the end
of the high curtain. The small breach on the extreme right was left for general Bradford's Portuguese who were drawn up on the Chofre hills;
some large boats filled with troops, were directed
to make a demonstration against the sea-line of the

Monte Orgullo, and sir Thomas Graham overlooked
the whole operations from the right bank of the
river.

The morning of the 31st broke heavily, a thick fog
hid every object, and the besiegers' batteries could
not open until eight o'clock.   From that hour a
constant shower of heavy missiles was poured upon
the besieged until eleven, when Robinson's brigade
getting out of the trenches passed through the
openings in the sea-wall and was launched bodily
against the breaches.   While the head of the column was still gathering on the strand, about thirty
yards from the salient angle of the horn-work,
twelve men, commanded by a serjeant whose heroic
death has not sufficed to preserve his name, running
violently forward leaped upon the covered way with
intent to cut the sausage of the enemy's mines. The
French startled by this sudden assault fired the
train prematurely, and though the serjeant and his
brave followers were all destroyed and the high sea-
wall was thrown with a dreadful crash upon the
head of the advancing column, not more than forty
men were crushed by the ruins and the rush of the
troops was scarcely checked. The forlorn hope
had already passed beyond the play of the mine,
and now speeded along the strand amidst a shower
of grape and shells, the leader lieutenant Macguire
of the fourth regiment, conspicuous from his long Memoirs
of Captain
Cooke.
white plume his fine figure and his swiftness,
bounded far ahead of his men in all the pride of
youthful strength and courage, but at the foot of
the great breach he fell dead, and the stormers went
sweeping like a dark surge over his body ; many
died however with him and the trickling of
wounded men to the rear was incessant.

This time there was a broad strand left by the
retreating tide and the sun had dried the rocks,
yet they disturbed the order and closeness of the
formation, the distance to the main breach was
still nearly two hundred yards, and the French,
seeing the first mass of assailants pass the horn-
work regardless of its broken bastion, immediately
abandoned the front and crowding on the river face
of that work, poured their musketry into the flank
of the second column as it rushed along a few
yards below them; but the soldiers still running
forward towards the breach returned this fire without slackening their speed. The batteries of the
Monte Orgullo and the St. Elmo now sent their
showers of shot and shells, the two pieces on the
cavalier swept the face of the breach in the bastion
of St. John, and the four-pounder in the horn-
work being suddenly mounted on the broken bastion poured grape-shot into their rear.

Thus scourged with fire from all sides, the
stormers, their array broken alike by the shot and
by the rocks they passed over, reached their destinations, and the head of the first column gained the
top of the great breach; but the unexpected gulf
below could only be passed at a few places where
meagre parcels of the burned houses were still attached to the rampart, and the deadly clatter of the
French musquets from the loop-holed wall beyond
soon strewed the narrow crest of the ruins with
dead. In vain the following multitude covered the
ascent seeking an entrance at every part; to advance was impossible and the mass of assailants,
slowly sinking downwards remained stubborn and
immoveable on the lower part of the breach. Here
they were covered from the musquetry in front, but

from several isolated points, especially the tower of
Las Hornos under which the great mine was placed,
the French still smote them with small arms, and
the artillery from the Monte Orgullo poured shells
and grape without intermission.

Such was the state of affairs at the great breach,
and at the half bastion of St. John it was even
worse. The access to the top of the high curtain
being quite practicable, the efforts to force a way
were more persevering and constant, and the
slaughter was in proportion ; for the traverse on the
flank, cutting it off from the cavalier, was defended
by French grenadiers who would not yield; the two
pieces on the cavalier itself swept along the front
face of the opening, and the four-pounder and the
musquetry from the horn-work, swept in like
manner along the river face. In the midst of this
destruction some sappers and a working party attached to the assaulting columns endeavoured to
form a lodgement, but no artificial materials had
been provided, and most of the labourers were
killed before they could raise the loose rocky frag-
ments into a cover.

During this time the besiegers' artillery kept up
a constant counter-fire which killed many of the
French, and the reserve brigades of the fifth division were pushed on by degrees to feed the attack
until the left wing of the ninth regiment only remained in the trenches. The volunteers also who
had been with difficulty restrained in the trenches,
" calling out to know, why they had been brought
there if they were not to lead the assault," these
men, whose presence had given such offence to
general Leith that he would have kept them altogether from the assault, being now let loose went like

a whirlwind to the breaches, and again the crowded masses swarmed up the face of the ruins, but reaching the crest line they came down like a falling wall; crowd after crowd were seen to mount, to totter, and to sink, the deadly French fire was unabated, the smoke floated away, and the crest of the breach bore no living man.

Sir Thomas Graham, standing on the nearest of the Chofre batteries, beheld this frightful destruction with a stern resolution to win at any cost; and he was a man to have put himself at the head of the last company and died sword in hand upon the breach rather than sustain a second defeat, but neither his confidence nor his resources were yet exhausted. He directed an attempt to be made on the horn-work, and turned all the Chofre batteries and one on the Isthmus, that is to say the concentrated fire of fifty heavy pieces upon the high curtain. The shot ranged over the heads of the troops who now were gathered at the foot of the breach, and the stream of missiles thus poured along the upper surface of the high curtain broke down the traverses, and in its fearful course shattering all things strewed the rampart with the mangled limbs of the defenders. When this flight of bullets first swept over the heads of the soldiers a cry arose, from some inexperienced people, " to retire because the batteries were firing on the stormers;" but the veterans of the light division under Hunt being at that point were not to be so disturbed, and in the very heat and fury of the cannonade effected a solid lodgement in some ruins of houses actually within the rampart on the right of the great breach.

For half an hour this horrid tempest smote upon the works and the houses behind, and then sud-

denly ceasing the small clatter of the French musquets shewed that the assailants were again in activity ; and at the same time the thirteenth Portuguese
regiment led by Major Snodgrass and followed by
a detachment of the twenty-fourth under colonel
Macbean entered the river from the Chofres. The
ford was deep the water rose above the waist, and
when the soldiers reached the middle of the stream
which was two hundred yards wide, a heavy gun
struck on the head of the column with a shower of
grape ; the havoc was fearful but the survivors
closed and moved on. A second discharge from the
same piece tore the ranks from front to rear, still
the regiment moved on, and amidst a confused fire
of musquetry from the ramparts, and of artillery
from St. Elmo, from the castle, and from the Mirador, landed on the left bank and rushed against
the third breach. Macbean's men who had followed with equal bravery then reinforced the great
breach, about eighty yards to the left of the other
although the line of ruins seemed to extend the
whole way. The fighting now became fierce and
obstinate again at all the breaches, but the French
musquetry still rolled with deadly effect, the heaps of
slain increased, and once more the great mass of
stormers sunk to the foot of the ruins unable to win ;
the living sheltered themselves as they could, but
the dead and wounded lay so thickly that hardly
could it be judged whether the hurt or unhurt were
most numerous.

It was now evident that the assault must fail
unless some accident intervened, for the tide was
rising, the reserves all engaged, and no greater
effort could be expected from men whose courage

had been already pushed to the verge of madness.
In this crisis fortune interfered. A number of powder
barrels, live shells, and combustible materials which
the French had accumulated behind the traverses
for their defence caught fire, a bright consuming
flame wrapped the whole of the high curtain, a succession of loud explosions were heard, hundreds of
the French grenadiers were destroyed, the rest were
thrown into confusion, and while the ramparts were
still involved with suffocating eddies of smoke the
British soldiers broke in at the first traverse. The
defenders bewildered by this terrible disaster yielded
for a moment, yet soon rallied, and a close desperate
struggle took place along the summit of the high
curtain, but the fury of the stormers whose numbers increased every moment could not be stemmed.
The French colours on the cavalier were torn away
by lieutenant Gethin of the eleventh regiment. The
horn-work and the land front below the curtain, and
the loop-holed wall behind the great breach were
all abandoned ; the light division soldiers who had
already established themselves in the ruins on the
French left, immediately penetrated to the streets,
and at the same moment the Portuguese at the small
breach, mixed with British who had wandered to that
point seeking for an entrance, burst in on their side.

Five hours the dreadful battle had lasted at the
walls and now the stream of war went pouring into
the town. The undaunted governor still disputed
the victory for a short time with the aid of his bar-
ricades, but several hundreds of his men being cut
off and taken in the horn-work, his garrison was so
reduced that even to effect a retreat behind the line
of defences which separated the town from the

Monte Orgullo was difficult.   Many of his troops
flying from the horn-work along the harbour flank
of the town broke through a body of the British
who had reached the vicinity of the fortified convent of Santa Téresa before them, and this post was
the only one retained by the French in the town.   It
was thought by some distinguished officers engaged
in the action that Monte Orgullo might have been
carried on this day, if a commander of sufficient rank
to direct the troops had been at hand; but whether
from wounds or accident no general entered the
place until long after the breach had been won, the
commanders of battalions were embarrassed for
want of orders, and a thunder-storm, which came
down from the mountains with unbounded fury immediately after the place was carried, added to the
confusion of the fight.

   This storm seemed to be the signal of hell for the
perpetration of villainy which would have shamed
the most ferocious barbarians of antiquity.   At
Ciudad Rodrigo intoxication and plunder had been
the principal object; at Badajos lust and murder
were joined to rapine and drunkenness; but at San
Sebastian, the direst, the most revolting cruelty was
added to the catalogue of crimes.   One atrocity of
which a girl of seventeen was the victim, staggers
the mind by its enormous, incredible, indescribable
barbarity.   Some order was at first maintained, but
the resolution of the troops to throw off discipline
was quickly made manifest.   A British staff-officer
was pursued with a volley of small arms and escaped
with difficulty from men who mistook him for the
provost-martial of the fifth division; a Portuguese
adjutant, who endeavoured to prevent some atrocity,
was put to death in the market-place, not with sud-

den violence from a single ruffian, but deliberately by a number of English soldiers. Many officers exerted themselves to preserve order, many men were well conducted, but the rapine and violence commenced by villains soon spread, the camp-followers crowded into the place, and the disorder continued until the flames following the steps of the plunderer put an end to his ferocity by destroying the whole town.

Three generals, Leith, Oswald, and Robinson, had been hurt in the trenches, sir Richard Fletcher the chief engineer, a brave man who had served his country honorably was killed, and colonel Burgoyne the next in command of that arm was wounded.

The carnage at the breaches was appalling. The volunteers, although brought late into the action, had nearly half their number struck down, most of the regiments of the fifth division suffered in the same proportion, and the whole loss since the renewal of the siege exceeded two thousand five hundred men and officers.

The town being thus taken, the Monte Orgullo was to be attacked, but it was very steep and difficult to assail. The castle served as a citadel and just below it four batteries connected with masonry stretched across the face of the hill. From the Mirador and Queen's batteries at the extremities of this line, ramps, protected by redans, led to the convent of Santa Teresa which was the most salient part of the defence. On the side of Santa Clara and behind the mountain were some sea batteries, and if all these works had been of good construction, the troops fresh and well supplied, the siege would have been long and difficult; but the garrison was shattered by the recent assault, most of the engineers

and leaders killed, the governor and many others
wounded, five hundred men were sick or hurt, the
soldiers fit for duty did not exceed thirteen hundred,
and they had four hundred prisoners to guard. The
castle was small, the bomb-proofs scarcely sufficed
to protect the ammunition and provisions, and only
ten guns remained in a condition for service, three
of which were on the sea line. There was very
little water and the troops were forced to lie out on
the naked rock exposed to the fire of the besiegers,
or only covered by the asperities of ground. General
Rey and his brave garrison were however still resolute to fight, and they received nightly by sea supplies of ammunition though in small quantities.

Lord Wellington arrived the day after the assault.
Regular approaches could not be carried up the
steep naked rock, he doubted the power of vertical
fire, and ordered batteries to be formed on the captured works of the town, intending to breach the
enemy's remaining lines of defence and then storm
the Orgullo. And as the convent of Santa Teresa
would enable the French to sally by the rampart on
the left of the allies' position in the town, he composed his first line with a few troops strongly barricaded, placing a supporting body in the market-
place, and strong reserves on the high curtain and
flank ramparts. Meanwhile from the convent, which
being actually in the town might have been easily
taken at first, the enemy killed many of the besiegers,
and when after several days it was assaulted, they
set the lower parts on fire and retired by a communication made from the roof to a ramp on the hill
behind. All this time the flames were destroying
the town, and the Orgullo was overwhelmed with
shells shot upward from the besiegers' batteries.

On the 3d of September, the governor being summoned to surrender demanded terms inadmissible, his resolution was not to be shaken, and the vertical fire was therefore continued day and night, though the British prisoners suffered as well as the enemy; for the officer commanding in the castle, irritated by the misery of the garrison cruelly refused to let the unfortunate captives make trenches to cover themselves. The French on the other hand complain that their wounded and sick men, although placed in an empty magazine with a black flag flying, were fired upon by the besiegers, although the English prisoners in their red uniforms were placed around it to strengthen the claim of humanity.

Jones'
Sieges.

Bellas'
Sieges.

The new breaching batteries were now commenced, one for three pieces on the isthmus, the other for seventeen pieces on the land front of the horn-work. These guns were brought from the Chofres at low water across the Urumea, at first in the night, but the difficulty of labouring in the water during darkness induced the artillery officers to transport the remainder in daylight, and within reach of the enemy's batteries, which did not fire a shot. In the town the besiegers' labours were impeded by the flaming houses, but near the foot of the hill the ruins furnished shelter for the musqueteers employed to gall the garrison, and the guns on the island of Santa Clara being reinforced were actively worked by the seamen. The besieged replied but little, their ammunition was scarce and the horrible vertical fire subdued their energy. In this manner the action was prolonged until the 8th of September when fifty-nine heavy battering pieces opened at once from the island the isthmus the horn-work and the Chofres. In two hours both the Mirador and the

Queen's battery were broken, the fire of the besieged
was entirely extinguished, and the summit and face
of the hill torn and furrowed in a frightful manner;
the bread-ovens were destroyed, a magazine exploded, and the castle, small and crowded with men,
was overlaid with the descending shells. Then the
governor proudly bending to his fate surrendered.
On the 9th this brave man and his heroic garrison,
reduced to one-third of their original number and
leaving five hundred wounded behind them in the
hospital, marched out with the honours of war.
The Spanish flag was hoisted under a salute of
twenty-one guns, and the siege terminated after
sixty-three days open trenches, precisely when the
tempestuous season, beginning to vex the coast,
would have rendered a continuance of the sea blockade impossible.

OBSERVATIONS.

1°. San Sebastian a third-rate fortress and in bad
condition when first invested, resisted a besieging
army, possessing an enormous battering train, for
sixty-three days. This is to be attributed partly to
the errors of the besiegers, principally to obstruc-
tions extraneous to the military operations. Amongst
the last are to be reckoned the misconduct of the
Admiralty, and the negligence of the government
relative to the battering train and supply of ammunition; the latter retarded the second siege for
sixteen days; the former enabled the garrison to
keep up and even increase its means as the siege
proceeded.

Next, in order and importance, was the failure of

the Spanish authorities, who neglected to supply carts and boats from the country, and even refused the use of their public buildings for hospitals. Thus between the sea and the shore, receiving aid from neither, lord Wellington had to conduct an operation of war which more than any other depends for success upon labour and provident care. It was probably the first time that an important siege was maintained by women's exertions; the stores of the besiegers were landed from boats rowed by Spanish girls!

Another impediment was Soult's advance towards Pampeluna, but the positive effect of this was slight since the want of ammunition would have equally delayed the attack. The true measure of the English government's negligence is thus obtained. It was more mischievous than the operations of sixty thousand men under a great general.

2°. The errors of execution having been before touched upon need no further illustration. The greatest difference between the first and second part of the siege preceding the assaults, was that in the latter, the approaches near the isthmus being carried further on and openings made in the sea-wall, the troops more easily and rapidly extricated themselves from the trenches, the distance to the breach was shortened, and the French fire bearing on the fronts of attack was somewhat less powerful. These advantages were considerable, but not proportionate to the enormous increase of the besiegers' means; and it is quite clear from the terrible effects of the cannonade during the assault, that the whole of the defences might have been ruined, even those of the castle, if this overwhelming fire had in compliance with the rules of art been first employed to silence the enemy's fire. A lodgement in the horn-work

could then have been made with little difficulty,
and the breach attacked without much danger.

3°. As the faults leading to failure in the first
part of the siege were repeated in the second,
while the enemy's resources had increased by the
gain of time, and because his intercourse with
France by sea never was cut off, it follows that
there was no reasonable security for success; not
even to make a lodgement on the breach, since no
artificial materials were prepared and the workmen
failed to effect that object. But the first arrangement and the change adopted in the council of war,
the option given to general Bradford, the remarkable
fact, that the simultaneous attack on the horn-work
was only thought of when the first efforts against
the breach had failed, all prove, that the enemy's
defensive means were underrated, and the extent of
the success exceeded the preparations to obtain it.

The place was won by accident. For first the
explosion of the great mine under the tower of Los
Hornos, was only prevented by a happy shot which
cut the sausage of the train during the fight, and
this was followed by the ignition of the French
powder-barrels and shells along the high curtain,
which alone opened the way into the town. Sir
Thomas Graham's firmness and perseverance in the
assault, and the judicious usage of his artillery
against the high curtain during the action, an operation however which only belonged to daylight,
were no mean helps to the victory. It was on such
sudden occasions that his prompt genius shone con-
spicuously, yet it was nothing wonderful that heavy
guns at short distances, the range being perfectly
known, should strike with certainty along a line of

rampart more than twenty-seven feet above the
heads of the troops.   Such practice was to be expected from British artillery, and Graham's genius
was more evinced by the promptness of the thought
and the trust he put in the valour of his soldiers.
It was far more extraordinary that the stormers did not
relinquish their attack when thus exposed to their own
guns, for it is a mistake to say that no mischief occurred ; a serjeant of the ninth regiment was killed
by the batteries close to his commanding officer, and
it is probable that other casualties also had place.

4°. The explosion on the ramparts is generally
supposed to have been caused by the cannonade from
the Chofre batteries, yet a cool and careful observer,
*Captain
Cooke,
forty-third
regiment.
Vide his
Memoirs.*
whose account I have adopted, because he was a
spectator in perfect safety and undisturbed by
having to give or receive orders, affirms that the
cannonade ceased before colonel Snodgrass forded
the river, whereas the great explosion did not happen
until half an hour after that event.   By some persons
that intrepid exploit of the Portuguese was thought
one of the principal causes of success, and it appears
certain that an entrance was made at the small
breach by several soldiers, British and Portuguese,
many of the former having wandered from the great
breach and got mixed with the latter, before the explosion happened on the high curtain.   Whether
those men would have been followed by greater
numbers is doubtful, but the lodgement made by
the light division volunteers within the great breach
was solid and could have been maintained.   The
Bellas.
French call the Portuguese attack a feint.   Sir
Thomas Graham certainly did not found much
upon it.   He gave general Bradford the option to
attack or remain tranquil, and colonel M'Bean

actually received counter-orders when his column was already in the river and too far advanced to be withdrawn.

5°. When the destruction of San Sebastian became known, it was used by the anti-British party at Cadiz to excite the people against England. The political chief of Guipuscoa publicly accused sir Thomas Graham, " that he sacked and burned the place because it had formerly traded entirely with France," his generals were said to have excited the furious soldiers to the horrid work, and his inferior officers to have boasted of it afterwards. A newspaper, edited by an agent of the Spanish government, repeating these accusations, called upon the people to avenge the injury upon the British army, and the Spanish minister of war, designated by lord Wellington as the abettor and even the writer of this and other malignant libels published at Cadiz, officially demanded explanations.

Lord Wellington addressed a letter of indignant denial and remonstrance to sir Henry Wellesley. " It was absurd," he said, " to suppose the officers of the army would have risked the loss of all their labours and gallantry, by encouraging the dispersion of the men while the enemy still held the castle. To him the town was of the utmost value as a secure place for magazines and hospitals. He had refused to bombard it when advised to do so, as he had previously refused to bombard Ciudad Rodrigo and Badajos, because the injury would fall on the inhabitants and not upon the enemy ; yet nothing could have been more easy, or less suspicious than this method of destroying the town if he had been so minded. It was the enemy who set fire to the houses, it was part of the defence ; the British officers strove to extinguish the flames, some in doing so lost their lives by the French musquetry from the castle, and the difficulty of communicating and working through the fire was so great, that he had been on the point of withdrawing the troops altogether. He admitted the plunder, observing, that he knew not whether that or the libels made him most angry; he had taken measures to stop it, but when two-thirds of the officers had been killed or wounded in the action, and when many of the inhabitants taking part with the enemy fired upon the troops, to prevent it was impossible. Moreover he was for several days unable from other circumstances to send fresh men to replace the stormers.

This was a solid reply to the scandalous libels circulated, but the broad facts remained. San Sebastian was a heap of smoking ruins, and atrocities degrading to human nature had been perpetrated by the troops. Of these crimes, the municipal and ecclesiastic bodies the consuls and principal persons of San Sebastian, afterwards published a detailed statement, solemnly affirming the truth of each case; and if Spanish declarations on this occasion are not to be heeded, four-fifths of the excesses attributed to the French armies must be effaced as resting on a like foundation. That the town was first set on fire behind the breaches during the operations, and that it spread in the tumult following the assault is undoubted; yet it is not improbable that plunderers, to forward their own views increased it, and certainly the great destruction did not befall until long after the town was in possession of the allies. I have been assured by a surgeon, that he was lodged the third day after the assault at a house well furnished, and in a street then untouched by fire

or plunderers, but house and street were afterwards
plundered and burned. The inhabitants could only
have fired upon the allies the first day, and it might
well have been in self-defence for they were barbarously treated. The abhorrent case alluded to was
notorious, so were many others. I have myself heard
around the picquet fires, when soldiers as every
experienced officer knows, speak without reserve of
their past deeds and feelings, the abominable actions mentioned by the municipality related with
little variation long before that narrative was published ; told however with sorrow for the sufferers
and indignation against the perpetrators, for these
last were not so numerous as might be supposed
from the extent of the calamities they inflicted.

It is a common but shallow and mischievous
notion, that a villain makes never the worse soldier
for an assault, because the appetite for plunder supplies the place of honour ; as if the compatability of
vice and bravery rendered the union of virtue and
courage unnecessary in warlike matters. In all the
host which stormed San Sebastian there was not a
man who being sane would for plunder only have
encountered the danger of that assault, yet under
the spell of discipline all rushed eagerly to meet it.
Discipline however has its root in patriotism, or how
could armed men be controuled at all, and it would
be wise and far from difficult to graft moderation
and humanity upon such a noble stock. The modern
soldier is not necessarily the stern bloody-handed
man the ancient soldier was, there is as much difference between them as between the sportsman and
the butcher ; the ancient warrior, fighting with the
sword and reaping his harvest of death when the
enemy was in flight, became habituated to the act

of slaying. The modern soldier seldom uses his bayonet, sees not his peculiar victim fall, and exults not over mangled limbs as proofs of personal prowess. Hence preserving his original feelings, his natural abhorrence of murder and crimes of violence, he differs not from other men unless often engaged in the assault of towns, where rapacity, lust, and inebriety, unchecked by the restraints of discipline, are excited by temptation. It is said that no soldier can be restrained after storming a town, and a British soldier least of all, because he is brutish and insensible to honor ! Shame on such calumnies ! What makes the British soldier fight as no other soldier ever fights? His pay ! Soldiers of all nations receive pay. At the period of this assault,

a serjeant of the twenty-eighth regiment, named Ball, had been sent with a party to the coast from Roncesvalles, to make purchases for his officers. He placed the money he was entrusted with, two thousand dollars, in the hands of a commissary and having secured a receipt persuaded his party to join in the storm. He survived, reclaimed the money, made his purchases, and returned to his regiment. And these are the men, these the spirits who are called too brutish to work upon except by fear. It is precisely fear to which they are most insensible.

Undoubtedly if soldiers hear and read, that it is impossible to restrain their violence they will not be restrained. But let the plunder of a town after an assault, be expressly made criminal by the articles of war, with a due punishment attached ; let it be constantly impressed upon the troops that such conduct is as much opposed to military honour and discipline as it is to morality ; let a select perma-

nent body of men receiving higher pay form a part
of the army, and be charged to follow storming
columns to aid in preserving order, and with power
to inflict instantaneous punishment, death if it be
necessary. Finally, as reward for extraordinary
valour should keep pace with chastisement for crimes
committed under such temptation, it would be fitting
that money, apportioned to the danger and importance of the service, should be insured to the successful troops and always paid without delay. This
money might be taken as ransom from enemies, but
if the inhabitants are friends, or too poor, government should furnish the amount. With such regulations the storming of towns would not produce
more military disorders than the gaining of battles
in the field.

CHAPTER III.

WHILE San Sebastian was being stormed Soult
fought a battle with the covering force, not willingly
nor with much hope of success, but he was averse
to let San Sebastian fall without another effort, and
thought a bold demeanour would best hide his real
weakness. Guided however by the progress of the
siege, which he knew perfectly through his sea
communication, he awaited the last moment of
action, striving meanwhile to improve his resources
and to revive the confidence of the army and of the
people. Of his dispersed soldiers eight thousand
had rejoined their regiments by the 12th of August,
and he was promised a reinforcement of thirty thousand conscripts; these last were however yet to be
enrolled, and neither the progress of the siege, nor
the general panic along the frontier which recurred
with increased violence after the late battles, would
suffer him to remain inactive.

He was in no manner deceived as to his enemy's
superior strength of position number and military
confidence; but his former efforts on the side of
Pampeluna had interrupted the attack of San Sebastian, and another offensive movement would necessarily produce a like effect; wherefore he hoped
by repeating the disturbance, as long as a free intercourse by sea enabled him to reinforce and supply

the garrison, to render the siege a wasting operation
for the allies. To renew the movement against
Pampeluna was most advantageous, but it required
fifty thousand infantry for the attack, and twenty
thousand as a corps of observation on the Lower
Bidassoa, and he had not such numbers to dispose
of. The subsistence of his troops also was uncertain, because the loss of all the military carriages
at Vittoria was still felt, and the resources of the
country were reluctantly yielded by the people. To
act on the side of St. Jean Pied de Port was therefore
impracticable. And to attack the allies' centre, at
Vera, Echallar, and the Bastan, was unpromising,
seeing that two mountain-chains were to be forced
before the movement could seriously affect lord
Wellington : moreover, the ways being impracticable for artillery, success if such should befall,
would lead to no decisive result. It only remained
to attack the left of the allies by the great road of
Irun.

Against that quarter Soult could bring more than
forty thousand infantry, but the positions were of
perilous strength. The Upper Bidassoa was in
Wellington's power, because the light division,
occupying Vera and the heights of Santa Barbara
on the right bank, covered all the bridges ; but the
Lower Bidassoa flowing from Vera with a bend to
the left separated the hostile armies, and against
this front about nine miles wide Soult's operations
were necessarily directed. On his right, that is to
say, from the broken bridge of Behobia in front of
Irun to the sea, the river, broad and tidal, offered
no apparent facility for a passage ; and between
the fords of Biriatu and those of Vera, a distance of
three miles, there was only the one passage of An-

darlassa about two miles below Vera; along this
space also the banks of the river, steep craggy
mountain ridges without roads, forbade any great
operations. Thus the points of attack were restricted to Vera and the fords between Biriatu and
the broken bridge of Behobia.

Plan 5.
　　To raise the siege it was only necessary to force
a way to Oyarzun, a small town about seven or
eight miles beyond the Bidassoa, from thence the
assailants could march at once upon Passages and
upon the Urumea. To gain Oyarzun was therefore
the object of the French marshal's combinations.
The royal road led directly to it by the broad valley
which separates the Peña de Haya from the Jaizquibel mountain. The latter was on the sea-coast,
but the Peña de Haya, commonly called the four-
crowned mountain, filled with its dependent ridges
all the space between Vera, Lesaca, Irun and Oyarzun. Its staring head bound with a rocky diadem
was impassable, but from the bridges of Vera and
Lesaca, several roads, one of them not absolutely
impracticable for guns, passed over its enormous
flanks to Irun at one side and to Oyarzun on the
other, falling into the royal road at both places.
Soult's first design was to unite Clauzel's and
D'Erlon's troops, drive the light division from the
heights of Santa Barbara, and then using the bridges
of Lesaca and Vera force a passage over the Peña
de Haya on the left of its summit, and push the
heads of columns towards Oyarzun and the Upper
Urumea; meanwhile Reille and Villatte, passing the
Bidassoa at Biriatu, were to fight their way also
Soult's Of-
ffioial Cor-
respon-
dence,
MSS.
to Oyarzun by the royal road. He foresaw that
Wellington might during this time collect his right
wing and seek to envelope the French army, or

march upon Bayonne; but he thought the general state of his affairs required bold measures, and the progress of the besiegers at San Sebastian soon drove him into action.

On the 29th Foy, marching by the road of Lohoussoa, crossed the Nive at Cambo and reached Espelette, leaving behind him six hundred men, and the national guards who were very numerous, with orders to watch the roads and valleys leading upon St. Jean Pied de Port. If pressed by superior forces, this corps of observation was to fall back upon that fortress, and it was supported with a brigade of light cavalry stationed at St. Palais.

In the night two of D'Erlon's divisions were secretly drawn from Ainhoa, Foy continued his march through Espelette, by the bridges of Amotz and Serres to San Jean de Luz, from whence the reserve moved forward, and thus in the morning of the 30th two strong French columns of attack were assembled on the Lower Bidassoa.

The first, under Clauzel, consisted of four divisions, furnishing twenty thousand men with twenty pieces of artillery. It was concentrated in the woods behind the Commissary and Bayonette mountains, above Vera.

The second, commanded by general Reille, was composed of two divisions and Villatte's reserve in all eighteen thousand men; but Foy's division and some light cavalry were in rear ready to augment this column to about twenty-five thousand, and there were thirty-six pieces of artillery and two bridge equipages collected behind the camp of Urogne on the royal road.

Reille's troops were secreted, partly behind the Croix des Bouquets mountain, partly behind that of Louis XIV. and the lower ridges of the Mandale near Biriatu. Meanwhile D'Erlon, having Conroux's and Abbe's divisions and twenty pieces of artillery under his command, held the camps in advance of Sarre and Ainhoa. If the allies in his front marched to reinforce their own left on the crowned mountain, he was to vex and retard their movements, always however avoiding a serious engagement, and feeling to his right to secure his connection with Clauzel's column; that is to say, he was with Abbe's division, moving from Ainhoa, to menace the allies towards Zagaramurdi and the Puerto de Echallar; and with Conroux's division, then in front of Sarre, to menace the light division, to seize the rock of Ivantelly if it was abandoned, and be ready to join Clauzel if occasion offered. On the other hand, should the allies assemble a large force and operate offensively by the Nive and Nivelle rivers, D'Erlon, without losing his connection with the main army, was to concentrate on the slopes descending from the Rhune mountains towards San Pe. Finally, if the attack on the Lower Bidassoa succeeded, he was to join Clauzel, either by Vera, or by the heights of Echallar and the bridge of Lesaca. Soult also desired to support D'Erlon with the two divisions of heavy cavalry, but forage could only be obtained for the artillery horses, two regiments of light horsemen, six chosen troops of dragoons and two or three hundred gensd'armes, which were all assembled on the royal road behind Reille's column.

It was the French marshal's intention to attack at daybreak on the 30th, but his preparations being incomplete he deferred it until the 31st, and took rigorous precautions to prevent intelligence passing

over to the allies' camps. Nevertheless Wellington's emissaries advised him of the movements in
the night of the 29th, the augmentation of troops
in front of Irun was observed in the morning of
the 30th, and in the evening the bridge equipage
and the artillery were descried on the royal road
beyond the Bidassoa. Thus warned he prepared
for battle with little anxiety. For the brigade of
English foot-guards, left at Oporto when the campaign commenced, was now come up; most of the
marauders and men wounded at Vittoria had rejoined; and three regiments just arrived from England formed a new brigade under lord Aylmer,
making the total augmentation of British troops in
this quarter little less than five thousand men.

The extreme left was on the Jaizquibel. This
narrow mountain ridge, seventeen hundred feet
high, runs along the coast, abutting at one end
upon the Passages harbour and at the other upon
the navigable mouth of the Bidassoa. Offering no
mark for an attack it was only guarded by a
flanking detachment of Spaniards, and at its foot
the small fort of Figueras commanding the
entrance of the river was garrisoned by seamen
from the naval squadron. Fuenterabia a walled
place, also at its base, was occupied, and the low
ground between that town and Irun defended by a
chain of eight large field redoubts, which connected the position of Jaizquibel with the heights
covering the royal road to Oyarzun.

On the right of Irun, between Biriatu and the
burned bridge of Behobia, there was a sudden
bend in the river, the concave towards the French,
and their positions commanded the passage of the
fords below; but opposed to them was the exceed-

ingly stiff and lofty ridge, called San Marcial, terminating one of the great flanks of the Pena de
Haya. The water flowed round the left of this
ridge, confining the road leading from the bridge
of Behobia to Irun, a distance of one mile, to the
narrow space between its channel and the foot
of the height, and Irun itself, strongly occupied
and defended by a field-work, blocked this way.
It followed that the French, after forcing the passage of the river, must of necessity win San Marcial before their army could use the great road.

About six thousand men of the fourth Spanish
army now under general Freyre, were established
on the crest of San Marcial, which was strengthened by abbattis and temporary field-works.

Behind Irun the first British division, under
general Howard, was posted, and lord Aylmer's
brigade was pushed somewhat in advance of Howard's right to support the left of the Spaniards.

The right of San Marcial falling back from the
river was, although distinct as a position, connected
with the Pena de Haya, and in some degree exposed to an enemy passing the river above Biriatu,
wherefore Longa's Spaniards were drawn off from
those slopes of the Pena de Haya which descended
towards Vera, to be posted on those descending towards Biriatu. In this situation he protected and
supported the right of San Marcial.

Eighteen thousand fighting men were thus directly
opposed to the progress of the enemy, and the fourth
division quartered near Lesaca was still disposable.
From this body a Portuguese brigade had been
detached, to replace Longa on the heights opposite
Vera, and to cover the roads leading from the
bridge and fords of that place over the flanks of

the Pena de Haya. Meanwhile the British bri-

gades of the division were stationed up the mountain, close under the foundry of San Antonio and
commanding the intersection of the roads coming
from Vera and Lesaca; thus furnishing a reserve to
the Portuguese brigade to Longa and to Freyre, they
tied the whole together. The Portuguese brigade
was however somewhat exposed, and too weak to
guard the enormous slopes on which it was placed,
wherefore Wellington drew general Inglis's brigade
of the seventh division from Echallar to reinforce it,
and even then the flanks of the Pena de Haya were
so rough and vast that the troops seemed sprinkled
here and there with little coherence. The English
general aware that his positions were too extensive
had commenced the construction of several large
redoubts on commanding points of the mountain,
and had traced out a second fortified camp on a
strong range of heights, which immediately in
front of Oyarzun connected the Haya with the
Jaizquibel, but these works were unfinished.

During the night of the 30th Soult garnished
with artillery all the points commanding the fords
of Biriatu, the descent to the broken bridge and
the banks below it, called the Bas de Behobia.
This was partly to cover the passage of the fords
and the formation of his bridges, partly to stop
gun-boats coming up to molest the troops in crossing, and in this view also he spread Casa Palacio's Soult's
Official
Corres-
pondence,
MSS.
brigade of Joseph's Spanish guards along the river
as far down as Andaya, fronting Fuenterabia.

General Reille, commanding La Martiniere's, Maucune's, and Villatte's divisions, directed the attack.
His orders were to storm the camp of San Marcial,
and leaving there a strong reserve to keep in check

any reinforcement coming from the side of Vera
or descending from the Pena de Haya, to drive the
allies with the remainder of his force from ridge to
ridge, until he gained that flank of the great mountain which descends upon Oyarzun. The royal
Plan 5.   road being thus opened, Foy's division with the
cavalry and artillery in one column, was to cross
by bridges to be laid during the attack on San
Marcial. And it was Soult's intention under any
circumstances to retain this last-named ridge, and
to fortify it as a bridge-head with a view to subsequent operations.

To aid Reille's progress and to provide for the
concentration of the whole army at Oyarzun, Clauzel was directed to make a simultaneous attack from
Vera, not as at first designed by driving the allies
from Santa Barbara and seizing the bridges, but
leaving one division and his guns on the ridges
above Vera to keep the light division in check,
to cross the river by two fords just below the town
of Vera with the rest of his troops, and assail that
slope of the Pena de Haya where the Portuguese
brigade and the troops under general Inglis were
posted. Then forcing his way upwards to the forge
of San Antonio, which commanded the intersection
of the roads leading round the head of the mountain, he could aid Reille directly by falling on
the rear of San Marcial, or meet him at Oyarzun by turning the rocky summit of the Pena de
Haya.

August.   *Combat of San Marcial.* At daylight on the
31st, Reille, under protection of the French guns,
forded the river above Biriatu with two divisions
and two pieces of artillery. He quickly seized a detached ridge of inferior height just under San Mar-

cial, and leaving there one brigade as a reserve detached another to attack the Spanish left by a slope which descended in that quarter to the river. Meanwhile with La Martiniere's division he assailed their right. But the side of the mountain was covered with brushwood and remarkably steep, the French troops being ill-managed preserved no order, the supports and the skirmishers mixing in one mass got into confusion, and when two-thirds of the height were gained the Spaniards charged in columns and drove the assailants headlong down.

Soult's
Official
Report,
MSS.

During this action two bridges were thrown, partly on trestles partly on boats, below the fords, and the head of Villatte's reserve crossing ascended the ridge and renewed the fight more vigorously; one brigade even reached the chapel of San Marcial and the left of the Spanish line was shaken, but the eighty-fifth regiment belonging to lord Aylmer's brigade advanced a little way to support it, and at that moment lord Wellington rode up with his staff. Then the Spaniards who cared so little for their own officers, with that noble instinct which never abandons the poor people of any country acknowledged real greatness without reference to nation, and shouting aloud dashed their adversaries down with so much violence that many were driven into the river, and some of the French pontoon boats coming to their succour were overloaded and sunk. It was several hours before the broken and confused masses could be rallied and the bridges, which had been broken up to let the boats save the drowning men, repaired. When this was effected, Soult who overlooked the action from the summit of the mountain Louis XIV.,

sent the remainder of Villatte's reserve over the
river, and calling up Foy's division prepared a more
formidable and better arranged attack; and he
expected greater success, inasmuch as the operation from the side of Vera, of which it is time to
treat, was now making considerable progress up the
Pena de Haya on the allies' right.

Combat of Vera.   General Clauzel had descended
the Bayonette and Commissari mountains immediately after day-break, under cover of a thick fog,
but at seven o'clock the weather cleared, and three
divisions formed in heavy columns were seen, by
the troops on Santa Barbara, making for the fords
below Vera in the direction of two hamlets called
the Salinas and the Bario de Lesaca.   A fourth
division and the guns remained stationary on the
slopes of the mountain, and the artillery opened
now and then upon the little town of Vera, from
which the picquets of the light division were
recalled with exception of one post in a fortified
house commanding the bridge.

About eight o'clock the enemy's columns began
to pass the fords covered by the fire of their artillery,
but the first shells thrown fell into the midst of
their own ranks and the British troops on Santa
Barbara cheered the French battery with a derisive
shout.   Their march was however sure, and a battalion of chosen light troops, without knapsacks,

Soult's
Correspon-
dence,
MSS.

quickly commenced the battle on the left bank
of the river, with the Portuguese brigade, and by
their extreme activity and rapid fire forced the
latter to retire up the slopes of the mountain.

Manu-
script Me-
moir by ge-
neral In-
glis.

General Inglis then reinforced the line of skirmishers
and the whole of his brigade was soon afterwards
engaged, but Clauzel menaced his left flank from

the lower ford, and the French troops still forced their way upwards in front without a check, until the whole mass disappeared fighting amidst the asperities of the Pena de la Haya. Inglis lost two hundred and seventy men and twenty-two officers, but he finally halted on a ridge commanding the intersection of the roads leading from Vera and Lesaca to Irun and Oyarzun. That is to say somewhat below the foundry of Antonio, where the fourth division, having now recovered its Portuguese brigade, was, in conjunction with Longa's Spaniards, so placed as to support and protect equally the left of Inglis and the right of Freyre on San Marcial.

These operations, from the great height and asperity of the mountain, occupied many hours, and it was past two o'clock before even the head of Clauzel's columns reached this point. Meanwhile as the French troops left in front of Santa Barbara made no movement, and lord Wellington had before directed the light division to aid general Inglis, a wing of the forty-third and three companies of the riflemen from general Kempt's brigade, with three weak Spanish battalions drawn from O'Donnel's Andalusians at Echallar, crossed the Bidassoa by the Lesaca bridge, and marched towards some lower slopes on the right of Inglis where they covered another knot of minor communications coming from Lesaca and Vera. They were followed by the remainder of Kempt's brigade which occupied Lesaca itself, and thus the chain of connection and defence between Santa Barbara and the positions of the fourth division on the Pena de la Haya was completed.

Clauzel seeing these movements, and thinking Clauzel's Official Report, MSS.

the allies at Echallar and Santa Barbara were
only awaiting the proper moment to take him in
flank and rear, by the bridges of Vera and Lesaca,
if he engaged further up the mountain, now abated
his battle and sent notice of his situation and
views to Soult. This opinion was well-founded ;
lord Wellington was not a general to let half his
army be paralyzed by D'Erlon's divisions. On the
30th, when he observed Soult's first preparations in
front of San Marcial, he had ordered attacks to be
made upon D'Erlon from the Puerto of Echallar
Zagaramurdi and Maya ; general Hill was also
directed to shew the heads of columns towards
St. Jean Pied de Port. And on the 31st when the
force and direction of Clauzel's columns were known,
he ordered lord Dalhousie to bring the remainder
of the seventh division by Lesaca to aid Inglis.

Following these orders Giron, who commanded
the Spaniards O'Donnel being sick, slightly skirmished on the 30th with Conroux's advanced posts
in front of Sarre, and on the 31st at day-break the
whole of the French line was assailed. That is to
say, Giron again fought with Conroux, feebly as
before, but two Portuguese brigades of the sixth
and seventh divisions, directed by lord Dalhousie
and general Colville from the passes of Zagaramurdi
and Maya, drove the French from their camp
behind Urdax and burned it. Abbé who commanded there being thus pressed, collected his
whole force in front of Ainhoa on an entrenched
position, and making strong battle repulsed the
allies with some loss of men by the sixth division.
Thus five combats were fought in one day at
different points of the general line, and D'Erlon,
who had lost three or four hundred men, seeing a

fresh column coming from Maya as if to turn his
left, judged that a great movement against Bayonne
was in progress and sent notice to Soult. He was
mistaken. Lord Wellington being entirely on the
defensive, only sought by these demonstrations to
disturb the plan of attack, and the seventh division,
following the second order sent to lord Dalhousie,
marched towards Lesaca; but the fighting at Urdax
having lasted until mid-day the movement was not
completed that evening.

D'Erlon's despatch reached Soult at the same
time that Clauzel's report arrived. All his arrangements for a final attack on San Marcial were then
completed, but these reports and the ominous cannonade at San Sebastian, plainly heard during the
morning, induced him to abandon this object and
hold his army ready for a general battle on the
Nivelle. In this view he sent Foy's division which
had not yet crossed the Bidassoa to the heights of
Serres, behind the Nivelle, as a support to D'Erlon,
and caused six chosen troops of dragoons to march
upon San Pé higher up on that river. Clauzel received orders to arrest his attack and repass the Bidassoa in the night. He was to leave Maransin's
division upon the Bayonette mountain and the Col
de Bera, and with the other three divisions to march
by Ascain and join Foy on the heights of Serres.

Notwithstanding these movements Soult kept
Reille's troops beyond the Bidassoa, and the battle
went on sharply, for the Spaniards continually
detached men from the ridge, endeavouring to drive
the French from the lower positions into the river,
until about four o'clock when their hardihood
abating they desired to be relieved; but Wellington
careful of their glory seeing the French attacks

were exhausted and thinking it a good opportunity to fix the military spirit of his allies, refused to relieve or to aid them; yet it would not be just to measure their valour by this fact. The English general blushed while he called upon them to fight, knowing that they had been previously famished by their vile government, and that there were no hospitals to receive no care for them when wounded. The battle was however arrested by a tempest which commencing in the mountains about three o'clock, raged for several hours with wonderful violence. Huge branches were torn from the trees and whirled through the air like feathers on the howling winds, while the thinnest streams swelling into torrents dashed down the mountains, rolling innumerable stones along with a frightful clatter. Amidst this turmoil and under cover of night the French re-crossed the river, and the head-quarters were fixed at St. Jean de Luz.

Clauzel's retreat was more unhappy. Having received the order to retire early in the evening when the storm had already put an end to all fighting, he repassed the fords in person and before dark at the head of two brigades, ordering general Vandermaesen to follow with the remainder of his divisions. It would appear that he expected no difficulty, since he did not take possession of the bridge of Vera nor of the fortified house covering it; and apparently ignorant of the state of his own troops on the other bank of the river occupied himself with suggesting new projects displeasing to Soult. Meanwhile Vandermaesen's situation became critical. Many of his soldiers attempting to cross were drowned by the rising waters, and finally, unable to effect a passage at the fords, that general marched up the stream to seize the bridge of Vera.

His advanced guard surprising a corporal's picquet rushed over, but was driven back by a rifle company posted in the fortified house. This happened about three o'clock in the morning and the riflemen defended the passage until daylight when a second company and some Portuguese Caçadores came to their aid. But the French reserve left at Vera seeing how matters stood opened a fire of guns against the fortified house from a high rock just above the town, and their skirmishers approached it on the right bank while Vandermaesen plied his musquetry from the left bank. The two rifle captains and many men fell under this cross fire, and the passage was forced, but Vandermaesen urging the attack in person was killed, and more than two hundred of his soldiers were hurt.

Soult now learning from D'Erlon that all offen- sive movements on the side of Maya had ceased at twelve o'clock on the 31st, contemplated another attack on San Marcial, but in the course of the day general Rey's report of the assault on San Sebastian
reached him, and at the same time he heard that general Hill was in movement on the side of St. Jean Pied de Port. This state of affairs brought reflection. San Sebastian was lost, a fresh attempt to carry off the wasted garrison from the castle would cost five or six thousand good soldiers, and the safety of the whole army would be endangered by pushing headlong amongst the terrible asperities of the crowned mountain. For Wellington could throw his right wing and centre, forming a mass of at least thirty-five thousand men, upon the French left during the action, and he would be nearer to

Bayonne than the French right when once the
battle was engaged beyond the Lower Bidassoa.
The army had lost in the recent actions three
thousand six hundred men. General Vandermaesen
had been killed, and four others, La Martiniere,
Menne, Remond, and Guy, wounded, the first
mortally; all the superior officers agreed that a
fresh attempt would be most dangerous, and serious
losses might draw on an immediate invasion of
France before the necessary defensive measures
were completed.

Yielding to these reasons he resolved to recover
his former positions and thenceforward remain
entirely on the defensive, for which his vast knowledge of war, his foresight, his talent for metho-
dical arrangement and his firmness of character,
peculiarly fitted him. Twelve battles or combats
fought in seven weeks, bore testimony that he had
strived hard to regain the offensive for the French
army, and willing still to strive if it might be so, he
had called upon Suchet to aid him and demanded
fresh orders from the emperor; but Suchet helped
him not, and Napoleon's answer indicated at once his
own difficulties and his reliance upon the duke of
Dalmatia's capacity and fidelity.

" *I have given you my confidence and can add
neither to your means nor to your instructions.*"

The loss of the allies was one thousand Anglo-
Portuguese, and sixteen hundred Spaniards. Wherefore the cost of men on this day, including the
storming of San Sebastian, exceeded five thousand,
but the battle in no manner disturbed the siege.
The French army was powerless against such strong
positions. Soult had brought forty-five thousand
men to bear in two columns upon a square of less

than five miles, and the thirty thousand French
actually engaged, were repulsed by ten thousand,
for that number only of the allies fought.

But the battle was a half measure and ill-judged on
Soult's part. Lord Wellington's experience of French
warfare, his determined character, coolness and
thorough acquaintance with the principles of his
art, left no hope that he would suffer two-thirds of
his army to be kept in check by D'Erlon's two divisions; and accordingly, the moment D'Erlon was
menaced Soult stopped his own attack to make a
counter-movement and deliver a decisive battle on
favourable ground. Perhaps his secret hope was
to draw his opponent to such a conclusion, but if so,
the combat of San Marcial was too dear a price to
pay for the chance.

A general who had made up his mind to force a
way to San Sebastian, would have organized his
rear so that no serious embarrassment could arise
from any partial incursions towards Bayonne; he
would have concentrated his whole army, and have
calculated his attack so as to be felt at San Sebastian before his adversary's counter-movement could
be felt towards Bayonne. In this view D'Erlon's
two divisions should have come in the night of
the 30th to Vera, which without weakening the
reserve opposed to the light division would have
augmented Clauzel's force by ten thousand men;
and on the most important line, because San Marcial offered no front for the action of great numbers,
and the secret of mountain warfare is, by surprise or
the power of overwhelming numbers, to seize such
commanding points as shall force an enemy either
to abandon his strong position, or become the assailant to recover those he has thus lost. Now the

difficulty of defending the crowned mountain was evinced by the rapid manner in which Clauzel at once gained the ridges as far as the foundry of San Antonio; with ten thousand additional men he might have gained a commanding position on the rear and left flank of San Marcial, and forced the allies to abandon it. That lord Wellington thought himself weak on the Haya mountain is proved by his calling up the seventh division from Echallar, and by his orders to the light division.

Soult's object was to raise the siege, but his plan involved the risk of having thirty-five thousand of the allies interposed during his attack between him and Bayonne, clearly a more decisive operation than the raising of the siege, therefore the enterprise may be pronounced injudicious. He admitted indeed, that excited to the enterprise, partly by insinuations, whether from the minister of war or his own lieutenants does not appear, partly by a generous repugnance to abandon the brave garrison, he was too precipitate, acting contrary to his judgment; but he was probably tempted by the hope of obtaining at least the camp of San Marcial as a bridge-head, and thus securing a favourable point for after combinations.

Lord Wellington having resolved not to invade France at this time, was unprepared for so great an operation as throwing his right and centre upon Soult's left; and it is obvious also that on the 30th he expected only a partial attack at San Marcial. The order he first gave to assail D'Erlon's position, and then the counter-order for the seventh division to come to Lesaca, prove this, because the latter was issued after Clauzel's numbers and the direction of his attack were ascertained. The efforts

of two Portuguese brigades against D'Erlon sufficed
therefore to render null the duke of Dalmatia's great
combinations, and his extreme sensitiveness to their
operations marks the vice of his own.   Here it may
be observed, that the movement of the forty-third the
rifle companies and the Spaniards, to secure the
right flank of Inglis, was ill-arranged.   Dispatched
by different roads without knowing precisely the
point they were to concentrate at, each fell in with
the enemy at different places; the Spaniards got
under fire and were forced to alter their route; the
forty-third companies stumbling on a French division
had to fall back half a mile ; it was only by thus
feeling the enemy at different points that the destined position was at last found, and a disaster was
scarcely prevented by the fury of the tempest.   Nevertheless those detachments were finally well placed
to have struck a blow the next morning, because
their post was only half an hour's march from the
high ground behind Vandermaesen's column when
he forced the bridge at Vera, and the firing would
have served as a guide.   The remainder of Kempt's
brigade could also have moved upon the same point
from Lesaca.   It is however very difficult to seize
such occasions in mountain warfare where so little
can be seen of the general state of affairs.

A more obvious advantage was neglected by general Skerrit.   The defence of the bridge at Vera by a
single company of rifles lasted more than an hour,
and four brigades of the enemy, crossing in a tumultuous manner, could not have cleared the narrow
passage after it was won in a moment.   Lord Wellington's despatch erroneously describes the French
as passing under the fire of great part of general
Skerrit's brigade, whereas that officer remained in

order of battle on the lower slopes of Santa Barbara, half a mile distant, and allowed the enemy to
escape. It is true that a large mass of French
troops were on the counter slopes of the Bayonette
mountain, beyond Vera, but the seventh division,
being then close to San Barbara, would have prevented any serious disaster if the blow had failed.
A great opportunity was certainly lost, but war in
rough mountains is generally a series of errors.

CHAPTER IV.

SOULT, now on the defensive, was yet so fearful of
an attack along the Nive, that his uneasy movements
made the allies think he was again preparing for
offensive operations. This double misunderstanding
did not however last long, and each army resumed
its former position.

The fall of San Sebastian had given Lord Wellington a new port and point of support, had
increased the value of Passages as a depôt, and let
loose a considerable body of troops for field operations; the armistice in Germany was at an end,
Austria had joined the allies, and it seemed therefore certain that he would immediately invade France.
The English cabinet had promised the continental
sovereigns that it should be so when the French
were expelled from Spain, meaning Navarre and
Guipuscoa; and the newspaper editors were, as
usual, actively deceiving the people of all countries
by their dictatorial absurd projects and assump-
tions. Meanwhile the partizans of the Bourbons
were secretly endeavouring to form a conspiracy in
the south, and the duke of Berri desired to join the
British army, pretending that twenty thousand
Frenchmen were already armed and organized at
the head of which he would place himself. In fine
all was exultation and extravagance. But lord

Wellington, well understanding the inflated nature of such hopes and promises, while affecting to rebuke the absurdity of the newspapers, took the opportunity to check similar folly in higher places, by observing, " *that if he had done all that was ex-pected he should have been before that period in the moon.*"

With respect to the duke of Berri's views, it was for the sovereigns he said to decide whether the restoration of the Bourbons should form part of their policy, but as yet no fixed line of conduct on that or any other political points was declared.   It was for their interest to get rid of Napoleon, and there could be no question of the advantage or propriety of accepting the aid of a Bourbon party without pledging themselves to dethrone the emperor.   The Bourbons might indeed decline, in default of such a pledge, to involve their partizans in rebellion, and he advised them to do so, because Napoleon's power rested internally upon the most extensive and ex-pensive system of corruption ever established in any country, externally upon his military force which was supported almost exclusively by foreign contri-butions ; once confined to the limits of France he would be unable to bear the double expense of his government and army, the reduction of either would be fatal to him, and the object of the Bourbons would thus be obtained without risk.   But, if they did not concur in this reasoning, the allies in the north of Europe must declare they would dethrone Napoleon before the duke of Berri should be allowed to join the army ; and the British government must make up its mind upon the question.

This reasoning put an end to the project, because neither the English cabinet nor the allied sovereigns

were ready to adopt a decisive open line of policy.
The ministers exulting at the progress of aristocratic domination, had no thought save that of wasting England's substance by extravagant subsidies
and supplies, taken without gratitude by the continental powers who held themselves no-ways bound
thereby to uphold the common cause, which each
secretly designed to make available for peculiar
interests. Moreover they all still trembled before
the conqueror and none would pledge themselves to
a decided policy. Lord Wellington alone moved
with a firm composure, the result of profound and
well-understood calculations ; yet his mind, naturally
so dispassionate, was strangely clouded at this time
by personal hatred of Napoleon.

Where is the proof, or even probability, of that
great man's system of government being internally
dependent upon " *the most extensive corruption ever
established in any country*"?

The annual expenditure of France was scarcely
half that of England, and Napoleon rejected public
loans which are the very life-blood of state corruption. He left no debt. Under him no man de-
voured the public substance in idleness merely
because he was of a privileged class; the state
servants were largely paid but they were made to
labour effectually for the state. They did not eat
their bread and sleep. His system of public accounts, remarkable for its exactness simplicity and
comprehensiveness, was vitally opposed to public
fraud, and therefore extremely unfavourable to
corruption. Napoleon's power was supported in
France by that deep sense of his goodness as a
sovereign, and that admiration for his genius which
pervaded the poorer and middle classes of the

people; by the love which they bore towards him, and still bear for his memory because he cherished the principles of a just equality. They loved him also for his incessant activity in the public service, his freedom from all private vices, and because his public works, wondrous for their number their utility and grandeur, never stood still; under him the poor man never wanted work. To France he gave noble institutions, a comparatively just code of laws, and glory unmatched since the days of the Romans. His *Cadastre*, more extensive and perfect than the Doomsday Book, that monument of the wisdom and greatness of our Norman Conqueror, was alone sufficient to endear him to the nation. Rapidly advancing under his vigorous superintendence, it registered and taught every man the true value and nature of his property, and all its liabilities public or private. It was designed and most ably adapted to fix and secure titles to property, to prevent frauds, to abate litigation, to apportion the weight of taxes equally and justly, to repress the insolence of the tax-gatherer without injury to the revenue, and to secure the sacred freedom of the poor man's home. The French *Cadastre*, although not original, would from its comprehensiveness, have been when completed the greatest boon ever conferred upon a civilized nation by a statesman.

To say that the emperor was supported by his soldiers, is to say that he was supported by the people; because the law of conscription, that mighty staff on which France leaned when all Europe attempted to push her down, the conscription, without which she could never have sustained the dreadful war of antagonist principles entailed upon her by the revolution; that energetic law,

which he did not establish but which he freed from
abuse, and rendered great, national, and endurable
by causing it to strike equally on all classes, the
conscription made the soldiers the real representa-
tives of the people.   The troops idolized Napoleon,
well they might, and to assert that their attachment
commenced only when they became soldiers, is to
acknowledge that his excellent qualities and greatness of mind turned hatred into devotion the moment he was approached.   But Napoleon never
was hated by the people of France; he was their
own creation and they loved him so as never monarch was loved before.   His march from Cannes
to Paris, surrounded by hundreds of thousands of
poor men, who were not soldiers, can never be
effaced or even disfigured.   For six weeks, at any
moment, a single assassin might by a single shot
have acquired the reputation of a tyrannicide, and
obtained vast rewards besides from the trembling
monarchs and aristocrats of the earth, who scrupled
not to instigate men to the shameful deed.   Many
there were base enough to undertake but none so
hardy as to execute the crime, and Napoleon,
guarded by the people of France, passed unharmed
to a throne from whence it required a million of
foreign bayonets to drive him again.   From the
throne they drove him, but not from the thoughts
and hearts of men.

Lord Wellington having shaken off the weight
of the continental policy, proceeded to consider the
question of invading France simply as a military
operation, which might conduce to or militate
against the security of the Peninsula while Napoleon's power was weakened by the war in Germany ; and such was his inflexible probity of cha-

racter, that no secret ambitious promptings, no facility of gaining personal reputation, diverted him
from this object, all the renown of which he already
enjoyed, the embarrassments mortifications and difficulties, enormous, although to the surface-seeing
public there appeared none, alone remaining.

The rupture of the congress of Prague, Austria's
accession to the coalition, and the fall of San Sebastian were favourable circumstances; but he
relied not much on the military skill of the banded
sovereigns, and a great defeat might at any moment
dissolve their alliance. Napoleon could then reinforce Soult and drive the allies back upon Spain,
where the French still possessed the fortresses of
Santona, Pampeluna, Jaca, Venasque, Monzon,
Fraga, Lerida, Mequinenza, Figueras, Gerona, Hos-
talrich, Barcelona, Tortoza, Morella, Peniscola,
Saguntum and Denia. Meanwhile lord William
Bentinck, misled by false information, had committed a serious error in sending Del Parque's army
to Tudela, because the Ordal disaster and subsequent retreat shewed that Suchet was strong
enough, if it so pleased him, to drive the Anglo-
Sicilian army back even to the Xucar and recover
all his strong places. In fine the affairs of Catalonia were in the same unsatisfactory state they
had been in from the first. It was not even certain
that a British army would remain there at all, for
lord William assured of Murat's defection was intent upon invading Italy; and the ministers seemed
to have leaned towards the project, since Wellington
now seriously desired to know whether the Anglo-
Sicilians were to go or stay in Spain.

Lord William himself had quitted that army,
making the seventh change in fifteen months;

this alone was sufficient to account for its misfortunes, and the Spanish generals, who had been placed under the English commander, ridiculed the latter's ill success and spoke vauntingly of themselves. Strenuously did lord Wellington urge the appointment of some commander for the Anglo-Sicilian troops who would devote his whole attention to his business, observing that at no period of the war would he have quitted his own army even for a few days without danger to its interests. But the English minister's ignorance of every thing relating to war was profound, and at this time he was himself being stript of generals. Graham, Picton, Leith, lord Dalhousie, H. Clinton, and Skerrit, had gone or were going to England on account of ill health wounds or private business; and marshal Beresford was at Lisbon, where dangerous intrigues to be noticed hereafter menaced the existence of the Portuguese army. Castaños and Giron had been removed by the Spanish regency from their commands, and O'Donnel, described as an able officer but of the most impracticable temper, being denied the chief command of Elio's, Copons', and Del Parque's troops, quitted the army under pretext that his old wounds had broken out; whereupon, Giron was placed at the head of the Andalusians. The operations in Catalonia were however so important, that lord Wellington thought of going there himself; and he would have done so, if the after misfortunes of Napoleon in Germany, had not rendered it impossible for that monarch to reinforce his troops on the Spanish frontier.

These general reasons for desiring to operate on the side of Catalonia were strengthened also by the

Wellington's Dispatches,
MSS.

consideration, that the country, immediately beyond the Bidassoa, being sterile, the difficulty of feeding the army in winter would be increased; and the twenty-five thousand half-starved Spaniards in his army, would certainly plunder for subsistence and incense the people of France. Moreover Soult's actual position was strong, his troops still numerous, and his entrenched camp furnished a secure retreat. Bayonne and St. Jean Pied de Port were so placed that no serious invasion could be made until one or both were taken, or blockaded, which, during the tempestuous season and while the admiralty refused to furnish sufficient naval means, was scarcely possible; even to get at those fortresses would be a work of time difficult against Soult alone, impracticable if Suchet, as he well might, came to the other's support. Towards Catalonia therefore lord Wellington desired to turn when the frontier of the western Pyrenees should be secured by the fall of Pampeluna. Yet he thought it not amiss meanwhile to yield something to the allied sovereigns, and give a spur to public feeling by occupying a menacing position within the French territory. A simple thing this seemed but the English general made no slight concession when he thus bent his military judgment to political considerations.

The French position was the base of a triangle of which Bayonne was the apex, and the great roads leading from thence to Irun and St. Jean Pied de Port, were the sides. A rugged mass of mountains intervened between the left and centre, but nearly all the valleys and communications, coming from Spain beyond the Nive, centred at St. Jean Pied de Port and were embraced by an entrenched camp which Foy occupied in front of that fortress. That general could, without calling upon Paris who was at Oleron, bring fifteen thousand men including the national guards into action, and serious dispositions were necessary to dislodge him; but these could not be made secretly, and Soult calculated upon having time to aid him and deliver a general battle on chosen ground. Meanwhile Foy barred any movement along the right bank of the Nive, and he could, either by the great road leading to Bayonne or by shorter communications through Bidaray, reach the bridge of Cambo on the Nive and so gain Espelette behind the camps of Ainhoa. From thence, passing the Nivelle by the bridges at Amotz and Serres he could reach St. Jean de Luz, and it was by this route he moved to aid in the attack of San Marcial. However, the allies marching from the Alduides and the Bastan could also penetrate by St. Martin D'Arosa and the Gorospil mountain to Bidaray, that is to say, between Foy's and D'Erlon's positions. Yet the roads were very difficult, and as the French sent out frequent scouring detachments and the bridge of Cambo was secured by works, Foy could not be easily cut off from the rest of the army.

D'Erlon's advanced camps were near Urdax, and on the Mondarain and Choupera mountains, but his main position was a broad ridge behind Ainhoa, the right covering the bridge of Amotz. Beyond that bridge Clauzel's position extended along a range of strong hills, trending towards Ascain and Serres, and as the Nivelle swept with a curve quite round his rear his right flank rested on that river also. The redoubts of San Barbe and the camp of Sarre, barring the roads leading from Vera and the Puerto

Plans 5
and 6.

de Echallar, were in advance of his left, and the greater Rhune, whose bare rocky head lifted two thousand eight hundred feet above the sea level overtopped all the neighbouring mountains, formed, in conjunction with its dependants the Commissary and Bayonette, a mask for his right.

From the Bayonette the French position run along the summit of the Mandale or Sulcogain mountain, on a single line, but from thence to the sea the ridges suddenly abated and there were two lines of defence; the first along the Bidassoa, the second commencing near St. Jean de Luz stretched from the heights of Bordegain towards Ascain, having the camps of Urogne and the Sans Culottes in advance. Reille's divisions guarded these lines, and the second was connected with Clauzel's position by Villatte's reserve which was posted at Ascain. Finally the whole system of defence was tied to that of St. Jean Pied de Port, by the double bridge-head at Cambo which secured the junction of Foy with the rest of the army.

The French worked diligently on their entrenchments, yet they were but little advanced when the castle of San Sebastian surrendered, and Wellington had even then matured a plan of attack as daring as any undertaken during the whole war. This was to seize the great Rhune mountain and its dependents, and at the same time to force the passage of the Lower Bidassoa and establish his left wing in the French territory. He would thus bring the Rhune Commissary and Bayonette mountains, forming a salient menacing point of great altitude and strength towards the French centre, within his own system, and shorten his communications by gaining the command of the road running along

the river from Irun to Vera. Thus also he would
obtain the port of Fuentarabia, which, though bad
in winter, was some advantage to a general whose
supplies came from the ocean, and who with scanty
means of land-transport had to encounter the perverse negligence and even opposition of the Spanish
authorities. Moreover Passages, his nearest port,
was restricted in its anchorage-ground, hard to
make from the sea and dangerous when full of
vessels.

CHAP.
IV.

1813.
September

He designed this operation for the middle of
September, immediately after the castle of San
Sebastian fell and before the French works acquired strength, but some error retarded the arrival
of his pontoons, the weather became bad, and the
attack, which depended as we shall find upon the
state of the tides and fords, was of necessity deferred until the 7th of October. Meanwhile to
mislead Soult, to ascertain Foy's true position
about St. Jean Pied de Port, and to strengthen his
own right, he brought part of Del Parque's force
up from Tudela to Pampeluna. The Andalusian
division which had remained at the blockade after
the battle of Sauroren then rejoined Giron at
Echallar, and at the same time Mina's troops
gathered in the neighbourhood of Roncesvalles.
Wellington himself repaired to that quarter on the
1st of October, and in his way, passing through
the Alduides, he caused general Campbell to surprize some isolated posts on the rock of Airola,
a French scouting detachment was also cut off near
the foundry of Baygorry, and two thousand sheep
were swept from the valley.

October.

Foy's re-
port to
Soult, 2d
October,
MSS.

These affairs awaked Soult's jealousy. He was
in daily expectation of an attack without being

BOOK
XXII.
———
1813.
October.

Soult's
Official
Correspon-
dence,
MSS.

able to ascertain on what quarter the blow would
fall, and at first, deceived by false information that
the fourth division had reinforced Hill, he thought
the march of Mina's troops and the Andalusians
was intended to mask an offensive movement by
the Val de Baygorry.   The arrival of light cavalry in the Bastan, lord Wellington's presence at
Roncesvalles, and the loss of the post at Airola
seemed to confirm this ; but he knew the pontoons
were at Oyarzun, and some deserters told him that
the real object of the allies was to gain the great
Rhune.   On the other hand a French commissary,
taken at San Sebastian and exchanged after remaining twelve days at Lesaca, assured him, that
nothing at Wellington's head-quarters indicated a
serious attack, although the officers spoke of one
and there were many movements of troops ; and
this weighed much with the French general, because the slow march of the pontoons and the wet
weather had caused a delay contradictory to the
reports of the spies and deserters.   It was also
beyond calculation that Wellington should, against
his military judgment, push his left wing into
France merely to meet the wishes of the allied
sovereigns in Germany, and as the most obvious
line for a permanent invasion was by his right and
centre, there was no apparent cause for deferring
his operations.

The true reason of the procrastination, namely
the state of the tides and fords on the Lower Bidassoa, was necessarily hidden from Soult, who
finally inclined to the notion that Wellington only
designed to secure his blockade at Pampeluna from
interruption by menacing the French and imped-
ing their labours, the results of which were now

becoming visible.   However, as all the deserters
and spies came with the same story he recommended increased vigilance along the whole line.
And yet so little did he anticipate the nature of
his opponent's project, that on the 6th he reviewed
D'Erlon's divisions at Ainhoa, and remained that
night at Espelette, doubting if any attack was intended and no way suspecting that it would be
against his right. But Wellington could not diminish his troops on the side of Roncesvalles and
the Alduides, lest Foy and Paris and the light
cavalry under Pierre Soult should unite at St. Jean
Pied de Port to raise the blockade of Pampeluna ;
the troops at Maya were already posted offensively,
menacing Soult between the Nive and the Nivelle,
and it was therefore only with his left wing and
left centre, and against the French right that he
could act.

Early in October a reinforcement of twelve hundred British soldiers arrived from England.   Mina
was then in the Ahescoa, on the right of general
Hill, who was thus enabled to relieve Campbell's
Portuguese in the Alduides ; and the latter marching to Maya replaced the third division, which,
shifting to its left occupied the heights above
Zagaramurdi, to enable the seventh division to
relieve Giron's Andalusians in the Puerto de
Echallar.

These dispositions were made with a view to the
attack of the great Rhune and its dependents, the
arrangements for which shall now be described.

Giron, moving with his Andalusians from the
Ivantelly, was to assail a lofty ridge or saddle,
uniting the Commissari and the great Rhune.   A

BOOK
XXII.
———
1813.
October.

Welling-
ton's Order
of Move-
ments,
MSS.

Plan 5.

battalion, stealing up the slopes and hollows on his right flank, was to seize the rocky head of the last-named mountain, and after placing detachments there in observation of the roads leading round it from Sarre and Ascain, was to descend upon the saddle and menace the rear of the enemy's position at the Puerto de Vera. Meanwhile the principal attack was to be made in two columns, but to protect the right and rear against a counter-attack from Sarre, the Spanish general was to leave one brigade in the narrow pass leading from Vera, between the Ivantelly and the Rhune to that place.

On the left of Giron the light division was to assail the Bayonette mountain and the Puerto de Vera, connecting its right with Giron's left by skirmishers.

Longa, who had resumed his old positions above the Salinas de Lesaca, was to move in two columns across the Bidassoa. One passing by the ford of Salinas was to aid the left wing of the light division in its attack on the Bayonette; the other passing by the bridge of Vera, was to move up the ravine separating the slopes of the Bayonette from the Puerto de Vera, and thus connect the two attacks of the light division. During these operations Longa was also to send some men over the river at Andarlasa, to seize a telegraph which the French used to communicate between the left and centre of their line.

Behind the light division general Cole was to take post with the fourth division on Santa Barbara, pushing forward detachments to secure the commanding points gained by the fighting troops in front. The sixth division was meanwhile to make a demonstration on the right by Urdax and Zagaramurdi, against D'Erlon's advanced posts. Thus without weakening his line between Ronces-valles and Echallar lord Wellington put nearly twenty thousand men in motion against the Rhune mountain and its dependents, and he had still twenty-four thousand disposable to force the passage of the Lower Bidassoa.

It has been already shewn that between Andar-lasa and Biriatu, a distance of three miles, there were neither roads nor fords nor bridges. The French trusting to this difficulty of approach, and to their entrenchments on the craggy slopes of the Mandale, had collected their troops principally, where the Bildox or green mountain, and the en-trenched camp of Biriatu overlooked the fords. Against these points Wellington directed general Freyre's Spaniards, who were to descend from San Marcial, cross the upper fords of Biriatu, assail the Bildox and Mandale mountains, and turn the left of that part of the enemy's line which being prolonged from Biriatu crossed the royal road and passed behind the town of Andaya.

Between Biriatu and the sea the advanced points of defence were the mountain of *Louis* XIV., the ridge called the *Caffé Republicain,* and the town of Andaya. Behind these the *Calvaire d'Urogne,* the *Croix des Bouquets,* and the camp of the *Sans Culottes,* served as rallying posts.

For the assault on these positions Wellington designed to employ the first and fifth divisions and the unattached brigades of Wilson and Lord Ayl-mer, in all about fifteen thousand men. By the help of Spanish fishermen he had secretly dis-

covered three fords, practicable at low water, between the brige of Behobia and the sea, and his
intent was to pass his column at the old fords above,
and at the new fords below the bridge, and this
though the tides rose sixteen feet, leaving at the
ebb open heavy sands not less than half a mile
broad. The left bank of the river also was completely exposed to observation from the enemy's
hills, which though low in comparison of the mountains above the bridge, were nevertheless strong
ridges of defence; but relying on his previous
measures to deceive the enemy the English general
disdained these dangers, and his anticipations were
not belied by the result.

The unlikelihood that a commander, having a
better line of operations, would pass such a river
as the Bidassoa at its mouth, deceived the French
general. Meanwhile his lieutenants were negligent.
Of Reille's two divisions La Martiniere's, now
commanded by general Boyer, was at the camp of
Urogne, and on the morning of the seventh was
dispersed as usual to labour at the works; Villatte's
reserve was at Ascain and Serres; the five thousand
men composing Maucune's division were indeed on
the first line but unexpectant of an attack, and
though the works on the Mandale were finished and
those at Biriatu in a forward state, from the latter
to the sea they were scarcely commenced.

Passage of the Bidassoa. The night set in heavily. A sullen thunder-storm gathering about the
craggy summit of the Pena de Haya came slowly
down its flanks, and towards morning rolling over
the Bidassoa fell in its greatest violence upon the
French positions. During this turmoil Wellington
whose pontoons and artillery were close up to Irun,

disposed a number of guns and howitzers along
the crest of San Marcial, and his columns attained
their respective stations along the banks of the
river. Freyre's Spaniards one brigade of the
guards and Wilson's Portuguese, stretching from
the Biriatu fords to that near the broken bridge of
Behobia, were ensconced behind the detached ridge
which the French had first seized in the attack of
the 31st. The second brigade of guards and the
Germans of the first division were concealed near
Irun, close to a ford below the bridge of Behobia
called the great Jonco. The British brigades of
the fifth division covered themselves behind a large
river embankment opposite Andaya; Sprye's Portuguese and lord Aylmer's brigade were posted in
the ditch of Fuenterabia.

Plan 5.

As all the tents were left standing in the camps
of the allies, the enemy could perceive no change
on the morning of the 7th, but at seven o'clock,
the fifth division and lord Aylmer's brigade emerging from their concealment took the sands in two
columns, that on the left pointing against the
French camp of the Sans Culottes, that on the
right against the ridge of Andaya. No shot was
fired, but when they had passed the fords of the
low-water channel a rocket was sent up from the
steeple of Fuenterabia as a signal. Then the guns
and howitzers opened from San Marcial, the troops
near Irun, covered by the fire of a battery, made
for the Jonco ford, and the passage above the
bridge also commenced. From the crest of San
Marcial seven columns could be seen at once, attacking on a line of five miles, those above the
bridge plunging at once into the fiery contest,
those below it appearing in the distance like huge

sullen snakes winding over the heavy sands. The
Germans missing the Jonco ford got into deep
water but quickly recovered the true line, and the
French, completely surprised, permitted even the
brigades of the fifth division to gain the right
bank and form their lines before a hostile musket
flashed.

The cannonade from San Marcial was heard by
Soult at Espelette, and at the same time the sixth
division, advancing beyond Urdax and Zagaramurdi,
made a false attack on D'Erlon's positions; the
Portuguese brigade under colonel Douglas, were
however pushed too far and repulsed with the loss
of one hundred and fifty men, and the French marshal instantly detecting the true nature of this attack hurried to his right, but his camps on the
Bidassoa were lost before he arrived.

When the British artillery first opened, Maucune's
troops had assembled at their different posts of
defence, and the French guns, established principally near the mountain of Louis XIV. and the
Caffé Republicain, commenced firing. The alarm
spread, and Boyer's marched from the second line
behind Urogne to support Maucune without waiting
for the junction of the working parties; but his brigades moved separately as they could collect, and
before the first came into action, Sprye's Portuguese,
forming the extreme left of the allies, menaced the
camp of the Sans Culottes; thither therefore one
of Boyer's regiments was ordered, while the others
advanced by the royal road towards the Croix des
Bouquets. But Andaya, guarded only by a piquet,
was abandoned, and Reille thinking the camp of the
Sans Culottes would be lost before Boyer's men
reached it, sent a battalion there from the centre,

thus weakening his force at the chief point of attack;

for the British brigades of the fifth division, were now
advancing left in front from Andaya, and bearing
under a sharp fire of artillery and musquetry towards
the Croix des Bouquets.

By this time the columns of the first division had
passed the river, one above the bridge, preceded by
Wilson's Portuguese, one below, preceded by Colin
Halkett's German light troops, who aided by the
fire of the guns on San Marcial, drove back the
enemy's advanced posts, won the Caffé Republicain,
the mountain of Louis XIV. and drove the French
from those heights to the Croix des Bouquets : this
was the key of the position, and towards it guns and
troops were now hastening from every side. The
Germans who had lost many men in the previous
attacks were here brought to a check, for the heights
were very strong, and Boyer's leading battalions were
now close at hand; but at this critical moment
colonel Cameron arrived with the ninth regiment of
the fifth division, and passing through the German
skirmishers rushed with great vehemence to the summit of the first height. The French infantry instantly
opened their ranks to let their guns retire, and then
retreated themselves at full speed to a second ridge,
somewhat lower but where they could only be
approached on a narrow front. Cameron as quickly
threw his men into a single column and bore against
this new position, which curving inwards enabled
the French to pour a concentrated fire upon his regiment; nor did his violent course seem to dismay
them until he was within ten yards, when appalled
by the furious shout and charge of the ninth they
gave way, and the ridges of the Croix des Bouquets
were won as far as the royal road. The British

regiment however lost many men and officers, and
during the fight the French artillery and scattered
troops, coming from different points and rallying on
Boyer's battalions, were gathered on the ridges to
the French left of the road.

The entrenched camp above Biriatu and the
Bildox, had been meanwhile defended with success
in front, but Freyre turned them with his right wing,
which being opposed only by a single battalion soon
won the Mandale mountain, and the French fell
back from that quarter to the Calvaire d'Urogne
and Jollimont.   Reille thus beaten at the Croix des
Bouquets, and his flanks turned, the left by the
Spaniards on the Mandale, the right by the allies
along the sea-coast, retreated in great disorder along
the royal causeway and the old road of Bayonne.
He passed through the village of Urogne and the
British skirmishers at first entered it in pursuit, but
they were beaten out again by the second brigade of
Boyer's division, for Soult now arrived with part of
Villatte's reserve and many guns, and by his presence and activity restored order and revived the
courage of the troops at the moment when the
retreat was degenerating into a flight.

Reille lost eight pieces of artillery and about four
hundred men, the allies did not lose more than six
hundred of which half were Spaniards, so slight
and easy had the skill of the general rendered this
stupendous operation.   But if the French commander penetrating Wellington's design, and avoiding the surprize, had opposed all his troops, amounting with what Villatte could spare to sixteen
thousand, instead of the five thousand actually
engaged, the passage could scarcely have been
forced ; and a check would have been tantamount

to a terrible defeat, because in two hours the returning tide would have come with a swallowing flood
upon the rear.

Equally unprepared and equally unsuccessful
were the French on the side of Vera, although the
struggle there proved more fierce and constant.

At day-break Giron had descended from the
Ivantelly rocks and general Alten from Santa Barbara; the first to the gorge of the pass leading from
Vera to Sarre, the last to the town of Vera, where
he was joined by half of Longa's force.

One brigade, consisting of the forty-third the
seventeenth Portuguese regiment of the line and the
first and third battalions of riflemen, drew up in
column on an open space to the right of Vera. The
other brigade under colonel Colborne, consisting of
the fifty-second two battalions of Caçadores and a
battalion of British riflemen, was disposed on the left
of Vera. Half of Longa's division was between these
brigades, the other half after crossing the ford of
Salinas drew up on Colborne's left. The whole of
the narrow vale of Vera was thus filled with
troops ready to ascend the mountains, and general
Cole displaying his force to advantage on the
heights of Santa Barbara presented a formidable
reserve.

Taupin's division guarded the enormous positions
in front of the allies. His right was on the Bayonette, from whence a single slope descended to a
small plain about two parts down the mountain. Plan 5.
From this platform three distinct tongues shot into
the valley below, each was defended by an advanced
post, and the platform itself secured by a star
redoubt, behind which, about half way up the single
slope, there was a second retrenchment with abbatis.

Another large redoubt and an unfinished breast-work
on the superior crest completed the system of defence
for the Bayonette.

The Commissari, which is a continuation of the
Bayonette towards the great Rhune, was covered by
a profound gulf thickly wooded and defended with
skirmishers, and between this gulf and another of
the same nature the main road, leading from Vera
over the Puerto, pierced the centre of the French
position.   Rugged and ascending with short abrupt
turns this road was blocked at every uncovered
point with abbatis and small retrenchments ; each
obstacle was commanded, at half musquet shot, by
small detachments placed on all the projecting parts
overlooking the ascent, and a regiment, entrenched
above on the Puerto itself, connected the troops on
the crest of the Bayonette and Commissari with
those on the saddle ridge, against which Giron's
attack was directed.

But between Alten's right and Giron's left was
an isolated ridge called by the soldiers the *Boar's
back*, the summit of which, about half a mile long
and rounded at each end, was occupied by four
French companies.   This huge cavalier, thrown as
it were into the gulf to cover the Puerto and saddle
ridges, although of mean height in comparison of
the towering ranges behind, was yet so great that the
few warning shots fired from the summit by the enemy, reached the allies at its base with that slow sing-
ing sound which marks the dying force of a musquet-
ball.   It was essential to take the Boar's back before
the general attack commenced, and five companies
of British riflemen, supported by the seventeenth
Portuguese regiment, were ordered to assail it at the
Vera end, while a battalion of Giron's Spaniards

preceded by a detached company of the forty-third
attacked it on the other.

At four o'clock in the morning Clauzel had received
intelligence that the Bayonette was to be assaulted
that day or the next, and at seven o'clock he heard
from Conroux, who commanded at Sarre, that Giron's
camps were abandoned although the tents of the
seventh division were still standing; at the same time
the sound of musquetry was heard on the side of
Urdax, a cannonade on the side of Irun, and then
came Taupin's report that the vale of Vera was filled
with troops. To this last quarter Clauzel hurried.
The Spaniards had already driven Conroux's outposts from the gorge leading to Sarre, and a detachment was creeping up towards the unguarded head
of the great Rhune. He immediately ordered four
regiments of Conroux's division to occupy the summit the front and the flanks of that mountain, and
he formed a reserve of two other regiments behind.
With these troops he designed to secure the mountain and support Taupin, but ere they could reach
their destination that general's fate was decided.

Second Combat of Vera.—Soon after seven o'clock
a few cannon-shot from some mountain-guns, of
which each side had a battery, were followed by
the Spanish musquetry on the right, and the next
moment the " *Boar's back*" was simultaneously assailed at both ends. The riflemen on the Vera side
ascended to a small pine-wood two-thirds of the
way up and there rested, but soon resuming their
movement with a scornful gallantry they swept the
French off the top, disdaining to use their rifles
beyond a few shots down the reverse side, to show
that they were masters of the ridge. This was the
signal for the general attack. The seventeenth Por-

tuguese followed the victorious sharp-shooters, the
forty-third, preceded by their own skirmishers and
by the remainder of the riflemen of the right wing,
plunged into the rugged pass, Longa's troops entered the gloomy wood of the ravine on the left,
and beyond them Colborne's brigade moving by
narrow paths and throwing out skirmishers assailed
the Bayonette, the fifty-second took the middle
tongue, the Caçadores and riflemen the two outer-
most and all bore with a concentric movement
against the star redoubt on the platform above.
Longa's second brigade should have flanked the left
of this attack with a wide skirting movement, but
neither he nor his starved soldiers knew much of
such warfare, and therefore quietly followed the
riflemen in reserve.

Soon the open slopes of the mountains were
covered with men and with fire, a heavy confused
sound of mingled shouts and musquetry filled the
deep hollows between, and the white smoke came
curling up above the dark forest trees which covered
their gloomy recesses. The French compared with
their assailants seemed few and scattered on the
mountain side, and Kempt's brigade soon forced its
way without a check through all the retrenchments
on the main pass, his skirmishers spreading wider
and breaking into small detachments of support as
the depth of the ravine lessened and the slopes melted
into the higher ridges. When about half-way up
an open platform gave a clear view over the Bayonette slopes, and all eyes were turned that way.
Longa's right brigade, fighting in the gulf between, seemed labouring and over-matched, but
beyond, on the broad open space in front of the
star fort, the Caçadores and riflemen of Colborne's

brigade, were seen coming out, in small bodies, from a forest which covered the three tongues of land up to the edge of the platform. Their fire was sharp, their pace rapid, and in a few moments they closed upon the redoubt in a mass as if resolved to storm it. The fifty-second were not then in sight, and the French thinking from the dark clothing that all were Portuguese rushed in close order out of the entrenchment; they were numerous and very sudden; the rifle as a weapon is overmatched by the musket and bayonet, and this rough charge sent the scattered assailants back over the rocky edge of the descent. With shrill cries the French followed, but just then the fifty-second appeared, partly in line partly in column, on the platform, and raising their shout rushed forward. The red uniform and full career of this regiment startled the hitherto adventurous French, they stopped short, wavered, and then turning fled to their entrenchment; the fifty-second following hard entered the works with them, the riflemen and Caçadores who had meanwhile rallied passed it on both flanks, and for a few moments every thing was hidden by a dense volume of smoke. Soon however the British shout pealed again and the whole mass emerged on the other side, the French, now the fewer, flying the others pursuing, until the second entrenchment, half-way up the parent slope, enabled the retreating troops to make another stand.

The exulting and approving cheers of Kempt's brigade now echoed along the mountain side, and with renewed vigour the men continued to scale the craggy mountain, fighting their toilsome way to the top of the Puerto. Meanwhile Colborne after

having carried the second entrenchment above the
star fort, was brought to a check by the works on
the very crest of the mountain, from whence the
French not only plied his troops with musquetry at
a great advantage, but rolled huge stones down the
steep.

These works were extensive well lined with men
and strengthened by a large redoubt on the right,
but the defenders soon faltered, for their left flank
was turned by Kempt and the effects of lord Wellington's skilful combinations were now felt in another quarter.   Freyre's Spaniards after carrying
the Mandale mountain, between Biriatu and the
Bayonette, had pushed to a road leading from the
Plan 5.   latter by Jollimont to St. Jean de Luz, and this
was the line of retreat from the crest of the
Bayonette for Taupin's right wing; but Freyre's
Spaniards got there first, and if Longa's brigade
instead of slowly following Colborne had spread
out widely on the left, a military line would have
been completed from Giron to Freyre.   Still Taupin's right was cut off on that side, and he was
forced to file it under fire along the crest of the
Bayonette to reach the Puerto de Vera road, where
he was joined by his centre.   He effected this but
lost his mountain battery and three hundred men.
These last, apparently the garrison of the large
fort on the extreme right of the Bayonette crest,
were captured by Colborne in a remarkable manner.
Accompanied by only one of his staff and half-a-
dozen riflemen, he crossed their march unexpectedly,
and with great presence of mind and intrepidity
ordered them to lay down their arms, an order which
they thinking themselves entirely cut off obeyed.
Meanwhile the French skirmishers in the deep

ravine, between the two lines of attack, being
feebly pushed by Longa's troops, retreated too
slowly and getting amongst some rocks from whence
there was no escape surrendered to Kempt's brigade.

The right and centre of Taupin's division being
now completely beaten fled down the side of the
mountain towards Olette, they were pursued by a
part of the allies until they rallied upon Villatte's
reserve, which was in order of battle on a ridge
extending across the gorge of Olette between
Urogne and Ascain. The Bayonette and Commissari, with the Puerto de Vera, were thus won
after five hours' incessant fighting and toiling up
their craggy sides. Nevertheless the battle was
still maintained by the French troops on the Rhune.

Giron after driving Conroux's advanced post from
the gorge leading from Vera to Sarre had, following
his orders, pushed a battalion from that side towards
the head of the great Rhune, and placed a reserve
in the gorge to cover his rear from any counter-
attack which Conroux might make. And when his
left wing was rendered free to move by the capture
of the " *Boar's back*" he fought his way up abreast
with the British line until near the saddle-ridge, a
little to his own right of the Puerto. There however he was arrested by a strong line of abbattis from
behind which two French regiments poured a heavy
fire. The Spaniards stopped, and though the ad-
venturer Downie, now a Spanish general, encouraged them with his voice and they kept their ranks,
they seemed irresolute and did not advance. There
happened to be present an officer of the forty-third
regiment named Havelock, who being attached to
general Alten's staff was sent to ascertain Giron's

progress. His fiery temper could not brook the
check. He took off his hat, he called upon the
Spaniards to follow him, and putting spurs to his
horse, at one bound cleared the abbattis and went
headlong amongst the enemy. Then the soldiers,
shouting for "*El chico blanco*" "*the fair boy*" so they
called him, for he was very young and had light
hair, with one shock broke through the French, and
this at the very moment when their centre was
flying under the fire of Kempt's skirmishers from
the Puerto de Vera.

The two regiments thus defeated by the Spaniards
retired by their left along the saddle-ridge to the
flanks of the Rhune, so that Clauzel had now eight
regiments concentrated on this great mountain. Two
occupied the crest including the highest rock called
the Hermitage; four were on the flanks, descending towards Ascain on one hand, and towards Sarre
on the other; the remaining two occupied a lower
and parallel crest behind called the small Rhune.
In this situation they were attacked at four o'clock
by Giron's right wing. The Spaniards first dislodged a small body from a detached pile of crags
about musket-shot below the summit, and then assailed the bald staring rocks of the Hermitage itself,
endeavouring at the same time to turn it by their
right. In both objects they were defeated with
loss. The Hermitage was impregnable, the French
rolled down stones large enough to sweep away
a whole column at once, and the Spaniards resorted
to a distant musketry which lasted until night.
This day's fighting cost Taupin's division two generals and four hundred men killed and wounded,
and five hundred prisoners. The loss of the allies
was nearly a thousand, of which about five hun-

dred were Spaniards, and the success was not complete, for while the French kept possession of the summit of the Rhune the allies' new position was insecure.

The front and the right flank of that great mountain were impregnable, but lord Wellington observing that the left flank, descending towards Sarre, was less inaccessible, concentrated the Spaniards on that side on the 8th, designing a combined attack against the mountain itself, and against the camp of Sarre. At three o'clock in the afternoon the rocks which studded the lower parts of the Rhune slope were assailed by the Spaniards, and at the same time detachments of the seventh division descended from the Puerto de Echallar upon the fort of San Barbe, and other outworks covering the advanced French camp of Sarre. The Andalusians soon won the rocks and an entrenched height that commanded the camp, for Clauzel, too easily alarmed at some slight demonstrations made by the sixth division towards the bridge of Amotz in Plan 6. rear of his left, thought he should be cut off from his great camp, and very suddenly abandoned not only the slope of the mountain but all his advanced works in the basin below, including the fort of San Barbe. His troops were thus concentrated on the height behind Sarre still holding with their right the smaller Rhune, but the consequences of his error were soon made apparent. Wellington immediately established a strong body of the Spanish troops close up to the rocks of the Hermitage, and the two French regiments there, seeing the lower slopes and the fort of San Barbe given up, imagined they also would be cut off, and without orders abandoned the impregnable rocks of the Hermitage

and retired in the night to the smaller Rhune. The
next morning some of the seventh division rashly
pushed into the village of Sarre, but they were
quickly repulsed and would have lost the camp and
works taken the day before if the Spaniards had not
succoured them.

The whole loss on the three days of fighting was
about fourteen hundred French and sixteen hundred
of the allies, one half being Spaniards, but many
of the wounded were not brought in until the third
day after the actions, and several perished miserably
where they fell, it being impossible to discover
them in those vast solitudes. Some men were also
lost from want of discipline; having descended into
the French villages they got drunk and were taken
the next day by the enemy. Nor was the number
small of those who plundered in defiance of lord
Wellington's proclamation; for he thought it necessary to arrest and send to England several officers,
and renewed his proclamation, observing that if he
had five times as many men he could not venture
to invade France unless marauding was prevented.
It is remarkable that the French troops on the same
day acted towards their own countrymen in the
same manner, but Soult also checked the mischief
with a vigorous hand, causing a captain of some
reputation to be shot as an example, for having
suffered his men to plunder a house in Sarre during
the action.

With exception of the slight checks sustained at
Sarre and Ainhoa, the course of these operations
had been eminently successful, and surely the bravery of troops who assailed and carried such stupendous positions must be admired. To them the
unfinished state of the French works was not visible.

Day after day, for more than a month, entrenchment
had risen over entrenchment, covering the vast
slopes of mountains which were scarcely accessible
from their natural steepness and asperity. This
they could see, yet cared neither for the growing
strength of the works, the height of the mountains,
nor the breadth of the river with its heavy sands,
and its mighty rushing tide; all were despised, and
while they marched with this confident valour, it
was observed that the French fought in defence of
their dizzy steeps with far less fierceness than,
when, striving against insurmountable obstacles,
they attempted to storm the lofty rocks of Sauroren.
Continual defeat had lowered their spirit, but the
feebleness of the defence on this occasion may be
traced to another cause. It was a general's not a
soldier's battle. Wellington had with overmaster-
ing combinations overwhelmed each point of attack.
Taupin's and Maucune's divisions were each less
than five thousand strong, and they were separately
assailed, the first by eighteen the second by fifteen
thousand men, and at neither point were Reille and
Clauzel able to bring their reserves into action
before the positions were won.

Soult complained that he had repeatedly told
his lieutenants an attack was to be expected, and
recommended extreme vigilance; yet they were
quite unprepared, although they heard the noise of
the guns and pontoons about Irun on the night of
the 5th and again on the night of the 6th. The
passage of the river he said had commenced at
seven o'clock, long after daylight, the allies' masses
were then clearly to be seen forming on the banks,
and there was full time for Boyer's division to arrive
before the Croix des Bouquets was lost. The

Soult's
Official
Correspon-
dence with
the Minis-
ter of War,
MSS.

battle was fought in disorder with less than five thousand men, instead of with ten thousand in good order, and supported by a part of Villatte's reserve. To this negligence the generals added also discouragement. They had so little confidence in the strength of their positions, that if the allies had pushed vigorously forward before the marshal's arrival from Espelette, they would have entered St. Jean de Luz, turned the right of the second position and forced the French army back upon the Nive and the Adour.

This reasoning of Soult was correct, but such a stroke did not belong to lord Wellington's system. He could not go beyond the Adour, he doubted whether he could even maintain his army during the winter in the position he had already gained, and he was averse to the experiment, while Pampeluna held out and the war in Germany bore an undecided aspect.

CHAPTER V.

SOULT was apprehensive for some days that lord CHAP. V.
Wellington would push his offensive operations
further, but when he knew by Foy's reports, and 1813. October. Official Correspondence, MSS.
by the numbers of the allies assembled on his right,
that there was no design of attacking his left, he
resumed his labours to advance the works covering
St. Jean de Luz. He also kept a vigilant watch
from his centre, holding his divisions in readiness to
concentrate towards Sarre, and when he saw the
heavy masses in his front disperse by degrees into
different camps, he directed Clauzel to recover the
fort of San Barbe. This work was constructed on
a comparatively low ridge barring issue from the
gorge leading out of the vale of Vera to Sarre, and
it defended the narrow ground between the Rhunes
and the Nivelle river. Abandoned on the 8th
without reason by the French, since it did not naturally belong to the position of the allies, it was now
occupied by a Spanish picquet of forty men. Some
battalions were also encamped in a small wood close
behind; but many officers and men slept in the fort,
and on the night of the 12th, about eleven o'clock,
three battalions of Conroux's division reached the
platform on which the fort stood without being perceived. The work was then escaladed, the troops
behind it went off in confusion at the first alarm,

and two hundred soldiers with fifteen officers were made prisoners. The Spaniards ashamed of the surprize made a vigorous effort to recover the fort at daylight, they were repulsed, and repeated the attempt with five battalions, but Clauzel brought up two guns, and a sharp skirmish took place in the wood which lasted for several hours, the French endeavouring to regain the whole of their old entrenchments and the Spaniards to recover the fort. Neither succeeded and San Barbe, too near the enemy's position to be safely held, was resigned with a loss of two hundred men by the French and five hundred by the Spaniards. Soon after this isolated action a French sloop freighted with stores for Santona attempted to run from St. Jean de Luz, and being chased by three English brigs and cut off from the open sea, her crew after exchanging a few distant shots with one of the brigs, set her on fire and escaped in their boats to the Adour.

Head-quarters were now fixed in Vera, and the allied army was organized in three grand divisions. The right having Mina's and Morillo's battalions attached to it was commanded by sir Rowland Hill, and extended from Roncesvalles to the Bastan. The centre occupying Maya, the Echallar, Rhune, and Bayonette mountains, was given to marshal Beresford. The left extending from the Mandale mountain to the sea was under sir John Hope. This officer succeeded Graham who had returned to England. Commanding in chief at Coruña after sir John Moore's death, he was superior in rank to lord Wellington during the early part of the Peninsular war, but when the latter obtained the baton of field-marshal at Vittoria, Hope with a patriotism and modesty worthy of the pupil of Abercrombie

the friend and comrade of Moore offered to serve as
second in command, and lord Wellington joyfully
accepted him, observing that he was the " *ablest*
officer in the army."

The positions of the right and centre were offensive and menacing, but the left was still on the
defensive, and the Bidassoa, impassable at high
water below the bridge, was close behind. However the ridges were strong, a powerful artillery
was established on the right bank, field-works were
constructed, and although the fords below Behobia
furnished but a dangerous retreat even at low water,
those above were always available, and a pontoon
bridge laid down for the passage of the guns during
the action was a sure resource. The front was
along the heights of the Croix des Bouquets facing
Urogne and the camp of the Sans Culottes, and
there was a reserve in an entrenched camp above
Andaya. The right of the line rested on the Mandale, and from that mountain and the Bayonette
the allies could descend upon the flank of an attacking army.

Soult had however no intention of renewing the
offensive. He had now lost many thousand men in
battle, and the old soldiers remaining did not exceed
seventy-nine thousand present under arms including officers and artillery-men. Of this number
the garrisons absorbed about thirteen thousand,
leaving sixty-six thousand in the field, whereas the
allies, counting Mina's and Del Parque's troops,
now at Tudela, Pampeluna, and the Val de Irati,
exceeded one hundred thousand, seventy-three Appendix
7, sect. 2.
thousand, including officers, sergeants, and artillery-
men, being British and Portuguese. And this was
below the calculation of the French general, for

deceived by the exaggerated reports which the
Spaniards always made of their forces, he thought
Del Parque had brought up twenty thousand men
and that there were one hundred and forty thousand
combatants in his front. But it was not so, and
as conscripts of a good description were now
joining the French army rapidly, and the national
guards of the Pyrenees were many, it was in the
number of soldiers rather than of men, that the
English general had the advantage.

In this state of affairs Soult's policy was to
maintain a strict defensive, under cover of which the
spirit of the troops might be revived, the country in
the rear organized, and the conscripts disciplined
and hardened to war. The loss of the Lower Bidassoa
was in a political view mischievous to him, it had
an injurious effect upon the spirit of the frontier
departments, and gave encouragement to the secret
partizans of the Bourbons; but in a military view
it was a relief. The great development of the
mountains bordering the Bidassoa had rendered
their defence difficult; while holding them he
had continual fear that his line would be pierced
and his army suddenly driven beyond the Adour.
His position was now more concentrated.

The right, under Reille, formed two lines. One
across the royal road on the fortified heights of
Urogne and the camp of the Sans Culottes; the
Plan 6. other in the entrenched camps of Bourdegain and
Belchena, covering St. Jean de Luz and barring the
gorges of Olhette and Jollimont.

The centre under Clauzel was posted on the
ridges between Ascain and Amotz holding the
smaller Rhune in advance; but one division was
retained by Soult in the camp of Serres on the

right of the Nivelle, overhanging Ascain. To replace
it one of D'Erlon's divisions crossed to the left of
the Nivelle and reinforced Clauzel's left flank above
Sarre.

Villatte's reserve was about St. Jean de Luz but
having the Italian brigade in the camp of Serres.

D'Erlon's remaining divisions continued in their
old position, the right connected with Clauzel's line
by the bridge of Amotz; the left, holding the Choupera and Mondarin mountains, bordered on the Nive.

Behind Clauzel and D'Erlon Soult had commenced a second chain of entrenched camps, prolonged from the camp of Serres up the right bank
of the Nivelle to San Pé, thence by Suraide to the
double bridge-head of Cambo on the Nive, and
beyond that river to the Ursouia mountain, covering
the great road from Bayonne to St. Jean Pied de
Port. He had also called general Paris up from
Oleron to the defence of the latter fortress and its
entrenched camp, and now drew Foy down the
Nive to Bidarray half-way between St. Jean Pied
de Port and Cambo. There watching the issues
from the Val de Baygorry he was ready to occupy
the Ursouia mountain on the right of the Nive, or,
moving by Cambo, to reinforce the great position
on the left of that river according to circumstances.

To complete these immense entrenchments, which
between the Nive and the sea were double and on
an opening of sixteen miles, the whole army
laboured incessantly, and all the resources of the
country whether of materials or working men
were called out by requisition. Nevertheless this
defensive warfare was justly regarded by the duke
of Dalmatia as unsuitable to the general state of
affairs. Offensive operations were most consonant

to the character of the French soldiers, and to the
exigencies of the time.   Recent experience had
shown the impregnable nature of the allies' positions
against a front attack, and he was too weak singly
to change the theatre of operations.   But when he
looked at the strength of the armies appropriated
by the emperor to the Spanish contest, he thought
France would be ill-served if her generals could not
resume the offensive successfully.   Suchet had just
proved his power at Ordal against lord William
Bentinck, and that nobleman's successor, with
inferior rank and power, with an army unpaid
and feeding on salt meat from the ships, with
jealous and disputing colleagues amongst the
Spanish generals, none of whom were willing to
act cordially with him upon a fixed and well-considered plan, was in no condition to menace the
French seriously.   And that he was permitted at
this important crisis to paralyze from fifty to sixty
thousand excellent French troops possessing all the
strong places of the country, was one of the most
singular errors of the war.

Exclusive of national guards and detachments of
the line, disposed along the whole frontier to guard
the passes of the Pyrenees against sudden marauding excursions, the French armies counted at this
time about one hundred and seventy thousand men
Appendix
8, sect. 2. and seventeen thousand horses.   Of these one hundred and thirty-eight thousand were present under
arms, and thirty thousand conscripts were in march
to join them.   They held all the fortresses of Valencia and Catalonia, and most of those in Aragon
Navarre and Guipuscoa, and they could unite
behind the Pyrenees for a combined effort in safety.
Lord Wellington could not, including the Anglo-

Sicilians and all the Spaniards in arms on the eastern coast, bring into line one hundred and fifty thousand men; he had several sieges on his hands, and to unite his forces at any point required great dispositions to avoid an attack during a flank march. Suchet had above thirty thousand disposable men, he could increase them to forty thousand by relinquishing some unimportant posts, his means in artillery were immense, and distributed in all his strong places, so that he could furnish himself from almost any point. It is no exaggeration therefore to say that two hundred pieces of artillery and ninety thousand old soldiers might have united at this period upon the flank of lord Wellington, still leaving thirty thousand conscripts and the national guards of the frontier, supported by the fortresses and entrenched camps of Bayonne and St. Jean Pied de Port, the castles of Navarens and Jaca on one side, and the numerous garrisons of the fortresses in Catalonia on the other, to cover France from invasion.

To make this great power bear in a right direction was the duke of Dalmatia's object, and his plans were large, and worthy of his reputation. Yet he could never persuade Suchet to adopt his projects, and that marshal's resistance would appear to have sprung from personal dislike contracted during Soult's sojourn near Valencia in 1812. It has been already shown how lightly he abandoned Aragon and confined himself to Catalonia after quitting Valencia. He did not indeed then know that Soult had assumed the command of the army of Spain and was preparing for his great effort to relieve Pampeluna; but he was aware that Clauzel and Paris were on the side of Jaca, and

he was too good a general not to know that operating on the allies' flank was the best mode of
palliating the defeat of Vittoria. He might have
saved both his garrison and castle of Zaragoza;
the guns and other materials of a very large field-
artillery equipment were deposited there, and from
thence, by Jaca, he could have opened a sure and
short communication with Soult, obtained information of that general's projects, and saved Pampeluna.

It may be asked why the duke of Dalmatia did
not endeavour to communicate with Suchet. The
reason was simple. The former quitted Dresden
suddenly on the 4th of July, reached Bayonne the
12th, and on the 20th his troops were in full march
towards St. Jean Pied de Port, and it was during this
very rapid journey that the other marshal abandoned
Valencia. Soult therefore knew neither Suchet's plans
nor the force of his army, nor his movements, nor his
actual position, and there was no time to wait for
accurate information.   However between the 6th
and the 16th of August, that is to say, immediately after his own retreat from Sauroren, he
earnestly prayed that the army of Aragon should
march upon Zaragoza, open a communication by
Jaca, and thus drawing off some of Wellington's
forces facilitate the efforts of the army of Spain to
relieve San Sebastian.   In this communication he
stated, that his recent operations had caused troops
actually in march under general Hill towards Catalonia to be recalled. This was an error.   His
emissaries were deceived by the movements, and
counter-movements in pursuit of Clauzel immediately after the battle of Vittoria, and by the
change in Wellington's plans as to the siege of

Pampeluna. No troops were sent towards Catalonia, but it is remarkable that Picton, Hill, Graham,
and the Conde de La Bispal were all mentioned, in
this correspondence between Soult and Suchet, as
being actually in Catalonia, or on the march, the
three first having been really sounded as to taking
the command in that quarter, and the last having
demanded it himself.

Suchet treated Soult's proposal as chimerical. His
movable troops he said did not exceed eleven
thousand, and a march upon Zaragoza with so few
men would be to renew the disaster of Baylen,
unless he could fly into France by Venasque where
he had a garrison. An extraordinary view of affairs
which he supported by statements still more extraordinary !

" *General Hill had joined lord William Bentinck
with twenty-four thousand men.*" " *La Bispal had
arrived with fifteen thousand.*" " *There were more
than two hundred thousand men on the Ebro.*"
" *The Spanish insurrection was general and strongly
organized.*" " *He had recovered the garrison of
Taragona and destroyed the works, and he must re-
vitual Barcelona and then withdraw to the vicinity
of Gerona and remain on the defensive*"!

This letter was written on the 23d of August,
when lord William Bentinck had just retreated from
the Gaya into the mountains above Hospitalet. The
imperial muster-rolls prove that the two armies of
Catalonia and Aragon, both under his command,
exceeded sixty-five thousand men, fifty-six thousand being present under arms. Thirty thousand
were united in the field when he received Soult's
letter. There was nothing to prevent him march
ing upon Tortoza, except lord William Ben

Appendix
8. Sect. 2.

tinck's army which had just acknowledged by a
retreat its inability to cope with him; there was
nothing at all to prevent him marching to Lerida.
The count of Bispal had thrown up his command
from bad health, leaving his troops under Giron on
the Echallar mountains. Sir Rowland Hill was at
Roncesvalles, and not a man had moved from Wellington's army. Elio and Roche were near Valencia in a starving condition. The Anglo-Sicilian
troops only fourteen thousand strong including
Whittingham's division, were on the barren mountains above Hospitalet, where no Spanish army
could remain; Del Parque's troops and Sarzfield's
division had gone over the Ebro, and Copons' Catalans had taken refuge in the mountains of Cer-
vera. In fine not two hundred thousand but less
than thirty-five thousand men, half-organized ill-
fed and scattered from Vich to Vinaros were
opposed to Suchet; and their generals had different
views and different lines of operations. The Anglo-
Sicilians could not abandon the coast, Copons could
not abandon the mountains. Del Parque's troops
soon afterwards marched to Navarre, and to use
lord Wellington's phrase there was nothing to prevent Suchet " *tumbling lord William Bentinck back
even to the Xucar.*" The true nature of the great
insurrection which the French general pretended to
dread shall be shown when the political condition
of Spain is treated of.

Suchet's errors respecting the allies were easily
detected by Soult, those touching the French in
Catalonia he could not suspect and acquiesced
in the objections to his first plan; but fertile of
resource he immediately proposed another, akin to
that which he had urged Joseph to adopt in 1812

after the battle of Salamanca, namely, to change the theatre of war. The fortresses in Spain would he said, inevitably fall before the allies in succession if the French armies remained on the defensive, and the only mode of rendering offensive operations successful was a general concentration of means and unity of action. The levy of conscripts under an imperial decree, issued in August, would furnish, in conjunction with the depôts of the interior, a reinforcement of forty thousand men. Ten thousand would form a sufficient corps of observation about Gerona. The armies of Aragon and Catalonia could, he hoped, by sacrificing some posts produce twenty thousand infantry in the field. The imperial muster-rolls prove that they could have produced forty thousand, but Soult misled by Suchet's erroneous statements assumed only twenty thousand, and he calculated that he could himself bring thirty-five or forty thousand good infantry and all his cavalry to a given point of junction for the two bodies between Tarbes and Pau. Fifteen thousand of the remaining conscripts were also to be directed on that place, and thus seventy or seventy-five thousand infantry all the cavalry of both armies and one hundred guns, would be suddenly assembled, to thread the narrow pass of Jaca and descend upon Aragon. Once in that kingdom they could attack the allied troops in Navarre if the latter were dispersed, and if they were united retire upon Zaragoza, there to fix a solid base and deliver a general battle upon the new line of operations. Meanwhile the fifteen thousand unappropriated conscripts might reinforce the twenty or twenty-five thousand old soldiers left to cover Bayonne.

An army so great and strongly constituted appearing in Aragon would, Soult argued, necessarily raise the blockades of Pampeluna, Jaca, Fraga, and Monzon, the two last being now menaced by the bands, and it was probable that Tortoza and even Saguntum would be relieved. The great difficulty was to pass the guns by Jaca, yet he was resolved to try, even though he should convey them upon trucks to be made in Paris and sent by post to Pau. He anticipated no serious inconvenience from the union of the troops in France since Suchet had already declared his intention of retiring towards Gerona; and on the Bayonne side the army to be left there could dispute the entrenched line between Cambo and St. Jean de Luz. If driven from thence it could take a flanking position behind the Nive, the right resting upon the entrenched camp of Bayonne, the left upon the works at Cambo and holding communication by the fortified mountain of Ursouia with St. Jean Pied de Port. But there could be little fear for this secondary force when the great army was once in Aragon. That which he most dreaded was delay, because a fall of snow, always to be expected after the middle of October, would entirely close the pass of Jaca.

This proposition written the 2d of September, immediately after the battle of San Marcial, reached Suchet the 11th and was peremptorily rejected. If he withdrew from Catalonia discouragement, he said, would spread, desertion would commence, and France be immediately invaded by lord William Bentinck at the head of fifty thousand men. The pass of Jaca was impracticable and the power of man could not open it for carriages under a year's labour. His wish was to act on the de-

fensive, but if an offensive movement was abso- lutely necessary, he offered a counter project; that is, he would first make the English in his front re-embark at Taragona, or he would drive them over the Ebro and then march with one hundred guns and thirty thousand men by Lerida to the Gallego river near Zaragoza. Soult's army, coming by Jaca without guns, might there meet him, and the united forces could then do what was fitting. But to effect this he required a reinforcement of conscripts, and to have Paris's division and the artillery-men and draft horses of Soult's army sent to Catalonia; he demanded also that two thousand bullocks for the subsistence of his troops should be provided to meet him on the Gallego. Then touching upon the difficulties of the road from Sanguessa to Pampeluna, he declared, that after forcing Wellington across the Ebro, he would re- turn to Catalonia to revictual his fortresses and prevent an invasion of France. This plan he judged far less dangerous than Soult's, yet he enlarged upon its difficulties and its dangers if the combined movements were not exactly executed. In fine, he continued, " The French armies are entangled amongst rocks, and the emperor should direct a third army upon Spain, to act between the Pyrenees and the Ebro in the centre, while the army of Spain sixty thousand strong and that of Aragon thirty thousand strong operate on the flanks. Thus *the reputation of the English army, too easily acquired at Salamanca and Vittoria, will be abated.*"

This illiberal remark combined with the defects of his project, proves that the duke of Albufera was far below the duke of Dalmatia's standard both in magnanimity and in capacity. The one giving his adversary just praise, thought the force already supplied by the emperor sufficient to dispute for victory; the other, with an unseemly boast, desired overwhelming numbers.

Soult's letter reached Suchet the day before the combat of Ordal, and in pursuance of his own plan he should have driven lord William Bentinck over the Ebro, as he could well have done, because the Catalan troops there separated from the Anglo-Sicilians. In his former letters he had estimated the enemies in his front at two hundred thousand fighting men, and affirmed that his own disposable force was only eleven thousand, giving that as a reason why he could not march to Aragon. Now, forgetful of his previous objections and estimates, he admitted that he had thirty thousand disposable troops, and proposed the very movement which he had rejected as madness when suggested by the duke of Dalmatia. And the futility of his arguments relative to the general discouragement, the desertion of his soldiers, and the temptation to an invasion of France if he adopted Soult's plan, is apparent; for these things could only happen on the supposition that he was retreating from weakness, a notion which would have effectually covered the real design until the great movement in advance should change the public opinion. Soult's plan was surer better imagined and grander than his; it was less dangerous in the event of failure and more conformable to military principles. Suchet's project involved double lines of operation without any sure communications, and consequently without any certainty of just cooperation;

his point of junction was within the enemy's power, and the principal army was to be deprived of its artillery. There was no solidity in this design; a failure would have left no resource. But in Soult's project the armies were to be united at a point beyond the enemy's reach, and to operate afterwards in mass with all arms complete, which was conformable to the principles of war. Suchet indeed averred the impracticability of moving the guns by Jaca, yet Soult's counter-opinion claims more respect. Clauzel and Paris who had lately passed with troops through that defile were in his camp, he had besides made very exact inquiries of the country people, had caused the civil engineers of roads and bridges on the frontiers to examine the route, and from their reports he judged the difficulty to be not insurmountable.

Neither the inconsistency, nor the exaggerations of Suchet's statements, escaped Soult's observation, but anxious to effect something while Pampeluna still held out, and the season permitted operations in the mountains he frankly accepted the other's modification, and adopted every stipulation, save that of sending the artillery-men and horses of his army to Catalonia which he considered dangerous. Moreover he doubted not to pass his own guns by Jaca. The preparations for this great movement were therefore immediately commenced, and Suchet on his part seemed equally earnest although he complained of increasing difficulties, pretended that Longa's and Morillo's divisions had arrived in Catalonia, that general Graham was also in march with troops to that quarter, and deplored the loss of Fraga from whence the Empecinado had just driven his garrison. This post commanded indeed a bridge over the Cinca a river lying in his way and dangerous from its sudden and great floods but he still possessed the bridge of Monzon.

During this correspondence between the French marshals, Napoleon remained silent, yet at a later period he expressed his discontent at Suchet's inactivity, and indirectly approved of Soult's plans by recommending a movement towards Zaragoza which Suchet however did not execute. It would appear that the emperor having given all the reinforcements he could spare, and full powers to both marshals to act as they judged fitting for his service, would not, at a distance and while engaged in such vast operations as those he was carrying on at Dresden, decide so important a question. The vigorous execution essential to success was not to be expected if either marshal acted under constraint and against his own opinion; Soult had adopted Suchet's modification and it would have been unwise to substitute a new plan which would have probably displeased both commanders. Meanwhile Wellington passed the Bidassoa, and Suchet's project was annulled by the approach of winter and by the further operations of the allies.

If the plan of uniting the two armies in Aragon had been happily achieved, it would certainly have forced Wellington to repass the Ebro or fight a great battle with an army much less strongly constituted than the French army. If he chose the latter, victory would have profited him little, because his enemy strong in cavalry could have easily retired on the fortresses of Catalonia. If he received a check he must have gone over the Ebro, perhaps back to Portugal, and the French would have recovered Aragon, Navarre,

and Valencia. It is not probable however that such
a great operation could have been conducted without being discovered in time by Wellington. It has
been already indicated in this History, that besides
the ordinary spies and modes of gaining intelligence employed by all generals, he had secret
emissaries amongst Joseph's courtiers, and even
amongst French officers of rank; and it has been
shown that Soult vainly endeavoured to surprise him
on the 31st of August when the combinations were
only two days old. It is true that the retreat of
Suchet from Catalonia and his junction with Soult
in France at the moment when Napoleon was pressed
in Germany, together with the known difficulty of
passing guns by Jaca, would naturally have led to
the belief that it was a movement of retreat and
fear; nevertheless the secret must have been known
to more than one person about each marshal, and
the English general certainly had agents who were
little suspected. Soult would however still have
had the power of returning to his old positions, and,
with his numbers increased by Suchet's troops,
could have repeated his former attack by the Roncesvalles. It might be that his secret design was
thus to involve that marshal in his operations, and
being disappointed he was not very eager to
adopt the modified plan of the latter, which the
approach of the bad season, and the menacing
position of Wellington, rendered each day less promising. His own project was hardy, and dangerous
for the allies, and well did it prove lord Wellington's
profound acquaintance with his art. For he had
entered France only in compliance with the wishes
of the allied sovereigns, and always watched closely
for Suchet, averring that the true military line of

operations was towards Aragon and Catalonia. Being now however actually established in France, and the war in Germany having taken a favourable turn for the allies, he resolved to continue the operations on his actual front awaiting only the

FALL OF PAMPELUNA.

This event was produced by a long blockade, less fertile of incident than the siege of San Sebastian yet very honourable to the firmness of the governor general Cassan.

The town, containing fifteen thousand inhabitants, stood on a bold table-land on which a number of valleys opened, and where the great roads, coming from St. Jean Pied de Port, Sanguessa, Tudela, Estella, Vittoria, and Irurzun, were concentrated. The northern and eastern fronts of the fortress were covered by the Arga, and the defences there consisted of simple walls edging the perpendicular rocky bank of the river, but the other fronts were regularly fortified with ditches, covered way, and half-moons. Two bad unfinished outworks were constructed on the south front, but the citadel which stood on the south west was a regular pentagon, with bomb-proofs and magazines, vaulted barracks for a thousand men, and a complete system of mines.

Pampeluna had been partially blockaded by Mina for eighteen months previous to the battle of Vittoria, and when Joseph arrived after the action, the place was badly provisioned. The stragglers of his army increased the garrison to something more than three thousand five hundred men of all arms, who were immediately invested by the allies. Many of the inhabitants went off during the short interval between the king's arrival and departure, and general Cassan, finding his troops too few for action and yet too many for the food, abandoned the two outwarks on the south, demolished everything which could interfere with his defence outside, and commenced such works as he deemed necessary to improve it inside. Moreover forseeing that the French army might possibly make a sudden march without guns to succour the garrison, he prepared a field-train of forty pieces to meet the occasion.

It has been already shown that Wellington, although at first inclined to besiege Pampeluna, finally established a blockade and ordered works of contravallation to be constructed. Cassan's chief object was then to obtain provisions, and on the 28th and 30th of June he sustained actions outside the place to cover his foragers. On the 1st of July he burned the suburb of Madalina, beyond the river Arga, and forced many inhabitants to quit the place before the blockaders' works were completed. Skirmishes now occurred almost daily, the French always seeking to gather the grain, and vegetables which were ripe and abundant beyond the walls, and the allies endeavouring to set fire to the standing corn within range of the guns of the fortress.

On the 14th of July, O'Donnel's Andalusians were permanently established as the blockading force, and the next day the garrison made a successful forage on the south side of the town. This operation was repeated towards the east beyond the Arga on the 19th, when a sharp engagement of cavalry took place, during which the remainder of the garrison carried away a great deal of corn.

The 26th the sound of Soult's artillery reached the place, and Cassan, judging rightly that the

marshal was in march to succour Pampeluna, made
a sally in the night by the Roncesvalles road ; he
was driven back, but the next morning he came out
again with eleven hundred men and two guns, over-
threw the Spanish outguards, and advanced towards
Villalba at the moment when Picton was falling
back with the third and fourth divisions.   Then
O'Donnel, as I have before related, evacuated some
of the entrenchments, destroyed a great deal of
ammunition, spiked a number of guns, and but for
the timely arrival of Carlos d'España's division, and
the stand made by Picton at Huarte, would have
abandoned the blockade altogether.

Soon the battle on the mountains of Oricain commenced, the smoke rose over the intervening heights
of Escava and San Miguel, the French cavalry
appeared on the slopes above El Cano, and the baggage of the allies was seen filing in the opposite direction by Berioplano along the road of Irurzun. The
garrison thought deliverance sure, and having reaped
a good harvest withdrew into the place.   The
bivouac fires of the French army cheered them
during the night, and the next morning a fresh
sally being made with the greatest confidence,
a great deal of corn was gathered with little loss of
men.   Several deserters from the foreign regiments
in the English service also came over with intelligence exaggerated and coloured after the manner
of such men, and the French re-entered the place
elated with hope ; but in the evening the sound of
the conflict ceased and the silence of the next day
shewed that the battle was not to the advantage of
Soult.   However the governor losing no time made
another sally and again obtained provisions from the
south side.

The 30th the battle recommenced but the retreating fire of the French told how the conflict was
decided and the spirit of the soldiers fell. Nevertheless their indefatigable officers led another
sally on the south side, whence they carried off
grain and some ammunition which had been left in
one of the abandoned outworks.

On the 31st Carlos d'España's troops and two
thousand of O'Donnel's Andalusians, in all about
seven thousand men, resumed the blockade, and
maintained it until the middle of September, when
the Prince of Anglona's division of Del Parque's
army, relieved the Andalusians who rejoined their
own corps near Echallar. The allies' works of contravallation were now augmented, and when Paris
retired into France from Jaca, part of Mina's troops
occupied the valleys leading from the side of Sanguessa to Pampeluna and made entrenchments to
bar the escape of the garrison that way.

In October Cassan put his fighting men upon
rations of horse-flesh, four ounces to each, with
some rice, and he turned more families out of the
town, but this time they were fired upon by their
countrymen and forced to re-enter.

On the 9th of September baron Maucune, who
had conducted most of the sallies during the
blockade, attacked and carried some fortified houses
on the east side of the place; he was immediately
assailed by the Spanish cavalry, but he beat them
and pursued the fugitives close to Villalba. Carlos
D'España then advanced to their aid in person with
a greater body and the French were driven in with
the loss of eighty men, yet the Spaniards lost a far
greater number, Carlos D'España himself was

wounded, and the garrison obtained some corn which was their principal object.

The soldiers were now feeding on rats and other disgusting animals ; seeking also for roots beyond the walls many in their hunger poisoned themselves with hemlock, and a number of others unable to bear their misery deserted. In this state Cassan made a general sally on the 10th of October, to ascertain the strength of the lines around him, with a view to breaking through, but after some fighting, his troops were driven in with the loss of seventy men and all hope of escape vanished. Yet he still spoke of attempting it, and the public manner in which he increased the mines under the citadel induced Wellington to reinforce the blockade, and to bring up his cavalry into the vicinity of Pampeluna.

The scurvy now invaded the garrison. One thousand men were sick, eight hundred had been wounded, the deaths by battle and disease exceeded four hundred, one hundred and twenty had deserted, and the governor moved by the great misery, offered on the 26th to surrender if he was allowed to retire into France with his troops and six pieces of cannon. This being refused he proposed to yield on condition of not serving for a year and a day, which being also denied, he broke off the negociation, giving out that he would blow up the works of the fortress and break through the blockade. To deter him a menacing letter was thrown to his outposts, and lord Wellington being informed of his design denounced it as contrary to the laws of war, and directed Carlos d'España to put him, all his officers and non-commissioned officers, and a tenth of the

soldiers to death when the place should be taken
if any damage were done to the works.

Cassan's object being merely to obtain better
terms this order remained dormant, and happily so,
for the execution would never have borne the test
of public opinion. To destroy the works of Pampeluna and break through the blockading force, as
Brennier did at Almeida, would have been a very
noble exploit, and a useful one for the French army
if Soult's plan of changing the theatre of war by
descending into Aragon had been followed. There
could therefore be nothing contrary to the laws of
war in a resolute action of that nature. On the
other hand if the governor, having no chance whatever of success, made a hopeless attempt the pretence for destroying a great fortress belonging to
the Spaniards and depriving the allies of the fruits
of their long blockade and glorious battles, the
conquerors might have justly exercised that severe
but undoubted right of war, refusing quarter to an
enemy.   But lord Wellington's letter to España
involved another question, namely the putting of
prisoners to death. For the soldiers could not be
decimated until captured, and their crime would
have been only obedience to orders in a matter of
which they dared not judge. This would have been
quite contrary to the usages of civilized nations, and
the threat must undoubtedly be considered only as
a device to save the works of Pampeluna and to
avoid the odium of refusing quarter.

A few days longer the governor and garrison
endured their distress and then capitulated, having
defended themselves more than four months with
great constancy. The officers and soldiers became
prisoners of war. The first were allowed to keep

their arms and baggage, the second their knapsacks, expressly on the ground that they had treated the inhabitants well during the investment.   This compliment was honourable to both sides, but there was another article, enforced by España without being accepted by the garrison, for which it is difficult to assign any motive but the vindictive ferocity of the Spanish character.   No person of either sex was permitted to follow the French troops, and women's affections were thus barbarously brought under the action of the sword.

There was no stronghold now retained by the French in the north of Spain except Santona, and as the blockade of that place had been exceedingly tedious, lord Wellington, whose sea communications were interrupted by the privateers from thence, formed a small British corps under lord Aylmer with a view to attack Laredo, which being on the opposite point of the harbour to Santona commanded the anchorage.   Accidental circumstances however prevented this body from proceeding to its destination and Santona remained in the enemy's possession.   With this exception the contest in the northern parts of Spain was terminated and the south of France was now to be invaded; but it is fitting first to show with what great political labour Wellington brought the war to this state, what contemptible actions and sentiments, what a faithless alliance, and what vile governments his dazzling glory hid from the sight of the world.

CHAPTER VI.

Political state of Portugal. In this country the national jealousy which had been compressed by the force of invasion expanded again with violence as danger receded, and the influence of England sunk precisely in the measure that her army assured the safety of Portugal. When Wellington crossed the Ebro, the Souza faction, always opposed in the council to the British policy, became elate ; and those members of the government who had hitherto cherished the British ascendancy because it sustained them against the Brazilian court intrigues, now sought popularity by taking an opposite direction. Each person of the regency had his own line of opposition marked out. Noguera vexatiously resisted or suspended commercial and financial operations ; the Principal Souza wrangled more fiercely and insolently at the council-board ; the Patriarch fomented ill-will at Lisbon and in the northern provinces ; Forjas, ambitious to command the national troops, became the organ of discontent upon military matters. The return of the prince-regent, the treaty of commerce, the Oporto company, the privileges of the British factory merchants, the mode of paying the subsidy, the means of military transport, the convention with Spain relative to the supply of the Portuguese troops in that country, the recruiting,

CHAP.
VI.

1813.

Mr. Stuart's Corresponbdence,
MSS.

the organization, the command of the national
army, and the honours due to it, all furnished occasions for factious proceedings, which were conducted with the ignoble subtlety that invariably
characterizes the politics of the Peninsula. Moreover the expenditure of the British army had been
immense, the trade and commerce dependent upon
it, now removed to the Spanish ports, enormous.
Portugal had lived upon England. Her internal
taxes carelessly or partially enforced were vexatious
to the people without being profitable to the government. Nine-tenths of the revenue accrued
from duties upon British trade, and the sudden
cessation of markets and of employment, the absence of ready money, the loss of profit, public
and private, occasioned by the departure of the
army while the contributions and other exactions
remained the same, galled all classes, and the
whole nation was ready to shake off the burthen
of gratitude.

In this state of feeling emissaries were employed
to promulgate in various directions tales, some
true some false, of the disorders perpetrated by
the military detachments on the lines of communication, adding that they were the result of secret
orders from Wellington to satisfy his personal hatred of Portugal! At the same time discourses
and writings against the British influence abounded
in Lisbon and at Rio Janeiro, and were re-echoed
or surpassed by the London newspapers, whose
statements overflowing of falsehood could be
traced to the Portuguese embassy in that capital.
It was asserted that England intending to retain
her power in Portugal opposed the return of the
prince-regent; that the war itself being removed

to the frontier of France was become wholly a
Spanish cause ; that it was not for Portugal to levy
troops, and exhaust her resources to help a nation
whose aggressions she must be called upon sooner
or later to resist.

Mr. Stuart's diplomatic intercourse with the government always difficult was now a continual remonstrance and dispute ; his complaints were met
with insolence or subterfuge, and illegal violence
against the persons and property of British subjects was pushed so far, that Mr. Sloane, an English gentleman upon whom no suspicion rested,
was cast into prison for three months because he
had come to Lisbon without a passport. The
rights of the English factory were invaded, and
the Oporto company which had been established
as its rival in violation of treaty was openly cherished. Irresponsible and rapacious, this pernicious company robbed every body, and the
prince-regent promising either to reform or totally
abolish it ordered a preparatory investigation, but
to use the words of Mr. Stuart, the regency acted
on the occasion no less unfairly by their sovereign
than unjustly by their ally.

Especial privileges claimed by the factory merchants were another cause of disquiet. They pretended to exemption from certain taxes, and from
billets, and that a fixed number of their clerks
domestics and cattle should be exonerated of military service. These pretensions were disputed.
The one touching servants and cattle, doubtful at
best, had been grossly abused, and that relating to
billets unfounded ; but the taxes were justly resisted, and the merchants offered a voluntary con-
tribution to the same amount. The government

rudely refused this offer, seized their property, imprisoned their persons, impressed their cattle to transport supplies that never reached the troops, and made soldiers of their clerks and servants without any intention of reinforcing the army. Mr. Stuart immediately deducted from the subsidy the amount of the property thus forcibly taken, and repaid the sufferers. The regency then commenced a dispute upon the fourth article of the treaty of commerce, and the prince, though he openly ordered it to be executed, secretly permitted count Funchal, his prime minister, to remain in London as ambassador until the disputes arising upon this treaty generally were arranged. Funchal who disliked to quit London took care to interpose many obstacles to a final decision, always advising delay under pretence of rendering ultimate concession of value in other negociations then depending.

When the battle of Vittoria became known, the regency proposed to entreat the return of the prince from the Brazils, hoping thereby to excite the opposition of Mr. Stuart; but when he, contrary to their expectations, approved of the proposal they deferred the execution. The British cabinet which had long neglected Wellington's suggestions on this head, then pressed the matter at Rio Janeiro, and Funchal who had been at first averse now urged it warmly, fearing that if the prince remained he could no longer defer going to the Brazils. However few of the Portuguese nobles desired the return of the royal family, and when the thing was proposed to the regent he discovered no inclination for the voyage.

But the most important subject of discord was

the army. The absence of the sovereign and the
intrigues which ruled the court of Rio Janeiro had
virtually rendered the government at Lisbon an
oligarchy without a leader, in other words, a government formed for mischief. The whole course
of this history has shewn that all Wellington's
energy and ability, aided by the sagacity and firmness of Mr. Stuart and by the influence of England's power and riches, were scarcely sufficient to
meet the evils flowing from this foul source. Even
while the French armies were menacing the capital
the regency was split into factions, the financial
resources were neglected or wasted, the public
servants were insolent incapable and corrupt, the
poorer people oppressed, and the military force for
want of sustenance was at the end of 1812 on the
point of dissolving together. The strenuous interference of the English general and envoy, seconded
by the extraordinary exertions of the British officers
in the Portuguese service, restored indeed the
efficiency of the army, and in the campaign of
1813 the spirit of the troops was surpassing. Even
the militia-men, who had been deprived of their
colours and drafted into the line to punish their
bad conduct at Guarda under general Trant in
1812, nobly regained their standards on the Pyrenees.

But this state of affairs acting upon the naturally sanguine temperament and vanity of the Portuguese, created a very exaggerated notion of their
military prowess and importance, and withal a Mr. Stu-
morbid sensitiveness to praise or neglect. General art's Cor-
respon-
Picton had thrown some slur upon the conduct of dence, MSS.
a regiment at Vittoria, and marshal Beresford com-

plained that full justice had not been done to their merits. The eulogiums passed in the English parliament and in the despatches upon the conduct of the British and Spanish troops, but not extended to the Portuguese, galled the whole nation, and the remarks and omissions of the London newspapers were as wormwood.

Meanwhile the regency, under pretext of a dispute with Spain relative to a breach of the military convention of supply, neglected the subsistence of the army altogether; and at the same time so many obstacles to the recruiting were raised, that the depôts, which ought to have furnished twelve thousand men to replace the losses sustained in the campaign, only contained four thousand, who were also without the means of taking the field. This matter became so serious that Beresford quitting the army in October came to Lisbon, to propose a new regulation which should disregard the exemptions claimed by the nobles the clergy and the English merchants for their servants and followers. On his arrival Forjas urged the public discontent at the political position of the Portuguese troops. They were, he said, generally incorporated with the British divisions, commanded by British officers, and having no distinct recognized existence their services were unnoticed and the glory of the country suffered. The world at large knew not how many men Portugal furnished for the war. It was known indeed that there were Portuguese soldiers, as it was known that there were Brunswickers and Hanoverians, but as a national army nothing was known of them; their exertions, their courage, only went to swell the general triumph of

England, while the Spaniards, inferior in numbers, and far inferior in all military qualities, were flattered, praised, thanked in the public despatches, in the English newspapers, and in the discourses and votes of the British parliament. He proposed therefore to have the Portuguese formed into a distinct army acting under lord Wellington.

It was objected that the brigades incorporated with the British divisions were fed by the British commissariat the cost being deducted from the subsidy, an advantage the loss of which the Portuguese could not sustain. Forjas rejoined that they could feed their own troops cheaper if the subsidy was paid in money, but Beresford referred him to his scanty means of transport, so scanty that the few stores they were then bound to furnish for the unattached brigades depending upon the Portuguese commissariat were not forwarded. Foiled on this point Forjas proposed gradually to withdraw the best brigades from the English divisions, to incorporate them with the unattached brigades of native troops and so form an auxiliary corps; but the same objection of transport still applied and this matter dropped for the moment. The regency then agreed to reduce the legal age of men liable to the conscription for the army, but the islands, which ought to have given three hundred men yearly, were exempt from their controul, and the governors supported by the prince-regent refused to permit any levies in their jurisdictions, and even granted asylums to all those who wished to avoid the levy in Portugal. In the islands also the persons so unjustly and cruelly imprisoned in 1810 were still kept in durance, although the regency yield-

ing to the persevering remonstrances of Mr. Stuart
and lord Wellington had released those at Lisbon.

Soon after this Beresford desired to go to England, and the occasion was seized by Forjas to
renew his complaints and his proposition for a separate army which he designed to command himself.　General Sylveira's claim to that honour was
however supported by the Souzas, to whose faction
he belonged, and the only matter in which all
agreed was the display of ill-will towards England.
Lord Wellington became indignant.　The English
newspapers, he said, did much mischief by their
assertions, but he never suspected they could by
their omissions alienate the Portuguese nation and
government.　The latter complained that their
troops were not praised in parliament, nothing
could be more different from a debate within the
house than the representation of it in the newspapers.　The latter seldom stated an event or
transaction as it really occurred, unless when they
absolutely copied what was written for them ; and
even then their observations branched out so far
from the text, that they appeared absolutely incapable of understanding much less of stating the
trnth upon any subject.　The Portuguese people
should therefore be cautious of taking English
newspapers as a test of the estimation in which
the Portuguese army was held in England, where
its character stood high and was rising daily.
" Mr. Forjas is," said lord Wellington, " the ablest
man of business I have met with in the Peninsula,
it is to be hoped he will not on such grounds have
the folly to alter a successful military system.　I
understand something of the organization and feed-

ing of troops, and I assure him that separated
from the British, the Portuguese army could not
keep the field in a good state although their government were to incur ten times the expense under
the actual system; and if they are not in a fitting
state for the field they can gain no honour, they
must suffer dishonour! The vexatious disputes
with Spain are increasing daily, and if the omissions or assertions of newspapers are to be the
causes of disagreement with the Portuguese *I will
quit the Peninsula for ever"!*

This remonstrance being read to the regency,
Forjas replied officially.

" The Portuguese government demanded nothing
unreasonable. The happy campaign of 1813 was
not to make it heedless of sacrifices beyond its
means. It had a right to expect greater exertions
from Spain, which was more interested than Portugal in the actual operations since the safety of
the latter was obtained. Portugal only wanted a
solid peace, she did not expect increase of territory, nor any advantage save the consideration
and influence which the services and gallantry of
her troops would give her amongst European nations, and which, unhappily, she would probably
require in her future intercourse with Spain. The
English prince-regent his ministers and his generals, had rendered full justice to her military services in the official reports, but that did not suffice
to give them weight in Europe. Official reports
did not remove this inconvenience. It was only
the public expressions of the English prince and
his ministers that could do justice. The Portuguese army was commanded by Marshal Beresford,
Marquis of Campo Mayor. It ought always to be

so considered and thanked accordingly for its exploits, and with as much form and solemnity by
the English parliament and general as was used
towards the Spanish army.   The more so that the
Portuguese had sacrificed their national pride to
the common good, whereas the Spanish pride had
retarded the success of the cause and the liberty
of Europe.   It was necessary also to form good
native generals to be of use after the war; but
putting that question aside, it was only demanded
to have the divisions separated by degrees and
given to Portuguese officers.   Nevertheless such
grave objections being advanced they were willing,
he said, to drop the matter altogether."

The discontent however remained, for the argument had weight, and if any native officers' reputation had been sufficient to make the proceeding
plausible, the British officers would have been
driven from the Portuguese service, the armies
separated, and both ruined.   As it was, the regency terminated the discussion from inability to
succeed ; from fear not from reason.   The persons who pretended to the command were Forjas
and Sylveira; but the English officers who were
as yet well-liked by the troops, would not have
served under the former, and Wellington objected
strongly to the latter, having by experience discovered that he was an incapable officer seeking
a base and pernicious popularity by encouraging
the views of the soldiers.   Beresford then relinquished his intention of going to England, and the
justice of the complaint relative to the reputation
of the Portuguese army being obvious, the general orders became more marked in favour of the
troops.   But the most effectual check to the pro-

ject of the regency was the significant intimation
of Mr. Stuart, that England, being bound by no
conditions in the payment of the subsidy, had a
right if it was not applied in the manner most
agreeable to her, to withdraw it altogether.

To have this subsidy in specie and to supply
their own troops continued to be the cry of the
regency, until their inability to effect the latter
became at last so apparent that they gave the matter
up in despair. Indeed Forjas was too able a man
ever to have supposed, that the badly organized
administration of Portugal, was capable of supporting an efficient army in the field five hundred miles
from its own country ; the real object was to shake
off the British influence if possible without losing
the subsidy. For the honour of the army or the
welfare of the soldiers neither the regency nor the
prince himself had any care. While the former
were thus disputing for the command, they suffered
their subordinates to ruin an establishment at Ruña,
the only asylum in Portugal for mutilated soldiers,
and turned the helpless veterans adrift. And the
prince while he lavished honours upon the dependents and creatures of his court at Rio Janeiro,
placed those officers whose fidelity and hard fighting had preserved his throne in Portugal at the
bottom of the list, amongst the menial servants of
the palace who were decorated with the same ri-
bands ! Honour, justice, humanity, were alike
despised by the ruling men and lord Wellington
thus expressed his strong disgust.

" *The British army which I have the honour to
command has met with nothing but ingratitude from
the government and authorities in Portugal for
their services, every thing that could be done has*

*been done by the civil authorities lately to op-
press the officers and soldiers on every occasion in
which it has by any accident been in their power.
I hope however that we have seen the last of Portugal"!*

Such were the relations of the Portuguese government with England, and with Spain they were
not more friendly. Seven envoys from that country
had succeeded each other at Lisbon in three years.
The Portuguese regency dreaded the democratic
opinions which had obtained ground in Spain, and
the leading party in the Cortez were intent to
spread those opinions over the whole Peninsula.
The only bond of sympathy between the two governments was hatred of the English who had
saved both. On all other points they differed. The
exiled bishop of Orense, from his asylum on the
frontier of Portugal, excited the Gallicians against
the Cortez so vigorously. that his expulsion from
Portugal, or at least his removal from the northern
frontier, was specially demanded by the Spanish
minister; but though a long and angry discussion
followed the bishop was only civilly requested by
the Portuguese government to abstain from acts
disagreeable to the Spanish regency. The latter
then demanded that he should be delivered up as a
delinquent, whereupon the Portuguese quoted a
decree of the Cortez which deprived the bishop of
his rights as a Spanish citizen and denaturalized
him. However he was removed twenty leagues
from the frontier, nor was the Portuguese government itself quite free from ecclesiastic troubles.
The bishop of Braganza preached doctrines which
were offensive to the patriarch and the government; he was confined but soon released and an

ecclesiastical sentence pronounced against him, which only increased his followers and extended the influence of his doctrines.

Another cause of uneasiness, at a later period, was the return of Ballesteros from his exile at Ceuta. He had been permitted towards the end of 1813, and as lord Wellington thought with no good intent, to reside at Fregenal. The Portuguese regency, fearing that he would rally round him other discontented persons, set agents to watch his proceedings, and under pretence of putting down robbers who abounded on that frontier, established a line of cavalry and called out the militia, thus making it manifest that but a little was wanting to kindle a war between the two countries.

Political state of Spain. Lord Wellington's victories had put an end to the intercourse between Joseph and the Spaniards who desired to make terms with the French; but those people not losing hope, formed a strong anti-English party and watched to profit by the disputes between the two great factions at Cadiz, which had now become most rancorous and dangerous to the common cause. The serviles extremely bigoted both in religion and politics had the whole body of the clergy on their side. They were the most numerous in the Cortez and their views were generally in accord with the feelings of the people beyond the Isla de Leon, although their doctrines were comprised in two sentences—*An absolute king, An intolerant church.* The liberals supported and instigated by all ardent innovators, by the commercial body and populace of Cadiz, had also partizans beyond the Isla; and taking as guides the revolutionary writings of the French philosophers were hastening onwards to a democracy, without regard to ancient usages or feelings, and without practical ability to carry their theories into execution. There was also a fourth faction in the Cortez, formed by the American deputies, who were secretly labouring for the independence of the colonies; they sometimes joined the liberals, sometimes the serviles, as it suited their purposes, and thus often produced anomalous results, because they were numerous enough to turn the scale in favour of the side which they espoused. Jealousy of England was however common to all, and " *Inglesismo*" was used as a term of contempt. Posterity will scarcely believe, that when lord Wellington was commencing the campaign of 1813 the Cortez was with difficulty, and by threats rather than reason, prevented from passing a law forbidding foreign troops to enter a Spanish fortress. Alicant, Tarifa, Cadiz itself where they held their sittings, had been preserved; Ciudad Rodrigo, Badajos, had been retaken for them by British valour; English money had restored their broken walls and replenished their exhausted magazines; English and Portuguese blood still smoked from their ramparts; but the men from whose veins that blood had flowed, were to be denied entrance at gates which they could not approach, without treading on the bones of slaughtered comrades who had sacrificed their lives to procure for this sordid ungrateful assembly the power to offer the insult.

The subjection of the bishops and other clergy, who had in Gallicia openly opposed the abolition

of the inquisition and excited the people to resistance, was an object of prominent interest with an
active section of the liberals called the Jacobins.
And this section generally ruled the Cortez, because the Americanos leaned strongly towards their
doctrines, and the interest of the anti-English, or
French party, was to produce dissensions which
could be best effected by supporting the most violent public men. A fierce and obstinate faction
they were, and they compelled the churchmen to
submit for the time, but not until the dispute became so serious that lord Wellington when in the
Pyrenees expected a civil war on his communications, and thought the clergy and the peasantry
would take part with the French. This notion
which gives his measure for the patriotism of both
parties, proved however unfounded; his extreme
discontent at the progress of liberal doctrines had
somewhat warped his judgment; the people were
less attached to the church than he imagined, the
clergy of Gallicia, meeting with no solid support,
submitted to the Cortez, and the archbishop of San-
tiago fled to Portugal.

Deep unmitigated hatred of democracy was indeed the moving spring of the English tories'
policy. Napoleon was warred against, not as they
pretended because he was a tyrant and usurper,
for he was neither; not because his invasion of
Spain was unjust, but because he was the powerful
and successful enemy of aristocratic privileges.
The happiness and independence of the Peninsula
were words without meaning in their state-papers
and speeches, and their anger and mortification
were extreme when they found success against the

emperor had fostered that democracy it was their
object to destroy. They were indeed only prevented by the superior prudence and sagacity of
their general, from interfering with the internal
government of Spain in so arrogant and injudicious
a manner, that an open rupture wherein the Spaniards would have had all appearance of justice,
must have ensued. This folly was however stifled
by Wellington, who desired to wait until the blow
could be given with some effect, and he was quite
willing to deal it himself; yet the conduct of the
Cortez, and that of the executive government
which acted under its controul, was so injurious
to Spain and to his military operations, and so
unjust to him personally, that the warmest friends
of freedom cannot blame his enmity. Rather
should his moderation be admired, when we find
his aristocratic hatred of the Spanish constitution
exacerbated by a´ state of affairs thus described by
Vegas, a considerable member of the Cortez and
perfectly acquainted with the subject.

Speaking of the " *Afrancesados*" or French
party, more numerous than was supposed and active

to increase their numbers, he says, " The thing
which they most enforced and which made most
progress was the diminution of the English influence. Amongst the serviles they gained pro-
selytes, by objecting the English religion and constitution which restricted the power of the sovereign. With the liberals, they said the same constitution gave the sovereign too much power ; and
the Spanish constitution having brought the king's
authority under that of the Cortez was an object
of jealousy to the English cabinet and aristocracy,

who, fearing the example would encourage the reformers of England, were resolved that the Spanish constitution should not stand. To the Americans they observed that lord Wellington opposed them, because he did not help them and permitted expeditions to be sent from Spain; but to the Europeans who wished to retain the colonies and exclude foreign trade, they represented the English as fomenters and sustainers of the colonial rebellion, because they did not join their forces with Spain to put it down. To the honest patriots of all parties they said, that every concession to the English general was an offence against the dignity and independence of the nation. If he was active in the field, he was intent to subjugate Spain rather than defeat the enemy; if he was careful in preparation, his delay was to enable the French to conquer; if he was vigorous in urging the government to useful measures, his design was to impose his own laws; if he neglected the Spanish armies, he desired they should be beaten; if he meddled with them usefully, it was to gain the soldiers turn the army against the country and thus render Spain dependent on England. And these perfidious insinuations were effectual because they flattered the national pride, as proving that the Spaniards could do every thing for themselves without the aid of foreigners. Finally that nothing could stop the spread of such dangerous doctrines but new victories, which would bring the simple honesty and gratitude of the people at large into activity. Those victories came and did indeed stifle the French party in Spain, but many of their arguments were too well founded to be stifled with their party.

The change of government which had place
in the beginning of the year, gave hope that the
democratic violence of the Cortez would decline
under the control of the cardinal Bourbon; but that
prince, who was not of true royal blood in the
estimation of the Spaniards, because his father had
married without the consent of the king, was from
age, and infirmity, and ignorance, a nullity. The
new regency became therefore more the slaves of
the Cortez than their predecessors, and the Cadiz
editors of newspapers, pre-eminent in falsehood
and wickedness even amongst their unprincipled
European brotherhood, being the champions of the
Jacobins directed the populace of that city as they
pleased. And always the serviles yielded under
the dread of personal violence. Their own crimes
had become their punishment. They had taught
the people at the commencement of the contest that
murder was patriotism, and now their spirit sunk
and quailed, because at every step to use the
terribly significant expression of Wellington, " *The
ghost of Solano was staring them in the face.*"

The principal points of the Jacobins' policy in
support of their crude constitution, which they
considered as perfect as an emanation from the
Deity, were, 1°. The abolition of the Inquisition,
the arrest and punishment of the Gallician bishops,
and the consequent warfare with the clergy. 2°. The
putting aside the claim of Carlotta to the regency.
3°. The appointment of captain-generals and other
officers to suit their factious purposes. 4°. The
obtaining of money for their necessities, without
including therein the nourishment of the armies.
5°. The control of the elections for a new Cortez
so as to procure an assembly of their own way of

thinking, or to prevent its assembling at the legal period in October.

The matter of the bishops as we have seen nearly involved them in a national war with Portugal, and a civil war with Gallicia. The affair of the princess was less serious, but she had never ceased intriguing, and her pretensions, wisely opposed by the British ministers and general while the army was cooped up in Portugal, were, although she was a declared enemy to the English alliance, now rather favoured by sir Henry Wellesley as a mode of checking the spread of democracy. Lord Wellington however still held aloof, observing that if appointed according to the constitution, she would not be less a slave to the Cortez than her predecessors, and England would have the discredit of giving power to the " worst woman in existence."

To remove the seat of government from the influence of the Cadiz populace was one mode of abating the power of the democratic party, and the yellow fever, coming immediately after the closing of the general Cortez in September, had apparently given the executive government some freedom of action, and seemed to furnish a favourable opportunity for the English ambassador to effect its removal. The regency, dreading the epidemic, suddenly resolved to proceed to Madrid, telling sir Henry Wellesley, who joyfully hastened to offer pecuniary aid, that to avoid the sickness was their sole motive. They had secretly formed this resolution at night and proposed to commence the journey next day, but a disturbance arose in the city and the alarmed regents convoked the extraordinary Cortez; the ministers were immediately called before it and bending in fear before their masters, declared

BOOK
XXII.
────────
1813.
Appendix
No. 2.

with a scandalous disregard of truth, that there was no intention to quit the Isla without consulting the Cortez.   Certain deputies were thereupon appointed to inquire if there was any fever, and a few cases being discovered, the deputation, apparently to shield the regents, recommended that they should remove to Port St. Mary.

This did not satisfy the assembly.   The government was commanded to remain at Cadiz until the new general Cortez should be installed, and a committee was appointed to probe the whole affair or rather to pacify the populace, who were so offended with the report of the first deputation, that the speech of Arguelles on presenting it was hissed from the galleries, although he was the most popular and eloquent member of the Cortez. The more moderate liberals thus discovered that they were equally with the serviles the slaves of the newspaper writers. Nevertheless the inherent excellence of freedom, though here presented in such fantastic and ignoble shapes, was involuntarily admitted by lord Wellington when he declared, that wherever the Cortez and government should fix themselves the press would follow to control, and the people of Seville, Granada, or Madrid, would become as bad as the people of Cadiz.

The composition of the new Cortez was naturally an object of hope and fear to all factions, and the result being uncertain, the existing assembly took such measures to prolong its own power that it was expected two Cortez would be established, the one at Cadiz, the other at Seville, each striving for mastery in the nation.   However the new body after many delays was installed at Cadiz in November, and the Jacobins, strong in the violence of the populace, still swayed the assembly, and kept the seat of government at Cadiz until the rapid spread of the fever brought a stronger fear into action. Then the resolution to repair to Madrid was adopted, and the sessions in the Isla closed on the 29th of November. Yet not without troubles. For the general belief being, that no person could take the sickness twice, and almost every resident family had already suffered from former visitations, the merchants with an infamous cupidity declaring that there was no fever, induced the authorities flagitiously to issue clean bills of health to ships leaving the port, and endeavoured by intimidation to keep the regency and Cortez in the city.

Appendix,
No. 2.

An exact and copious account of these factions and disputes, and of the permanent influence which these discussions of the principles of government, this constant collision of opposite doctrines, had upon the character of the people, would, if sagaciously traced, form a lesson of the highest interest for nations. But to treat the subject largely would be to write a political history of the Spanish revolution, and it is only the effect upon the military operations which properly appertains to a history of the war. That effect was one of unmitigated evil, but it must be observed that this did not necessarily spring from the democratic system, since precisely the same mischiefs were to be traced in Portugal, where arbitrary power, called legitimate government, was prevalent. In both cases alike, the people and the soldiers suffered for the crimes of factious politicians.

It has been shewn in a former volume, that one Spanish regency contracted an engagement with lord Wellington on the faith of which he took the

command of their armies in 1813.   It was scrupu-
lously adhered to by him, but systematically violated by the new regency and minister of war, almost
as soon as it was concluded.   His recommendations
for promotion after Vittoria were disregarded, orders
were sent direct to the subordinate generals, and
changes were made in the commands and in the
destinations of the troops without his concurrence,
and without passing through him as generalissimo.
Scarcely had he crossed the Ebro when Castaños,
captain-general of Gallicia, Estremadura, and Castile, was disgracefully removed from his government
under pretence of calling him to assist in the council
òf state.   His nephew general Giron was at the
same time deprived of his command over the Gallician army, although both he and Castaños had
been largely commended for their conduct by lord
Wellington.   General Frere, appointed captain-
general of Castile and Estremadura, succeeded
Giron in command of the troops, and the infamous
Lacy replaced Castaños in Gallicia, chosen, it was
believed, as a fitter tool to work out the measures
of the Jacobins against the clergy in that kingdom.   Nor was the sagacity of that faction at
fault, for Castaños would, according to lord Wellington, have turned his arms against the Cortez
if an opportunity had offered.   He and others were
now menaced with death, and the Cortez contemplated an attack upon the tithes, upon the
feudal and royal tenths, and upon the estates of the
grandees.   All except the last very fitting to do if
the times and circumstances had been favourable
for a peaceful arrangement; but most insane when
the nation generally was averse, and there was an
invader in the country to whom the discontented

could turn.   The clergy were at open warfare with
the government, many generals were dissatisfied,
and menacing in their communications with the
superior civil authorities, the soldiers were starving
and the people tired of their miseries only desired
to get rid of the invaders, and to avoid the burthen of supplying the troops of either side.   The
English cabinet, after having gorged Spain with
gold and flattery was totally without influence.   A
terrible convulsion was at hand if the French could
have maintained the war with any vigour in Spain
itself; and the following passages, from Wellington's
letters to the ministers, prove, that even he contemplated a forcible change in the government and
constitution.

" If the mob of Cadiz begin to remove heads
from shoulders as the newspapers have threatened
Castaños, and the assembly seize upon landed property to supply their necessities, I am afraid we
must do something more than discountenance them."
—" It is quite impossible such a system can last.
What I regret is that I am the person that maintains it.   If I was out of the way there are
plenty of generals who would overturn it.   Ballesteros positively intended it, and I am much
mistaken if O'Donnel and even Castaños, and probably others are not equally ready.   If the king
should return he also will overturn the whole fabric
if he has any spirit."—" I wish you would let me
know whether if I should find a fair opportunity of
striking at the democracy the government would
approve of my doing it."   And in another letter he
seriously treated the question of withdrawing from
the contest altogether.   " The government were
the best judges," he said, " of whether they could

or ought to withdraw, but he did not believe that
Spain could be a useful ally, or at all in alliance
with England, if the republican system was not put
down.   Meanwhile he recommended to the English
government and to his brother, to take no part
either for or against the princess of Brazil, to discountenance the democratical principles and measures of the Cortez, and if their opinion was
asked regarding the formation of a new regency,
to recommend an alteration of that part of the constitution which lodged all power with the Cortez,
and to give instead, some authority to the executive
government whether in the hands of king or regent.
To fill the latter office one of royal blood uniting
the strongest claims of birth with the best capacity
should he thought be selected, but if capacity
was wanting in the royal race then to choose the
Spaniard who was most deserving in the public
estimation !   Thus necessity teaches privilege to
bend before merit.

The whole force of Spain in arms was at this period
about one hundred and sixty thousand men. Of this
number not more than fifty thousand were available
for operations in the field, and those only because
they were paid clothed and armed by England,
and kept together by the ability and vigour of the
English general.   He had proposed when at Cadiz
an arrangement for the civil and political government of the provinces rescued from the French,
with a view to the supply of the armies, but his
plan was rejected and his repeated representations
of the misery the army and the people endured
under the system of the Spanish government were
unheeded.   Certain districts were allotted for the
support of each army, yet, with a jealous fear

of military domination, the government refused
the captain-generals of those districts the necessary powers to draw forth the resources of the
country, powers which lord Wellington recommended that they should have, and wanting which
the whole system was sure to become a nullity.
Each branch of administration was thus conducted
by chiefs independent in their attributes, yet each
too restricted in authority, generally at variance
with one another, and all of them neglectful of
their duty. The evil effect upon the troops was
thus described by the English general as early as
August.

" More than half of Spain has been cleared of
the enemy above a year, and the whole of Spain
excepting Catalonia and a small part of Aragon
since the months of May and June last. The most
abundant harvest has been reaped in all parts of
the country; millions of money spent by the contending armies are circulating every where, and
yet your armies however weak in numbers are
literally starving. The allied British and Portuguese armies under my command have been sub-
sisted, particularly latterly, almost exclusively upon
the magazines imported by sea, and I am concerned
to inform your excellency, that besides money for
the pay of all the armies, which has been given
from the military chest of the British army and has
been received from no other quarter, the British
magazines have supplied quantities of provisions to
all the Spanish armies in order to enable them to
remain in the field at all. And notwithstanding
this assistance I have had the mortification of seeing the Spanish troops on the outposts, obliged to

plunder the nut and apple-trees for subsistence, and to know that the Spanish troops, employed in the blockade of Pampeluna and Santona, were starving upon half an allowance of bread, while the enemy whom they were blockading were at the same time receiving their full allowance. The system then is insufficient to procure supplies for the army and at the same time I assure your excellency that it is the most oppressive and injurious to the country that could be devised. It cannot be pretended that the country does not produce the means of maintaining the men necessary for its defence ; those means are undoubtedly superabundant, and the enemy has proved that armies can be maintained in Spain, at the expense of the Spanish nation, infinitely larger than are necessary for its defence.

These evils he attributed to the incapacity of the public servants, and to their overwhelming numbers, that certain sign of an unprosperous state ; to the disgraceful negligence and disregard of public duties, and to there being no power in the country for enforcing the law ; the collection of the revenue cost in several branches seventy and eighty per cent. Meanwhile no Spanish officers capable of commanding a large body of troops or keeping it in an efficient state had yet appeared, no efficient staff, no system of military administration had been formed, and no shame for these deficiencies, no exertions to amend were visible.

From this picture two conclusions are to be drawn, 1°. that the provinces, thus described as superabounding in resources, having been for several years occupied by the French armies, the warfare of the latter could not have been so devastating and barbarous as it was represented. 2°. That Spain, being now towards the end as helpless as she had been at the beginning and all through the war, was quite unequal to her own deliverance either by arms or policy ; that it was English valour English steel, directed by the genius of an English general, which rising superior to all obstacles, whether presented by his own or the peninsular governments or by the perversity of national character, worked out her independence. So utterly inefficient were the Spaniards themselves, that now, at the end of six years' war, lord Wellington declared thirty thousand of their troops could not be trusted to act separately ; they were only useful when mixed in the line with larger numbers of other nations. And yet all men in authority to the lowest alcalde were as presumptuous as arrogant and as perverse as ever. Seeming to be rendered callous to public misery by the desperate state of affairs, they were reckless of the consequences of their actions and never suffered prudential considerations or national honour to check the execution of any project. The generals from repeated failures had become insensible to misfortunes, and without any remarkable display of personal daring, were always ready to deliver battle on slight occasions, as if that were a common matter instead of being the great event of war.

The government agents were corrupt, and the government itself was as it had ever been tyrannical faithless mean and equivocating to the lowest degree. In 1812 a Spaniard of known and active patriotism thus commenced an elaborate plan of defence for the provinces. " Catalonia abhors France as her oppressor but she abhors still more the despotism which has been carried on in all the branches of her administration since the beginning of the war." In fine there was no healthy action in any part of the body politic, every thing was rotten except the hearts of the poorer people. Even at Cadiz Spanish writers compared the state to a vessel in a hurricane without captain, pilot, compass, chart sails or rudder, and advised the crew to cry to heaven as their sole resource. But they only blasphemed.

When Wellington, indignant at the systematic breach of his engagement, remonstrated, he was answered that the actual regency did not hold itself bound by the contracts of the former government. Hence it was plain no considerations of truth, for they had themselves also accepted the contract, nor of honest policy, nor the usages of civilized states with respect to national faith, had any influence on their conduct. Enraged at this scandalous subterfuge, he was yet conscious how essential it was he should retain his command. And seeing all Spanish generals more or less engaged in political intrigues, none capable of co-operating with him, and that no Spanish army could possibly subsist as a military body under the neglect and bad arrangement of the Spanish authorities, conscious also that public opinion in Spain would, better than the menaces of the English government, enable him to obtain a counterpoise to the democratic party, he tendered indeed his resignation if the government engagement was not fulfilled, but earnestly endeavoured by a due mixture of mildness argument and reproof to reduce the ruling authorities to reason. Nevertheless there were, he told them, limits to his forbearance to his submission under injury, and he had been already most unworthily treated, even as a gentleman, by the Spanish government.

From the world these quarrels were covered by an appearance of the utmost respect and honour. He was made a grandee of the first class, and the estate of Soto de Roma in Grenada, of which the much-maligned and miserable Prince of Peace had been despoiled, was settled upon him. He accepted the gift, but, as he had before done with his Portuguese and Spanish pay, transferred the proceeds to the public treasury during the war. The regents however, under the pressure of the Jacobins, and apparently bearing some personal enmity, although one of them, Ciscar, had been instrumental in procuring him the command of the Spanish army, were now intent to drive him from it; and the excesses committed at San Sebastian served their factious writers as a topic for exciting the people not only to demand his resignation, but to commence a warfare of assassination against the British soldiers. Moreover, combining extreme folly with wickedness, they pretended amongst other absurdities that the nobility had offered, if he would change his religion, to make him king of Spain. This tale was eagerly adopted by the English newspapers, and three Spanish grandees thought it necessary to declare that they were not among the nobles who made the proposition. His resignation was accepted in the latter end of September, and he held the command only until the assembling of the new Cortez, but the attempt to render him odious failed even at Cadiz, owing chiefly to the personal ascendancy which all great minds so surely attain over the masses in troubled times.　Both the people and the soldiers respected him more than they did their own government, and the Spanish officers had generally yielded as ready obedience to his wishes before he was appointed generalissimo, as they did to his orders when holding that high office.　It was this ascendancy which enabled him to maintain the war with such troublesome allies; and yet so little were the English ministers capable of appreciating its importance, that after the battle of Vittoria they entertained the design of removing him from Spain to take part in the German operations.　His answer was short and modest, but full of wisdom.

"Many might be found to conduct matters as well as I can both here and in Germany, but nobody would enjoy the same advantages here, and I should be no better than another in Germany."

The egregious folly which dictated this proposition was thus checked, and in December the new Cortez decided that he should retain the command of the armies and the regency be bound to fulfil its predecessor's engagements.　Nevertheless so deeply had he been offended by the libels relative to San Sebastian that a private letter to his brother terminated thus:—"*It will rest with the king's government to determine what they will do upon a consideration of all the circumstances of the case, but if I was to decide I would not keep the army in Spain for one hour.*"　And to many other persons at different times he expressed his fears and conviction that the cause was lost and that he should fail at last.　It was under these and other enormous difficulties he carried on his military operations.　It was with an enemy at his back more to be dreaded than the foe in his front that he invaded the south of France ; and that is the answer to those French writers who have described him as being at the head of more than two hundred thousand well-furnished soldiers, supported by a well-organized insurrection of the Spanish people, unembarrassed in his movements, and luxuriously rioting in all the resources of the Peninsula and of England.

BOOK XXIII.

CHAPTER I.

WAR IN THE SOUTH OF FRANCE.

WHILE Pampeluna held out, Soult laboured to complete his works of defence, especially the entrenched camp of St. Jean Pied de Port, that he might be free to change the theatre of war to Aragon. He pretended to entertain this project as late as November; but he must have secretly renounced all hope before that period, because the snows of an early and severe winter had rendered even the passes of the Lower Pyrenees impracticable in October. Meanwhile his political difficulties were not less than lord Wellington's, all his efforts to draw forth the resources of France were met with apathy, or secret hostility, and there was no money in the military chest to answer the common daily expenses. A junta of the leading merchants in Bayonne voluntarily provided for the most pressing necessities of the troops, but their means were limited and Soult vainly urged the merchants of Bordeaux and Toulouse to follow the patriotic example. It required therefore all his firmness of character to support the crisis; and if the English naval force had been sufficient to intercept the coasting vessels between Bordeaux and

Bayonne, the French army must have retired beyond the Adour. As it was, the greatest part of
the field artillery and all the cavalry were sent so
far to the rear for forage, that they could not be
counted a part of the fighting troops; and the infantry, in addition to their immense labours, were
forced to carry their own provisions from the
navigable points of the rivers to the top of the
mountains.

Soult was strongly affected. " *Tell the emperor,*"
he wrote to the minister of war, " *tell him when you
make your next report that on the very soil of France,
this is the situation of the army destined to defend
the southern provinces from invasion; tell him also
that the unheard-of contradictions and obstacles I
meet with shall not make me fail in my duty.*"

The French troops suffered much, but the privations of the allies were perhaps greater, for being on
higher mountains, more extended, more dependent
upon the sea, their distress was in proportion to
their distance from the coast. A much shorter line
had been indeed gained for the supply of the centre,
and a bridge was laid down at Andarlassa which
gave access to the roots of the Bayonette mountain, yet the troops were fed with difficulty ; and
so scantily, that lord Wellington in amends reduced
the usual stoppage of pay, and invoked the army
by its military honour to sustain with firmness the
unavoidable pressure. The effect was striking.
The murmurs, loud in the camps before, were
hushed instantly, although the soldiers knew that
some commissaries leaguing with the speculators
upon the coast, secretly loaded the provision mules
with condiments and other luxuries, to sell on the
mountains at enormous profit. The desertion was

however great, more than twelve hundred men went
over to the enemy in less than four months; and
they were all Germans, Englishmen or Spaniards,
for the Portuguese who abandoned their colours invariably went back to their own country.

This difficulty of feeding the Anglo-Portuguese,
the extreme distress of the Spaniards and the certainty that they would plunder in France and so
raise the people in arms, together with the uneasy
state of the political affairs in the Peninsula, rendered lord Wellington very averse to further offensive operations while Napoleon so tenaciously
maintained his positions on the Elbe against the
allied sovereigns. It was impossible to make a
formidable and sustained invasion of France with
the Anglo-Portuguese alone, and he had neither
money nor means of transport to feed the Spaniards,
even if policy warranted such a measure. The
nature of the country also forbad a decisive victory,
and hence an advance was attended with the risk
of returning to Spain again during the winter,
when a retreat would be dangerous and dishonouring.
But on the 20th of October a letter from the
governor of Pampeluna was intercepted, and lord
Fitzroy Somerset, observing that the compliment of
ceremony at the beginning was also in numerals,
ingeniously followed the cue and made out the
whole. It announced that the place could not hold
out more than a week, and as intelligence of Napoleon's disasters in Germany became known at the
same time, lord Wellington was induced to yield
once more to the wishes of the allied sovereigns and
the English ministers, who were earnest that he
should invade France.

His intent was to attack Soult's entrenched camp

on the 29th, thinking Pampeluna would fall before
that period. In this he was mistaken; and bad
weather stopped his movements, for in the passes
above Roncesvalles the troops were knee-deep in
snow. The preparations however continued and
strict precautions were taken to baffle the enemy's
emissaries. Soult was nevertheless perfectly informed by the deserters of the original design and the
cause of the delay; and he likewise obtained from
a serjeant-major of artillery who losing his road was
taken on the 29th, certain letters and orders indicating
an attack in the direction of the bridge of Amotz,
between D'Erlon's right and Clauzel's left. Some
French peasants also who had been allowed to pass
the allied outposts declared they had been closely
questioned about that bridge and the roads leading
to it. The defences there were therefore augmented with new redoubts and abbatis, and Soult
having thus as he judged, sufficiently provided for
its safety, and being in no pain for his right, nor
for Clauzel's position, covered as the latter was by
the smaller Rhune, turned his attention towards
Foy's corps.

That general had been posted at Bidarray, half
way between St. Jean Pied de Port and Cambo, to
watch certain roads, which leading to the Nive from
Val Baigorry by St. Martin d'Arosa, and from the
Bastan by Yspegui and the Gorospil mountain, gave
Soult anxiety for his left; but now expecting the principal attack at the bridge of Amotz, and not by these
roads, nor by St. Jean Pied de Port, as he at first
supposed and as lord Wellington had at one time
designed, he resolved to use Foy's division offensively. In this view on the 3d of November he
instructed him if St. Jean Pied de Port should be

only slightly attacked, to draw all the troops he
could possibly spare from its defence to Bidarray,
and when the allies assailed D'Erlon, he was to
seize the Gorospil mountain and fall upon their
right as they descended from the Puerto de Maya.
If on the other hand he was himself assailed by
those lines, he was to call in all his detached troops
from St. Jean Pied de Port, repass the Nive by the
bridge of Bidarray, make the best defence possible
behind that river, and open a communication with
Pierre Soult and Trielhard, whose divisions of cavalry
were at St. Palais and Orthes.

On the 6th Foy, thinking the Gorospil difficult
to pass, proposed to seize the Col de Yspegui from
the side of St. Jean Pied de Port, and so descend
into the Bastan. Soult however preferred Bidarray
as a safer point and more united with the main body
of the army; but he gave Foy a discretionary
power to march along the left of the Nive upon
Itzatzu and Espelette, if he judged it fitting to
reinforce D'Erlon's left rather than to attack the
enemy.

Having thus arranged his regular defence, the
French general directed the prefect of the Lower
Pyrenees to post the organized national guards at
the issues of all the valleys about St. Jean Pied de
Port, but to keep the mass of the people quiet until
the allies penetrating into the country should at
once provoke and offer facilities for an irregular
warfare.

On the 9th, being still uneasy about the San
Martin d'Arosa and Gorospil roads, he brought up
his brother's cavalry from St. Palais to the heights
above Cambo, and the next day the long-expected
storm burst.

Allured by some fine weather on the 6th and 7th
of November, lord Wellington had moved sir Rowland Hill's troops from the Roncesvalles to the Bastan with a view to attack Soult, leaving Mina on
the position of Altobiscar and in the Alduides.
The other corps had also received their orders, and
the battle was to commence on the 8th, but general
Freyre suddenly declared, that unable to subsist on
the mountains he must withdraw a part of his
troops. This was a scheme to obtain provisions
from the English magazines, and it was successful,
for the projected attack could not be made without
his aid. Forty thousand rations of flour with a
formal intimation that if he did not cooperate the
whole army must retire again into Spain, contented
Freyre for the moment ; but the extravagant abuses
of the Spanish commissariat were plainly exposed
when the chief of the staff declared that the flour
would only suffice for two days, although there were
less than ten thousand soldiers in the field. Spain
therefore furnished at the rate of two rations for
every fighting man and yet her troops were starving !

When this difficulty was surmounted heavy
rain caused the attack to be again deferred, but
on the 10th ninety thousand combatants of all Appendix,
7, No. 3.
arms and ranks above seventy-four thousand being
Anglo-Portuguese, descended to the battle, and
with them went ninety-five pieces of artillery, which
under the command of colonel Dickson were all
with inconceivable vigour and activity thrown into
action. Nor in this host do I reckon four thousand
five hundred cavalry, nor the Spaniards of the blockading division which remained in reserve. On the
other hand the French numbers were now increased
by the new levy of conscripts, but many had de-

BOOK
XXIII.
———
1813.
November

Appendix,
No. 8.
serted again into the interior, and the fighting men
did not exceed seventy-nine thousand including the
garrisons   Six thousand of these were cavalry, and
as Foy's operations were extraneous to the line of
defence scarcely sixty thousand infantry and artillery were opposed to the allies.

Lord Wellington seeing that the right of Soult's
line could not be forced without great loss, resolved
to hold it in check while he turned it by forcing the
centre and left, pushing down the Nivelle to San
Pé.   In this view the second and sixth British
division, Hamilton's Portuguese, Morillo's Spaniards,
four of Mina's battalions, and Grant's brigade of
light cavalry, in all twenty-six thousand fighting
men and officers with nine guns, were collected
under general Hill in the Bastan to attack D'Erlon.
The position of Roncesvalles was meanwhile occupied by the remainder of Mina's troops supported
by the blockading force under Carlos d'España.

The third fourth and seventh divisions, and
Giron's Andalusians, the whole under the command
of marshal Beresford, were disposed about Zagaramurdi, the Puerto de Echallar, and the lower parts
of those slopes of the greater Rhune which descended upon Sarre.   On the left of this body the
light division and Longa's Spaniards, both under
Charles Alten, were disposed on those slopes of the
greater Rhune which led down towards Ascain.
Victor Alten's brigade of light cavalry and three
British batteries, were placed on the road to Sarre,
and six mountain guns followed Giron's and Charles
Alten's troops.   Thus thirty-six thousand fighting
men and officers, with twenty-four guns, were concentrated in this quarter to attack Clauzel.

General Freyre's Spaniards, about nine thousand

strong, with six guns, were disposed on Alten's left,
at the fort of Calvary and towards Jollimont, ready
to fall upon any troops which might be detached
from the camp of Serres by the bridge of Ascain,
to support Clauzel.

General Hope having the first and fifth divisions,
Wilson's, Bradford's, and lord Aylmer's brigades of
infantry, Vandeleur's brigade of light dragoons, and
the heavy German cavalry, in all about nineteen
thousand men and officers with fifty-four guns, was
opposed to Soult's right wing; and the naval squadron hovering on Hope's left flank was to aid the
land operations.

On the French side each lieutenant-general had
a special position to defend. D'Erlon's first line,
its left resting on the fortified rocks of Mondarin
which could not be turned, run from thence along
the Choupera and Atchuleguy mountains by the
forge of Urdax to the Nivelle. This range was
strongly entrenched and occupied by one of Abbé's
and one of D'Armagnac's brigades, Espelette being
behind the former and Ainhoa behind the latter.
The second line or main position was several miles
distant on a broad ridge, behind Ainhoa, and it was
occupied by the remaining brigades of the two
divisions. The left did not extend beyond the
centre of the first line, but the right reaching to
the bridge of Amotz stretched with a wider flank,
because the Nivelle flowing in a slanting direction
towards the French gave greater space as their
positions receded. Three great redoubts were constructed in a line on this ridge, and a fourth had
been commenced close to the bridge.

On the right of D'Erlon's second line, that is to
say beyond the bridge of Amotz, Clauzel's position

extended to Ascain, also along a strong range of
heights fortified with many redoubts trenches and
abbatis, and as the Nivelle after passing Amotz
swept in a curve completely round the range to
Ascain, both flanks rested alike upon that river,
having communication by the bridges of Amotz and
Ascain on the right and left, and a retreat by the
bridges of San Pé and Harastagui which were in
rear of the centre. Two of Clauzel's divisions
reinforced by one of D'Erlon's under general Maransin were here posted. In front of the left were
the redoubts of St. Barbe and Grenada covering
the village and ridge of Sarre. In front of the
right was the smaller Rhune which was fortified
and occupied by a brigade of Maransin's division.
A new redoubt with abbatis was also commenced to
cover the approaches to the bridge of Amotz.

On the right of this line beyond the bridge of
Ascain, Daricau's division belonging to Clauzel's
corps, and the Italian brigade of San Pol drawn
from Villatte's reserve, were posted to hold the
entrenched camp of Serres and to connect Clauzel's
position with Villatte's, which was as I have before
said on a ridge crossing the gorges of Olette and
Jollimont. The French right wing under Reille,
strongly fortified on the lower ground and partially
covered by inundations, was nearly impregnable.

Soult's weakest point of general defence was
certainly the opening between the Rhune mountains and the Nivelle. Gradually narrowing as it
approached the bridge of Amotz this space was the
most open, the least fortified, and the Nivelle being
fordable above that bridge could not hamper the
allies' movements. Wherefore a powerful force acting
in this direction could pass by D'Erlon's first line

and breaking in upon the main position, between the right of that general's second line and Clauzel's left, turn both by the same attack.

Lord Wellington thus designed his battle. General Hill, leaving Mina's four battalions on the Gorospil mountain facing the rocks of Mondarin, moved in the night by the different passes of the Puerto de Maya, Morillo's Spaniards being to menace the French on the Choupera and Atchuleguy mountains, the second division to attack Ainhoa and Urdax. The sixth division and Hamilton's Portuguese were to assault the works covering the bridge of Amotz, either on the right or left bank of the Nivelle according to circumstances. Thus the action of twenty-six thousand men was combined against D'Erlon's position, and on their left Beresford's corps was assembled. The third division under general Colville, descending from Zagaramurdi, was to move against the unfinished redoubts and entrenchments covering the approaches to the bridge of Amotz on the left bank of the Nivelle, thus turning D'Erlon's right at the moment when it was attacked in front by Hill's corps. On the left of the third division, the seventh, descending from the mouth of the Echallar pass, was to storm the Grenada redoubt, and then passing the village of Sarre assail Clauzel's main position abreast with the attack of the third division. On the left of the seventh, the fourth division, assembling on the lower slopes of the greater Rhune, was to descend upon the redoubt of San Barbe, and then moving through Sarre also to assail Clauzel's main position abreast with the seventh division. On the left of the fourth division, Giron's Spaniards, gathered higher up on the flank of the great Rhune, were to move abreast

with the others leaving Sarre on their right.   They
were to drive the enemy from the lower slopes of
the smaller Rhune and then in concert with the rest
attack Clauzel's main position.   In this way Hill's
and Beresford's corps, forming a mass of more than
forty thousand infantry were to be thrust, on both
sides of the bridge of Amotz, between Clauzel and
D'Erlon to break their line of battle.

Charles Alten with the light division and Longa's
Spaniards, furnishing together about eight thousand
men, was likewise to attack Clauzel's line on the
left of Giron, while Freyre's Gallicians approached
the bridge of Ascain to prevent reinforcements
coming from the camp of Serres.   But ere Alten
could assail Clauzel's right the smaller Rhune which
covered it was to be stormed.   This mountain outwork was a hog's-back ridge rising abruptly out of
table-land and parallel with the greater Rhune.   It
was inaccessible along its front, which was precipitous and from fifty to two hundred feet high;
but on the enemy's left these rocks gradually de-
creased, descending by a long slope to the valley
of Sarre, and about two-thirds of the way down
the thirty-fourth French regiment was placed, with
an advanced post on some isolated crags situated
in the hollow between the two Rhunes.   On the
enemy's right the hog's-back sunk by degrees into
the plain or platform.   It was however covered at
that point by a marsh scarcely passable, and the
attacking troops were therefore first to move up
against the perpendicular rocks in front, and then to
file to their left under fire, between the marsh and
the lower crags, until they gained an accessible
point from whence they could fight their way along
the narrow ridge of the hog's-back.   But the

bristles of the latter were huge perpendicular crags connected with walls of loose stones so as to form several small forts or castles communicating with each other by narrow foot-ways, and rising one above another until the culminant point was attained. The table-land beyond this ridge was extensive and terminated in a very deep ravine on every side, save a narrow space on the right of the marsh, where the enemy had drawn a traverse of loose stones, running perpendicularly from behind the hog's-back and ending in a star fort which overhung the edge of the ravine.

This rampart and fort, and the hog's back itself, were defended by Barbot's brigade of Maransin's division, and the line of retreat was towards a low narrow neck of land, which bridging the deep ravine linked the Rhune to Clauzel's main position: a reserve was placed here, partly to sustain the thirty-fourth French regiment posted on the slope of the mountain towards Sarre, partly to protect the neck of land on the side of that village. As this neck was the only approach to the French position in that part, to storm the smaller Rhune was a necessary preliminary to the general battle, wherefore Alten, filing his troops after dark on the 9th from the Hermitage, the Commissary mountain, and the Puerto de Vera, collected them at midnight on that slope of the greater Rhune which descended towards Ascain. The main body of the light division, turning the marsh by the left, was to assail the stone traverse and lap over the star fort by the ravine beyond; Longa, stretching still farther on the left, was to turn the smaller Rhune altogether; and the forty-third regiment supported by the seventeenth Portuguese was to assail the hog's back.

One battalion of riflemen and the mountain-guns were however left on the summit of the greater Rhune, with orders to assail the craggy post between the Rhunes and connect Alten's attack with that of Giron's Spaniards. All these troops gained their respective stations so secretly that the enemy had no suspicion of their presence, although for several hours the columns were lying within half musket-shot of the works. Towards morning indeed five or six guns, fired in a hurried manner from the low ground near the sea, broke the stillness, but the French on the Rhune remained quiet, and the British troops awaited the rising of the sun when three guns fired from the Atchubia mountain were to give the signal of attack.

BATTLE OF THE NIVELLE.

The day broke with great splendour, and as the first ray of light played on the summit of the lofty Atchubia the signal guns were fired in rapid succession from its summit. The soldiers instantly leaped up, and the French beheld with astonishment several columns rushing forward from the flank of the great Rhune. Running to their defences with much tumult they opened a few pieces, which were answered from the top of the greater Rhune by the mountain-artillery, and at the same moment two companies of the forty-third were detached to cross the marsh if possible, and keep down the enemy's fire from the lower part of the hog's back. The action being thus commenced the remainder of the regiment, formed partly in line partly in a column of reserve, turned the marsh by the right and advanced against the high rocks. From these crags the French shot fast and thickly, but the quick

even movement of the British line deceived their
aim, and the soldiers, running forward very swiftly
though the ground was rough, turned suddenly
between the rocks and the marsh, and were immediately joined by the two companies which had passed
that obstacle notwithstanding its depth.   Then all
together jumped into the lower works, but the men
exhausted by their exertions, for they had passed
over half a mile of very difficult ground with a wonderful speed, remained for a few minutes inactive
within half pistol-shot of the first stone castle from
whence came a sharp and biting musketry.   When
they had recovered breath they arose and with a
stern shout commenced the assault.

The defenders were as numerous as the assailants,
and for six weeks they had been labouring on their
well-contrived castles; but strong and valiant in arms
must the soldiers have been who stood in that hour
before the veterans of the forty-third.   One French
grenadier officer only dared to sustain the rush.
Standing alone on the high wall of the first castle and
flinging large stones with both his hands, a noble
figure, he fought to the last and fell, while his men
shrinking on each side sought safety among the rocks
on his flanks. Close and confused then was the action,
man met man at every turn, but with a rattling fire
of musketry, sometimes struggling in the intricate
narrow paths sometimes climbing the loose stone
walls, the British soldiers won their desperate way
until they had carried the second castle, called by
the French the place of arms, and the magpie's nest,
because of a lofty pillar of rock which rose above
it and on which a few marksmen were perched.
From these points the defenders were driven into
their last castle, which being higher and larger

than the others and covered by a natural ditch or cleft in the rocks, fifteen feet deep, was called the Donjon. Here they made a stand, and the assailants, having advanced so far as to look into the rear of the rampart and star fort on the table-land below, suspended the vehement throng of their attack for a while, partly to gather a head for storming the Donjon, partly to fire on the enemy beneath them, who were now warmly engaged with the two battalions of riflemen, the Portuguese Caçadores, and the seventeenth Portuguese. This last regiment was to have followed the forty-third but seeing how rapidly and surely the latter were carrying the rocks, had moved at once against the traverse on the other side of the marsh; and very soon the French defending the rampart, being thus pressed in front, and warned by the direction of the fire that they were turned on the ridge above, seeing also the fifty-second, forming the extreme left of the division, now emerging from the deep ravine beyond the star fort on the other flank, abandoned their works. Then the forty-third gathering a strong head stormed the Donjon. Some leaped with a shout down the deep cleft in the rock, others turned it by the narrow paths on each flank, and the enemy abandoned the loose walls at the moment they were being scaled. Thus in twenty minutes six hundred old soldiers were hustled out of this labyrinth; yet not so easily but that the victors lost eleven officers and sixty-seven men.

The whole mountain was now cleared of the French, for the riflemen dropping perpendicularly down from the greater Rhune upon the post of crags in the hollow between the Rhunes seized it with small loss; but they were ill-seconded by

Giron's Spaniards and were hardly handled by the thirty-fourth French regiment, which maintaining its post on the slope, covered the flight of the confused crowd which came rushing down the mountain behind them towards the neck of land leading to the main position. At that point they all rallied and seemed inclined to renew the action, but after some hesitation continued their retreat. This favourable moment for a decisive stroke had been looked for by the commander of the forty-third, but the officer entrusted with the reserve companies of the regiment had thrown them needlessly into the fight, thus rendering it impossible to collect a body strong enough to assail such a heavy mass.

The contest at the stone rampart and star fort, being shortened by the rapid success on the hog's back, was not very severe, but general Kempt, always conspicuous for his valour, was severely wounded, nevertheless he did not quit the field and soon reformed his brigade on the platform he had thus so gallantly won. Meanwhile the fifty-second having turned the position by the ravine was now approaching the enemy's line of retreat, when general Alten, following his instructions, halted the division partly in the ravine itself to the left of the neck, partly on the table-land, and during this action Longa's Spaniards having got near Ascain were in connection with Freyre's Gallicians. In this position with the enemy now and then cannonading Longa's people and the troops in the ravine, Alten awaited the progress of the army on his right, for the columns there had a long way to march and it was essential to regulate the movements.

The signal-guns from the Atchubia which sent the light division against the Rhune, had also put

the fourth and seventh divisions in movement against
the redoubts of San Barbe and Grenada. Eighteen
guns were immediately placed in battery against
the former, and while they poured their stream of
shot the troops advanced with scaling ladders and
the skirmishers of the fourth division got into the
rear of the work, whereupon the French leaped out
and fled. Ross's battery of horse artillery galloping to a rising ground in rear of the Grenada
fort drove the enemy from there also, and then the
fourth and seventh divisions carried the village of
Sarre and the position beyond it and advanced to the
attack of Clauzel's main position.

It was now eight o'clock and from the smaller
Rhune a splendid spectacle of war opened upon the
view. On one hand the ships of war slowly sailing to
and fro were exchanging shots with the fort of Socoa;
Hope menacing all the French lines in the low ground
sent the sound of a hundred pieces of artillery
bellowing up the rocks, and they were answered by
nearly as many from the tops of the mountains.
On the other hand the summit of the great Atchu-
bía was just lighted by the rising sun, and fifty
thousand men rushing down its enormous slopes
with ringing shouts, seemed to chase the receding
shadows into the deep valley. The plains of France
so long overlooked from the towering crags of the
Pyrenees were to be the prize of battle, and the half-
famished soldiers in their fury, broke through the
iron barrier erected by Soult as if it were but a
screen of reeds.

The principal action was on a space of seven or
eight miles, but the skirts of battle spread wide,
and in no point had the combinations failed. Far
on the right general Hill after a long and difficult

night march had got within reach of the enemy a
little before seven o'clock. Opposing Morillo's and

Mina's Spaniards to Abbé's troops on the Mondarain
and Atchuleguy rocks, he directed the second division against D'Armagnac's brigade and brushed it
back from the forge of Urdax and the village of
Ainhoa. Meanwhile the aid of the sixth division
and Hamilton's Portuguese being demanded by him,
they passed the Nivelle lower down and bent their
march along the right bank towards the bridge of
Amotz. Thus while Mina's battalion and Morillo's
division kept Abbé in check on the mountains, the
three Anglo-Portuguese divisions, marching left
flank in advance, approached D'Erlon's second position, but the country being very rugged it was
eleven o'clock before they got within cannon-shot of
the French redoubts. Each of these contained five
hundred men, and they were placed along the summit of a high ridge which being thickly clothed
with bushes, and covered by a deep ravine was
very difficult to attack. However general Clinton,
leading the sixth division on the extreme left, turned
this ravine and drove the enemy from the works
covering the approaches to the bridge, after which
wheeling to his right he advanced against the nearest redoubt, and the garrison not daring to await
the assault abandoned it. Then the Portuguese
division passing the ravine and marching on the right
of the sixth menaced the second redoubt, and the
second division in like manner approached the third
redoubt. D'Armagnac's troops now set fire to their
hutted camp and retreated to Helbacen de Borda
behind San Pé, pursued by the sixth division. Abbé's
second brigade forming the French left was separated by a ravine from D'Armagnac's ground, but

hé also after some hesitation retreated towards Espelette and Cambo, where his other brigade, which
had meanwhile fallen back from the Mondarain
before Morillo, rejoined him.

It was the progress of the battle on the left of
the Nive that rendered D'Erlon's defence so feeble.
After the fall of the St. Barbe and Grenada redoubts Conroux's right and centre endeavoured to
defend the village and heights of Sarre; but while
the fourth and seventh divisions, aided by the ninety-
fourth regiment detached from the third division, attacked and carried those points, the third division
being on their right and less opposed pushed rapidly
towards the bridge of Amotz, forming in conjunction
with the sixth division the narrow end of the wedge
into which Beresford's and Hill's corps were now
thrown. The French were thus driven from all their
new unfinished works covering the approaches to that
bridge on both sides of the Nivelle, and Conroux's
division, spreading from Sarre to Amotz, was broken
by superior numbers at every point. That general
indeed vigorously defended the old works around
the bridge itself, but he soon fell mortally wounded,
his troops were again broken, and the third division
seized the bridge and established itself on the
heights between that structure and the redoubt of
Louis the XIV. which having been also lately commenced was unfinished. This happened about eleven o'clock and D'Erlon fearing to be cut off from
St. Pé yielded as we have seen at once to the
attack of the sixth division, and at the same time the
remainder of Conroux's troops fell back in disorder
from Sarre, closely pursued by the fourth and
seventh divisions, which were immediately established on the left of the third. Thus the com-

munication between Clauzel and D'Erlon was cut, the left flank of one and the right flank of the other broken, and a direct communication between Hill and Beresford secured by the same blow,

D'Erlon abandoned his position, but Clauzel stood firm with Taupin's and Maransin's divisions. The latter now completed by the return of Barbot's brigade from the smaller Rhune, occupied the re- doubt of Louis the XIV. and supported with eight field-pieces attempted to cover the flight of Con- roux's troops. The guns opened briskly but they were silenced by Ross's battery of horse artillery, the only one which had surmounted the difficulties of the ground after passing Sarre, the infantry were then assailed, in front by the fourth and se- venth divisions, in flank by the third division, the redoubt of Louis XIV. was stormed, the garri- son bayonetted, Conroux's men continued to fly, Maransin's after a stiff combat were cast headlong into the ravines behind their position, and Maran- sin himself was taken but escaped in the confusion. Giron's Spaniards now came up on the left of the fourth division, somewhat late however, and after having abandoned the riflemen on the lower slopes of the smaller Rhune.

On the French side Taupin's division and a large body of conscripts forming Clauzel's right wing still remained to fight. The left rested on a large work called the signal redoubt, which had no ar- tillery but overlooked the whole position ; the right was covered by two redoubts overhanging a ravine which separated them from the camp of Serres, and some works in the ravine itself protected the commu- nication by the bridge of Ascain. Behind the signal redoubt, on a ridge crossing the road to San Pé and

along which Maransin and Conroux's beaten divisions were now flying in disorder, there was another
work called the redoubt of Harastaguia, and Clauzel
thinking he might still dispute the victory, if his
reserve division, posted in the camp of Serres,
could come to his aid, drew the thirty-first French
regiment from Taupin, and posted it in front of
this redoubt of Harastaguia. His object was to
rally Maransin's and Conroux's troops there and so
form a new line, the left on the Harastaguia, the
right on the signal redoubt, into which last he threw
six hundred of the eighty-eighth regiment. In this
position having a retreat by the bridge of Ascain
he resolved to renew the battle, but his plan failed
at the moment of conception, because Taupin could
not stand before the light division which was now
again in full action.

About half-past nine, general Alten, seeing the
whole of the columns on his right, as far as the eye
could reach, well engaged with the enemy, had
crossed the low neck of land in his front. It was
first passed by the fifty-second regiment with a
rapid pace and a very narrow front, under a destructive cannonade and fire of musketry from the
entrenchments which covered the side of the opposite mountain ; a road coming from Ascain by the
ravine led up the position, and as the fifty-second
pushed their attack along it the enemy abandoned
his entrenchments on each side, and forsook even
his crowning works above. This formidable regiment
was followed by the remainder of Alten's troops,
and Taupin, though his division was weak from its
losses on the 7th of October and now still further
diminished by the absence of the thirty-first regiment, awaited the assault above, being supported

by the conscripts drawn up in his rear. But at CHAP. I. this time Longa, having turned the smaller Rhune, approached Ascain, and being joined by part of Freyre's troops their skirmishers opened a distant musketry against the works covering that bridge on Taupin's right; a panic immediately seized the French, the seventieth regiment abandoned the two redoubts above, and the conscripts were withdrawn. Clauzel ordered Taupin to retake the forts but this only added to the disorder, the seventieth regiment instead of facing about disbanded entirely and were not reassembled until next day. There remained only four regiments unbroken, one, the eighty-eighth, was in the signal redoubt, two under Taupin in person kept together in rear of the works on the right, and the thirty-first covered the fort of Harastaguia now the only line of retreat.

1813. November

Clauzel's Official Report to Soult, MSS.

Taupin's Official Report, MSS.

In this emergency, Clauzel, anxious to bring off the eighty-eighth regiment, ordered Taupin to charge on one side of the signal redoubt, intending to do the same himself on the other at the head of the thirty-first regiment; but the latter was now vigorously attacked by the Portuguese of the seventh division, and the fourth division was rapidly interposing between that regiment and the signal redoubt. Moreover Alten previous to this had directed the forty-third, preceded by Barnard's riflemen, to turn at the distance of musquet shot the right flank of the signal redoubt, wherefore Taupin instead of charging, was himself charged in front by the riflemen, and being menaced at the same time in flank by the fourth division, retreated, closely pursued by Barnard until that intrepid officer fell dangerously wounded. During this struggle the seventh division broke the thirty-first, the

rout was complete; the French fled to the different
bridges over the Nivelle and the signal redoubt
was left to its fate.

This formidable work barred the way of the
light division, but it was of no value to the defence
when the forts on its flanks were abandoned.
Colborne approached it in front with the fifty-
second regiment, Giron's Spaniards menaced it on
Colborne's right, the fourth division was passing to
its rear, and Kempt's brigade was as we have seen
turning it on the left. Colborne whose military
judgment was seldom at fault, halted under the
brow of the conical hill on which the work was
situated, but some of Giron's Spaniards making a
vaunting though feeble demonstration of attacking
it on his right were beaten back, and at that moment
a staff-officer without warrant, for general Alten on
the spot assured the Author of this History that he
sent no such order, rode up and directed Colborne
to advance. It was not a moment for remonstrance
and his troops covered by the steepness of the hill
reached the flat top which was about forty yards
across to the redoubt; then they made their rush,
but a wide ditch, thirty feet deep well fraised and
pallisaded, stopped them short, and the fire of the
enemy stretched all the foremost men dead. The
intrepid Colborne, escaping miraculously for he was
always at the head and on horseback, immediately
led the regiment under cover of the brow to another
point, and thinking to take the French unawares made
another rush, yet with the same result. At three
different places did he rise to the surface in this
manner, and each time the French fire swept away the
head of his column. Resorting then to persuasion
he held out a white handkerchief and summoned the

commandant, pointing out to him how his work was surrounded and how hopeless his defence, whereupon the garrison yielded having had only one man killed, whereas on the British side there fell two hundred soldiers of a regiment never surpassed in arms since arms were first borne by men.

During this affair Clauzel's divisions had crossed the Nivelle in great disorder, Maransin's and Conroux's troops near San Pé, the thirty-first regiment at Harastaguia, Taupin between that place and the bridge of Serres. They were pursued by the third and seventh divisions, and the skirmishers of the former crossing by Amotz and a bridge above San Pé entered that place while the French were in the act of passing the river below. It was now past two o'clock, Conroux's troops pushed on to Helbacen de Borda, a fortified position on the road from San Pé to Bayonne, where they were joined by Taupin and by D'Erlon with D'Armagnac's division, but Clauzel rallied Maransin's men and took post on some heights immediately above San Pé. Meanwhile Soult had hurried from St. Jean de Luz to the camp of Serres with all his reserve artillery and spare troops to menace the allies' left flank by Ascain, and Wellington thereupon halted the fourth and light divisions, and Giron's Spaniards, on the reverse slopes of Clauzel's original position, facing the camp of Serres, waiting until the sixth division, then following D'Armagnac's retreat on the right of the Nivelle, was well advanced. When he was assured of Clinton's progress he crossed the Nivelle with the third and seventh divisions and drove Maransin from his new position after a hard struggle, in which general Inglis was wounded and the fifty-

first and sixty-eighth regiments handled very roughly.
This ended the battle in the centre, for darkness was
coming on and the troops were exhausted, especially
the sixth division which had been marching or
fighting for twenty-four hours. However three divisions were firmly established in rear of Soult's right
wing of whose operations it is now time to treat.

In front of Reille's entrenchments were two advanced positions, the camp of the Sans Culottes on
the right, the Bons Secours in the centre covering
Urogne. The first had been attacked and carried
early in the morning by the fifth division, which
advanced to the inundation covering the heights of
Bordegain and Ciboure. The second after a short
cannonade was taken by Halket's Germans and the
guards, and immediately afterwards the eighty-fifth
regiment, of lord Aylmer's brigade, drove a French
battalion out of Urogne. The first division, being
on the right, then menaced the camp of Belchena,
and the German skirmishers passed a small stream
covering this part of the line, but they were driven
back by the enemy whose musketry and cannonade
were brisk along the whole front. Meanwhile
Freyre, advancing in two columns from Jollimont
and the Calvaire on the right of the first division,
placed eight guns in battery against the Nassau
redoubt, a large work constructed on the ridge
occupied by Villate to cover the approaches to Ascain.
The Spaniards were here opposed by their own
countrymen under Casa Palacio who commanded
the remains of Joseph's Spanish guards, and during
the fight general Freyre's skirmishers on the right
united with Longa's men. Thus a kind of false
battle was maintained along the whole line to the
sea until nightfall, with equal loss of men but

great advantage to the allies, because it entirely occupied Reille's two divisions and Villatte's
reserve, and prevented the troops in the camp of
Serres from passing by the bridge of Ascain to aid
Clauzel, who was thus overpowered. When that
event happened and lord Wellington had passed the
Nivelle at San Pé, Daricau and the Italian brigade
withdrew from Serres, and Villatte's reserve occupied it, whereupon Freyre and Longa entered the
town of Ascain. Villatte however held the camp
above until Reille had withdrawn into St. Jean de
Luz and destroyed all the bridges on the Lower
Nivelle; when that was effected the whole retired
and at daybreak reached the heights of Bidart on
the road to Bayonne.

During the night the allies halted on the position
they had gained in the centre, but an accidental
conflagration catching a wood completely separated
the picquets towards Ascain from the main body,
and spreading far and wide over the heath lighted
up all the hills, a blazing sign of war to France.

On the 11th the army advanced in order of
battle. Sir John Hope on the left, forded the
river above St. Jean de Luz with his infantry, and
marched on Bidart. Marshal Beresford in the
centre moved by the roads leading upon Arbonne.
General Hill, communicating by his right with
Morillo who was on the rocks of Mondarain,
brought his left forward into communication with
Beresford, and with his centre took possesion of
Suraide and Espelette facing towards Cambo. The
time required to restore the bridges for the artillery
at Ciboure, and the change of front on the right
rendered these movements slow, and gave the duke
of Dalmatia time to rally his army upon a third

line of fortified camps which he had previously
commenced, the right resting on the coast at Bidart,
the centre at Helbacen Borda, the left at Ustaritz
on the Nive. This front was about eight miles, but
the works were only slightly advanced and Soult
dreading a second battle on so wide a field drew
back his centre and left to Arbonne and Arauntz,
broke down the bridges on the Nive at Ustaritz, and
at two o'clock a slight skirmish, commenced by the
allies in the centre, closed the day's proceedings.
The next morning the French retired to the ridge
of Beyris, having their right in advance at Anglet
and their left in the entrenched camp of Bayonne
near Marac. During this movement a dense fog
arrested the allies, but when the day cleared sir John
Hope took post at Bidart on the left, and Beresford
occupied Ahetze, Arbonne, and the hill of San Barbe,
in the centre. General Hill endeavoured to pass
the fords and restore the broken bridges of Ustaritz
and he also made a demonstration against the works
at Cambo, but the rain which fell heavily in the
mountains on the 11th rendered the fords impassable
and both points were defended successfully by Foy
whose operations had been distinct from the rest.

In the night of the 9th D'Erlon, mistrusting the
strength of his own position, had sent that general
orders to march from Bidaray to Espelette, but the
messenger did not arrive in time and on the morning of the 10th about eleven o'clock Foy, following
Soult's previous instructions, drove Mina's battalions from the Gorospil mountain; then pressing
against the flank of Morillo he forced him also back
fighting to the Puerto de Maya. However D'Erlon's
battle was at this period receding fast, and Foy
fearing to be cut off retired with the loss of a colonel

and one hundred and fifty men, having however taken a quantity of baggage and a hundred prisoners. Continuing his retreat all night he reached Cambo and Ustaritz on the 11th, just in time to relieve Abbé's division at those posts, and on the 12th defended them against general Hill. Such were the principal circumstances of the battle of the Nivelle, whereby Soult was driven from a mountain position which he had been fortifying for three months. He lost four thousand two hundred and sixty-five men and officers including twelve or fourteen hundred prisoners, and one general was killed. His field-magazines at St. Jean de Luz and Espelette fell into the hands of the victors, and fifty-one pieces of artillery were taken, the greater part having been abandoned in the redoubts of the low country to sir John Hope. The allies had two generals, Kempt and Byng, wounded, and they lost two thousand six hundred and ninety-four men and officers.

OBSERVATIONS.

1°. Soult fared in this battle as most generals will who seek by extensive lines to supply the want of numbers or of hardiness in the troops. Against rude commanders and undisciplined soldiers lines may avail, seldom against accomplished generals, never when the assailants are the better soldiers. Cæsar at Alesia resisted the Gauls, but his lines served him not at Dyrrachium against Pompey. Crassus failed in Calabria against Spartacus, and in modern times the duke of Marlborough broke through all the French lines in Flanders. If Wel-

lington triumphed at Torres Vedras it was perhaps
because his lines were not attacked, and, it may be,
Soult was seduced by that example. His works
were almost as gigantic and upon the same plan,
that is to say a river on one flank, the ocean on the
other, and the front upon mountains covered with
redoubts and partially protected by inundations.
But the duke of Dalmatia had only three months to
complete his system, his labours were under the
gaze of his enemy, his troops, twice defeated during
the execution, were inferior in confidence and numbers to the assailants. Lord Wellington's lines at
Torres Vedras had been laboured for a whole year.
Massena only knew of them when they stopped his
progress, and his army inferior in numbers had
been repulsed in the recent battle of Busaco.

It is not meant by this to decry entrenched
camps within compass, and around which an
active army moves as on a pivot, delivering or
avoiding battle according to circumstances. The
objection applies only to those extensive covering
lines by which soldiers are taught to consider themselves inferior in strength and courage to their
enemies. A general is thus precluded from shewing
himself at important points and at critical periods;
he is unable to encourage his troops or to correct
errors; his sudden resources and the combinations
of genius are excluded by the necessity of adhering
to the works, while the assailants may make whatever dispositions they like, menace every point
and select where to break through. The defenders,
seeing large masses directed against them and unable to draw confidence from a like display of numbers, become fearful, knowing there must be some
weak point which is the measure of strength for the

whole. The assailants fall on with that heat
and vehemence which belongs to those who act
voluntarily and on the offensive; each mass strives
to outdo those on its right and left, and failure is
only a repulse, whereas the assailed having no resource but victory look to their flanks, and are more
anxious about their neighbours' fighting than their
own.

All these disadvantages were experienced at the
battle of the Nivelle. D'Erlon attributed his defeat
to the loss of the bridge of Amotz by Conroux's
division, and to this cause also Maransin traced his
misfortunes. Taupin laid his defeat at Maran-
sin's door, but Clauzel on the other hand ascribed it Official
Reports of
at once to want of firmness in the troops, although the French
generals to
he also asserted that if Daricau's division had come Soult,
MSS.
to his aid from the camp of Serres, he would have
maintained his ground. Soult however traced
Clauzel's defeat to injudicious measures. That ge- Soult's
Official
neral he said attempted to defend the village of Sarre Report to
the Minis-
after the redoubts of San Barbe and Grenada were ter of War,
MSS.
carried, whereby Conroux's division was overwhelmed
in detail and driven back in flight to Amotz. Clauzel
should rather have assembled his three divisions at
once in the main position which was his battle-
ground, and there, covered by the smaller Rhune,
ought to have been victorious. It was scarcely
credible he observed that such entrenchments as
Clauzel's and D'Erlon's should have been carried.
For his part he relied on their strength so confidently as to think the allies must sacrifice twenty-
five thousand men to force them and perhaps fail
then. He had been on the right when the battle
began, no reports came to him, he could judge of
events only by the fire, and when he reached the

camp of Serres with his reserve troops and
artillery Clauzel's works were lost! His arrival
had however paralyzed the march of three divisions. This was true, yet there seems some
foundation for Clauzel's complaint, namely, that he
had for five hours fought on his main position, and
during that time no help had come, although the
camp of Serres was close at hand, the distance
from St. Jean de Luz to that place only four miles,
and the attack in the low ground evidently a feint.
This then was Soult's error. He suffered sir John
Hope to hold in play twenty-five thousand men in
the low ground, while fifteen thousand under
Clauzel lost the battle on the hills.

2º. The French army was inferior in numbers
and many of the works were unfinished ; and yet two
strong divisions, Daricau's and Foy's, were quite
thrown out of the fight, for the slight offensive
movement made by the latter produced no effect
whatever. Vigorous counter-attacks are no doubt
essential to a good defence, and it was in allusion
to this that Napoleon, speaking of Joseph's position
behind the Ebro in the beginning of the war, said,
" if a river were as broad and rapid as the Danube
it would be nothing without secure points for passing to the offensive." The same maxim applies to
lines, and Soult grandly conceived and applied this
principle when he proposed the descent upon
Aragon to Suchet. But he conceived it meanly
and poorly when he ordered Foy to attack by the
Gorospil mountain. That general's numbers were
too few, and the direction of the march false ; one
regiment in the field of battle at the decisive moment
would have been worth three on a distant and secondary point. Foy's retreat was inevitable if

D'Erlon failed, and wanting the other's aid he did
fail. What success could Foy obtain? He might
have driven Mina's battalions over the Puerto de
Maya and quite through the Bastan ; he might have
defeated Morillo and perhaps have taken general
Hill's baggage ; yet all this would have weighed
little against the allies' success at Amotz ; and the
deeper he penetrated the more difficult would
have been his retreat. The incursion into the Bastan by Yspegui proposed by him on the 6th, although properly rejected by Soult would probably
have produced greater effects than the one executed
by Gorospil on the 10th. A surprise on the 6th,
Hill's troops being then in march by brigades
through the Alduides, might have brought some
advantages to the French, and perhaps delayed the
general attack beyond the 10th, when the heavy
rains which set in on the 11th would have rendered
it difficult to attack at all : Soult would thus have
had time to complete his works.

3°. It has been observed that a minor cause of
defeat was the drawing up of the French troops in
front instead of in rear of the redoubts. This may
possibly have happened in some places from error
and confusion, not by design, for Clauzel's report
expressly states that Maransin was directed to form
in rear of the redoubts and charge the allies when
they were between the works and the abbatis. It
is however needless to pry closely into these matters when the true cause lies broad on the surface.
Lord Wellington directed superior numbers with
superior skill. The following analysis will prove
this, but it must be remembered that the conscripts
are not included in the enumeration of the French

force : being quite undisciplined they were kept in masses behind and never engaged.

Abbé's division, furnishing five thousand old soldiers, was posted in two lines one behind the other, and they were both paralyzed by the position of Morillo's division and Mina's battalions. Foy's division was entirely occupied by the same troops. Six thousand of Wellington's worst soldiers therefore sufficed to employ twelve thousand of Soult's best troops during the whole day. Meanwhile Hill fell upon the decisive point where there was only D'Armagnac's division to oppose him, that is to say, five thousand against twenty thousand. And while the battle was secured on the right of the Nivelle by this disproportion, Beresford on the other bank thrust twenty-four thousand against the ten thousand composing Conroux's and Maransin's divisions. Moreover as Hill and Beresford, advancing, the one from his left the other from his right, formed a wedge towards the bridge of Amotz, forty-four thousand men composing the six divisions under those generals, fell upon the fifteen thousand composing the divisions of D'Armagnac Conroux and Maransin ; and these last were also attacked in detail, because part of Conroux's troops were defeated near Sarre, and Barbot's brigade of Maransin's corps was beaten on the Rhune by the light division before the main position was attacked. Finally Alten with eight thousand men, having first defeated Barbot's brigade, fell upon Taupin who had only three thousand while the rest of the French army was held in check by Freyre and Hope. Thus more than fifty thousand troops full of confidence from repeated victories were suddenly thrown upon the decisive point where there were only eighteen thousand dispirited by previous reverses to oppose them. Against such a thunderbolt there was no defence in the French works. Was it then a simple matter for Wellington so to combine his battle? The mountains on whose huge flanks he gathered his fierce soldiers, the roads he opened, the horrid crags he surmounted, the headlong steeps he descended, the wild regions through which he poured the destructive fire of more than ninety guns, these and the reputation of the French commander furnish the everlasting reply.

And yet he did not compass all that he designed. The French right escaped, because when he passed the Nivelle at San Pé he had only two divisions in hand, the sixth had not come up, three were in observation of the camp at Serres, and before he could assemble enough men to descend upon the enemy in the low ground the day had closed. The great object of the battle was therefore unattained, and it may be a question, seeing the shortness of the days and the difficulty of the roads were not unexpected obstacles, whether the combinations would not have been surer if the principal attack had been directed entirely against Clauzel's position. Carlos D'España's force and the remainder of Mina's battalions could have reinforced Morillo's division with five thousand men to occupy D'Erlon's attention; it was not essential to defeat him, for though he attributed his retreat to Clauzel's reverse that general did not complain that D'Erlon's retreat endangered his position. This arrangement would have enabled the rest of Hill's troops to reinforce Beresford and have given lord Wellington three

additional divisions in hand with which to cross the
Nivelle before two o'clock. Soult's right wing
could not then have escaped.

4°. In the report of the battle lord Wellington
from some oversight did but scant and tardy justice
to the light division. Acting alone, for Longa's
Spaniards went off towards Ascain and scarcely
fired a shot, this division furnishing only four thousand seven hundred men and officers, first carried
the smaller Rhune defended by Barbot's brigade,
and then beat Taupin's division from the main
position, thus driving superior numbers from the
strongest works. In fine being less than one-sixth
of the whole force employed against Clauzel, they
defeated one-third of that general's corps. Many
brave men they lost, and of two who fell in this
battle I will speak.

The first, low in rank for he was but a lieutenant,
rich in honour for he bore many scars, was young
of days. He was only nineteen. But he had
seen more combats and sieges than he could
count years. So slight in person, and of such
surpassing and delicate beauty that the Spaniards
often thought him a girl disguised in man's clothing,
he was yet so vigorous, so active, so brave, that
the most daring and experienced veterans watched
his looks on the field of battle, and implicitly
following where he led, would like children obey his
slightest sign in the most difficult situations. His
education was incomplete, yet were his natural
powers so happy, the keenest and best-furnished in-
tellects shrunk from an encounter of wit, and every
thought and aspiration was proud and noble, indicating future greatness if destiny had so willed it.

Such was Edward Freer of the forty-third one of
three brothers who covered with wounds have all
died in the service. Assailed the night before the
battle with that strange anticipation of coming
death so often felt by military men, he was pierced
with three balls at the first storming of the Rhune
rocks, and the sternest soldiers in the regiment
wept even in the middle of the fight when they
heard of his fate.

On the same day and at the same hour was killed
colonel Thomas Lloyd. He likewise had been a
long time in the forty-third. Under him Freer had
learned the rudiments of his profession, but in the
course of the war promotion placed Lloyd at the
head of the ninety-fourth, and it was leading that
regiment he fell. In him also were combined
mental and bodily powers of no ordinary kind.
A graceful symmetry combined with Herculean
strength, and a countenance at once frank and
majestic gave the true index of his nature, for his
capacity was great and commanding, and his military knowledge extensive both from experience and
study. On his mirth and wit, so well known in the
army, I will not dwell, save to remark, that he used
the latter without offence, yet so as to increase his
ascendancy over those with whom he held intercourse, for though gentle he was valiant, ambitious,
and conscious of his fitness for great exploits. He
like Freer was prescient of, and predicted his
own fall, yet with no abatement of courage. When
he received the mortal wound, a most painful one,
he would not suffer himself to be moved but
remained watching the battle and making observations upon the changes in it until death came. It
was thus at the age of thirty, that the good the

BOOK
XXIII.

1813.
November
Welling-
ton's Des-
patches.
TheEvent-
ful Life of a
Sergeant.
brave the generous Lloyd died. Tributes to his
merit have been published by lord Wellington and
by one of his own poor soldiers! by the highest and
by the lowest! To their testimony I add mine, let
those who served on equal terms with him say
whether in aught I have exceeded his deserts.

CHAPTER II.

Soult having lost the Nivelle, at first designed to leave part of his forces in the entrenched camp of Bayonne, and with the remainder take a flanking position behind the Nive, half-way between Bayonne and St. Jean Pied de Port, securing his left by the entrenched mountain of Ursouia, and his right on the heights above Cambo, the bridge-head of which would give him the power of making offensive movements. He could thus keep his troops together and restore their confidence, while he confined the allies to a small sterile district of France between the river and the sea, and rendered their situation very uneasy during the winter if they did not retire. However he soon modified this plan. The works of the Bayonne camp were not complete and his presence was necessary to urge their progress. The camp on the Ursouia mountain had been neglected contrary to his orders, and the bridge-head at Cambo was only commenced on the right bank. On the left it was indeed complete but constructed on a bad trace. Moreover he found that the Nive in dry weather was fordable at Ustaritz below Cambo, and at many places above that point. Remaining therefore at Bayonne himself with six divisions and Villatte's reserve, he sent D'Erlon with three divisions to reinforce Foy at Cambo. Yet neither D'Erlon's divisions nor Soult's whole army could have stopped lord Wellington at this time if other circumstances had permitted the latter to follow up his victory as he designed.

The hardships and privations endured on the mountains by the Anglo-Portuguese troops had been beneficial to them as an army. The fine air and the impossibility of the soldiers committing their usual excesses in drink had rendered them unusually healthy, while the facility of enforcing a strict discipline, and their natural impatience to win the fair plains spread out before them, had raised their moral and physical qualities in a wonderful degree. Danger was their sport, and their experienced general in the prime and vigour of life was as impatient for action as his soldiers. Neither the works of the Bayonne camp nor the barrier of the Nive, suddenly manned by a beaten and dispirited army, could have long withstood the progress of such a fiery host, and if Wellington could have let their strength and fury loose in the first days succeeding the battle of the Nivelle France would have felt his conquering footsteps to her centre. But the country at the foot of the Pyrenees is a deep clay, quite impassable after rain except by the royal road near the coast and that of St. Jean Pied de Port, both of which were in the power of the French. On the bye-roads the infantry sunk to the mid leg, the cavalry above the horses' knees, and even to the saddle-girths in some places. The artillery could not move at all. The rain had commenced on the 11th, the mist in the early part of the 12th had given Soult time to regain his camp and secure the high road to St. Jean Pied de Port, by which his troops easily gained their proper posts on the Nive, while his adversary fixed in the swamps could only make the ineffectual demonstration at Ustaritz and Cambo already noticed.

Wellington uneasy for his right flank while the French commanded the Cambo passage across the Nive directed general Hill to menace it again on the 16th. Foy had received orders to preserve the bridge-head on the right bank in any circumstances, but he was permitted to abandon the work on the left bank in the event of a general attack ; however at Hill's approach the officer placed there in command destroyed all the works and the bridge itself. This was a great cross to Soult, and the allies' flank being thus secured they were put into cantonments to avoid the rain, which fell heavily. The bad weather was however not the only obstacle to the English general's operations. On the very day of the battle Freyre's and Longa's soldiers entering Ascain pillaged it and murdered several persons ; the next day the whole of the Spanish troops continued these excesses in various places, and on the right Mina's battalions, some of whom were also in a state of mutiny, made a plundering and murdering incursion from the mountains towards Hellette. The Portuguese and British soldiers of the left wing had commenced the like outrages and two French persons were killed in one town, however the adjutant-general Pakenham arriving at the moment saw and instantly put the perpetrators to death thus nipping this wickedness in the bud, but at his own risk for legally he had not that power. This general whose generosity humanity and chivalric spirit excited the admiration of every honourable person who approached him, is the man who afterwards fell at New Orleans and who has been so foully traduced by American

writers. He who was pre-eminently distinguished
by his detestation of inhumanity and outrage has
been with astounding falsehood represented as in-
stigating his troops to the most infamous excesses.
But from a people holding millions of their fellow-
beings in the most horrible slavery while they prate
and vaunt of liberty until all men turn with loath-
ing from the sickening folly, what can be expected?

Terrified by these excesses the French people
fled even from the larger towns, but Wellington
quickly relieved their terror. On the 12th, although expecting a battle, he put to death all the
Spanish marauders he could take in the act, and
then with many reproaches and despite of the discontent of their generals, forced the whole to withdraw into their own country. He disarmed the
insubordinate battalions under Mina, quartered Giron's Andalusians in the Bastan where O'Donnel
resumed the command; sent Freyre's Gallicians to
the district between Irun and Ernani, and Longa
over the Ebro. Morillo's division alone remained
with the army. These decisive proceedings marking the lofty character of the man proved not less
politic than resolute. The French people immediately returned, and finding the strictest discipline
preserved and all things paid for adopted an amicable intercourse with the invaders. However the
loss of such a mass of troops and the effects of
weather on the roads reduced the army for the
moment to a state of inactivity; the head-quarters
were suddenly fixed at St. Jean de Luz, and the
troops were established in permanent cantonments
with the following line of battle.

Plan 7.　　　The left wing occupied a broad ridge on both
sides of the great road beyond Bidart, the principal

post being at a mansion belonging to the mayor of
Biaritz. The front was covered by a small stream
spreading here and there into large ponds or tanks
between which the road was conducted. The
centre posted partly on the continuation of this
ridge in front of Arcangues, partly on the hill of
San Barbe, extended by Arrauntz to Ustaritz, the
right being thrown back to face count D'Erlon's
position, extended by Cambo to Itzassu. From
this position which might stretch about six miles
on the front and eight miles on the flank, strong
picquets were pushed forwards to several points,
and the infantry occupied all the villages and towns
behind as far back as Espelette, Suraide, Ainhoa,
San Pé, Sarre, and Ascain.   One regiment of Vandeleur's cavalry was with the advanced post on the
left, the remainder were sent to Andaya and Urogne,
Victor Alten's horsemen were about San Pé, and
the heavy cavalry remained in Spain.

In this state of affairs the establishment of the
different posts in front led to several skirmishes.
In one on the 18th, general John Wilson and general Vandeleur were wounded; but on the same day
Beresford drove the French from the bridge of Urdains, near the junction of the Ustaritz and San
Pé roads, and though attacked in force the next
day he maintained his acquisition. A more serious action occurred on the 23d in front of
Arcangues. This village held by the picquets of the
light division was two or three miles in front of
Arbonne where the nearest support was cantoned.
It is built on the centre of a crescent-shaped ridge,
and the sentries of both armies were so close that
the reliefs and patroles actually passed each other in
their rounds, so that a surprise was inevitable if it

BOOK
XXIII.
———
1813.
November
suited either side to attempt it. Lord Wellington
visited this post and the field-officer on duty made
known to him its disadvantages, and the means of
remedying them by taking entire possession of the
village, pushing picquets along the horns of the
crescent, and establishing a chain of posts across the
valley between them. He appeared satisfied with
this project, and two days afterwards the forty-third
and some of the riflemen were employed to effect
it, the greatest part of the division being brought up
in support. The French after a few shots abandoned Arcangues, Bussussary, and both horns of
the crescent, retiring before the picquets to a large
fortified house situated at the mouth of the valley.
The project suggested by the field-officer was thus
executed with the loss of only five men wounded
and the action should have ceased, but the picquets
of the forty-third suddenly received orders to attack
the fortified house, and the columns of support
were shewn at several points of the semicircle ; the
French then conceiving they were going to be seriously assailed reinforced their post ; a sharp skirmish ensued and the picquets were finally withdrawn to the ground they had originally gained and
beyond which they should never have been pushed.
This ill-managed affair cost eighty-eight men and
officers of which eighty were of the forty-third.

Lord Wellington, whose powerful artillery and
cavalry, the former consisting of nearly one hundred field-pieces and the latter furnishing more than
Original
Morning
States,
MSS.
eight thousand six hundred sabres, were paralysed
in the contracted space he occupied, was now anxious to pass the Nive, but the rain which continued
to fall baffled him, and meanwhile Mina's Spaniards
descending once more from the Alduides to plunder

Baigorry were beaten by the national guards of that valley. However early in December the wea- ther amended, forty or fifty pieces of artillery were brought up, and other preparations made to sur- prize or force the passage of the Nive at Cambo and Ustaritz. And as this operation led to san- guinary battles it is fitting first to describe the exact position of the French.

Bayonne situated at the confluence of the Nive Plans 7 and 8. and the Adour commands the passage of both. A weak fortress of the third order its importance was in its position, and its entrenched camp, exceedingly strong and commanded by the fortress could not be safely attacked in front, wherefore Soult kept only six divisions there. His right composed of Reille's two divisions and Villatte's reserve touched on the Lower Adour where there was a flotilla of gun-boats. It was covered by a swamp and artifi- cial inundation, through which the royal road led to St. Jean de Luz, and the advanced posts, well entrenched, were pushed forward beyond Anglet on this causeway. His left under Clauzel, composed of three divisions, extended from Anglet to the Nive ; it was covered partly by the swamp, partly by the large fortified house which the light division assailed on the 23d, partly by an inundation spread- ing below Urdains towards the Nive. Thus en- trenched the fortified outposts may be called the front of battle, the entrenched camp the second line, and the fortress the citadel. The country in front a deep clay soil, enclosed and covered with small wood and farm-houses, was very difficult to move in.

Beyond the Nive the entrenched camp stretching

from that river to the Adour was called the front of
Mousseroles. It was in the keeping of D'Erlon's
four divisions, which were also extended up the
right bank of the Nive; that is to say, D'Armagnac's troops was in front of Ustaritz, and Foy prolonged the line to Cambo. The remainder of D'Erlon's corps was in reserve, occupying a strong range
of heights about two miles in front of Mousseroles,
the right at Villefranque on the Nive, the left at
Old Moguerre towards the Adour. D'Erlon's communications with the rest of the army were double,
one circuitous through Bayonne, the other direct
by a bridge of boats thrown above that place.

After the battle of the Nivelle Soult brought
general Paris's division from St. Jean Pied de Port to
Lahoussoa close under the Ursouia mountain, where
it was in connection with Foy's left, communicating
by the great road to St. Jean Pied de Port which
ran in a parallel direction to the river.

The Nive, the Adour, and the Gave de Pau which
falls into the latter many miles above Bayonne, were
all navigable, the first as far as Ustaritz, the second to
Dax, the third to Peyrehorade, and the great French
magazines were collected at the two latter places.
But the army was fed with difficulty, and hence
to restrain Soult from the country beyond the
Nive, to intercept his communications with St. Jean
Pied de Port, to bring a powerful cavalry into activity, and to obtain secret intelligence from the
interior of Spain were Wellington's inducements to
force a passage over the Nive. Yet to place the
troops on both sides of a navigable river with communications bad at all times and subject to entire
interruptions from rain; to do this in face of an

army possessing short communications good roads
and entrenched camps for retreat, was a delicate
and dangerous operation.

On the 7th orders were issued for forcing the
passage on the 9th. On that day Sir John Hope
and Charles Alten, with the first, fifth, and light
divisions, the unattached brigades of infantry, Vandeleur's cavalry and twelve guns, in all about twenty-
four thousand combatants, were to drive back the
French advanced posts along the whole front of the
entrenched camp between the Nive and the sea. This
movement was partly to examine the course of the
Lower Adour with a view to subsequent operations,
but principally to make Soult discover his dispositions of defence on that side, and to keep his troops
in check while Beresford and Hill crossed the Nive.
To support this double operation the fourth and
seventh divisions were secretly brought up from
Ascain and Espelette on the 8th, the latter to the
hill of St. Barbe, from whence it detached one
brigade to relieve the posts of the third division.
There remained the second the third and the sixth
divisions, Hamilton's Portuguese, and Morillo's
Spaniards, for the passage. Beresford leading the
third and sixth reinforced with six guns and a
squadron of cavalry, was to cross at Ustaritz with
pontoons, Hill having the second division, Hamilton's Portuguese, Vivian's and Victor Alten's cavalry, and fourteen guns, was to ford the river at
Cambo and Larressore. Both generals were then
to repair the bridges at these respective points
with materials prepared beforehand ; and to cover
Hill's movement on the right and protect the valley
of the Nive from Paris, who being at Lahoussoa
might have penetrated to the rear of the army

during the operations, Morillo's Spaniards were to cross at Itzassu. At this time Foy's division was extended from Halzou in front of Larressore, to the fords above Cambo, the Ursouia mountain being between his left and Paris. The rest of D'Erlon's troops remained on the heights of Moguerre in front of Mousserolles.

PASSAGE OF THE NIVE

AND

BATTLES IN FRONT OF BAYONNE.

At Ustaritz the French had broken both bridges, but the island connecting them was in possession of Plans 7 and 8. the British. Beresford laid his pontoons down on the hither side in the night of the 8th and in the morning of the 9th a beacon lighted on the heights above Cambo gave the signal of attack. The passage was immediately forced under the fire of the artillery, the second bridge was laid, and D'Armagnac's brigade was driven back by the sixth division ; but the swampy nature of the country between the river and the high road retarded the allies' march and gave the French time to retreat with little loss. At the same time Hill's troops, also covered by the fire of artillery, forced the passage in three columns above and below Cambo with slight resistance, though the fords were so deep that several horsemen were drowned, and the French strongly posted, especially at Halzou where there was a deep and strong mill-race to cross as well as the river.

Foy seeing, by the direction of Beresford's fire, that his retreat was endangered, retired hastily with his left leaving his right wing under general Berlier at Halzou without orders. Hence when general Pringle attacked the latter from Larressore, the sixth division was already on the high road between Foy and Berlier, who escaped by cross roads towards Hasparen, but did not rejoin his division until two o'clock in the afternoon. Meanwhile Morillo crossed at Itzassu, and Paris retired to Hellette where he was joined by a regiment of light cavalry belonging to Pierre Soult who was then on the Bidouse river. Morillo followed, and in one village near Hellette his troops killed fifteen peasants, amongst them several women and children.

General Hill having won the passage, placed a brigade of infantry at Urcurray to cover the bridge of Cambo, and to support the cavalry which he despatched to scour the roads towards Lahoussoa, St. Jean Pied de Port, and Hasparen, and to observe Paris and Pierre Soult. With the rest of his troops he marched to the heights of Lormenthoa in front of the hills of Moguerre and Villefranque, and was there joined by the sixth division, the third remaining to cover the bridge of Ustaritz. It was now about one o'clock, and Soult, coming hastily from Bayonne, approved of the disposition made by D'Erlon, and offered battle, his line being extended so as to bar the high road. D'Armagnac's brigade which had retired from Ustaritz was now in advance at Villefranque and a heavy cannonade and skirmish ensued along the front, but no general attack was made because the deep roads had retarded the rear of Hill's columns. However the Portuguese of the sixth division, descending from Lormenthoa about three o'clock, drove D'Armagnac's brigade with sharp fighting and after one repulse out of Villefranque. A brigade of the second division was then established in advance connecting

Hill's corps with the troops in Villefranque. Thus
three divisions of infantry, wanting the brigade
left at Urcurray, hemmed up four French divisions;
and as the latter, notwithstanding their superiority
of numbers, made no advantage of the broken movements of the allies caused by the deep roads, the
passage of the Nive may be judged a surprize. Wellington thus far overreached his able adversary, yet
he had not trusted to this uncertain chance alone.

The French masses falling upon the heads of
his columns at Lormenthoa while the rear was still
labouring in the deep roads, might have caused
some disorder, but could not have driven either Hill
or Beresford over the river again, because the third
division was close at hand to reinforce the sixth, and
the brigade of the seventh, left at San Barbe, could
have followed by the bridge of Ustaritz, thus giving
the allies the superiority of numbers. The greatest
danger was, that Paris, reinforced by Pierre Soult's
cavalry, should have returned and fallen either upon
Morillo or the brigade left at Urcurray in the rear,
while Soult, reinforcing D'Erlon with fresh divisions
brought from the other side of the Nive, attacked
Hill and Beresford in front. It was to prevent this
that Hope and Alten whose operations are now to be
related pressed the enemy on the left bank.

The first-named general having twelve miles to
march from St. Jean de Luz before he could reach
the French works, put his troops in motion during
the night, and about eight o'clock passed between
the tanks in front of Barrouilhet with his right,
while his left descended from the platform of Bidart
and crossed the valley towards Biaritz. The French
outposts retired fighting, and Hope sweeping with
a half circle to his right, and being preceded by

the fire of his guns and many skirmishers, arrived
in front of the entrenched camp about one o'clock.
His left then rested on the Lower Adour, his centre
menaced a very strong advanced work on the ridge
of Beyris beyond Anglet, and his right was in communication with Alten. That general having a
shorter distance to move, halted about Bussussary
and Arcangues until Hope's fiery crescent was
closing on the French camp, and then he also advanced, but with the exception of a slight skirmish
at the fortified house there was no resistance. Three
divisions, some cavalry, and the unattached brigades,
equal to a fourth division, sufficed therefore to keep
six French divisions in check on this side.

When evening closed the allies fell back towards
their original positions, but under heavy rain, and
with great fatigue to Hope's wing, for even the
royal road was knee-deep of mud and his troops
were twenty-four hours under arms. The whole
day's fighting cost about eight hundred men for each
side, the loss of the allies being rather greater on
the left bank of the Nive than on the right.

Wellington's wings being now divided by the
Nive the French general resolved to fall upon one
of them with the whole of his forces united; and
misled by the prisoners who assured him that the
third and fourth divisions were both on the heights
of Lormenthoa, he resolved, being able to assemble
his troops with greater facility on the left of the
Nive where also the allies' front was most extended,
to choose that side for his counter-stroke. The garrison of Bayonne was eight thousand strong, partly
troops of the line partly national guards, with which
he ordered the governor to occupy the entrenched
camp of Mousserolles; then stationing ten gun-boats
on the Upper Adour to watch that river as high

BOOK
XXIII.
———
1813.
December.

as the confluence of the Gave de Pau, he made D'Erlon file his four divisions over the bridge of boats between the fortress and Mousserolles, directing him to gain the camp of Marac and take post behind Clauzel's corps on the other side of the river. He thus

Imperial
Muster-
rolls, MSS.

concentrated nine divisions of infantry and Villatte's reserve, a brigade of cavalry and forty guns, furnishing in all about sixty thousand combatants, including conscripts, to assail a quarter where the allies, although stronger by one division than the

Original
Morning
States.

French general imagined, had yet only thirty thousand infantry with twenty-four pieces of cannon.

The French marshal's first design was to burst

Correspon-
dence with
the minis-
ter of war,
MSS.

with his whole army on the table-land of Bussussary and Arcangues, and then to act as circumstances should dictate ; and he judged so well of his position that he desired the minister of war to expect good news for the next day. Indeed the situation of the allies although better than he knew of gave him some right to anticipate success. On no point was there any expectation of this formidable counter-attack. Lord Wellington was on the left of the Nive preparing to assault the heights where he had last seen the French the evening before. Hope's troops, with the exception of Wilson's Portuguese now commanded by general Campbell and posted at Barrouilhet, had retired to their cantonments ; the first division was at St. Jean de Luz and Ciboure more than six miles distant from the outposts; the fifth division was between those places and Bidart, and all exceedingly fatigued. The light division had orders to retire from Bussussary to Arbonne a distance of four miles, and part of the second brigade had already marched, when fortunately general Kempt, somewhat suspicious of the enemy's movements, delayed obedience until he could see what was going on in his front, he thus as the event proved saved the position.

The extraordinary difficulty of moving through the country even for single horsemen, the numerous enclosures and copses which denied any distinct view, the easy success of the operation to cross the Nive, and a certain haughty confidence the sure attendant of a long course of victory, seems to have rendered the English general at this time somewhat negligent of his own security. Undoubtedly the troops were not disposed as if a battle was expected. The general position, composed of two distinct parts was indeed very strong; the ridge of Barrouilhet could only be attacked along the royal road on a narrow front between the tanks, and he had directed entrenchments to be made; but there was only one brigade there, and a road made with difficulty by the engineers supplied a bad flank communication with the light division. This Barrouilhet ridge was prolonged to the platform of Bussussary, but in its winding bulged out too near the enemy's works in the centre to be safely occupied in force, and behind it there was a deep valley or basin extending to Arbonne.

The ridge of Arcangues on the other side of this basin was the position of battle for the centre. Three tongues of land shot out from this part to the front, and the valleys between them as well as their slopes were covered with copse-woods almost impenetrable. The church of Arcangues, a gentleman's house, and parts of the village, furnished rallying points of defence for the picquets, which were necessarily numerous because of the extent of front. At this time the left-hand ridge or tongue of land was occupied by the fifty-second regiment which had also posts in the great basin separating the Arcangues position from that of Barrouilhet; the central tongue was held by the picquets of the forty-third with supporting companies placed in succession towards Bussussary, where was an open common across which troops in retreat would have to pass to the church of Arcangues. The third tongue was guarded, partly by the forty-third, partly by the riflemen, but the valley between was not occupied, and the picquets on the extreme right extended to an inundation, across a narrow part of which, near the house of the senator Garrat, there was a bridge : the facility for attack was there however small.

One brigade of the seventh division continued this line of posts to the Nive, holding the bridge of Urdains, the rest of the division was behind San Barbe and belonged rather to Ustaritz than to this front. The fourth division was several miles behind the right of the light division.

In this state of affairs if Soult had, as he first designed, burst with his whole army upon Bussussary and Arcangues it would have been impossible for the light division, scattered as it was over such an extent of difficult ground, to have stopped him for half an hour ; and there was no support within several miles, no superior officer to direct the concentration of the different divisions. Lord Wellington had indeed ordered all the line to be entrenched, but the works were commenced on a great scale, and, as is common when danger does not spur, the soldiers had laboured so carelessly that beyond a few abbatis, the tracing of some lines and redoubts, and the opening of a road of communication, the ground remained in its natural state. The French

general would therefore quickly have gained the
broad open hills beyond Arcangues, separated the
fourth and seventh divisions from the light division,
and cut them off from Hope. Soult however, in
the course of the night, for reasons which I do not
find stated, changed his project, and at day-break
Reille marched with Boyer's and Maucune's divisions, Sparre's cavalry and from twenty to thirty
guns against Hope by the main road. He was
followed by Foy and Villatte, but Clauzel assembled his troops under cover of the ridges near the
fortified house in front of Bussussary, and one of
D'Erlon's divisions approached the bridge of
Urdains.

Combat of the 10th.—A heavy rain fell in the
night yet the morning broke fair, and soon after
dawn the French infantry were observed by the
picquets of the forty-third pushing each other about
as if at gambols, yet lining by degrees the nearest
ditches; a general officer was also seen behind a farm-
house close to the sentinels, and at the same time the
heads of columns could be perceived in the rear.
Thus warned some companies of the forty-third
were thrown on the right into the basin to prevent
the enemy from penetrating that way to the small
plain between Bussussary and Arcangues. General
Kempt was with the picquets, and his foresight in
delaying his march to Arbonne now saved the
position, for he immediately placed the reserves of
his brigade in the church and mansion-house of
Arcangues. Meanwhile the French breaking forth
with loud cries, and a rattling musquetry, fell at
a running pace upon the picquets of the forty-
third both on the tongue and in the basin, and a
cloud of skirmishers descending on their left, pene-

trating between them and the fifty-second regiment, sought to turn both. The right tongue was in like manner assailed and at the same time the picquets at the bridge near Garrat's house were driven back.

The assault was so strong and rapid, the enemy so numerous, and the ground so extensive, that it would have been impossible to have reached the small plain beyond Bussussary in time to regain the church of Arcangues if any serious resistance had been attempted; wherefore delivering their fire at pistol-shot distance the picquets fell back in succession, and never were the steadiness and intelligence of veteran soldiers more eminently displayed; for though it was necessary to run at full speed to gain the small plain before the enemy, who was constantly outflanking the line of posts by the basin, though the ways were so deep and narrow that no formation could be preserved, though the fire of the French was thick and close, and their cries vehement as they rushed on in pursuit, the instant the open ground at Bussussary was attained, the apparently disordered crowd of fugitives became a compact and well-formed body defying and deriding the fruitless efforts of their adversaries.

The fifty-second being about half a mile to the left, though only slightly assailed fell back also to the main ridge, for though the closeness of the country did not permit colonel Colborne to observe the strength of the enemy he could see the rapid retreat of the forty-third, and thence judging how serious the affair was, so well did the regiments of the light division understand each other's qualities, withdrew his outposts to secure the main position. And in good time he did so.

On the right-hand tongue the troops were not so

fortunate, for whether they delayed their retreat too
long, or that the country was more intricate, the
enemy moving by the basin, reached Bussussary
before the rear arrived, and about a hundred of the
forty-third and riflemen were thus intercepted. The
French were in a hollow road and careless, never
doubting that the officer of the forty-third, ensign
Campbell, a youth scarcely eighteen years of age,
would surrender; but he with a shout broke into
their column sword in hand, and though the struggle
was severe and twenty of the forty-third and thirty
of the riflemen with their officer remained prisoners,
reached the church with the rest.

D'Armagnac's division of D'Erlon's corps now
pushed close up to the bridge of Urdains, and
Clauzel assembled his three divisions by degrees
at Bussussary, opening meanwhile a sharp fire of
musquetry. The position was however safe. The
mansion-house on the right, covered by abbatis and
not easily accessible, was defended by a rifle battalion and the Portuguese. The church and church-
yard were occupied by the forty-third who were supported with two mountain-guns, their front being
covered by a declivity of thick copse-wood, filled with
riflemen, and only to be turned by narrow hollow
roads leading on each side to the church. On the
left the fifty-second now supported by the remainder
of the division, spread as far as the great basin
which separated the right wing from the ridge of
Barrouilhet, towards which some small posts were
pushed, but there was still a great interval between Alten's and Hope's positions.

The skirmishing fire grew hot, Clauzel brought
up twelve guns to the ridge of Bussussary,
with which he threw shot and shells into the

church-yard of Arcangues, and four or five hundred
infantry then made a rush forwards, but a heavy
fire from the forty-third sent them back over the
ridge where their guns were posted. Yet the practice
of the latter, well directed at first, would have been
murderous if this musquetry from the church-yard
had not made the French gunners withdraw their
pieces a little behind the ridge, which caused their
shot to fly wild and high. General Kempt thinking
the distance too great, was at first inclined to stop
this fire, but the moment it lulled the French gunners
pushed their pieces forwards again and their shells
knocked down eight men in an instant. The small
arms then recommenced and the shells again flew
high. The French were in like manner kept at
bay by the riflemen in the village and mansion-
house, and the action, hottest where the fifty-second
fought, continued all day. It was not very severe
but it has been noticed in detail because both
French and English writers, misled perhaps by an
inaccurate phrase in the public despatch, have
represented it as a desperate attack by which the
light division was driven into its entrenchments,
whereas it was the picquets only that were forced
back, there were no entrenchments save those made
on the spur of the moment by the soldiers in the
church-yard, and the French can hardly be said to
have attacked at all. The real battle was at Barrouilhet.

On that side Reille advancing with two divisions
about nine o'clock, drove Campbell's Portuguese
from Anglet, and Sparre's cavalry charging during
the fight cut down a great many men. The French
infantry then assailed the ridge at Barrouilhet, but
moving along a narrow ridge and confined on each

flank by the tanks, only two brigades could get into
action by the main road, and the rain of the preceding night had rendered all the bye-roads so deep
that it was mid-day before the French line of battle
was filled. This delay saved the allies, for the
attack here also was so unexpected, that the first
division and lord Aylmer's brigade were at rest in
St. Jean de Luz and Bidart when the action commenced. The latter did not reach the position
before eleven o'clock; the foot-guards did not
march from St. Jean until after twelve, and only
arrived at three o'clock in the afternoon when the
fight was done; all the troops were exceedingly fatigued, only ten guns could be brought into play,
and from some negligence part of the infantry were
at first without ammunition.

Robinson's brigade of the fifth division first arrived to support Campbell's Portuguese, and fight
the battle. The French spread their skirmishers
along the whole valley in front of Biaritz, but their
principal effort was directed by the great road and
against the platform of Barrouilhet about the
mayor's house, where the ground was so thick of
hedges and coppice-wood that a most confused fight
took place. The assailants cutting ways through
the hedges poured on in smaller or larger bodies as
the openings allowed, and were immediately engaged with the defenders; at some points they were
successful at others beaten back, and few knew
what was going on to the right or left of where they
stood. By degrees Reille engaged both his divisions, and some of Villatte's reserve also entered
the fight, and then Bradford's Portuguese and lord
Aylmer's brigade arrived on the allies' side, which
enabled colonel Greville's brigade of the fifth divi-

sion, hitherto kept in reserve, to relieve Robinson's ;
that general was however dangerously wounded
and his troops suffered severely.

And now a very notable action was performed
by the ninth regiment under colonel Cameron.
This officer was on the extreme left of Greville's
brigade, Robinson's being then shifted in second
line and towards the right, Bradford's brigade was
at the mayor's house some distance to the left of the
ninth regiment, and the space between was occupied by a Portuguese battalion. There was in
front of Greville's brigade a thick hedge, but immediately opposite the ninth was a coppice-wood
possessed by the enemy, whose skirmishers were
continually gathering in masses and rushing out as
if to assail the line, they were as often driven
back, yet the ground was so broken that nothing
could be seen beyond the flanks and when some
time had passed in this manner, Cameron, who had
received no orders, heard a sudden firing along the
main road close to his left. His adjutant was sent
to look out and returned immediately with intelligence that there was little fighting on the road,
but a French regiment, which must have passed
unseen in small bodies through the Portuguese between the ninth and the mayor's house, was rapidly
filing into line on the rear. The fourth British

Manu-
script note
by lieute-
nant-gene-
ral sir John
Cameron.
regiment was then in close column at a short distance, and its commander colonel Piper was directed
by Cameron to face about, march to the rear, and
then bring up his left shoulder when he would
infallibly fall in with the French regiment. Piper
marched, but whether he misunderstood the order,
took a wrong direction, or mistook the enemy for
Portuguese, he passed them. No firing was heard,

the adjutant again hurried to the rear, and returned with intelligence that the fourth regiment was not to be seen, but the enemy's line was nearly formed. Cameron leaving fifty men to answer the skirmishing fire which now increased from the copse, immediately faced about and marched in line against the new enemy, who was about his own strength, as fast as the rough nature of the ground would permit. The French fire, slow at first, increased vehemently as the distance lessened, but when the ninth, coming close up, sprung forwards to the charge the adverse line broke and fled to the flanks in the utmost disorder. Those who made for their own right brushed the left of Greville's brigade, and even carried off an officer of the royals in their rush, yet the greatest number were made prisoners, and the ninth having lost about eighty men and officers resumed their old ground.

The final result of the battle at Barrouilhet was the repulse of Reille's divisions, but Villatte still menaced the right flank, and Foy, taking possession of the narrow ridge connecting Bussussary with the platform of Barrouilhet, threw his skirmishers into the great basin leading to Arbonne, and connecting his right with Reille's left menaced Hope's flank at Barrouilhet. This was about two o'clock, Soult, whose columns were now all in hand gave orders to renew the battle, and his masses were beginning to move when Clauzel reported that a large body of fresh troops, apparently coming from the other side of the Nive, was menacing D'Armagnac's division from the heights above Urdains. Unable to account for this, Soult, who saw the guards and Germans moving up fast from St. Jean de Luz and all the unattached brigades already in line, hesitated,

BOOK
XXIII.
———
1813.
December.
Soult's
Official
Report,
MSS.

suspended his own attack, and ordered D'Erlon, who had two divisions in reserve, to detach one to the support of D'Armagnac : before this disposition could be completed the night fell.

The fresh troops seen by Clauzel were the third fourth sixth and seventh divisions, whose movements during the battle it is time to notice. When lord Wellington, who remained on the right of the Nive during the night of the 9th, discovered at daybreak, that the French had abandoned the heights in Hill's front, he directed that officer to occupy them, and push parties close up to the entrenched camp of Mousseroles while his cavalry spread beyond Hasparen and up the Adour. Meanwhile, the cannonade on the left bank of the Nive being heard, he repaired in person to that side, first making the third and sixth divisions repass the river, and directing Beresford to lay another bridge of communication lower down the Nive, near Villefranque, to shorten the line of movement. When he reached the left of the Nive and saw how the battle stood, he made the seventh division close to the left from the hill of San Barbe, placed the third division at Urdains, and brought up the fourth division to an open heathy ridge on a hill about a mile behind the church of Arcangues. From this point general Cole sent Ross's brigade down into the basin on the left of Colborne, to cover Arbonne, being prepared himself to march with his whole division if the enemy attempted to penetrate in force between Hope and Alten. These dispositions were for the most part completed about two o'clock, and thus Clauzel was held in check at Bussussary, and the renewed attack by Foy, Villatte, and Reille's divisions on Barrouilhet prevented.

This day's battle cost the Anglo-Portuguese more than twelve hundred men killed and wounded, two generals were amongst the latter and about three hundred men were made prisoners. The French had one general, Villatte, wounded, and lost about two thousand men, but when the action terminated two regiments of Nassau and one of Frankfort, the whole under the command of a colonel Kruse, came over to the allies. These men were not deserters. Their prince having abandoned Napoleon in Germany sent secret instructions to his troops to do so likewise, and in good time, for orders to disarm them reached Soult the next morning. The generals on each side, the one hoping to profit the other to prevent mischief, immediately transmitted notice of the event to Catalonia where several regiments of the same nations were serving. Lord Wellington failed for reasons to be hereafter mentioned, but Suchet disarmed his Germans with reluctance thinking they could be trusted, and the Nassau troops at Bayonne were perhaps less influenced by patriotism than by an old quarrel; for when belonging to the army of the centre they had forcibly foraged Soult's district early in the year, and carried off the spoil in defiance of his authority, which gave rise to bitter disputes at the time and was probably not forgotten by him.

Combat of the 11th.—In the night of the 10th Reille withdrew behind the tanks as far as Pucho, Foy and Villatte likewise drew back along the connecting ridge towards Bussussary, thus uniting with Clauzel's left and D'Erlon's reserve, so that on the morning of the 11th the French army, with the exception of D'Armagnac's division which remained in front of Urdains, was concentrated, for Soult feared a counter-attack. The French deserters indeed declared that Clauzel had formed a body of two thousand choice grenadiers to assault the village and church of Arcangues, but the day passed without any event in that quarter save a slight skirmish in which a few men were wounded. Not so on the side of Barrouilhet. There was a thick fog, and lord Wellington, desirous to ascertain what the French were about, directed the ninth regiment about ten o'clock to open a skirmish beyond the tanks towards Pucho, and to push the action if the French augmented their force. Cameron did so and the fight was becoming warm, when colonel Delancy, a staff-officer, rashly directed the ninth to enter the village. The error was soon and sharply corrected, for the fog cleared up, and Soult, who had twenty-four thousand men at that point, observing the ninth unsupported, ordered a counter-attack which was so strong and sudden that Cameron only saved his regiment with the aid of some Portuguese troops hastily brought up by sir John Hope. The fighting then ceased and lord Wellington went to the right, leaving Hope with orders to push back the French picquets and re-establish his former outposts on the connecting ridge towards Bussussary.

Soult had hitherto appeared undecided, but roused by this second insult, he ordered Darricau's division to attack Barrouilhet along the connecting ridge, while Boyer's division fell on by the main road between the tanks. This was about two o'clock and the allies expecting no battle had dispersed to gather fuel, for the time was wet and cold. In an instant the French penetrated in all directions, they outflanked the right, they passed the tanks, seized the out-buildings of the mayor's house, and occupied the coppice in front of it; they were indeed quickly driven from the out-buildings by the royals, but the tumult was great and the coppice was filled with men of all nations intermixed and fighting in a perilous manner. Robinson's brigade was very hardly handled, the officer commanding it was wounded, a squadron of French cavalry suddenly cut down some of the Portuguese near the wood, and on the right the colonel of the eighty-fourth having unwisely engaged his regiment in a hollow road where the French possessed the high bank, was killed with a great number of men. However the ninth regiment posted on the main road plied Boyer's flank with fire, the eighty-fifth regiment of lord Aylmer's brigade came into action, and sir John Hope conspicuous from his gigantic stature and heroic courage, was seen wherever danger pressed rallying and encouraging the troops; at one time he was in the midst of the enemy, his clothes were pierced with bullets, and he received a severe wound in the ankle, yet he would not quit the field and by his great presence of mind and calm intrepidity restored the battle. The French were finally beaten back from the position of Barrouilhet yet they had recovered their original posts, and continued to gall the allies with a fire of shot and shells until the fall of night. The total loss in this fight was about six hundred men of a side, and as the fifth division was now considerably reduced in numbers the first division took its place on the front line. Meanwhile Soult sent his cavalry over the Nive to Mousseroles to check the incursions of Hill's horsemen.

Combat of the 12th.—The rain fell heavily in the night, and though the morning broke fair neither side seemed inclined to recommence hostilities. The

BOOK
XXIII.
───────
1813.
December.

Soult's
Official
Despatches
MSS.

advanced posts were however very close to each
other and about ten o'clock a misunderstanding
arose.   The French general observing the fresh regiments of the first division close to his posts, imagined the allies were going to attack him and immediately reinforced his front ; this movement causing
an English battery to fall into a like error it opened
upon the advancing French troops, and in an instant
the whole line of posts was engaged.   Soult then
brought up a number of guns, the firing continued
without an object for many hours, and three or four
hundred men of a side were killed and wounded,
but the great body of the French army remained
concentrated and quiet on the ridge between Barrouilhet and Bussussary.

Lord Wellington as early as the 10th had expected Soult would abandon this attack to fall upon
Hill, and therefore had given Beresford orders to
carry the sixth division to that general's assistance
by the new bridge and the seventh division by
Ustaritz, without waiting for further instructions, if
Hill was assailed ; now observing Soult's tenacity
at Barrouilhet he drew the seventh division towards
Arbonne.   Beresford had however made a movement towards the Nive, and this with the march of
the seventh division and some changes in the position of the fourth division, caused Soult to believe
the allies were gathering with a view to attack his
centre on the morning of the 13th ; and it is remarkable that the deserters at this early period told
him the Spaniards had re-entered France although
orders to that effect were not as we shall find given
until the next day.   Convinced then that his bolt
was shot on the left of the Nive, he left two divisions and Villatte's reserve in the entrenched camp,

and marched with the other seven to Mousseroles intending to fall upon Hill.

That general had pushed his scouting parties to the Gambouri, and when general Sparre's horsemen arrived at Mousseroles on the 12th, Pierre Soult advanced from the Bidouze with all the light cavalry. He was supported by the infantry of general Paris and drove the allies' posts from Hasparen. Colonel Vivian, who commanded there, immediately ordered major Brotherton to charge with the fouteenth dragoons across the bridge, but it was an ill-judged order, and the impossibility of succeeding so manifest, that when Brotherton, noted throughout the army for his daring, galloped forward, only two men and one subaltern, lieutenant Southwell, passed the narrow bridge with him, and they were all taken. Vivian then seeing his error charged with his whole brigade to rescue them, yet in vain, he was forced to fall back upon Urcuray where Morillo's Spaniards had relieved the British infantry brigade on the 11th. This threatening movement induced general Hill to put the British brigade in march again for Urcuray on the 12th, but he recalled it at sunset, having then discovered Soult's columns passing the Nive by the boat-bridge above Bayonne.

Lord Wellington now feeling the want of numbers, brought forward a division of Gallicians to St. Jean de Luz, and one of Andalusians from the Bastan to Itzassu, and to prevent their plundering fed them from the British magazines. The Gallicians were to support Hope, the Andalusians to watch the upper valley of the Nive and protect the rear of the army from Paris and Pierre Soult, who could easily be reinforced with a strong body of national guards.

Meanwhile Hill had taken a position of battle on a
front of two miles.

His left, composed of the twenty-eighth, thirty-
fourth, and thirty-ninth regiments under general
Pringle, occupied a wooded and broken range
crowned by the chateau of Villefranque; it covered
the new pontoon bridge of communication, which was
a mile and a half higher up the river, but it was
separated from the centre by a small stream forming a chain of ponds in a very deep and marshy
valley.

The centre placed on both sides of the high road
Plan 8. near the hamlet of St. Pierre, occupied a crescent-
shaped height, broken with rocks and close brushwood on the left hand, and on the right hand enclosed
with high and thick hedges, one of which, covering,
at the distance of a hundred yards, part of the line,
was nearly impassable. Here Ashworth's Portuguese
and Barnes's British brigade of the second division
were posted. The seventy-first regiment was on the
left, the fiftieth in the centre, the ninety-second on
the right. Ashworth's Portuguese were posted in
advance immediately in front of St. Pierre, and
their skirmishers occupied a small wood covering
their right. Twelve guns under the colonels Ross
and Tullock were concentrated in front of the centre, looking down the great road, and half a mile
in rear of this point Lecor's Portuguese division
was stationed with two guns as a reserve.

The right under Byng was composed of the third,
fifty-seventh, thirty-first, and sixty-sixth. One of
these regiments, the third, was posted on a height
running nearly parallel with the Adour called
the ridge of Partouhiria, or Old Moguerre, because

a village of that name was situated upon the summit.
This regiment was pushed in advance to a point
where it could only be approached by crossing the
lower part of a narrow swampy valley which separated Moguerre from the heights of St. Pierre. The
upper part of this valley was held by Byng with the
remainder of his brigade, and his post was well
covered by a mill-pond leading towards the enemy
and nearly filling all the valley.

One mile in front of St. Pierre was a range of
counter heights belonging to the French, but the
basin between was broad open and commanded in
every part by the fire of the allies, and in all parts
the country was too heavy and too much enclosed
for the action of cavalry. Nor could the enemy
approach in force, except on a narrow front of battle and by the high road, until within cannon-shot,
when two narrow difficult lanes branched off to the
right and left, and crossing the swampy valleys on
each side, led, the one to the height where the third
regiment was posted on the extreme right of the
allies, the other to general Pringle's position on the
left.

In the night of the 12th the rain swelled the Nive
and carried away the allies' bridge of communication. It was soon restored, but on the morning of
the 13th general Hill was completely cut off from
the rest of the army; and while seven French divisions of infantry, furnishing at least thirty-five thousand combatants, approached him in front, an eighth
under general Paris and the cavalry division of
Pierre Soult menaced him in rear. To meet the Appendix 7, sect. 4.
French in his front he had less than fourteen
thousand, men and officers with fourteen guns in

position ; and there were only four thousand
Spaniards with Vivian's cavalry at Urcuray.

Battle of St. Pierre.—The morning broke with a
heavy mist under cover of which Soult formed his
order of battle. D'Erlon, having D'Armagnac's
Abbé's and Daricau's divisions of infantry, Sparre's
cavalry and twenty-two guns, marched in front ; he
was followed by Foy and Maransin, but the remainder of the French army was in reserve, for the roads
would not allow of any other order. The mist hung
heavily and the French masses, at one moment
quite shrouded in vapour, at another dimly seen or
looming sudden and large and dark at different
points, appeared like thunder-clouds gathering before the storm. At half-past eight Soult pushed back
the British picquets in the centre, the sun burst out
at that moment, the sparkling fire of the light troops
spread wide in the valley, and crept up the hills on
either flank, while the bellowing of forty pieces of
artillery shook the banks of the Nive and the Adour.
Darricau marching on the French right was directed
against general Pringle. D'Armagnac, moving on
their left and taking Old Moguerre as the point of
direction, was ordered to force Byng's right. Abbé
assailed the centre at St. Pierre, where general
Stewart commanded, for Sir Rowland Hill had taken
his station on a commanding mount in the rear, from
whence he could see the whole battle and direct the
movements.

Abbé, a man noted for vigour, pushed his attack
with great violence and gained ground so rapidly
with his light troops, on the left of Ashworth's Portuguese, that Stewart sent the seventy-first regiment
and two guns from St. Pierre to the latter's aid ; the

French skirmishers likewise won the small wood on Ashworth's right, and half of the fiftieth regiment was also detached from St. Pierre to that quarter. The wood was thus retaken, and the flanks of Stewart's position secured, but his centre was very much weakened, and the fire of the French artillery was concentrated against it. Abbé then pushed on a column of attack there with such a power that in despite of the play of musquetry on his flanks and a crashing cannonade in his front, he gained the top of the position, and drove back the remainder of Ashworth's Portuguese and the other half of the fiftieth regiment which had remained in reserve.

General Barnes who had still the ninety-second regiment in hand behind St. Pierre, immediately brought it on with a strong counter-attack. The French skirmishers fell back on each side leaving two regiments composing the column to meet the charge of the ninety-second; it was rough and pushed home, the French mass wavered and gave way. Abbé immediately replaced it and Soult redoubling the heavy play of his guns from the height he occupied, sent forward a battery of horse artillery which galloping down into the valley opened its fire close to the allies with most destructive activity. The cannonade and musquetry rolled like a prolonged peal of thunder, and the second French column, regardless of Ross's guns, though they tore the ranks in a horrible manner, advanced so steadily up the high road that the ninety-second yielding to the tempest slowly regained its old position behind St. Pierre. The Portuguese guns, their British commanding officer having fallen wounded, then limbered up to retire and the French skirmishers reached the impenetrable hedge in front of Ashworth's right.

General Barnes now seeing that hard fighting only could save the position, made the Portuguese guns resume their fire, and the wing of the fiftieth and the Caçadores gallantly held the small wood on the right; but Barnes was soon wounded, the greatest part of his and general Stewart's staff were hurt, and the matter seemed desperate. For the light troops overpowered by numbers were all driven in except those in the wood, the artillerymen were falling at the guns, Ashworth's line of Portuguese crumbled away rapidly before the musquetry and cannonade, the ground was strewed with the dead in front, and the wounded crawling to the rear were many.

If the French light troops could then have penetrated through the thick hedge in front of the Portuguese, defeat would have been inevitable on this point, for the main column of attack still steadily advanced up the main road, and a second column launched on its right was already victorious, because the colonel of the seventy-first had shamefully withdrawn that gallant regiment out of action and abandoned the Portuguese. Pringle was indeed fighting strongly against Daricau's superior numbers on the hill of Villefranque, but on the extreme right the colonel of the third regiment had also abandoned his strong post to D'Armagnac, whose leading brigade was thus rapidly turning Byng's other regiments on that side. And now Foy's and Maransin's divisions, hitherto retarded by the deep roads, were coming into line ready to support Abbé, and this at the moment when the troops opposed to him were deprived of their reserve. For when general Hill beheld the retreat of the third and seventy-first regiments he descended in haste from his mount, met, and turned the latter back to renew the fight, and then in person

leading one brigade of Le Cor's reserve division to
the same quarter sent the other against D'Armagnac
on the hill of Old Moguerre. Thus at the decisive
moment of the battle the French reserve was augmented and that of the allies thrown as a last resource into action. However the right wing of the
fiftieth and Ashworth's Caçadores, both spread as
skirmishers, never lost the small wood in front, up-
holding the fight there and towards the high road
with such unflinching courage that the ninety-second
regiment had time to reform behind the hamlet of
St. Pierre. Then its gallant colonel Cameron once
more led it down the road with colours flying and
music playing resolved to give the shock to whatever stood in the way. At this sight the British
skirmishers on the flanks, suddenly changing from
retreat to attack, rushed forward and drove those of
the enemy back on each side; yet the battle seemed
hopeless for Ashworth was badly wounded, his line
was shattered to atoms, and Barnes who had not
quitted the field for his former hurt was now shot
through the body.

The ninety-second was but a small body compared
with the heavy mass in its front, and the French
soldiers seemed willing enough to close with the
bayonet; but an officer riding at their head suddenly
turned his horse waved his sword and appeared to
order a retreat, then they faced about and immediately
retired across the valley to their original position,
in good order however and scarcely pursued by the
allies, so exhausted were the victors. This retrograde movement, for there was no panic or disorder,
was produced partly by the gallant advance of the
ninety-second and the returning rush of the skirm-

Published
Memoir on
the battle
by captain
Pringle,
engineers.

ishers, partly by the state of affairs immediately on
the right of the French column. For the seventy-
first indignant at their colonel's conduct had returned
to the fight with such alacrity, and were so well
aided by Le Cor's Portuguese, generals Hill and
Stewart each in person leading an attack, that the
hitherto victorious French were overthrown there
also in the very moment when the ninety-second
came with such a brave shew down the main road :
Le Cor was however wounded.

This double action in the centre being seen from
the hill of Villefranque, Daricau's division, already
roughly handled by Pringle, fell back in confusion;
and meantime on the right, Buchan's Portuguese,
detached by Hill to recover the Moguerre or Partouhiria ridge, crossed the valley, and ascending
under a heavy flank fire from Soult's guns rallied
the third regiment; in happy time, for D'Armagnac's first brigade having already passed the
flank of Byng's regiments at the mill-pond was
actually in rear of the allies' lines. It was now
twelve o'clock, and while the fire of the light troops
in the front and the cannonade in the centre continued the contending generals restored their respective orders of battle. Soult's right wing had
been quite repulsed by Pringle, his left was giving
way before Buchan, and the difficult ground forbad
his sending immediate succour to either; moreover
in the exigency of the moment he had called
D'Armagnac's reserve brigade to sustain Abbé's
retiring columns. However that brigade and Foy's
and Maransin's divisions were in hand to renew the
fight in the centre, and the allies could not, unsuc-
coured, have sustained a fresh assault; for their ranks

were wasted with fire, nearly all the staff had been
killed or wounded, and three generals had quitted
the field badly hurt.

In this crisis general Hill seeing that Buchan
was now well and successfully engaged on the Partouhiria ridge, and that Byng's regiments were quite
masters of their ground in the valley of the mill-
pond, drew the fifty-seventh regiment from the
latter place to reinforce his centre. At the same
time the bridge above Villefranque having been
restored, the sixth division, which had been marching since daybreak, appeared in order of battle on
the mount from whence Hill had descended to rally
the seventy-first. It was soon followed by the
fourth division, and that again by the brigades
of the third division; two other brigades of the
seventh division were likewise in march. With the
first of these troops came lord Wellington who had
hurried from Barrouilhet when the first sound of
the cannon reached him, yet he arrived only to
witness the close of the battle, the crisis was past,
Hill's day of glory was complete. Soult had,
according to the French method, made indeed another
attack, or rather demonstration, against the centre,
to cover his new dispositions, an effort easily repulsed,
but at the same moment Buchan drove D'Armagnac
headlong off the Partouhiria ridge. The sixth division then appeared on the commanding mount in the
rear of St. Pierre, and though the French masses
still maintained a menacing position on the high
road, and on a hillock rising between the road and
the mill-pond, they were quickly dispossessed. For
the English general being now supported by the
sixth division, sent Byng with two battalions against
the hillock, and some troops from the centre against

those on the high road. At this last point the
generals and staff had been so cut down that colonel
Currie, the aid-de-camp who brought the order, could
find no superior officer to deliver it to and led the
troops himself to the attack, but both charges were successful; and two guns of the light battery sent down
in the early part of the fight by Soult, and which had
played without ceasing up to this moment, were taken.

The battle now abated to a skirmish of light
troops, under cover of which the French endeavoured
to carry off their wounded and rally their stragglers,
but at two o'clock lord Wellington commanded a
general advance of the whole line. Then the
French retreated fighting, and the allies following
close on the side of the Nive plied them with musquetry until dark. Yet they maintained their line
towards the Adour, for Sparre's cavalry passing
out that way rejoined Pierre Soult on the side of
Hasparen. This last-named general and Paris had
during the day menaced Morillo and Vivian's cavalry
at Urcuray, however not more than thirty men of
a side were hurt, and when Soult's ill success became known the French retired to Bonloc.

In this bloody action Soult had designed to employ seven divisions of infantry with one brigade of
cavalry on the front, and one brigade of infantry
with a division of cavalry on the rear; but the state
of the roads and the narrow front he was forced to
move upon did not permit more than five divisions
to act at St. Pierre, and only half of those were
seriously engaged. His loss was certainly three
thousand, making a total on the five days' fighting
of six thousand men with two generals, Villatte and
Maucomble, wounded. The estimate made by the
British at the time far exceeded this number, and

one French writer makes their loss ten thousand
including probably the Nassau and Frankfort regiments. The same writer however estimates the loss
of the allies at sixteen thousand! Whereas Hill
had only three generals and about fifteen hundred
men killed and wounded on the 13th and Morillo
lost but twenty-six men at Urcuray. The real
loss of the allies in the whole five days' fighting
was only five thousand and nineteen, including
however five generals, Hope, Robinson, Barnes,
Lecor, and Ashworth. Of this number five hundred
were prisoners.

The duke of Dalmatia, baffled by the unexpected
result of the battle of St. Pierre, left D'Erlon's
three divisions in front of the camp of Mousseroles, sent two others over the Nive to Marac, and
passing the Adour himself during the night with
Foy's division, spread it along the right bank of
that river as far as the confluence of the Gave de
Pau.

OBSERVATIONS.

1°. The French general's plan was conceived
with genius but the execution offers a great contrast
to the conception. What a difference between the
sudden concentration of his whole army on the
platforms of Arcangues and Bussussary, where
there were only a few picquets to withstand him,
and from whence he could have fallen with the roll
of an avalanche upon any point of the allies' line!
what a difference between that and the petty attack
of Clauzel, which a thousand men of the light division sufficed to arrest at the village and church of
Arcangues. There beyond question was the weak

part of the English general's cuirass. The spear
pushed home there would have drawn blood. For the
disposition and movements of the third fourth and
seventh divisions, were made more with reference to
the support of Hill than to sustain an attack from
Soult's army, and it is evident that Wellington,
trusting to the effect of his victory on the 10th of
November, had treated the French general and
his troops, more contemptuously than he could
have justified by arms without the aid of fortune. I know not what induced marshal Soult to
direct his main attack by Anglet and the connecting
ridge of Bussussary, against Barrouilhet, instead of
assailing Arcangues as he at first proposed; but
this is certain, that for three hours after Clauzel first
attacked the picquets at the latter place, there were
not troops enough to stop three French divisions,
much less a whole army. And this point being
nearer to the bridge by which D'Erlon passed the
Nive, the concentration of the French troops could
have been made sooner than at Barrouilhet, where
the want of unity in the attack caused by the difficulty of the roads ruined the French combinations.

The allies were so unexpectant of an attack, that
the battle at Barrouilhet which might have been
fought with seventeen thousand men, was actually
fought by ten thousand. And those were not
brought into action at once, for Robinson's brigade
and Campbell's Portuguese, favoured by the narrow
opening between the tanks, resisted Reille's divisions for two hours, and gave time for the rest of the
fifth division and Bradford's brigade to arrive. But
if Foy's division and Villatte's reserve had been
able to assail the flank at the same time, by the
ridge coming from Bussussary, the battle would

have been won by the French ; and meanwhile three
divisions under Clauzel and two under D'Erlon remained hesitating before Urdains and Arcangues, for the cannonade and skirmishing at the latter place were the very marks and signs of indecision.

2⁰. On the 11th the inactivity of the French during the morning may be easily accounted for. The defection of the German regiments, the necessity of disarming and removing those that remained, the care of the wounded, and the time required to re-examine the allies' position and ascertain what changes had taken place during the night, must have given ample employment to the French general. His attack in the afternoon also was well judged because already he must have seen from the increase of troops in his front, from the intrenched battery and other works rapidly constructed at the church of Arcangues, that no decisive success could be expected on the left of the Nive, and that his best chance was to change his line of attack again to the right bank. To do this with effect, it was necessary, not only to draw all lord Wellington's reserves from the right of the Nive but to be certain that they had come, and this could only be done by repeating the attacks at Barrouilhet. The same cause operated on the 12th, for it was not until the fourth and seventh divisions were seen by him on the side of Arbonne that he knew his wile had succeeded. Yet again the execution was below the conception, for first, the bivouac fires on the ridge of Bussussary were extinguished in the evening, and then others were lighted on the side of Mousseroles, thus plainly indicating the march, which was also begun too early, because the lead-

ing division was by Hill seen to pass the bridge of
boats before sun-set.

These were serious errors yet the duke of Dalmatia's generalship cannot be thus fairly tested.
There are many circumstances which combine to
prove, that when he complained to the emperor of
the contradictions and obstacles he had to encounter
he alluded to military as well as to political and
financial difficulties. It is a part of human nature
to dislike any disturbance of previous habits, and
soldiers are never pleased at first with a general,
who introduces and rigorously exacts a system of
discipline differing from what they have been accustomed to. Its utility must be proved and confirmed by habit ere it will find favour in their eyes.
Now Soult suddenly assumed the command of
troops, who had been long serving under various
generals and were used to much license in Spain.
They were therefore, men and officers, uneasy at
being suddenly subjected to the austere and resolute command of one who, from natural character
as well as the exigency of the times, the war being
now in his own country, demanded a ready and
exact obedience, and a regularity which long habits
of a different kind rendered onerous. Hence we
find in all the French writers, and in Soult's own
reports, manifest proofs that his designs were frequently thwarted or disregarded by his subordinates
when circumstances promised impunity. His greatest and ablest military combinations were certainly
rendered abortive by the errors of his lieutenants in
the first operations to relieve Pampeluna, and on
the 31st of August a manifest negligence of his
earnest recommendations to vigilance led to serious
danger and loss at the passage of the Lower

Bidassoa. Complaint and recrimination were rife
in all quarters about the defeat on the 10th of November, and on the 19th the bridge-head of Cambo
was destroyed contrary to the spirit of his instructions. These things, joined to the acknowledged
jealousy and disputes prevalent amongst the French
generals employed in Spain, would indicate that
the discrepancy between the conception and execution of the operations in front of Bayonne was not
the error of the commander-in-chief. Perhaps king
Joseph's faction, so inimical to the duke of Dalmatia, was still powerful in the army and difficult
to deal with.

3°. Lord Wellington has been blamed for putting
his troops in a false position, and no doubt he
under-valued, it was not the first time, the military
genius and resources of his able adversary, when he
exposed Hill's troops on the left of the Nive to a
species of surprize. But the passage of the Nive
itself, the rapidity with which he moved his divisions from bank to bank, and the confidence with
which he relied upon the valour of his troops, so
far from justifying the censures which have been
passed upon him by French writers, emphatically
mark his mastery in the art. The stern justice of
sending the Spaniards back into Spain after the
battle of the Nivelle is apparent, but the magnanimity of that measure can only be understood by
considering lord Wellington's military situation at
the time. The battle of the Nivelle was delivered
on political grounds, but of what avail would his
gaining it have been if he had remained enclosed
as it were in a net between the Nive and the sea,
Bayonne and the Pyrenees, unable to open communications with the disaffected in France, and having

the beaten army absolutely forbidding him to forage or even to look beyond the river on his right. The invasion of France was not his own operation, it was the project of the English cabinet and the allied sovereigns; both were naturally urging him to complete it, and to pass the Nive and free his flanks was indispensable if he would draw any profit from his victory of the 10th of November. But he could not pass it with his whole army unless he resigned the sea-coast and his communications with Spain. He was therefore to operate with a portion only of his force and consequently required all the men he could gather to ensure success. Yet at that crisis he divested himself of twenty-five thousand Spanish soldiers!

Was this done in ignorance of the military glory awaiting him beyond the spot where he stood?

" *If I had twenty thousand Spaniards paid and fed,*" he wrote to lord Bathurst, " *I should have Bayonne. If I had forty thousand I do not know where I should stop. Now I have both the twenty thousand and the forty thousand, but I have not the means of paying and supplying them, and if they plunder they will ruin all.*"

Requisitions which the French expected as a part of war would have enabled him to run this career, but he looked further; he had promised the people protection and his greatness of mind was disclosed in a single sentence. " *I must tell your lordship that our success and every thing depends upon our moderation and justice.*" Rather than infringe on either, he sent the Spaniards to the rear and passed the Nive with the British and Portuguese only, thus violating the military rule which forbids a general to disseminate his troops before an enemy who remains in mass lest he should be beaten in detail. But genius begins where rules end. A great general always seeks moral power in preference to physical force. Wellington's choice here was between a shameful inactivity or a dangerous enterprise. Trusting to the influence of his reputation, to his previous victories, and to the ascendancy of his troops in the field, he chose the latter, and the result, though he committed some errors of execution, justified his boldness. He surprised the passage of the Nive, laid his bridges of communication, and but for the rain of the night before, which ruined the roads and retarded the march of Hill's columns, he would have won the heights of St. Pierre the same day. Soult could not then have withdrawn his divisions from the right bank without being observed. Still it was an error to have the troops on the left bank so unprepared for the battle of the 10th. It was perhaps another error not to have occupied the valley or basin between Hope and Alten, and surely it was negligence not to entrench Hill's position on the 10th, 11th, and 12th. Yet with all this so brave so hardy so unconquerable were his soldiers that he was successful at every point, and that is the justification of his generalship. Hannibal crossed the Alps and descended upon Italy, not in madness but because he knew himself and his troops.

4°. It is agreed by French and English that the battle of St. Pierre was one of the most desperate of the whole war. Lord Wellington declared that he had never seen a field so thickly strewn with dead, nor can the vigour of the combatants be well denied where five thousand men were killed or wounded in three hours upon a space of one mile square. How then did it happen, valour being so conspicuous on both sides, that six English and Portuguese bri-

BOOK
XXIII.

1813.

December.

Appendix
7. Sect. 4.
gades, furnishing less than fourteen thousand men
and officers with fourteen guns, were enabled to
withstand seven French divisions, certainly furnishing thirty-five thousand men and officers with twenty-two guns? The analysis of this fact shows upon
what nice calculations and accidents war depends.

If Hill had not observed the French passing
their bridge on the evening of the 12th, and their
bivouac fires in the night, Barnes's brigade, with
which he saved the day, would have been at Urcuray, and Soult could not have been stopped. But
the French general could only bring five divisions
into action, and those only in succession, so that in
fact three divisions or about sixteen thousand men
with twenty-two guns actually fought the battle.
Foy's and Maransin's troops did not engage until
after the crisis had passed. On the other hand the
proceedings of colonel Peacocke of the seventy-first,
and colonel Bunbury of the third, for which they
were both obliged to quit the service, forced general
Hill to carry his reserve away from the decisive
point at that critical period which always occurs in a
well-disputed field and which every great general
watches for with the utmost anxiety. This was no
error, it was a necessity, and the superior military
quality of the British troops rendered it successful.

The French officer who rode at the head of the
second attacking column might be a brave man,
doubtless he was ; he might be an able man, but
he had not the instinct of a general. On his right
flank indeed Hill's vigorous counter-attack was
successful, but the battle was to be won in the centre ; his column was heavy, undismayed, and
only one weak battalion, the ninety-second, was
before it; a short exhortation, a decided ges-
ture, a daring example, and it would have over-

borne the small body in its front, Foy's, Maransin's,
and the half of D'Armagnac's divisions would
then have followed in the path thus marked out.
Instead of this he weighed chances and retreated.
How different was the conduct of the British generals, two of whom and nearly all their staff fell at
this point, resolute not to yield a step at such a critical period ; how desperately did the fiftieth and
Portuguese fight to give time for the ninety-second
to rally and reform behind St. Pierre; how glo-
riously did that regiment come forth again to charge
with their colours flying and their national music
playing as if going to a review. This was to understand war. The man who in that moment and immediately after a repulse thought of such military
pomp was by nature a soldier.

I have said that Sir Rowland Hill's employment
of his reserve was no error, it was indeed worthy of
all praise. From the commanding mount on which
he stood, he saw at once, that the misconduct of the
two colonels would cause the loss of his position
more surely than any direct attack upon it, and
with a promptness and decision truly military he
descended at once to the spot, playing the soldier
as well as the general, rallying the seventy-first and
leading the reserve himself; trusting meanwhile with
a noble and well-placed confidence to the courage
of the ninety-second and the fiftieth to sustain the
fight at St. Pierre. He knew indeed that the sixth
division was then close at hand and that the battle
might be fought over again, but like a thorough
soldier he was resolved to win his own fight with
his own troops if he could. And he did so after a
manner that in less eventful times would have rendered him the hero of a nation.

CHAPTER III.

To understand all the importance of the battle of
St. Pierre, the nature of the country and the relative
positions of the opposing generals before and after
that action must be considered.　Bayonne although
a mean fortress in itself was at this period truly designated by Napoleon as one of the great bulwarks
of France.　Covered by its entrenched camp, which
the inundations and the deep country rendered impregnable while there was an army to defend it, this
place could not be assailed until that army was
drawn away, and it was obviously impossible to pass
it and leave the enemy to act upon the communications with Spain and the sea-coast.　To force
the French army to abandon Bayonne was therefore
Lord Wellington's object, and his first step was the
passage of the Nive ; he thus cut Soult's direct
communication with St. Jean Pied de Port, obtained an intercourse with the malcontents in France,
opened a large tract of fertile country for his cavalry, and menaced the navigation of the Adour so
as to render it difficult for the French general to receive supplies.　This was however but a first step,
because the country beyond the Nive was still the
same deep clayey soil with bad roads ; and it was traversed by many rivers more or less considerable,
which flooding with every shower in the mountains,

formed in their concentric courses towards the
Adour a number of successive barriers, behind which
Soult could maintain himself on Lord Wellington's
right and hold communication with St. Jean Pied de
Port. He could thus still hem in the allies as
before; upon a more extended scale however and
with less effect, for he was thrown more on the
defensive, his line was now the longest, and his
adversary possessed the central position.

On the other hand, Wellington could not, in that
deep impracticable country, carry on the wide operations necessary to pass the rivers on his right, and
render the French position at Bayonne untenable,
until fine weather hardened the roads, and the winter
of 1813 was peculiarly wet and inclement.

From this exposition it is obvious that to nourish
their own armies and circumvent their adversaries
in that respect were the objects of both generals,
Soult aimed to make Wellington retire into Spain,
Wellington to make Soult abandon Bayonne entirely, or so reduce his force in the entrenched
camp that the works might be stormed. The
French general's recent losses forbad him to maintain his extended positions except during the wet
season; three days' fine weather made him tremble;
and the works of his camp were still too unfinished
to leave a small force there. The difficulty of the
roads and want of military transport threw his army
almost entirely upon water-carriage for subsistence,
and his great magazines were therefore established
at Dax on the Adour, and at Peyrehorade on the
Gave of Pau, the latter being about twenty-four
miles from Bayonne. These places he fortified to
resist sudden incursions, and he threw a bridge
across the Adour at the port of Landes, just above

its confluence with the Gave de Pau. But the navigation of the Adour below that point, especially
at Urt, the stream being confined there, could be
interrupted by the allies who were now on the left
bank. To remedy this Soult ordered Foy to pass
the Adour at Urt and constrnct a bridge with a
head of works, but the movement was foreseen by
Wellington, and Foy, menaced with a superior force,
recrossed the river. The navigation was then carried on at night by stealth, or guarded by the
French gun-boats and exposed to the fire of the
allies. Thus provisions became scarce, and the
supply would have been quite unequal to the demand if the French coasting trade, now revived
between Bordeaux and Bayonne, had been interrupted by the navy, but lord Wellington's representations on this head were still unheeded.

Soult was embarrassed by Foy's failure at Urt.
He reinforced him with Boyer's and D'Armagnac's
divisions, which were extended to the Port de
Lannes; then leaving Reille with four divisions
to guard the entrenched camp and to finish the
works, he completed the garrison of Bayonne and
transferred his head-quarters to Peyrehorade.
Clauzel with two divisions of infantry and the light
cavalry now took post on the Bidouze, being supported with Trielhard's heavy dragoons, and having
his left in communication with Paris and with St.
Jean Pied de Port where there was a garrison of
eighteen hundred men besides national guards. He
soon pushed his advanced posts to the Joyeuse
or Gambouri, and the Aran, streams which unite to
fall into the Adour near Urt, and he also occupied
Hellette, Mendionde, Bonloc, and the Bastide de
Clerence. A bridge-head was constructed at

Peyrehorade, Hastingues was fortified on the Gave de Pau, Guiche, Bidache and Came, on the Bidouze, and the works of Navarens were augmented. In fine Soult with equal activity and intelligence profited from the rain which stopped the allies' operations in that deep country.

Lord Wellington also made some changes of position. Having increased his works at Barrouilhet he was enabled to shift some of Hope's troops towards Arcangues, and he placed the sixth division on the heights of Villefranque, which permitted general Hill to extend his right up the Adour to Urt. The third division was posted near Urcuray, the light cavalry on the Joyeuse facing Clauzel's outposts, and a chain of telegraphs was established from the right of the Nive by the hill of San Barbe to St. Jean de Luz. Freyre's Gallicians were placed in reserve about St. Pé, and Morillo was withdrawn to Itzassu where supported by the Andalusian division and by Freyre, he guarded the valley of the Upper Nive and watched general Paris beyond the Ursouia mountain. Such was the state of affairs in the beginning of January, but some minor actions happened before these arrangements were completed.

In December the allies seized the island of Holriague near La Honce on the Adour, which gave them a better command of that river, but Foy kept possession of the islands of Berens and Broc above Holriague. The allies' bridges of communication on the Nive were now carried away by floods which occasioned some embarrassment, and meanwhile, without any orders from lord Wellington, probably with a view to plunder, for his troops were exceedingly licentious, Morillo obtained from Victor Alten

two squadrons of the eighteenth hussars, under pretence of exploring the enemy's position towards
Mendionde and Maccaye. Their commander, major
Hughes, having with difficulty ascertained that he
was to form an advanced guard in a close wooded
country, demanded the aid of some Spanish Caçadores, and then moving forwards drove in the
picquets, crossed the bridge of Mendionde and
commenced a skirmish. But during this action
Morillo withdrew his division without giving any
notice, and at the same time the Caçadores fled in
a shameful manner from the left, the cavalry were
thus turned and escaped with difficulty, having had
one captain killed, two other captains and a lieutenant, and Hughes himself, badly wounded. The
unfortunate issue of this skirmish was attributed at
the time to the bad conduct of the eighteenth hussars, against whom lord Wellington was by mali-
cious misrepresentation previously prejudiced ; for
at Vittoria they were unjustly accused of being more
licentious than others in plundering the captured
property on the field, whereas they had fought well
and plundered less than many who were praised for
their orderly demeanour.

About the same time that this disaster occurred
at Mendionde, Mina, acting independently, and
being pressed for provisions in the mountains, invaded the Val de Baigorry and the Val des Osses,
where his men committed the greatest enormities,
plundering and burning, and murdering men women
and children without distinction. The people of
these valleys, distinguished amongst the Basques for
their warlike qualities, immediately took arms under
the command of one of their principal men, named
Etchevery, and being reinforced with two hundred

and fifty men from St. Jean Pied de Port, surprised
one of Mina's battalions, and attacked the rest with
great vigour. This event gave Soult hopes of exciting the Basques to commence such a war as they
had carried on at the commencement of the French
revolution. His efforts to accomplish it were unceasing, and he had for two months been expecting
the arrival of general Harispe an officer whose
courage and talents have been frequently noticed
in this History, and who being the head of an ancient Basque family had great local influence,
which was increased by his military reputation. It
was thought that if he had come when first expected, about November, lord Wellington's strict
discipline being then unknown to the people, he
would have raised a formidable partizan war in the
mountains. But now the English general's attention to all complaints, his proclamation, and the
proof he gave of his sincerity by sending the Spaniards back when they misconducted themselves,
had, in conjunction with the love of gain that
master passion with all mountaineers, tamed the
Basque spirit and disinclined them to exchange
ease and profit for turbulence and ravage. Nevertheless this incursion by Mina and the licentious
conduct of Morillo's troops, awakened the warlike
propensities of the Val de Baygorry Basques, and
Harispe was enabled to make a levy with which he
immediately commenced active operations, and was
supported by general Paris.

Soult with a view to aid Harispe, to extend his
own cantonments, and to restrict those of the allies,
now resolved to drive the latter's detachments alto- Clauzel's
gether from the side of St. Jean Pied de Port, and Official Reports
fix Clauzel's left at Hellette, the culminant point of and Orders MSS.

the great road to that fortress. To effect this, on the 3d of January, he caused Clauzel to establish two divisions of infantry at the heights of La Costa, near the Bastide de Clerence and beyond the Joyeuse river. Buchan's Portuguese brigade, placed in observation there, was thus forced to retreat upon Briscons, and at the same time Paris advancing to Bonloc connected his right with Clauzel's left at Ayherre, while the light cavalry menaced all the allies' line of outposts. Informed of this movement by telegraph, Wellington, thinking Soult was seeking a general battle on the side of Hasparen, made the fifth division, and lord Aylmer's brigade relieve the light division which marched to Arauntz; the fourth division then passed the Nive at Ustaritz, and the sixth division made ready to march from Ville-franque, by the high road of St. Jean Pied de Port, towards Hasparen, as a reserve to the third fourth and seventh divisions. The latter were concentrated beyond Urcuray on the 4th, their left in communication with Hill's right at Briscons, and their right, supported by Morillo, who advanced from Itzassu for this purpose.

The English general's intent was to fall upon the enemy at once, but the swelling of the small rivers prevented him. However on the 5th having ascertained the true object and dispositions of the French general, and having twenty-four thousand infantry in hand with a division of cavalry and four or five brigades of artillery, he resolved to attack Clauzel's divisions on the heights of La Costa. In this view Le Cor's Portuguese marched against the French right, the fourth division marched against their centre, the third division supported by cavalry against their left; the remainder of the cavalry and

the seventh division, the whole under Stapleton
Cotton, were posted at Hasparen to watch Paris on
the side of Bonloc. Soult was in person at the
Bastide de Clerence and a general battle seemed
inevitable, but the intention of the English general
was merely to drive back the enemy from the
Joyeuse, and the French general, thinking the whole
allied army was in movement resolved to act on the
defensive, and directed the troops at La Costa to
retire fighting upon the Bidouze : the affair terminated therefore with a slight skirmish on the
evening of the 6th. The allies then resumed their old
positions on the right of the Nive, the Andalusians were ordered back to the Bastan, and Carlos
D'Españo's Gallicians were brought up to Ascain in
their place.

When Clauzel saw that nothing serious was designed he sent his horsemen to drive away general
Hill's detachments, which had taken advantage of
the great movements to forage on the lower parts
of the Joyeuse and Aran rivers. Meanwhile Soult
observing how sensitive his adversary was to any
demonstration beyond the Bidouze resolved to maintain the line of those two rivers. In this view he
reduced his defence of the Adour to a line
drawn from the confluence of the Aran to Bayonne,
which enabled him to reinforce Clauzel with Foy's
division and all the light cavalry. Meantime general
Harispe having the division of Paris and the brigade of general Dauture placed under his orders
to support his mountaineers, fixed his quarters
at Hellette and commenced an active partizan warfare. On the 8th he fell upon Mina in the Val des
Osses and drove him with loss into Baygorry. On
the 10th returning to Hellette he surprised Morillo's

foragers with some English dragoons on the side of
Maccaye, and took a few prisoners. On the 12th
he again attacked Mina and drove him up into the
Alduides. During these affairs at the outposts
lord Wellington might have stormed the entrenched
camp in front of Bayonne, but he could not hold it
except under the fire of the fortress, and not being
prepared for a siege avoided that operation. Nor
would the weather, which was again become terrible,
permit him to make a general movement to drive
Harispe from his position in the upper country ;
wherefore he preferred leaving that general in quiet
possession to irritating the mountaineers by a coun-
ter-warfare. He endeavoured however to launch
some armed boats on the Adour above Bayonne,
where Soult had increased the flotilla to twenty
gun-boats for the protection of his convoys, which
were notwithstanding forced to run past Urt under
the fire of a battery constructed by general Hill.

Lord Wellington now dreading the bad effect
which the excesses committed by Mina's and Morillo's men were likely to produce, for the Basques
were already beginning to speak of vengeance, put
forth his authority in repression. Rebuking Morillo
for his unauthorized and disastrous advance upon
Mendionde, and for the excesses of his troops, he
ordered him to keep the latter constantly under arms.
This was resented generally by the Spanish officers,
and especially by Morillo whose savage untractable
and bloody disposition, since so horribly displayed in
South America, prompted him to encourage violence.
He asserted falsely that his troops were starving,
declared that a settled design to ill-use the Spaniards existed, and that the British soldiers were
suffered to commit every crime with impunity. The

English general in reply explained himself both to
Morillo, and to Freyre, who had alluded to the
libels about San Sebastian, with a clearness and
resolution that showed how hopeless it would be to
strive against him.

" He had not," he said, "lost thousands of men
to pillage and ill-treat the French peasantry, he
preferred a small army obedient to a large one dis-
obedient and undisciplined. If his measures to
enforce good order deprived him of the Spanish
troops the fault would rest with those who suffered
their soldiers to commit disorders. Professions
without corresponding actions would not do, he
was determined to enforce obedience one way or
another and would not command insubordinate
troops. The question between them was whether
they should or should not pillage the French peasants. His measures were taken to prevent it and
the conduct which called them forth was more dishonouring to the Spaniards than the measures
themselves. For libels he cared not, he was used
to them and he did not believe the union of the
two nations depended upon such things; but if it
did he desired no union founded upon such an infamous interest as pillage. He had not lost twenty
thousand men in the campaign to enable Morillo to
plunder and he would not permit it. If the Spaniards were resolved to do so let them march their
great armies into France under their own generals,
he would meanwhile cover Spain itself and they
would find they could not remain in France for
fifteen days. They had neither money nor magazines, nothing to maintain an army in the field, the
country behind was incapable of supporting them
and were he scoundrel enough to permit pillage

France rich as it was could not sustain the burthen. Even with a view to living on the enemy by contribu- tions it would be essential to prevent plunder ; and yet in defiance of all these reasons he was called an enemy by the Spanish generals because he op- posed such conduct, and his measures to prevent it were considered dishonouring !

" Something also he could say against it in a poli- tical point of view, but it was unnecessary because careless whether he commanded a large or a small army he was resolved that it should obey him and should not pillage.

" General Morillo expressed doubts of his right to interfere with the Spaniards. It was his right and his duty, and never before did he hear that to put soldiers under arms was a disgrace. It was a measure to prevent evil and misfortunes. Mina could tell by recent experience what a warfare the French peasants could carry on, and Morillo was openly menaced with a like trial. It was in vain for that general to palliate or deny the plundering of his division, after having acknowledged to general Hill that it was impossible to prevent it because the officers and soldiers received by every post letters from their friends, congratulating them upon their good luck in entering France and urging them to seize the opportunity of making fortunes. General Morillo asserted that the British troops were allowed to commit crimes with impunity. Neither he nor any other man could produce an instance of injury done where proof being adduced the perpetrators had escaped punishment. Let him enquire how many soldiers had been hanged, how many stricken with minor chastisements and made to pay for damages done. But had the English troops no cause of complaint against the Spaniards? Officers and soldiers were frequently shot and robbed on the high roads and a soldier had been lately murdered between Oyarzun and Lesaca; the English stores and convoys were plundered by the Spanish soldiers, a British officer had been put to death at Vittoria and others were ill-treated at Santander."

A sullen obedience followed this correspondence for the moment, but the plundering system was soon renewed, and this with the mischief already done was sufficient to rouse the inhabitants of Bidarray as well as those of the Val de Baygorry into action. They commenced and continued a partizan warfare until lord Wellington, incensed by their activity, issued a proclamation calling upon them to take arms openly and join Soult or stay peaceably at home, declaring that he would otherwise burn their villages and hang all the inhabitants. Thus it appeared that notwithstanding all the outcries made against the French for resorting to this system of repressing the warfare of peasants in Spain, it was considered by the English general both justifiable and necessary. However the threat was sufficient for this occasion. The Basques set the pecuniary advantages to be derived from the friendship of the British and Portuguese troops and the misery of an avenging warfare against the evils of Spanish plunder, and generally disregarded Harispe's appeals to their patriotism.

Meanwhile Soult who expected reinforcements seeing that little was to be gained by insurrection and being desirous to resume the offensive, ordered Harispe to leave only the troops absolutely necessary for the defence of St. Jean Pied de Port and

its entrenched camp with a few Basques as scouts
in the valleys, and to concentrate the remainder of
his force at Mendionde, Hellette and La Houssoa,
thus closely hemming in the right of the allies' line
with a view to making incursions beyond the
Upper Nive. This was on the 14th, on the 23rd
Harispe, getting information that Morillo was to
forage in force on the side of Bidarray, endeavoured
to cut him off, the supporting troops consisting
of Spanish infantry and some English hussars
repulsed his first attack, but they were finally
pushed back with some loss in horses and mules.
About the same time one of Hill's posts near the
confluence of the Aran with the Adour was surprised by some French companies who remained
in advance until fresh troops detached from Urt
forced them to repass the river again. This affair
was a retaliation for the surprise of a French post a
few days before by the sixth division, which was
attended with some circumstances repugnant to the
friendly habits long established between the French
and British troops at the outposts. The value of
such a generous intercourse old soldiers well
understand, and some illustrations of it at this period may be quoted.

On the 9th of December, the forty-third was assembled in column on an open space within twenty
yards of the enemy's out-sentry, yet the latter continued to walk his beat for an hour without concern,
relying so confidently on the customary system that
he placed his knapsack on the ground to ease his
shoulders. When at last the order to advance was
given, one of the British soldiers stepping out told
him to go away and helped him to replace his pack,
the firing then commenced ; the next morning the

French in like manner warned a forty-third sentry to retire. But the most remarkable instance happened on the occasion of lord Wellington's being desirous of getting to the top of a hill occupied by the enemy near Bayonne. He ordered the riflemen who escorted him to drive the French away, and seeing the former stealing up, as he thought too close, called out to commence firing; with a loud voice one of those old soldiers replied " *no firing!* " and then holding up the butt of his rifle towards the French, tapped it in a peculiar way. At the well-understood signal which meaned " *we must have the hill for a short time,* " the French who though they could not maintain would not have relinquished the post without a fight if they had been fired upon, quietly retired. And this signal would never have been made if the post had been one capable of a permanent defence, so well do veterans understand war and its proprieties.

The English general now only waited until the roads were practicable, to take the offensive with an army superior in every point of view to Soult's. That general's numbers were also about to be reduced. His conscripts were deserting fast, and the inclemency of the weather was filling his hospitals, while the bronzed veterans of Wellington's army impassive to fatigue, patient to endure, fierce in execution, were free from serious maladies, ready and able to plant their colours wherever their general listed. At this time however the country was a vast quagmire; it was with difficulty that provisions or even orders could be conveyed to the different quarters, and a Portuguese brigade on the right of the Nive, was several days without food from the swelling of the rivulets which stopped the commissariat mules. At the sea-side the troops were better off, yet with a horrible counterpoise, for on that iron-bound coast storms and shipwrecks were so frequent, that scarcely a day passed but some vessel, sometimes many together, were seen embayed and drifting towards the reefs which shoot out like needles for several miles. Once in this situation there was no human help! a faint cry might be heard at intervals, but the tall ship floated slowly and solemnly onwards until the first rock arrested her, a roaring surge then dashed her to pieces and the shore was strewed with broken timbers and dead bodies. December and January were thus passed by the allies, but February saw Wellington break into France the successful invader of that mighty country. Yet neither his nor Soult's military operations can be understood without a previous description of political affairs which shall be given in the next chapter.

CHAPTER IV.

Portugal. — It has been shewn that marshal Beresford's arrival at Lisbon put a momentary check upon the intrigues of the regency relative to the command of the troops, when he rejoined the army the vexatious conduct of the government was renewed with greater violence, and its ill-will was vented upon the English residents, whose goods were arbitrarily seized and their persons imprisoned without regard to justice or international law. The supply and reinforcing of the army were the pretences for these exactions, yet the army was neither supplied nor recruited, for though the new regulations had produced nine thousand trained soldiers, they were, in contempt of the subsidizing treaty, retained in the depôts. At first this was attributed to the want of transport to enable them to march through Spain, but though lord Wellington obtained in the beginning of 1814 shipping to convey them to the army, the Portuguese government still withheld the greatest number, alleging in excuse the ill-conduct of the Spaniards relative to the military convention established between the two countries.

This convention had been concluded in 1812 to enable the Portuguese troops to establish hospitals and to draw certain resources from Spain upon fixed conditions. One of these was that all sup-

CHAP.
IV.

1814.

Mr.
Stuart's
Correspon-
dence,
MSS.

plies might be purchased, half with ready money
half with bills on the Portuguese treasury; nevertheless in December 1813 the Spanish envoy at
Lisbon informed the Portuguese government, that to
give up the shells of certain public buildings for
hospitals was the only effect they would give to the
convention. Wherefore as neither troops nor horses
could march through Spain, and the supply of
those already with the army became nearly impossible, the regency detained the reinforcements. Lord
Wellington strongly reproached the Spanish government for this foul conduct, yet observed with great
force to the Portuguese regency, that the treaty by
which a certain number of soldiers were to be constantly in the field was made with England, not
with Spain; and as the government of the former
country continued to pay the subsidy and provided
ships for the transport of the troops there was no
excuse for retaining them in Portugal.

His remonstrances, Beresford's orders, and Mr.
Stuart's exertions although backed by the menaces
of lord Castlereagh, were however alike powerless;
the regency embarked only three thousand men out
of nine thousand, and those not until the month of
March when the war was on the point of terminating. Thus instead of thirty thousand Portuguese under arms lord Wellington had less than
twenty thousand, and yet Mr. Stuart affirmed that
by doing away with the militia and introducing
the Prussian system of granting furloughs, one
hundred thousand troops of the line might have
been furnished and supported by Portugal, without
pressing more severely on the finances of the country
than the actual system which supplied these twenty
thousand. The regency were now more than usually

importunate to have the subsidy paid in specie in

which case their army would have disappeared
altogether. Mr. Stuart firmly opposed this, knowing
the money would be misapplied if it fell into their
hands, and thinking their importunity peculiarly
ill-timed when their quota of troops was withheld,
and when lord Wellington, forced to pay ready
money for his supplies in France, wanted all the
specie that could be procured for the military chest.
Such was the countenance assumed by Portugal
towards England in return for the independence
which the latter had secured for her; and it is obvious that if the war had not terminated immediately afterwards the alliance could not have continued. The British army deserted by Portugal
and treated hostilely, as we shall find, by the Spaniards, must then have abandoned the Peninsula.

Spain.—The malice evinced towards lord Wellington by the Spanish government, the libels upon
him and upon the Anglo-Portuguese army, the vices
of the system by which the Spanish troops were
supplied, and their own evil propensities fostered
by long and cruel neglect and suffering, the activity
of those intriguing politicians who were inimical to
the British alliance, the insolence and duplicity of
the minister of war, the growing enmity between
Spain and Portugal, the virulence of all parties
and the absolute hostility of the local authorities
towards the British army, the officers and soldiers
of which were on all occasions treated as if they
were invaders rather than friends, drove lord Wellington in the latter end of November to extremity. He judged the general disposition of the
Spanish people to be still favourable to the English
alliance, and with the aid of the serviles hoped to

put down the liberals; but an open rupture with
the government he thought inevitable, and if the
liberal influence should prove most powerful with
the people he might be unable to effect a retreat
into Portugal. Wherefore he recommended the
British ministers to take measures with a view to a
war against Spain! And this at the very moment
when, victorious in every battle, he seemed to have
placed the cause he supported beyond the power of
fortune. Who when Napoleon was defeated at
Leipsic, when all Europe and even part of Asia
were pouring their armed hordes into the northern
and eastern parts of France, when Soult was unable
to defend the western frontier ; who then looking
only on the surface could have supposed that Wellington, the long-enduring general, whose profound
calculations and untiring vigour in war had brought
the affairs of the Peninsula to their apparently
prosperous state, that he the victorious commander
could with truth thus describe his own uneasy situation to his government?

" Matters are becoming so bad between us and
the Spaniards that I think it necessary to draw
your attention seriously to the subject. You will
have seen the libels about San Sebastian, which I
know were written and published by an officer of
the war department and I believe under the direction of the minister at war Don Juan O'Donoju.
Advantage has been taken of the impression made
by these libels to circulate others in which the old
stories are repeated about the outrages committed
by sir John Moore's army in Gallicia, and endeavours are made to irritate the public mind about
our still keeping garrisons in Cadiz and Carthagena, and particularly in Ceuta. They exaggerate

the conduct of our traders in South America, and every little concern of a master of a ship who may behave ill in a Spanish port is represented as an attack upon the sovereignty of the Spanish nation. I believe these libels all proceed from the same source, the government and their immediate servants and officers ; and although I have no reason to believe that they have as yet made any impression on the nation at large they certainly have upon the officers of the government, and even upon the principal officers of the army. These persons must see that if the libels are not written or encouraged by the government they are at least not discouraged, they know that we are odious to the government and they treat us accordingly. The Spanish troops plunder every thing they approach, neither their own nor our magazines are sacred. Until recently there was some semblance of inquiry and of a desire to punish offenders, lately these acts of disorder have been left entirely unnoticed, unless when I have interfered with my authority as commander-in-chief of the Spanish army. The civil magistrates in the country have not only refused us assistance but have particularly ordered the inhabitants not to give it for payment, and when robberies have been discovered and the property proved to belong to the commissariat the law has been violated and possession withheld. This was the case lately at Tolosa.

" Then what is more extraordinary and more difficulf to understand is a transaction which occurred lately at Fuenterabia. It was settled that the British and Portuguese hospitals should go to that town. There is a building there which has been a Spanish hospital, and the Spanish authority who gave it over wanted to carry off, in order to burn as fire-wood, the beds, that our soldiers might not have the use of them ; and these are people to whom we have given medicines instruments and other aids, who when wounded and sick we have taken into our hospitals, and to whom we have rendered every service in our power after having recovered their country from the enemy ! These are not the people of Spain but the officers of government, who would not dare to conduct themselves in this manner if they did not know that their conduct was agreeable to their employers. If this spirit is not checked, if we do not show that we are sensible of the injury done to our characters, and of the injustice and unfriendly nature of such proceedings, we must expect that the people at large will soon behave towards us in the same manner, and that we shall have no friend or none who will dare to avow him as such in Spain. Consider what will be the consequence of this state of affairs if any reverse should happen, or if an aggravation of the insults and injuries or any other cause should cause the English army to be withdrawn. I think I should experience great difficulty, the Spanish people being hostile, in retiring through Spain into Portugal from the peculiar nature of our equipments, and I think I might be able to embark the army at Passages in spite of all the French and Spanish armies united. But I should be much more certain of getting clear off as we ought if we had possession of San Sebastian, and this view of the subject is the motive for the advice I am about to give you as the remedy for the evils with which I have made you acquainted.

" First then I recommend to you to alter the nature of your political relations with Spain and to

have nothing there but a *"chargé d'affaires."* Secondly to complain seriously of the conduct of the
government and their servants, to remind them that
Cadiz, Carthagena, and I believe, Ceuta, were garrisoned by British troops at their earnest request,
and that the troops were not sent to the two former
till the government agreed to certain conditions. If
we had not garrisoned the last it would before now
have fallen into the hands of the Moors. Thirdly
to demand, as security for the safety of the king's
troops against the criminal disposition of the government and of those in authority under them,
that a British garrison should be admitted into San
Sebastian, giving notice that unless this demand
was complied with the troops should be withdrawn.
Fourthly. To withdraw the troops if this demand
be not complied with, be the consequences what
they may, and to be prepared accordingly. You
may rely upon this, that if you take a firm decided
line and shew your determination to go through
with it, you will have the Spanish nation with you,
and will bring the government to their senses, and
you will put an end at once to all the petty cabals
and counter-action existing at the present moment,
and you will not be under the necessity of bringing
matters to extremities ; if you take any other than
a decided line and one which in its consequences
will involve them in ruin you may depend upon it
you will gain nothing and will only make matters
worse. I recommend these measures whatever may
be the decision respecting my command of the
army. They are probably the more necessary if I
should keep my command. The truth is that a
crisis is approaching in our connection with Spain
and if you do not bring the government and nation

to their senses before they go too far, you will
inevitably lose all the advantages which you might
expect from services rendered to them."

Thus it appears that lord Wellington at the end
of the war described the Spaniards precisely as sir
John Moore described them at the beginning. But
the seat of government was now transferred to
Madrid and the new Cortez, as I have already
noticed, decided, against the wishes of the regency, that the English general should keep the
command of the Spanish armies. The liberals indeed with great diligence had previously sought to
establish a system of controul over the Cortez by
means of the populace of Madrid as they had done
at Cadiz, and they were so active and created so
much alarm by their apparent success, that the serviles, backed by the Americans, were ready to make
the princess Carlotta sole regent as the only resource for stemming the progress of democracy.
However when they had proved their strength upon
the question of lord Wellington's command, they
deferred the princess's affair and resolved to oppose
their adversaries more vigorously in the assembly.
They were encouraged also by a tumult which happened at Madrid, where the populace instigated
by their agents, or disliking the new constitution,
for the measures of the democratic party were generally considered evil in the great towns beyond the
Isla, rose and forced the authorities to imprison a
number of obnoxious persons ; the new Cortez then
arrived, the serviles got the upper hand and being
resolved to change the regency took as their ground
of attack its conduct towards the English general.
Pursuing this scheme of opposition with ardour
they caused the minister of war to be dismissed, and

were ready to attack the regency itself, expecting
full success, when to their amazement and extreme anger lord Wellington, far from desiring to have his personal enemies thus thrust out of power, expressed his earnest desire to keep them in their stations.

To men who were alike devoid of patriotism or principle, and whose only rule of action was the momentary impulse of passion, such a proceeding was incomprehensible ; yet it was a wise and well-considered political change on his part, shewing that private feelings were never the guides of his conduct in public matters, and that he ever seemed to bear in mind the maxim which Sophocles has put into the mouth of Ajax, *" carrying himself towards his friends as if they might one day become enemies and treating his foes as men who might become friends."* The new spirit had given him no hopes of any general alteration of the system, nor was he less convinced that sooner or later he must come to extremities with the Spaniards ; but he was averse to any appearance of disunion becoming public at the moment he was invading France, lest it should check his projects of raising an anti-Napoleon party in that country. He therefore advised the British government to keep his hostile propositions in abeyance, leaving it to him and to his brother to put them in execution or not as events might dictate. Meanwhile he sent orders to evacuate Cadiz and Carthagena, and opposed the projected change in the Spanish government, observing that " the minister of war being dismissed, the most obnoxious opponent of military arrangement was gone ; that the mob of Madrid, being worked upon by the same press in the hands of the same people who had made the mob of Cadiz so ungovernable, would become as

bad as these last, and though the mercantile interest
would not have so much power in the capital they
would not want partizans when desirous of carrying
a question by violence. The grandees were too poor
to retain their former natural influence, and the constitution gave them no political power. The only
chance which the serviles had was to conduct
themselves with prudence, and when in the right
with a firm contempt for the efforts of the press and
the mob; but this was what no person in Spain
ever did and the smaller party being wiser bolder
and more active would soon govern the Cortez at
Madrid as they did that at Cadiz."

No permanent change for the better could be
expected, and meanwhile the actual government,
alarmed by the tumults in the capital, by the
strength of the serviles in the Cortez, by the rebukes and remonstrances of the English general
and ministers, and by the evident danger of an open
rupture with England, displayed, according to lord
Wellington, the utmost prudence and fairness in a
most important affair which occurred at this time.
That is to say, their own views and interests coin-
ciding with those of the English commander and
government there was a momentary agreement, and
Wellington wisely preferred this opening for con-
ciliation to the more dangerous mode he had before
recommended.

The event which called forth his approval of their
conduct was the secret arrival of the duke of San
Carlos at Madrid in December. He brought with
him a treaty of peace, proposed by Napoleon and
accepted by Ferdinand, called the treaty of Valençay. It acknowledged Ferdinand as king of
Spain and the Indies, and the integrity of the

Spanish empire was recognized. He was in return to make the English evacuate Spain, and the French troops were to abandon the country at the same time. The contracting powers were to maintain their respective maritime rights as they had been stipulated by the treaty of Utrecht and observed until 1792. The sales of the national domains made by Joseph were to be confirmed; all the Spaniards who had attached themselves to the French cause were to be reinstated in their dignities and property, those who chose to quit Spain were to have ten years to dispose of their possessions. Prisoners, including all those delivered up by Spain to the English, were to be sent home on both sides. The king was to pay annually thirty millions of reals to his father Charles IV., and two millions to his widow; a treaty of commerce was to be arranged.

Ferdinand being entirely devoid of principle acted with that cunning which marked his infamous career through life. He gave the duke of San Carlos secret instructions to tell the serviles, if he found them all-powerful in the Cortez, to ratify this treaty with a secret resolution to break it when time served; but if the Jacobins were strongest San Carlos was merely to ask them to ratify it, Ferdinand in that case reserving to himself the task of violating it on his own authority. These instructions were made known to the English ministers and the English general, but they, putting no trust in such a negociator, and thinking his intention was rather to deceive the allies than Napoleon, thwarted him as much as they could, and in this they were joined by the Por- Mr.
tuguese government. The British authorities were Stuart's Corres-
naturally little pleased with the prospect of being pondence MSS.

forced to abandon Spain under a treaty, which would necessarily give Napoleon great influence over that country in after times, and for the present enable him to concentrate all the old troops on the eastern frontier of his empire; nor was the Jacobinical Spanish government more content to have a master. Wherefore, all parties being agreed, the regency, keeping the matter secret, dismissed San Carlos on the 8th of January with a copy of the decree passed by the Cortez, which rendered null and void all acts of Ferdinand while a prisoner, and forbad negociation for peace while a French army remained in the Peninsula. And that the king might fully understand them, they told him " *the monster despotism had been driven from the throne of Spain.*" Meanwhile Joseph Palafox, who had been a prisoner ever since the siege of Zaragoza, was by the French emperor first sent to Valençay, after which he was to follow San Carlos and he arrived at Madrid four days after the latter's departure. But his negociations were equally fruitless with the regency, and in the secret sittings of the Cortez measures were discussed for watching the king's movements and forcing him to swear to the constitution and to the Cortez before he passed the frontier.

Lord Wellington was alarmed at the treaty of Valençay. He had, he said, long suspected Napoleon would adopt such an expedient and if he had shewn less pride and more common sense it would have succeeded. This sarcasm was perhaps well applied to the measure as it appeared at the time, but the emperor's real proceedings he was unacquainted with, and this splenetic ebullition only indicated his own vexation at approaching mischief, for he was forced to acknowledge that the project was not unlikely even then to succeed, because the misery of Spain was so great and so clearly to be traced to the views of the government and of the new constitution, that many persons must have been desirous to put an end to the general suffering under the sanction of this treaty. " If Napoleon," he said, " had withdrawn the garrisons from Catalonia and Valencia and sent Ferdinand who must be *as useless a person in France as he would probably be in Spain* at once to the frontier, or into the Peninsula, peace would have been made or the war at least rendered so difficult as to be almost impracticable and without hope of great success." Now this was precisely what Napoleon had designed, and it seems nearly certain that he contemplated the treaty of Valençay and the restoration of Ferdinand as early as the period of the battle of Vittoria, if not before.

The scheme was one which demanded the utmost secrecy, that it might be too sudden for the English influence to defeat it; the emperor had therefore arranged that Ferdinand should enter Spain early in November, that is at the very moment when it would have been most injurious to the English interest, because then the disputes in the Cortez between the serviles and Jacobins were most rancorous, and the hostility of the regencies both in Portugal and Spain towards the English general and English influence undisguised. Suchet had then also proved his superiority to the allies in Catalonia, and Soult's gigantic lines being unessayed seemed impregnable. But in Napoleon's council were persons seeking only to betray him. It was the great misfortune of his life to have been

driven by circumstances to suffer such men as Talleyrand and Fouché, whose innate treachery has
become proverbial, to meddle in his affairs or even
to approach his court. Mischief of this kind,
however, necessarily awaits men who like Napoleon
and Oliver Cromwell have the courage to attempt
after great convulsions and civil wars the rebuilding
of the social edifice without spilling blood. Either
to create universal abhorrence by their cruelty, or
to employ the basest of men, the Talleyrands,
Fouchés, and Monks, of revolutions, is their inevitable fate; and never can they escape the opposition, more dangerous still, of honest and resolute
men, who unable to comprehend the necessity of the
times see nothing but tyranny in the vigour which
prevents anarchy.

The treaty of Valençay was too important a
measure to escape the sagacity of the traitors
around Napoleon, and when their opposition in the
council and their secret insinuations proved unavailing to dissuade him from it, they divulged the
secret to the partizans of the Bourbons. Taking advantage of the troubled state of public affairs which
occupied the emperor's time and distracted his
attention, they contrived that Ferdinand's emissaries
should precede him to Madrid, and delayed his
own departure until March when the struggle was
at an end. Nevertheless the chances of success for
this scheme, even in its imperfect execution, were
so many and so alarming that lord Wellington's
sudden change from fierce enmity to a warm
support of the regency, when he found it resolute
and frank in its rejection of the treaty, although it
created so much surprize and anger at the moment,
cannot be judged otherwise than as the wise and

prudent proceeding of a consummate statesman.
Nor did he fail to point out to his own government
the more distant as well as the immediate danger to
England and Spain involved in this singularly
complicated and important affair.

The evils as affecting the war and English alliance
with Spain were obvious, but the two articles relating to the provision for Ferdinand's father and
mother, and to the future state of the Spaniards who
had joined the French involved great interests. It
was essential, he said, that the Spanish government
should explicitly declare its intentions. Negociations for a general peace were said to be commenced, of that he knew nothing, but he supposed
such being the case that a basis would be
embodied in a preliminary treaty which all the
belligerents would ratify, each power then to
arrange its own peculiar treaty with France under
protection of the general confederation. Napoleon would necessarily put forward his treaty
with Ferdinand. It could be got rid of by the
statement that the latter was a prisoner when negociating; but new articles would then have to be
framed and therefore the Spanish government
should be called upon previously to declare what
their intentions were as to the two articles in the
treaty of Valençay. His objections to them were
that the allowance to Charles IV. was beyond the
financial means of Spain, and were it not so, Napoleon should not be allowed to stipulate for any
provision for him. Neither should he be suffered
to embody or establish a permanent French party
in Spain, under protection of a treaty, an article of
which provided for the restoration of the Spaniards
who had taken part with the French. It would

give him the right, which he would not fail to
exercise, of interfering in their favour in every
question of property, or other interest, and the
Spanish government would be involved in perpetual
disputes wtth France.   It was probable the allied
sovereigns would be desirous of getting rid of this
question and would think it desirable that Spain
should pardon her rebellious subjects.   For this
reason he had before advised the Spanish government to publish a general amnesty, with the view of
removing the difficulty when a general peace should
come to be negociated, and this difficulty and danger
be enhanced, if not before provided for, by the
desire which each of the allied powers would feel,
when negociating on their separate grounds, to save
their finances by disbanding their armies.

This suggestion of an amnesty, made ten days
before the battle of Vittoria, illustrates Wellington's
sagacity, his long and provident reach of mind, his
discriminating and magnanimous mode of viewing
the errors and weaknesses of human nature.   Let it
be remembered that in the full tide of success, after
having passed the Douro, and when Joseph surprised
and bewildered was flying before him, that he
who had been called the iron duke in the midst of
his bivouac fires, found time to consider, and had
sufficient humanity and grandeur of mind thus to
address the Spanish government on this subject.

" A large number of Spaniards who have taken
the side of the French are now with the enemy's
army, many of these are highly meritorious and have
rendered most essential service to the cause even
during the period in which they have been in the
service of the enemy.   It is also a known fact that
fear, the misery and distress which they suffered

during the contest, and despair of the result, were
the motives which induced many of these unfortunate persons to take the part which they have taken,
and I would suggest for consideration whether it is
expedient to involve the country in all the consequences of a rigid adherence to the existing law in
order to punish such persons. I am the last man
who will be found to diminish the merit of those
Spaniards who have adhered to the cause of the
country during the severe trial which I hope has
passed, particularly of those, who, having remained
amongst the enemy without entering their service,
have served their country at the risk of their lives.
But at the same time that I can appreciate the
merits of these individuals and of the nation at large
I can forgive the weakness of those who have been
induced by terror by distress or by despair to pursue
a different line of conduct.

" I entreat the government to advert to the circumstances of the commencement and of the different
stages of this eventful contest, and to the numerous
occasions in which all men must have imagined that
it was impossible for the powers of the Peninsula,
although aided by Great Britain, to withstand the
colossal power by which they were assailed and
nearly overcome. Let them reflect upon the weakness of the country at the commencement of the
contest, upon the numerous and almost invariable
disasters of the armies, and upon the ruin and dis-
organization that followed, and let them decide
whether those who were witnesses of these events
are guilty because they could not foresee what has
since occurred. The majority are certainly not
guilty in any other manner, and many now deemed
guilty in the eye of the law as having served the

pretended king have by that very act acquired the
means of serving and have rendered important services to their country. It is my opinion that the
policy of Spain should lead the government and the
Cortez to grant a general amnesty with certain
exceptions. This subject deserves consideration in
the two views of failing or succeeding in freeing the
country from its oppressors. If the effort fail the
enemy will by an amnesty be deprived of the principal means now in his hands of oppressing the
country in which his armies will be stationed; he
will see clearly that he can place no reliance on
any partizans in Spain, and he will not have even a
pretence for supposing that the country is divided
in opinion. If the effort succeed the object of the
government should be to pacify the country and to
heal the divisions which the contest has unavoidably
occasioned. It is impossible to accomplish this
object while there exists a great body of the
Spanish nation, some possessing the largest property in the country and others endowed with
considerable talents, who are proscribed for their
conduct during the contest, conduct which has been
caused by the misfortunes to which I have above
adverted. These persons their friends and relations
will if persecuted naturally endeavour to perpetuate
the divisions in the country in the hope at some
time to take advantage of them, and adverting to
their number and to that power which they must
derive from their property and connections it must
be feared that they will be too successful.

   " But there are other important views of this
question. First should the effort to free the country
from its oppressors succeed, at some time or other
approaches to peace must be made between the two

nations and the amnesty to the persons above described will remove the greatest difficulty in the way of such an arrangement. Secondly, should even Spain be at peace with France and the proscription against these persons be continued, they will remain in France a perpetual instrument in the hands of that restless power to disturb the internal tranquillity of Spain ; and in case of a renewal of the war, which will be their wish and object, they will be the most mischievous and most inveterate enemies of their country, of that country which with mistaken severity aggravates her misfortunes by casting off from her thousands of her useful subjects. On every ground then it is desirable that the measure should be adopted and the present moment should be seized for adopting it."

Then pointing out with great accuracy and justice those who should be exempted from an amnesty he thus terminated this record of his own true greatness, and of the littleness of the people to whom it was fruitlessly addressed.

" In bringing this subject under the consideration of the government I am perhaps intruding my opinion on a subject in which as a stranger I have no concern, but having had an advantage enjoyed by few of being acquainted with the concerns of the country since the commencement of the contest, and having been sensible both in the last and present campaign of the disadvantages suffered by Spain from the want of a measure of this description, I have thought it proper as a well-wisher to the cause to bring it under the consideration of the government assuring them at the same time that I have never had the slightest communication on the subject with the government of my country, nor do

I believe that they have ever turned their attention
to it. What I have above stated are my own
opinions to which I may attribute more weight than
they merit but they are founded upon a sincere devotion to the interests of the country."

Such was the general political state of the Peninsula as bearing upon the military operations at the
close of the year 1813, and the state of England
and France shall be shewn in the next chapters.
But however hateful and injurious to England the
conduct of the Peninsular government appears, and
however just and well-founded were the greatest
part of lord Wellington's complaints, it is not
to be assumed that the Spanish government and
Cortez were totally without excuse for their
hostility or ingratitude. It was not solely upon
military grounds that they were obnoxious to the
English general. He united heartily with the
English government in hatred of democratic institutions as opposed to aristocratic domination. Spain
with the former seemed scarcely worth saving from
France, and in a letter written about that period to
the Conde de la Bispal, who it would appear proposed some immediate stroke of violence against
the regency, he openly avows that he was inimical
to the constitution, because it admitted a free press
and refused to property any political influence
beyond what naturally belonged to it. That is, it
refused to heap undue honours privileges and power
upon those who already possessed all the luxury
and happiness which riches can bestow; it refused
to admit the principle that those who have much
should have more, that the indolence corruption and
insolence naturally attendant upon wealth should
be supported and increased by irresponsible power;

that those who laboured and produced all things should enjoy nothing, that the rich should be tyrants and the poor slaves. But these essential principles of aristocratic government have never yet been, and never will be quietly received and submitted to by any thinking people : where they prevail there is no real freedom. Property inevitably confers power on its possessors, and far from adding to that natural power by political privileges it should be the object of all men who love liberty to balance it by raising the poorer classes to political importance : the influence and insolence of riches ought to be tamed and subdued instead of being inflated and excited by political institutions. This was the guiding principle of the most celebrated Greek legislators, the opposite principle produced the domestic dissensions of the Romans, and was the ruin of Carthage. It was the cause also of the French revolution. But after many years of darkness, the light of reason is now breaking forth again, and that ancient principle of justice which places the right of man in himself, above the right of property, is beginning to be understood. A clear perception of it has produced the American republic. France and Spain have admitted it and England ripens for its adoption. Yet pure and bright and beautiful and healthful as the light of freedom is in itself, it fell at this time on such foul and stagnant pools, such horrid repulsive objects, that millions turned at first from its radiance with disgust and wished for darkness again.

CHAPTER V.

THE force and energy of Napoleon's system of government was evinced in a marvellous manner by the rapidity with which he returned to Germany, at the head of an enormous army, before his enemies had time even to understand the extent of his misfortunes in the Russian campaign. The victories of Lutzen and Bautzen then seemed to reinstate him as the arbiter of Europe. Bnt those battles were fought with the heads of columns the rear of which were still filing out of France. They were fought also with young troops. Wherefore the emperor when he had given himself a fixed and menacing position in Germany more readily listened to the fraudful negociations of his trembling opponents, partly in hopes of attaining his object without further appeal to arms, partly to obtain time to organize and discipline his soldiers, confident in his own unmatched skill in directing them if war was finally to decide his fate. He counted also upon the family ties between him and Austria, and believed that power willing to mediate sincerely. Not that he was so weak as to imagine the hope of regaining some of its former power and possessions was not uppermost, nor was he unprepared to make concessions ; but he seems to have been quite unsuspecting of the long course of treachery and deceit followed by the Austrian politicians.

It has been already shewn that while negociating with France an offensive and defensive treaty in 1812, the Austrian cabinet was cognizant of, and secretly aiding the plan of a vast insurrection extending from the Tyrol to Calabria and the Illyrian provinces. The management of this scheme was entrusted by the English cabinet to general Nugent and Mr. King who were at Vienna ; their agents went from thence to Italy and the Illyrian coast, many Austrian officers were engaged in the project ; and Italians of great families entered into commercial houses to enable them with more facility to carry on this plan. Moreover Austria while actually signing the treaty with Napoleon was with unceasing importunity urging Prussia to join the Russians in opposition to him. The feeble operations of Prince Swartzenberg, the manner in which he uncovered the emperor's right flank and permitted Tchitchagoff to move to the Beresina in the Russian campaign, were but continuations of this deceitful policy. And it was openly advanced as a merit by the Austrian cabinet that her offer of mediation after the battle of Bautzen was made solely with the view of gaining time to organize the army which was to join the Russians and Prussians. Finally the armistice itself was violated, hostilities being commenced before its termination, to enable the Russian troops safely to join the Austrians in Bohemia.

Nevertheless Napoleon's genius triumphed at Dresden over the unskilful operations of the allies, directed by Swartzenberg, whose incapacity as a commander was made manifest in this campaign.

Vol.v.p.49

Appendix,
No. 1.

Nor would the after misfortunes of Vandamme and
Marshal Macdonald, or the defeat of Oudinot and
Ney have prevented the emperor's final success but
for the continuation of a treachery, which seemed
at the time to be considered a virtue by sovereigns
who were unceasingly accusing their more noble
adversary of the very baseness that they were
practising so unblushingly. He had conceived a
project so vast so original so hardy, so far above
the imaginations of his contemporary generals, that
even Wellington's sagacity failed to pierce it, and he
censured the emperor's long stay on the Elbe as an
obstinacy unwarranted by the rules of art. But
Napoleon had more profoundly judged his own
situation. The large forces he left at Dresden at
Torgau, and Wittemberg, for which he has been so
much blamed by shallow military critics as lessening
his numbers on the field of Leipsic, were essential
parts of his gigantic plan. He quitted Dresden,
apparently in retreat, to deceive his enemies, but
with the intention of marching down the Elbe, re-
crossing that river and throwing his opponents into
a false position. Then he would have seized Berlin
and reopening his communications with his garrisons both on the Elbe and the Oder have operated
between those rivers; and with an army much augmented in power, because he would have recovered
many thousand old soldiers cooped up in the garrisons; an army more compact and firmly established also, because he would have been in direct
communication with the Danes and with Davoust's
force at Hamburgh, and both his flanks would have
been secured by his chains of fortresses on the two
rivers. Already had Blucher and the Swedes felt
his first stroke, the next would have taught the

allies that the lion was still abroad in his strength,
if at the very moment of execution without any
previous declaration the Bavarians, upon whose
operations he depended for keeping the Austrians
in the valley of the Danube in check, had not formed
common cause with his opponents and the whole
marched together towards the Rhine. The battle
of Leipsic followed, the well-known treason of the
Saxon troops led to the victory gained there by the
allies, and Napoleon, now the prey of misfortune,
reached France with only one-third of his army,
having on the way however trampled in the dust
the Bavarian Wrede who attempted to stop his
passage at Hannau.

Meanwhile the allied sovereigns, by giving hopes
to their subjects that constitutional liberty would
be the reward of the prodigious popular exertions against France, hopes which with the most
detestable baseness they had previously resolved to
defraud, assembled greater forces than they were
able to wield, and prepared to pass the Rhine.
But distrusting even their immense superiority of
numbers they still pursued their faithless system.
When Napoleon in consequence of the Bavarian
defection marched to Leipsic, he sent orders to
Gouvion St. Cyr to abandon Dresden and unite
with the garrisons on the Lower Elbe, the messengers were intercepted, and St. Cyr, too little
enterprising to execute such a plan of his own
accord, surrendered on condition of being allowed
to regain France. The capitulation was broken
and general and soldiers remained prisoners.

After the Lepsic battle, Napoleon's adherents fell
away by nations. Murat the husband of his sister
joined Austria and thus forced prince Eugene to

abandon his position on the Adige. A successful insurrection in favour of the prince of Orange broke out in Holland. The neutrality of Switzerland was violated, and more than half a million of armed men were poured across the frontiers of France in all the violence of brute force, for their military combinations were contemptible and their course marked by murder and devastation. But previous to this the allies gave one more notable example of their faithless cunning.

St. Aignan the French resident minister at Gotha had been taken at Leipsic and treated at first as a prisoner of war. He remonstrated and being known to entertain a desire for peace was judged a good tool with which to practise deception. Napoleon had offered on the field of battle at Leipsic to negociate, no notice was taken of it at the time, but now the Austrian Metternich and the Russian Nesselrode had an interview with St. Aignan at Frankfort, and they assured him the Prussian minister agreed in all things with them. They had previously arranged that Lord Aberdeen should come in during the conference as if by accident; nothing was put down in writing, yet St. Aignan was suffered to make minutes of their proposals in reply to the emperor's offer to negociate. These were generally that the alliance of the sovereigns was indissoluble—that they would have only a general peace—that France was to be confined to her natural limits, viz. the Alps the Rhine and the Pyrenees—that the independence of Germany was a thing not to be disputed—that the Spanish Peninsula should be free and the Bourbon dynasty be restored—that Austria must have a frontier in Italy the line of which could be afterwards discussed,

Diplomatic Correspondence, MSS.

but Italy itself was to be independent of any preponderating power—that Holland was also to be independent and her frontier to be matter for after discussion—that England was ready to make great sacrifices for peace upon these bases and would acknowledge that freedom of commerce and of navigation which France had a right to pretend to. St. Aignan here observed that Napoleon believed England was resolved to restrict France to the possession of thirty sail of the line, lord Aberdeen replied that it was not true.

This conference had place at the emperor of Austria's head-quarters on the 10th of November, and lord Aberdeen inclosed the account of it in a despatch dated at Smalcalde the 16th of November. He had objected verbally to the passage relating to the maritime question with England, nevertheless he permitted it to remain in St. Aignan's minutes. It was decided also that the military operations should go on notwithstanding the negociation, and in truth the allies had not the slightest design to make peace. They thought Napoleon would refuse the basis proposed, which would give them an opportunity to declare he was opposed to all reasonable modes of putting an end to the war and thus work upon the French people. This is proved by what followed. For when contrary to their expectations the emperor's minister signified, on the 16th of November, that he accepted the propositions, observing that the independence of all nations at sea as well as by land had been always Napoleon's object, Metternich in his reply, on the 25th of November, pretended to consider this answer as avoiding the acceptation of the basis. The emperor however put that obstacle aside, on the 2d of December, by

accepting explicitly the basis, generally and sum-
marily, such as it had been presented to him,
adding, that France would make great sacrifices
but the emperor was content if by like sacrifices on
the part of England, that general peace which was
the declared object of the allies could be obtained.
Metternich thus driven from his subterfuge required
Napoleon to send a like declaration to each of the
allies separately when negociations might, he said,
commence.

Meanwhile lord Aberdeen, who had permitted
St. Aignan to retain the article relating to maritime
rights in his minutes of conference, presented to
Metternich on the 27th of November a note declaring that England would not admit the turn
given by France to her share of the negociation;
that she was ready to yield all the rights of commerce and navigation which France had a right to
pretend to, but the question would turn upon what
that right was. England would never permit her
navigation laws to be discussed at a congress, it
was a matter essentially foreign to the object of
such an assembly, and England would never depart
from the great principle thereby announced as to
her maritime rights. Metternich approved of lord
Aberdeen's views, saying they were his own and
those of his court, thus proving that the negociation had been a deceit from the beginning. This
fact was however placed beyond doubt by lord
Castlereagh's simultaneous proceedings in London.

In a note dated the 30th November that minister
told lord Aberdeen England admitted as a basis,
that the Alps the Rhine and the Pyrenees should
be the frontier of France, subject to such modi-
fications as might be necessary to give a secure

frontier to Holland, and to Switzerland also, although
the latter had not been mentioned in the proposals
given by St. Aignan. He applauded the resolution
to pursue military operations notwithstanding the
negociations, and he approved of demanding nothing
but what they were resolved to have. Nevertheless
he said that any sacrifice to be made by England
was only to secure the independence of Holland
and Switzerland, and the former having already
declared for the house of Nassau was now out of
the pale of discussion. Finally he recommended
that any unnecessary delay or equivocation on the
part of the enemy should be considered as tantamount to a rejection of the basis, and that the allies
*should then put forward the offer of peace to show
that it was not they but France that opposed an
honourable termination of the war.* Having thus
thrown fresh obstacles in the way of that peace
which the allies pretended to have so much at
heart, he, on the 21st December, sent notes to the
different ambassadors of the allied powers then in
London demanding explicit answers about the intentions of their courts as to England's maritime code.
To this they all responded that their cabinets would
not suffer any question relative to that code to be
entertained at a congress in which England was
represented, and this on the express ground that it
would mar the great object of peace.

Lord Castlereagh thus provided, declared that
France should be informed of their resolutions
before negociations commenced, but twenty days
before this Napoleon having decreed a fresh levy
of three hundred thousand conscripts the allies had
published a manifesto treating this measure, so
essentially a defensive one since they would not

suspend their military operations, as a fresh provo-
cation on his part, because the motives assigned for
the conscription contained a just and powerful
description of their past deceits and violence with
a view to rouse the national spirit of France. Thus
having first by a pretended desire for peace and a
willingness on the part of England to consent to an
arrangement about her maritime code, inveigled the
French emperor into negociations and thereby ascertained that the maritime question was uppermost in
his mind and the only obstacle to peace, they declared that vital question should not even be discussed. And when by this subtlety they had
rendered peace impossible proclaimed that Napoleon alone resisted the desire of the world for tranquillity. And at this very moment Austria was secretly
endeavouring to obtain England's consent to her
seizing upon Alsace a project which was stopped
by lord Wellington who forcibly pointed out the
danger of rousing France to a general insurrection
by such a proceeding.

The contrast between these wiles to gain a momentary advantage, and the manly, vigorous policy of
lord Wellington must make honest men of all nations
blush for the cunning which diplomatists call policy.
On one side the arts of guileful negociation masked
with fair protestations but accompanied by a savage
and revolting system of warfare ; on the other a
broad open hostility declared on manly and just
grounds followed up with a strict regard to humanity and good faith ; nothing put forward with
an equivocal meaning and the actions true to the
word.   On the eastern frontier the Cossack let
loose to ravage with all the barbarity of Asiatic
warfare. On the western frontier the Spaniards

turned back into their own country in the very
midst of triumph, for daring to pass the bounds of
discipline prescribed by the wise and generous
policy of their commander. Terror and desolation
and the insurrection of a people rendered frantic by
the cruelty of the invaders marked the progress of
the ferocious multitudes who crossed the Rhine.
Order and tranquillity, profound even on the very
edge of the battle-field, attended the march of the
civilized army which passed the Bidassoa. And
what were the military actions? Napoleon rising
even above himself hurtled against the armed
myriads opposed to him with such a terrible energy
that though ten times his number they were rolled
back on every side in confusion and dismay. But
Wellington advanced without a check, victorious in
every battle, although one half of the veterans opposed to him would have decided the campaign
on the eastern frontier. Nor can this be gainsaid,
since Napoleon's career in this campaign was only
stayed by the defection of his brother-in-law Murat,
and by the sickening treachery of two marshals to
whom he had been prodigal of benefits. It is
undeniable that lord Wellington with sixty thousand
Anglo-Portuguese acting in the south, effected more
than half a million of the allies were able to effect
on the opposite side of France; and yet Soult's army
on the 10th of November was stronger than that
with which Napoleon fought the battle of Brienne.

That great man was never personally deceived by
the allies' pretended negociations. He joined issue
with them to satisfy the French people that he was
not averse to peace, but his instructions dated the
4th of January and addressed to Caulaincourt prove
at once his sagacity and firmness. " I think," he

said, " that both the allies good faith and the wish
of England to make peace is doubtful; for my part
I desire peace but it must be solid and honourable.
I have accepted the basis proposed at Frankfort yet
it is more than probable the allies have other notions.　These propositions are but a mask, the negociations are placed under the influence of the
military operations and it is easy to foresee what
the consequences of such a system must be.　It is
necessary therefore to listen to and observe every
thing.　It is not certain even that you will be admitted to the head-quarters of the allies.　The
Russians and the English watch to prevent any
opening for explanation and reconciliation with the
emperor of Austria.　You must therefore endeavour
to ascertain the real views of the allies and let me
know day by day what you learn that I may frame
instructions for which at present I have no sure
grounds."

The internal state of France was more disquieting
to his mind than foreign negociations or the number of invaders.　The sincere republicans were
naturally averse to him as the restorer of monarchy,
yet they should have felt that the sovereign whose
ruin was so eagerly sought by the legitimate kings
and nobles of Europe could not be really opposed to
liberty.　Meanwhile the advocates of legitimacy
shrunk from him as an usurper, and all those tired
of war, and they were a majority of the nation,
judging from the stupendous power of his genius
that he had only to will peace to attain it with
security, blamed his tardiness in negociation.　An unexpected opposition to his wishes was also displayed
in the legislative body, and the partizans of the Bourbons were endeavouring to form a great conspiracy

in favour of that house. There were many traitors
likewise to him and to their country, men devoid of
principle, patriotism, or honour, who with instinctive
hatred of a failing cause plotted to thwart his projects for the defence of the nation. In fine the men
of action and the men of theories were alike combined for mischief. Nor is this outbreak of passion to be wondered at when it is considered how
recently Napoleon had stopped the anarchy of the
revolution and rebuilt the social and political structure in France. But of all who by their untimely
opposition to the emperor hurt their country, the
most pernicious were those silly politicians, whom
he so felicitously described as " *discussing abstract
systems of government when the battering ram was
at the gates.*"

Such however has been in all ages the conduct
of excited and disturbed nations, and it seems to be
inherent in human nature, because a saving policy
can only be understood and worked to good by
master-spirits, and they are few and far between,
their time on earth short, their task immense. They
have not time to teach, they must command although
they know that pride and ignorance and even
honesty will carp at the despotism which brings
general safety. It was this vain short-sighted
impatience that drove Hannibal into exile, caused
the assassination of Cæsar, and strewed thorns
beneath the gigantic footsteps of Oliver Cromwell.
It raged fiercely in Spain against lord Wellington,
and in France against Napoleon, and always with
the most grievous injury to the several nations.
Time only hallows human institutions. Under that
guarantee men will yield implicit obedience and
respect to the wildest caprices of the most stupid

tyrant that ever disgraced a throne, and wanting it
they will cavil at and reject the wisest measures of
the most sublime genius. The painful notion is
thus excited, that if governments are conducted
with just the degree of stability and tranquillity
which they deserve and no more, the people of all
nations, much as they may be oppressed, enjoy upon
an average of years precisely the degree of liberty
they are fitted for. National discontents mark,
according to their bitterness and constancy, not so
much the oppression of the rulers as the real progress of the ruled in civilization and its attendant
political knowledge. When from peculiar circumstances those discontents explode in violent revolutions, shattering the fabric of society and giving
free vent and activity to all the passions and follies
of mankind, fortunate is the nation which possesses
a Napoleon or an Oliver Cromwell " *to step into
their state of dominion with spirit to controul and
capacity to subdue the factions of the hour and re-
construct the frame of reasonable government.*"

For great as these two men were in the field of
battle, especially the former, they were infinitely
greater when they placed themselves in the seat of
power, and put forth the gigantic despotism of genius essential to the completion of their holy work.
Nor do I hold the conduct of Washington to be
comparable to either of those men. His situation
was one of infinitely less difficulty, and there is no
reason to believe that his capacity would have been
equal to the emergencies of a more formidable
crisis than he had to deal with. Washington could
not have made himself master of all had it been
necessary and he so inclined, for he was neither the
foremost general nor the foremost statesman of his

nation. His forbearance was a matter of necessity,
and his love of liberty did not prevent him from
bequeathing his black slaves to his widow.

Such was Napoleon's situation, and as he read the
signs of the times truly he knew that in his military
skill and the rage of the peasants at the ravages of
the enemy he must find the means to extricate himself from his difficulties, or rather to extricate his
country, for self had no place in his policy save as his
personal glory was identified with France and her
prosperity. Never before did the world see a man,
soaring so high and devoid of all selfish ambition.
Let those who honestly seeking truth doubt this,
study Napoleon carefully ; let them read the record
of his second abdication published by his brother
Lucien, that stern republican who refused kingdoms
as the price of his principles, and they will doubt
no longer. It is not however with these matters
that this History has to deal but with the emperor's
measures affecting his lieutenants on the Spanish
frontier of France. There disaffection to his government was extensive but principally from local
causes. The conscription was peculiarly hateful
to the wild mountaineers, who like most borderers
cherish very independent notions. The war with
England had ruined the foreign commerce of their
great towns, and the advantage of increased traffic
by land on the east was less directly felt in the
south. There also the recollection of the Vendean
struggle still lingered and the partizans of the
Bourbons had many connections. But the chief
danger arose from the just and politic conduct
of lord Wellington which, offering no cause of
anger and very much of private advantage to the

people, gave little or no hope of insurrection from
sufferings.

While France was in this state England presented a scene of universal exultation. Tory politics
were triumphant, opposition in the parliament was
nearly crushed by events, the press was either subdued by persecution or in the pay of the ministers,
and the latter with undisguised joy hailed the
coming moment when aristocratic tyranny was to be
firmly established in England. The most enormous
subsidies and military supplies were poured into
the continent, and an act was passed to enable
three-fourths of the militia to serve abroad. They
were not however very forward to volunteer, and a
new army which ought to have reinforced Wellington was sent, under the command of general
Graham, to support the insurrection of Holland,
where it was of necessity engaged in trifling or
unsuccessful operations in no manner affecting the
great objects of the war. Meanwhile the importance of lord Wellington's army and views was quite
overlooked or misunderstood. The ministers perse-
vered in the foolish plan of removing him to another quarter of Europe, and at the same time, instigated by the ambassadors of the allied sovereigns, were continually urging him to push his
operations with more vigour in France. As if he
was the man who had done least!

His letters were filled with strong and well-
founded complaints that his army was neglected.
Let his real position be borne in mind. He had,
not as a military man but with a political view
and to meet the wishes of the allied sovereigns
backed by the importunities of his own government,

placed himself in a confined and difficult district of France, where his operations were cramped by rivers and fortresses and by a powerful army occupying strong positions on his front and flanks. In this situation, unable to act at all in wet weather, he was necessarily dependent upon the ocean for supplies and reinforcements, and upon the Spanish authorities for his hospitals, depôts, and communications. Numbers were requisite to balance the advantages derived by the enemy from the peculiar conformation of the country and the position of the fortresses. Money also was wanted to procure supplies which he could not carry with him, and must pay for exactly, if he would avoid a general insurrection and the consequent ruin of the political object for which he had adopted such critical military operations. But though he had undertaken the invasion of France at the express desire of the government the latter seemed to be alike ignorant of its importance and of the means to accomplish it, at one moment urging progress beyond reason, at another ready to change lightly what they had proposed ignorantly. Their unsettled policy proved their incapacity even to comprehend the nature of the great tide of events on which they floated rather than sailed. Lord Wellington was forced day by day to teach them the value of their own schemes, and to show them how small their knowledge was of the true bearing of the political and military affairs they pretended to direct.

" Assure," he wrote on the 21st of December to lord Bathurst, in reply to one of their ill-founded remonstrances, " Assure the Russian ambassador there is nothing I can do to forward the general interest that I will not do. What do they require ?

I am already further advanced on the French territory than any of the allied powers, and better prepared to take advantage of any opportunities which
might offer as a consequence of my own situation
or of their proceedings."—"In military operations
there are some things which can not be done, and
one is to move troops in this country during or immediately after a violent fall of rain. To attempt
it will be to lose more men than can be replaced, a
guilty waste of life."

"The proper scene of action for the army was undoubtedly a question for the government to decide,
but with thirty thousand men in the Peninsula, he
had for five years held two hundred thousand of
Napoleon's best soldiers in check, since it was ridi-
culous to suppose that the Spaniards and Portuguese could have resisted for a moment if the
British troops had been withdrawn. The French
armies actually employed against him could not be
less than one hundred thousand men, more if he
included garrisons, and the French newspapers
spoke of orders to form a fresh reserve of one hundred thousand at Bordeaux. Was there any man
weak enough to suppose one-third of the number
first mentioned would be employed against the
Spaniards and Portuguese if the British were withdrawn? They would if it were an object with
Buonaparte to conquer the Peninsula and he would
in that case succeed; but he was more likely to
give peace to the Peninsula and turn against the
allied sovereigns his two hundred thousand men of
which one hundred thousand were such troops as
their armies had not yet dealt with. The war every
day offered a crisis the result of which might affect
the world for ages, and to change the scene of

operations for the British army would render it incapable of fighting for four months, even if the scene were Holland, and it would even then be a deteriorated machine."

" The ministers might reasonably ask how by remaining where he was he could induce Napoleon to make peace. The answer was ready. He held a commanding situation on the most vulnerable frontier of France, probably the only vulnerable one, and if he could put twenty thousand Spaniards in activity, and he could do it if he had money and was properly supported by the fleet, Bayonne the only fortress on the frontier, if it could be called a fortress, would fall to him in a short time. If he could put forty thousand Spaniards in motion his posts would soon be on the Garonne, and did any man believe that Napoleon would not feel an army in such a position more than he would feel thirty or forty thousand British troops laying siege to one of his fortresses in Holland? The resources in men and money of which the emperor would be thus deprived, and the loss of reputation would do ten times more to procure peace than ten armies on the side of Flanders. But if he was right in believing a strong Bourbon party existed in France and that it preponderated in the south, what mischief would not an advance to the Garonne do Napoleon! What sacrifices would he not make to get rid of the danger!"

" It was for the government not for him to dispose of the nation's resources, he had no right to give an opinion upon the subject, but military operations in Holland and in the Peninsula could not be maintained at the same time with British troops; one or other must be given up, the British military establishment was not equal to maintain two armies in

the field.   He had begun the recent campaign with
seventy thousand Anglo-Portuguese, and if the men
got from the English militia, and the Portuguese
recruits which he expected, had been added to his
force, even though the Germans were removed from
his army according to the ministers' plan, he might
have taken the field early in 1814 with eighty thousand men. That was now impossible. The formation
of a Hanoverian army was the most reasonable plan
of acting on the continent but the withdrawal of the
Germans would reduce his force to fifty thousand
men unless he received real and efficient assistance
to bring up the Portuguese recruits.   This would
increase his numbers to fifty-five or even sixty thousand if his own wounded recovered well and he had
no more battles, but he would even then be twenty
thousand less than he had calculated upon, and it
was certain that if the government extended their
operations to other countries new means must be put
in activity or the war must be stinted on the old
stage.   He did not desire to complain but every
branch of the service in the Peninsula was already
stinted especially in what concerned the navy and
the supplies which came directly from England !"

While thus combating the false views of the
English cabinet as to the general state of affairs he
had also to struggle with its negligence and even
opposition to his measures in details.

The general clothing of the Spanish troops and
the great coats of the British soldiers for 1813, were
not ready in January 1814, because the inferior departments could not comprehend that the opening
of new scenes of exertion required new means, and
the soldiers had to brave the winter half naked, first
on the snowy mountains, then in the more chilling

damps of the low country about Bayonne. The clothing of the British soldiers for 1814 should have arrived in the end of 1813 when the army lying inactive near the coast by reason of the bad weather could have received and fitted it without difficulty. It did not however arrive until the troops were in progress towards the interior of France, wherefore, there being no means of transporting it by land, many of the best regiments were obliged to return to the coast to receive it, and the army as we shall find had to fight a critical battle without them.

He had upon commencing the invasion of France issued a proclamation promising protection to persons and property. This was construed by the French to cover their vessels in the Nivelle when the battle of that name gave the allies St. Jean de Luz. Lord Wellington sacrificing personal profit to the good of the service admitted this claim as tending to render the people amicable, but it clashed with the prize-money pretensions of lord Keith who commanded the fleet of which Collier's squadron formed a detached portion. The serious evils endured by the army in default of sufficient naval assistance had been treated as of very slight importance, the object of a trifling personal gain for the navy excited a marvellous activity, and vigorous interference on the part of the government. Upon these subjects, and others of a like vexatious nature affecting his operations, lord Wellington repeatedly and forcibly declared his discontent during the months of December, January, and February.

"As to the naval affairs," he said, " the reports of the number of ships on the stations striking off those coming out and going home would shew whether he had just ground of complaint, and whatever their

numbers there remained the right of complaint because they did not perform the service required.
The French had recommenced their coast navigation
from Bordeaux to Bayonne, and if the blockade of
Santona had been maintained the place would have
been forced to surrender at an early period. The proclamation of protection which he had issued, and
the licenses which he had granted to French vessels,
every act of that description, and two-thirds of the
acts which he performed every day could not he
knew be considered of any avail as affecting the
king's government, unless approved of and confirmed
by the prince regent ; and he knew that no power
short of the regent's could save the property of
French subjects on the seas from the British navy.
For that reason he had requested the sanction of the
government to the sea passports which he had
granted. His proclamation of protection had been
construed whether rightfully or wrongfully to protect the French ships in the rivers ; his personal
interest, greater than others, would lead him to deny
this, but he sacrificed his profit to the general good.

" Were lord Keith and sir George Collier because
the latter happened to have a brig or two cruizing
off the coast, to claim as prizes all the vessels lying
in every river which the army might pass in its
operations ? and this to the detriment of the cause
which required the strictest respect for private property. For the last five years he had been acting
in the confidence that his conduct would be approved
of and supported, and he concluded it would be so
still ; but he was placed in a novel situation and
asked for legal advice to determine, whether lord
Keith and the channel fleet, were to be considered
as engaged in a conjoint expedition with the army

under his command against the subjects of France,

neither having any specific instructions from government, and the fleet having nothing to do with the
operations by land. He only required that fleet to
give him a free communication with the coast of
Spain, and prevent the enemy's sea communication
between the Garonne and the Adour, and this last
was a part of its duty before the army arrived. Was
his proclamation of protection to hold good as regarded
the ships in the rivers ? He desired to have it sancti-
oned by the prince regent, or that he might be permitted to issue another declaring that it was of no value."

This remonstrance produced so much effect that
lord Keith relinquished his claims, and admiral Penrose was sent to command upon the station instead
of sir George Collier. The immediate intercourse of
lord Wellington with the navy was thus ameliorated
by the superior power of this officer, who was remarkable for his suavity. Yet the licenses given
to French vessels were strongly condemned by the
government, and rendered null, for we find him
again complaining that "he had granted them
only in hopes of drawing money and supplies
from France, and of interesting the French mercantile men to aid the army ; but he feared the government were not aware of, and did not feel the
difficulties in which he was placed at all times for
want of money, and judged his measures without
adverting to the necessity which occasioned them ;
hence their frequent disapprobation of what he did."

Strange this may sound to those who seeing the
duke of Wellington in the fulness of his glory have
been accustomed to regard him as the star of
England's greatness ; but those who at that period
frequented the society of ministers know well that

he was then looked upon by those self-sufficient men as a person whose views were wild and visionary, requiring the corroboration of older and wiser heads before they could be assented to. Yea! even thus at the eleventh hour was the giant Wellington measured by the political dwarfs.

Although he gained something by making San Jean de Luz a free port for all nations not at war with France, his financial situation was nearly intolerable, and at the moment of greatest pressure Colonel Bunbury, under-secretary of state, was sent out to protest against his expenses. One hundred thousand pounds a month was the maximum in specie which the government would consent to supply, a sum quite inadequate to his wants. And this remonstrance was addressed to this victorious commander at the very crisis of his stupendous struggle, when he was overwhelmed with debts and could scarcely stir out of his quarters on account of the multitude of creditors waiting at his door for payment of just claims.

" Some of his muleteers he said were twenty-six months in arrears, and recently, instigated by British merchants, they had become so clamorous that rather than lose their services he had given them bills on the treasury for a part of their claims, though he knew they would sell these bills at a discount to the *sharks*, who had urged them to be thus importunate and who were waiting at the ports to take advantage of the public distresses. A dangerous measure which he desired not to repeat.

" It might be true that the supply of one hundred thousand pounds a month had been even exceeded for some time past, but it was incon-

testible that the English army and all its departments, and the Spanish and Portuguese armies
were at the moment paralyzed for want of money.
The arrears of pay to the soldiers was entering
the seventh month, the debt was immense, and
the king's engagements with the Spanish and Portuguese governments were not fulfilled. Indebted
in every part of Spain he was becoming so in
France, the price of all commodities was increasing
in proportion to the delay of payment, to the difficulty of getting food at all, and the want of credit
into which all the departments of the army had
fallen. Of two hundred thousand dollars given to
marshal Beresford for the pay of his troops on
account of the Portuguese subsidy he had been
forced to take back fifty thousand to keep the
Spaniards together, and was even then forced to
withhold ten thousand to prevent the British cavalry
from perishing. Money to pay the Spaniards had
sailed from Cadiz, but the vessel conveying it, and
another containing the soldiers' great coats, were by
the admiralty arrangements obliged to go first to
Corunna, and neither had arrived there in January
although the money had been ready in October.
But the ship of war designed to carry it did not
arrive at Cadiz until the end of December. Sixteen
thousand Spanish troops were thus rendered useless
because without pay they could not be trusted in
France."

" The commissary-in-chief in England had been
regularly informed of the state of the supplies of
the military chest and of the wants and prospects of
the army, but those wants were not attended to.
The monthly hundred thousand pounds spoken of
as the maximum, even if it had been given regularly, would not cover the ordinary expenses of the

troops, and there were besides the subsidies other
outlays requiring ready money, such as meat for the
soldiers, hospital expenses, commissariat labourers,
and a variety of minor engagements. The Portuguese government had been reduced to a monthly
sum of two hundred thousand dollars out of a subsidy of two millions sterling. The Spanish government got what they could out of a subsidy of one
million. And when money was obtained for the
government in the markets of Lisbon and Cadiz, it
came not in due time, because, such were the admiralty arrangements, there were no ships to convey
the treasure to the north coast of Spain. The whole
sum which had passed through the military chest
during the past year was scarcely more than two
millions four hundred thousand pounds, out of
which part of the subsidies had been paid. This
was quite inadequate, the Government had desired
him to push his operations to the Garonne during
the winter, he was prepared to do so in every point
excepting money, and he knew the greatest advantages would accrue from such a movement but
he could not stir. His posts were already so distant
from the coast that his means of transport were
daily destroyed by the journeys, he had not a
shilling to pay for any thing in the country and
his credit was gone. He had been obliged privately
to borrow the expense of a single courier sent to
general Clinton. It was not his duty to suggest
the fitting measures for relief, but it was obvious
that an immediate and large supply from England
was necessary and that ships should be provided
to convey that which was obtained at Lisbon and
Cadiz to the army."

Such was the denuded state of the victorious
Wellington at a time when millions, and the worth

of more millions were being poured by the English ministers into the continent; when every petty German sovereign, partizan, or robber, who raised a band, or a cry against Napoleon, was supplied to satiety. And all this time there was not in England one public salary reduced, one contract checked, one abuse corrected, one public servant rebuked for negligence; not a writer dared to expose the mischief lest he should be crushed by persecution; no minister ceased to claim and to receive the boasting congratulations of the tories, no whig had sense to discover or spirit to denounce the iniquitous system, no voice of reprehension was heard from that selfish faction unless it were in sneering contempt of the general whose mighty genius sustained England under this load of folly.

Nor were these difficulties all that lord Wellington had to contend with. We have seen that the Portuguese regency withheld his reinforcements even when he had provided transports for their conveyance. The duke of York meanwhile insisted upon withdrawing his provisional battalions, which being all composed of old soldiers, the remains of regiments reduced by the casualties of war, were of more value in a winter campaign than three times their numbers of new men. With respect to the English militia regiments, he had no desire for them, because they possessed, he said, all the worst faults of the regulars and some peculiar to themselves besides. What he desired was that eight or ten thousand men should be drafted from them to fill up his ranks, he could then without much injury let his foreign battalions be taken away to reform a Hanoverian army on the continent; and this plan he was inclined to, because the Germans, brave and

strong soldiers, were yet extremely addicted to
desertion and in that particular set a bad example
to the British : this suggestion was however disregarded, and other reinforcements were promised to
him.

But the most serious of all the secondary
vexations he endured sprung from the conduct of
the Spanish authorities. His hospitals and depôts
were for the most part necessarily in the Spanish
territories and principally at Santander. To avoid
inconvenience to the inhabitants he had caused por-
table wooden houses to be brought from England in
which to shelter his sick and wounded men ; and he
paid extravagantly and regularly for every aid demanded from the natives. Nevertheless the natural
arrogance or ill-will which produced the libels
about St. Sebastian the insolence of the minister of
war and the sullen insubordination of Morillo and
other generals broke out here also. After much
underhand and irritating conduct at different times,
the municipality, resolute to drive the hospitals
from their town, suddenly, and under the false pretext that there was a contagious fever, placed all the
British hospitals with their officers and attendants
under quarantine. This was in the middle of
January. Thirty thousand men had been wounded
since June in the service of Spain, and the return
was to make those wounded men close prisoners
and drive their general to the necessity of fixing his
hospitals in England. Vessels coming from Santander were thus rendered objects of dread, and the
municipalities of the other ports, either really
fearing or pretending to fear the contagion, would
not suffer them to enter their waters. To such a
height did this cowardice and villainy attain that

the political chief of Guipuscoa, without giving any notice to lord Wellington, shut all the ports of that province against vessels coming from Santander, and the alcalde of Fuenterabia endeavoured to prevent a Portuguese military officer from assisting an English vessel which was about to be and was afterwards actually cast away, because she came from Santander.

Now in consequence of the difficulties and dangers of navigating the Bay of Biscay in the winter and the badness of the ports near the positions of the army, all the stores and provisions coming by sea went in the first instance to Santander, the only good port, there to wait until favourable opportunities occurred for reaching the more eastern harbours. Moreover all the provision magazines of the Spanish army were there, but this blow cut them off, the army was reduced to the smaller magazines at Passages which could only last for a few days, and when that supply was expended lord Wellington would have had no resource but to withdraw across the Pyrenees! " *Here,*" *he exclaimed,* " *here are the consequences of the system by which these provinces are governed! Duties of the highest description, military operations, political interests, and the salvation of the state, are made to depend upon the caprices of a few ignorant individuals, who have adopted a measure unnecessary and harsh without adverting to its objects or consequences, and merely with a view to their personal interests and convenience.*"

They carried it into execution also with the utmost hardness caprice and injustice, regardless of the loss of ships and lives which must follow, and finally desired lord Wellington to relinquish the harbour and town of Santander altogether as a depôt! However his vigorous remonstrances stopped this nefarious proceeding in time to avert the danger which it menaced.

Be it remembered now, that these dangers and difficulties, and vexations, although related in succession, happened, not one after another, but altogether ; that it was when crossing the Bidassoa, breaking through the mountain fortifications of Soult, passing the Nive, fighting the battles in front of Bayonne, and when still greater and more intricate combinations were to be arranged, that all these vials of folly and enmity were poured upon his head. Who then shall refuse to admire the undaunted firmness, the unwearied temper and vigilance, the piercing judgement with which he steered his gallant vessel and with a flowing sail, unhurt through this howling storm of passion this tumultuous sea of folly.

CHAPTER VI.

CONTINUATION OF THE WAR IN THE EASTERN PARTS OF SPAIN.

WHEN general Clinton succeeded lord William Bentinck, his whole force, composed of the Anglo-Sicilians, Whittingham's and Sarzfield's Spaniards, and two battalions of Roche's division, did not furnish quite nineteen thousand men under arms. Copons, blockading Mequinenza Lerida and Monzon and having garrisons in Cardona and the Seo d'Urgel, the only places in his possession, could not bring more than nine thousand men into the field. Elio had nominally twenty-five thousand, but this included Sarzfield's and Roche's troops the greater part of which were with Clinton. It included likewise the bands of Villa Campa Duran and the Empecinado, all scattered in Castile Aragon and Valencia, and acting according to the caprices of their chiefs. His force, daily diminishing also from the extreme unhealthiness of the country about Tortoza, was scarcely sufficient to maintain the blockades of the French fortresses beyond the Ebro.

Copons' army having no base but the mountains about Vich and Monserrat, having no magazines or depôts or place of arms, having very little artillery and scarcely any cavalry, lived as it could from day to day ; in like manner lived Sarzfield's and Whittingham's troops, and Clinton's army was chiefly

fed on salt provisions from the ships. The two
former having no means of transport were unable
to make even one day's march with ease, they were
continually upon the point of starvation and could
never be reckoned as a moveable force. Nor indeed
could the Anglo-Sicilians, owing to their scanty
means of transport, make above two or three marches
from the sea; and they were at this time more than
usually hampered, being without pay and shut out
from their principal depôts at Gibraltar and Malta,
by plague at the first and yellow fever at the second
place. In fine, the courage and discipline of the
British and Germans set aside, it would be difficult
to find armies less efficient for an offensive campaign
than those of the allies in Catalonia. Moreover
lord William Bentinck had been invested with the
command of all the Spanish armies, but Clinton had
only Whittingham's and Sarzfield's troops under
him, and notwithstanding his constant endeavours to
conciliate Copons, the indolence and incapacity of
that general impeded or baffled all useful operations: and to these disqualifications he added an
extreme jealousy of Eroles and Manso, men designated by the public voice as the most worthy of
command.

This analysis shows that Elio being entirely
engaged in Valencia, and Sarzfield and Whittingham unprovided with the means of movement, the
army of Copons and the Anglo-Sicilians, together
furnishing, when the posts and escorts and the
labourers employed on the fortifications of Taragona
were deducted, not more than eighteen thousand
men in line of battle, were the only troops to be
counted on to oppose Suchet, who having sixty-five
thousand men, of which fifty-six thousand were

present under arms, could without drawing a man from his garrisons attack them with thirty thousand. But Copons and Clinton could not act together above a few days because their bases and lines of retreat were on different sides. The Spaniard depended upon the mountains and plains of the interior for security and subsistence, the English-man's base was Taragona and the fleet. Hence the only mode of combining on a single line was to make Valencia a common base, and throwing bridges over the Ebro construct works on both sides to defend them. This was strongly recommended by lord Wellington to lord William and to Clinton; but the former had several times lost his bridges partly from the rapidity of the stream, partly from the activity of the garrison of Tortoza. And for general Clinton the difficulty was enhanced by dis-tance, because Taragona, where all his materials were deposited was sixty miles from Amposta, and all his artificers were required to restore the defences of the former place. The blockade of Tortoza was therefore always liable to be raised, and the troops employed there exposed to a sudden and fatal attack, since Suchet, sure to separate the Anglo-Sicilians from Copons when he advanced, could penetrate between them; and while the former rallied at Taragona and the latter at Igualada his march would be direct upon Tortoza. He could thus either carry off his strong garrison, or passing the Ebro by the bridge of the fortress, move with-out let or hindrance upon Peniscola, Saguntum, and Valencia, and driving Elio back upon Alicant col-lect his garrisons and return too powerful to be meddled with.

In these circumstances lord Wellington's opinion

was, that the blockade of Tortoza should be given
up and the two armies acting on their own peculiar
lines, the one from Taragona the other from the
mountains, harass in concert the enemy's flanks and
rear, alternately if he attacked either, but together
if he moved upon Tortoza.   To besiege or blockade
that place with safety it was necessary to throw two
bridges over the Ebro below, to enable the armies
to avoid Suchet, by either bank when he should
succour the place, as he was sure to do.   But it
was essential that Copons should not abandon
Catalonia and difficult for him to do so, wherefore
it would be advisable to make Taragona the point
of retreat for both armies in the first instance, after
which they could separate and infest the French
rear.

The difficulties of besieging Tortoza he thought
insuperable, and he especially recommended that
they should be well considered before-hand, and if
it was invested, that the troops should be entrenched
around it.   In fine all his instructions tended
towards defence and were founded upon his conviction of the weak and dangerous position of the
allies, yet he believed them to have more resources
than they really had, and to be superior in number
to the French, a great error as I have already shewn.
Nothing therefore could be more preposterous than
Suchet's alarm for the frontier of France at this
time, and it is unquestionable that his personal
reluctance was the only bar to aiding Soult either
indirectly by marching on Tortoza and Valencia,
or directly by adopting that marshal's great project of uniting the two armies in Aragon.   So certain indeed is this that general Clinton, seeing the
difficulties of his own situation, only retained the

command from a strong sense of duty, and lord
Wellington despairing of any advantage in Catalonia
recommended that the Anglo-Sicilian army should
be broken up and employed in other places. The
French general's inactivity was the more injurious to the interests of his sovereign, because any
reverse or appearance of reverse to the allies would
at this time have gone nigh to destroy the alliance
between Spain and England; but personal jealousy,
the preference given to local and momentary interests
before general considerations, hurt the French cause
at all periods in the Peninsula and enabled the
allies to conquer.

General Clinton had no thoughts of besieging
Tortoza, his efforts were directed to the obtaining
a secure place of arms, yet, despite of his intrinsic
weakness, he resolved to show a confident front,
hoping thus to keep Suchet at arm's length. In
this view he endeavoured to render Taragona
once more defensible notwithstanding the nineteen
breaches which had been broken in its walls; the
progress of the work was however tedious and vexatious because he depended for his materials upon
the Spanish authorities. Thus immersed in difficulties of all kinds he could make little change
in his positions which were generally about the
Campo, Sarzfield's division only being pushed to
Villafranca. Suchet meanwhile held the line of the
Llobregat, and apparently to colour his refusal to
join Soult, grounded on the great strength of the
allies in Catalonia, he suffered general Clinton to
remain in tranquillity.

Towards the end of October reports that the
French were concentrating, for what purpose was
not known, caused the English general, although

Taragona was still indefensible to make a forward
movement. He dared not indeed provoke a battle,
but unwilling to yield the resources which Villafranca and other districts occupied by the allies still
offered, he adopted the resolution of pushing an
advanced guard to the former place. He even
fixed his head-quarters there, appearing ready to
fight, yet his troops were so disposed in succession
at Arbos, Vendrills and Torredembarra that he
could retreat without dishonour if the French advanced in force, or could concentrate at Villafranca
in time to harass their flank and rear if they attempted to carry off their garrisons on the Segre.
In this state of affairs Suchet made several demonstrations, sometimes against Copons sometimes
against Clinton, but the latter maintained his offensive attitude with firmness, and even in opposition
to lord Wellington's implied opinion that the line
of the Ebro was the most suitable to his weakness;
for he liked not to abandon Taragona the repairs of
which were now advancing though slowly to completion. His perseverance was crowned with success; he preserved the few resources left for the
support of the Spanish troops, and furnished Suchet
with that semblance of excuse which he desired for
keeping aloof from Soult.

In this manner October and November were
passed, but on the 1st of December the French
general attempted to surprise the allies' cantonments at Villafranca, as he had before surprised
them at Ordal. He moved in the same order. One
column marched by San Sadurni on his right,
another by Bejer and Avionet on his left, and the
main body kept the great road. But he did not
find colonel Adam there. Clinton had blocked the

Ordal so as to render a night surprise impossible,
and the natural difficulties of the other roads delayed the flanking columns.   Hence when the
French reached Villafranca, Sarzfield was in full
march for Igualada, and the Anglo-Sicilians, who
had only three men wounded at one of the advanced
posts, were on the strong ground about Arbos,
where being joined by the supporting divisions they
offered battle ; but Suchet retired to the Llobregat
apparently so mortified by his failure that he has
not even mentioned it in his Memoirs.

Clinton now resumed his former ground, yet his
embarrassments increased, and though he transferred two of Whittingham's regiments to Copons
and sent Roche's battalions back to Valencia, the
country was so exhausted that the enduring constancy of the Spanish soldiers under privations
alone enabled Sarzfield to remain in the field : more
than once, that general, a man of undoubted firmness and courage, was upon the point of re-crossing
the Ebro to save his soldiers from perishing of
famine.   Here as in other parts, the Spanish
government not only starved their troops but would
not even provide a piece of ordnance or any stores
for the defence of Taragona, now, by the exertions of
the English general, rendered defensible.   Nay! when
admiral Hallowell in conjunction with Quesada the
Spanish commodore at Port Mahon, brought some
ship-guns from that place to the fortress, the minister
of war, O'Donoju, expressed his disapprobation, observing with a sneer that the English might provide
the guns wanting from the Spanish ordnance moved
into Gibraltar by general Campbell when he destroyed the lines of San Roque!

The 9th Suchet pushed a small corps by Bejer

between the Ordal and Sitjes, and on the 10th surprised at the Ostel of Ordal an officer and thirty men of the Anglo-Sicilian cavalry. This disaster was the result of negligence. The detachment after patroling to the front had dismounted without examining the buildings of the inn, and some French troopers who were concealed within immediately seized the horses and captured the whole party.

On the 17th, French troops appeared at Martorel, the Ordal, and Bejer, with a view to mask the march of a large convoy coming from Upper Catalonia to Barcelona ; they then resumed their former positions, and at the same time Soult's and lord Wellington's respective letters announcing the defection of the Nassau battalions in front of Bayonne arrived. Lord Wellington's came first, and enclosed a communication from colonel Kruse to his countryman, colonel Meder, who was serving in Barcelona and as Kruse supposed willing to abandon the French. But when Clinton by the aid of Manso transmitted the letter to Meder, that officer handed it to general Habert who had succeeded Maurice Mathieu in the command of the city. All the German regiments, principally cavalry, were immediately disarmed and sent to France. Severoli's Italians were at the same time recalled to Italy and a number of French soldiers, selected to fill the wasted ranks of the imperial guards, marched with them ; two thousand officers and soldiers were likewise detached to the depôts of the interior to organize the conscripts of the new levy destined to reinforce the army of Catalonia. Besides these drafts a thousand gens-d'armes hitherto employed on the Spanish frontier in aid of the regular troops were withdrawn ; Suchet

thus lost seven thousand veterans, yet he had still
an overwhelming power compared to the allies.
It was in this state of affairs that the duke of
San Carlos, bearing the treaty of Valençay, arrived
secretly at the French head-quarters on his way ot
Madrid. Copons knew this, and it seems certain was
only deterred from openly acceding to the views of
the French emperor and concluding a military convention, by the decided conduct of the Cortez, and
the ascendancy which lord Wellington had obtained over him in common with the other Spanish officers : an ascendancy which had not escaped
Soult's sagacity, for he early warned the French
minister that nothing could be expected from them
while under the powerful spell of the English
general. Meanwhile Clinton, getting information
that the French troops were diminished in numbers,
especially in front of Barcelona and on the Llobregat, proposed to pass that river and invest Barcelona
if Copons, who was in the mountains, would undertake to provision Sarzfield's division and keep the
French troops between Barcelona and Gerona in
check. For this purpose he offered him the aid of
a Spanish regiment of cavalry which Elio had lent
for the operations in Catalonia; but Copons,
whether influenced by San Carlos' mission and his
secret wishes for its success, or knowing that the
enemy were really stronger than Clinton imagined,
declared that he was unable to hold the French
troops between Gerona and Barcelona in check, and
that he could not provision either Sarzfield's division
or the regiment of cavalry. He suggested instead of
Clinton's plan, a combined attack upon some of
Suchet's posts on the Llobregat, promising to send
Manso to Villafranca to confer upon the execution.

Clinton's proposal was made early in January yet
it was the middle of that month before Copons
replied, and then he only sent Manso to offer the
aid of his brigade in a combined attack upon two
thousand French who were at Molino del Rey. It
was however at last arranged that Manso should at
day-break on the 16th seize the high ground above
Molino, on the left of the Llobregat, to intercept
the enemy's retreat upon Barcelona, while the
Anglo-Sicilians fell upon them from the right bank.

Success depended upon Clinton's remaining quiet
until the moment of execution, wherefore he could
only use the troops immediately in hand about Villafranca, in all six thousand men with three pieces
of artillery; but with these he made a night march
of eighteen miles, and was close to the ford of San
Vicente about two miles below the fortified bridge
of Molino del Rey before daylight. The French
were tranquil and unsuspicious, and he anxiously
but vainly awaited the signal of Manso's arrival.
When the day broke, the French piquets at
San Vicente descrying his troops commenced a
skirmish, and at the same time a column with
a piece of artillery, coming from Molino, advanced
to attack him thinking there was only a patroling
detachment to deal with, for he had concealed his
main body. Thus pressed he opened his guns per
force and crippled the French piece, whereupon
the reinforcements retired hastily to the entrenchments at Molino; he could then easily have forced
the passage at the ford and attacked the enemy's
works in the rear, but this would not have ensured
the capture of their troops, wherefore he still
awaited Manso's arrival relying on that partizan's
zeal and knowledge of the country. He appeared

at last, not, as agreed upon, at St. Filieu, between Molino and Barcelona, but at Papiol above Molino, and the French immediately retreated by San Filieu. Sarzfield, and the cavalry, which Clinton now detached across the Llobregat, followed them hard, but the country was difficult, the distance short, and they soon gained a second entrenched camp above San Filieu. A small garrison remained in the masonry-works at Molino, general Clinton endeavoured to reduce them but his guns were not of a calibre to break the walls and the enemy was strongly reinforced towards evening from Barcelona; whereupon Manso went off to the mountains, and Clinton returned to Villafranca having killed and wounded about one hundred and eighty French, and lost only sixty-four men, all Spaniards.

Manso's failure surprized the English general, because that officer, unlike the generality of his countrymen, was zealous, skilful, vigilant, modest, and humane, and a sincere cooperator with the British officers. He however soon cleared himself of blame, assuring Clinton that Copons, contrary to his previous declarations, had joined him with four thousand men, and taking the controul of his troops not only commenced the march two hours too late, but without any reason halted for three hours on the way. Nor did that general offer any excuse or explanation of his conduct, merely observing, that the plan having failed nothing more could be done and he must return to his mountainous asylum about Vich. A man of any other nation would have been accused of treachery, but with the Spaniards there is no limit to absurdity, and from their actions no conclusion can be drawn as to their motives.

The great events of the general war were now
beginning to affect the struggle in Catalonia. Suchet finding that Copons dared not agree to the
military convention dependent upon the treaty of
Valençay, resigned all thoughts of carrying off his
garrisons beyond the Ebro, and secretly instructed
the governor of Tortoza, that when his provisions,
calculated to last until April, were exhausted, he
should march upon Mequinenza and Lerida, unite
the garrisons there to his own, and make way by
Venasque into France. Meanwhile he increased
the garrison of Barcelona to eight thousand men
and prepared to take the line of the Fluvia; for
the allied sovereigns were in France and Napoleon
had recalled more of his cavalry and infantry, in
all ten thousand men with eighty pieces of artillery,
from Catalonia, desiring that they should march
as soon as the results expected from the mission of
San Carlos were felt by the allies. Suchet prepared the troops but proposed that instead of waiting for the uncertain result of San Carlos' mission,
Ferdinand should himself be sent to Spain through
Catalonia and be trusted on his faith to restore the
garrisons in Valencia. Then he said he could
march with his whole army to Lyons which
would be more efficacious than sending detachments.
The restoration of Ferdinand was the Emperor's
great object, but this plausible proposition
can only be viewed as a colourable counter-
project to Soult's plan for a junction of the two
armies in Bearn, since the Emperor was undoubtedly the best judge of what was required for the
warfare immediately under his own direction.

It was in the midst of these operations that Clinton
attacked Molino del Rey and as we have seen

would but for the interference of Copons have

stricken a great blow, which was however soon inflicted in another manner.

There was at this time in the French service a Spaniard of Flemish descent called Van Halen. This man, of fair complexion, handsome person, and a natural genius for desperate treasons, appears to have been at first attached to Joseph's court. After that monarch's retreat from Spain he was placed by the duke de Feltre on Suchet's staff; but the French party was now a failing one and Van Halen only sought by some notable treachery to make his peace with his country. Through the medium of a young widow, who followed him without suffering their connection to appear, he informed Eroles of his object. He transmitted through the same channel regular returns of Suchet's force and other matters of interest, and at last having secretly opened Suchet's portfolio he copied the key of his cypher, and transmitted that also, with an intimation that he would now soon pass over and endeavour to perform some other service at the same time. The opportunity soon offered. Suchet went to Gerona to meet the duke of San Carlos, leaving Van Halen at Barcelona, and the latter immediately taking an escort of three hussars went to Granollers where the cuirassiers were quartered. Using the marshal's name he ordered them to escort him to the Spanish outposts, which being in the mountains could only be approached by a long and narrow pass where cavalry would be helpless. In this pass he ordered the troops to bivouac for the night, and when their colonel expressed his uneasiness, Van Halen quieted him and made a solitary mill their common quarters. He

Memoir
by Sir Wm.
Clinton,
MSS.

had before this, however, sent the widow to give Eroles information of the situation into which he would bring the troops and now with anxiety awaited his attack ; but the Spanish general failed to come and at daybreak Van Halen, still pretending he carried a flag of truce from Suchet, rode off with his first escort of hussars and a trumpeter to the Spanish lines. There he ascertained that the widow had been detained by the outposts and immediately delivered over his escort to their enemies, giving notice also of the situation of the cuirassiers with a view to their destruction, but they escaped the danger.

Van Halen and Eroles now forged Suchet's signature, and the former addressed letters in cypher to the governors of Tortoza, Lerida, Mequinenza, and Monzon, telling them that the emperor in consequence of his reverses required large drafts of men from Catalonia, and had given Suchet orders to negotiate a convention by which the garrisons south of the Llobregat were to join the army with arms and baggage and followers. The result was uncertain, but if the treaty could not be effected the governors were to join the army by force, and they were therefore immediately to mine their principal bastions and be prepared to sally forth at an appointed time. The marches and points of junction were all given in detail, yet they were told that if the convention took place the marshal would immediately send an officer of his staff to them, with such verbal instructions as might be necessary. The document finished with deploring the necessity which called for the sacrifice of conquests achieved by the valour of the troops.

Spies and emissaries who act for both sides are

common in all wars, but in the Peninsula so many
pretended to serve the French and were yet true to the Spaniards, that to avoid the danger of betrayal Suchet had recourse to the ingenious artifice of placing a very small piece of light-coloured hair in the cyphered paper, the latter was then enclosed in a quill sealed and wrapped in lead. When received, the small parcel was carefully opened on a sheet of white paper and if the hair was discovered the communication was good, if not, the treachery was apparent because the hair would escape the vigilance of uninitiated persons and be lost by any intermediate examination. Van Halen knew this secret also, and when his emissaries had returned after delivering the preparatory communication, he proceeded in person with a forged convention, first to Tortoza, for Suchet has erroneously stated in his Memoirs that the primary attempts were made at Lerida and Mequinenza. He was accompanied by several Spanish officers and by some French deserters dressed in the uniforms of the hussars he had betrayed to the Spanish outposts. The governor Robert though a vigilant officer was deceived and prepared to evacuate the place. During the night however a true emissary arrived with a letter from Suchet of later date than the forged convention. Robert then endeavoured to entice Van Halen into the fortress, but the other was too wary and proceeded at once to Mequinenza and Lerida where he completely overreached the governors and then went to Monzon.

This small fortress had now been besieged since the 28th of September 1813, by detachments from the Catalan army and the bands from Aragon. Its

means of defence were slight, but there was within
a man of resolution and genius called St. Jacques.
He was a Piedmontese by birth and only a private
soldier of engineers, but the commandant appreciating his worth was so modest and prudent as to
yield the direction of the defence entirely to him.
Abounding in resources, he met, and at every point
baffled the besiegers who worked principally by
mines, and being as brave as he was ingenious
always led the numerous counter-attacks which he
contrived to check the approaches above and below
ground. The siege continued until the 18th
of February when the subtle Van Halen arrived,
and by his Spanish wiles obtained in a few hours
what Spanish courage and perseverance had vainly
strived to gain for one hundred and forty days.
The commandant was suspicious at first, but when
Van Halen suffered him to send an officer to ascertain that Lerida and Mequinenza were evacuated,
he was beguiled like the others and marched to join
the garrisons of those places.

Sir William Clinton had been informed of this
project by Eroles as early as the 22d of January
and though he did not expect any French general
would be so egregiously misled, readily promised
the assistance of his army to capture the garrisons
on their march. But Suchet was now falling back
upon the Fluvia, and Clinton, seeing the fortified
line of the Llobregat weakened and being uncertain
of Suchet's real strength and designs, renewed
his former proposal to Copons for a combined attack
which should force the French general to discover
his real situation and projects. Ere he could
obtain an answer, the want of forage obliged him to

refuse the assistance of the Spanish cavalry lent to
him by Elio, and Sarzfield's division was reduced to
its last ration. The French thus made their retreat
unmolested, for Clinton's project necessarily involved the investment of Barcelona after passing
the Llobregat, and the Anglo-Sicilian cavalry, being
mounted on. small Egyptian animals the greatest
part of which were foundered or unserviceable from
sand-cracks, a disease very common amongst the
horses of that country, were too weak to act without
the aid of Elio's horsemen. Moreover as a division
of infantry was left at Taragona awaiting the
effect of Van Halen's wiles against Tortoza the aid
of Sarzfield's troops was indispensable.

Copons accepted the proposition towards the end
of the month, the Spanish cavalry was then
gone to the rear, but Sarzfield having with great
difficulty obtained some provisions the army was
put in movement on the 3d of February, and as
Suchet was now near Gerona, it passed the Llobregat at the bridge of Molino del Rey without resistance. On the 5th Sarzfield's picquets were vigorously attacked at San Filieu by the garrison of
Barcelona, he however supported them with his whole
division and being reinforced with some cavalry
repulsed the French and pursued them to the walls.
On the 7th the city was invested on the land
side by Copons who was soon aided by Manso ; on
the sea-board by admiral Hallowell, who following
the movements of the army with the fleet blockaded
the harbour with the Castor frigate, and anchored
the Fame a seventy-four off Mataro. On the 8th
intelligence arrived of Van Halen's failure at Tortoza,
but the blockade of Barcelona continued uninterrupted until the 16th when Clinton was informed

by Copons of the success at Lerida, Mequinenza, and Monzon. The garrisons, he said, would march upon Igualada, and Eroles who, under pretence of causing the convention to be observed by the Somatenes, was to follow in their rear, proposed to undeceive and disarm them at that place. On the 17th however he sent notice that Martorel had been fixed upon in preference to Igualada for undeceiving and disarming the French, and as they would be at the former place that evening general Clinton was desired to send some of his troops there to ensure the success of the project.

This change of plan and the short warning, for Martorel was a long march from Barcelona, together with the doubts and embarrassments which Copons' conduct always caused, inclined the English general to avoid meddling with the matter at all; yet fearing that it would fail in the Spaniard's hands he finally drafted a strong division of troops and marched in person to Martorel. There he met Copons who now told him that the French would not pass Esparaguera that night, that Eroles was close in their rear, and another division of the Catalan army at Bispal blocking the bridge of Martorel. Clinton immediately undertook to pass the Llobregat, meet the French column, and block the road of San Sadurni; and he arranged with Copons the necessary precautions and signals.

About nine o'clock general Isidore La Marque arrived with the garrisons at Martorel, followed at a short distance by Eroles. No other troops were to be seen and after a short halt the French continued their march on the right bank of the Llobregat, where the Barcelona road enters a narrow pass between the river and a precipitous hill. When

they were completely entangled Clinton sent an
officer to forbid their further progress and referred
them to Copons who was at Martorel for an explanation, then giving the signal all the heights around
were instantly covered with armed men. It was in
vain to offer resistance, and two generals, having
two thousand six hundred men, four guns, and a
rich military chest, capitulated, but upon conditions,
which were granted and immediately violated with
circumstances of great harshness and insult to the
prisoners. The odium of this baseness which was
quite gratuitous, since the French helpless in the
defile must have submitted to any terms, attaches
entirely to the Spaniards. Clinton refused to meddle
in any manner with the convention, he had not
been a party to Van Halen's deceit, he appeared
only to ensure the surrender of an armed force in
the field which the Spaniards could not have subdued without his aid, he refused even to be present
at any consultation previous to the capitulation,
and notwithstanding an assertion to the contrary in
Suchet's Memoirs no appeal on the subject from
that marshal ever reached him.

During the whole of these transactions the in-
fatuation of the French leaders was extreme. The
chief of one of the battalions more sagacious than
his general told Lamarque in the night of the 16th
at Igualada that he was betrayed, at the same time
urging him vainly to abandon his artillery and
baggage and march in the direction of Vich, to
which place they could force their way in despite
of the Spaniards. It is remarkable also that Robert
when he had detected the imposture and failed to
entice Van Halen into Tortoza did not make a sud-

den sally upon him and the Spanish officers who were with him, all close to the works. And still more notable is it that the other governors, the more especially as Van Halen was a foreigner, did not insist upon the bearer of such a convention remaining to accompany their march. It has been well observed by Suchet that Van Halen's refusal to enter the gates was alone sufficient to prove his treachery.

The detachment recalled by Napoleon now moved into France, and in March was followed by a second column of equal force which was at first directed upon Lyons, but the arrival of lord Wellington's troops on the Garonne caused, as we shall hereafter find, a change in its destination. Meanwhile by order of the minister at war Suchet entered into a fresh negociation with Copons, to deliver up all the fortresses held by his troops except Figueras and Rosas, provided the garrisons were allowed to rejoin the army. The Spanish commander assented and the authorities generally were anxious to adopt the proposal, but the regency referred the matter to lord Wellington who rejected it without hesitation, as tending to increase the force immediately opposed to him. Thus baffled and over-reached at all points, Suchet destroyed the works of Olot, Besalu, Bascara and Palamos, dismantled Gerona and Rosas, and concentrated his forces at Figueras. He was followed by Copons, but though he still had twelve thousand veterans besides the national guards and dépôts of the French departments, he continued most obstinately to refuse any aid to Soult, and yet remained inactive himself. The blockade of Barcelona was therefore maintained by the allies without difficultry or danger save what

arose from their commissariat embarrassments and the efforts of the garrison.

On the 23d of February Habert made a sally with six battalions, thinking to surprize Sarzfield, he was however beaten, and colonel Meder the Nassau officer who had before shewn his attachment to the French cause was killed. The blockade was thus continued until the 12th of March when Clinton received orders from lord Wellington to break up his army, send the foreign troops to lord William Bentinck in Sicily, and march with the British battalions by Tudela to join the great army in France. Clinton at first prepared to obey but Suchet was still in strength, Copons appeared to be provoking a collision though he was quite unable to oppose the French in the field; and to maintain the blockade of Barcelona in addition, after the Anglo-Sicilians should depart, was quite impossible. The latter therefore remained and on the 19th of March king Ferdinand reached the French frontier.

This event, which happening five or even three months before would probably have changed the fate of the war, was now of little consequence. Suchet first proposed to Copons to escort Ferdinand with the French army to Barcelona and put him in possession of that place, but this the Spanish general dared not assent to, for he feared lord Wellington and his own regency, and was closely watched by colonel Coffin who had been placed near him by sir William Clinton. The French general then proposed to the king a convention for the recovery of his garrisons, to which Ferdinand agreed with the facility of a false heart. His great anxiety was to

reach Valencia, because the determination of the
Cortez to bind him to conditions before he recovered
his throne was evident, the Spanish generals were
apparently faithful to the Cortez, and the British
influence was sure to be opposed to him while he
was burthened with French engagements.

Suchet had been ordered to demand securities
for the restoration of his garrisons previous to Ferdinand's entry into Spain, but time was precious
and he determined to escort him at once with the
whole French army to the Fluvia, having first received a promise to restore the garrisons. He also
Suchet's
Memoirs.
retained his brother Don Carlos as a hostage for
their return, but even this security he relinquished
when the king in a second letter written from Gerona
solemnly confirmed his first promise. On the 24th
therefore in presence of the Catalan and French
armies, ranged in order of battle on either bank of the
Fluvia, Ferdinand passed that river and became once
more king of Spain. He had been a rebellious son in
the palace, a plotting traitor at Aranjuez, a dastard at
Bayonne, an effeminate superstitious fawning slave at
Valençay, and now after six years' captivity he returned to his own country an ungrateful and cruel
tyrant. He would have been the most odious and
contemptible of princes if his favourite brother
Don Carlos had not existed. Reaching the camp
at Barcelona on the 30th he dined with sir William
Clinton, reviewed the allied troops and then proceeded first to Zaragoza and finally to Valencia.
Memoirs
by sir Wm.
Clinton,
MSS.
Marshal Suchet says the honours of war were paid
to him by all the French garrisons but this was not
the case at Barcelona: no man appeared, even on
the walls. After this event the French marshal
repassed the Pyrenees leaving only one division at

Figueras and Clinton proceeded to break up his army, but was again stopped by the vexatious conduct of Copons who would not relieve the Anglo-Sicilians at the blockade, nor indeed take any notice of the English general's communications on the subject before the 11th of April. On the 14th however the troops marched, part to embark at Taragona, part to join lord Wellington. Copons then became terrified lest general Robert, abandoning Tortoza, should join Habert at Barcelona, and enclose him between them and the division at Figueras, wherefore Clinton once more halted to protect the Spaniards.

Copons had indeed some reason to fear, for Habert about this time received, and transmitted to Robert, the emperor's orders to break out of Tortoza and gain Barcelona instead of passing by the valley of Venasque as Suchet had before prescribed : the twelve thousand men thus united were then to push into France. This letter was intercepted, copied, and sent on to Robert, whose answer being likewise intercepted shewed that he was not prepared and had no inclination for the enterprise. This seen Clinton continued his embarkation and thus completed his honourable but difficult task. With a force weak in numbers, and nearly destitute of every thing that constitutes strength in the field, he had maintained a forward and dangerous position for eight months ; and though Copons' incapacity and ill-will, and other circumstances beyond control, did not permit him to perform any brilliant actions, he occupied the attention of a very superior army, suffered no disaster and gained some advantages.

While his troops were embarking, Habert, in furtherance of the emperor's project, made a vigorous

sally on the 18th, and though repulsed with loss he killed or wounded eight hundred Spaniards. This was a lamentable combat. The war had terminated long before, yet intelligence of the cessation of hostilities only arrived four days later. Habert was now repeatedly ordered by Suchet and the duke of Feltre to give up Barcelona, but warned by the breach of former conventions he held it until he was assured that all the French garrisons
in Valencia had returned safely to France, which did not happen until the 28th of May, when he yielded up the town and marched to his own country. This event, the last operation of the whole war, released the duchess of Bourbon. She and the old prince of Conti had been retained prisoners in the city during the Spanish struggle, the prince died early in 1814, the duchess survived, and now returned to France.

How strong Napoleon's hold of the Peninsula had been, how little the Spaniards were able of their own strength to shake him off, was now apparent to all the world. For notwithstanding lord Wellington's great victories, notwithstanding the invasion of France, six fortresses, Figueras, Barcelona, Tortoza, Morella, Peniscola, Saguntum and Denia were recovered, not by arms but by the general peace. And but for the deceits of Van Halen there would have been three others similarly situated in the eastern parts alone, while in the north Santona was recovered in the same manner; for neither the long blockade nor the active operations against that place, of which some account shall now be given, caused it to surrender.

The site of Santona is one of those promontories frequent on the coast of Spain which connected by

low sandy necks with the main land offer good harbours. Its waters deep and capacious furnished
two bays. The outer one or roadstead was commanded by the works of Santona itself, and by
those of Laredo, a considerable town lying at the
foot of a mountain on the opposite point of the
harbour. A narrow entrance to the inner port
was between a spit of land, called the Puntal, and
the low isthmus on which the town of Santona is
built. The natural strength of the ground was
very great, but the importance of Santona arose
from its peculiar situation as a harbour and fort of
support in the Montaña de Santander. By holding
it the French shut out the British shipping from
the only place which being defensible on the land
side furnished a good harbour between San Sebastian and Coruña; they thus protected the sea-flank
of their long line of invasion, obtained a port of
refuge for their own coasting vessels, and a post of
support for the moveable columns sent to chase the
partidas which abounded in that rough district.
And when the battle of Vittoria placed the allies
on the Bidassoa, from Santona issued forth a
number of privateers who, as we have seen, intercepted lord Wellington's supplies and interrupted
his communication with Coruña, Oporto, Lisbon,
and even with England.

The advantages of possessing Santona were felt
early by both parties; the French seized it at once
and although the Spaniards recovered possession of
it in 1810 they were driven out again immediately.
The English ministers then commenced deliberating
and concocting extensive and for that reason injudicious and impracticable plans of offensive operations, to be based upon the possession of Santona;

Vol. 3.
Book XI.
Chapter V.

Ibid.
Book XII.
Chapter I.

meanwhile Napoleon fortified it and kept it to the
end of the war. In August 1812 its importance
was better understood by the Spaniards, and it was
continually menaced by the numerous bands of
Biscay, the Asturias and the Montaña. Fourteen
hundred men, including the crew of a corvette,
then formed its garrison, the works were not very
strong and only forty pieces of artillery were
mounted. Napoleon however, foreseeing the disasters which Marmont was provoking, sent general
Lameth, a chosen officer, to take charge of the
defence. He immediately augmented the works
and constructed advanced redoubts on two hills,
called the Gromo and the Brusco, which like San
Bartolomeo at San Sebastian closed the isthmus
inland. He also erected a strong redoubt and
blockhouse on the Puntal to command the straits,
and to sweep the roadstead in conjunction with the
fort of Laredo which he repaired. This done he
formed several minor batteries and cast a chain to
secure the narrow entrance to the inner harbour,
and then covered the rocky promontory of Santona
itself with defensive works.

Some dismounted guns remained in the arsenal,
others which had been thrown into the sea by the
Spaniards when they took the place in 1810 were
fished up, and the garrison felling trees in the vicinity made carriages for them ; by these means a
hundred and twenty guns were finally placed in
battery and there was abundance of ammunition.
The corvette was not sea-worthy, but the governor
established a flotilla of gun-boats, and other small
craft, which sallied forth whenever the signal-posts
on the head-land gave notice of the approach of
vessels liable to attack, or of French coasters

bringing provisions and stores. The garrison had

previously lost many men, killed in a barbarous
manner by the partidas, and in revenge they never
gave quarter to their enemies. Lameth shocked
at their inhumanity resolutely forbad under pain of
death any farther reprisals, rewarded those men
who brought in prisoners and treated the latter
with gentleness : the Spaniards discovering this
also changed their system and civilization resumed
its rights. From this time military operations were
incessant, the garrison sometimes made sallies,
sometimes sustained partial attacks, sometimes aided
the moveable columns employed by the different
generals of the army of the north to put down
the partizan warfare, which was seldom even lulled
in the Montaña.

After the battle of Vittoria Santona being left to
its own resources was invested on the land side by a
part of the troops composing the Gallician or fourth
Spanish army. It was blockaded on the sea-board
by the English ships of war, but only nominally,
for the garrison received supplies, and the flotilla
vexed lord Wellington's communications, took
many of his store-ships and other vessels, delayed
his convoys, and added greatly to the difficulties
of his situation. The land blockade thus also became a nullity and the Spanish officers complained
with reason that they suffered privations and endured hardships without an object. These complaints and his own embarassments, caused by lord
Melville's neglect, induced lord Wellington in
October, 1813, when he could ill spare troops, to
employ a British brigade under lord Aylmer in the
attack of Santona ; the project for reasons already
mentioned was not executed, but an English en-

BOOK
XXIII.

1814.

Victoires et
Conquêtes.

February.

gineer, captain Wells, was sent with some sappers and miners to quicken the operations of the Spanish officers, and his small detachment has been by a French writer magnified into a whole battalion.

Captain Wells remained six months, for the Spanish generals though brave and willing were tainted with the national defect of procrastination. The siege made no progress until the 13th of February 1814 when general Barco the Spanish commander carried the fort of Puntal in the night by escalade, killing thirty men and taking twenty-three prisoners, yet the fort being under the heavy fire of the Santona works was necessarily dismantled and abandoned the next morning. A picquet was however left there and the French opened their batteries, but as this did not dislodge the Spaniards Lameth embarked a detachment and recovered his fort. Howewer in the night of the 21st general Barco ordered an attack to be made with a part of his force upon the outposts of El Grumo and Brusco, on the Santona side of the harbour, and led the remainder of his troops in person to storm the fort and town of Laredo. He carried the latter and also some outer defences of the fort, which being on a rock was only to be approached by an isthmus so narrow as to be closed by a single fortified house. In the assault of the body of this fort Barco was killed and the attack ceased, but the troops retained what they had won and established themselves' at the foot of the rock where they were covered from fire. The attack on the other side, conducted by colonel Llorente, was successful; he carried the smallest of the two outworks on the Brusco, and closely invested the largest after an ineffectual at-

tempt by mine and assault to take it. A large
breach was however made and the commandant
seeing he could no longer defend his post, valiantly
broke through the investment and gained the work
of the Grumo. He was however aided by the appearance on the isthmus of a strong column which sallied'
at the same time from the works on the Santona
promontory, and the next day the Grumo itself was
abandoned by the French.

Captain Wells, who had been wounded at the
Puntal escalade, now strenuously urged the Spaniards to crown the counter-scarp of the fort at
Laredo and attack vigorously, but they preferred
establishing four field-pieces to batter it in form at
the distance of six hundred yards. These guns as
might be expected were dismounted the moment
they began to fire, and thus corrected, the Spanish
generals committed the direction of the attack to
Wells. He immediately opened a heavy musquetry
fire on the fort to stifle the noise of his workmen,
then pushing trenches up the hill close to the
counterscarp in the night, he was proceeding to burst
open the gate with a few field-pieces and to cut down
the pallisades, when the Italian garrison, whose musquets from constant use had become so foul that few
would go off, mutinied against their commander and
making him a prisoner surrendered the place. This
event gave the allies the command of the entrance
to the harbour, and Lameth offered to capitulate in
April upon condition of returning to France with
his garrison. Lord Wellington refused the condition, Santona therefore remained a few days longer in
possession of the enemy, and was finally evacuated
at the general cessation of hostilities.

Having now terminated the narrative of all mili-

tary and political events which happened in the
Peninsula, the reader will henceforth be enabled to
follow without interruption the events of the war
in the south of France which shall be continued
in the next book.

BOOK XXIV.

CHAPTER I.

LORD Wellington's difficulties have been described. CHAP.
Those of his adversary were even more embarrassing I.
because the evil was at the root; it was not January.
misapplication of power but the want of power
itself which paralyzed Soult's operations. Napoleon
trusted much to the effect of his treaty with Ferdinand who, following his intentions, should have
entered Spain in November, but the intrigues to
retard his journey continued, and though Napoleon,
when the refusal of the treaty by the Spanish government became known, permitted him to return without any conditions, as thinking his presence would
alone embarrass and perhaps break the English
alliance with Spain, he did not as we have seen
arrive until March. How the emperor's views were
frustrated by his secret enemies is one of the obscure
parts of French history, at this period, which time
may possibly clear but probably only with a feeble
and uncertain light. For truth can never be expected in the memoirs, if any should appear, of such
men as Talleyrand, Fouché, and other politicians of
their stamp, whose plots rendered his supernatural
efforts to rescue France from her invaders abortive.
Meanwhile there is nothing to check and expose the
political and literary empirics who never fail on
such occasions to poison the sources of history.

CHAP.
I.
1814.
January.

Relying upon the effect which the expected
journey of Ferdinand would produce, and pressed
by the necessity of augmenting his own weak army,
Napoleon gave notice to Soult that he must ultimately take from him, two divisions of infantry and
one of cavalry. The undecided nature of his first
battle at Brienne caused him to enforce this notice
in the beginning of February, but he had previously
sent imperial commissaries to the different departments of France, with instructions to hasten the new
conscription, to form national and urban guards, to draw
forth all the resources of the country, and to aid the
operations of the armies by the action of the people.
These measures however failed generally in the
south.   The urban cohorts were indeed readily
formed as a means of police, and the conscription
was successful, but the people remained sullen and
apathetic ; and the civil commissaries are said to

have been, with some exceptions, pompous, declama-
tory, and affecting great state and dignity without
energy and activity.   Ill-will was also produced by
the vexatious and corrupt conduct of the subordinate government agents, who seeing in the general
distress and confusion a good opportunity to forward
their personal interests, oppressed the people for
their own profit.   This it was easy to do, because
the extreme want of money rendered requisitions
unavoidable, and under the confused direction of
civilians, partly ignorant and unused to difficult
times, partly corrupt, and partly disaffected to the
emperor, the abuses inevitably attendant upon such
a system were numerous; and to the people so offensive, that numbers to avoid them passed with their
carts and utensils into the lines of the allies.   An
official letter written from Bayonne at this period

run thus : " The English general's policy and the
good discipline he maintains does us more harm than
ten battles. Every peasant wishes to be under his
protection."

Another source of anger was Soult's works near
Bayonne, where the richer inhabitants could not
bear to have their country villas and gardens destroyed by the engineer, he who spares not for
beauty or for pleasure where his military traces are
crossed. The merchants, a class nearly alike in all
nations, with whom profit stands for country,
had been with a few exceptions long averse to
Napoleon's policy which from necessity interfered
with their commerce. And this feeling must have
been very strong in Bayonne and Bordeaux, for one
Batbedat, a banker of the former place, having obtained leave to go to St. Jean de Luz under pretence
of settling the accounts of English officers, prisoners
of war, to whom he had advanced money, offered lord
Wellington to supply his army with various commodities and even provide money for bills on the
English treasury. In return he demanded licenses
for twenty vessels to go from Bordeaux, Rochelle
and Mants, to St. Jean de Luz, and they were given
on condition that he should not carry back colonial
produce. The English navy however shewed so
little inclination to respect them that the banker and
his coadjutors hesitated to risk their vessels, and
thus saved them, for the English ministers refused to
sanction the licenses and rebuked their general.

During these events the partizans of the Bourbons,
coming from Brittany and La Vendée, spread themselves all over the south of France and entered into
direct communication with lord Wellington. One
of the celebrated family of La Roche Jacquelin

arrived at his head-quarters, Bernadotte sent an
agent to those parts, and the count of Grammont,
then serving as a captain in the British cavalry, was
at the desire of the marquis de Mailhos, another of
the malcontents, sent to England to call the princes
of the house of Bourbon forward.   Finally the duke
of Angoulême arrived suddenly at the head-quarters,
and he was received with respect in private though
not suffered to attend the movements of the army.
The English general indeed, being persuaded that
the great body of the French people especially in
the south, were inimical to Napoleon's government,
was sanguine as to the utility of encouraging a
Bourbon party.   Yet he held his judgment in
abeyance, sagaciously observing that he could not
come to a safe conclusion merely from the feelings
of some people in one corner of France ; and as the
allied sovereigns seemed backward to take the
matter in hand unless some positive general movement in favour of the Bourbons was made, and there
were negociations for peace actually going on, it
would be, he observed, unwise and ungenerous to
precipitate the partizans of the fallen house into a
premature outbreak and then leave them to the
vengeance of the enemy.

That lord Wellington should have been convinced
the prevailing opinion was against Napoleon is not
surprising, because every appearance at the time
would seem to prove it so ; and certain it is that a
very strong Bourbon party and one still stronger
averse to the continuation of war existed.   But in
civil commotions nothing is more dangerous, nothing
more deceitful, than the outward show and declarations on such occasions.   The great mass of men
in all nations are only endowed with moderate ca-

pacity and spirit, and as their thoughts are intent upon the preservation of their families and property they must bend to circumstances; thus fear and suspicion, ignorance baseness and good feeling, all combine to urge men in troubled times to put on the mask of enthusiasm for the most powerful, while selfish knaves ever shout with the loudest. Let the scene change and the multitude will turn with the facility of a weathercock. Lord Wellington soon discovered that the count of Viel Chastel, Bernadotte's agent, while pretending to aid the Bourbons was playing a double part, and only one year after this period Napoleon returned from Elba, and neither the presence of the duke of Angoulême, nor the energy of the duchess, nor all the activity of their partizans, could raise in this very country more than the semblance of an opposition to him. The tricolor was every where hoisted and the Bourbon party vanished. And this was the true test of national feeling, because in 1814 the white colours were supported by foreign armies, and misfortune had bowed the great democratic chief to the earth; but when rising again in his wondrous might he came back alone from Elba, the poorer people, with whom only patriotism is ever really to be found, and that because they are poor and therefore unsophisticated, crowded to meet and hail him as a father. Not because they held him entirely blameless. Who born of woman is? They demanded redress of grievances even while they clung instinctively to him as their stay and protection against the locust tyranny of aristocracy.

There was however at this period in France enough of discontent passion and intrigue, enough of treason, and enough of grovelling spirit in adver-

sity, added to the natural desire of escaping the
ravages of war, a desire so carefully fostered by the
admirable policy of the English general, as to render
the French general's position extremely difficult
and dangerous. Nor is it the least remarkable circumstance of this remarkable period, that while Soult
expected relief by the Spaniards falling away from
the English alliance, lord Wellington received from
the French secret and earnest warnings to beware of
some great act of treachery meditated by the Spaniards. It was at this period also that Morillo and
other generals encouraged their soldiers' licentious-
ness, and displayed their own ill-will by sullen discontent and captious complaints, while the civil
authorities disturbed the communications and made
war in their fashion against the hospitals and
magazines.

His apprehensions and vigilance are plainly to be
traced in his correspondence. Writing about general
Copons he says, " his conduct is quite unjustifiable
both in concealing what he knew of the duke de
San Carlos' arrival and the nature of his mission."
In another letter he observes, that the Spanish military people about himself desired peace with Napoleon according to the treaty of Valençay ; that they
all had some notion of what had occurred and yet
had been quite silent about it ; that he had repeated
intelligence from the French of some act of treachery
meditated by the Spaniards ; that several persons
of that nation had come from Bayonne to circulate
reports of peace, and charges against the British
which he knew would be well received on that
frontier ; that he had arrested a man calling himself
an agent of and actually bearing a letter of credence
from Ferdinand.

But the most striking proof of the alarm he felt was his great satisfaction at the conduct of the Spanish government in rejecting the treaty brought by San Carlos and Palafox. Sacrificing all his former great and just resentment he changed at once from an enemy to a friend of the regency, supported the members of it even against the serviles, spoke of the matter as being the most important concern of all that had engaged his attention, and when the count of La Bispal, the deadly enemy of the regency, proposed some violent and decided action of hostility which a few weeks before would have been received with pleasure, he checked and softened him, observing, that the conduct of the government about the treaty should content every Spaniard, that it was not possible to act with more frankness and loyalty, and that they had procured honour for themselves and for their nation not only in England but all over Europe. Such is the light mode in which words are applied by public men, even by the noblest and greatest, when their wishes are fulfilled. This glorious and honourable conduct of the regency was simply a resolution to uphold their personal power and that of their faction, both of which would have been destroyed by the arrival of the king.

Napoleon hoping much from the effect of these machinations not only intimated to Soult, as I have already shewn, that he would require ten thousand of his infantry immediately, but that twice that number with a division of cavalry would be called away if the Spaniards fell off from the English alliance. The duke of Dalmatia then foreseeing the ultimate result of his own operations against Wellington, conceived a vast general plan of action which showed how capable a man he was to treat the greatest questions of military policy.

" Neither his numbers nor means of supply after Wellington had gained the banks of the Adour above Bayonne would, he said, suffice to maintain his positions covering that fortress and menacing the allies' right flank ; the time therefore approached when he must, even without a reduction of force, abandon Bayonne to its own resources and fight his battles on the numerous rivers which run with concentric courses from the Pyrenees to the Adour. Leval's and Boyer's divisions of infantry were to join the grand army on the eastern frontier, Abbé's division was to reinforce the garrison of Bayonne and its camp to fourteen thousand men, but he considered this force too great for a simple general of division and wished to give it to general Reille whose corps would be broken up by the departure of the detachments. That officer was however altogether averse, and as an unwilling commander would be half beaten before the battle commenced he desired that count D'Erlon should be appointed in Reille's place.

" The active army remaining could not then be expected to fight the allies in pitched battles, and he therefore recommended the throwing it as a great partizan corps on the left, touching always upon the Pyrenees and ready to fall upon lord Wellington's flank and rear if he should penetrate into France. Clauzel a native of those parts and speaking the country language was by his military qualities and knowledge the most suitable person to command. General Reille could then march with the troops called to the great army, and as there would be nothing left for him, Soult, to do in these parts he desired to be employed where he could aid the emperor with more effect. This he pressed urgently because, notwithstanding the refusal of the Cortez to receive the treaty of Valençay, it was probable the war on the eastern frontier would oblige the emperor to recall all the troops designated. It would then become imperative to change from a regular to an irregular warfare, in which a numerous corps of partizans would be more valuable than the shadow of a regular army without value or confidence, and likely to be destroyed in the first great battle. For these partizans it was necessary to have a central power and director. Clauzel was the man most fitted for the task. He ought to have under his orders all the generals who were in command in the military departments between the Garonne and the Pyrenees, with power to force all the inhabitants to take arms and act under his directions.

" I am sensible," he continued, " that this system, one of the least unhappy consequences of which would be to leave the enemy apparently master of all the country between the mountains and the Garonne, can only be justified by the necessity of forming an army in the centre of France sufficiently powerful to fend off the multitude of our enemies from the capital; but if Paris falls all will be lost, whereas if it be saved the loss of a few large towns in the south can be repaired. I propose then to form a great army in front of Paris by a union of all the disposable troops of the armies on the different frontiers, and at the same time to spread what remains of the latter as partizans wherever the enemy penetrates or threatens to penetrate. All the marshals of France the generals and other officers, either in activity or in retirement, who shall not be

attached to the great central army, should then
repair to their departments to organize the partizan
corps and bring those not actively useful as such
up to the great point of union, and they should have
military power to make all men able to bear arms,
find them at their own expense." " This measure
is revolutionary but will infallibly produce important results, while none or at least a very feeble effect
will be caused by the majority of the imperial commissioners already sent to the military divisions.
They are grand persons, they temporize, make proclamations and treat every thing as civilians instead
of acting with vigour to obtain promptly a result
which would astonish the world ; for notwithstanding the cry to the contrary, the resources of France
are not exhausted, what is wanted is to make those
who possess resources use them for the defence of the
throne and the emperor."

Having thus explained his views, he again requested
to be recalled to Paris to serve near the emperor, but
declared that he was ready to obey any order and
serve in any manner ; all he demanded was clear instructions with reference to the events that might
occur. 1°. What he should do if the treaty arrangements with Ferdinand had no effect and the
Spanish troops remained with lord Wellington.
2°. If those troops retired and the British seeing
the French weakened by detachments should alone
penetrate into France. 3°. If the changes in Spain
should cause the allies to retire altogether.

Such was Soult's plan of action but his great
project was not adopted and the emperor's reasons
for neglecting it have not been made known. Nor
can the workings of that capacious mind be judged
of without a knowledge of all the objects and con-

ditions of his combinations. Yet it is not improbable that at this period he did not despair of
rejecting the allies beyond the Rhine either by
force of arms, by negociation, or by working upon
the family pride of the emperor of Austria. With
this hope he would be naturally averse to incur the
risk of a civil war by placing France under martial
law, or of reviving the devouring fire of revolution
which it had been his object for so many years to
quell; and this is the more probable because it
seems nearly certain, that one of his reasons for re-
placing Ferdinand on the Spanish throne was his
fear lest the republican doctrines which had gained
ground in Spain should spread to France. Was he
wrong? The fierce democrat will answer Yes! But
the man who thinks that real liberty was never
attained under a single unmixed form of government
giving no natural vent to the swelling pride of
honour birth or riches; those who measure the
weakness of pure republicanism by the miserable
state of France at home and abroad when Napoleon
by assuming power saved her; those who saw
America with all her militia and her licentious
liberty unable to prevent three thousand British
soldiers from passing three thousand miles of
ocean and burning her capital, will hesitate to condemn him. And this without detriment to the democratic principle which in substance may and
should always govern under judicious forms. Napoleon early judged, and the event has proved he
judged truly, that the democratic spirit of France
however violent was unable to overbear the aristocratic and monarchic tendencies of Europe; wisely
therefore while he preserved the essence of the
first by fostering equality, he endeavoured to blend

it with the other two ; thus satisfying as far as the nature of human institutions would permit the conditions of the great problem he had undertaken to solve. His object was the reconstruction of the social fabric which had been shattered by the French revolution, mixing with the new materials all that remained of the old sufficiently unbroken to build with again. If he failed to render his structure stable it was because his design was misunderstood, and the terrible passions let loose by the previous stupendous explosion were too mighty even for him to compress.

To have accepted Soult's project would have been to endanger his work, to save himself at the expense of his system, and probably to plunge France again into the anarchy from which he had with so much care and labour drawn her. But as I have before said, and it is true, Napoleon's ambition was for the greatness and prosperity of France, for the regeneration of Europe, for the stability of the system which he had formed with that end, never for himself personally ; and hence it is that the multitudes of many nations instinctively revere his memory. And neither the monarch nor the aristocrat, dominant though they be by his fall, feel themselves so easy in their high places as to rejoice much in their victory.

Whatever Napoleon's motive was he did not adopt Soult's project, and in February two divisions of infantry and Trielhard's cavalry with many batteries were withdrawn. Two thousand of the best soldiers were also selected to join the imperial guards, and all the gensd'armes were sent to the interior. The total number of old soldiers left, did not, including the division of General Paris, ex-

ceed forty thousand exclusive of the garrison of
Bayonne and other posts, and the conscripts, beard-
less youths, were for the most part unfit to enter
the line nor were there enough of musquets in the
arsenals to arm them. It is remarkable also, as
shewing how easily military operations may be
affected by distant operations, that Soult expected
and dreaded at this time the descent of a great
English army upon the coast of La Vendée, led
thereto by intelligence of an expedition preparing
in England, under Sir Thomas Graham, really to aid
the Dutch revolt.

While the French general's power was thus diminished, lord Wellington's situation was as suddenly
ameliorated. First by the arrival of reinforcements,
next by the security he felt from the rejection of the
treaty of Valençay, lastly by the approach of better
weather, and the acquisition of a very large sum in
gold which enabled him not only to put his Anglo-
Portuguese in activity but also to bring the Spaniards again into line with less danger of their
plundering the country. During the forced cessation of operations he had been actively engaged
preparing the means to enter France with power
and security, sending before him the fame of a just
discipline and a wise consideration for the people
who were likely to fall under his power, for there
was nothing he so much dreaded as the partizan and
insurgent warfare proposed by Soult. The peasants
of Baygorry and Bidarray had done him more mischief than the French army, and his terrible menace
of destroying their villages, and hanging all the population he could lay his hands upon if they ceased
not their hostility, marks his apprehensions in the
strongest manner. Yet he left all the local autho-

rities free to carry on the internal government, to draw their salaries, and raise the necessary taxes in the same mode and with as much tranquillity as if perfect peace prevailed ; he opened the ports and drew a large commerce which served to support his own army and engage the mercantile interests in his favour ; he established many sure channels for intelligence political and military, and would have extended his policy further and to more advantage if the English ministers had not so abruptly and ignorantly interfered with his proceedings. Finally foreseeing that the money he might receive would, being in foreign coin, create embarrassment, he adopted an expedient which he had before practised in India to obviate this. Knowing that in a British army a wonderful variety of knowledge and vocations good and bad may be found, he secretly caused the coiners and die-sinkers amongst the soldiers to be sought out, and once assured that no mischief was intended them, it was not difficult to persuade them to acknowledge their peculiar talents. With these men he established a secret mint at which he coined gold Napoleons, marking them with a private stamp and carefully preserving their just fineness and weight with a view of enabling the French govern ment when peace should be established to call them in again. He thus avoided all the difficulties of exchange, and removed a very fruitful source of quarrels and ill-will between the troops and the country people and shopkeepers ; for the latter are always fastidious in taking and desirous of abating the current worth of strange coin, and the former attribute to fraud any declination from the value at which they receive their money. This sudden increase of the current coin tended also to diminish the pressure necessarily attendant upon troubled times.

Nor was his provident sagacity less eminently displayed in purely military matters than in his administrative and political operations. During the bad weather he had formed large magazines at the ports, examined the course of the Adour, and carefully meditated upon his future plans. To penetrate into France and rally a great Bourbon party under the protection of his army was the system he desired to follow; and though the last point depended upon the political proceedings and successes of the allied sovereigns the military operations most suitable at the moment did not clash with it. To drive the French army from Bayonne and either blockade or besiege that place were the first steps in either case. But this required extensive and daring combinations. For the fortress and its citadel, comprising in their circuit the confluence of the Nive and the Adour, could not be safely invested with less than three times the number necessary to resist the garrison at any one point, because the communications of the invested being short internal and secure, those of the investers external difficult and unsafe, it behoved that each division should be able to resist a sally of the whole garrison. Hence, though reduced to the lowest point, the whole must be so numerous as seriously to weaken the forces operating towards the interior.

How and where to cross the Adour with a view to the investment was also a subject of solicitude. It was a great river with a strong current and well guarded by troops and gun-boats above Bayonne; still greater was it below the town; there the ebb tide run seven miles an hour, there also there were gun-boats, a sloop of war, and several merchant-vessels which could be armed and employed to interrupt the passage. The number of pontoons or other boats required to bridge the stream across either above or below, and the carriage of them, an immense operation in itself, would inevitably give notice of the design and render it abortive, unless the French army were first driven away, and even then the garrison of Bayonne nearly fifteen thousand strong might be sufficient to baffle the attempt. Nevertheless in the face of these difficulties he resolved to pass, the means adopted being proportionate to the greatness of the design.

He considered, that, besides the difficulty of bringing the materials across the Nive and through the deep country on each side of that river, he could not throw his bridge above Bayonne without first driving Soult entirely from the confluents of the Adour and from the Adour itself; that when he had effected this his own communications between the bridge and his magazines at the sea-ports would still be difficult and unsafe, because his convoys would have a flank march, passing the Nive as well as the Adour and liable to interruption from the overflowing of those rivers; finally, that his means of transport would be unequal to the wear and tear of the deep roads and be interrupted by rain. But throwing his bridge below the town he would have the Adour itself as a harbour; while his land convoys used the royal causeway leading close to the river and not liable to be interrupted by weather. His line of retreat also would then be more secure if any unforeseen misfortune should render it necessary to break up the investment. He had no fear that Soult, while retiring before the active force he intended to employ against

him on the upper parts of the rivers, would take his
line of retreat by the great Bordeaux road and fall
upon the investing force : that road led behind
Bayonne through the sandy wilderness called the
Landes, into which the French general would not
care to throw himself, lest his opponent's operations
along the edge of the desert should prevent him
from ever getting out. To draw the attention of the
French army by an attack on their left near the
roots of the Pyrenees would be sure to keep the
lower Adour free from any formidable defensive
force, because the rapidity and breadth of the stream
there denied the use of common pontoons, and the
mouth, about six miles below Bayonne, was so
barred with sand, so beaten by surges, and so difficult of navigation even with the help of the land-
marks, some of which had been removed, that the
French would never expect small vessels fit for
constructing a bridge could enter that way. Yet it
was thus lord Wellington designed to achieve his
object. He had collected forty large sailing boats
of from fifteen to thirty tons burthen, called *chasse
marées*, as if for the commissariat service, but he
secretly loaded them with planks and other materials for his bridge. These and some gun-boats he
designed, with the aid of the navy, to run up the
Adour to a certain point upon which he meant also
to direct the troops and artillery, and then with
hawsers, and pontoons formed into rafts, to throw
over a covering body and destroy a small battery
near the mouth of the river. He trusted to the
greatness and danger of the attempt for success and
in this he was favoured by fortune.

The French trading vessels in the Adour had
offered secretly to come out upon licenses and enter

the service of his commissariat, but he was obliged
to forego the advantage because of the former interference and dissent of the English ministers about
the passports he had previously granted.   This
added greatly to the difficulty of the enterprize.
He was thus forced to maltreat men willing to be
friends, to prepare grates for heating shot, and a
battery of Congreve rockets with which to burn
their vessels and the sloop of war, or at least to drive
them up the river, after which he proposed to protect his bridge with the gun-boats and a boom.

While he was thus preparing for offensive
operations the French general was active in defensive measures.   He had fortified all the main
passes of the rivers by the great roads leading
against his left, but the diminution of his force in
January obliged him to withdraw his outposts from
Anglet, which enabled lord Wellington to examine
the whole course of the Adour below Bayonne
and arrange for the passage with more facility.
Soult then in pursuance of Napoleon's system of
warfare, which always prescribed a recourse to
moral force to cover physical weakness, immediately
concentrated his left wing against the allies' right
beyond the Nive, and redoubled that harassing
partizan warfare which I have already noticed,
endeavouring to throw his adversary entirely upon
the defensive.   Thus on the 26th of January, Morillo having taken possession of an advanced post
near Mendionde not properly belonging to him,
Soult, who desired to ascertain the feelings of the
Spaniards about the English alliance, caused Harispe
under pretence of remonstrating to sound him ;
he did not respond and Harispe then drove him,
not without a vigorous resistance, from the post.

The French marshal had however no hope of checking the allies long by these means. He judged justly
that Wellington was resolved to obtain Bordeaux
and the line of the Garonne, and foreseeing that his
own line of retreat must ultimately be in a parallel
direction with the Pyrenees, he desired to organize
in time a strong defensive system in the country
behind him and to cover Bordeaux if possible. In
this view he sent general Darricau a native of the
Landes to prepare an insurgent levy in that wilderness, and directed Maransin to the High Pyrenees
to extend the insurrection of the mountaineers already commenced in the Lower Pyrenees by Harispe.
The castle of Jaca was still held by eight hundred
men but they were starving, and a convoy collected at Navarrens being stopped by the snow in
the mountain-passes made a surrender inevitable.
Better would it have been to have withdrawn
the troops at an early period; for though the
Spaniards would thus have gained access to the
rear of the French army and perhaps ravaged a part
of the frontier, they could have done no essential
mischief to the army; and their excesses would have
disposed the people of those parts who had not yet
felt the benefit of lord Wellington's politic discipline to insurrection.

At Bordeaux there was a small reserve commanded
by general La Huillier, Soult urged the minister of
war to increase it with conscripts from the interior.
Meanwhile he sent artillery-men from Bayonne,
ordered fifteen hundred national guards to be
selected as a garrison for the citadel of Blaye, and
desired that the Médoc and Paté forts and the batteries along the banks of the Garonne should be put
in a state of defence. The vessels in that river fit

for the purpose he desired might be armed, and a flotilla of fifty gun-boats established below Bordeaux, with a like number to navigate that river above the city as far as Toulouse. But these orders were feebly carried into execution or entirely neglected, for there was no public spirit, and treason and disaffection were rife in the city.

On the side of the Lower Pyrenees Soult enlarged and improved the works of Navarrens and designed to commence an entrenched camp in front of it. The castle of Lourdes in the High Pyrenees was already defensible, and he gave orders to fortify the castle of Pau, thus providing a number of supporting points for the retreat which he foresaw. At Mauleon he put on foot some partizan corps, and the imperial commissary Caffarelli gave him hopes of being able to form a reserve of seven or eight thousand national guards, *gensd'armes*, and artillery-men, at Tarbes. Dax containing his principal depôts was already being fortified, and the communication with it was maintained across the rivers by the bridges and bridge-heads at Port de Lannes, Hastingues, Pereyhorade, and Sauveterre; but the floods in the beginning of February carried away his bridge at the Port de Lannes, and the communication between Bayonne and the left of the army was thus interrupted until he established a flying bridge in place of the one carried away.

Such was the situation of the French general when lord Wellington advanced, and as the former supposed with one hundred and twenty thousand infantry and fifteen thousand cavalry, for he knew nothing of the various political and financial difficulties which had reduced the English general's power and prevented all the reinforcements he ex-

pected from joining him. His emissaries told him
that Clinton's force was actually broken up, and the
British part in march to join Wellington ; that the
garrisons of Carthagena Cadiz and Ceuta were on
the point of arriving and that reinforcements were
coming from England and Portugal. This information made him conclude that there was no intention of pressing the war in Catalonia and that all
the allied troops would be united and march against
him ; wherefore with more earnestness than before
he urged that Suchet should be ordered to join him
that their united forces might form a " dike against
the torrent" which threatened to overwhelm the
south of France. The real power opposed to him
was however very much below his calculations.
The twenty thousand British and Portuguese reinforcements promised had not arrived, Clinton's army
was still in Catalonia ; and though it is impossible to
fix the exact numbers of the Spaniards, their regular
forces available, and that only partially and with
great caution on account of their licentious conduct,
did not exceed the following approximation.

Twelve thousand Gallicians under Freyre including Carlos d'España's division; four thousand
under Morillo ; six thousand Andalusians under
O'Donnel ; eight thousand of Del Parque's troops
under the prince of Anglona. In all thirty thousand.
The Anglo-Portuguese present under arms were by
the morning states on the 13th of February, the day
on which the advance commenced, about seventy
thousand men and officers of all arms, nearly ten
thousand being cavalry. The whole force, exclusive
of Mina's bands which were spread as we have seen
from Navarre to the borders of Catalonia, was therefore, one hundred thousand men and officers, with

one hundred pieces of field-artillery of which ninety-five were Anglo-Portuguese.

It is difficult to fix with precision the number of the French army at this period, because the imperial muster-rolls, owing to the troubled state of the emperor's affairs were either not continued beyond December 1813 or have been lost. But from Soult's correspondence and other documents it would appear, that exclusive of his garrisons, his reserves and detachments at Bordeaux and in the department of the High Pyrenees, exclusive also of the conscripts of the second levy which were now beginning to arrive, he could place in line of battle about thirty-five thousand soldiers of all arms, three thousand being cavalry, with forty pieces of artillery. But Bayonne alone without reckoning the fortresses of St. Jean Pied de Port and Navarrens occupied twenty-eight thousand of the allies ; and by this and other drains lord Wellington's superiority in the field was so reduced, that his penetrating into France, that France which had made all Europe tremble at her arms, must be viewed as a surprising example of courage and fine conduct, military and political.

PASSAGE OF THE GAVES.

In the second week of February the weather set in with a strong frost, the roads became practicable and the English general, eagerly seizing the long-expected opportunity, advanced at the moment when general Paris had again marched with the convoy from Navarrens to make a last effort for the relief of Jaca. But the troops were at this time receiving the clothing which had been so long delayed in England, and the regiments wanting the means of carriage,

marched to the stores; the English general's first
design was therefore merely to threaten the French
left and turn it by the sources of the rivers with
Hill's corps, which was to march by the roots of the
Pyrenees, while Beresford kept the centre in check
upon the lower parts of the same rivers. Soult's attention would thus he hoped be drawn to that side while
the passage of the Adour was being made below
Bayonne. And it would seem that uncertain if he
should be able to force the passage of the tributary
rivers with his right, he intended, if his bridge was
happily thrown, to push his main operations on that
side and thus turn the Gaves by the right bank of
the Adour: a fine conception by which his superiority of numbers would have best availed him to
seize Dax and the Port de Landes and cut Soult off
from Bordeaux.

On the 12th and 13th Hill's corps, which including Picton's division and five regiments of cavalry
furnished twenty thousand combatants with sixteen
guns, being relieved by the sixth and seventh divisions in front of Mousseroles and on the Adour, was
concentrated about Urcurray and Hasparen. The
14th it marched in two columns. One by Bonloc Plan 9.
to drive the French posts beyond the Joyeuse; another by the great road of St. Jean Pied de Port
against Harispe who was at Hellette. This second
column had the Ursouia mountain on the right, and
a third, composed of Morillo's Spaniards, having
that mountain on its left marched from La Houssoa
against the same point. Harispe who had only three
brigades, principally conscripts, retired skirmishing
in the direction of St. Palais and took a position for
the night at Meharin. Not more than thirty men
on each side were hurt but the line of the Joyeuse

was turned by the allies, the direct communication with St. Jean Pied de Port cut, and that place was immediately invested by Mina's battalions.

On the 15th Hill, leaving the fifty-seventh regiment at Hellette to observe the road to St. Jean Pied de Port, marched through Meharin upon Garris, eleven miles distant, but that road being impracticable for artillery the guns moved by Armendaritz more to the right. Harispe's rear-guard was overtaken and pushed back fighting, and meanwhile lord Wellington directed Beresford to send a brigade of the seventh division from the heights of La Costa across the Gamboury to the Bastide de Clerence. The front being thus extended from Urt by Briscons, the Bastide and Isturitz, towards Garris, a distance of more than twenty miles, was too attenuated; wherefore he caused the fourth division to occupy La Costa in support of the troops at the Bastide. At the same time learning that the French had weakened their force at Mousseroles, and thinking that might be to concentrate on the heights of Anglet, which would have frustrated his plan for throwing a bridge over the Adour, he directed Hope secretly to occupy the back of those heights in force and prevent any intercourse between Bayonne and the country.

Soult knew of the intended operations against his left on the 12th, but hearing the allies had collected boats and constructed a fresh battery near Urt on the Upper Adour, and that the pontoons had reached Urcurray, he thought lord Wellington designed to turn his left with Hill's corps, to press him on the Bidouze with Beresford's, and to keep the garrison of Bayonne in check with the Spaniards while Hope crossed the Adour above that fortress.

Wherefore, on the 14th, when Hill's movement commenced, he repaired to Passarou near the Bastide
de Clerence and made his dispositions to dispute
the passage, first of the Bidouze and the Soissons or
Gave of Mauleon, and then of the Gave of Oleron.
He had four divisions in hand with which he occupied a position on the 15th along the Bidouze; and he
recalled general Paris, posting him on the road between St. Palais and St. Jean Pied de Port, with a
view to watch Mina's battalions which he supposed to
be more numerous than they really were. Jaca thus
abandoned capitulated on the 17th, the garrison returning to France on condition of not serving until
exchanged. This part of the capitulation it appears
was broken by the French, but the recent violation
by the Spaniards of the convention made with the
deluded garrisons of Lerida, Mequinenza, and Monzon, furnished a reply.

Harispe, having Paris under his command and
being supported by Pierre Soult with a brigade of
light cavalry, now covered the road from St. Jean
Pied de Port with his left, and the upper line of the
Bidouze with his right. Lower down that river,
Villatte occupied Ilharre, Taupin was on the heights
of Bergoney below Villatte, and Foy guarded the
banks of the river from Came to its confluence with
the Adour. The rest of the army remained under
D'Erlon on the right of the latter river.

Combat of Garris.—Harispe had just taken a position in advance of the Bidouze, on a height called
the Garris mountain which stretched to St. Palais,
when his rear-guard came plunging into a deep
ravine in his front closely followed by the light
troops of the second division. Upon the parallel
counter-ridge thus gained by the allies general

BOOK
XXIV.
———
1814.
February. Hill's corps was immediately established, and though the evening was beginning to close the skirmishers descended into the ravine, and two guns played over it upon Harispe's troops. These last to the number of four thousand were drawn up on the opposite mountain, and in this state of affairs Wellington arrived. He was anxious to turn the line of the Bidouze before Soult could strengthen himself there, and seeing that the communication with general Paris by St. Palais was not well maintained, sent Morillo by a flank march along the ridge now occupied by the allies towards that place; then menacing the enemy's centre with Le Cor's Portuguese division he at the same time directed the thirty-ninth and twenty-eighth regiments forming Pringle's brigade to attack, observing with a concise energy, " *you must take the hill before dark.*"

Memoir of
the action
published
in the
United
Service
Journal. The expression caught the attention of the troops, and it was repeated by colonel O'Callaghan as he and general Pringle placed themselves at the head of the thirty-ninth, which, followed by the twenty-eighth, rushed with loud and prolonged shouts into the ravine. The French fire was violent, Pringle fell wounded and most of the mounted officers had their horses killed, but the troops covered by the thick wood gained with little loss the summit of the Garris mountain, on the right of the enemy who thought from the shouting that a larger force was coming against them and retreated. The thirty-ninth then wheeled to their own right intending to sweep the summit, but soon the French discovering their error came back at a charging pace, and receiving a volley without flinching tried the bayonet. Colonel O'Callaghan distinguished

by his strength and courage received two strokes of
that weapon but repaid them with fatal power in
each instance, and the French, nearly all conscripts,
were beaten off. Twice however they came back
and fought until the fire of the twenty-eighth was
beginning to be felt, when Harispe seeing the remainder of the second division ready to support the
attack, Le Cor's Portuguese advancing against the
centre, and the Spaniards in march towards St.
Palais, retreated to that town and calling in Paris See Plan.
from the side of Mauleon immediately broke down
the bridges over the Bidouze. He lost on this day
nearly five hundred men, of whom two hundred
were prisoners, and he would hardly have escaped
if Morillo had not been slow. The allies lost only
one hundred and sixty of whom not more than fifty
fell at Garris, and these chiefly in the bayonet contest, for the trees and the darkness screened them at
first.

During these operations at Garris Picton moved
from Bonloc to Oreque, on Hill's left, menacing
Villatte, but though Beresford's scouting parties,
acting on the left of Picton, approached the Bidouze facing Taupin and Foy, his principal force
remained on the Gamboury, the pivot upon which
Wellington's line hinged while the right sweeping
forward turned the French positions. Foy however
though in retreat observed the movement of the
fourth and seventh divisions on the heights between
the Nive and the Adour, pointing their march as he
thought towards the French left, and his reports to
that effect reached Soult at the moment that general
Blondeau gave notice of the investment of St. Jean
Pied de Port. The French general being thus con-

vinced that lord Wellington's design was not to pass
the Adour above Bayonne, but to gain the line of
that river by constantly turning the French left,
made new dispositions.

The line of the Bidouze was strong, if he could
have supported Harispe at St. Palais, and guarded
at the same time the passage of the Soissons at
Mauleon ; but this would have extended his front,
already too wide, wherefore he resolved to abandon
both the Bidouze and the Soissons and take the line
of the Gave d'Oleron, placing his right at Peyrehorade and his left at Navarrens. In this view
D'Erlon was ordered to pass the Adour by the
flying bridge at the Port de Landes and take post
on the left bank of that river, while Harispe, having
Paris' infantry still attached to his division, defended the Gave de Mauleon and pushed parties on
his left towards the town of that name. Villatte
occupied Sauveterre, where the bridge was fortified
with a head on the left bank, and from thence
Taupin lined the right bank to Sordes near the
confluence of the Gave de Pau. Foy occupied the
works of the bridge-head at Peyrehorade and Hastingues guarding that river to its confluence with
the Adour ; this line was prolonged by D'Erlon
towards Dax, but Soult still kept advanced parties
on the lower Bidouze at the different entrenched
passages of that river. One brigade of cavalry
was in reserve at Sauveterre, another distributed
along the line. Head-quarters were transported to
Orthes, and the parc of artillery to Aire. The
principal magazines of ammunition were however
at Bayonne, Navarrens, and Dax, and the French
general seeing that his communications with all

these places were likely to be intercepted before he
could remove his stores, anticipated distress and
wrote to the minister of war to form new dépôts.

On the 16th lord Wellington repaired the broken
bridges of St. Palais, after a skirmish in which a
few men were wounded. Hill then crossed the
Bidouze, the cavalry and artillery by the repaired
bridge, the infantry by the fords, but the day
being spent in the operation the head of the column only marched beyond St. Palais. Meanwhile
the fourth and part of the seventh divisions occupied the Bastide de Clerence on the right of the
Joyeuse, and the light division came up in support
to the heights of La Costa on the left bank of that
river.

The 17th Hill, marching at eight o'clock, passed
through Domenzain towards the Soissons, while the
third division advancing from Oreque on his left
passed by Masparraute to the heights of Somberraute, both corps converging upon general Paris, who
was in position at Arriveriete to defend the Soissons
above its confluence with the Gave d'Oleron. The
French outposts were immediately driven across
the Gave. General Paris attempted to destroy the
bridge of Arriveriete but lord Wellington was too
quick; the ninety-second regiment covered by the
fire of some guns crossed at a ford above the
bridge, and beating two French battalions from the
village secured the passage. The allies then halted
for the day near Arriveriete having marched only
five miles and lost one man killed with twenty-three
wounded. Paris relinquished the Soissons but remained between the two rivers during the night
and retired on the morning of the 18th. The allies
then seized the great road, which here runs from

BOOK
XXIV.
——————
1814.
February.
Soult's
Official
Correspon-
dence,
MSS.
Sauveterre to Navarrens up the left bank of the
Oleron Gave.

Harispe, Villatte, and Paris, supported by a brigade of cavalry were now at Sauveterre occupying
the bridge-head on the left bank, Taupin's division
was opposite the Bastide de Bearn lower down on
the right, Foy on the right of Taupin, and D'Erlon
on the left of the Adour above its confluence with
the Gave de Pau. Meanwhile the fourth division
advanced to Bidache on the Bidouze, and the light
division followed in support to the Bastide de Clerence, the seventh division remaining as before,
partly in that vicinity partly extended on the left to
the Adour. The cavalry of the centre, under sir
Stapleton Cotton, arrived also on the banks of the
Bidouze connecting the fourth with the third division at Somberraute. In this state of affairs Hill
sent Morillo up the Soissons to guard the fords as
high as Nabas, then spreading Fane's cavalry and
the British and Portuguese infantry between that
river and the Gave d'Oleron, he occupied all the
villages along the road to Navarrens and at the
same time cannonaded the bridge-head of Sauveterre.

Soult thrown from the commencement of the
operations entirely upon the defensive was now at a
loss to discover his adversary's object. The situation of the seventh division, and the march of the
fourth and light divisions, led him to think his
works at Hastingues and Peyrehorade would be
assailed. The weakness of his line, he having only
Taupin's division to guard the river between
Sauveterre and Sordes a distance of ten miles,
made him fear the passage of the Gave would be
forced near the Bastide de Bearn, to which post

there was a good road from Came and Bidache.
On the other hand the prolongation of Hill's line
up the Gave towards Navarrens indicated a design
to march on Pau, or it might be to keep him in
check on the Gaves while the camp at Bayonne was
assaulted. In this uncertainty he sent Pierre Soult,
with a cavalry brigade and two battalions of infantry to act between Oleron and Pau, and keep
open a communication with the partizan corps forming at Mauleon. That done he decided to hold the
Gaves as long as he could, and when they were
forced, to abandon the defensive concentrate his
whole force at Orthes and fall suddenly upon the
first of the allies' converging columns that approached him.

CHAPTER II.

THE French general's various conjectures embraced every project but the true one of the English general. The latter did indeed design to keep him in check upon the rivers, not to obtain an opportunity of assaulting the camp of Bayonne but to throw his stupendous bridge over the Adour; yet were his combinations so made that failing in that he could still pursue his operations on the Gaves. When therefore he had established his offensive line strongly beyond the Soissons and the Bidouze, and knew that his pontoon train was well advanced towards Garris, he on the 19th returned rapidly to St. Jean de Luz. Everything there depending on man was ready, but the weather was boisterous with snow for two days, and Wellington, fearful of letting Soult strengthen himself on the Gave of Oleron, returned on the 21st to Garris, having decided to press his operations on that side in person and leave to sir John Hope and admiral Penrose the charge of effecting

THE PASSAGE OF THE ADOUR.

The heights of Anglet had been occupied since the 15th by the guards and Germans, small parties were cautiously pushed towards the river through the pine-forest called the wood of Bayonne, and the

fifth division, now commanded by general Colville, CHAP. II.
occupied Bussussary and the bridge of Urdains. ───
On the 21st Colville relieved the sixth division in 1814. February.
the blockade of Mousseroles on the right of the Nive.
To replace these troops at Bussussary, Freyre's
Spaniards passed the Bidassoa, but the Andalusians and Del Parque's troops and the heavy
British and Portuguese cavalry were still retained
within the frontiers of Spain. Sir John Hope had
therefore only two British and two Spanish divi-
sions, three independent brigades of Anglo-Portu- Original Morning
guese infantry and Vandeleur's brigade of cavalry, States. MSS.
furnishing altogether about twenty-eight thousand
men and officers with twenty pieces of artillery.
There were however two regiments which had been
sent to the rear sick and several others expected
from England destined to join him.

In the night of the 22d the first division, six
eighteen pounders, and the rocket battery, were
cautiously filed from the causeway near Anglet
towards the Adour, but the road was deep and
heavy and one of the guns falling into a ditch
delayed the march. Nevertheless at daybreak the
whole reached some sand-downs which extended Plan 7.
behind the pine-forest to the river. The French
picquets were then driven into the entrenched camp
at Beyris, the pontoon train and the field-artillery
were brought down to the Adour opposite to the
village of Boucaut, and the eighteen-pounders were
placed in battery on the bank. The light troops
meanwhile closed to the edge of the marsh which
covered the right of the French camp, and Carlos
España's division taking post on the heights of
Anglet, in concert with the independent brigades,
which were at Arcangues and the bridge of Urdains,

attracted the enemy's attention by false attacks which were prolonged beyond the Nive by the fifth division.

It was intended that the arrival of the gun-boats and chasse-marées at the mouth of the Adour should have been simultaneous with that of the troops, but the wind having continued contrary none were to be seen, and sir John Hope whose firmness no untoward event could ever shake resolved to attempt the passage with the army alone. The French flotilla opened its fire on his columns about nine o'clock, his artillery and rockets retorted upon the French gun-boats and the sloop of war so fiercely, that three of the former were destroyed and the sloop so hardly handled that about one o'clock the whole took refuge higher up the river. Meanwhile sixty men of the guards were rowed in a pontoon across the mouth of the river in the face of a French picquet, which, seemingly bewildered, retired without firing. A raft was then formed with the remainder of the pontoons and a hawser being stretched across, six hundred of the guards and the sixtieth regiment, with a part of the rocket battery, the whole under colonel Stopford, passed, yet slowly, and at slack water only, for the tide run strongly and the waters were wide.

During this operation general Thouvenot deceived by spies and prisoners thought that the light division was with Hope as well as the first division, and that fifteen thousand men were embarked at St. Jean de Luz to land between Cape Breton and the Adour. Wherefore fearing to endanger his garrison by sending a strong force to any distance down the river, when he heard Stopford's detachment was on the right bank, he detached only two

Thouvenot's Official Report

battalions under general Macomble to ascertain the
state of affairs, for the pine-forest and a great bending of the river prevented him from obtaining any
view from Bayonne. Macomble made a show of
attacking Stopford, but the latter, flanked by the
field-artillery from the left bank, received him with
a discharge of rockets, projectiles which like the
elephants in ancient warfare often turn upon their
own side. This time however, amenable to their
directors they smote the French column and it fled,
amazed, and with a loss of thirty wounded. It is
nevertheless obvious that if Thouvenot had kept
strong guards, with a field-battery, on the right bank
of the Adour, sir John Hope could not have passed
over the troops in pontoons, nor could any vessels
have crossed the bar; no resource save that of disembarking troops between the river and Cape Breton
would then have remained. This error was fatal to
the French. The British continued to pass all night,
and until twelve o'clock on the 24th, when the flotilla was seen under a press of sail making with a
strong breeze for the mouth of the river.

To enter the Adour is from the flatness of the
coast never an easy task, it was now most difficult, because the high winds of the preceding days
had raised a great sea and the enemy had removed
one of the guiding flag-staves by which the navigation was ordinarily directed. In front of the flotilla
came the boats of the men of war, and ahead of all,
the naval captain, O'Reilly, run his craft, a chosen
Spanish vessel, into the midst of the breakers, which
rolling in a frightful manner over the bar dashed
her on to the beach. That brave officer stretched
senseless on the shore would have perished with his
crew but for the ready succour of the soldiers,

however a few only were drowned and the remainder with an intrepid spirit launched their boat again to aid the passage of the troops which was still going on. O'Reilly was followed and successfully by lieutenant Debenham in a six-oared cutter, but the tide was falling, wherefore the remainder of the boats, the impossibility of passing until high water being evident drew off, and a pilot was landed to direct the line of navigation by concerted signals.

When the water rose again the crews were promised rewards in proportion to their successful daring and the whole flotilla approached in close order, but with it came black clouds and a driving gale which covered the whole line of coast with a rough tumbling sea, dashing and foaming without an interval of dark water to mark the entrance of the river. The men-of-war's boats first drew near this terrible line of surge and Mr. Bloye of the Lyra, having the chief pilot with him, heroically led into it, but in an instant his barge was engulphed and he and all with him were drowned. The Lyra's boat thus swallowed up the following vessels swerved in their course, and shooting up to the right and left kept hovering undecided on the edge of the tormented waters. Suddenly lieutenant Cheyne of the Woodlark pulled ahead, and striking the right line, with courage and fortune combined safely passed the bar. The wind then lulled, the waves as if conquered abated somewhat of their rage, and the chasse-marées, manned with Spanish seamen but having an engineer officer with a party of sappers in each who compelled them to follow the men-of-war's boats, came plunging one after another through the huge breakers and reached the point designed for the bridge. Thus was achieved this perilous and glorious exploit, but captain Elliot of the Martial with his launch and crew and three transports' boats, perished close to the shore in despite of the most violent efforts made by the troops to save them ; three other vessels cast on the beach lost part of their crews; and one large chasse-marée, full of men, after passing the line of surf safely was overtaken by a swift bellying wave which breaking on her deck dashed her to pieces.

The whole of the first division and Bradford's Portuguese, in all eight thousand men, being now on the right bank took post on the sand-hills for the night. The next morning, sweeping in a half circle round the citadel and its entrenchments, they placed their left on the Adour above the fortress, and their right on the same river below the place ; for the water here made such a bend in their favour that their front was little more than two miles wide, and for the most part covered by a marshy ravine. This nice operation was effected without opposition because the entrenched camps, menaced by the troops on the other side of the Adour, were so enormous that Thouvenot's force was scarcely sufficient to maintain them. Meanwhile the bridge was constructed, about three miles below Bayonne, at a place where the river was contracted to eight hundred feet by strong retaining walls, built with the view of sweeping away the bar by increasing the force of the current. The plan of the bridge and boom were the conception of colonel Sturgeon and major Todd, but the execution was confided entirely to the latter, who, with a mind less brilliant than Sturgeon's but more indefatigable, very ably and usefully served his country throughout this war.

Twenty-six of the chasse-marées moored head
and stern at distances of forty feet, reckoning from
centre to centre, were bound together with ropes,
two thick cables were then carried loosely across
their decks, and the ends being cast over the walls
on each bank were strained and fastened in various
modes to the sands. They were sufficiently slack to
meet the spring-tides which rose fourteen feet, and
planks were laid upon them without any supporting
beams. The boom, moored with anchors above and
below, was a double line of masts connected with
chains and cables, so as to form a succession of
squares, in the design that if a vessel broke through
the outside, it should by the shock turn round in the
square and become entangled with the floating
wrecks of the line through which it had broken.
Gun-boats, with aiding batteries on the banks,
were then stationed to protect the boom, and to
keep off fire-vessels, many row-boats were furnished
with grappling irons. The whole was by the united
labour of seamen and soldiers finished on the 26th.
And contrary to the general opinion on such matters,
major Todd assured the Author of this History that
he found the soldiers, with minds quickened by the
wider range and variety of knowledge attendant on
their service, more ready of resource and their
efforts, combined by a more regular discipline, of
more avail, with less loss of time, than the irregular activity of the seamen.

The agitation of the water in the river from the
force of the tides was generally so great that to
maintain a pontoon bridge on it was impossible.
A knowledge of this had rendered the French officers
too careless of watch and defence, and this year the
shifting sands had given the course of the Adour

such a slanting direction towards the west that it
run for some distance almost parallel to the shore;
the outer bank thus acting as a breakwater lessened
the agitation within and enabled the large two-
masted boats employed, to ride safely and support
the heaviest artillery and carriages. Nevertheless
this fortune, the errors of the enemy, the matchless
skill and daring of the British seamen, and the discipline and intrepidity of the British soldiers, all
combined by the genius of Wellington, were necessary to the success of this stupendous undertaking
which must always rank amongst the prodigies of
war.

When the bridge was finished sir John Hope
resolved to contract his line of investment round
the citadel. This was a serious affair. The position
of the French outside that fort was exceedingly
strong, for the flanks were protected by ravines the
sides of which were covered with fortified villas ;
and in the centre a ridge, along which the great
roads from Bordeaux and Peyrehorade led into
Bayonne, was occupied by the village and church of
St. Etienne, both situated on rising points of ground
strongly entrenched and under the fire of the citadel
guns. The allies advanced in three converging columns covered by skirmishers. Their wings easily
attained the edges of the ravines at either side, resting their flanks on the Adour above and below the
town, at about nine hundred yards from the enemy's
works. But a severe action took place in the centre.
The assailing body composed of Germans and a
brigade of guards was divided into three parts
which should have attacked simultaneously, the
guards on the left, the light battalions of Germans
on the right, and their heavy infantry in the centre.

The flanks were retarded by some accident and the centre first attacked the heights of St. Etienne. The French guns immediately opened from the citadel and the skirmishing fire became heavy, but the Germans stormed church and village, forced the entrenched line of houses, and took a gun, which however they could not carry off under the close fire from the citadel. The wings then gained their positions and the action ceased for a time, but the people of Bayonne were in such consternation that Thouvenot to re-assure them sallied at the head of the troops. He charged the Germans twice and fought well but was wounded and finally lost his gun and the position of St. Etienne. There is no return of the allies' loss, it could not have been less than five hundred men and officers of which four hundred were Germans, and the latter were dissatisfied that their conduct was unnoticed in the despatch: an omission somewhat remarkable because their conduct was by sir John Hope always spoken of with great commendation.

The new position thus gained was defended by ravines on each flank, and the centre being close to the enemy's works on the ridge of St. Etienne was entrenched. Preparations for besieging the citadel were then commenced under the direction of the German colonel Hartmann, a code of signals was established, and infinite pains taken to protect the bridge and to secure a unity of action between the three investing bodies. The communications however required complicated arrangements, for the ground on the right bank of the river being low was overflowed every tide, and would have occasioned great difficulty but for the retaining wall which being four feet thick was made use of as a carriage road.

While these events were in progress at Bayonne lord Wellington pushed his operations on the Gaves with great vigour. On the 21st he returned as we have seen to Garris, the pontoons had already reached that place and on the 23d they were carried beyond the Gave de Mauleon. During his absence the sixth and light divisions had come up, and thus six divisions of infantry and two brigades of cavalry were concentrated beyond that river on the Gave d'Olero͂, between Sauveterre and Navarrens. Beresford meanwhile held the line of the Bidouze down to its confluence with the Adour, and apparently to distract the enemy threw a battalion over the latter river near Urt, and collected boats as if to form a bridge there. In the evening he recalled this detachment, yet continued the appearance of preparations for a bridge until late in the 23d, when he moved forward and drove Foy's posts from the works at Oeyergave and Hastingues, on the lower parts of the Oleron Gave, into the entrenchments of the bridge-head at Peyrehorade. The allies lost fifty men, principally Portuguese, but Soult's right and centre were thus held in check, for Beresford having the fourth and seventh divisions and Vivian's cavalry was strong enough for Foy at Peyrehorade and Taupin at the Bastide of Bearn. The rest of the French army was distributed at Orthes and Sauveterre, feeling towards Navarrens, and on the 24th Wellington put his troops in motion to pass the Gave d'Oleron.

During the previous days his movements and the arrival of his reinforcements had again deceived the French general, who seems to have known nothing

French Official Correspondence, MSS.

of the presence of the light division, and imagined the first division was at Came on the 22d as well as the fourth and seventh divisions. However his dispositions remained the same, he did not expect to hold the Gave and looked to a final concentration at Orthes.

On the 24th Morillo reinforced with a strong detachment of cavalry moved to the Laussette, a small river running in front of Navarrens, where rough ground concealed his real force, while his scouters beat back the French outposts, and a battalion marching higher up menaced the fords of the Gave at Doguen, with a view to draw the attention of the garrison of Navarrens from the ford of Ville Nave. This ford about three miles below Doguen was the point where lord Wellington designed really to pass, and a great concentric movement was now in progress towards it.   Le Cor's Portuguese division marched from Gestas, the light division from Aroue crossing the Soissons at Nabas; the second division, three batteries of artillery, the pontoons, and four regiments of cavalry moved from other points. Favoured by the hilly nature of the country the columns were well concealed from the enemy, and at the same time the sixth division advanced towards the fords of Montfort about three miles below that of Ville Nave.   A battalion of the second division was sent to menace the ford of Barraute below Monfort, while the third division, reinforced with a brigade of hussars and the batteries of the second division, marched by Osserain and Arriveriette against the bridge-head of Sauveterre, with orders to make a feint of forcing a passage there.   The bulk of the light cavalry remained in reserve under Cotton, but Vivian's hussars coming up from

Beresford's right, threatened all the fords between
Picton's left and the Bastide of Bearn; and below
this Bastide some detachments were directed upon
the fords of Sindos Castagnhede and Hauterive.
During this movement Beresford keeping Foy in
check at Peyrehorade with the seventh division,
sent the fourth towards Sordes and Leren above the
confluence of the Gaves to seek a fit place to throw
a bridge. Thus the whole of the French front was
menaced on a line of twenty-five miles, but the great
force was above Sauveterre.

The first operations were not happily executed.
The columns directed on the side of Sindos missed
the fords. Picton opened a cannonade against
the bridge-head of Sauveterre and made four
companies of Keane's brigade and some cavalry
pass the Gave in the vicinity of the bridge; they
were immediately assailed by a French regiment
and driven across the river again with a loss of
ninety men and officers, of whom some were drowned
and thirty were made prisoners, whereupon the
cavalry returned to the left bank and the cannonade
ceased. Nevertheless the diversion was complete
and the general operations were successful. Soult
on the first alarm drew Harispe from Sauveterre and
placed him on the road to Orthes at Monstrueig,
where a range of hills running parallel to the Gave
of Oleron separates it from that of Pau; thus only
a division of infantry and Berton's cavalry remained
under Villatte at Sauveterre, and that general, notwithstanding his success against the four companies, alarmed by the vigour of Picton's demonstrations, abandoned his works on the left bank and
destroyed the bridge. Meanwhile the sixth division
passed without opposition at Montfort above Sauve-

terre, and at the same time the great body of the other troops coming down upon the ford of Villenave met only with a small cavalry picquet and crossed with no more loss than two men drowned : a happy circumstance for the waters were deep and rapid, the cold intense, and the ford so narrow that the passage was not completed before dark. To have forced it in face of an enemy would have been exceedingly difficult and dangerous, and it is remarkable that Soult who was with Harispe, only five miles from Montfort and about seven from Villenave, should not have sent that general down to oppose the passage. The heads of the allies' columns immediately pushed forward to the range of hills before spoken of, the right being established near Loubeing, the left towards Sauveterre, from whence Villatte and Berton had been withdrawn by Clauzel, who commanding at this part seems to have kept a bad watch when Clinton passed at Montfort.

The French divisions now took a position to give time for Taupin to retire from the lower parts of the Gave of Oleron, towards the bridge of Berenx on the Gave of Pau, for both he and Foy had received orders to march upon Orthes and break down all the bridges as they passed. When the night fell Soult sent Harispe's division also over the bridge of Orthes and D'Erlon was already established in that town, but general Clauzel remained until the morning at Orion to cover the movement. Meanwhile Pierre Soult, posted beyond Navarrens with his cavalry and two battalions of infantry to watch the road to Pau, was pressed by Morillo, and being cut off from the army by the passage of the allies at Villenave was forced to retreat by Monein.

On the 25th at daylight, lord Wellington with some cavalry and guns pushed Clauzel's rear-guard from Magret into the suburb of Orthes, which covered the bridge of that place on the left bank. He also cannonaded the French troops beyond the river, and the Portuguese of the light division, skirmishing with the French in the houses to prevent the destruction of the bridge, lost twenty-five men.

The second sixth and light divisions, Hamilton's Portuguese, five regiments of cavalry, and three batteries were now massed in front of Orthes; the third division and a brigade of cavalry was in front of the broken bridge of Berenx about five miles lower down the Gave; the fourth and seventh divisions with Vivian's cavalry were in front of Peyrehorade, from whence Foy retired by the great Bayonne road to Orthes. Affairs being in this state Morillo was directed to invest Navarrens. And as Mina's battalions were no sure guarantee against the combined efforts of the garrison of St. Jean Pied de Port and the warlike inhabitants of Baygorry, five British regiments, which had gone to the rear for clothing and were now coming up separately, were ordered to halt at St. Palais in observation, relieving each other in succession as they arrived at that place.

On the morning of the 26th, Beresford, finding that Foy had abandoned the French works at Peyrehorade, passed the Gave, partly by a pontoon bridge partly by a ford, where the current run so strong that a column of the seventh division was like to have been carried away bodily. He had previously detached the eighteenth hussars to find another ford higher up, and this being effected under the guidance of a miller, the hussars gained the high road about

BOOK
XXIV.
———
1814.
February.
Memoir by
colonel
Hughes,
eighteenth
hussars,
MSS.

half-way between Peyrehorade and Orthes, and drove some French cavalry through Puyoo and Ramous. The French rallying upon their reserves turned and beat back the foremost of the pursuers, but they would not await the shock of the main body now reinforced by Vivian's brigade and commanded by Beresford in person. In this affair major Sewell, an officer of the staff, who had frequently distinguished himself by his personal prowess, happening to be without a sword, pulled a large stake from a hedge and with that weapon overthrew two hussars in succession, and only relinquished the combat when a third had cut his club in twain.

Beresford now threw out a detachment to Habas on his left to intercept the enemy's communication with Dax, and lord Wellington immediately ordered lord Edward Somerset's cavalry and the third division to cross the Gave by fords below the broken bridge of Berenx. Then directing Beresford to take a position for the night on some heights near the village of Baïghts he proceeded to throw a pontoon bridge at Berenx, and thus after a circuitous march of more than fifty miles with his right wing he again united it with his centre and secured a direct communication with Hope.

During the 25th and 26th he had carefully examined Soult's position. The bridge of Orthes could not be easily forced. That ancient and beautiful structure consisted of several irregular arches, with a high tower in the centre the gateway of which was built up by the French, the principal arch in front of the tower was mined, and the houses on both sides contributed to the defence. The river above and below was deep and full of tall pointed rocks, but above the town the water spread-

ing wide with flat banks presented the means of
crossing. Lord Wellington's first design was to pass
there with Hill's troops and the light division, but
when he heard that Beresford had crossed the Gave
he suddenly changed his design, and as we have seen
passed the third division over and threw his bridge
at Berenx. This operation was covered by Beresford,
while Soult's attention was diverted by the continual skirmish at the suburbs of Orthes, by the
appearance of Hill's columns above, and by Wellington's taking cognizance of the position near the
bridge so openly as to draw a cannonade.

The English general did not expect Soult would,
when he found Beresford and Picton were over the
Gave, await a battle, and his emissaries reported
that the French army was already in retreat, a
circumstance to be borne in mind because the next
day's operation required success to justify it. Hope's
happy passage of the Adour being now known that
officer was instructed to establish a line of communication to the port of Lannes, where a permanent bridge was to be formed with boats brought
up from Urt. A direct line of intercourse was
thus secured with the army at Bayonne. But lord
Wellington felt that he was pushing his operations
beyond his strength if Suchet should send reinforcements to Soult; wherefore he called up Freyre's
Spaniards, ordering that general to cross the Adour
below Bayonne, with two of his divisions and a
brigade of Portuguese nine-pounders, and join him
by the port of Lannes. O'Donnel's Andalusians
and the prince of Anglona's troops were also
directed to be in readiness to enter France.

These orders were given with the greatest reluctance.

The feeble resistance made by the French in the
difficult country already passed, left him without
much uneasiness as to the power of Soult's army in
the field, but his disquietude was extreme about
the danger of an insurgent warfare. " Maintain
the strictest discipline, *without that we are lost*,"
was his expression to general Freyre, and he issued
a proclamation authorizing the people of the districts he had overrun to arm themselves for the
preservation of order under the direction of their
mayors. He invited them to arrest all straggling
soldiers and followers of the army, and all plunderers and evil-doers and convey them to head-quarters
with proof of their crimes, promising to punish the
culpable and to pay for all damages. At the same
time he confirmed all the local authorities who
chose to retain their offices, on the sole condition
of having no political or military intercourse with
the countries still possessed by the French army.
Nor was his proclamation a dead letter, for in the
night of the 25th the inhabitants of a village,
situated near the road leading from Sauveterre to
Orthes, shot one English soldier dead and wounded
a second who had come with others to plunder.
Lord Wellington caused the wounded man to be
hung as an example, and he also forced an English
colonel to quit the army for suffering his soldiers
to destroy the municipal archives of a small town.

Soult had no thought of retreating. His previous
retrograde movements had been effected with order,
his army was concentrated with its front to the Gave,
and every bridge, except the noble structure at
Orthes the ancient masonry of which resisted his
mines, had been destroyed. One regiment of
cavalry was detached on the right to watch the

fords as far as Peyrehorade, three others with two CHAP. II.
battalions of infantry under Pierre Soult watched
those between Orthes and Pau, and a body of horse- February.
men and gens-d'armes covered the latter town from Official
Report,
Morillo's incursions. Two regiments of cavalry re- MSS.
Memoir by
mained with the army, and the French general's general
Berton,
intention was to fall upon the head of the first MSS.
Canevas'
column which should cross the Gave. But the negli- de faits par
general
gence of the officer stationed at Puyoo, who had Reille et
colonel de
suffered Vivian's hussars, as we have seen, to pass on la Chasse,
MS.
the 26th without opposition and without making
any report of the event, enabled Beresford to make
his movement in safety when otherwise he would
have been assailed by at least two-thirds of the
French army. It was not until three o'clock in the
evening that Soult received intelligence of his march,
and his columns were then close to Baïghts on the
right flank of the French army, his scouters were
on the Dax road in its rear, and at the same time
the sixth and light divisions were seen descending
by different roads from the heights beyond the river
pointing towards Berenx.

In this crisis the French marshal hesitated whether
to fall upon Beresford and Picton while the latter
was still passing the river, or take a defensive position, but finally judging that he had not time to form
his columns of attack he decided upon the latter. Soult's
Official
Wherefore under cover of a skirmish, sustained Report,
MSS.
near Baïghts by a battalion of infantry which
coming from the bridge of Berenx was joined by
the light cavalry from Puyoo, he hastily threw D'Erlon's and Reille's divisions on a new line across the
road from Peyrehorade. The right extended to the
heights of San Boes along which run the road
from Orthes to Dax, and this line was prolonged by

Clauzel's troops to Castetarbe a village close to the
Gave. Having thus opposed a temporary front to
Beresford he made his dispositions to receive battle
the next morning, bringing Villatte's infantry and
Pierre Soult's cavalry from the other side of Orthes
through that town, and it was this movement that
led lord Wellington's emissaries to report that the
army was retiring.

Soult's new line was on a ridge of hills partly
wooded partly naked.

In the centre was an open rounded hill from
whence long narrow tongues were pushed out, on
the French left towards the high road of Peyrehorade, on their right by St. Boës towards the high
church of Baïghts, the whole presenting a concave
to the allies.

The front was generally covered by a deep and
marshy ravine broken by two short tongues of land
which jutted out from the principal hill.

The road from Orthes to Dax passed behind the
front to the village of St. Boës and thence along
the ridge forming the right flank.

Behind the centre a succession of undulating
bare heathy hills trended for several miles to the rear,
but behind the right the country was low and deep.

The town of Orthes, receding from the river up
the slope of a steep hill and terminating with an
ancient tower, was behind the left wing.

General Reille, having Taupin's, Roguet's, and
Paris's divisions under him, commanded on the right,
and occupied all the ground from the village of St.
Boës to the centre of the position.

Count D'Erlon, commanding Foy's and D'Armagnac's divisions, was on the left of Reille. He placed
the first along a ridge extending towards the road of

Peyrehorade, the second in reserve. In rear of
this last Villatte's division and the cavalry were
posted above the village of Rontun, that is to say,
on the open hills behind the main position. In this
situation with the right overlooking the low country
beyond St. Boës, and the left extended towards
Orthes this division furnished a reserve to both
D'Erlon and Reille.

Harispe, whose troops as well as Villatte's were
under Clauzel, occupied Orthes and the bridge, having a regiment near the ford of Souars above the town.
Thus the French army extended from St. Boës to
Orthes, but the great mass was disposed towards the
centre.   Twelve guns were attached to general Harispe's troops, twelve were upon the round hill in the
centre, sweeping in their range the ground beyond
St. Boës, and sixteen were in reserve on the Dax road.

The 27th at day-break the sixth and light divisions, having passed the Gave near Berenx by the
pontoon bridge thrown in the night, wound up a
narrow way between high rocks to the great road
of Peyrehorade. The third division and lord Edward
Somerset's cavalry were already established there
in columns of march with skirmishers pushed forwards to the edge of the wooded height occupied by
D'Erlon's left, and Beresford with the fourth and seventh divisions and Vivian's cavalry had meanwhile
gained the ridge of St. Boës and approached the
Dax road beyond.   Hill remained with the second British, and Le Cor's Portuguese divisions
menacing the bridge of Orthes and the ford of
Souars   Between Beresford and Picton, a distance
of a mile and a half, there were no troops; but
about half-way, exactly in front of the French
centre, was a Roman camp crowning an isolated

peering hill of singular appearance and nearly as lofty as the centre of Soult's position.

On this camp, now covered with vineyards, but then open and grassy with a few trees, lord Wellington, after viewing the country on Beresford's left, stopped for an hour or more to examine the enemy's disposition for battle. During this time the two divisions were coming up from the river, but so hemmed in by rocks that only a few men could march abreast, and their point of union with the third division was little more than cannon-shot from the enemy's position. The moment was critical, Picton did not conceal his disquietude, but Wellington undisturbed as the deep sea continued his observations without seeming to notice the dangerous position of his troops. When they had reached the main road he reinforced Picton with the sixth, and drew the light division by cross roads behind the Roman camp, thus connecting his wings and forming a central reserve. From this point byeways led, on the left to the high church of Baïghts and the Dax road, on the right to the Peyrehorade road ; and two others led straight across the marsh to the French position.

This marsh, the open hill about which Soult's guns and reserves were principally gathered, the form and nature of the ridges on the flanks, all combined to forbid an attack in front, and the flanks were scarcely more promising. The extremity of the French left sunk indeed to a gentle undulation in crossing the Peyrehorade road, yet it would have been useless to push troops on that line towards Orthes, between D'Erlon and Caste Tarbe, for the town was strongly occupied by Harispe and was there covered by an ancient wall and the bed of a

torrent. It was equally difficult to turn the St.
Boës flank because of the low marshy country into
which the troops must have descended beyond the
Dax road; and the brows of the hills trending
backwards from the centre of the French position
would have enabled Soult to oppose a new and
formidable front at right angles to his actual position. The whole of the allied army must therefore have made a circuitous flank movement within
gun-shot and through a most difficult country, or
Beresford's left must have been dangerously extended and the whole line weakened. Nor could
the movement be hidden, because the hills although
only moderately high were abrupt on that side, af-
fording a full view of the low country, and Soult's
cavalry detachments were in observation on every
brow.

It only remained to assail the French flanks along
the ridges, making the principal efforts on the side
of St. Boës, with intent if successful to overlap
the French right beyond, and seize the road of
St. Sever while Hill passed the Gave at Souars
and cut off the road to Pau, thus enclosing the
beaten army in Orthes. This was however no
slight affair. On Picton's side it was easy to obtain
a footing on the flank ridge near the high road, but
beyond that the ground rose rapidly and the French
were gathered thickly with a narrow front and
plenty of guns. On Beresford's side they could
only be assailed along the summit of the St. Boës
ridge, advancing from the high church of Baïghts
and the Dax road. But the village of St. Boës was
strongly occupied, the ground immediately behind it
was strangled to a narrow pass by the ravine, and the
French reserve of sixteen guns, placed on the Dax

road, behind the hill in the centre of Soult's line, and well covered from counter-fire, was in readiness to crush the head of any column which should emerge from the gorge of St. Boës.

BATTLE OF ORTHES.

During the whole morning a slight skirmish with now and then a cannon-shot had been going on with the third division on the right, and the French cavalry at times pushed parties forward on each flank, but at nine o'clock Wellington commenced the real attack. The third and sixth divisions won without difficulty the lower part of the ridges opposed to them, and endeavoured to extend their left along the French front with a sharp fire of musquetry ; but the main battle was on the other flank. There general Cole, keeping Anson's brigade of the fourth division in reserve, assailed St. Boës with Ross's British brigade and Vasconcellos' Portuguese ; his object was to get on to the open ground beyond it, but fierce and slaughtering was the struggle. Five times breaking through the scattered houses did Ross carry his battle into the wider space beyond ; yet ever as the troops issued forth the French guns from the open hill smote them in front, and the reserved battery on the Dax road swept through them with grape from flank to flank. And then Taupin's supporting masses rushed forwards with a wasting fire, and lapping the flanks with skirmishers, which poured along the ravines on either hand, forced the shattered columns back into the village. It was in vain that with desperate valour the allies time after time broke through the

narrow way and struggled to spread a front beyond,
Ross fell dangerously wounded, and Taupin, whose
troops were clustered thickly and well supported
defied their utmost efforts. Nor was Soult less happy
on the other side. The nature of the ground
would not permit the third and sixth divisions to
engage many men at once, so that no progress was
made ; and one small detachment which Picton extended to his left, having made an attempt to gain
the smaller tongue jutting out from the central hill,
was suddenly charged, as it neared the summit, by
Foy, and driven down again in confusion, losing several prisoners.

When the combat had thus continued with unabated fury on the side of St. Boës for about three
hours, lord Wellington sent a caçadore regiment of
the light division from the Roman camp to protect
the right flank of Ross's brigade against the French
skirmishers ; but this was of no avail, for Vasconcellos' Portuguese, unable to sustain the violence
of the enemy any longer, gave way in disorder,
and the French pouring on, the British troops retreated through St. Boës with difficulty. As this
happened at the moment when the detachment on
Picton's left was repulsed, victory seemed to declare
for the French, and Soult, conspicuous on his commanding open hill, the knot of all his combinations,
seeing his enemies thus broken and thrown backwards on each side put all his reserves in movement
to complete the success. It is said that in the exultation of the moment he smote his thigh exclaim-
ing, " At last I have him." Whether this be so or
not it was no vain-glorious speech, for the moment
was most dangerous. There was however a small
black cloud rising just beneath him, unheeded at

first amidst the thundering din and tumult that now shook the field of battle, but which soon burst with irresistible violence. Wellington seeing that St. Boës was inexpugnable had suddenly changed his plan of battle. Supporting Ross with Anson's brigade which had not hitherto been engaged, he backed both with the seventh division and Vivian's cavalry now forming one heavy body towards the Dax road. Then he ordered the third and sixth divisions to be thrown in mass upon Foy's left flank, and at the same time sent the fifty-second regiment down from the Roman camp with instructions to cross the marsh in front, to mount the French ridge beyond, and to assail the flank and rear of the troops engaged with the fourth division at St. Boës.

Colonel Colborne, so often distinguished in this war, immediately led the fifty-second down and crossed the marsh under fire, the men sinking at every step above the knees, in some places to the middle, but still pressing forwards with that stern resolution and order to be expected from the veterans of the light division, soldiers who had never yet met their match in the field. They soon obtained footing on firm land and ascended the heights in line at the moment that Taupin was pushing vigorously through St. Boës, Foy and D'Armagnac, hitherto more than masters of their positions, being at the same time seriously assailed on the other flank by the third and sixth divisions. With a mighty shout and a rolling fire the fifty-second soldiers dashed forwards between Foy and Taupin, beating down a French battalion in their course and throwing everything before them into disorder. General Bechaud was killed in Taupin's division, Foy was dangerously wounded, and his troops, discouraged by his fall and by this sud-

den burst from a quarter where no enemy was expected, for the march of the fifty-second had been
hardly perceived save by the skirmishers, got into
confusion, and the disorder spreading to Reille's wing
he also was forced to fall back and take a new position
to restore his line of battle. The narrow pass behind
St. Boës was thus opened, and Wellington seizing
the critical moment thrust the fourth and seventh
divisions, Vivian's cavalry, and two batteries of artillery through, and spread a front beyond.

The victory was thus secured. For the third and
sixth divisions had now won D'Armagnac's position
and established a battery of guns on a knoll, from
whence their shot ploughed through the French
masses from one flank to another. Suddenly a
squadron of French chasseurs came at a hard gallop
down the main road of Orthes to charge these guns,
and sweeping to their right they rode over some of
the sixth division which had advanced too far ; but
pushing this charge too madly got into a hollow
lane and were nearly all destroyed. The third and
seventh divisions then continued to advance and the
wings of the army were united. The French general
rallied all his forces on the open hills beyond the
Dax road, and with Taupin's, Roguet's, Paris', and
D'Armagnac's divisions made strong battle to cover
the reformation of Foy's disordered troops, but
his foes were not all in front. This part of the
battle was fought with only two-thirds of the
allied army. Hill who had remained with twelve
thousand combatants, cavalry and infantry, before
the bridge of Orthes, received orders, when Wellington changed his plan of attack, to force the passage
of the Gave, partly in the view of preventing Harispe
from falling upon the flank of the sixth division,

2 o

partly in the hope of a successful issue to the attempt: and so it happened. Hill though unable to force the bridge, forded the river above at Souars, and driving back the troops posted there seized the heights above, cut off the French from the road to Pau, and turned the town of Orthes. He thus menaced Soult's only line of retreat by Salespice, on the road to St. Sever, at the very moment when the fifty-second having opened the defile of St. Boës the junction of the allies' wings was effected on the French position.

Clauzel immediately ordered Harispe to abandon Orthes and close towards Villatte on the heights above Rontun, leaving however some conscript battalions on a rising point beyond the road of St. Sever called the " *Motte de Turenne*." Meanwhile in person he endeavoured to keep general Hill in check by the menacing action of two cavalry regiments and a brigade of infantry; but Soult arrived at the moment and seeing that the loss of Souars had rendered his whole position untenable, gave orders for a general retreat.

This was a perilous matter. The heathy hills upon which he was now fighting, although for a short distance they furnished a succession of parallel positions favourable enough for defence, soon resolved themselves into a low ridge running to the rear on a line parallel with the road to St. Sever ; and on the opposite side of that road about cannon-shot distance was a corresponding ridge along which general Hill, judging by the firing how matters went, was now rapidly advancing. Five miles distant was the *Luy de Bearn*, and four miles beyond that the *Luy de France*, two rivers deep and with difficult banks. Behind these the Lutz, the Gabas, and the

Adour, crossed the line, and though once beyond
the wooden bridge of Sault de Navailles on the *Luy*
de Bearn, these streams would necessarily cover the
retreat, to carry off by one road and one bridge a
defeated army still closely engaged in front seemed
impossible. Nevertheless Soult did so. For Paris
sustained the fight on his right until Foy and Taupin's
troops rallied, and when the impetuous assault of the
fifty-second and the rush of the fourth and seventh
divisions drove Paris back, D'Armagnac interposed
to cover him until the union of the allies' wings was
completed, then both retired, being covered in turn
by Villatte. In this manner the French yielded,
step by step and without confusion, the allies advancing with an incessant deafening musketry and
cannonade, yet losing many men especially on the
right where the third division were very strongly
opposed. However as the danger of being cut off
at Salespice by Hill became more imminent the
retrograde movements were more hurried and confused; Hill seeing this, quickened his pace until
at last both sides began to run violently, and so many
men broke from the French ranks making across the
fields towards the fords, and such a rush was necessarily made by the rest to gain the bridge of Sault de
Navailles, that the whole country was covered with
scattered bands. Sir Stapleton Cotton then breaking with lord Edward Somerset's hussars through a
small covering body opposed to him by Harispe
sabred two or three hundred men, and the seventh
hussars cut off about two thousand who threw down
their arms in an enclosed field ; yet some confusion
or mismanagement occurring the greatest part recovering their weapons escaped, and the pursuit
ceased at the Luy of Bearn.

The French army appeared to be entirely dispersed, but it was more disordered in appearance
than reality, for Soult passed the Luy of Bearn and
destroyed the bridge with the loss of only six guns
and less than four thousand men killed wounded
and prisoners. Many thousands of conscripts however threw away their arms, and we shall find one
month afterwards the stragglers still amounting to
three thousand. Nor would the passage of the river
have been effected so happily if lord Wellington had
not been struck by a musket-ball just above the
thigh, which caused him to ride with difficulty,
whereby the vigour and unity of the pursuit was
necessarily abated. The loss of the allies was two
thousand three hundred, of which fifty with three
officers were taken, but among the wounded were
lord Wellington, general Walker, general Ross, and
the duke of Richmond, then lord March. He had
served on lord Wellington's personal staff during the
whole war without a hurt, but being made a captain
in the fifty-second, like a good soldier joined his regiment the night before the battle. He was shot
through the chest a few hours afterwards, thus learning by experience, the difference between the labours
and dangers of staff and regimental officers, which
are generally in the inverse ratio to their promotions.

General Berton, stationed between Pau and Orthes during the battle, had been cut off by Hill's
movement, yet skirting that general's march he retreated by Mant and Samadet with his cavalry,
picking up two battalions of conscripts on the road.
Meanwhile Soult having no position to rally upon,
continued his retreat in the night to St. Sever, breaking down all the bridges behind him. Lord Wellington pursued at daylight in three columns, the

right by Lacadée and St. Medard to Samadet, the
centre by the main road, the left by St. Cricq.   At
St. Sever he hoped to find the enemy still in confusion, but he was too late; the French were across
the river, the bridge was broken, and the army halted.
The result of the battle was however soon made
known far and wide, and Darricau who with a few
hundred soldiers was endeavouring to form an insurgent levy at Dax, the works of which were incomplete and still unarmed, immediately destroyed part
of the stores, the rest had been removed to Mont
Marsan, and retreated through the Landes to Langon
on the Garonne.

From St. Sever which offered no position Soult
turned short to the right and moved upon Barcelona higher up the Adour; but he left D'Erlon with
two divisions of infantry some cavalry and four guns
at Caceres on the right bank, and sent Clauzel to
occupy Aire on the other side of the river.   He thus
abandoned his magazines at Mont Marsan and left
open the direct road to Bordeaux, but holding
Caceres with his right he commanded another road
by Rocquefort to that city, while his left being at
Aire protected the magazines and artillery parc at
that place and covered the road to Pau.   Meanwhile
the main body at Barcelona equally supported
Clauzel and D'Erlon, and covered the great roads
leading to Agen and Toulouse on the Garonne, and
to the mountains by Tarbes.

In this situation it was difficult to judge what
line of operations he meant to adopt.   Wellington
however passed the Adour about one o'clock, partly
by the repaired bridge of St. Sever partly by a deep
ford below, and immediately detached Beresford
with the light division and Vivian's cavalry to seize

the magazines at Mont Marsan ; at the same time
he pushed the head of a column towards Caceres
where a cannonade and charge of cavalry had place,
and a few men and officers were hurt on both
sides.   The next day Hill's corps marching from
Samadet reached the Adour between St. Sever
and Aire, and D'Erlon was again assailed on the
right bank and driven back skirmishing to Barcelona.   This event proved that Soult had abandoned
Bordeaux, but the English general could not push
the pursuit more vigorously, because every bridge
was broken and a violent storm on the evening of
the 1st had filled the smaller rivers and torrents,
carried away the pontoon bridges, and cut off all
communication between the troops and the supplies.

   The bulk of the army was now necessarily halted
on the right bank of the Adour until the bridges
could be repaired, but Hill who was on the left bank
marched to seize the magazines at Aire.   Moving in
two columns from St. Savin and St. Gillies on the
2d, he reached his destination about three o'clock
with two divisions of infantry a brigade of cavalry
and a battery of horse-artillery ; he expected no
serious opposition, but general Clauzel had arrived
a few hours before and was in order of battle covering the town with Villatte's and Harispe's divisions
and some guns.   The French occupied a steep ridge
in front of Aire, high and wooded on the right
where it overlooked the river, but merging on the
left into a wide table-land over which the great road
led to Pau.   The position was strong for battle yet
it could be readily outflanked on the left by the
table-land, and was an uneasy one for retreat on the
right where the ridge was narrow, the ravine behind steep and rugged with a mill-stream at the

bottom between it and the town.   A branch of the
Adour also flowing behind Aire cut it off from Bar-
celona, while behind the left wing was the greater
Lees a river with steep banks and only one bridge.

COMBAT OF AIRE.

General Hill arriving about two o'clock attacked without hesitation.   General Stewart with
two British brigades fell on the French right, a
Portuguese brigade assailed their centre, and the
other brigades followed in columns of march.   The
action was however very sudden, the Portuguese
were pushed forward in a slovenly manner by
general Da Costa, a man of no ability, and the
French under Harispe met them on the flat summit
of the height with so rough a charge that they gave
way in flight.   The rear of the allies' column being
still in march the battle was like to be lost, but
general Stewart having by this time won the
heights on the French right, where Villatte, fearing
to be enclosed made but a feeble resistance, immediately detached general Barnes with the fiftieth and
ninety-second regiments to the aid of the Portuguese.
The vehement charge of these troops turned the
stream of battle, the French were broken in turn and
thrown back on their reserves, yet they rallied and
renewed the action with great courage, fighting
obstinately until General Byng's British brigade
came up, when Harispe was driven towards the
river Lees, and Villate quite through the town of
Aire into the space between the two branches of
the Adour behind.
General Reille who was at Barcelona when the

action began, brought up Roguet's division to support Villatte, the combat was thus continued until
night at that point, meanwhile Harispe crossed
the Lees and broke the bridge, but the French lost
many men. Two generals, Dauture and Gasquet,
were wounded, a colonel of engineers was killed, a
hundred prisoners were taken, many of Harispe's
conscripts threw away their arms and fled to their
homes, and the magazines fell into the conqueror's
hands. The loss of the British troops was one hundred and fifty, general Barnes was wounded and
colonel Hood killed. The loss of the Portuguese was
never officially stated, yet it could not have been
less than that of the British, and the vigour of the
action proved that the French courage was very
little abated by the battle of Orthes. Soult immediately retreated up the Adour by both banks towards Maubourget and Marciac, and he was not
followed for new combinations were now opened
to the generals on both sides.

OBSERVATIONS.

1°. On the 14th of February the passage of the
Gaves was commenced, by Hill's attack on Harispe
at Hellette. On the 2d of March the first series of
operations was terminated by the combat at Aire.
In these sixteen days lord Wellington traversed
with his right wing eighty miles, passed five large
and several small rivers, forced the enemy to abandon two fortified bridge-heads and many minor
works, gained one great battle and two combats,
captured six guns and about a thousand prisoners,
seized the magazines at Dax, Mont Marsan, and

Aire, forced Soult to abandon Bayonne and cut him off from Bordeaux. And in this time he also threw his stupendous bridge below Bayonne and closely invested that fortress after a sharp and bloody action. Success in war like charity in religion covers a multitude of sins; but success often belongs to fortune as much as skill, and the combinations of Wellington, profound and sagacious, might in this manner be confounded with the lucky operations of the allies on the other side of France, where the presumption and the vacillation of ignorance alternately predominated.

2°. Soult attributed the loss of his positions to the superior forces of the allies. Is this well-founded? The French general's numbers cannot be determined exactly, but after all his losses in December, after the detachments made by the emperor's order in January, and after completing the garrison of Bayonne to fourteen thousand men, he informed the minister of war that thirty thousand infantry, three thousand cavalry and forty pieces of artillery were in line. This did not include the conscripts of the new levy, all youths indeed and hastily sent to the army by battalions as they could be armed, but brave and about eight thousand of them might have joined before the battle of Orthes. Wherefore deducting the detachments of cavalry and infantry under Berton on the side of Pau, and under Daricau on the side of Dax, it may be said that forty thousand combatants of all arms were engaged in that action. Thirty-five thousand were very excellent soldiers, for the conscripts of the old levy who joined before the battle of the Nivelle were stout men; their vigorous fighting at Garris and Aire proved it, for of them was Harispe's division composed.

Official
Corres-
pondence,
MSS.

Now lord Wellington commenced his operations
with the second third fourth and seventh British
divisions, the independent Portuguese division under
Le Cor, Morillo's Spaniards, forty-eight pieces of
artillery, and only four brigades of light cavalry,
for Vandaleur's brigade remained with Hope and all
the heavy cavalry and the Portuguese were left in
Spain.   Following the morning states of the army,
this would furnish, exclusive of Morillo's Spaniards,
something more than forty thousand fighting men
and officers of all arms, of which four thousand were
horsemen.   But five regiments of infantry, and
amongst them two of the strongest British regiments
of the light division, were absent to receive their
clothing ; deduct these and we have about thirty-
seven thousand Anglo-Portuguese combatants.   It
is true that Mina's battalions and Morillo's aided in
the commencement of the operations, but the first
immediately invested St. Jean Pied de Port and the
latter invested Navarrens.   Lord Wellington was
therefore in the battle superior by a thousand horsemen and eight guns, but Soult outnumbered him in
infantry by four or five thousand, conscripts it is
true, yet useful.   Why then was the passage of the
Gaves so feebly disputed ?   Because the French
general remained entirely on the defensive in positions too extended for his numbers.

3°. *Offensive operations must be the basis of a good
defensive system.*   Let Soult's operations be tried by
this rule.   On the 12th he knew that the allies were
in motion for some great operation and he judged
rightly that it was to drive him from the Gaves.
From the 14th to the 18th his left was continually
assailed by very superior numbers, but during part
of that time Beresford could only oppose to his right

and centre, the fourth and a portion of the seventh
divisions with some cavalry; and those not in a
body and at once but parcelled and extended, for
it was not until the 16th that the fourth seventh
and light divisions were so closed towards the Bidouze as to act in one mass. On the 15th lord Wellington admitted that his troops were too extended,
Villatte's, Taupin's, and Foy's divisions, were never
menaced until the 18th, and there was nothing to
prevent D'Erlon's divisions which only crossed the
Adour on the 17th from being on the Bidouze the
15th. Soult might therefore by rapid and well-di-
gested combinations have united four divisions of
infantry and a brigade of cavalry to attack Beresford on the 15th or 16th between the Nive and the
Adour. If successful the defeated troops, pushed
back upon the sixth division, must have fought for
life with the rivers on their flanks, Soult in front,
and the garrison of Bayonne issuing from the works
of Mousseroles on their rear. If unsuccessful the
French retreat behind the Gave of Oleron could not
have been prevented.

It is however to be pleaded that Soult was not
exactly informed of the numbers and situation of
his opponents. He thought Beresford had the first Soult's
Official
Reports,
MSS.
division also on the Lower Bidouze; he knew that
Wellington had large reserves to employ, and, that
general's design of passing the Adour below Bayonne being unknown to him, he naturally supposed
they would be used to support the operations on the
Gaves : he therefore remained on the defensive. It
might possibly also have been difficult to bring
D'Erlon's division across the Adour by the Port de
Lannes before the 17th, because the regular bridge
had been carried away and the communications in-

terrupted a few days before by the floods. In fine
there are many matters of detail in war known only
to a general-in-chief which forbid the best combinations, and this it is that makes the art so difficult
and uncertain. Great captains worship Fortune.

On the 24th the passage of the Gave d'Oleron
was effected. Soult then recognised his error and
concentrated his troops at Orthes to retake the offensive. It was a fine movement and effected with ability, but he suffered another favourable opportunity
of giving a counter-blow to escape him. The infantry under Villatte, Harispe, and Paris, supported
by a brigade of cavalry, were about Sauveterre, that
is to say, four miles from Montfort and only seven
from Villenave, where the principal passage was
effected, where the ford was deep, the stream rapid,
and the left bank although favourable for the passage not entirely commanding the right bank. How
then did it happen that the operation was effected
without opposition? Amongst the allies it was
rumoured at the time that Soult complained of the
negligence of a general who had orders to march
against the passing troops. The position of Harispe's division at Monstrueig, forming a reserve at
equal distances from Sauveterre and Villenave, would
seem to have been adopted with that view, but I
find no confirmation of the report in Soult's correspondence, and it is certain he thought Picton's
demonstrations at Sauveterre was a real attack.

4°. The position adopted by the French general
at Orthes was excellent for offence. It was not so
for defence, when Beresford and Picton had crossed
the Gave below in force. Lord Wellington could
then throw his whole army on that side, and secure
his communication with Hope, after which out-

flanking the right of the French he could seize the CHAP. II.
defile of Sault de Navailles, cut them off from
their magazines at ´Dax, Mont Marsan and Aire, 1814.
and force them to retreat by the Pau road leaving open the way to Bordeaux. To await this
attack was therefore an error, but Soult's original Official Correspondence, MSS.
design was to assail the head of the first column
which should come near him and Beresford's approach to Baïghts on the 26th furnished the opportunity. It is true that the French light cavalry
gave intelligence of that general's march too late
and marred the combination, but there was still time
to fall on the head of the column while the third
division was in the act of passing the river and entangled in the narrow way leading from the ford to
the Peyrehorade road : it is said the French mar- Notes by general Reille and colonel De la Chasse, MSS.
shal appeared disposed to do this at first, but finally
took a defensive position in which to receive battle.
However when the morning came he neglected
another opportunity. For two hours the third division and the hussars remained close to him, covering
the march of the sixth and light divisions through the
narrow ways leading from the bridge of Berenx up
to the main road ; the infantry had no defined position, the cavalry had no room to extend, and there
were no troops between them and Beresford who
was then in march by the heights of Baïghts to the
Dax road. If the French general had pushed a
column across the marsh to seize the Roman camp
he would have separated the wings of the allies ; then
pouring down the Peyrehorade road with Foy's, D'Armagnac's and Villatte's divisions he would probably
have overwhelmed the third division before the other
two could have extricated themselves from the defiles. Picton therefore had grounds for uneasiness.

With a subtle skill did Soult take his ground of
battle at Orthes, fiercely and strongly did he fight,
and wonderfully did he effect his retreat across the
Luy of Bearn, but twice in twenty-four hours he
had neglected those happy occasions which in war
take birth and flight at the same instant; and as
the value of his position, essentially an offensive one,
was thereby lost, a slowness to strike may be objected to his generalship. Yet there is no commander, unless a Hannibal or a Napoleon surpassing
the human proportions, but will abate something of
his confidence and hesitate after repeated defeats,
Soult in this campaign as in many others proved
himself a hardy captain full of resources.

5°. Lord Wellington with a vastness of conception
and a capacity for arrangement and combination
equal to his opponent, possessed in a high degree that daring promptness of action, that faculty
of inspiration for suddenly deciding the fate of whole
campaigns with which Napoleon was endowed beyond all mankind. It is this which especially constitutes military genius. For so vast so complicated
are the combinations of war, so easily and by such
slight causes are they affected, that the best generals
do but grope in the dark, and they acknowledge the
humiliating truth. By the number and extent of
their fine dispositions then, and not by their errors,
the merit of commanders is to be measured.

In this campaign lord Wellington designed to
penetrate France, not with a hasty incursion but
solidly, to force Soult over the Garonne, and if possible in the direction of Bordeaux, because it was
the direct line, because the citizens were inimical
to the emperor, and the town, lying on the left bank
of the river, could not be defended; because a junc-

tion with Suchet would thus be prevented.   Finally
if by operating against Soult's left he could throw
the French army into the Landes, where his own
superior cavalry could act, it would probably be
destroyed.

To operate against Soult's left in the direction of
Pau was the most obvious method of preventing a
junction with Suchet, and rendering the positions
which the French general had fortified on the Gaves
useless.   But the investment of Bayonne required a
large force, which was yet weak against an outer
attack because separated in three parts by the rivers;
hence if lord Wellington had made a wide movement on Pau, Soult might have placed the Adour
between him and the main army and then fallen upon
Hope's troops on the right side of that river.   The
English general was thus reduced to act upon a
more contracted line,. and to cross all the Gaves.
To effect this he collected his principal mass on his
right by the help of the great road leading to St.
Jean Pied de Port, then by rapid marches and reiterated attacks he forced the passage of the rivers
above the points which Soult had fortified for defence, and so turned that general's left with the view
of finally cutting him off from Suchet and driving
him into the wilderness of the Landes.   During these
marches he left Beresford on the lower parts of the
rivers to occupy the enemy's attention and cover the
troops blockading Mousseroles.   Meanwhile by the
collection of boats at Urt and other demonstrations
indicating a design of throwing a bridge over the
Adour above Bayonne, he diverted attention from
the point chosen below the fortress for that operation, and at the same time provided the means of
throwing another bridge at the Port de Lannes to

secure the communication with Hope by the right
bank whenever Soult should be forced to abandon
the Gaves. These were fine combinations.

I have shown that Beresford's corps was so weak
at first that Soult might have struck a counter-
blow. Lord Wellington admitted the error. Writing on the 15th he says, " If the enemy stand upon
the Bidouze I am not so strong as I ought to
be," and he ordered up the fourth and light divisions ; but this excepted, his movements were conformable to the principles of war. He chose the
best strategic line of operations, his main attack
was made with heavy masses against the enemy's
weakest points, and in execution he was prompt and
daring. His conduct was conformable also to his
peculiar situation. He had two distinct operations
in hand, namely to throw his bridge below Bayonne
and to force the Gaves. He had the numbers required to obtain these objects but dared not use
them lest he should put the Spanish troops into
contact with the French people ; yet he could not entirely dispense with them ; wherefore bringing Freyre
up to Bayonne, Morillo to Navarrens, and Mina to
St. Jean Pied de Port, he seemed to put his whole
army in motion, thus gaining the appearance of
military strength with as little political danger as
possible. Nevertheless so terrible had the Spaniards already made themselves by their cruel law-
less habits that their mere return across the frontier
threw the whole country into consternation.

6°. When in front of Orthes it would at first sight
appear as if lord Wellington had changed his plan
of driving the enemy upon the Landes, but it was
not so. He did not expect a battle on the 27th.
This is proved by his letter to sir John Hope in

which he tells that general that he anticipated no
difficulty in passing the Gave of Pau, that on the
evening of the 26th the enemy were retiring, and
that he designed to visit the position at Bayonne.
To pass the Gave in the quickest and surest manner,
to re-establish the direct communications with Hope
and to unite with Beresford, were his immediate
objects ; if he finally worked by his left it was a
sudden act and extraneous to the general design,
which was certainly to operate with Hill's corps and
the light division by the right.

It was after passing the Gave at Berenx on the
morning of the 27th lord Wellington first discovered Soult's intention to fight, and that consequently he was himself in a false position.   Had he
shewn any hesitation, any uneasiness, had he endeavoured to take a defensive position with either
Beresford's or Picton's troops, he would inevitably
have drawn the attention of the enemy to his dangerous situation.   Instead of this, judging that
Soult would not on the instant change from the
defensive to the offensive, he confidently pushed
Picton's skirmishers forward as if to assail the left
of the French position, and put Beresford in movement against their right, and this with all the
coolness imaginable.   The success was complete.
Soult who supposed the allies stronger than they
really were, naturally imagined the wings would not
be so bold unless well supported in the centre where
the Roman camp could hide a multitude.   He therefore held fast to his position until the movement
was more developed, and in two hours the sixth
and light divisions were up and the battle commenced.   It was well fought on both sides but the
crisis was decided by the fifty-second, and when

that regiment was put in movement only a single
Portuguese battalion was in reserve behind the
Roman camp : upon such nice combinations of time
and place does the fate of battles turn.

7°. Soult certainly committed an error in receiving battle at Orthes, and it has been said that lord
Wellington's wound at the most critical period of
the retreat alone saved the hostile army. Nevertheless the clear manner in which the French general carried his troops away, his prompt judgement, shown in the sudden change of his line of
retreat at St. Sever, the resolute manner in which
he halted and showed front again at Caçeres, Barcelonne, and Aire, were all proofs of no common
ability. It was Wellington's aim to drive the French
on to the Landes, Soult's to avoid this, he therefore
shifted from the Bordeaux line to that of Toulouse, not in confusion but with the resolution of a
man ready to dispute every foot of ground. The

Soult's
Official
Corres-
pondence,
MSS.

loss of the magazines at Mont Marsan was no fault
of his ; he had given orders for transporting them
towards the Toulouse side fifteen days before, but
the matter depending upon the civil authorities was
neglected. He was blamed by some of his officers
for fighting at Aire, yet it was necessary to cover
the magazines there, and essential to his design of
keeping up the courage of the soldiers under the
adverse circumstances which he anticipated. And
here the palm of generalship remained with him,
for certainly the battle of Orthes was less decisive
than it should have been. I speak not of the pursuit to Sault de Navailles, nor of the next day's
march upon St. Sever, but of Hill's march on the
right. That general halted near Samade the 28th,
reached St. Savin on the Adour the 1st and fought

the battle of Aire on the evening of the 2d of March.

But from Samadet to Aire is not longer than from
Samadet to St. Savin where he was on the 1st. He
could therefore, if his orders had prescribed it so,
have seized Aire on the 1st before Clauzel arrived,
and thus spared the obstinate combat at that place.
It may also be observed that his attack did not
receive a right direction. It should have been
towards the French left, because they were more
weakly posted there, and the ridge held by their
right was so difficult to retire from, that no troops
would stay on it if any progress was made on the
left. This was however an accident of war, general
Hill had no time to examine the ground, his orders
were to attack, and to fall without hesitation upon
a retiring enemy after such a defeat as Orthes was
undoubtedly the right thing to do ; but it cannot
be said that lord Wellington pushed the pursuit
with vigour. Notwithstanding the storm on the
evening of the 1st he could have reinforced Hill
and should not have given the French army time to
recover from their recent defeat. " The secret of
war," says Napoleon, " is to march twelve leagues,
fight a battle and march twelve more in pursuit."

CHAPTER III.

BOOK
XXIV.
————
1814.
March. EXTREMELY perilous and disheartening was the situation of the French general. His army was greatly reduced by his losses in battle and by the desertion of the conscripts, and three thousand stragglers, old soldiers who ought to have rejoined their eagles, were collected by different generals, into whose districts they had wandered, and employed to strengthen detached corps instead of being restored to the army. All his magazines were taken, discontent the natural offspring of misfortune prevailed amongst his officers, a powerful enemy was in front, no certain resources of men or money behind, and his efforts were ill-seconded by the civil authorities. The troops indignant at the people's apathy behaved with so much violence and insolence, especially during the retreat from St. Sever, that Soult's
Official
Correspon-
dence,
MSS. Soult, who wanted officers very badly, proposed to fill the vacancies from the national guards that he might have " men who would respect property." On the other hand the people comparing the conduct of their own army with the discipline of the Anglo-Portuguese, and contrasting the requisitions necessarily imposed by their countrymen with the ready and copious disbursements in gold made by their enemies, for now one commissary preceded each division to order rations for the troops and another followed to arrange and pay on the spot, were

become so absolutely averse to the French army
that Soult writing to the minister of war thus
expressed himself. " If the population of the departments of the Landes of Gers, and the Lower
Pyrenees, were animated with a good spirit, this is
the moment to make the enemy suffer by carrying
off his convoys and prisoners, but they appear more
disposed to favour the invaders than to second the
army. It is scarcely possible to obtain a carriage
for transport and I shall not be surprised to find in
a short time these inhabitants taking arms against
us." Soult was however a man formed by nature
and by experience to struggle against difficulties,
always appearing greater when in a desperate condition than when more happily circumstanced. At
Genoa under Massena, at Oporto, and in Andalusia,
he had been inured to military distress, and probably for that reason the emperor selected him to
sustain this dangerous contest in preference to
others accounted more ready tacticians on a field of
battle.

On the 3d and 4th he retreated by Plaissance
and Madiran to Rabastens, Marciac, and Maubourget where he halted, covering Tarbes, for his
design was to keep in mass and await the development of the allies' plans. In this view he called in
the detachments of cavalry and infantry which had
been left on the side of Pau before the battle of
Orthes, and hearing that Darricau was at Langon
with a thousand men he ordered him to march by
Agen and join the army immediately. He likewise
put the national guards and *gens-d'armes* in activity
on the side of the Pyrenees, and directed the
commanders of the military districts in his rear to
keep their old soldiers, of which there were many

scattered through the country, in readiness to aid the army.

While thus acting he received from the minister of war a note dictated by the emperor.

" Fortresses," said Napoleon, " are nothing in themselves when the enemy having the command of the sea can collect as many shells and bullets and guns as he pleases to crush them. Leave therefore only a few troops in Bayonne, the way to prevent the siege is to keep the army close to the place. Resume the offensive, fall upon one or other of the enemy's wings, and though you should have but twenty thousand men if you seize the proper moment and attack hardily you ought to gain some advantage. You have enough talent to understand my meaning."

This note came fourteen days too late. But what if it had come before? Lord Wellington after winning the battle of St. Pierre the 13th of December was firmly established on the Adour above Bayonne, and able to interrupt the French convoys as they descended from the Port de Landes. It was evident then that when dry weather enabled the allies to move Soult must abandon Bayonne to defend the passage of the Gaves, or risk being turned and driven upon the Landes from whence it would be difficult for him to escape. Napoleon however desired him to leave only a few men in Bayonne, another division would thus have been added to his field army, and this diminution of the garrison would not have increased lord Wellington's active forces, because the investment of Bayonne would still have required three separate corps : moreover until the bridge-head at Peyrehorade was abandoned to concentrate at Orthes, Bayonne was not rigorously speaking left to its own defence.

To the emperor's observations Soult therefore replied, that several months before, he had told the minister of war Bayonne was incapable of sustaining fifteen days open trenches unless the entrenched camp was well occupied, and he had been by the minister authorised so to occupy it. Taking that as his base he had left a garrison of thirteen thousand five hundred men, and now that he knew the emperor's wishes it was no longer in his power to withdraw them. With respect to keeping close to the place he had done so as long as he could without endangering the safety of the army; but lord Wellington's operations had forced him to abandon it, and he had only changed his line of operations at St. Sever when he was being pushed back upon Bordeaux with little prospect of being able to pass the Garonne in time. He had for several months thought of establishing a pivot of support for his movements at Dax, in the design of still holding by Bayonne, and with that view had ordered the old works of the former place to be repaired and a camp to be fortified; but from poverty of means even the body of the place was not completed or armed at the moment when the battle of Orthes forced him to relinquish it. Moreover the insurgent levy of the Landes upon which he depended to man the works had failed, not more than two hundred men had come forward. Neither was he very confident of the advantage of such a position, because Wellington with superior numbers would probably have turned his left and forced him to retire precipitately towards Bordeaux by the desert of the greater Landes.

The emperor ordered him to take the offensive were it only with twenty thousand men. He would

obey with this observation, that from the 14th of
February to that moment he had had no power to
take the initiatory movement, having been constantly attacked by infinitely superior numbers. He
had defended himself as he could, but had not expected to succeed against the enormous disproportion of force. It being thus impossible, even though
he sacrificed his last man in the attempt, to stop the
enemy, he now sought to prolong the war as much
as possible on the frontier, and by defending every
position to keep the invaders in check and prevent
them from attacking Bordeaux or Toulouse, save by
detachments. He had taken his line of operations
by the road of Tarbes, St. Gaudens, and Toulouse,
that is to say, by the roots of the Pyrenees, calculating that if lord Wellington sent small detachments
against Bordeaux or Toulouse, the generals commanding at those places would be able if the national
guards would fight for their country to defend them.

If the enemy made large detachments, an attack
in front while he was thus weakened would bring
them back again. If he marched with his whole
army upon Bordeaux he could be followed and
forced to face about. If he attempted to march by
Auch against Toulouse he might be stopped by an
attack in flank. If he remained stationary he should
be provoked by an advance to develope his objects.
But if, as was to be expected, the French army
was itself attacked it would defend its position
vigorously, and then retreating by St. Gaudens draw
the allies into a difficult mountain country, where
the ground might be disputed step by step the
war be kept still on the frontier and the passage
of the Garonne be delayed. He had meditated
deeply upon his task and could find no better mode.

But his army was weakened by combats, still more by desertion; the conscripts went off so fast that of five battalions lately called up from Toulouse two-thirds were already gone without having seen an enemy.

Soult was mistaken as to the real force of the allies in the recent operations. In other respects he displayed clear views and great activity. He reorganized his army in six divisions, called in his detachments, urged the imperial commissioners and local authorities to hasten the levies and restore deserters, and he prepared a plan of action for the partizans which had been organized towards the mountains. Nevertheless his difficulties increased. The conscripts who did arrive were for the most part unarmed and he had none to spare. The imperial commissary Cornudet, and the prefect of the Gironde, quitted Bordeaux, and when general L'Huillier attempted to remove the military stores belonging to the army from Langon, Podensac, and Bordeaux, the inferior authorities opposed him. There was no money they said to pay the expense, but in truth Bordeaux was the focus of Bourbon conspiracy, and the mayor, count Lynch, was eager to betray his sovereign.

Nor was Wellington without embarrassments. The storms prevented him following up his victory while the French army was in confusion. Now it was reorganized on a new line and could retreat for many days in a direction parallel to the Pyrenees with strong defensive positions. Should he press it closely? His army weakened at every step would have to move between the mountains and the Garonne exposing its flanks and rear to the operations of any force which the French might be able to collect on those boundaries; that is to say all the power of

France beyond the Garonne. It was essential to find some counterpoise, and to increase his field army. To establish a Bourbon party at Bordeaux was an obvious mode of attaining the first object. Should he then seize that city by a detachment? He must employ twelve thousand men and remain with twenty-six thousand to oppose Soult, who he erroneously believed was being joined by the ten thousand men which Suchet had sent to Lyons. The five regiments detached for their clothing had rejoined the army and all the reserves of cavalry and artillery were now called up, but the reinforcements from England and Portugal, amounting to twenty thousand men, upon which he had calculated were detained by the respective governments. Wherefore, driven by necessity he directed Freyre to join him by the Port de Landes with two divisions of the Gallician army, a measure which was instantly followed by innumerable complaints of outrages and excesses, although the Spaniards were entirely provided from the English military chest. Now also Clinton was ordered to send the British and Germans of the Anglo-Sicilian army to St. Jean de Luz. This done he determined to seize Bordeaux. Meanwhile he repaired the destroyed bridges, brought up one of Morillo's brigades from Navarrens to the vicinity of Aire, sent Campbell's Portuguese dragoons to Rocquefort, general Fane with two regiments of cavalry and a brigade of infantry to Pau, and pushed posts towards Tarbes and Vic Bigorre.

Soult, now fearing the general apathy and ill-will of the people would become fatal to him, endeavoured to arouse the energies of the people and the army by the following proclamation which has been unreasonably railed at by several English

writers, for it was a judicious well-timed and powerful address.

" Soldiers, at the battle of Orthes you did your duty, the enemy's losses surpassed yours, his blood moistened all the ground he gained. You may consider that feat of arms as an advantage. Other combats are at hand, no repose for us until his army, formed of such extraordinary elements, shall evacuate the French territory or be annihilated. Its numbers and progress may be great, but at hand are unexpected perils. Time will teach the enemy's general that French honour is not to be outraged with impunity."

" Soldiers, he has had the indecency to provoke you and your countrymen to revolt and sedition, he speaks of peace but firebrands of discord follow him! He speaks of peace and excites the French to a civil war! Thanks be to him for making known his projects, our forces are thereby centupled ; and he himself rallies round the imperial eagles all those who deceived by appearances believed our enemies would make a loyal war. No peace with the disloyal and perfidious nation! no peace with the English and their auxiliaries until they quit the French territory! they have dared to insult the national honour, the infamy to incite Frenchmen to become perjured towards the emperor. Revenge the offence in blood. To arms! Let this cry resound through the south of France, the Frenchman that hesitates abjures his country and belongs to her enemies."

" Yet a few days and those who believe in English delicacy and sincerity will learn to their cost that cunning promises are made to abate their courage and subjugate them. They will learn also that if the English pay to-day and are generous,

they will to-morrow retake and with interest in contributions what they disburse. Let the pusillanimous
beings who calculate the cost of saving their country
remember that the English have in view to reduce
Frenchmen to the same servitude as the Spaniards
Portuguese and Sicilians who groan under their domination. Past history will recall to those unworthy
Frenchmen who prefer momentary enjoyment to
the safety of the great family, the English making
Frenchmen kill Frenchmen at Quiberon; it will
show them at the head of all conspiracies, all odious
political intrigues plots and assassinations, aiming
to overthrow all principles, to destroy all grand
establishments of trade to satisfy their immeasura-
ble ambition, their insatiable cupidity. Does there
exist upon the face of the globe a point known to
the English where they have not destroyed by sedi-
dions and violence all manufactures which could
rival their own? Thus they will do to the French
establishments if they prevail.

" Devote then to opprobrium and execration all
Frenchmen who favour their insidious projects,
aye! even those who are under his power if they
seek not to hurt him. Devote to opprobrium and
reject as Frenchmen those who think under spe-
cious pretexts to avoid serving their country; and
those also who from corruption or indolence hide
deserters instead of driving them back to their
colours. With such men we have nothing in common, and history will pass their names with ex-
ecrations to posterity. As to us soldiers our duty
is clear. Honour and fidelity. This is our motto
and we will fight to the last the enemies of our
emperor and France. Respect persons and property. Grieve for those who have momentarily
fallen under the enemy's yoke, and hasten the

moment of their deliverance. Be obedient and disciplined, and bear implacable hatred towards traitors and enemies of the French name! War to death against those who would divide us to destroy us; and to those cowards who desert the imperial eagles to range themselves under another banner. Remember always that fifteen ages of glory, triumphs innumerable, have illustrated our country. Contemplate the prodigious efforts of our great sovereign, his signal victories which immortalize the French name. Let us be worthy of him and we can then bequeath without a taint to our posterity the inheritance we hold from our fathers. Be in fine Frenchmen and die arms in hand sooner than survive dishonour."

Let the time and the occasion of this proclamation be considered. Let it be remembered that no English writer orator or politician, had for many years used milder terms than robbers, murderers, atheists, and tyrant, when speaking of Frenchmen and their sovereign, that lord Wellington even at this time refused that sovereign his title of emperor, calling him Buonaparte; that on entering France he had published an order of the day accusing the French commanders of authorising and encouraging the cruelties of their soldiers in Spain; finally that for six years the Spanish Portuguese and English state papers were filled with most offensive ribald abuse of Napoleon his ministers and commanders. Let all this be remembered and the acrimony of Soult's proclamation cannot be justly blamed, while the noble energy, the loyalty of the sentiments, the exciting passionate feeling of patriotism which pervades it must be admired. Was he, sprung from the ranks, a soldier of the

republic, a general of the empire, after fighting
thirty years under the tri-colour, to be tame and
measured to squeamishness in his phrases when he
saw his country invaded by foreigners, and a pre-
tender to the throne stalking behind their bayonets
beckoning his soldiers to desert their eagles, invit-
ing his countrymen to betray their sovereign and
dishonour their nation! Why the man was surrounded by traitors, and proud and scornful of
danger was his spirit to strive so mightily against
defeat and treason combined.

It has been said in condemnation of him that
the English general did not encourage the Bourbon
party. Is that true? Did it so appear to the French
general? Had not the duke of Angoulême come to
the English head-quarters with mystery, and following the invading army and protected by its arms
assemble round him all the ancient partizans of
his house, sending forth agents, scattering proclamations even in Soult's camp, endeavouring to
debauch his soldiers and to aid strangers to subjugate France. Soult not only knew this but was
suffering under the effects. On every side he met
with opposition and discontent from the civil authorities, his movements were made known to the
enemy and his measures thwarted in all directions. At Bordeaux a party were calling aloud with
open arms to the invaders. At Tarbes the fear of
provoking an action near the town had caused the
dispersion of the insurrectional levy organized by
the imperial commissioner Caffarelli. At Pau the
aristocracy had secretly assembled to offer homage
to the duke of Angoulême, and there was a rumour
that he was to be crowned at the castle of Henry IV.
Was the French general to disregard these facts

and symptoms because his opponent had avoided
any public declaration in favour of the Bourbon
family? Lord Wellington would have been the first
to laugh at his simplicity if he had.

And what was the reason that the English general did not openly call upon the Bourbon partizans
to raise the standard of revolt? Simply that Napoleon's astounding genius had so baffled the
banded sovereigns and their innumerable hordes
that a peace seemed inevitable to avoid fatal disasters; and therefore lord Wellington, who had instructions from his government not to embarrass Secret in-
any negociation for peace by pledges to a Bourbon structions from Lord
party, acting as an honest statesman and com- Bathurst, MSS.
mander, would not excite men to their own ruin
for a momentary advantage. But so far from dis-
couraging treason to Napoleon on any other ground Published Des-
he avowed his anxious desire for it, and his readi- patches.
ness to encourage every enemy of that monarch.
He had seen and consulted with La Roche Jacquelin, with de Mailhos and other vehement partizans
for an immediate insurrection; and also with Viel
Castel an agent of Bernadotte's until he found
him intriguing against the Bourbons. He advised
the duke of Angoulême to form regular battalions,
promised him arms and actually collected eighty
thousand stand, to arm the insurgents. Finally he
rebuked the timid policy of the English ministers
who having such an opportunity of assailing Napoleon refrained from doing it. Before Soult's proclamation appeared he thus wrote to lord Bathurst.

" I find the sentiment as we advance in the
country still more strong against the Buonaparte
dynasty and in favour of the Bourbons, but I am

quite certain there will be no declaration on the part of the people if the allies do not in some manner declare themselves." " *I cannot discover the policy of not hitting one's enemy as hard as one can and in the most vulnerable place. I am certain that he would not so act by us, he would certainly overturn the British authority in Ireland if it were in his power.*"

Soult and Wellington acted and wrote, each in the manner most suitable to their situation, but it was not a little remarkable that Ireland should so readily occur to the latter as a parallel case.

It was in this state of affairs that the English general detached Beresford with twelve thousand men against Bordeaux, giving him instructions to occupy that city and acquire the Garonne as a port for the allies, but to make the French authorities declare whether they would or would not continue to exercise their functions under the conditions announced by proclamation. For hitherto lord Wellington had governed the country as he advanced in this public manner, thus nullifying the misrepresentations of political intriguers, obviating the dangers of false reports and rumours of his projects, making his justice and moderation known to the poorest peasant, and securing the French local authorities who continued to act under him from any false and unjust representation of their conduct to the imperial government if peace should be made with Napoleon. This expedition against Bordeaux however involved political as well as military interests. Beresford was instructed that there were many partizans of the Bourbons in that city who might propose to hoist the white standard and proclaim Louis the Eighteenth under protection of the troops. They were to be told that the British nation and its allies wished well to their cause, and while public tranquillity was maintained in the districts occupied by the troops there would be no hindrance to their political proceedings: they or any party opposed to Napoleon would receive assistance. Nevertheless, as the allied sovereigns were negociating with the French emperor, however well inclined the English general might be to support a party against the latter during war, he could give no help if peace were concluded, and this they must weigh well before they revolted. Beresford was therefore not to meddle with any declaration in favour of Louis the Eighteenth; but he was not to oppose it, and if revolt took place he was to supply the revolters with the arms and ammunition collected at Dax.

On the 8th Beresford marched towards Langon with the fourth and seventh divisions, Vivian's horsemen, and some guns; he was joined on the road by some of Vandeleur's cavalry from Bayonne, and he had orders to observe the enemy's movements towards Agen, for it was still in Soult's power by a forced march on that side to cross the Garonne and enter Bordeaux before him. La Roche Jacquelin preceded the troops and the duke of Angoulême followed closely, but his partizans in the city frightened at the danger of their enterprize now besought Beresford to delay his march. La Roche Jacquelin vehemently condemned their hesitation, and his influence supported by the consternation which the battle of Orthes had created amongst the Napoleonists decided the question in favour of revolt.

Long before this epoch, Soult, foreseeing that the probable course of the war would endanger Bordeaux, had given orders to place the forts in a state of defence, to arm the flotilla and to organize the national guards and the urban legions; he had urged these measures again when the imperial commissioner Cornudet first arrived, but according to the usual habits of civilians who have to meddle with military affairs every thing was promised and nothing done. Cornudet and the prefect quitted the city as early as the 4th, first burning with a silly affectation of vigour some ships of war upon the stocks; general L'Huillier, unable to oppose the allies, then destroyed the fort of Medoc on the left bank of the Garonne, disarmed some of the river batteries, and passing in the night of the 11th to the right bank occupied the fortress of Blaye, the Paté and other points. Meanwhile Beresford who reached Langon the 10th, left lord Dalhousie there with the bulk of the forces and advanced with eight hundred cavalry.

Entering Bordeaux the 12th, he met the municipality and a great body of Bourbonists, at the head of whom was the mayor count Lynch, decorated with the scarf of his office and the legion of honour, both conferred upon him, and probably at his own solicitation, by the sovereign he was then going to betray. After some formal discourse in which Beresford explicitly made known his instructions Lynch very justly tore the tricolor, the emblem of his country's glory, from his own shoulders, the white flag was then displayed and the allies took peaceable possession of the city. The duke of Angoulême arrived on the same day and Louis the Eighteenth was formally proclaimed. This event, the act of a party, was not generally approved, and the mayor

conscious of weakness immediately issued with the
connivance of the duke of Angoulême a proclamation, in which he asserted, that "the British Portuguese and Spanish armies were united in the south,
as the other nations were united in the north, solely
to destroy Napoleon and replace him by a Bourbon
king who was conducted thither by these generous
allies, and only by accepting that king could the
French appease the resentment of the Spaniards."
At the same time the duke of Angoulême, as if
quite master of the country, appointed prefects and
other authorities in districts beyond the limits of
Bordeaux.

Both the duke and the mayor soon repented of
their precipitancy. The English fleet which should
have acted simultaneously with the troops had not arrived; the Regulus a French seventy-four with several
inferior vessels of war were anchored below Blaye, and
Beresford was recalled with the fourth division and Vivian's cavalry. Lord Dalhousie remained with only
the seventh division and three squadrons to oppose
L'Huillier's troops and other French corps which were
now on the Garonne. He could not guard the river
below Bordeaux, and some French troops recrossing
again took possession of the fort of Grave near the
mouth; a new army was forming under general Decaen
beyond the Garonne, the Napoleonists recovering from
their first stupor began to stir themselves, and a partizan officer coming down to St. Macaire on the 18th
surprised fifty men which lord Dalhousie had sent
across the Garonne from Langon to take possession
of a French magazine. In the Landes the peasants
forming bands burned the houses of the gentlemen
who had joined the white standard, and in Bordeaux

itself a counter-insurrection was preparing whenever Decaen should be ready to advance.

The prince frightened at these symptoms of reaction desired lord Dalhousie to bring his troops into Bordeaux to awe the Napoleonists, and meanwhile each party strove to outvie the other in idle rumours and falsehoods relating to the emperor. Victories and defeats were invented or exaggerated, Napoleon was dead from illness, had committed suicide, was poisoned, stabbed; and all these things were related as certain with most circumstantial details. Meanwhile Wellington, writing to the duke of Angoulême, denied the veracity of the mayor's proclamation and expressed his trust that the prince was not a party to such a mendacious document. The latter however with some excuses about hurry and confusion avowed his participation in its publication, and defended the mayor's conduct. He also forwarded a statement of the danger his party was exposed to and demanded aid of men and money, supporting his application by a note of council in which with more ingenuity than justice, it was argued, that as civil government could not be conducted without executive power, and as lord Wellington had suffered the duke of Angoulême to assume the civil government at Bordeaux without an adequate executive force, he was bound to supply the deficiency from his army, and even to furnish money until taxes could be levied under the protection of the soldiers.

The English general was not a man to bear with such sophistry in excuse for a breach of faith. Sorry he was he said to find that the principle by which he regulated his conduct towards the Bour-

bon party, though often stated, had made so little
impression that the duke could not perceive how
inconsistent it was with the mayor's proclamation.
Most cautious therefore must be his future conduct,
seeing that as the chief of an army and the confidential agent of three independent nations, he could not
permit his views to be misrepresented upon such an
important question. He had occupied Bordeaux as
a military point, but certain persons contrary to his
advice and opinion thought proper to proclaim Louis
the Eighteenth. Those persons made no exertions,
subscribed not a shilling, raised not a soldier, yet
because he would not extend the posts of his army
beyond what was proper and convenient, merely to
protect their families and property, exposed to danger, not on account of their exertions for they had
made none, but on account of their premature declaration contrary to his advice, they took him to
task in a document delivered to lord Dalhousie by
the prince himself. The writer of that paper and
all such persons however might be assured that
nothing should make him swerve from what he
thought his duty to the sovereigns who employed
him, he would not risk even a company of infantry
to save properties and families placed in a state of
danger contrary to his advice. The duke had better then conduct his policy and compose his mani-
festos in such a manner as not to force a public
contradiction of them. His royal highness was free
to act as he pleased for himself, but he was not free
to adduce the name and authority of the allied
governments in support of his measures when they
had not been consulted, nor of their general when
he had been consulted but had given his opinion
against those measures.

He had told him that if any great town or extensive district declared in favour of the Bourbons he
would not interfere with the government of that
town or district, and if there was a general declaration in favour of his house he would deliver the civil
government of all the country overrun by the army
into his hands, but the fact was that even at Bordeaux the movement in favour of the Bourbons was
not unanimous. The spirit had not spread elsewhere, not even to La Vendée, nor in any part occupied by the army. The events contemplated had
not therefore occurred, and it would be a great
breach of duty towards the allied sovereigns and
cruel to the inhabitants if he were to deliver them
over to his royal highness prematurely or against
their inclinations. He advised him therefore to
withdraw his prefects and confine his government to
Bordeaux. He could give him no money and after
what had passed he was doubtful if he should afford
him any countenance or protection. The argument
of the note of council, affirming that he was bound
to support the civil government of his royal highness, only rendered it more incumbent upon him to
beware how he gave farther encouragement, or to
speak plainly, *permission* to the Bourbonists to declare themselves. It was disagreeable to take any
step which should publicly mark a want of good
understanding between himself and the duke, but
count Lynch had not treated him with common fairness or with truth, wherefore as he could not allow
the character of the allied sovereigns or his own to
be doubted, if his royal highness did not within ten
days contradict the objectionable parts of the mayor's
proclamation he would do so himself.

Thus it appeared that with the French as with the

Spaniards and Portuguese neither enthusiastic declarations nor actual insurrection offered any guarantee for sense truth or exertion ; and most surely
all generals and politicians of every country who
trust to sudden popular commotions will find that
noisy declamations, vehement demonstrations of feeling, idle rumours and boasting, the life-blood of
such affairs, are essentially opposed to useful public
exertions.

When Beresford marched to rejoin the army the
line of occupation was too extensive for lord Dalhousie and lord Wellington ordered him to keep
clear of the city and hold his troops together, observing that his own projected operations on the
Upper Garonne would keep matters quiet on the
lower part of that river. Nevertheless if the war
had continued for a month that officer's situation
would have been critical. For when Napoleon
knew that Bordeaux had fallen he sent Decaen by
post to Libourne to form the " *army of the Gironde.*"
For this object general Despeaux acting under Soult's
orders collected a body of gensd'armes custom-
house officers and national guards on the Upper
Garonne, between Agen and La Reolle, and it was
one of his detachments that surprised lord Dalhousie's men at St. Macaire on the 18th. A battery of eight guns was sent down from Narbonne,
other batteries were despatched from Paris to arrive
at Perigueux on the 11th of April, and three or four
hundred cavalry coming from the side of Rochelle
joined Le Huillier who with a thousand infantry was
in position at St. André de Cubsac beyond the Dordogne. Behind these troops all the national guards
custom-house officers and gensd'armes of five departments were ordered to assemble, and march to

Official Re-
ports and
Correspon-
dence of
general
Decaen
upon the
formation
of the army
of the Gi-
ronde,
1814,
MSS.

the Dordogne ; but the formidable part of the in-. tended army was a body of Suchet's veterans, six thousand in number under general Beurman, who had been turned from the road of Lyons and directed upon Libourne.

Decaen entered Mucidan on the 1st of April but Beurman's troops had not then reached Perigeaux, and lord Dalhousie's cavalry were in Libourne between him and L'Huillier. The power of concentration was thus denied to the French and meanwhile admiral Penrose had secured the command

Published despatches

of the Garonne. It appears lord Wellington thought this officer dilatory, but on the 27th he arrived with a seventy-four and two frigates, whereupon the Regulus, and other French vessels then at Royan, made sail up the river and were chased to the shoal of Talmont, but they escaped through the narrow channel on the north side and cast anchor under some batteries. Previous to this event Mr.

Official Report by Mr. Ogilvie, MSS.

Ogilvie a commissary, being on the river in a boat manned with Frenchmen, discovered the Requin sloop, half French half American, pierced for twenty-two guns, lying at anchor not far below Bordeaux, at the same time he saw a sailor leap hastily into a boat above him and row for the vessel. This man being taken proved to be the armourer of the Requin, he said there were not many men on board, and Mr. Ogilvie observing his alarm and judging that the crew would also be fearful, with ready resolution bore down upon the Requin, boarded, and took her without any opposition either from her crew or that of his own boat, although she had fourteen guns mounted and eleven men with two officers on board.

The naval cooperation being thus assured lord

Dalhousie crossed the Garonne above the city, drove the French posts beyond the Dordogne, pushed scouring parties to La Reolle and Marmande, and sending his cavalry over the Dordogne intercepted Decaen's and La Huilhier's communications ; the former was thus forced to remain at Mucidan with two hundred and fifty gensd'armes awaiting the arrival of Beurman, and he found neither arms nor ammunition nor a willing spirit to enable him to organize the national guards.

The English horsemen repassed the Dordogne on the 2d of April, but on the 4th lord Dalhousie crossed it again lower down, near St. André de Cubzac, with about three thousand men, intending to march upon Blaye, but hearing that L'Huillier had halted at Etauliers he turned suddenly upon him. The French general formed his line on an open common occupying some woods in front with his detachments. Overmatched in infantry he had three hundred cavalry opposed to one weak squadron, and yet his troops would not stand the shock of the battle. The allied infantry cleared the woods in a moment, the artillery then opened upon the main body which retired in disorder, horsemen and infantry together, through Etauliers, leaving behind several scattered bodies upon whom the British cavalry galloped and made two or three hundred men and thirty officers prisoners.

If the six thousand old troops under Beurman had, according to Napoleon's orders, arrived at this time in lord Dalhousie's rear, his position would have been embarrassing but they were delayed on the road until the 10th. Meanwhile admiral Penrose, having on the 2d observed the French flotilla, consisting of fifteen armed vessels and gun-boats, coming down from Blaye to join the Regulus at Talmont sent the boats of his fleet to attack them, whereupon the French vessels run on shore and the crews aided by two hundred soldiers from Blaye lined the beach to protect them. Lieutenant Dunlop who commanded the English boats landing all his seamen and marines, beat these troops and carried off or destroyed the whole flotilla with a loss to himself of only six men wounded and missing. This operation completed and the action at Etauliers known, the admiral, now reinforced with a second ship of the line, resolved to attack the French squadron and the shore batteries, but in the night of the 6th the enemy set fire to their vessels. Captain Harris of the Belle Poule frigate then landed with six hundred seamen and marines and destroyed the batteries and forts on the right bank from Talmont to the Courbe point. Blaye still held out, but at Paris treason had done its work and Napoleon, the man of mightiest capacity known for good, was overthrown to make room for despots, who with minds enlarged only to cruelty avarice and dissoluteness, were at the very moment of triumph intent to defraud the people, by whose strength and suffering they had conquered, of the only reward they demanded, *just government*. The war was virtually over, but on the side of Toulouse, Bayonne, and Barcelona, the armies ignorant of this great event were still battling with unabated fury.

CHAPTER IV.

WHILE Beresford was moving upon Bordeaux Soult and Wellington remained in observation, each thinking the other stronger than himself. For the English general having intelligence of Beurman's march, believed that his troops were intended to reinforce and had actually joined Soult. On the other hand that marshal, who knew not of Beresford's march until the 13th, concluded Wellington still had the twelve thousand men detached to Bordeaux. The numbers on each side were however nearly equal. The French army was thirty-one thousand, infantry and cavalry, yet three thousand being stragglers detained by the generals of the military districts, Soult could only put into line, exclusive of conscripts without arms, twenty-eight thousand sabres and bayonets with thirty-eight pieces of artillery. On the allies' side twenty-seven thousand sabres and bayonets were under arms, with forty-two guns, but from this number detachments had been sent to Pau on one side, Roquefort on the other, and the cavalry scouts were pushed into the Landes and to the Upper Garonne.

Lord Wellington expecting Soult would retreat upon Auch and designing to follow him, had caused Beresford to keep the bulk of his troops towards

the Upper Garonne that he might the sooner rejoin
the army ; but the French general having early fixed
his line of retreat by St. Guadens was only prevented from retaking the offensive on the 9th or
10th by the loss of his magazines, which forced
him first to organize a system of requisition for
the subsistence of his army. Meanwhile his
equality of force passed away, for on the 13th
Freyre came up with eight thousand Spanish infantry, and the next day Ponsonby's heavy cavalry arrived.   Lord Wellington was then the strongest, yet
he still awaited Beresford's troops, and was uneasy
about his own situation.   He dreaded the junction
See Chap.
VI., Book
XXIII. of Suchet's army, for it was at this time the Spanish
regency referred the convention, proposed by that
marshal for the evacuation of the fortresses, to his
decision.   He gave a peremptory negative, observing that it would furnish twenty thousand veterans for Soult while the retention of Rosas and
Figueras would bar the action of the Spanish armies
of Catalonia in his favour.   But his anxiety was great
because he foresaw that Ferdinand's return and
his engagement with Suchet, already related, together with the evident desire of Copons that the garrisons should be admitted to a convention would
finally render that measure inevitable.   Meanwhile
the number of his own army was likely to decrease.
The English cabinet, less considerate even than the
Spanish government, had sent the militia, permitted
by the recent act of parliament to volunteer for
foreign service, to Holland, and with them the
other reinforcements originally promised for the
army in France : two or three regiments of militia
only came to the Garonne when the war was over.
To make amends the ministers proposed that lord

William Bentinck should send four thousand men
from Sicily to land at Rosas, or some point in
France, and so join lord Wellington, who was
thus expected to extend his weakened force from
the Bay of Biscay to the Mediterranean in order to
cover the junction of this uncertain reinforcement.
In fine experience had taught the English states-
men so little that we find their general thus ad-
dressing them only one week previous to the
termination of the war.

Having before declared that he should be, contrary to his wishes, forced to bring more Spaniards
into France, he says : —

" There are limits to the numbers with which
this army can contend and I am convinced your
lordship would not wish to see the safety and honour
of this handful of brave men depend upon the
doubtful exertions and discipline of an undue proportion of Spanish troops."—" The service in Holland may doubtless be more important to the
national interest than that in this country, but I
hope it will be considered that that which is most
important of all is not *to lose* the brave army which
has struggled through its difficulties for nearly six
years."

The French infantry was now re-organized in six
divisions commanded by Darricau, D'Armagnac,
Taupin, Maransin, Villatte and Harispe ; general
Paris' troops hitherto acting as an unattached Soult's
Official
body were thus absorbed, the cavalry composed of Report,
MSS.
Berton's and Vial's brigades was commanded
by Pierre Soult, and there was a reserve division of seven thousand conscripts, infantry under
general Travot. The division into wings and a
centre, each commanded by a lieutenant-general

continued, yet this distinction was not attended to in the movements. Reille though commanding the right wing was at Maubourget on the left of the line of battle; D'Erlon commanding the centre was at Marsiac on the right covering the road to Auch; Clauzel was at Rabastens forming a reserve to both. The advanced guards were towards Plaissance on the right, Madiran in the centre, and Lembege on the left. Soult thus covered Tarbes, and could move on a direct line by good roads either to Auch or Pau.

Lord Wellington driven by necessity now sent orders to Giron's Andalusians and Del Parque's troops to enter France from the Bastan, although Freyre's soldiers had by their outrages already created a wide-spread consternation. His headquarters were fixed at Aire, his army was in position on each side of the Adour, he had repaired all the bridges behind him, restored that over the Lees in his front, and dispersed some small bands which had appeared upon his left flank and rear: Soult had however organized a more powerful system of partizans towards the mountains and only wanted money to put them in activity. The main bodies of the two armies were a long day's march asunder, but their advanced posts were not very distant, the regular cavalry had frequent encounters and both generals claimed the superiority though neither made any particular report.

On the night of the 7th Soult thinking to find only some weak parties at Pau sent a strong detachment there to arrest the nobles who had assembled to welcome the duke of Angoulême, but general Fane getting there before him with a brigade of infantry and two regiments of cavalry the stroke failed; however the French returning by another road made prisoners of an officer and four or five English dragoons. Meanwhile a second detachment penetrating between Pau and Aire carried off a post of correspondence; and two days after, when Fane had quitted Pau, a French officer accompanied by only four hussars captured there thirty-four Portuguese with their commander and ten loaded mules. The French general having by these excursions obtained exact intelligence of Beresford's march to Bordeaux resolved to attack the allies, and the more readily that Napoleon had recently sent him instructions to draw the war to the side of Pau keeping his left resting on the Pyrenees, which accorded with his own designs.

Lord Wellington's main body was now concentrated round Aire and Barcelone, yet divided by the Adour and the advanced guards were pushed to Garlin, Conchez, Viella, Riscle and Pouydraguien, that is to say, on a semicircle to the front and about half a march in advance. Soult therefore thought to strike a good blow, and gathering his divisions on the side of Maubourget the 12th, marched on the 13th, designing to throw himself upon the high tabular land between Pau and Aire, and then act according to circumstances.

The country was suited to the action of all arms, offering a number of long and nearly parallel ridges of moderate height, the sides of which were sometimes covered with vineyards, but the summits commonly so open that troops could move along them without much difficulty, and between these ranges a number of small rivers and muddy fords descended from the Pyrenees to the Adour. This conformation determined the order of

the French general's march which followed the
courses of these rivers. Leaving one regiment of
cavalry to watch the valley of the Adour he moved
with the rest of his army by Lembege upon
Conchez down the smaller Lees. Clauzel thus seized
the high land of Daisse and pushed troops to Portet;
Reille supported him at Conchez; D'Erlon remained behind that place in reserve.   In this
position the head of the columns, pointing direct
upon Aire, separated Viella from Garlin which was
the right of general Hill's position, and menaced that
general's posts on the great Lees. Meanwhile Pierre
Soult marching with three regiments of cavalry
along the high land between the two Lees; reached
Mascaras and the castle of Sault, he thus covered
the left flank of the French army and pushed
Fane's cavalry posts back with the loss of two
officers taken and a few men wounded. During this
movement Berton advancing from Madiran with
two regiments of cavalry towards Viella, on the
right flank of the French army, endeavoured to

Memoirs
by general
Berton,
MSS.
cross the Saye river at a difficult muddy ford near
the broken bridge. Sir John Campbell leading a
squadron of the fourth Portuguese cavalry over-

Note by
sir John
Campbell,
MSS.
threw the head of his column, but the Portuguese
horsemen were too few to dispute the passage
and Berton finally getting a regiment over higher
up, gained the table-land above, and charging the
rear of the retiring troops in a narrow way leading to
the Aire road killed several and took some prisoners,
amongst them Bernardo de Sà the since well-known
count of Bandeira.

This terminated the French operations for the
day, and lord Wellington imagining the arrival of
Suchet's troops had made Soult thus bold, resolved

to keep on the defensive until his reinforcements
and detachments could come up. Hill however
passed the greater Lees partly to support his posts
partly to make out the force and true direction of
the French movement, but he recrossed that river
during the night and finally occupied the strong
platform between Aire and Garlin which Soult
had designed to seize. Lord Wellington immediately brought the third and sixth division and
the heavy cavalry over the Adour to his support,
leaving the light division with the hussar brigade
still on the right bank. The bulk of the army thus
occupied a strong position parallel with the Pau
road. The right was at Garlin, the left at Aire, the
front covered by the greater Lees a river difficult
to pass; Fane's cavalry was extended along the
Pau road as far as Boelho, and on the left of the
Adour the hussars pushed the French cavalry
regiment left there back upon Plaissance.

On the morning of the 14th Soult intending to
fall on Hill, whose columns he had seen the evening
before on the right of the Lees, drove in the advanced posts which had been left to cover the
retrograde movement, and then examined the allies'
new position ; but these operations wasted the day,
and towards evening he disposed his army on the
heights between the two Lees, placing Clauzel and
D'Erlon at Castle Pugon opposite Garlin, and
Reille in reserve at Portet. Meanwhile Pierre
Soult carried three regiments of cavalry to Clarac,
on the Pau road, to intercept the communications
with that town and to menace the right flank of the
allies, against which the whole French army was
now pointing. Fane's outposts being thus assailed
retired with some loss at first but they were soon

supported and drove the French horsemen in disorder clear off the Pau road to Carere.

Soult now seeing the strength of the position
above Aire, and hearing from the peasants that
forty or fifty thousand men were concentrated there,
feared to attack, but changing his plan resolved to
hover about the right flank of the allies in the hopes
of enticing them from their vantage-ground. Lord
Wellington on the other hand drew his cavalry
posts down the valley of the Adour, and keeping
close on that side massed his forces on the right in
expectation of an attack. In fine each general acting
upon false intelligence of the other's strength was
afraid to strike. The English commander's error
as to the junction of Suchet's troops was encouraged
by Soult, who had formed his battalions upon two
ranks instead of three to give himself an appearance
of strength, and in the same view had caused his
reserve of conscripts to move in rear of his line of
battle. And he also judged the allies' strength by
what it might have been rather than by what it
Morning
States,
MSS.
was; for though Freyre's Spaniards and Ponsonby's
dragoons were now up, the whole force did not
exceed thirty-six thousand men, including the light
division and the hussars who were on the right
bank of the Adour. This number was however
increasing every hour by the arrival of detachments
and reserves; and it behoved Soult, who was entangled in a country extremely difficult if rain
should fall, to watch that Wellington while holding
the French in check with his right wing did not
strike with his left by Maubourget and Tarbes, and
thus cast them upon the mountains about Lourdes.

This danger, and the intelligence now obtained of
the fall of Bordeaux, induced the French general to

retire before day on the 16th to Lembege and Sima-
courbe, where he occupied both sides of the two
branches of the Lees and the heights between them;
however his out-posts remained at Conchez, and
Pierre Soult again getting upon the Pau road detached a hundred chosen troopers against the allies'
communication with Orthes. Captain Dania commanding these men making a forced march reached
Hagetnau at nightfall, surprised six officers and
eight medical men with their baggage, made a
number of other prisoners and returned on the
evening of the 18th. This enterprize extended to
such a distance from the army was supposed to be
executed by the bands, and seemed to indicate a
disposition for insurrection; wherefore lord Wellington to check it seized the civil authorities at
Hagetnau, and declared that he would hang all the
peasants caught in arms and burn their villages.

The offensive movement of the French general
had now terminated, he sent his conscripts at once
to Toulouse and prepared for a rapid retreat on that
place. His recent operations had been commenced
too late, he should have been on the Lees the 10th
or 11th when there were not more than twenty
thousand infantry and two thousand five hundred
cavalry to oppose him between Aire and Garlin.
On the other hand the passive state of Wellington,
which had been too much prolonged, was now also at
an end, all his reinforcements and detachments were
either up or close at hand, and he could put in motion six Anglo-Portuguese and three Spanish divisions of infantry, furnishing forty thousand bayonets, Morning
with five brigades of cavalry, furnishing nearly six States,
thousand sabres, and from fifty to sixty pieces of MSS.
artillery.

On the evening of the 17th, the English general pushed the hussars up the valley of the Adour, towards Plaissance, supporting them with the light division, which was followed at the distance of half a march by the fourth division coming from the side of Roquefort, on its return from Langon.

The 18th at daylight the whole army was in movement, the hussars with the light and the fourth division, forming the left, marched upon Plaissance ; Hill's troops forming the right marched from Garlin upon Conchez, keeping a detachment on the road to

Pau in observation of Pierre Soult's cavalry. The main body moved in the centre, under Wellington in person, to Viella, by the high road leading from Aire to Maubourget. The French right was thus turned by the valley of the Adour, while general Hill with a sharp skirmish, in which about eighty British and Germans were killed and wounded, drove back their outposts upon Lembege.

Soult retired during the night to a strong ridge having a small river with rugged banks, called the Laiza, in his front, and his right under D'Erlon was extended towards Vic Bigorre on the great road of Tarbes. Meanwhile Berton's cavalry, one regiment

of which retreating from Viella on the 16th disengaged itself with some difficulty and loss, reached Maubourget, and took post in column behind that place, the road being confined on each side by deep and wide ditches. In this situation pressed by Bock's cavalry, which preceded the centre column of the allies, the French horsemen suddenly charged the Germans, at first with success, taking an officer and some men, but finally they were beaten and retreated through Vic Bigorre. Soult thinking a flanking column only was on this side in the valley of the Adour,

resolved to fall upon it with his whole army ; but he
recognised the skill of his opponent when he found
that the whole of the allies' centre, moving by Madiran, had been thrown on to the Tarbes road while
he was retiring from Lembege. This heavy mass was
now approaching Vic Bigorre, the light division, coming from Plaissance up the right bank of the Adour,
were already near Auriebat, pointing to Rabastens,
upon which place the hussars had already driven
the French cavalry left in observation when the
army first advanced : Vic Bigorre was thus turned,
Berton's horsemen had passed it in retreat and the
danger was imminent. The French general immediately ordered Berton to support the cavalry regiment at Rabastens and cover that road to Tarbes.
Then directing D'Erlon to take post at Vic Bigorre
and check the allies on the main road, he marched,
in person and in all haste, with Clauzel's and
Reille's divisions to Tarbes by a circuitous road
leading through Ger-sur-landes.

D'Erlon not seeming to comprehend the crisis
moved slowly, with his baggage in front, and having
the river Lechez to cross, rode on before his troops
expecting to find Berton at Vic Bigorre, but he
met the German cavalry there. Then indeed he
hurried his march yet he had only time to place
Darricau's division, now under general Paris,
amongst some vineyards, two miles in front of Vic
Bigorre, when hither came Picton to the support of
the cavalry and fell upon him.

Combat of Vic Bigorre.—The French left flank
was secured by the Lechez river, but their right,
extending towards the Adour, being loose was menaced by the German cavalry while the front was
attacked by Picton. The action commenced about

two o'clock, and Paris was soon driven back in disorder, but then D'Armagnac's division entered the
line and extending to the Adour renewed the fight,
which lasted until D'Erlon, after losing many men,
saw his right turned, beyond the Adour, by the light
division and by the hussars who were now close to
Rabastens, whereupon he likewise fell back behind Vic Bigorre, and took post for the night. The
action was vigorous. About two hundred and fifty
Anglo-Portuguese, men and officers, fell, and
amongst them died colonel Henry Sturgeon so often
mentioned in this history. Skilled to excellence in
almost every branch of war and possessing a variety
of accomplishments, he used his gifts so gently for
himself and so usefully for the service that envy
offered no bar to admiration, and the whole army
felt painfully mortified that his merits were passed
unnoticed in the public despatches.

Soult's march through the deep sandy plain of
Ger was harassing, and would have been dangerous
if lord Wellington had sent Hill's cavalry, now reinforced by two regiments of heavy dragoons, in pursuit; but the country was unfavorable for quick observation and the French covered their movements
with rear-guards whose real numbers it was difficult
to ascertain. One of these bodies was posted on a
hill the end of which abutted on the high road, the
slope being clothed with trees and defended by skirmishers. Lord Wellington was desirous to know
whether a small or a large force thus barred his
way, but all who endeavoured to ascertain the fact
were stopped by the fire of the enemy. At last
captain William Light, distinguished by the variety
of his attainments, an artist, musician, mechanist,
seaman, and soldier, made the trial. He rode for-

ward as if he would force his way through the
French skirmishers, but when in the wood dropt his
reins and leaned back as if badly wounded ; his
horse appeared to canter wildly along the front of
the enemy's light troops, and they thinking him
mortally hurt ceased their fire and took no further
notice. He thus passed unobserved through the
wood to the other side of the hill, where there were
no skirmishers, and ascending to the open summit
above, put spurs to his horse and galloped along
the French main line counting their regiments as he
passed. His sudden appearance, his blue undress,
his daring confidence and his speed, made the
French doubt if he was an enemy, and a few shots
only were discharged, while he, dashing down the
opposite declivity, broke from the rear through the
very skirmishers whose fire he had first essayed
in front. Reaching the spot where lord Wellington
stood he told him there were but five battalions on
the hill.

Soult now felt that a rapid retreat upon Toulouse
by St. Gaudens was inevitable, yet determined to
dispute every position which offered the least advantage, his army was on the morning of the 20th
again in line of battle on the heights of Oleac, two
or three miles behind Tarbes, and covering Tournay
on the road to St. Gaudens : however he still held
Tarbes with Clauzel's corps, which was extended on
the right towards Trie, as if to retain a power of
retreat by that road to Toulouse. The plain of
Tarbes although apparently open was full of deep
ditches which forbad the action of horsemen, wherefore he sent his brother with five regiments of
cavalry to the Trie road, with orders to cover the
right flank and observe the route to Auch, for he

feared lest Wellington should intercept his retreat
by that line.

At day-break the allies again advanced in two
columns. The right under Hill moved along the
high road. The left under Wellington in person
was composed of the light division and hussars,
Ponsonby's heavy cavalry, the sixth division and
Freyre's Spaniards. It marched by the road from
Rabastens, and general Cole still making forced
marches with the fourth division and Vivian's
cavalry, followed from Beaumarchez and La Deveze,
sending detachments through Marciac to watch
Pierre Soult on the side of Trie.

Combat of Tarbes.—The Adour separated Wellington's columns, but when the left approached

Tarbes, the light division and the hussars bringing
up their right shoulders attacked the centre of
Harispe's division, which occupied the heights of
Orliex and commanded the road from Rabastens
with two guns. Under cover of this attack general
Clinton made a flank movement to his left through
the village of Dours, and opening a cannonade
against Harispe's right endeavoured to get between that general and Soult's main position at
Oleac. Meanwhile general Hill moving by the
other bank of the Adour assailed the town and
bridge of Tarbes, which was defended by Villatte's
division. These operations were designed to envelope and crush Clauzel's two divisions, which seemed
the more easy because there appeared to be only a
fine plain, fit for the action of all the cavalry, between him and Soult. The latter however, having sent
his baggage and encumbrances off during the night,
saw the movement without alarm, he was better
acquainted with the nature of the plain behind

Harispe and had made roads to enable him to retreat upon the second position without passing
through Tarbes. Nevertheless Clauzel was in
some danger, for while Hill menaced his left at
Tarbes, the light division supported with cavalry
and guns fell upon his centre at Orleix, and general
Clinton opening a brisk cannonade passed through
the villages of Oleat and Boulin, penetrated between
Harispe and Pierre Soult, and cut the latter off from
the army.

The action was begun about twelve o'clock.
Hill's artillery thundered on the right, Clinton's
answered it on the left, and Alten threw the light
division in mass upon the centre where Harispe's
left brigade posted on a strong hill was suddenly
assailed by the three rifle battalions. Here the fight
was short yet wonderfully fierce and violent, for the
French, probably thinking their opponents to be
Portuguese on account of their green dress, charged
with great hardiness, and being encountered by
men not accustomed to yield, they fought muzzle
to muzzle, and it was difficult to judge at first who
would win. At last the French gave way, and
Harispe's centre being thus suddenly overthrown
he retired rapidly through the fields, by the ways
previously opened, before Clinton could get into
his rear. Meanwhile Hill forced the passage of
the Adour at Tarbes and Villatte also retreated
along the high road to Tournay, but under a continued cannonade. The flat country was now
covered with confused masses of pursuers and pursued, all moving precipitately with an eager musquetry, the French guns also replying as they
could to the allies' artillery. The situation of the
retreating troops seemed desperate, but as Soult

BOOK
XXIV.
———
1814.
March.
had foreseen, the deep ditches and enclosures and
the small copses, villages, and farm-houses, prevented the British cavalry from acting; Clauzel
therefore extricating his troops with great ability
from their dangerous situation, finally gained the
main position, where four fresh divisions were drawn
up in order of battle and immediately opened all
their batteries on the allies. The pursuit was thus
checked, and before lord Wellington could make
arrangements for a new attack darkness came on
and the army halted on the banks of the Larret and
Larros rivers. The loss of the French is unknown,
that of the allies did not exceed one hundred and
twenty, but of that number twelve officers and
eighty men were of the rifle battalions.

Official
Report,
MSS.
During the night Soult retreated in two columns,
one by the main road, the other on the left of it,
guided by fires lighted on different hills as points
of direction. The next day he reached St. Gau-
Clauzel's
Orders,
MSS.
dens with D'Erlon's and Reille's corps, while Clauzel, who had retreated across the fields, halted at
Monrejean and was there rejoined by Pierre
Soult's cavalry. This march of more than thirty
miles was made with a view to gain Toulouse in
the most rapid manner. For the French general,
having now seen nearly all Wellington's infantry
and his five thousand horsemen, and hearing from
his brother that the fourth division and Vivian's
cavalry were pointing towards Mielan on his right,
feared that the allies would by Trie and Castlenau
suddenly gain the plains of Muret and intercept
his retreat upon Toulouse, which was his great depôt,
the knot of all his future combinations, and the only
position where he could hope to make a successful
stand with his small army.

The allies pursued in three columns by St. Gaudens, Galan, and Trie, but their marches were short.

On the 21st Beresford who had assumed the command of the left column was at Castlenau, Hill in the vicinity of Lannemezan, Wellington at Tournay.

The 22d Beresford was at Castlenau, Wellington at Galan, Hill at Monrejean, and Fane's horsemen pushed forwards to St. Gaudens. Here four squadrons of French cavalry were drawn up in front of the town. Overthrown by two squadrons of the thirteenth dragoons at the first shock, they galloped in disorder through St. Gaudens, yet rallied on the other side and were again broken and pursued for two miles, many being sabred and above a hundred taken prisoners. In this action the veteran major Dogherty of the thirteenth was seen charging between his two sons at the head of the leading squadron.

On the 23d Hill was at St. Gaudens, Beresford at Puymauren, Wellington at Boulogne.

The 24th Hill was in St. Martory, Beresford in Lombez, Wellington at Isle en Dodon.

The 25th Hill entered Caceres, Beresford reached St. Foy, and Wellington was at Samatan.

The 26th Beresford entered St. Lys and marching in order of battle by his left, while his cavalry skirmished on the right, took post on the Auch road behind the Aussonnelle stream, facing the French army, which was on the Touch covering Toulouse. The allies thus took seven days to march what Soult had done in four.

This tardiness, idly characterized by French military writers as the sign of timidity and indecision of character, has been by English writers excused on the score of wet weather and the encumbrance of a large train of artillery and pontoons; yet the rain equally affected the French, and the pontoons might have been as usefully waited for on the Garonne after the French army had been pressed in its retreat of ninety miles. It is more probable that the English general, not exactly informed of Soult's real numbers nor of his true line of retreat, nor perfectly acquainted with the country, was cautious; because being then acrimoniously disputing with the duke of Angoulême he was also uneasy as to the state of the country behind him and on his flanks. The partizans were beginning to stir, his reinforcements from England and Portugal were stopped, and admiral Penrose had not yet entered the Garonne. On the other hand Ferdinand had entered Spain and formed that engagement with Suchet about the garrisons already mentioned. In fine, lord Wellington found himself with about forty-five thousand men composed of different nations, the Spaniards being almost as dangerous as useful to him, opposed to an able and obstinate enemy, and engaged on a line of operations running more than a hundred and fifty miles along the French frontier. His right flank was likely to be vexed by the partizans forming in the Pyrenees, his left flank by those behind the Garonne on the right bank of which a considerable regular force was also collecting, while the generals commanding the military districts beyond Toulouse were forming corps of volunteers national guards and old soldiers of the regular depôts: and ever he expected Suchet to arrive on his front and overmatch him in numbers. He was careful therefore to keep his troops well in hand, and to spare them fatigue that the hospitals might not increase. In battle their

bravery would he knew bring him through any
crisis, but if wearing down their numbers by
forced marches he should cover the country with
small posts and hospital stations, the French people
would be tempted to rise against him. So little
therefore was his caution allied to timidity that it
was no slight indication of daring to have advanced
at all.

It does seem however that with an overwhelming cavalry, and great superiority of artillery he
should not have suffered the French general so to
escape his hands. It must be admitted also that
Soult proved himself a very able commander. His
halting on the Adour, his success in reviving the
courage of his army, and the front he shewed in
hopes to prevent his adversary from detaching
troops against Bordeaux, were proofs not only of a
firm unyielding temper but of a clear and ready
judgment. For though, contrary to his hopes, lord
Wellington did send Beresford against Bordeaux, it
was not on military grounds but because treason
was there to aid him. Meanwhile he was forced to
keep his army for fifteen days passive within a few
miles of an army he had just defeated, permitting
his adversary to reorganize and restore the discipline and courage of the old troops, to rally the
dispersed conscripts, to prepare the means of a
partizan warfare, to send off all his encumbrances
and sick to Toulouse, and to begin fortifying that
city as a final and secure retreat : for the works
there were commenced on the 3d or 4th of March,
and at this time the entrenchments covering the
bridge and suburb of St. Cyprien were nearly completed. The French general was even the first to
retake the offensive after Orthes, too late indeed,

and he struck no important blow, and twice placed
his army in dangerous situations; but his delay
was a matter of necessity arising from the loss of
his magazines, and if he got into difficulties they
were inseparable from his operations and he extricated himself again.

That he gained no advantages in fight is rather
argument for lord Wellington than against Soult.
The latter sought but did not find a favourable opportunity to strike, and it would have been unwise,
because his adversary gave him no opening, to have
fallen desperately upon superior numbers in a
strong position with an army so recently defeated,
and whose restored confidence it was so essential
not to shake again by a repulse. He increased
that confidence by appearing to insult the allied
army with an inferior force, and in combination
with his energetic proclamation encouraged the
Napoleonists and alarmed the Bourbonists; lastly,
by his rapid retreat from Tarbes he gained two
days to establish and strengthen himself on his
grand position at Toulouse. And certainly he deceived his adversary, no common general and at
the head of no common army; for so little did
Wellington expect him to make a determined stand
there, that in a letter written on the 26th to Sir
John Hope, he says, " I fear the Garonne is too
full and large for our bridge, if not we shall be in
that town (Toulouse) I hope immediately."

The French general's firmness and the extent of
his views cannot however be fairly judged by
merely considering his movements in the field.
Having early proved the power of his adversary,
he had never deceived himself about the ultimate
course of the campaign and therefore struggled

without hope, a hard and distressing task; yet he
showed no faintness, fighting continually, and always for delay as thinking Suchet would finally
cast personal feelings aside and strike for his
country. Nor did he forbear importuning that
marshal to do so. Notwithstanding his previous
disappointments he wrote to him again on the 9th
of February, urging the danger of the crisis, the
certainty that the allies would make the greatest
effort on the western frontier, and praying him to
abandon Catalonia and come with the bulk of his
troops to Bearn : in the same strain he wrote to
the minister of war, and his letters reached their
destinations on the 13th. Suchet, having no orders
to the contrary, could therefore have joined him with
thirteen thousand men before the battle of Orthes ;
but that marshal giving a deceptive statement of
his forces in reply, coldly observed, that if he
marched anywhere it would be to join the emperor
and not the duke of Dalmatia. The latter continued notwithstanding to inform him of all his
battles and his movements, and his accumulating
distresses, yet in vain, and Suchet's apathy would
be incredible but for the unequivocal proofs of it
furnished in the work of the French engineer
Choumara.

CHAPTER V.

BOOK
XXIV.
———
1814.
March. THE two armies being now once more in presence of each other and with an equal resolution to fight, it is fitting to show the peculiar calculations upon which the generals founded their respective combinations. Soult, born in the vicinity, knew the country and chose Toulouse as a strategic post, because that ancient capital of the south contained fifty thousand inhabitants, commanded the principal passage of the Garonne, was the centre of a great number of roads on both sides of that river, and the chief military arsenal of the south of France. Here he could most easily feed his troops, assemble arm and discipline the conscripts, controul and urge the civil authorities, and counteract the machinations of the discontented. Posted at Toulouse he was master of various lines of operations. He could retire upon Suchet by Carcassone, or towards Lyons by Alby. He could take a new position behind the Tarn and prolong the contest by defending successively that river and the Lot, retreating if necessary upon Decaen's army of the Gironde, and thus drawing the allies down the right bank of the Garonne as he had before drawn them up the left bank, being well assured that lord Wellington must follow him, and with weakened forces as it would be necessary to leave troops in observation of Suchet.

His first care was to place a considerable body of

troops, collected from the depots and other parts of the interior at Montauban, under the command of general Loverdo, with orders to construct a bridge-head on the left of the Tarn. The passage of that river, and a strong point of retreat and assembly for all the detachments sent to observe the Garonne below Toulouse, was thus secured, and withal the command of a number of great roads leading to the interior of France, consequently the power of making fresh combinations. To maintain himself as long as possible in Toulouse was however a great political object. It was the last point which connected him at once with Suchet and with Decaen; and while he held it, both the latter general and the partizans in the mountains about Lourdes could act, each on their own side, against the long lines of communications maintained by Wellington with Bordeaux and Bayonne. Suchet also could do the same, either by marching with his whole force or sending a detachment through the Arriege department to the Upper Garonne, where general Lafitte having seven or eight hundred men, national guards and other troops, was already in activity. These operations Soult now strongly urged Suchet to adopt, but the latter treated the proposition, as he had done all those before made from the same quarter, with contempt.

Toulouse was not less valuable as a position of battle.

The Garonne, flowing on the west, presented to the allies a deep loop, at the bottom of which was the bridge, completely covered by the suburb of St. Cyprien, itself protected by an ancient brick wall three feet thick and flanked by two massive towers : these defences Soult had improved and he added a line of exterior entrenchments.

Beyond the Garonne was the city, surrounded by
an old wall flanked with towers, and so thick as to
admit sixteen and twenty-four pound guns.

The great canal of Languedoc, which joined the
Garonne a few miles below the town, wound for the
most part within point-blank shot of the walls, covering them on the north and east as the Garonne
and St. Cyprien did on the west.

The suburbs of St. Stephen and Guillermerie,
built on both sides of this canal, furnished outworks
on the west, for they were entrenched and connected
with and covered by the hills of Sacarin and Cambon, also entrenched and flanking the approaches to
the canal both above and below these suburbs.

Eight hundred yards beyond these hills a strong
ridge, called the Mont Rave, run nearly parallel
with the canal, its outer slope was exceedingly
rugged and overlooked a marshy plain through
which the Ers river flowed.

The south side of the town opened on a plain, but
the suburb of St. Michel lying there, between the
Garonne and the canal, furnished another advanced
defence, and at some distance beyond, a range of
heights called the Pech David commenced, trending
up the Garonne in a direction nearly parallel to
that river.

Such being the French general's position, he calculated, that as lord Wellington could not force the
passage by the suburb of St. Cyprien without an
enormous sacrifice of men, he must seek to turn the
flanks above or below Toulouse, and leave a sufficient
force to blockade St. Cyprien under pain of having
the French army issue on that side against his communications. If he passed the Garonne above its
confluence with the Arriege, he would have to cross

that river also, which could not be effected nearer
than Cintegabelle, one march higher up. Then he
must come down by the right of the Arriege, an
operation not to be feared in a country which
the recent rains had rendered impracticable for
guns. If the allies passed the Garonne below the
confluence of the Arriege, Soult judged that he
could from the Pech David, and its continuation,
overlook their movements, and that he should be in
position to fall upon the head of their column while
in the disorder of passing the river : if he failed in
this he had still Toulouse and the heights of Mont
Rave to retire upon, where he could fight again,
his retreat being secure upon Montauban.

For these reasons the passage of the Garonne
above Toulouse would lead to no decisive result and
he did not fear it, but a passage below the city was
a different matter. Lord Wellington could thus cut
him off from Montauban and attack Toulouse from
the northern and eastern quarters ; and if the French
then lost the battle they could only retreat by Carcassonne to form a junction with Suchet in Roussil-
lon, where having their backs to the mountains and
the allies between them and France they could not
exist. Hence feeling certain the attack would finally
be on that side, Soult lined the left bank of the Garonne with his cavalry as far as the confluence of
the Tarn, and called up general Despeaux's troops
from Agen in the view of confining the allies to the
space between the Tarn and the Garonne : for his
first design was to attack them there rather than
lose his communication with Montauban.

On the other hand lord Wellington whether from
error from necessity or for the reasons I have before
touched upon, having suffered the French army to

gain three days' march in the retreat from Tarbes, had now little choice of operations. He could not halt until the Andalusians and Del Parque's troops should join him from the Bastan, without giving Soult all the time necessary to strengthen himself and organize his plan of defence, nor without appearing fearful and weak in the eyes of the French people, which would have been most dangerous. Still less could he wait for the fall of Bayonne. He had taken the offensive and could not resume the defensive with safety, the invasion of France once begun it was imperative to push it to a conclusion. Leading an army victorious and superior in numbers his business was to bring his adversary to battle as soon as possible, and as he could not force his way through St. Cyprien in face of the whole French army, nothing remained but to pass the Garonne above or below Toulouse.

It has been already shown that in a strategic view this passage should have been made below that town, but seeing that the south side of the city was the most open to attack, the English general resolved to cast his bridge at Portet, six miles above Toulouse, designing to throw his right wing suddenly into the open country between the Garonne and the canal of Languedoc, while with his centre and left he assailed the suburb of St. Cyprien. With this object, at eight o'clock in the evening of the 27th, one of Hill's brigades marched up from Muret, some men were ferried over and the bridge was commenced, the remainder of that general's troops being to pass at midnight. But when the river was measured the width was found too great for the pontoons and there were no means of substituting trestles, where fore this plan was abandoned. Had it been exe-

cuted some considerable advantage would probably
have been gained, since it does not appear that Soult knew of the attempt until two days later, and then
only by his emissaries, not by his scouts.

Wellington thus baffled tried another scheme, he drove the enemy from the Touch river on the 28th, and collected the infantry of his left and centre about Portet, masking the movement with his cavalry. In the course of the operation a single squadron of the eighteenth hussars, under major Hughes, being inconsiderately pushed by colonel Vivian across the bridge of St. Martyn de la Touch, suddenly came upon a whole regiment of French cavalry; the rashness of the act, as often happens in war, proved the safety of the British, for the enemy thinking that a strong support must be at hand discharged their carbines and retreated at a canter. Hughes followed, the speed of both sides increased, and as the nature of the road did not admit of any egress to the sides, this great body of French horsemen was pushed head-long by a few men under the batteries of St. Cyprien.

During these movements Hill's troops were with-drawn to St. Roques, but in the night of the 30th a new bridge being laid near Pensaguel, two miles above the confluence of the Arriege, that general passed the Garonne with two divisions of infantry, Morillo's Spaniards, Gardiner's and Maxwell's artil-lery, and Fane's cavalry, in all thirteen thousand sabres and bayonets, eighteen guns, and a rocket brigade. The advanced guard moved with all ex-pedition by the great road, having orders to seize the stone bridge of Cintegabelle, fifteen miles up the Arriege, and, on the march, to secure a ferry-boat known to be at Vinergue. The remainder of the troops followed, the intent being to pass the Arriege

French Official Correspon-dence, MSS.

Memoir by colonel Hughes, MSS.

river hastily at Cintegabelle, and so come down the right bank to attack Toulouse on the south while lord Wellington assailed St. Cyprien. This march was to have been made privily in the night, but the bridge, though ordered for the evening of the 30th, was not finished until five o'clock in the morning of the 31st. Soult thus got notice of the enterprise in time to observe from the heights of Old Toulouse the strength of the column, and to ascertain that the great body of the army still remained in front of St. Cyprien. The marshy nature of the country on the right of the Arriege was known to him, and the suburbs of St. Michel and St. Etienne being now in a state to resist a partial attack, the matter appeared a feint to draw off a part of his army from Toulouse while St. Cyprien was assaulted, or the Garonne passed below the city. In this persuasion he kept his infantry in hand, and sent only his cavalry up the right bank of the Arriege to observe the march of the allies; but he directed general Lafitte, who had collected some regular horsemen and the national guards of the department, to hang upon their skirts and pretend to be the van of Suchet's army. He was however somewhat disquieted, because the baggage, which to avoid encumbering the march had been sent up the Garonne to cross at Carbonne, being seen by his scouts, was reported to be a second column, increasing Hill's force to eighteen thousand men.

Official
Correspon-
dence,
MSS.

While in this uncertainty he heard of the measurement of the river made at Portet on the night of the 27th, and that many guns were still collected there, wherefore, being ignorant of the cause why the bridge was not thrown, he concluded there was a design to cross there also when Hill should descend

the Arriege. To meet this danger, he put four
divisions under Clauzel, with orders to fall upon
the head of the allies if they should attempt the
passage before Hill came down, resolving in the
contrary case to fight in the suburbs of Toulouse
and on the Mont-Rave, because the positions on the
right of the Arriege were all favourable to the
assailants. He was however soon relieved from
anxiety. General Hill effected indeed the passage
of the Arriege at Cintegabelle and sent his cavalry
towards Villefranche and Nailloux, but his artillery
were quite unable to move in the deep country
there, and as success and safety alike depended on
rapidity he returned during the night to Pinsaguel,
recrossed the Garonne, and taking up his pontoons
left only a flying bridge with a small guard of
infantry and cavalry on the right bank. His retreat
was followed by Lafitte's horsemen who picked up
a few stragglers and mules, but no other event occurred, and Soult remained well pleased that his
adversary had thus lost three or four important
days.

1814.
April.
Official
Corres-
pondence,
MSS.

The French general was now sure the next attempt
would be below Toulouse, yet he changed his design
of marching down the Garonne to fight between
that river and the Tarn rather than lose his communications with Montauban. Having completed
his works of defence for the city and the suburbs,
and fortified all the bridges over the canal, he concluded not to abandon Toulouse under any circumstances, and therefore set his whole army and all
the working population to entrench the Mont
Rave, between the canal and the Ers river, thinking
he might thus securely meet the shock of battle let
it come on which side it would. Meanwhile the

Garonne continued so full and rapid that lord Wellington was forced to remain inactive before St. Cyprien until the evening of the 3d; then the waters falling, the pontoons were carried in the night to Grenade, fifteen miles below Toulouse, where the bridge was at last thrown and thirty guns placed in battery on the left bank to protect it. The third fourth and sixth divisions of infantry and three brigades of cavalry, the whole under Beresford, immediately passed, and the cavalry being pushed out two leagues on the front and flanks captured a large herd of bullocks destined for the French army. But now the river again swelled so fast, that the light division and the Spaniards were unable to follow, the bridge got damaged and the pontoons were taken up.

This passage was made known to Soult immediately by his cavalry scouts, yet he knew not the exact force which had crossed, and as Morillo's Spaniards, whom he mistook for Freyre's, had taken the outposts in front of St. Cyprien he imagined Hill also had moved to Grenade, and that the greatest part of the allied army was over the Garonne. Wherefore merely observing Beresford with his cavalry he continued to strengthen his field of battle about Toulouse, his resolution to keep that city being confirmed by hearing on the 7th that the allied sovereigns had entered Paris.

On the 8th the waters subsided, the allies' bridge was again laid down, Freyre's Spaniards and the Portuguese artillery crossed, and lord Wellington taking the command in person advanced to the heights of Fenoulhiet within five miles of Toulouse. Marching up both banks of the Ers his columns were separated by that river, which was impassable without pontoons, and it was essential to secure as soon as possible one of the stone bridges. Hence when his left approached the heights of Kirie Eleison, on the great road of Alby, Vivian's horsemen drove Berton's cavalry up the right of the Ers towards the bridge of Bordes, and the eighteenth hussars descended towards that of Croix d'Orade. The latter was defended by Vial's dragoons, and after some skirmishing the eighteenth was suddenly menaced by a regiment in front of the bridge, the opposite bank of the river being lined with dismounted carbineers. The two parties stood facing each other, hesitating to begin, until the approach of some British infantry, when both sides sounded a charge at the same moment, but the English horses were so quick the French were in an instant jammed up on the bridge, their front ranks were sabred, and the mass breaking away to the rear went off in disorder, leaving many killed and wounded and above a hundred prisoners in the hands of the victors. They were pursued through the village of Croix d'Orade, but beyond it they rallied on the rest of their brigade and advanced again, the hussars then recrossed the bridge, which was now defended by the British infantry whose fire stopped the French cavalry. The communication between the allied columns was thus secured.

The credit of this brilliant action was given to Colonel Vivian in the despatch, incorrectly, for that officer was wounded by a carbine shot previous to the charge at the bridge : the attack was conceived and conducted entirely by major Hughes of the eighteenth.

Lord Wellington from the heights of Kirie Eleison, carefully examined the French general's position and resolved to attack on the 9th. Meanwhile to shorten his communications with general Hill he directed the pontoons to be removed from Grenade and relaid higher up at Seilh. The light division were to cross at the latter place at daybreak, but the bridge was not relaid until late in the day, and the English general extremely incensed at the failure was forced to defer his battle until the 10th.

Soult's combinations were now crowned with success. He had by means of his fortresses, his battles, the sudden change of his line of operations after Orthes, his rapid retreat from Tarbes, and his clear judgment in fixing upon Toulouse as his next point of resistance, reduced the strength of his adversary to an equality with his own. He had gained seventeen days for preparation, had brought the allies to deliver battle on ground naturally adapted for defence, and well fortified; where one-third of their force was separated by a great river from the rest, where they could derive no advantage from their numerous cavalry, and were overmatched in artillery notwithstanding their previous superiority in that arm.

His position covered three sides of Toulouse. Defending St. Cyprien on the west with his left, he guarded the canal on the north with his centre, and with his right held the Mont Rave on the east. His reserve under Travot manned the ramparts of Toulouse, and the urban guards while maintaining tranquillity aided to transport the artillery and ammunition to different posts. Hill was opposed to his left, but while the latter, well fortified at St. Cyprien, had short and direct communication with the centre by the great bridge of Toulouse, the former could only communicate with the main body under

Wellington by the pontoon bridge at Seilh, a circuit of ten or twelve miles.

The English general was advancing from the north, but his intent was still to assail the city on the south side, where it was weakest in defence. With this design he had caused the country on the left of the Ers to be carefully examined, in the view of making, under cover of that river, a flank march round the eastern front and thus gaining the open ground which he had formerly endeavoured to reach by passing at Portet and Pinsaguel. But again he was baffled by the deep country, which he could not master so as to pass the Ers by force, because all the bridges with the exception of that at Croix d'Orade were mined or destroyed by Soult, and the whole of the pontoons were on the Garonne. There was then no choice save to attack from the northern and eastern sides. The first, open and flat, and easily approached by the great roads of Montauban and Alby, was yet impregnable in defence, because the canal, the bridges over which were strongly defended by works, was under the fire of the ramparts of Toulouse, and for the most part within musquet-shot. Here then, as at St. Cyprien, it was a fortress and not a position which was opposed to him, and his field of battle was necessarily confined to the Mont Rave or eastern front.

This range of heights, naturally strong and rugged, and covered by the Ers river, which as we have seen was not be forded, presented two distinct platforms, that of Calvinet, and that of St. Sypiere on which the extreme right of the French was posted. Between them, where the ground dipped a little, two roads leading from Lavaur and Caraman were conducted to Toulouse, passing the canal behind the ridge at the suburbs of Guillemerie and St. Etienne.

The Calvinet platform was fortified on its extreme left with a species of horn-work, consisting of several open retrenchments and small works, supported by two large redoubts, one of which flanked the approaches to the canal on the north : a range of abbatis was also formed there by felling the trees on the Alby road. Continuing this line to the right, two other large forts, called the Calvinet and the Colombette redoubts, terminated the works on this platform.

On that of St. Sypiere there were also two redoubts, one on the extreme right called St. Sypiere, the other without a name nearer to the road of Caraman.

The whole range of heights occupied was about two miles long, and an army attacking in front would have to cross the Ers under fire, advance through ground, naturally steep and marshy, and now rendered almost impassable by means of artificial inundations, to the assault of the ridge and the works on the summit ; and if the assailants should even force between the two platforms, they would, while their flanks were battered by the redoubts above, come upon the works of Cambon and Saccarin. If these fell the suburbs of Guillemerie and St. Steven, the canal, and finally the ramparts of the town, would still have to be carried in succession. But it was not practicable to pass the Ers except by the bridge of Croix d'Orade which had been seized so happily on the 8th. Lord Wellington was therefore reduced to make a flank march under fire, between the Ers and the Mont Rave, and then to carry the latter with a view of crossing the

Manuscript
Notes by
the Duke
of Wellington.

canal above the suburb of Guillemerie, and establishing his army on the south side of Toulouse, where only the city could be assailed with any hope of success.

To impose this march upon him all Soult's dispositions had been directed. For this he had mined all the bridges on the Ers, save only that of Croix d'Orade, thus facilitating a movement between the Ers and the Mont Rave, while he impeded one beyond that river by sending half his cavalry over to dispute the passage of the numerous streams in the deep country on the right bank. His army was now disposed in the following order. General Reille defended the suburb of St. Cyprien with Taupin's and Maransin's divisions. Daricau's division lined the canal on the north from its junction with the Garonne to the road of Alby, defending with his left the bridge-head of Jumeaux, the convent of the Minimes with his centre, and the Matabiau bridge with his right. Harispe's division was established in the works on the Mont-Rave. His right at St. Sypiere looked towards the bridge of Bordes, his centre was at the Colombette redoubt, about which Vial's horsemen were also collected ; his left looked down the road of Alby towards the bridge of Croix d'Orade. On this side a detached eminence within cannon-shot, called the Hill of Pugade, was occupied by St. Pol's brigade, drawn from Villatte's division. The two remaining divisions of infantry Plan 10. were formed in columns at certain points behind the Mont Rave, and Travot's reserve continued to man the walls of Toulouse behind the canal. This line of battle presented an angle towards the Croix d'Orade, each side about two miles in length and the apex covered by the brigade on the Pugade.

Wellington having well observed the ground on the 8th and 9th, made the following disposition of attack for the 10th. General Hill was to menace St. Cyprien, augmenting or abating his efforts to draw the enemy's attention according to the progress of the battle on the right of the Garonne, which he could easily discern. The third and light divisions and Freyre's Spaniards, being already on the left of the Ers, were to advance against the northern front of Toulouse. The two first supported by Bock's German cavalry were to make demonstrations against the line of canal defended by Daricau. That is to say, Picton was to menace the bridge of Jumeaux and the convent of the Minimes, while Alten maintained the communication between him and Freyre who, reinforced with the Portuguese artillery, was to carry the hill of Pugade and then halt to cover Beresford's column of march. This last composed of the fourth and sixth division with three batteries was, after passing the bridge of Croix d'Orade, to move round the left of the Pugade and along the low ground between the French heights and the Ers, until the rear should pass the road of Lavaur, when the two divisions were to wheel into line and attack the platform of St. Sypiere. Freyre was then to assail that of Calvinet, and Ponsonby's dragoons following close were to connect that general's left with Beresford's column. Meanwhile lord Edward Somerset's hussars were to move up the left of the Ers, while Vivian's cavalry moved up the right of that river, each destined to observe Berton's cavalry, which, having possession of the bridges of Bordes and Montaudran higher up, could pass from the right bank to the left, and destroying the bridge fall upon the head of Beresford's troops while in march.

BATTLE OF TOULOUSE.

The 10th of April at two o'clock in the morning the light division passed the Garonne by the bridge at Seilh, and about six o'clock the whole army moved forwards in the order assigned for the different columns. Picton and Alten, on the right, drove the French advanced posts behind the works at the bridge over the canal. Freyre's columns, marching along the Alby road, were cannonaded by St. Pol with two guns until they had passed a small stream by the help of some temporary bridges, when the French general following his instructions retired to the horn-work on the Calvinet platform. The Spaniards were thus established on the Pugade, from whence the Portuguese guns under major Arentschild opened a heavy cannonade against Calvinet. Meanwhile Beresford, preceded by the hussars, marched from Croix d'Orade in three columns abreast. Passing behind the Pugade, through the village of Montblanc, he entered the marshy ground between the Ers river and the Mont Rave, but he left his artillery at Montblanc, fearing to engage it in that deep and difficult country under the fire of the enemy. Beyond the Ers on his left, Vivian's cavalry, now under colonel Arentschild, drove Berton's horsemen back with loss, and nearly seized the bridge of Bordes which the French general passed and destroyed with difficulty at the last moment. However the German hussars succeeded in gaining the bridge of Montaudran higher up, though it was barricaded, and defended by a detachment of cavalry sent there by Berton who remained himself in

Memoir by general Berton, MSS.

Memoir by colonel Hughes, MSS.

position near the bridge of Bordes, looking down the left of the Ers.

While these operations were in progress, general Freyre who had asked as a favour to lead the battle at Calvinet, whether from error or impatience assailed the horn-work on that platform about eleven o'clock and while Beresford was still in march. The Spaniards, nine thousand strong, moved in two lines and a reserve, and advanced with great resolution at first, throwing forwards their flanks so as to embrace the end of the Calvinet hill. The French musquetry and great guns thinned the ranks at every step, yet closing upon their centre they still ascended the hill, the formidable fire they were exposed to increasing in violence until their right wing, which was also raked from the bridge of Matabiau, unable to endure the torment wavered. The leading ranks rushing madly onwards jumped for shelter into a hollow road, twenty-five feet deep in parts, and covering this part of the French entrenchments; but the left wing and the second line run back in great disorder, the Cantabrian fusiliers under colonel Leon de Sicilia alone maintaining their ground under cover of a bank which protected them. Then the French came leaping out of their works with loud cries, and lining the edge of the hollow road poured an incessant stream of shot upon the helpless crowds entangled in the gulph below, while the battery from the bridge of Matabiau, constructed to rake this opening, sent its bullets from flank to flank hissing through the quivering mass of flesh and bones.

The Spanish generals rallying the troops who had fled, led them back again to the brink of the

fatal hollow, but the frightful carnage below and
the unmitigated fire in front filled them with horror.
Again they fled, and again the French bounding
from their trenches pursued, while several battalions sallying from the bridge of Matabiau and from
behind the Calvinet followed hard along the road of
Alby. The country was now covered with fugitives whose headlong flight could not be restrained,
and with pursuers whose numbers and vehemence
increased, until lord Wellington, who was at that
point, covered the panic-stricken troops with Ponsonby's cavalry, and the reserve artillery which
opened with great vigour. Meanwhile the Portuguese guns on the Pugade never ceased firing, and a
brigade of the light division, wheeling to its left,
menaced the flank of the victorious French who
immediately retired to their entrenchments on Calvinet: but more than fifteen hundred Spaniards
had been killed or wounded and their defeat was
not the only misfortune.

General Picton, regardless of his orders, which,
his temper on such occasions being known were especially given, had turned his false attack into a
real one against the bridge of Jumeaux, and the
enemy fighting from a work too high to be forced
without ladders and approachable only along an
open flat, repulsed him with a loss of nearly four
hundred men and officers: amongst the latter
colonel Forbes of the forty-fifth was killed, and
general Brisbane who commanded the brigade was
wounded. Thus from the hill of Pugade to the
Garonne the French had completely vindicated
their position, the allies had suffered enormously,
and beyond the Garonne, although general Hill
had now forced the first line of entrenchments co-

vering St. Cyprien and was menacing the second
line, the latter being much more contracted and
very strongly fortified could not be stormed.
The musquetry battle therefore subsided for a time,
but a prodigious cannonade was kept up along the
whole of the French line, and on the allies' side
from St. Cyprien to Montblanc, where the artillery
left by Beresford, acting in conjunction with the
Portuguese guns on the Pugade, poured its shot incessantly against the works on the Calvinet platform : injudiciously it has been said because the
ammunition thus used for a secondary object was
afterwards wanted when a vital advantage might
have been gained.

It was now evident that the victory must be won
or lost by Beresford, and yet from Picton's error
lord Wellington had no reserves to enforce the decision ; for the light division and the heavy cavalry only remained in hand, and these troops were
necessarily retained to cover the rallying of the
Spaniards, and to protect the artillery employed to
keep the enemy in check. The crisis therefore
approached with all happy promise to the French
general. The repulse of Picton, the utter dispersion of the Spaniards, and the strength of the second line of entrenchments at St. Cyprien, enabled
him to draw, first Taupin's whole division, and then
one of Maransin's brigades from that quarter, to
reinforce his battle on the Mont Rave. Thus
three divisions and his cavalry, that is to say nearly
fifteen thousand combatants, were disposable for an
offensive movement without in any manner weakening the defence of his works on Mont Rave or on
the canal. With this mass he might have fallen upon
Beresford, whose force, originally less than thirteen

thousand bayonets, was cruelly reduced as it made
slow and difficult way for two miles through a deep
marshy country crossed and tangled with water-
courses.   For sometimes moving in mass, sometimes
filing under the French musquetry, and always
under the fire of their artillery from the Mont Rave,
without a gun to reply, the length of the column
had augmented so much at every step from the
difficulty of the way that frequent halts were necessary to close up the ranks.

The flat miry ground between the river and the
heights became narrower and deeper as the troops
advanced, Berton's cavalry was ahead, an impassable river was on the left, and three French
divisions supported by artillery and horsemen over-
shadowed the right flank!   Fortune came to their
aid.   Soult always eyeing their march, had, when
the Spaniards were defeated, carried Taupin's division to the platform of St. Sypiere, and supporting
it with a brigade of D'Armagnac's division disposed the whole about the redoubts.   From thence
after a short hortative to act vigorously he ordered
Taupin to fall on with the utmost fury, at the
same time directing a regiment of Vial's cavalry to
descend the heights by the Lavaur road and intercept the line of retreat, while Berton's horsemen
assailed the other flank from the side of the bridge
of Bordes.   But this was not half of the force
which the French general might have employed.
Taupin's artillery, retarded in its march, was still in
the streets of Toulouse, and that general instead
of attacking at once took ground to his right,
waiting until Beresford having completed his flank
march had wheeled into lines at the foot of the
heights.

Taupin's infantry, unskilfully arranged for action it is said, at last poured down the hill, but
some rockets discharged in good time ravaged the
ranks and with their noise and terrible appearance,
unknown before, dismayed the French soldiers;
then the British skirmishers running forwards plied
them with a biting fire, and Lambert's brigade of
the sixth division, aided by Anson's brigade and
some provisional battalions of the fourth division,
for it is an error to say the sixth division alone repulsed this attack, Lambert's brigade I say, rushed
forwards with a terrible shout, and the French turning fled back to the upper ground. Vial's horsemen trotting down the Lavaur road now charged
on the right flank, but the second and third lines of
the sixth division being thrown into squares repulsed them, and on the other flank general Cole
had been so sudden in his advance up the heights,
that Berton's cavalry had no opportunity to charge.
Lambert, following hard upon the beaten infantry
in his front, killed Taupin, wounded a general of
brigade, and without a check won the summit of
the platform, his skirmishers even descended in pursuit on the reverse slope, and meanwhile, on his
left, general Cole meeting with less resistance had
still more rapidly gained the height at that side :
so complete was the rout that the two redoubts
were abandoned from panic, and the French with the
utmost disorder sought shelter in the works of Sacarin and Cambon.

Soult astonished at this weakness in troops from
whom he had expected so much, and who had but
just before given him assurances of their resolution
and confidence, was in fear that Beresford pushing
his success would seize the bridge of the Demoi-

selles on the canal. Wherefore, covering the flight
as he could with the remainder of Vial's cavalry, he
hastily led D'Armagnac's reserve brigade to the
works of Sacarin, checked the foremost British skirmishers and rallied the fugitives ; Taupin's guns
arrived from the town at the same moment, and the
mischief being stayed a part of Travot's reserve
immediately moved to defend the bridge of the
Demoiselles. A fresh order of battle was thus organized, but the indomitable courage of the British
soldiers overcoming all obstacles and all opposition,
had decided the first great crisis of the fight.

Lambert's brigade immediately wheeled to its
right across the platform on the line of the Lavaur
road, menacing the flank of the French on the
Calvinet platform, while Pack's Scotch brigade
and Douglas's Portuguese, composing the second
and third lines of the sixth division, were disposed
on the right with a view to march against the Colombette redoubts on the original front of the enemy.
And now also the eighteenth and German hussars,
having forced the bridge of Montaudran on the
Ers river, came round the south end of the Mont
Rave, where in conjunction with the skirmishers of
the fourth division they menaced the bridge of the
Demoiselles, from whence and from the works of
Cambon and Sacarin the enemy's guns played
incessantly.

The aspect and form of the battle were thus entirely changed. The French thrown entirely on the
defensive occupied three sides of a square. Their
right, extending from the works of Sacarin to the redoubts of Calvinet and Colombette, was closely menaced by Lambert, who was solidly posted on the platform of St. Sypiere while the redoubts themselves

were menaced by Pack and Douglas. The French left thrown back to the bridge-head of Matabiau awaited the renewed attack of the Spaniards, and the whole position was very strong, not exceeding a thousand yards on each side with the angles all defended by formidable works. The canal and city of Toulouse, its walls and entrenched suburbs, offered a sure refuge in case of disaster, while the Matabiau on one side, Sacarin and Cambon on the other, insured the power of retreat.

In this contracted space were concentrated Vial's cavalry, the whole of Villatte's division, one brigade of Maransin's, another of D'Armagnac's, and with the exception of the regiment driven from the St. Sypiere redoubt the whole of Harispe's division. On the allies' side therefore defeat had been staved off, but victory was still to be contended for, and with apparently inadequate means; for Picton being successfully opposed by Darricau was so far paralyzed, the Spaniards rallying slowly were not to be depended upon for another attack, and there remained only the heavy cavalry and the light division, which lord Wellington could not venture to thrust into the action under pain of being left without any reserve in the event of a repulse. The final stroke therefore was still to be made on the left, and with a very small force, seeing that Lambert's brigade and the fourth division were necessarily employed to keep in check the French troops at the bridge of the Demoiselles, Cambon and Sacarin. This heavy mass, comprising one brigade of Travot's reserve, the half of D'Armagnac's division and all of Taupin's, together with the regiment belonging to Harispe which had abandoned the forts of St. Sypiere, was commanded by general Clauzel, who disposed the greater part in advance of the entrenchments as if to retake the offensive.

Such was the state of affairs about half-past two o'clock, when Beresford renewed the action with Pack's Scotch brigade, and the Portuguese of the sixth division under colonel Douglas. These troops, ensconced in the hollow Lavaur road on Lambert's right, had been hitherto well protected from the fire of the French works, but now scrambling up the steep banks of that road, they wheeled to their left by wings of regiments as they could get out, and ascending the heights by the slope facing the Ers, under a wasting fire of cannon and musquetry carried all the French breast-works, and the Colombette, and Calvinet redoubts. It was a surprising action when the loose disorderly nature of the attack imposed by the difficulty of the ground is considered ; but the French although they yielded at first to the thronging rush of the British troops soon rallied and came back with a reflux. Their cannonade was incessant, their reserves strong, and the struggle became terrible. For Harispe, who commanded in person at this part, and under whom the French seemed always to fight with redoubled vigour, brought up fresh men, and surrounding the two redoubts with a surging multitude absolutely broke into the Colombette, killed or wounded four-fifths of the forty-second, and drove the rest out. The British troops were however supported by the seventy-first and ninety-first, and the whole clinging to the brow of the hill fought with a wonderful courage and firmness, until so many men had fallen that their order of battle was reduced to a thin line of skirmishers. Some of the British cavalry then rode up from the low ground and attempted a

charge, but they were stopped by a deep hollow
road, of which there were many, and some of the
foremost troopers tumbling headlong in perished.
Meanwhile the combat about the redoubts continued fiercely, the French from their numbers had
certainly the advantage, but they never retook the
Calvinet fort, nor could they force their opponents
down from the brow of the hill.   At last when the
whole of the sixth division had rallied and again
assailed them, flank and front, when their generals
Harispe and Baurot had fallen dangerously wounded
and the Colombette was retaken by the seventy-
ninth, the battle turned, and the French finally
abandoned the platform, falling back partly by their
right to Sacarin, partly by their left towards the
bridge of Matabiau.

It was now about four o'clock.   The Spaniards
during this contest had once more partially attacked,
but they were again put to flight, and the French
thus remained masters of their entrenchments in
that quarter; for the sixth division had been very
hardly handled, and Beresford halted to reform
his order of battle and receive his artillery : it
came to him indeed about this time, yet with great
difficulty and with little ammunition in consequence
of the heavy cannonade it had previously furnished
from Montblanc.   However Soult seeing that the
Spaniards, supported by the light division, had
rallied a fourth time, that Picton again menaced the
bridge of Jumeaux and the Minime convent, while
Beresford, master of three-fourths of Mont Rave,
was now advancing along the summit, deemed farther resistance useless and relinquished the northern
end of the Calvinet platform also.   About five o'clock
he withdrew his whole army behind the canal,

still however holding the advanced works of Sacarin and Cambon. Lord Wellington then established
the Spaniards in the abandoned works and so
became master of the Mont Rave in all its extent.
Thus terminated the battle of Toulouse. The French
had five generals, and perhaps three thousand men
killed or wounded and they lost one piece of
artillery. The allies lost four generals and four
thousand six hundred and fifty-nine men and
officers, of which two thousand were Spaniards.
A lamentable spilling of blood, and a useless, for
before this period Napoleon had abdicated the
throne of France and a provisional government was
constituted at Paris.

During the night the French general, defeated
but undismayed, replaced the ammunition expended
in the action, re-organized and augmented his field
artillery from the arsenal of Toulouse, and made
dispositions for fighting the next morning behind
the canal. Yet looking to the final necessity of a
retreat he wrote to Suchet to inform him of the
result of the contest and proposed a combined plan
of operations illustrative of the firmness and perti-
nacity of his temper. " March," said he, " with
the whole of your forces by Quillan upon Carcassonne, I will meet you there with my army, we can
then retake the initiatory movement, transfer the
seat of war to the Upper Garonne, and holding on
by the mountains oblige the enemy to recall his
troops from Bordeaux, which will enable Decaen to
recover that city and make a diversion in our
favour."

On the morning of the 11th he was again ready
to fight, but the English general was not. The
French position, within musquet-shot of the walls

of Toulouse, was still inexpugnable on the northern and eastern fronts. The possession of Mont Rave was only a preliminary step to the passage of the canal at the bridge of the Demoiselles and other points above the works of Sacarin and Cambon, with the view of throwing the army as originally designed on to the south side of the town. But this was a great affair requiring fresh dispositions, and a fresh provision of ammunition only to be obtained from the parc on the other side of the Garonne. Hence to accelerate the preparations, to ascertain the state of general Hill's position, and to give that general farther instructions, lord Wellington repaired on the 11th to St. Cyprien; but though he had shortened his communications by removing the pontoon bridge from Grenade to Seilh, the day was spent before the ammunition arrived and the final arrangements for the passage of the canal could be completed. The attack was therefore deferred until daylight on the 12th.

Meanwhile all the light cavalry were sent up the canal, to interrupt the communications with Suchet and menace Soult's retreat by the road leading to Carcassonne. The appearance of these horsemen on the heights of St. Martyn, above Baziege, together with the preparations in his front, taught Soult that he could no longer delay if he would not be shut up in Toulouse. Wherefore, having terminated all his arrangements, he left eight pieces of heavy artillery, two generals, the gallant Harispe being one, and sixteen hundred men whose wounds were severe, to the humanity of the conquerors; then filing out of the city with surprising order and ability, he made a forced march of twenty-two miles, cut the bridges over the canal and the Upper

Ers, and the 12th established his army at Ville-franche. On the same day general Hill's troops were pushed close to Baziege in pursuit, and the light cavalry, acting on the side of Montlaur, beat the French with the loss of twenty-five men, and cut off a like number of gensd'armes on the side of Revel.

Lord Wellington now entered Toulouse in triumph, the white flag was displayed, and, as at Bordeaux, a great crowd of persons adopted the Bourbon colours, but the mayor, faithful to his sovereign, had retired with the French army. The British general, true to his honest line of policy, did not fail to warn the Bourbonists that their revolutionary movement must be at their own risk, but in the afternoon two officers, the English colonel Cooke, and the French colonel St. Simon, arrived from Paris. Charged to make known to the armies the abdication of Napoleon they had been detained near Blois by the officiousness of the police attending the court of the empress Louisa, and the blood of eight thousand brave men had overflowed the Mont Rave in consequence. Nor did their arrival immediately put a stop to the war. When St. Simon in pursuance of his mission reached Soult's quarters on the 13th, that marshal, not without just cause, demurred to his authority, and proposed to suspend hostilities until authentic information could be obtained from the ministers of the emperor: then sending all his incumbrances by the canal to Carcassonne, he took a position of observation at Castelnaudary and awaited the progress of events. Lord Wellington refused to accede to his proposal, and as general Loverdo, commanding at Montauban, acknowledged the authority of the provincial

government and readily concluded an armistice, he judged that Soult designed to make a civil
war and therefore marched against him.   The 17th
the outposts were on the point of engaging when
the duke of Dalmatia, who had now received official
information from the chief of the emperor's staff,
notified his adhesion to the new state of affairs
in France : and with this honourable distinction
that he had faithfully sustained the cause of his
great monarch until the very last moment.

A convention which included Suchet's army was
immediately agreed upon, but that marshal had
previously adopted the white colours of his own
motion, and lord Wellington instantly transmitted
the intelligence to general Clinton in Catalonia and
to the troops at Bayonne.   Too late it came for both
and useless battles were fought.   That at Barcelona
has been already described, but at Bayonne misfortune and suffering had fallen upon one of the
brightest soldiers of the British army.

SALLY FROM BAYONNE.

During the progress of the main army in the interior Sir John Hope conducted the investment of
Bayonne, with all the zeal the intelligence and un-
remitting vigilance and activity which the difficult
nature of the operation required.   He had gathered
great stores of gabions and fascines and platforms,
and was ready to attack the citadel when rumours
of the events at Paris reached him, yet indirectly
and without any official character to warrant a formal
communication to the garrison without lord Wellington's authority.   These rumours were however

made known at the outposts. and perhaps lulled the vigilance of the besiegers, but to such irregular communications which might be intended to deceive the governor naturally paid little attention.

The piquets and fortified posts at St. Etienne were at this time furnished by a brigade of the fifth division, but from thence to the extreme right the guards had charge of the line, and they had also one company in St. Etienne itself. General Hinuber's German brigade was encamped as a support to the left, the remainder of the first division was encamped in the rear, towards Boucaut. In this state, about one o'clock in the morning of the 14th, a deserter, coming over to general Hay who commanded the outposts that night, gave an exact account of the projected sally. The general not able to speak French sent him to general Hinuber, who immediately interpreting the man's story to general Hay, assembled his own troops under arms, and transmitted the intelligence to sir John Hope. It would appear that Hay, perhaps disbelieving the man's story, took no additional precautions, and it is probable that neither the German brigade nor the reserves of the guards would have been put under arms but for the activity of general Hinuber. However at three o'clock the French, commencing with a false attack on the left of the Adour as a blind, poured suddenly out of the citadel to the number of three thousand combatants. They surprised the piquets, and with loud shouts breaking through the chain of posts at various points, carried with one rush the church, and the whole of the village of St. Etienne with exception of a fortified house which was defended by captain Forster of the thirty-eighth regiment. Masters of every other part and overthrowing

Beamish's
History of
the German
Legion.

all who stood before them they drove the picquets
and supports in heaps along the Peyrehorade road,
killed general Hay, took colonel Townsend of the
guards prisoner, divided the wings of the investing
troops, and passing in rear of the right threw the
whole line into confusion. Then it was that Hinuber, having his Germans well in hand, moved up
on the side of St. Etienne, rallied some of the fifth
division, and being joined by a battalion of general
Bradford's Portuguese from the side of St. Esprit
bravely gave the counter-stroke to the enemy and
regained the village and church.

The combat on the right was at first even more
disastrous than in the centre, neither the piquets
nor the reserves were able to sustain the fury of the
assault and the battle was most confused and terrible ; for on both sides the troops, broken into small
bodies by the enclosures and unable to recover
their order, came dashing together in the darkness,
fighting often with the bayonet, and sometimes
friends encountered sometimes foes : all was tumult
and horror. The guns of the citadel vaguely guided
by the flashes of the musquetry sent their shot and
shells booming at random through the lines of
fight, and the gun-boats dropping down the river
opened their fire upon the flank of the supporting
columns, which being put in motion by sir John
Hope on the first alarm were now coming up from
the side of Boucaut. Thus nearly one hundred
pieces of artillery were in full play at once, and the
shells having set fire to the fascine depôts and to
several houses, the flames cast a horrid glare over
the striving masses.

Amidst this confusion sir John Hope suddenly
disappeared, none knew how or wherefore at the

time, but it afterwards appeared, that having
brought up the reserves on the right, to stem the
torrent in that quarter, he pushed for St. Etienne by
a hollow road which led close behind the line of
picquets; the French had however lined both banks,
and when he endeavoured to return a shot struck
him in the arm, while his horse, a large one as was
necessary to sustain the gigantic warrior, received
eight bullets and fell upon his leg. His followers
had by this time escaped from the defile, but two of
them, captain Herries, and Mr. Moore a nephew of
sir John Moore, seeing his helpless state turned
back and alighting endeavoured amidst the heavy
fire of the enemy to draw him from beneath the
horse. While thus engaged they were both struck
down with dangerous wounds, the French carried them all off, and sir John Hope was again
severely hurt in the foot by an English bullet before
they gained the citadel.

The day was now beginning to break and the
allies were enabled to act with more unity and
effect. The Germans were in possession of St.
Etienne, and the reserve brigades of the guards,
being properly disposed, by general Howard who
had succeeded to the command, suddenly raised a
loud shout, and running in upon the French drove
them back into the works with such slaughter
that their own writers admit a loss of one general
and more than nine hundred men. But on the British
side general Stopford was wounded, and the whole
loss was eight hundred and thirty men and officers.
Of these more than two hundred were taken, besides the commander-in-chief; and it is generally acknowledged that captain Forster's firm defence of the
fortified house first, and next the readiness and

gallantry with which general Hinuber and his Germans retook St. Etienne, saved the allies from a very terrible disaster.

A few days after this piteous event the convention made with Soult became known and hostilities ceased.

All the French troops in the south were now reorganized in one body under the command of Suchet, but they were so little inclined to acquiesce in the revolution, that prince Polignac, acting for the duke of Angoulême, applied to the British commissary-general Kennedy for a sum of money to quiet them.

The Portuguese army returned to Portugal. The Spanish army to Spain, the generals being it is said inclined at first to declare for the Cortez against the king, but they were diverted from their purpose by the influence and authority of lord Wellington.

The British infantry embarked at Bordeaux, some for America, some for England, and the cavalry marching through France took shipping at Boulogne.

Thus the war terminated, and with it all remembrance of the veteran's services.

CHAPTER VI.

GENERAL OBSERVATIONS.

Marshal Soult and General Thouvenot have
been accused of fighting with a full knowledge of
Napoleon's abdication. This charge circulated originally by the Bourbon party is utterly unfounded.
The extent of the information conveyed to Thouvenot through the advanced posts has been already
noticed ; it was not sufficiently authentic to induce
sir John Hope to make a formal communication,
and the governor could only treat it as an idle story
to insult or to deceive him, and baffle his defence
by retarding his counter-operations while the works
for the siege were advancing. For how unlikely,
nay impossible, must it not have appeared, that the
emperor Napoleon, whose victories at Mont-Mirail
and Champaubert were known before the close investment of Bayonne, should have been deprived
of his crown in the space of a few weeks, and the
stupendous event be only hinted at the outposts
without any relaxation in the preparations for the
siege.

As false and unsubstantial is the charge against
Soult.

The acute remark of an English military writer, Memoirs of
that if the duke of Dalmatia had known of the captain
Kincaid.
peace before he fought, he would certainly have announced it after the battle, were it only to maintain

himself in that city and claim a victory, is unanswerable : but there are direct proofs of the falsehood of the accusation.   How was the intelligence to reach him ?   It was not until the 7th that the provisional government wrote to him from Paris, and the bearer could not have reached Toulouse under three days even by the most direct way, which was through Montauban.   Now the allies were in possession of that road on the 4th, and on the 9th the French army was actually invested.   The intelligence from Paris must therefore have reached the allies first, as in fact it did, and it was not Soult it was lord Wellington who commenced the battle.   The charge would therefore bear more against the English general, who would yet have been the most insane as well as the wickedest of men to have risked his army and his fame in a battle where so many obstacles seemed to deny success.   He also was the person of all others called upon, by honour, gratitude, justice and patriotism, to avenge the useless slaughter of his soldiers, to proclaim the infamy and seek the punishment of his inhuman adversary.

Did he ever by word or deed countenance the calumny ?

Lord Aberdeen, after the passing of the English reform bill, repeated the accusation in the house of lords and reviled the minister for being on amicable political terms with a man capable of such a crime. Lord Wellington rose on the instant and emphatically declared that marshal Soult did not know, and that it was impossible he could know of the emperor's abdication when he fought the battle.   The detestable distinction of sporting with men's lives by wholesale attaches to no general on the records of history save the Orange William, the murderer of Glencoe.

And though marshal Soult had known of the emperor's abdication he could not for that have been
justly placed beside that cold-blooded prince, who
fought at St. Denis with the peace of Nimeguen in
his pocket, because *" he would not deny himself a safe
lesson in his trade."*

The French marshal was at the head of a brave
army and it was impossible to know whether Napoleon had abdicated voluntarily or been constrained.
The authority of such men as Talleyrand, Fouché,
and other intriguers, forming a provisional government, self-instituted and under the protection of
foreign bayonets, demanded no respect from Soult.
He had even the right of denying the emperor's
legal power to abdicate. He had the right, if he
thought himself strong enough, to declare, that he
would not suffer the throne to become the plaything
of foreign invaders, and that he would rescue France
even though Napoleon yielded the crown. In fine
it was a question of patriotism and of calculation,
a national question which the general of an army
had a right to decide for himself, having reference
always to the real will and desire of the people at
large.

It was in this light that Soult viewed the matter,
even after the battle and when he had seen colonel
St. Simon.

Writing to Talleyrand on the 22d, he says, " The Official
Correspon-
circumstances which preceded my act of adhesion dence,
MSS.
are so extraordinary as to create astonishment. The
7th the provisional government informed me of the
events which had happened since the 1st of April.
The 6th and 7th, count Dupont wrote to me on the
same subject. On the 8th the duke of Feltre, in his
quality of war minister, gave me notice, that having

left the military cipher at Paris he would immediately forward to me another.   The 9th the prince
Berthier vice-constable and major-general, wrote to
me from Fontainbleau, transmitting the copy of a
convention and armistice which had been arranged
at Paris with the allied powers; he demanded at the
same time a state of the force and condition of my
army; but neither the prince nor the duke of Feltre
mentioned events, we had then only knowledge of a
proclamation of the empress, dated the 3rd, *which
forbade us to recognize any thing coming from Paris.*

"The 10th I was attacked near Toulouse by the
whole allied army under the orders of lord Wellington.   This vigorous action, where the French army
the weakest by half showed all its worth, cost the
allies from eight to ten thousand men : lord Wellington might perhaps have dispensed with it.

" The 12th I received through the English the first
hint of the events at Paris.   I proposed an armistice,
it was refused, I renewed the demand it was again
refused.   At last I sent count Gazan to Toulouse,
and my reiterated proposal for a suspension of arms
was accepted and signed the 18th, the armies being
then in presence of each other.   The 19th I ratified
this convention and gave my adhesion to the re-es-
tablishment of Louis XVIII.   And upon this subject I ought to declare that I sought to obtain a suspension of arms before I manifested my sentiments
in order that my will and that of the army should be
free.   *That neither France nor posterity should have
power to say it was torn from us by force of arms.   To
follow only the will of the nation was a homage I
owed to my country.*"

The reader will observe in the above letter certain
assertions, relative to the numbers of the contending

armies and the loss of the allies, which are at variance
with the statements in this History; and this loose
but common mode of assuming the state of an adverse force has been the ground-work for great exaggeration by some French writers, who strangely
enough claim a victory for the French army although
the French general himself made no such claim at
the time, and so far as appears has not done so
since.

*Victories are determined by deeds and their conse-
quences.* By this test we shall know who won the
battle of Toulouse.

Now all persons, French and English, who have
treated the subject, including the generals on both
sides, are agreed, that Soult fortified Toulouse the
canal and the Mont Rave as positions of battle;
that he was attacked, that Taupin's division was
beaten, that the Mont Rave with all its redoubts
and entrenchments fell into the allies' power.
Finally that the French army abandoned Toulouse,
leaving there three wounded generals, sixteen hundred men, several guns and a quantity of stores at
the discretion of their adversaries: and this without
any fresh forces having joined the allies, or any remarkable event affecting the operations happening
elsewhere.

Was Toulouse worth preserving? Was the abandonment of it forced or voluntary? Let the French
general speak! " I have entrenched the suburb of Soult to
Suchet,
St. Cyprien which forms a good bridge-head. The 29th
March.
enemy will not I think attack me there unless he
desires to lose a part of his army. Two nights ago
he made a demonstration of passing the Garonne
two leagues above the city, but he will probably try
to pass it below, in which case I will attack him

whatever his force may be, because it is of the utmost importance to me not to be cut off from Montauban where I have made a bridge-head."—" I
think the enemy will not move on your side *unless I
move that way first, and I am determined to avoid
that as long as I can.*"—" If I could remain a month
on the Garonne I should be able to put six or eight
thousand conscripts into the ranks who now em-
barass me, and who want arms which I expect with
great impatience from Perpignan."—" I am resolved
to deliver battle near Toulouse whatever may be the

superiority of the enemy.   In this view I have fortified a *position*, which, *supported by the town and the
canal*, furnishes me with a retrenched camp susceptible of defence."—" I have received the unhappy
news of the enemy's entrance into Paris.   This misfortune strengthens my determination to defend
Toulouse whatever may happen.   The preservation
of the place which contains establishments of all
kinds is of the utmost importance to us, but if unhappily I am forced to quit it, my movements will
naturally bring me nearer to you.   In that case you
cannot sustain yourself at Perpignan because the
enemy will inevitably follow me."—" The enemy
appears astonished at the determination I have taken
to defend Toulouse, four days ago he passed the
Garonne and has done nothing since, perhaps the
bad weather is the cause."

From these extracts it is clear that Soult resolved
if possible not to fall back upon Suchet, and was
determined even to fight for the preservation of his
communications with Montauban; yet he finally
resigned this important object for the more important one of defending Toulouse.   And so intent
upon its preservation was he, that having on the

25th of March ordered all the stores and artillery
not of immediate utility, to be sent away, he on the
2d of April forbade further progress in that work
and even had those things already removed brought
back. Moreover he very clearly marks that to abandon the city and retreat towards Suchet will be the
signs and consequences of defeat.

These points being fixed, we find him on the evening of the 10th writing to the same general thus.

" The battle which I announced to you took place
to-day, the enemy has been horribly maltreated, but
he succeeded in *establishing himself upon a position
which I occupied to the right of Toulouse.* The general of division Taupin has been killed, general Harispe has lost his foot by a cannon-ball, and three
generals of brigade are wounded. I am prepared
to recommence to-morrow if the enemy attacks, but
*I do not believe I can stay in Toulouse, it might even
happen that I shall be forced to open a passage to get
out.*"

On the 11th of April he writes again:

" As I told you in my letter of yesterday I am in
the necessity of retiring from Toulouse, and I fear
being obliged to fight my way at Baziege where the
enemy is directing a column to cut my communications. To-morrow I will take a position at Ville-
franche, because I have good hope that this obstacle
will not prevent my passing."

To the minister of war he also writes on the
10th.

" To-day I rest in position. If the enemy attacks
me I will defend myself. I have great need to re-
plenish my means before I put the army in march,
yet I believe that in the coming night I shall be
forced to abandon Toulouse, and it is probable I

shall direct my movements so as to rally upon the troops of the duke of Albufera."

Soult lays no claim here to victory. He admits that all the events previously indicated by him as the consequences of defeat were fulfilled to the letter. That is to say, the loss of the position of battle, the consequent evacuation of the city, and the march to join Suchet. On the other hand lord Wellington clearly obtained all that he sought. He desired to pass the Garonne and he did pass it; he desired to win the position and works of Mont Rave and he did win them; he desired to enter Toulouse and he did enter it as a conqueror at the head of his troops.

Amongst the French writers who without denying these facts lay claim to a victory Choumara is most deserving of notice. This gentleman, known as an able engineer, with a praise-worthy desire to render justice to the great capacity of marshal Soult, shews very clearly that his genius would have shone in this campaign with far greater lustre if marshal Suchet had adopted his plans and supported him in a cordial manner. But Mr. Choumara heated by his subject completes the picture by a crowning victory at Toulouse which the marshal himself appears not to recognize. The work is a very valuable historical document with respect to the disputes between Soult and Suchet, but with respect to the battle of Toulouse it contains grave errors as to facts, and the inferences are untenable though the premises were admitted.

The substance of Mr. Choumara's argument is, that the position of Toulouse was of the nature of a fortress. That the canal was the real position of battle, the Mont Rave an outwork, the loss of

which weighed little in the balance, because the
French army was victorious at Calvinet against the
Spaniards, at the convent of the Minimes against
the light division, at the bridge of Jumeaux against
Picton, at St. Cyprien against General Hill. Finally that the French general certainly won the
victory because he offered battle the next day and
did not retreat from Toulouse until the following
night.

Now admitting that all these facts were established, the fortress was still taken.

But the facts are surprisingly incorrect. For
first marshal Soult himself tells Suchet that the
Mont Rave was his *position of battle*, and that the
town and the canal *supported it*. Nothing could
be more accurate than this description. For when
he lost the Mont Rave, the town and the canal
enabled him to rally his army and take measures
for a retreat. But the loss of the Mont Rave rendered the canal untenable, why else was Toulouse
abandoned? That the line of the canal was a
more formidable one to attack in front than the
Mont Rave is true, yet that did not constitute it
a position; it was not necessary to attack it, except
partially at Sacarin and Cambon and the bridge
of the Demoiselles; those points once forced the
canal would, with the aid of the Mont Rave, have
helped to keep the French in Toulouse as it had
before helped to keep the allies out. Lord Wellington once established on the south side of the
city and holding the Pech David could have removed the bridge from Seilh to Portet, above
Toulouse, thus shortening and securing his communication with Hill; the French army must then
have surrendered, or broken out, no easy matter in

such a difficult and strangled country.   The Mont
Rave was therefore not only the position of battle,
it was also the key of the position behind the canal,
and Mr. de Choumara is placed in this dilemma.
He must admit the allies won the fight, or confess
the main position was so badly chosen that a slight
reverse at an outwork was sufficient to make the
French army abandon it at every other point.

But were the French victorious at every other
point?   Against the Spaniards they were, and
Picton also was repulsed.   The order of movements for the battle proves indeed that this general's attack was intended to be a false one ; he dis-
obeyed his orders however, and one of his brigades
was repulsed ; but to check one brigade with a loss
of three or four hundred men, is a small matter
in a battle where more than eighty thousand combatants were engaged.

The light division made a demonstration against
the convent of the Minimes and nothing more.
Its loss on the whole day was only fifty-six men
and officers, and no French veteran of the Peninsula but would laugh at the notion that a real
attack by that matchless division could be so
stopped.

It is said the exterior line of entrenchments at
St. Cyprien was occupied with a view to offensive
movements, and to prevent the allies from establishing batteries to rake the line of the canal from
that side of the Garonne ; but whatever may have
been the object, General Hill got possession of it,
and was so far victorious.   He was ordered not to
assail the second line seriously and he did not, for
his whole loss scarcely exceeded eighty men and
officers.

From these undeniable facts, it is clear that the French gained an advantage against Picton, and a marked success against the Spaniards; but Beresford's attack was so decisive as to counterbalance these failures and even to put the defeated Spaniards in possession of the height they had originally contended for in vain.

Mr. Choumara attributes Beresford's success to Taupin's errors and to a vast superiority of numbers on the side of the allies. " Fifty-three thousand infantry, more than eight thousand cavalry, and a reserve of eighteen thousand men of all arms, opposed to twenty-five thousand French infantry, two thousand five hundred cavalry, and a reserve of seven thousand conscripts three thousand of which were unarmed." Such is the enormous disproportion assumed on the authority of general Vaudoncourt.

Now the errors of Taupin may have been great, and his countrymen are the best judges of his demerit; but the numbers here assumed are most inaccurate. The imperial muster-rolls are not of a later date than December 1813, yet an official table of the organization of Soult's army, published by the French military historian Kock, gives thirty-six thousand six hundred and thirty-five combatants on the 10th of March. Of these, in round numbers, twenty-eight thousand six hundred were infantry, two thousand seven hundred cavalry, and five thousand seven hundred were artillery-men, engineers, miners, sappers, gensd'armes, and military workmen. Nothing is said of the reserve division of conscripts commanded by general Travot, but general Vaudoncourt's table of the same army on the 1st of April, adopted by Choumara, supplies the de-

Kock's
Campaign
of 1814.

ficiency. The conscripts are there set down seven
thousand two hundred and sixty-seven, and this
cipher being added to Kock's, gives a total of
forty-three thousand nine hundred fighting men.
The loss in combats and marches from the 10th of
March to the 1st of April must be deducted, but
on the other hand we find Soult informing the
minister of war, on the 7th of March, that three
thousand soldiers dispersed by the battle of Orthes were still wandering behind the army: the
greatest part must have joined before the battle of
Toulouse. There was also the regular garrison of
that city, composed of the depôts of several regiments and the urban guards, all under Travot.
Thus little less than fifty thousand men were at
Soult's disposal.

Let twelve thousand be deducted for, 1°. the
urban guard which was only employed to maintain
the police of the town, 2°. the unarmed conscripts,
3°. the military workmen not brought into action,
4°. the detachments employed on the flanks to communicate with La Fitte in the Arriege, and to reinforce general Loverdo at Montauban. There will
remain thirty-eight thousand fighting men of all
arms. And with a very powerful artillery; for we
find Soult after the action, directing seven field-
batteries of eight pieces each to attend the army;
and the French writers mention, besides this field-
train, 1°. fifteen pieces which were transferred
during the battle from the exterior line of St. Cyprien to the northern and eastern fronts. 2°. Four
twenty-four pounders and several sixteen-pounders
mounted on the walls of the city. 3°. The arma-
ments of the bridge-heads, the works on Calvinet
and those at Sàccarin and Cambon. Wherefore

not less than eighty, or perhaps ninety, pieces of French artillery were engaged.

An approximation to the strength of the French army being thus made it remains to show the number of the allies, and with respect to the Anglo-Portuguese troops that can be done very exactly, not by approximative estimates but positively from the original returns.

The morning state delivered to lord Wellington on the 10th of April bears forty-three thousand seven hundred and forty-four British and Germans, and twenty thousand seven hundred and ninety-three Portuguese, in all sixty-four thousand five hundred and thirty-seven soldiers and officers present under arms, exclusive of artillery-men. Of this number nearly ten thousand were cavalry, eleven hundred and eighty-eight being Portuguese.

See note at the end of the Appendix.

The Spanish auxiliaries, exclusive of Mina's bands investing St. Jean Pied de Port, were 1°. Giron's Andalusians and the third army under O'Donnel, fifteen thousand. 2°. The Gallicians under general Freyre, fourteen thousand. 3°. Three thousand Gallicians under Morillo and as many more under Longa, making with the Anglo-Portuguese a total of ninety thousand combatants with somewhat more than a hundred pieces of field-artillery.

Of this force, O'Donnel's troops were in the valley of the Bastan, Longa's on the Upper Ebro; one division of Freyre's Gallicians was under Carlos D'Espagne in front of Bayonne; one half of Morillo's division was blockading Navarens, the other half and the nine thousand Gallicians remaining under Freyre, were in front of Toulouse. Of the Anglo-Portuguese, the first and fifth divisions, and three unattached brigades of infantry with one brigade of

cavalry, were with sir John Hope at Bayonne; the
seventh division was at Bordeaux; the household
brigade of heavy cavalry was on the march from the
Ebro where it had passed the winter; the Portuguese horsemen were partly employed on the communications in the rear, partly near Agen, where sir
John Campbell commanding the fourth regiment
had an engagement on the 11th with the celebrated
partizan Florian.   The second, third, fourth, sixth,
and light divisions of infantry, and Le Cor's Portuguese, called the unattached division, were with lord
Wellington, who had also Bock's, Ponsonby's, Fane's,
Vivian's, and lord E. Somerset's brigades of cavalry.

See note
at the end
of the
Appendix.

Appendix
7, sections
6 and 7.

These troops on the morning of the 10th mus-
tered under arms, in round numbers, thirty-one
thousand infantry, of which four thousand three hundred were officers sergeants and drummers, leaving
twenty-six thousand and six hundred bayonets.
Add twelve thousand Spaniards under Freyre and
Morillo, and we have a total of forty-three thousand
five hundred infantry.   The cavalry amounted to
seven thousand, and there were sixty-four pieces of
artillery.   Hence about fifty-two thousand of all
ranks and arms were in line to fight thirty-eight
thousand French with more than eighty pieces of
artillery, some being of the largest calibre.

But of the allies only twenty-four thousand men
with fifty-two guns can be said to have been seriously
engaged.   Thirteen thousand sabres and bayonets
with eighteen guns were on the left of the Garonne
under general Hill.   Neither the light division nor
Ponsonby's heavy cavalry, nor Bock's Germans were
really engaged.   Wherefore twelve thousand six
hundred sabres and bayonets under Beresford, nine
thousand bayonets under Freyre, and two thousand

five hundred of Picton's division really fought the battle. Thus the enormous disproportion assumed by the French writers disappears entirely; for if the allies had the advantage of numbers it was chiefly in cavalry, and horsemen were of little avail against the entrenched position and preponderating artillery of the French general.

The duke of Dalmatia's claim to the admiration of his countrymen is well-founded and requires no vain assumption to prop it up. Vast combinations, inexhaustible personal resources, a clear judgment, unshaken firmness and patience under difficulties, unwavering fidelity to his sovereign and his country, are what no man can justly deny him. In this cele-brated campaign of only nine months, although counteracted by the treacherous hostility of many of his countrymen, he repaired and enlarged the works of five strong places and entrenched five great camps with such works as Marius himself would not have disdained; once he changed his line of opera-tions and either attacking or defending delivered twenty-four battles and combats. Defeated in all he yet fought the last as fiercely as the first, re-maining unconquered in mind, and still intent upon renewing the struggle when peace came to put a stop to his prodigious efforts. Those efforts were fruitless because Suchet renounced him, because the people of the south were apathetic and fortune was adverse; because he was opposed to one of the greatest generals of the world at the head of uncon-querable troops. For what Alexander's Macedo-nians were at Arbela, Hannibal's Africans at Cannæ, Cæsar's Romans at Pharsalia, Napoleon's guards at Austerlitz, such were Wellington's British soldiers at this period. The same men who had fought at

Vimiera and Talavera contended at Orthes and Toulouse. Six years of uninterrupted success had en-
grafted on their natural strength and fierceness a
confidence which rendered them invincible. It is
by this measure Soult's firmness and the constancy
of his army is to be valued, and the equality to which
he reduced his great adversary at Toulouse is a
proof of ability which a judicious friend would put
forward rather than suppress.

Was he not a great general who being originally
opposed on the Adour by nearly double his own
numbers, for such was the proportion after the great
detachments were withdrawn from the French army
by the emperor in January, did yet by the aid of his
fortresses, by his able marches and combinations,
oblige his adversary to employ so many troops for
blockades sieges and detached posts, that at Toulouse his army was scarcely more numerous than the
French? Was it nothing to have drawn Wellington
from such a distance along the frontier, and force
him at last, either to fight a battle under the most
astonishing disadvantages or to retreat with dishonour. And this not because the English general
had committed any fault, but by the force of combinations which embracing all the advantages offered
by the country left him no option.

That Soult made some mistakes is true, and perhaps the most important was that which the emperor warned him against, though too late, the
leaving so many men in Bayonne. He did so he
says because the place could not hold out fifteen
days without the entrenched camp, and the latter
required men; but the result proved Napoleon's
sagacity, for the allies made no attempt to try the
strength of the camp, and on the 18th of March lord

Wellington knew not the real force of the garrison.
Up to that period Sir John Hope was inclined to
blockade the place only, and from the difficulty of
gathering the necessary stores and ammunition on
the right bank of the Adour, the siege though resolved upon was not even commenced on the 14th
of April when that bloody and most lamentable
sally was made. Hence the citadel could not even
with a weaker garrison have been taken before the
end of April, and Soult might have had Abbé's division of six thousand good troops in the battles of
Orthes and Toulouse. Had Suchet joined him, his
army would have been numerous enough to bar lord
Wellington's progress altogether, especially in the
latter position. Here it is impossible not to admire
the sagacity of the English general, who from the
first was averse to entering France and only did so
for a political object, under the promise of great reinforcements and in the expectation that he should
be allowed to organize a Bourbon army. What
could he have done if Soult had retained the twenty
thousand men drafted in January, or if Suchet had
joined, or the people had taken arms?

How well Soult chose his ground at Toulouse,
how confidently he trusted that his adversary would
eventually pass the Garonne below and not above
the city, with what foresight he constructed the
bridge-head at Montauban, and prepared the difficulties lord Wellington had to encounter have been
already touched upon. But Mr. Choumara has
assumed that the English general's reason for relinquishing the passage of the Garonne at Portet on
the night of the 27th, was not the want of pontoons
but the fear of being attacked during the operation,
adducing in proof Soult's orders to assail the heads

of his columns.　Those orders are however dated the 31st, three days after the attempt of which Soult appears to have known nothing at the time : they were given in the supposition that lord Wellington wished to effect a second passage at that point to aid general Hill while descending the Arriege.　And what reason has any man to suppose that the same general and troops who passed the Nive and defeated a like counter-attack near Bayonne, would be deterred by the fear of a battle from attempting it on the Garonne ?.　The passage of the Nive was clearly more dangerous, because the communication with the rest of the army was more difficult, Soult's disposable force larger, his counter-movements more easily hidden until the moment of execution.　At Portet the passage, designed for the night season, would have been a surprise, and the whole army, drawn close to that side could have been thrown over in three or four hours with the exception of the divisions destined to keep the French in check at St. Cyprien.　Soult's orders did not embrace such an operation.　They directed Clauzel to fall upon the head of the troops and crush them while in the disorder of a later passage which was expected and watched for.

General Clauzel having four divisions in hand was no doubt a formidable enemy, and Soult's notion of defending the river by a counter-attack was excellent in principle ; but to conceive is one thing to execute is another.　His orders were, as I have said, only issued on the 31st, when Hill was across both the Garonne and the Arriege.　Lord Wellington's design was then not to force a passage at Portet, but to menace that point, and really attack St. Cyprien when Hill should have descended the

Arriege. Nor did Soult himself much expect
Clauzel would have any opportunity to attack, for
in his letter to the minister of war he said, the positions between the Arriege and the canal were all
disadvantageous to the French and his intention
was to fight in Toulouse if the allies approached
from the south; yet he still believed Hill's movement to be only a blind and that lord Wellington
would finally attempt the passage below Toulouse.

The French general's views and measures were
profoundly reasoned but extremely simple. His
first care on arriving at Toulouse was to secure the
only bridge over the Garonne by completing the
works of St. Cyprien, which he had begun while
the army was still at Tarbes. He thus gained time,
and as he felt sure that the allies could not act in
the Arriege district, he next directed his attention
to the bridge-head of Montauban to secure a retreat behind the Tarn and the power of establishing
a fresh line of operations. Meanwhile contrary to
his expectation lord Wellington did attempt to act
on the Arriege, and the French general, turning of
necessity in observation to that side, entrenched a
position on the south; soon however he had proof
that his first notion was well-founded, that his adversary after losing much time must at last pass below
Toulouse; wherefore he proceeded with prodigious
activity to fortify the Mont Rave and prepare a field
of battle on the northern and eastern fronts of the
city. These works advanced so rapidly, while the
wet weather by keeping the rivers flooded reduced
lord Wellington to inactivity, that Soult became confident in their strength, and being influenced also by
the news from Paris, relinquished his first design of
opposing the passage of the Garonne and preserving

BOOK
XXIV.

1814.

the line of operations by Montauban. To hold Toulouse then became his great object, nor was he diverted from this by the accident which befel lord Wellington's bridge at Grenade. Most writers, French and English, have blamed him for letting slip that opportunity of attacking Beresford. It

Notes by
general
Berton,
MSS.

is said that general Reille first informed him of the rupture of the bridge, and strongly advised him to attack the troops on the right bank; but Choumara has well defended him on that point; the distance was fifteen miles, the event uncertain, the works on the Mount Rave would have stood still meanwhile, and the allies might perhaps have stormed St. Cyprien.

Lord Wellington was however under no alarm for Beresford, or rather for himself, because each day he passed the river in a boat and remained on

Morning
State of
lord Wel-
lington,
4th of
April,
MSS.

that side. His force was not less than twenty thousand including sergeants and officers, principally British; his position was on a gentle range the flanks covered by the Ers and the Garonne; he had eighteen guns in battery on his front, which was likewise flanked by thirty other pieces placed on the left of the Garonne. Nor was he without retreat. He could cross the Ers, and Soult dared not have followed to any distance lest the river should subside and the rest of the army pass on his rear, unless, reverting to his original design of operating by Montauban, he lightly abandoned his now matured plan of defending Toulouse. Wisely therefore he continued to strengthen his position round that city, his combinations being all directed to force the allies to attack him between the Ers and the Mount Rave where it seemed scarcely possible to succeed.

He has been also charged with this fault, that he
did not entrench the Hill of Pugade. Choumara
holds that troops placed there would have been endangered without adequate advantage. This does
not seem conclusive. The hill was under the shot
of the main height, it might have been entrenched
with works open to the rear, and St. Pol's brigade
would thus have incurred no more danger than
when placed there without any entrenchments. Beresford could not have moved up the left bank of
the Ers until these works were carried, and this
would have cost men. It is therefore probable that
want of time caused Soult to neglect this advantage.
He committed a graver error during the battle by
falling upon Beresford with Taupin's division only
when he could have employed D'Armagnac's and
Villatte's likewise in that attack. He should have
fallen on him also while in the deep country below,
and before he had formed his lines at the foot of
the heights. What hindered him? Picton was repulsed, Freyre was defeated, the light division was
protecting the fugitives, and one of Maransin's brigades withdrawn from St. Cyprien had reinforced
the victorious troops on the extreme left of the Calvinet platform. Beresford's column entangled in
the marshy ground, without artillery and menaced
both front and rear by cavalry, could not have resisted such an overwhelming mass, and lord Wellington can scarcely escape criticism for placing
him in that predicament.

A commander is not indeed to refrain from
high attempts because of their perilous nature, the
greatest have ever been the most daring, and the
English general who could not remain inactive
before Toulouse was not deterred by danger or difficulty: twice he passed the broad and rapid Ga-

ronne and reckless of his enemy's strength and skill worked his way to a crowning victory. This was hardihood, greatness. But in Beresford's particular attack he did not overstep the rules of art, he hurtled against them, and that he was not damaged by the shock is owing to his good fortune the fierceness of his soldiers and the errors of his adversary. What if Beresford had been overthrown on the Ers? Wellington must have repassed the Garonne, happy if by rapidity he could reunite in time with Hill on the left bank. Beresford's failure would have been absolute ruin and that alone refutes the French claim to a victory. Was there no other mode of attack? That can hardly be said. Beresford passed the Lavaur road to assail the platform of St. Sypiere, and he was probably so ordered to avoid an attack in flank by the Lavaur road, and because the platform of Calvinet on the side of the Ers river was more strongly entrenched than that of St. Sypiere. But for this gain it was too much to throw his column into the deep ground without guns, and quite separated from the rest of the army seeing that the cavalry intended to maintain the connection were unable to act in that miry labyrinth of water-courses. If the Spaniards were judged capable of carrying the strongest part of the Calvinet platform, Beresford's fine Anglo-Portuguese divisions were surely equal to attacking this same platform on the immediate left of the Spaniards, and an advanced guard would have sufficed to protect the left flank. The assault would then have been made with unity, by a great mass and on the most important point: for the conquest of St. Sypiere was but a step towards that of Calvinet, but the conquest of Calvinet would have rendered St. Sypiere untenable. It is however to be ob-

served that the Spaniards attacked too soon and their
dispersion exceeded all reasonable calculation : so
panic-stricken they were as to draw from lord Wellington at the time the bitter observation, that he
had seen many curious spectacles but never before
saw ten thousand men running a race.

Soult's retreat from Toulouse, a model of order
and regularity, was made in the night. This
proves the difficulty of his situation. Nevertheless
it was not desperate ; nor was it owing to his adversary's generous forbearance that he passed unmolested under the allies' guns as an English writer
has erroneously assumed. For first those guns had
no ammunition, and this was one reason why lord
Wellington though eager to fall upon him on the
11th could not do so. On the 12th Soult was gone,
and his march covered by the great canal could
scarcely have been molested, because the nearest
point occupied by the allies was more than a mile
and a half distant. Nor do I believe that Soult, as
some other writers have imagined, ever designed to
hold Toulouse to the last. It would have been an
avowal of military insolvency to which his proposal,
that Suchet should join him at Carcassone and retake
the offensive, written on the night of the 11th, is
quite opposed. Neither was it in the spirit of
French warfare. The impetuous valour and sus-
ceptibility of that people are ill-suited for stern
Numantian despair. Place an attainable object of
war before the French soldier and he will make
supernatural efforts to gain it, but failing he be-
comes proportionally discouraged. Let some new
chance be opened, some fresh stimulus applied to
his ardent sensitive temper, and he will rush forward
again with unbounded energy : the fear of death
never checks him he will attempt any thing. But

the unrelenting vigour of the British infantry in resistance wears his fury out; it was so proved in the
Peninsula, where the sudden deafening shout, rolling
over a field of battle more full and terrible than
that of any other nation, and followed by the strong
unwavering charge, often startled and appalled a
French column before whose fierce and vehement
assault any other troops would have given way.

Napoleon's system of war was admirably adapted
to draw forth and augment the military excellence
and to strengthen the weakness of the national character. His discipline, severe but appealing to the
feelings of hope and honour, wrought the quick
temperament of the French soldiers to patience
under hardships and strong endurance under fire;
he taught the generals to rely on their own talents,
to look to the country wherein they made war for
resources, and to dare every thing even with the
smallest numbers, that the impetuous valour of
France might have full play : hence the violence of
their attacks. But he also taught them to combine
all arms together, and to keep strong reserves that
sudden disorders might be repaired and the discouraged troops have time to rally and recover their
pristine spirit, certain that they would then renew
the battle with the same confidence as before. He
thus made his troops, not invincible indeed, nature
had put a bar to that in the character of the British
soldier, but so terrible and sure in war that the
number and greatness of their exploits surpassed
those of all other nations : the Romans not excepted
if regard be had to the shortness of the period, nor
the Macedonians if the quality of their opponents
be considered.

Let their amazing toils in the Peninsular war
alone, which though so great and important was but

an episode in their military history, be considered.
" *In Spain large armies will starve and small armies
will be beaten*" was the saying of Henry IV. of
France, and this was no light phrase of an indolent
monarch but the profound conclusion of a sagacious
general.   Yet Napoleon's enormous armies were so
wonderfully organized that they existed and fought
in Spain for six years, and without cessation, for to
them winters and summers were alike.   Their large
armies endured incredible toils and privations but
were not starved out, nor were their small armies
beaten by the Spaniards.   And for their daring and
resource a single fact recorded by lord Wellington
will suffice.   They captured more than one strong
place in Spain without any provision of bullets save
those fired at them by their enemies, having trusted
to that chance when they formed the siege!   Before
the British troops they fell, but how terrible was
the struggle! how many defeats they recovered
from, how many brave men they slew, what changes
and interpositions of fortune occurred before they
could be rolled back upon their own frontiers!   And
this is the glory of England, that her soldiers and
hers only were capable of overthrowing them in
equal battle.   I seek not to defraud the Portuguese
of his well-earned fame, nor to deny the Spaniard
the merit of his constancy.   England could not
alone have triumphed in the struggle, but for her
share in the deliverance of the Peninsula let this
brief summary speak.

    She expended more than one hundred millions
sterling on her own operations, she subsidised Spain
and Portugal besides, and with her supplies of
clothing arms and ammunition maintained the
armies of both even to the guerillas.   From thirty up

to seventy thousand British troops were employed
by her constantly, and while her naval squadrons
continually harassed the French with descents upon
the coasts, her land forces fought and won nineteen
pitched battles and innumerable combats ; they
made or sustained ten sieges, took four great fortresses, twice expelled the French from Portugal,
preserved Alicant, Carthagena, Cadiz, Lisbon ; they
killed wounded and took about two hundred thousand enemies, and the bones of forty thousand
British soldiers lie scattered on the plains and
mountains of the Peninsula.

Finally, for Portugal she re-organized a native
army and supplied officers who led it to victory, and
to the whole Peninsula she gave a general whose
like has seldom gone forth to conquer. And all
this and more was necessary to redeem the Peninsula from France !

The duke of Wellington's campaigns furnish
lessons for generals of all nations, but they must
always be peculiarly models for British commanders in future continental wars, because he
modified and reconciled the great principles of art
with the peculiar difficulties which attend generals
controlled by politicians who depending upon
private intrigue prefer parliamentary to national
interests. An English commander must not trust
his fortune. He dare not risk much however conscious he may be of personal resources when one
disaster will be his ruin at home. His measures
must therefore be subordinate to this primary consideration. Lord Wellington's caution, springing
from that source, has led friends and foes alike into
wrong conclusions as to his system of war. The
French call it want of enterprize, timidity ; the

English have denominated it the Fabian system. These are mere phrases. His system was the same as that of all great generals. He held his army in hand, keeping it with unmitigated labour always in a fit state to march or to fight; and thus prepared he acted indifferently as occasion offered on the offensive or defensive, displaying in both a complete mastery of his art. Sometimes he was indebted to fortune, sometimes to his natural genius, but always to his untiring industry, for he was emphatically a pains-taking man.

That he was less vast in his designs, less daring in execution, neither so rapid nor so original a commander as Napoleon must be admitted, and being later in the field of glory it is to be presumed that he learned something of the art from that greatest of all masters; yet something besides the difference of genius must be allowed for the difference of situation; Napoleon was never even in his first campaign of Italy so harassed by the French as Wellington was by the English Spanish and Portuguese governments. Their systems of war were however alike in principle, their operations being necessarily modified by their different political positions. Great bodily exertion, unceasing watchfulness, exact combinations to protect their flanks and communications without scattering their forces, these were common to both. In defence firm, cool, enduring; in attack fierce and obstinate; daring when daring was politic, but always operating by the flanks in preference to the front: in these things they were alike, but in following up a victory the English general fell short of the French emperor. The battle of Wellington was the stroke of a battering-ram, down went the wall in ruins. The

battle of Napoleon was the swell and dash of a
mighty wave, before which the barrier yielded and
the roaring flood poured onwards covering all.

Yet was there nothing of timidity or natural
want of enterprize to be discerned in the English
general's campaigns. Neither was he of the Fabian
school. He recommended that commander's system
to the Spaniards, but he did not follow it himself.
His military policy more resembled that of Scipio
Africanus. Fabius dreading Hannibal's veterans, red
with the blood of four consular armies, hovered on
the mountains, refused battle, and to the unmatched
skill and valour of the great Carthaginian opposed
the almost inexhaustible military resources of Rome.
Lord Wellington was never loath to fight when there
was any equality of numbers. He landed in Portugal
with only nine thousand men, with intent to attack
Junot who had twenty-four thousand. At Roliça
he was the assailant, at Vimiera he was assailed,
but he would have changed to the offensive during
the battle if others had not interfered. At Oporto
he was again the daring and successful assailant.
In the Talavera campaign he took the initiatory
movements, although in the battle itself he sustained
the shock. His campaign of 1810 in Portugal was
entirely defensive, because the Portuguese army
was young and untried, but his pursuit of Massena
in 1811 was as entirely aggressive although cautiously so, as well knowing that in mountain warfare those who attack labour at a disadvantage.
The operations of the following campaign, including
the battles of Fuentes Onoro and Albuera the first
siege of Badajos and the combat of Guinaldo, were
of a mixed character ; so was the campaign of Salamanca ; but the campaign of Vittoria and that in

the south of France were entirely and eminently offensive.

Slight therefore is the resemblance to the Fabian warfare. And for the Englishman's hardiness and enterprise bear witness the passage of the Douro at Oporto, the capture of Ciudad Rodrigo, the storming of Badajos, the surprise of the forts at Mirabete, the march to Vittoria, the passage of the Bidassoa, the victory of the Nivelle, the passage of the Adour below Bayonne, the fight of Orthes, the crowning battle of Toulouse! To say that he committed faults is only to say that he made war; but to deny him the qualities of a great commander is to rail against the clear midday sun for want of light. How few of his combinations failed. How many battles he fought, victorious in all! Iron hardihood of body, a quick and sure vision, a grasping mind, untiring power of thought, and the habit of laborious minute investigation and arrangement; all these qualities he possessed, and with them that most rare faculty of coming to prompt and sure conclusions on sudden emergencies. This is the certain mark of a master spirit in war, without it a commander may be distinguished, he may be a great man, but he cannot be a great captain: where troops nearly alike in arms and knowledge are opposed the battle generally turns upon the decision of the moment.

At the Somosierra, Napoleon's sudden and what to those about him appeared an insensate order, sent the Polish cavalry successfully charging up the mountain when more studied arrangements with ten times that force might have failed. At Talavera, if Joseph had not yielded to the imprudent heat of Victor, the fate of the allies would have been sealed. At the Coa, Montbrun's refusal to charge with his cavalry saved general Craufurd's division, the loss of which would have gone far towards producing the evacuation of Portugal. At Busaco, Massena would not suffer Ney to attack the first day, and thus lost the only favourable opportunity for assailing that formidable position. At Fuentes Onoro, the same Massena suddenly suspended his attack when a powerful effort would probably have been decisive. At Albuera, Soult's column of attack instead of pushing forward halted to fire from the first height they had gained on Beresford's right, which saved that general from an early and total defeat; again at a later period of that battle the unpremeditated attack of the fusileers decided the contest. At Barosa, general Graham with a wonderful promptitude snatched the victory at the very moment when a terrible defeat seemed inevitable. At Sabugal, not even the astonishing fighting of the light division could have saved it if general Reynier had possessed this essential quality of a general. At El Bodon, Marmont failed to seize the most favourable opportunity which occurred during the whole war for crushing the allies. At Orthes, Soult let slip two opportunities of falling upon the allies with advantage, and at Toulouse he failed to crush Beresford.

At Vimiera, lord Wellington was debarred by Burrard from giving a signal illustration of this intuitive generalship, but at Busaco and the heights of San Cristoval, near Salamanca, he suffered Massena and Marmont to commit glaring faults unpunished. On the other hand he has furnished many examples of that successful improvisation in which Napoleon seems to have surpassed a mankind. His sudden retreat from Oropesa across the Tagus by the bridge of Arzobispo; his passage of the Douro in 1809; his halt at Guinaldo in the face of Marmont's overwhelming numbers; the battle of Salamanca; his sudden rush with the third division to seize the hill of Arinez at Vittoria; his counter-stroke with the sixth division at Sauroren; his battle of the 30th two days afterwards; his sudden passage of the Gave below Orthes. Add to these his wonderful battle of Assye, and the proofs are complete that he possesses in an eminent degree that intuitive perception which distinguishes the greatest generals.

Fortune however always asserts her supremacy in war, and often from a slight mistake such disastrous consequences flow that in every age and every nation the uncertainty of arms has been proverbial. Napoleon's march upon Madrid in 1808 before he knew the exact situation of the British army is an example. By that march he lent his flank to his enemy. Sir John Moore seized the advantage and though the French emperor repaired the error for the moment by his astonishing march from Madrid to Astorga, the fate of the Peninsula was then decided. If he had not been forced to turn against Moore, Lisbon would have fallen, Portugal could not have been organized for resistance, and the jealousy of the Spaniards would never have suffered Wellington to establish a solid base at Cadiz: that general's after-successes would then have been with the things that are unborn. It was not so ordained. Wellington was victorious, the great conqueror was overthrown. England stood the most triumphant nation of the world. But with an enormous debt, a dissatisfied people, gaining peace without tranquillity, greatness without intrinsic strength, the present time uneasy, the future dark and threatening. Yet she rejoices in the glory of her arms! And it is a stirring sound! War is the condition of this world. From man to the smallest insect all are at strife, and the glory of arms which cannot be obtained without the exercise of honour, fortitude, courage, obedience, modesty and temperance, excites the brave man's patriotism and is a chastening corrective for the rich man's pride. It is yet no security for power. Napoleon the greatest man of whom history makes mention, Napoleon the most wonderful commander, the most sagacious politician, the most profound statesman, lost by arms, Poland, Germany, Italy, Portugal, Spain and France. Fortune, that name for the unknown combinations of infinite power, was wanting to him, and without her aid the designs of man are as bubbles on a troubled ocean.

APPENDIX.

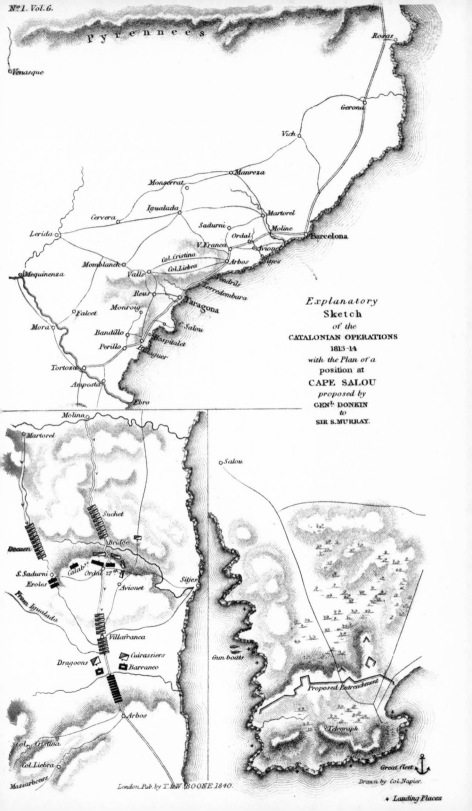

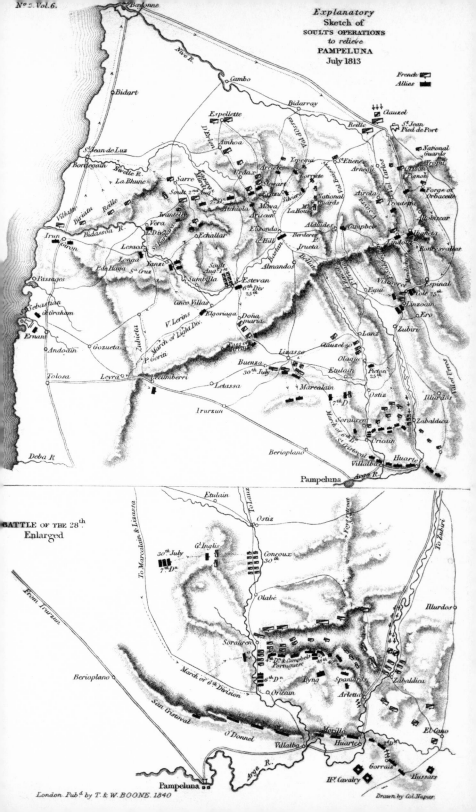

Explanatory
Sketch of
SOULT'S OPERATIONS
to relieve
PAMPELUNA
July 1813

French
Allies

Bayonne

Nive R.

Cambo

Bidart

Espellette

Bidarray

D'Erlan

Ainhoa

Clauzel

St Jean Pied de Port

St Jean de Luz

Urdax

Arretta

Ypegui

St Etienne

National Guards

Bordegain

La Rhune

Sarre

Stovart

Torrette

Arnegui

Tropal

Villate

Nivelle R.

Rolle

Soult 2nd Aug.t

Etzu

Mira

Schrozt

National Guards

Airola

Troutenia

Forge of Orbaceite

Briatte

Atchiola

Ariscun

Mt La House

Albinsear

Irun

Bidassoa R.

Wantelle

Elizondo

Aldudes

Berderez

Campbell

Hugueta

Ronesvalles

Vera

Echallar

C Hill

Irueta

Bellate

Zindous

Passages

Lesaca

Ste Cruz

Almandos

Clauzel 30

Vistavera

Espinal

Sebastian & Graham

Longa

Yanzi

Soult Aug.t 1st

Estevan

Equi

Ole 35

Ero

Ernani

Pd. Haya

Sumbilla

6th Div.

Minzoain

Zubiri

Andoain

Gozueta

Cinco Villas

Elgoriaga

Doña Ymaria

Clauzel 30

Lanz

Olague

Illurdos

Tolosa

Leyra

V Lerins

Buenza

Lizasso

Etulain

Picton

Ostiz

Zabalduca

Lecumberri

Letassa

30th July

Marcalain

7th D

Irurzun

Berioplano

Sorauren

Oricain

Huarte

Villalba

Arga R.

Pampeluna

BATTLE OF THE 28th
Enlarged

Etulain

Ostiz

To Zubiri

To Marcalain & Lizassa

G.l Inglis

Conroux 30

Forge Arias

30th July

7th Dn

Olabé

Illurdos

From Irurzun

Sorauren

D.n & Campbell Portuguese

Berioplano

March of 6th Division

7th Dn

Byng

Spaniards

Zabalduca

San Cristoval

Oricain

Arletta

El Caño

O'Donnel

Villalba

Morillo

Huarte

Gorraiz

Hussars

Pampeluna

Arga R.

H.l Cavalry

London. Pub.d by T. & W. BOONE. 1840.

Drawn by Col. Napier.

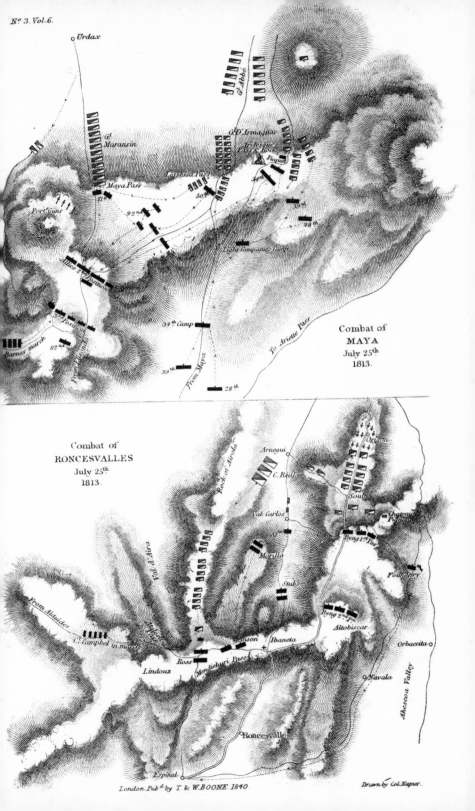

Urdax

G.ˡ Maransin

Maya Pass

21ˢᵗ

Port Guns

92ⁿᵈ

Allies 2.ᵈ Position

3.ᵈ Position

Barnes march

82ⁿᵈ

From Maya

G.ˡ L'Abbé

G.ᵈ D'Armagnac

Artesque
Elite Regts

Pegue

34ᵗʰ

39ᵗʰ

28ᵗʰ

50ᵗʰ

Light Companies Tarry

39ᵗʰ Camp

To Arette Pass

39ᵗʰ From Maya

28ᵗʰ

Combat of
MAYA
July 25ᵗʰ
1813.

Combat of
RONCESVALLES
July 25ᵗʰ
1813.

Rock of Airola

Arnegui

C. Reille

Val Carlos

Orisan

Soult

Chateau
Pignon

Byng 1ˢᵗ Pos.

Foundery

Val d'Arla

Nuttar Valley

From Aldudes

C.ˡ Campbel in march

Ross

Lindouz

Anison

Mendichuri Pass

Ibaneta

Stubs

Morillo

Byng 2.ᵈ Pos.

Altobiscar

Orbaceita

Navala

Abescoa Valley

Roncesvalle

Espinal

London Pub.ᵈ by T. & W. BOONE 1840

Drawn by Col. Napier.

Explanatory
Sketch
of the
ASSAULT OF Sᵀ SEBASTIAN
August 31ˢᵗ
1813.

London. Pubᵈ by T.& W.BOONE.1840.

Drawn by Col. Napier

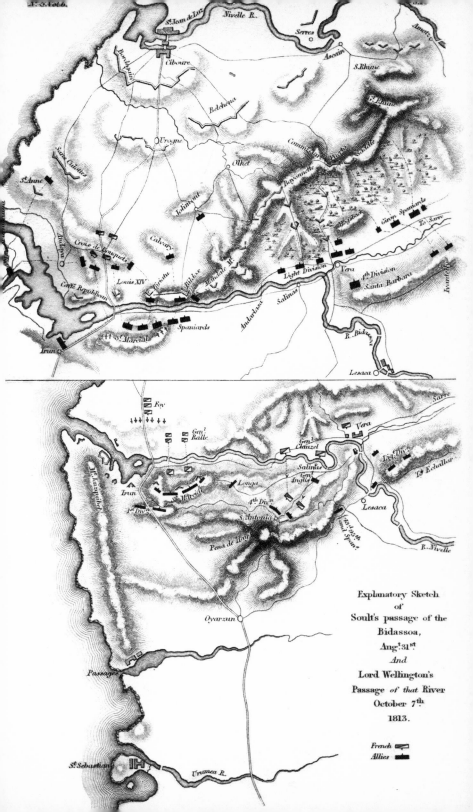

Explanatory Sketch
of
Soult's passage of the
Bidassoa,
Aug.t 31.st
And
Lord Wellington's
Passage of that River
October 7.th
1813.

French
Allies

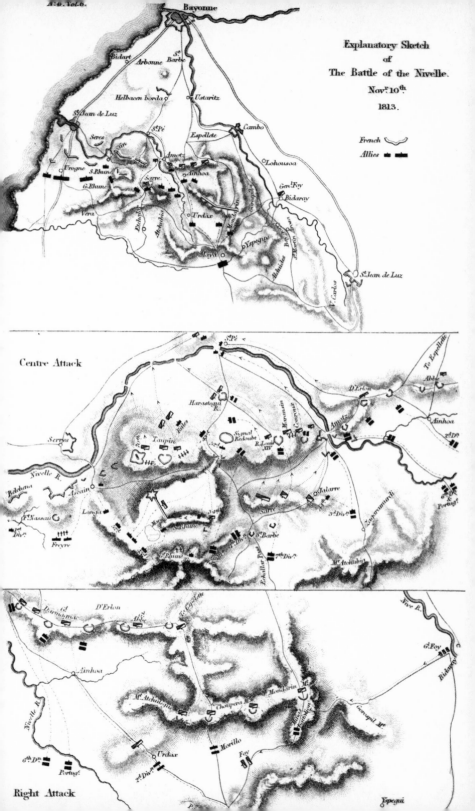

Bayonne

Explanatory Sketch
of
The Battle of the Nivelle.
Novr 10th
1813.

French
Allies

Bidart
Arbonne
Sta Barbe
Helbaen borda
Ustaritz
St Jean de Luz
Cambo
Seres
St Pé
Espellte
Sarin
Amot
Lohousoa
Urogne
S. Rhune
Genl Foy
G. Rhune
Sarre
Ainhoa
Bidaray
Vera
Echalar
Arbonhio
Urdax
Maya
Yspegu
Zuhainia
St Martin Arrosn
St Martin Arran
Banca
V. Carlos
St Jean de Luz

Centre Attack

St Pé
To Espellte
Abb
Harasteqa R.
D'Erlon
Serres
Zth
Taupin
Rolas
Signal Redoubt
R. Louis XIV
Morrain
Louvance
Amot
Ainhoa
2d Dn
Niville R.
Ascain
Belchena
Sa St
Jalarre
3d Dn & Portugl
Pd Nassau
Langa
1st Dn
Sare
Sd Divn
Mte Achubia
Freyre
Maca
Sadame
St Barbe
Echallar Pass
7th Divn
G. Rhune
Zaguramurdi

Right Attack

Cs
Gl Darmagnac
D'Erlon
Abbe
To Espellte
Nive R.
Gl Foy
Ainhoa
Bidray
Mte Achinegue
Chaupera Mr
Mondarin Mt
Atchu
Finodain
Carequil Mr
Niville R.
6th Dn
Urdax
Morillo
Foy
Portugl
2d Divn
P.
Yspegu

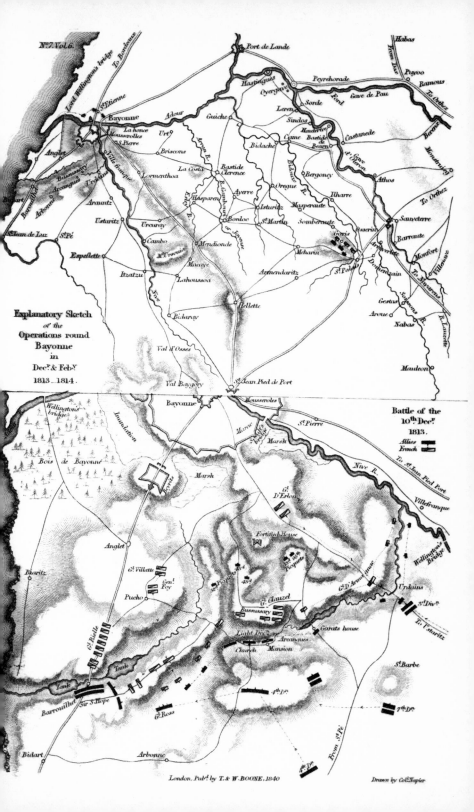

No.7. Vol.6.

Explanatory Sketch
of the
Operations round
Bayonne
in
Dec.r & Feb.y
1813 _ 1814.

Battle of the
10th Dec.r
1813.

Allies
French

London, Pub.d by T. & W. BOONE, 1840

Drawn by Col.l Napier

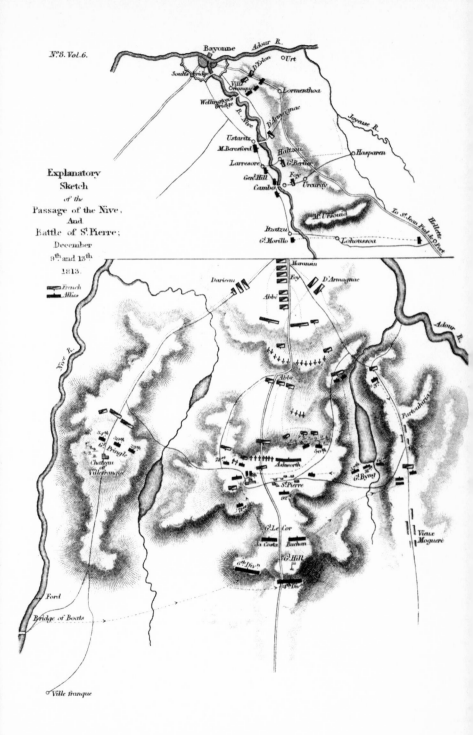

Bayonne

Adour R.

Soult's bridge

Ville Franque

Urt

D'Erlon

Lormenthoa

Wellington's Bridge

R. Nive

D'Armagnac

Joyeuse R.

Ustaritz

M. Beresford

Haltzou

Larresore

G.ᵉ Barbier

Gen.ˡ Hill

Foy

Hasparen

Cambo

Urcaray

M. Urcouid

Itzatzu

G.ˡ Morillo

Lohoussoa

To St Jean Pied de Port

Hallette

Explanatory
Sketch
of the
Passage of the Nive,
And
Battle of St Pierre;
December
9ᵗʰ and 13ᵗʰ
1813.

French
Allies

Marensin

Darieau

Foy

D'Armagnac

Abbe

Nive R.

Abbe

Adour R.

Partouharga

54ᵗʰ

39ᵗʰ

Pringle

Ashworth

G.ˡ Byng

Chateau
of
Villefranque

St Pierre

Vieux
Moguere

G.ˡ Le Cor

la Costa

Buchan

Ford

6ᵗʰ Div.ⁿ

G.ˡ Hill

Bridge of Boats

4ᵗʰ Div.ⁿ

Ville franque

London. Pub.ᵈ by T. & W. BOONE, 1840.

Drawn by Col.ˡ Napier

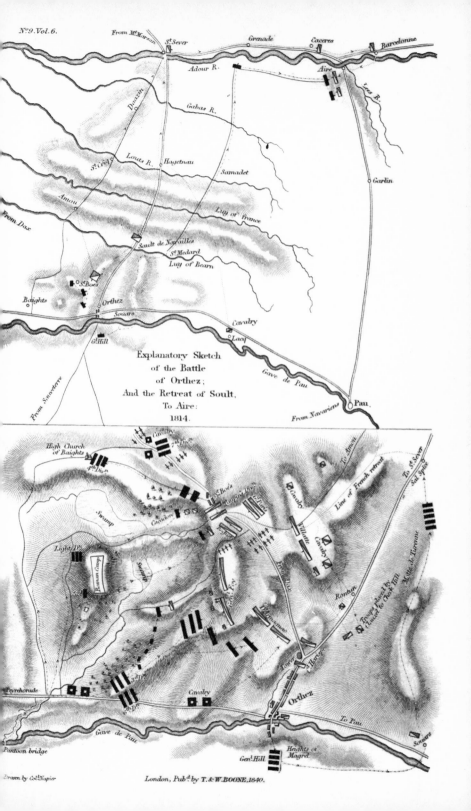

Explanatory Sketch
of the Battle
of Orthez;
And the Retreat of Soult,
To Aire:
1814.

Drawn by Colⁿ Napier

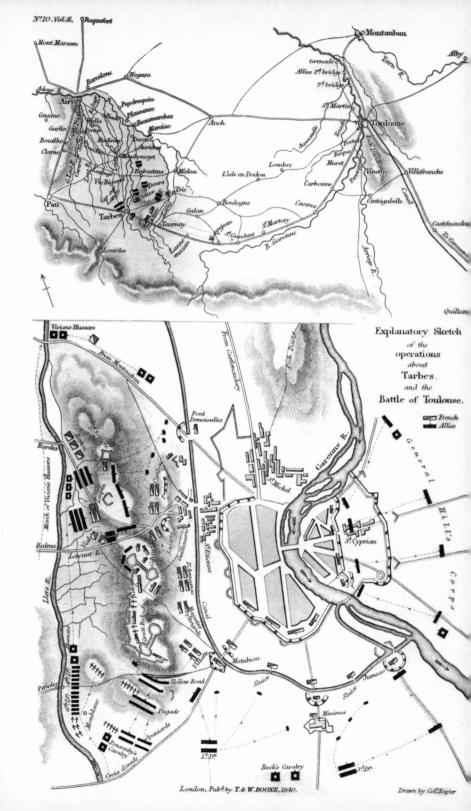

Explanatory Sketch
of the
operations
about
Tarbes,
and the
Battle of Toulouse.

⬒ French
▬ Allies

London, Publᵈ by T. & W. BOONE, 1840.

Drawn by Colⁿ Napier.

APPENDIX.

No. 1.

JUSTIFICATORY PIECES.

Lord William Bentinck to sir E. Pellew.
At sea, June 18*th,* 1813.

SIR,

Y. E. has seen the information I have received of a projected attack upon Sicily by Murat, in conjunction with the Toulon fleet. It seems necessary that the French fleet should leave Toulon, should reach the coast of Naples, embark the men and land them in Sicily, or cover their passage from Calabria or the Bay of Naples, if the intention be, as in the last instance, to transport them to Sicily in the tonnage and small craft of the country.— The most important question is, whether this can be effected by the enemy.— I have no difficulty in saying on my part, that in the present disposition of the Neapolitan army in Sicily, and in the non-existence of any national force, and the imperfect composition of the British force, if half the number intended for this expedition should land in Sicily the island would be conquered.

(Signed)   W. BENTINCK.

Sir E. Pellew to lord W. Bentinck.
H. M. S. Caledonia, June 19*th,* 1813.

MY LORD,

I feel it my duty to state to your lordship that in my judgment the Toulon fleet may evade mine without difficulty under a strong N. W. wind to carry them through the passage of the Hieres islands, without the possibility of my interrupting them, and that they may have from twelve to twenty-four hours' start of me in

chasing them. When blown off the coast, my look-out ships
would certainly bring me such information as would enable me to
follow them immediately to the Bay of Naples. Your lordship is
most competent to judge whether in the interval of their arrival
and my pursuit, the French admiral would be able to embark
Murat's army artillery and stores, and land them on the coast of
Sicily before I came up with them.—The facility of communication by telegraph along the whole coast of Toulon would certainly
apprize Murat of their sailing at a very short notice, but for my
own part, I should entertain very sanguine hopes of overtaking
them either in the Bay of Naples or on the coast of Sicily before
they could make good their landing.

Lord Wm. Bentinck to lord Wellington.
At sea, June 20th, 1813.

My lord,

By the perusal of the accompanying despatch to lord Castlereagh, your lordship will perceive that Murat has opened a
negociation with us, the object of which is friendship with us and
hostility to Buonaparte. You will observe in one of the conver-
sations with Murat's agent, that he informed me that Buonaparte
had ordered Murat to hold twenty thousand men in readiness for
the invasion of Sicily in conjunction with the Toulon fleet. I enclose the copy of a letter I have in consequence addressed to Sir
E. Pellew, together with his answer, upon the practicability of the
Toulon fleet sailing without the knowledge of the blockading fleet.
Your lordship will have received my letter of the 21st of May
enclosing a copy of my despatch to Lord Bathurst, relative to the
discontent of the Neapolitan troops in Sicily and the consequent
state of weakness if not of danger resulting from it to that island.
I stated also that this circumstance had induced me to detain in
Sicily the two battalions which had been withdrawn from Spain.

Lord Wellington to lord William Bentinck.
Huarte, July 1st, 1813.

My lord,

In answer to your lordship's despatch, I have to observe, that I
conceive that the island of Sicily is at present in no danger
whatever.

No. II.

Letter from general Nugent to lord William Bentinck.
Vienna, January 24th, 1812.

MY DEAR LORD WILLIAM,

I hope you have received the letter I wrote to you shortly after my arrival here by a person sent for that purpose. Soon after his departure the affair of La Tour happened, as King mentions in his letter. It required some time before I could judge of the result it would have and the manner it would be considered by the emperor and the government here, and then to settle again the manner of sending officers down to the Mediterranean, for some of those then destined to be sent were implicated. All these circumstances caused the delay of the present which otherwise you would have had much sooner. Another cause of the delay was that I wanted to inform you of the answer which would be given by this house to the speculations that I was commissioned by the prince-regent to propose relative to the arch-duke. There was no decisive answer given, and the only manner of forming an opinion upon that subject was by observing and getting information of their true intentions. I am now firmly convinced that these are such as we could wish, and that it is only fear of being committed that prevents them to speak in a more positive manner. Their whole conduct proves this, more particularly in La Tour's affair which has produced no change whatsoever nor led to any discovery of views or connexions. There is even now less difficulty than ever for officers going to the Mediterranean. They get passports from government here without its inquiring or seeming to know the real object. As it can do nothing else but connive, to which this conduct answers, I think a more explicit declaration is not even requisite and I am convinced that when the thing is once done they will gladly agree. This is likewise King's and Hardenberg's and Johnson's opinion upon the subject, and as such they desire me to express it to you, and to observe that the situation of things here makes the forwarding of the measures you may think expedient in the Mediterranean and the Adriatic the more desirable.

They are here extremely satisfied with the conduct of government in England, and by the accounts we have the latter is much pleased with the conduct of this country, particularly relative to the affairs of Prussia. These are however not decided yet. But

whatever the consequence may be and whatever this country may
do for the present, I am convinced that your measures will ultimately contribute much to the result. I am happy to perceive by
the last information from England that every thing seems to have
been settled there by you. The recruiting business of major
Burke is going on rapidly. As it was not begun at the time of
my departure I can only attribute it to your presence. The letters contain likewise that government is come to the most favorable
resolutions relative to the arch-duke, and I hope the formation of
the troops will soon be effectuated. The dispositions of the
Adriatic coasts and the Tyrol are as good as can be, but all depends upon establishing a basis and without that all partial exertions would be useless or destructive. At the same time that some
regiments would be formed, I think it would be very expedient, to
form at the same place a Dalmatian or a Croat regiment, particularly
as in the present state of things it will be much easier even than
the other. The men could be easily recruited in Bosnia, and sent
from Durazzo to the place you should appoint. The bearer will
give you every information upon the subject, and at all events, I
should propose to you to send him immediately back to Durazzo,
and, should you adopt the above, to give him the necessary orders
and the commission for recruiting and sending the men to the
place of formation. No person can be better qualified than he
is. He knows the languages, the country, and the character of
the people, and understands every thing that relates to commercial
affairs. As to the place of formation, I think I already proposed
Cephalonia to you. Lissa or one of the nearer islands would
give too much jealousy in the beginning in those parts, until our
capital increases so as to undertake an important enterprise, at all
events it is important to form a noyau of the three nations ; it is
then that we may hope to be joined by the whole of Dalmatia and
Croatia after a short time. Major and other officers will shortly
proceed to the Mediterranean. They will be directed to Messina
where I request you will send orders for them. It would be very
useful and saving to provide means for transporting them to that
place from Durazzo, and if possible to establish a more frequent
and regular intercourse between you and the latter. Johnson who
soon sets off from here will in the meantime establish a communication across Bosnia to Durazzo. His presence in those parts will
be productive of many good effects. You will find that he is an
able active and zealous man and will certainly be very useful in
forwarding your views. I can answer for his being worthy of

your full confidence, should you adopt the proposition relative to
the recruiting it would be necessary to put at his disposal the
requisite funds.

You will judge by the account the bearer of this will give you
whether cloth &c. can be had at a cheaper rate from this country
or where you are, and he will bring back your directions for this
object. Allow me to observe that it would be highly useful to
have clothes for a considerable number of men prepared before-
hand. Many important reasons have prevented me hitherto from
proceeding to the Mediterranean as speedily as I wished. I
hope however not to be detained much longer and soon to have
removed every obstacle. I think to set off from here in the beginning of March, and request you will be so kind as to provide
with the return of the bearer to Durazzo the means of my passage
from thence, where I shall come with a feigned name. I hope he
will be back there by the time of my arrival. I shall endeavour
to hasten my journey as I have important information in every
respect. By that time we shall know the decision relative to the
north. King has informed you of the reasons which made an alteration necessary in regard to Frozzi's journey. Part of your
object is in fact fulfilled already, and there are agents in Italy
&c. As to the other and principal part relative to connections in
the army, and the gaining an exact knowledge of it and of the
government in Italy, with other circumstances, I expect soon to
have a person of sufficient consequence and ability to execute
your instructions, and he will go to Milan &c. as soon as it can
be done with safety. His permanent residence in that country seems
to be necessary, that he may be able to accomplish fully the object,
and as the sum you have assigned for this purpose is sufficient for
a considerable time, you can determine whether he is to remain
there permanently or not. Frozzi will bring you an exact account
of what has been arranged relative to this business, and will himself be a very proper person for communications between you
and Italy or this country. He will for that purpose go back to
Italy, the obstacle that opposed it hitherto being now no more. I
cannot but repeat the importance of giving all possible extent to
the arch-duke's establishment, and particularly the raising of as
much troops as possible, for all will depend upon having the
means of landing. We are then sure of augmenting very speedily,
and finding the greatest assistance. The place for beginning cannot be determined on exactly, but there is much to be expected
in Dalmatia and Croatia where we could be joined by the in-

habitants and troops. The lower part would be best adapted in
case we begin with a small force. I shall send and bring officers particularly acquainted with the country and provide every
other assistance such as plans &c. and I think it would be expedient to prevent for the present any enterprize in that country
that would alarm them. Since I began my letter a courier has
arrived from Paris.

The contingent of the Rhenish confederacy have got orders to
be ready for marching. Reinforcements are sending from France
to the north and every preparation is making for war. Buonaparte told to Swartzenburg that he would begin in April and all
circumstances seem to agree with this. On the other side Russia
is very slow in making peace with Turkey. He entirely neglects
Prussia, and for this reason it is to be feared that the latter will
place his capital with Buonaparte notwithstanding that this cabinet
is endeavouring to prevent it. I should be then very much afraid for
the conduct of this house well inclined as the emperor is. Proposals were made by France but no resolution has been taken until
it is known how things turn out. The worst is that Romanzow
is still in credit with Alexander, which prevents all confidence in
other houses and makes Russia adopt half measures. This sketch
of the situation will give you some idea of the wavering and uncertain state people are in. There is no calculation to be made
as to the conduct of government, nor must we be surprised at any
thing they may do. On the other side our speculations are not
built upon them, but upon the disposition of the people ; and
whatever may happen I am convinced that this is a good foundation
if the measures are taken and the means prepared. A principal
object of mine in these parts has been to prepare the measures
for the case that it comes here to the very worst. The most important thing is the augmenting in every possible manner the force
at your disposition. The accounts we have to-day of your return
and the powers I hope you have give me the best hopes of your
overcoming every difficulty. I must yet observe that as Johnson's
proceedings are entirely subordinate to, and make a part of your
plans and operations in general, and that he cannot of course depend upon King, you will be so good as to give him decisive instructions to that purpose, and assign him the means and powers
for acting in consequence. I shall combine with him in my passage through Bosnia every thing in the hopes that you will approve
of this.

Letter from Mr. King to lord William Bentinck.
Vienna, January 24th, 1812.

MY LORD,

I have the honour to acknowledge the receipt of your lordship's letter of the 25th of August, which was delivered to me towards the latter end of October by captain Frizzi whom I should immediately have furnished with the means of proceeding to Italy for the purpose of carrying your lordship's instructions into effect, had it not appeared to me that the measures which I had taken on my arrival here had already in a great degree anticipated your lordship's intentions. As a confirmation of this, I beg leave to transmit for your lordship's perusal the reports (marked A) of three messengers whom I sent to the north of Italy for the purpose of ascertaining the state of the public mind, particularly in the ci-devant Venetian territories and adjacent districts. These reports confirm in a very satisfactory manner the assurances, which I have received through various other channels, that the inhabitants of those countries are ready and determined to avail themselves of the first opportunity to shake off a yoke which is become insupportable. I have also the honour to transmit to your lordship the copy of a letter from count Montgelas, the minister of foreign affairs in Bavaria, to the commissary-general at Nimpten, from which it appears that the Bavarian government is not altogether ignorant of the intentions of the Swiss and Tyroleze, but I am happy to have it in my power to inform your lordship that the persons who seem to have excited the suspicions of the Bavarian government do not enjoy the confidence of our friends in Switzerland, and have not been made acquainted with their intentions; it is nevertheless indispensably necessary that we should act with the greatest possible caution in the employment of emissaries, lest the French and Bavarian governments should take the alarm and adopt measures which would defeat our projects or at least occasion a premature explosion. On these grounds (having previously consulted with general N. to whom captain Frizzi was particularly addressed and who entirely coincides in my opinion) I think it eligible to send this officer back to Sicily and I trust that in so doing I shall meet with your lordship's approbation. I beg leave to observe that the only service captain Frizzi could render in Italy at the present moment would be to ascertain the number and distribution of the French forces in this country, but as these undergo continual changes I think it will be sufficient to despatch

a confidential agent to your lordship with the latest intelligence
from Italy, at a period when the northern war and consequent
occupation of the French troops will enable your lordship to derive
advantage from such intelligence.

The general opinion is that hostilities will commence between
France and Russia in the month of April at which period the
preparations of the French government will be completed, and there
is little reason to hope that the Russians will avail themselves of
the interval, either to annihilate the army of the duchy of
Warsaw or to advance to the assistance of the king of Prussia,
who will in all probability ally himself with France notwithstanding
his former declarations to the contrary. The latest intelligence
from Berlin states that count St. Marsan had presented the ulti-
matum of his government, which demands an unconditional surrender of all the Prussian fortresses, and insists on the military
force and resources of Prussia being placed at the disposal of
French generals. It is positively asserted that the king is inclined to submit to these humiliating proposals, but nothing has
been as yet definitively concluded. I am sorry to inform your
lordship that the aspect of affairs in this country is highly dis-
couraging ; the injudicial financial measures which count Wallis
has thought proper to adopt have rendered it impossible for government to place the army on a respectable footing, and have considerably increased the discontent of the people, who however still
retain their characteristic aversion to the French. The government is determined to maintain a strict neutrality during the
approaching crisis if possible.

In my former letter I mentioned to your lordship my intention
of establishing a person at Durazzo in order to forward messengers &c. &c. and to transmit to me occasionally intelligence of the
state of things in the Adriatic. But having received of late
repeated assurances of the increasing discontent of the inhabitants
of those parts of the coast who have the misfortune to be under
the dominion of the French, and of their willingness to make every
effort to shake off the yoke, and being aware how important it is
at the present moment not to neglect an object of this nature I
have desired Mr. Johnson to proceed thither in order to form
connections in Albania, Dalmatia, and to avail himself in every
possible manner of the spirit of discontent which has so decidedly
manifested itself. Mr. Johnson who has been employed on the
continent for some years past as an agent of government, and who
has given proofs of his zeal and abilities, will repair to Durazzo, or

according to circumstances to some other town in the neighbour-hood of the Adriatic and will there reside as agent of the British government. He will communicate his arrival to your lordship with as little delay as possible.

By the following piece of information which I have derived from an authentic source your lordship will perceive that the French and Swedish governments are far from being on friendly terms. An alliance has been proposed by the former to the latter and instantaneously rejected. The terms of the alliance were as follows, viz. 1st, a body of 30,000 Swedes to be placed at the disposal of France. 2nd, 3000 seamen to be furnished to the French marine, and 3rd, a regiment of Swedes to be raised for the service of France as was the case before the French revolution. I transmit this letter to your lordship by captain Steinberg and ensign Ferandi, two officers who have served creditably in the Austrian army. The former has connections and local knowledge in his native country which may become particularly useful. I fear it will not be in my power to send 50 subaltern officers to Sicily as your lordship desired. I shall however occasionally despatch some intelligent officers who will I think be extremely useful in the formation of new corps.

No. III.

Extracts from the correspondence of sir Henry Wellesley, sir Charles Stuart, and Mr. Vaughan.

Mr. Vaughan to sir Charles Stuart.
Cadiz, August 3d, 1813.

" The Spanish troops in Catalonia and elsewhere are starving, and the government are feeding them with proclamations to intendants. Since I have known Spain I have never known the seat of government in a worse state. There is a strong feeling against the English and a miserable jacobin party which is violent beyond measure."

Ditto to Ditto.
Chichana, Nov. 2d, 1813.

" Never was any thing so disgraceful in the annals of the world as the conduct of all the Spanish authorities on the occasion

of the sickness breaking out.   It is believed that no persons have
the sickness twice, and as almost every family in Cadiz has passed
the epidemic of the fever the interested merchants would not allow
it to be said that the epidemic existed, they have continued to issue
clear bills of health to vessels leaving the port in the height of the
mortality and did all they could to intimidate the government and
Cortez into remaining amongst them."

Sir Henry Wellesley to lord Wellington.

Sept. 13*th*, 1813.

   " A curious scene has been passing here lately.   The permanent deputation* having been appointed the Cortez closed their
session on the 14th.   There had been for some days reports of the
prevalence of the yellow fever which had excited alarm.   On the
16th in the evening, I received an official note from the ministers
of state apprizing me of the intention of the government to proceed
to Madrid on the following day, but without assigning any reason
for so sudden a resolution.   At night I went to the regency,
thinking this was an occasion when it would be right to offer them
some pecuniary assistance.   I found Agar and Ciscar together,
the cardinal being ill of the gout.   They told me that the prevalence of the disorder was the sole cause of their determination to
leave Cadiz; and Ciscar particularly dwelt upon the necessity of
removing, saying he had seen the fatal effects of delay at Carthagena.   They then told me that there was disturbance in the town,
in consequence of which they determined on summoning the
extraordinary Cortez.   I went from the regency to the Cortez.
A motion was made for summoning the ministers to account for
the proceedings of the regency.   Never was I witness to so disgraceful a scene of lying and prevarication.   The ministers insisted that it was not the intention of the regency to leave Cadiz
until the Cortez had been consulted, although I had in my pocket
the official note announcing their intention to do so, and had been
told by Ciscar that the extraordinary Cortez was assembled for no
other reason than because there were disturbances in the town."

Ditto to Ditto.

Cadiz, Dec. 10*th*, 1813.

   " The party for placing the princess at the head of the Spanish
regency is gaining strength, and I should not be surprised if that

* Called the Extraordinary Cortez.

measure were to be adopted soon after our arrival at Madrid, unless a peace and the return of Ferdinand should put an end to all such projects."

Mr. Stuart to lord Wellington.

June 11th, 1813.

" The repugnance of the Admiralty to adopt the measures suggested by your lordship at the commencement of the American war for the protection of the coast, has been followed by events which have fully justified your opinion. *Fifteen merchantmen have been taken off Oporto in a fortnight and a valuable Portuguese homeward-bound merchant ship was captured three days ago close to the bar of Lisbon.*"

No. IV.

Extract from a manuscript memoir by captain Norton, thirty-fourth regiment.

COMBAT OF MAYA.

The thirty-ninth regiment, commanded by the hon. col. O'Callaghan, then immediately engaged with the French and after a severe contest also retired, the fiftieth was next in succession and they also after a gallant stand retired, making way for the ninety-second which met the advancing French column first with its right wing drawn up in line, and after a most destructive fire and heavy loss on both sides the remnant of the right wing retired, leaving a line of killed and wounded that appeared to have no interval; the French column advanced up to this line and then halted, the killed and wounded of the ninety-second forming a sort of rampart, the left wing then opened its fire on the column, and as I was but a little to the right of the ninety-second I could not help reflecting painfully how many of the wounded of their right wing must have unavoidably suffered from the fire of their comrades. The left wing after doing good service and sustaining a loss equal to the first line retired.

COMBAT OF RONCESVALLES.

EXTRACTS FROM GENERAL COLE'S AND MARSHAL SOULT'S OFFICIAL REPORTS, MSS.

General Cole to lord Wellington.

Heights in front of Pampeluna, July 27th, 1813.

—————— " The enemy having in the course of the night turned those posts, were now perceived moving in very considerable force along the ridge leading to the Puerto de Mendichurri. I therefore proceeded in that direction and found that their advance had nearly reached the road leading from Roncesvalles pass to Los Alduides, from which it is separated by a small wooded valley. Owing to the difficulty of the communications the head of major-general Ross's brigade could not arrive there sooner; the major-general however, with great decision, attacked them with the Brunswick company and three companies of the twentieth, all he had time to form; these actually closed with the enemy and bayonetted several in the ranks. They were however forced to yield to superior numbers, and to retire across the valley, the enemy attempted to follow them but were repulsed with loss, the remainder of the brigade having come up."

Marshal Soult to the Minister of War.

" *Linzoin, 26 Juiller, 1813.*

" Leurs pertes ont également été considérables, soit à l'attaque du Lindouz par le général Reille ou le 20me regiment a été presque détruit à la suite d'une charge à la bayonnette executée par un bataillon du 6me leger, division Foy, soit à l'attaque d'Altobiscar par le général Clauzel."

Extract from the correspondence of the duke of Dalmatia with the Minister of War.

Ascain, 12 Août, 1813.

" Dés a présent V. E. voit la situation de l'armée, elle connait ses forces, celles de l'ennemi, et elle se fait sans doute une idée de ses projets, et d'avance elle peut apprécier ce qu'il est en notre pouvoir de faire; je ne charge point le tableau, je dis ma pensée sans détour, et j'avoue que si l'ennemi emploie tous ses moyens, ainsi que probablement il le fera, ceux que nous pourrons en ce moment lui opposer etant de beaucoup inferieurs, nous ne pourrons pas empêcher qu'ils ne fasse beaucoup de mal. Mon devoir est de le dire à V. E. quoique je tienne une autre language aux troupes et au pays, et que d'ailleurs je ne néglige aucun moyen pour remplir de mon mieux la tache qui m'est imposée."

No. V.

EXTRACTED FROM THE IMPERIAL MUSTER-ROLLS.

Report of the movements of the army of Arragon during the first fifteen days of September, 1813.

" Le 12eme toute l'armée d'Aragon se reunit a Molino del Rey; partie de celle de Catalonia et la garrison de Barcelonne se placent a droite a Ollessa et Martorel, pour partir tous ensemble a 8 heures du soir et se porter le droite par San Sadurni, le rest par le grande route d'Ordal sur Villa Franca, ou l'armée Anglaise etait rasemble. General Harispe rencontré a onze heures du soir un fort advant garde au Col d'Ordal *dans les anciens ratranchemens.* Un combat de plus vif s'engagea sous les ordres du general de l'avant garde Mesclop. Le 7eme et 44eme reg^{ns.} montrerent une haute valeur, ainsi qu'une partie d'116eme. Les positions sont prise et reprise, et nous restent enfin, couvert des morts et de blesses Anglais. Dans la pursuite le 4eme houssards se saissirent des 4 pieces de cannon Anglais, &c. avec trois ou quatre cents prisoniers, presque tous de la 27eme reg^{n.} Anglais. Le droit, ayant rencontrer des obstacles et quelques troupes ennemis a combattre dans les passages, est retarde dans sa marche, et n'arriva pas avec le jour au rendezvouz entre L'Ongat et Grenada. Un battalion de 117eme venant à gauche, par Bejas sur Avionet, rejoint l'armée en position, avec des prisoniers.

" Le marechal Suchet directé une movement de cavalrie et de l'artillerie qui tenaient la téte pour donner le tems à l'infanterie d'entrer en ligne. Les Anglais etaient en battaile sur trois lignes en avant de Villa Franca, ils commencerent aussitot leur retraite en bon ordre. On les poursuiverent et on les harcelerent, la cavalrie fit plusieurs charges assez vive. Ils opposerent de la resistance, essuyerent des pertes, surtout en cavalrie, precipiterent leur marche, brulerent un pont et s'eloignerent vers Arbos et Vendrils, laissant plus que 150 hommes pris et beaucoup des morts et des blesses, surtout des houssards de Brunswick. Nôtre avant garde va ce soir à Vendrils et plusieurs certaines de deserteurs sont ramassé."

No. VI.

No. 1.—Extract from the official state of the allied army, commanded by lieutenant-general sir John Murray, at the Col de Balaguer, 17th June, 1813. Exclusive of officers, sergeants, and drummers.

	Present fit for duty.	Sick.	Command.	Horses.	Mules.	Total men.
British and German cavalry	739	12	6	733	,,	757
British Portuguese and Sicilian artillery	783	8	199	362	604	990
British engineers and staff corps	78	5	36	,,	,,	119
British and German infantry	7,226	830	637	,,	,,	8,693
Whittingham's infantry	4,370	503	316	,,	,,	5,189
Sicilian infantry......... .	985	121	272	,,	,,	1,378
General Total........	14,181	1,479	1,466	1,095	604	17,126

No. 2.—Extract from the original weekly state of the Anglo-Sicilian force, commanded by lieutenant-general sir William Clinton. Head-quarters, Taragona, 25th September, 1813. Exclusive of officers, sergeants, and drummers.

	Present fit for duty.	Sick.	Command.	Horses.	Mules.	Total men.
Cavalry	663	61	215	875	40	939
Artillery, engineers, and staff corps	997	67	58	507	896	1,122
Infantry	9,124	1,390	1,019	115	429	11,533
General Total............	10,784	1,518	1,292	1,497	1,465	13,594

No. 3.—Extract from the original state of the Mallorquina division (Whittingham's.) Taragona, 15th of December, 1813.

	Under arms.	Sick.	Command.	Horses.	Mules.	Total men.
Infantry........................	4,014	400	627	110	21	5,041

No. 4.—Extract from the original state of the first army commanded by the camp-marshal, Don Francisco Copons et Navia. Head-quarters, Vich, 1st of August, 1813.

	Under arms.	Sick.	Command.	Horses.	Mules.	Total men.
Infantry disposable..........	10,219	1,535	2,207	586	,,	13,961
In Cardona....................	1,182	115	398	,,	,,	1,695
Seo d'Urgel....................	984	172	144	,,	,,	1,300
Artillery, &c.	877	7	59	6	,,	1,070
Grand total	13,262	1,829	2,808	592	,,	18,026

No. 5.—Extract from the original state of the second army commanded by the camp-marshal, Don Francisco Xavier Elio. Vinaros, 19th September, 1833.

	Present under arms.	Sick.	Command.	Total of men.	Horses.
Total of all arms	26,835	3,181	7,454	37,470	4,073

Note.—This state includes Villa Campa's, Sarzfield's, Duran's, the Empecinado's, and Roche's divisions, besides the troops immediately under Elio himself.

No. VII.

No. 1.—Force of the Anglo-Portuguese army under the marquis of Wellington's command. Extracted from the original morning state for the 24th of July, 1813.

	Officers, Sergeants, &c.	Rank and file.	Total. Men.	Horses.
British and German cavalry $\}$ Present under arms............ $\}$	916	5,834	6,750	5,834
Ditto infantry	4,665	29,926	34,581	,,
Portuguese cavalry	251	1,241	1,492	1,178
Ditto infantry	2,594	20,565	23,459	,,
Grand Total, exclusive of $\}$ sick and absent on command $\}$	8,726	57,566	66,282	7,012 $\{$ Infantry $\{$ and cavalry.

The artillerymen, &c. were about 4,000.

No. 2.—Anglo-Portuguese force. Extracted from the original morning state, 15th of October, 1813.

	Officers, Sergeants, &c.	Rank and file.	Total.
British and German cavalry and infantry.............................	5,859	37,250	43,109
Portuguese ditto	4,253	21,274	25,527
Grand Total, exclusive of sick, $\}$ absent on command. &c. &c... $\}$	10,112	58,524	68,636

The artillerymen and drivers about 4,000

Total........ 72,636

No. 3.—Anglo-Portuguese force, from the original morning state, 9th November, 1813.

	Officers, Sergeants, &c.	Rank and file.	Total.
British and German cavalry and infantry	5,356	39,687	45,043
Portuguese ditto	2,990	22,237	25,227
Grand Total, exclusive of sick, $\}$ absent on command, &c..... $\}$	8,346	61,924	70,270

The artillerymen, &c. &c. about...... 4,000

Total 74,270

No. 4.—Sir Rowland Hill's force at the battle of St. Pierre. Extracted from the original morning state, 13th December, 1813.

	Officers, Sergeants, &c.	Rank and file.	Total.
Second division .... { British	802	5,371	6,173
{ Portuguese.........	277	2,331	2,608
Lecor's Portuguese division	507	4,163	4,670
Total under arms, exclusive of artillerymen	1,586	11,865	13,451

No. 5.—Anglo-Portuguese force. Extracted from the original morning state, 13th February, 1814.

	Officers, Sergeants, &c.	Rank and file.	Total.	
British and German cavalry....	1,093	7,315	8,408	Cavalry.
Portuguese cavalry	280	1,210	1,490 }	9,898
				Infantry.
British and German infantry ..	4,853	29,714	34,567	
Portuguese infantry..............	2,828	18,911	21,739 }	56,306

General Total, present under arms 66,204

Artillerymen, &c. about 4,000

No. 6.—Anglo-Portuguese force. Extracted from the original morning state, 10th of April, 1814.

	Officers, Sergeants, &c.	Rank and file.	Total.	
British and German cavalry....	1,159	7,640	8,799 }	9,987
Portuguese cavalry	230	958	1,188	
British and German infantry..	4,946	29,999	34,945	54,550
Portuguese infantry	2,622	16,983	19,605 }	

General Total, present under arms 64,537

The artillerymen, &c. about............................ 4,000

No. 7.—Actual strength of the infantry divisions engaged in the battle of Toulouse. Extracted from the original morning state, 10th April, 1814.

Infantry, present under arms.		Officers, Sergeants, &c.	Rank and file.	Total.	
Second division,	British........	715	4,123	6,940	Grand Total infantry, officers and soldiers, present under arms.
Ditto	Portuguese ..	235	1,867 }		
Third division,	British........	529	2,741	4,679	
Ditto	Portuguese ..	226	1,183 }		
Fourth division,	British........	531	3,028	5,383	30,963
Ditto	Portuguese ..	239	1,855 }		
Sixth division,	British........	558	3,233	5,681	
Ditto	Portuguese ..	246	1,644 }		
Light division,	British	378	2,469	4,318	
Ditto	Portuguese ..	231	1,240 }		
Lecor's Portuguese division....		455	3,507	3,962	
		4,343	26,620		

Note.—There is no separate state for the cavalry on the 10th of April, but on the 15th of May, 1814, they stood as follows.

Cavalry, present under arms.	Officers, Sergeants, &c.	Rank and file.	
Bock's brigade of Germans	112	694	Total cavalry,
Ponsonby's brigade of British	188	1,921	present under arms.
Fane's brigade of British....	240	1,506	6,954
Vivian's brigade of British	128	960	
Lord Edw. Somerset's brigade of British	214	1,691	
	882	6,072	

Total of Anglo-Portuguese cavalry and infantry, present under arms ..	37,917
Add the Spaniards under Freyre and Morillo, together said to be ..	14,000
	51,917
Artillerymen, &c.	1,500
General Total	53,417

Note—My authority for the number of guns employed during this campaign are copies of the returns given to me by sir Alexander Dickson who commanded that arm. The number of artillerymen is not borne on the morning states, but in the original weekly state of the 15th of May, 1814, I find the artillerymen, engineers, drivers, and waggon-train, amounted to four thousand eight hundred and twenty-one, with five thousand and thirty horses and mules. This may be taken as the average strength during the campaign, but more than half were with sir John Hope and some with lord Dalhousie. Wherefore, the number at the battle of Toulouse could not have exceeded fifteen hundred, making a total of all ranks and arms of fifty-three thousand combatants.

No. VIII.

No. 1.—General state of the French armies under Soult and Suchet. Extracted from the Imperial Muster-rolls, July 1813. The armies of the north centre and south being by an imperial decree reorganised in one body, taking the title of the army of Spain.

	Present under arms.		Detached.		Hospitals.	Total.	
	Men.	Horses.	Men.	Horses.		Men.	Horses.
Army of Spain........	97,983	12,676	2,110	392	14,074	114,167	13,028
Arragon	32,362	4,919	3,621	551	3,201	39,184	5,470
Catalonia ..	25,910	1,869	168	,,	1,379	27,457	1,744
General Total	156,255	19,464	5,899	943	18,654	180,808	20,242

No. 2.—15th of September, 1813.

						Total.	
	Men.	Horses.	Men.	Horses.	Men.	Men.	Horses.
Army of Spain	81,351	11,159	4,004	1,438	22,488	107,843	11,272
Arragon......	32,476	4,447	2,721	320	3,616	38,813	6,305
Catalonia....	24,026	1,670	120	,,	2,137	26,283	2,497
General Total	137,853	17,276	6,845	1,758	28,241	172,939	20,074

Note.—The garrison of San Sebastian though captive is borne on this state.

This is the last general state of the French army in my possession but the two following notes were inserted in the Imperial Rolls.

" Ar.i.y of Spain, 16th November, 1813.—102 battalions. 74 squadrons, without garrisons 74,152 men present under arms. 100,212 effectives. 17,206 horses.

18,230 Hospital.
8,555 Troop horses.
1,809 Officers' horses.
5,384 Horses of draft.

" Army of Spain, 1st December.—93 battalions. 74 squadrons. 17,989 horses."

No. 3.—Detailed state of the army of Spain, July 1813, when Soult took the command.

Right wing.—Lieutenant-general Reille.

	Men.	Horses.			Effective and non-effective.	
					Men.	Total.
First division, Foy, 9 battalions......	5,922	189	Present under arms.		6,784	
Seventh ditto, Maucune, 7 ditto......	4,186	110	17,235	450	5,676	21,366
Ninth ditto, La Martiniere, 11 ditto	7,127	151	men.	horses.	8,906	

Centre.—Drouet, Count D'Erlon.

	Men.	Horses.				
Second division, D'Armagnac, 8 batt.	6,961	116			8,580	
Third ditto, Abbé, 9 ditto	8,030	285	20,957	624	8,728	23,935
Sixth ditto, Daricau, 8 ditto	5,966	223	men.	horses.	6,627	

Left wing.—Lieut.-general Clauzel.

	Men.	Horses.				
Fourth division, Conroux, 9 battalions	7,056	150			7,477	
Fifth ditto, Vandermaesen, 7 ditto	4,181	141	17,218	432	5,201	20,265
Eighth ditto, Taupin, 10 ditto	5,981	141	men.	horses.	7,587	

Reserve, General Villatte.

French..................	14,959	2,091	17,929
Foreign ...... 4 battalions of the Rhine, strength not given.			
4 ditto Italians, general St. Pol, ditto.			
4 ditto Spaniards, general Casabianca, ditto.			

Cavalry, Pierre Soult.

	Men.	Horses.		Effective and non-effective.	
22 squadrons	4,723	4,416	Present under arms.	5,098	
Ditto Trielhard........	2,358	2,275	7,081 men. 6,691 horses.	2,523	7,621
Total according to the organization, but exclusive of the foreign battalions ..	77,450			91,086	

Men under arms.

Troops not in the organization	14,938	16,946
Generals Garrison of St.Sebastian,1st July	2,731	3,086
Rey forming part of this number....		
Cassan.—Ditto of Pampeluna, 1st July....	2,951	3,121
Lameth.—Ditto of Santona, 1st May......	1,465	1,674
Second reserve, not in the above	5,595	6,105

	Men.	Horses.	Effective and non-effective. Men. Horses.
General Total............	97,983	12,676.	Present under arms.. 114,167 13,028

No. 4.—Detailed state of the army of Spain, 16th of September, 1813.

		Men.			Effective and non-effective
Right wing	Foy	5,002	14,875 present under arms.		Men.
	Maucune............	4,166			
	Menne	5,707			45,752
Centre.	D'Armagnac........	4,353	15,098 ditto		
	Abbé	5,903			
	Maranzin	4,842			
Left wing.	Conroux	4,736	15,789 ditto		
	Roguet	5,982			
	Taupin	5,071			
Reserve.	Villatte	8,256	The Italian brigade, about 2,000 ordered to Milan.		10,424
Provisional troops of the right wing, destined to reinforce the garrison of Bayonne		2,168			

		Men.	Horses.		Total. Men.
Cavalry.—Pierre Soult....................		4,456	4,617	}	
Ditto Trielhard		2,368	2,583		8,325
Gensd'armes	{ mounted................	291	247		
	{ dismountned	1,210	,,		
Parc..		895	885	}	1,399
Engineers		504	127		
Garrisons.	Pampeluna	3,805	191		
	San Sebastian............	2,356 prisoners of war.			
	Santona	1,633			
	Bayonne....................	4,631	137		15,164
	St. Jean Pied de Port..	1,786			
	Navarens	842			
	Castle of Lourdes	107			

81,064

Deduct garrison of San Sebastian.... 2,366

Total, present under arms................................... 78,698

No. IX.

Orders for the several divisions of the allied army for the attack of the enemy's fortified position in front of Toulouse for to-morrow, 1st April, 1814. Published in the United Service Journal, October 1838.

(EXTRACT.)

"*St. Jory, 9th April,* 1814.

" The front attack of the third division is to extend from the river Garonne to the great road which leads from the village of La Lande to Toulouse (the road from Montauban) inclusive of that road.

" The light division will be immediately on the left of the third division, and it will extend its front of attack from the great road above-mentioned until it connects its left flank with the right of the Spanish troops.

" The operations of these two divisions are meant, however, more as diversions than as real attacks ; it not being expected that they will be able to force any of the passes of the canal which covers Toulouse. The line of the canal is to be threatened chiefly at the bridges and at the locks or any other points where the form of the ground, or other circumstances most favour the advance of the troops. A considerable part both of the third and of the light divisions must be kept in reserve."

Note.—The analysis of the allied army on the 10th of April, given in Appendix VII. Sections 6 and 7, has been very carefully made and faithfully set down ; but as the real number of the allies has lately become a point of dispute between French and English writers, I here give the Morning State of the whole army, accurately printed from the original document delivered by the adjutant-general to lord Wellington on the morning of the 10th of April, 1814. The reader will thus be enabled, with the help of my text, to trace each division in its course and ascertain its true numbers.

MORNING STATE of the FORCES in the PENINSULA, under the Command of HIS EXCELLENCY FIELD-MARSHAL THE MARQUIS OF WELLINGTON, K.G. Head-Quarters, St. Jory, 10th April, 1814.

Date of last State received	DIVISIONS	Colonels	Lieut.-Colonels	Majors	Captains	Lieutenants	Cornets or Ensigns	Staff	Quarter-Masters of Cavalry	Serg. Present	Serg. Sick Present	Serg. Sick Absent	Serg. Command	Serg. Prs. of War & Missing	Serg. Total	Trump. Present	Trump. Sick Present	Trump. Sick Absent	Trump. Command	Trump. Prs. of War & Missing	Trump. Total	R&F Present	R&F Sick Present	R&F Sick Absent	R&F Command	R&F Prs. of War & Missing	R&F Total	Horses Present	Horses Sick	Horses Command	Horses Total	Joined	Dead	Discharged	Deserted	Transferred	Promoted	Reduced	Effective Rank and File, Portuguese included
7th Apr.	**BRITISH.** Cavalry	1	13	17	106	189	25	94	25	581	9	17	68	7	682	108		8	4	2	192	7640	106	406	1071	939	9456	7289	611	602	8502								8144
Do.	1st Dn. Infantry	3	16	6	64	53	36	48		433	13	40	38	4	528	142	4	3		3	152	5894	244	692	200	185	7155					**4	6		4	**10	***3	****4	5894
9th Do.	2d	2	16	10	45	123	59	41		320	5	89	68	18	500	143	1	23	3	8	178	4123	112	2251	474	716	7676						11			4		4	5990
Do.	3d		3	10	38	69	30	32		231	3	82	47	5	368	114		20	7	4	145	2741	75	1352	297	229	4694					*1	1					*1	3934
6th Do.	4th		3	9	42	86	27	30		232	3	76	56	4	371	102	1	15	5	6	129	3028	44	1700	279	201	5252										o 1		4613
7th Do.	5th	1	4	6	35	102	39	38		245	28	63	30	10	376	99	10	10	3	8	130	3277	363	1075	924	315	5954						2		2				4438
6th Do.	6th		4	6	41	74	24	31		236	4	59	41	1	341	101	1	19	3	1	124	3233	54	1923	309	103	4932										1		4877
5th Do.	7th	1	4	6	38	74	31	31		187	5	62	42	16	312	92	2	8	4	11	117	2738	114	1074	991	673	4990									*17			4474
9th Do.	Lt.	2	6	4	24	63	13	19		182	2	39	21	1	245	66	1	3	3		73	2469	77	696	131	146	3519					1	2			2		*1	3709
7th Do.	Ld. Aylmer's Bde.			7	37	74	19	26		188	7	7	8		210	72	1	4	4		77	2496		319	92		3112						2						2496
	TOTAL																					37639	1401	10721	3468	2801	56030	7289	611	602	8502	5	24		6	33	4	6	
7th Apr.	**PORTUGUESE.** Cavalry	2	4	4	17	39	15	41	4	64	2		28		94	40			10		50	958	5	598	598	16	1650	855	114	404	1373								
9th Do.	2d Dn. Infantry	2	2	2	16	16	28	10		192		19	52		173	39		1	4		44	1862	71	472	101		2511												
Do.	3d		2	2	9	17	23	14		101	5	20	39		165	58		5	6		71	1183	105	598	383		2269												
6th Do.	4th		1	3	10	12	24	51		103	3	27	23		153	36		6	5		47	1585	30	635	199		2449												
7th Do.	5th		1	2	13	13	16	49		105	3	25	19		151	33	2	6	2		42	1161	19	550	176		1900					1				2			
8th Do.	6th		1	3	12	13	17	47		110	4	12	20		154	33	1	6	2		42	1644	44	469	151		2308						3						
5th Do.	7th		1	4	17	11	26	43		101	3	12	30		149	51		3	7		63	1736	48	528	211	48	2271					69							
9th Do.	Lt.		2	7	13	90	51	29		197	7	6	47		197	93	3	6	6		93	1240	54	237	94	11	1936							o 1		2			
8th Do.	Unattached Dn.		1	6	25	92	90	29		197	1	10	20		278	64	3	6	2		76	3507	54	835	219	76	485												3507
8th Do.	1st Brigade	1	4	4	9	12	9	16		197	1	10	60		168	64	3	9	6	3	72	1510	68	928	146	213	2265						1						1510
Do.	10th			4	18	14	23	38		124	7	7	15		153	31		3	5	4	59	1530	115	351	89		2102												1530
	Total Portuguese																					17941	768	4776	2660	368	26513	855	114	404	1373	70	5	1		2	1	6	
	Total British																																						
	Grand Total																																						

3 Men deserted 2d Line Bn. K.G.L.
1 Do. ,, 1st Line Do.
1 Do. ,, 47th Foot.
1 Do. ,, 4th Do.

The Men transferred are Invalids sent home.

Note.—The figures belonging to the grand total are wanting in the original.